Mythras

MYTHIC ROME

DEVELOPED AND WRITTEN BY
Pete Nash

ADDITIONAL MATERIAL BY
Lawrence Whitaker

LATIN CORRECTIONS
Henri de Marcellus, D.Phil (Oxford)

EDITING
Brian Pivik

PROOFING
Charlotte Law

DESIGN AND LAYOUT
The Design Mechanism

ARTISTS
David Benzal, Dan MacKinnon, Colin Driver

FIND US AT
*www.thedesignmechanism.com and www.*MYTHRAS*rpg.com.*
Facebook: https://www.facebook.com/The-Design-Mechanism
G+: https://plus.google.com/communities/113034383032729983266

ISBN: 978-0-9947589-5-8

THE DESIGN MECHANISM

CONTENTS

INTRODUCTION

S P Q R

Senatus Populusque Romanus

"Ilia the fair, a priestess and a queen,
Who, full of Mars, in time, with kindly throes,
Shall at a birth two goodly boys disclose.
The royal babes a tawny wolf shall drain:
Then Romulus his grandsire's throne shall gain,
Of martial towers the founder shall become,
The people Romans call, the city Rome.
To them no bounds of empire I assign,
Nor term of years to their immortal line
Even haughty Juno, who, with endless broils,
Earth, seas, and heaven, and Jove himself turmoils;
At length atoned, her friendly power shall join,
To cherish and advance the Trojan line
The subject world shall Rome's dominion own,
And, prostrate, shall adore the nation of the gown.
An age is ripening in revolving fate
When Troy shall overturn the Grecian state,
And sweet revenge her conquering sons shall call,
To crush the people that conspired her fall
Then Cæsar from the Julian stock shall rise,
Whose empire ocean, and whose fame the skies
Alone shall bound; whom, fraught with eastern spoils,
Our heaven, the just reward of human toils,
Securely shall repay with rites divine;
And incense shall ascend before his sacred shrine
Then dire debate and impious war shall cease,
And the stern age be softened into peace:
Then banished Faith shall once again return,
And Vestal fires in hallowed temples burn;
And Remus with Quirinus shall sustain
The righteous laws, and fraud and force restrain.
Janus himself before his fane shall wait,
And keep the dreadful issues of his gate,
With bolts and iron bars: within remains
Imprisoned Fury, bound in brazen chains;
High on a trophy raised, of useless arms,
He sits, and threats the world with vain alarms."

Virgil, The Aeneid

Rome is the longest enduring civilisation in western European history. It is synonymous with empire, legions, dictators, gladiators and decadence. The Romans have been an inescapable influence on our lives. Much of modern law, European languages, and even some political systems, are based upon their legacy.

The efforts of this once mighty nation still echo in our psyche, making Rome a perfect setting for roleplaying campaigns. Whether you prefer the gritty underhanded corruption of Roman politics, fighting great battles against Rome's enemies, or participating in the spectacular excitements of chariot racing and gladiatorial combat, ancient Rome can cater to your needs.

In its own peculiar way, Rome is the archetypal metropolis, the original upon which our modern cultures are but a pale shadow. Welcome to the Eternal City and its treacherous depths...

ABOUT THIS BOOK

This book contains setting information for role-playing in Rome during its Monarchy and Republic. Although it includes some complementary rules and skills it is not a game in its own right and is designed for use with Design Mechanism's MYTHRAS system for play – although it should be easy to use with any percentile based role-playing game.

The content focuses on the city and culture of Rome from its legendary founding in 753 BC to the end of the Republic in 27 BC. 700 years is an incredible length of time, which makes it difficult to cover the period in any detail. Imagine how much modern society has changed in the last 100 years... women's suffrage, economic reforms, the rise and fall of communism, fashion, entertainment; the transformations have been profound. Although readers may find the following contents more comprehensive than any previous role-playing supplement on the era, it still only scratches the surface.

Despite the focus on the city itself – rather than its burgeoning empire – Games Masters should bear in mind that to a Roman, Rome was the centre of the world and the provinces merely places to conquer and reap taxes from. On a more practical level, there was simply not room to add any additional material covering the regions and enemies of the empire.

Most of this book contains dates and periods to indicate when certain historical events occurred. The author has used the following generalisations to break the era into four parts and utilises BC

A cane non magno saepe tenetur aper – A boar is often held by a not-so-large dog (Ovid)

instead of BCE out of old fashioned familiarity. For those who desire to use the more authentic Roman dating system of AUC ab urbe condita (from the founding of Rome), simply subtract the BC year from the value of 753 and add one.

Ω The Monarchy, 753-509 BC – The founding of the city to the overthrow of the Monarchy

Ω The Early Republic, 509-264 BC – The start of the Republic and conquering of Italy

Ω The Middle Republic, 264-133 BC – The Punic Wars to the Gracchi reforms

Ω The Late Republic, 133-27 BC – Political instability and civil wars leading the end of the Republic

QUICK LATIN GUIDE

Singular Ending	Plural Ending
-a (lupa)	-ae (lupae)
-us (gladius)	usually: -i (gladii), but sometimes -us (.)
-um (templum)	-a (templa)
-is (inauris)	-es (inaures)
-e (monile)	-ia (monilia)
-io (pugio)	-iones (pugiones)

HISTORICAL FLAVOUR

Since this is an historical setting, most of the information has been carefully researched to be as accurate as possible, drawing on the archaeological and historical theories current at the time of publication. Many of the cultural conventions described may seem odd, or even wrong, but where space permits their accuracy has been illustrated using quotes from Roman and Greek authors contemporary to the time or within a few generations of the period. Due to the dearth of written material surviving from earlier times, most of the information is skewed towards the lifestyle and culture at end of the Republic and, at best, are only generalisations.

Although primarily a historical guide to early Roman life, some supernatural and mythological elements are included in the Magic and Creatures chapters to provide for Games Masters desiring a mythic campaign. These aspects are more subtle than their earlier archaic Greek counterparts and demonstrate Roman superstition prevalent at the time.

The layout of the book places the cultural sections first, leaving the majority of chapters involving game mechanics and campaigns to the latter half.

QUICK LATIN GUIDE

Included throughout the book are Latin translations for commonplace objects, ideas or acts. These have been added to show the original source of many English words and it is hoped that, if used in play, the vocabulary will provide players with an increased level of immersion.

It should also be noted that although the author spells some Roman names and words with the letter 'J', the Romans used the letter 'I' instead.

In Latin, changing a word from singular to plural was not as straightforward as adding an 's'. Different kinds of words formed the plural in different ways. Here is a simplified table for those who need it:

SOCIETY

To be Roman was to be a member of a vibrant urban society; an expanding, conquering civilisation which gained authority over its neighbours – confident in its power, arrogant in its politics and egocentric in its laws and social divisions. A Roman separated from their city was akin to a fish out of water, seeing only barbarism or decadence about them.

Although many Romans were sophisticated enough to survive in foreign lands, or even briefly sojourn to the countryside, they were never wholly content there. A true Roman craved society, culture, gossip, wealth and promotion. Where else could this be found save Rome itself?

The following chapter attempts to describe the richly complex structure of Roman society.

SOCIAL STRUCTURE (MOS MAIORUM)

Towards the end of the Monarchy, the population of Rome was estimated to be 100,000 people. By the end of the Republic, it had grown to a staggering metropolis of nearly 1,000,000 souls, comprising of people divided into different layers of rank and status. These divisions defined social interaction, responsibility and access to legal rights.

A number of key fundamental ideas tied the populace together, maintaining social order.

THE FAMILY (FAMILIA)

The basic unit of Roman society is the family. A *familia* comprised of an entire household from the eldest living male, including all his offspring and their own families, down to even the slaves. Thus a home could contain an extensive number of people, which was the normal and accepted way to live.

The head of the household was the eldest living father, the Paterfamilias, who has absolute authority over all his descendants. This power (patria potestas) included the right to kill family members or even sell them into slavery, subject to the contemporary morals and customs at the time.

"As tribune of the people, Spurius Cassius was the first to propose laws redistributing land and gained great popularity through actions that pleased the masses. After he had stood down from office, his father Cassius followed the precedent of Brutus and called a meeting of friends and relatives. He condemned his son before the household for having tried to set up a tyranny, ordered him to be scourged and executed, and gave his wealth to the goddess Ceres."
Valerius Maximus - Memorabilia

The *paterfamilias* was the representative for the family in all things religious and in relations with the community. He led the rituals and sacrifices to the family ancestors and household gods. No matter their rank or status, Romans were expected to live up to the expectations of the head of the family.

The autocratic rights of a paterfamilias continued to hold sway over their own sons, despite the fact they may be adults or even grandfathers. Freedom from this authority only occurred when their father died, promoting each of the next generation of males to patres familiarum in their own right.

Normally however, once sons reached adulthood they were generally granted some independence by the paterfamilias so that they might own property or pursue careers free from the necessity of requiring their father's authority to enter into contracts.

Children (and even adults) unrelated by blood could be brought into the family by the paterfamilias. Once legally adopted, from that point onwards the child was considered a full member of the familia.

THE CLAN (GENS)

The *gentes* were groups of families who could all trace their descent back to a common ancestor. They were related by their gentile name (nomen) and acted like a clan. Since it is difficult to differentiate between the many members of the gentes by only their personal name (praenomen), it was sometimes necessary to add a further sub name (cognomen) to differentiate between individual families (stirpes) in the same gens. For example Caius Julius Caesar would be Caius of the Caesarian stirps of the gens Julii (see Roman Names page 123).

Many of the gens practice their own unique religious rituals, festivals and customs, which strengthened the clan bonds between them, often allowing an entire gens to act in concert during times of war or political unease. At these times the gens was led by the leading paterfamilias of its comprising families. If a paterfamilias died without an heir, then their property was left to the gens.

Membership in a particular gens conferred no nobility or authority. To gain this one must have served in high office, not be born or adopted to it. Indeed, even enfranchised slaves could become a member of a gens, since a freed man adopts the praenomen and nomen of their former master.

CLIENT SYSTEM (CLIENTELA)

The *client* system was an exclusive relationship where a patron offered protection and aid in exchange for the client's support and services. The tie was a moral rather than legal bond, where a free man was accepted into the 'good faith' (fides) of the patron.

The association, and the respect it involved, was two-way; a patron would not offer a favour to those who could not reciprocate, and in like manner a client would not continue in a relationship where the patron did not act on their behalf.

In the monarchic period, the system was originally based upon agriculture; clients (clientes) would farm small parcels of land for the patron in return for their livelihood. However, over the course of the republican era these services evolved into personal attendance upon the patron, primarily for protection and political support.

A faithful client resident in the city was expected to arrive at the residence of his patron every morning to see if their services are required. In return the patron might gift the client with a few coins, some cast-off clothing, old household goods, or at the very least one good meal, depending on their rank or financial status.

Successful client-patron bonds could become hereditary and were passed on to the sons on both sides of the relationship. The system was extremely important in a city where there was no state-supported protection from crime or law (see Law page 19). However, by the end of the Republic, this sense of duty had eroded to the point where some clients served several different patrons.

In general it is the members of the Roman aristocracy who granted their patronage to clients; although one need not be of higher status to offer such a relationship. Many gentes had great influence and power primarily because of their large numbers of dependent clients.

THE CENSUS (CENSUS)

The cornerstone of Roman civilisation, the census was the scrutiny of each citizen's personal wealth, which differentiated their rank in early Roman society, their voting block in the Comitia Centuriata (see The Assemblies page 15) and in turn their position in the army (see The Army during the Monarchy page 89). It also governed correct social behaviour, reinforcing Roman traditions and conformity.

The census was held in Rome every fifth year and each male Roman citizen was forced to register his family members, possessions and slaves; else have them confiscated and be sold into slavery, including even himself.

Despite the aggravation of registration, the census defined freedom. Being listed as a citizen (civis) ensured one's identity and status

---

COMPREHENDING CULTURAL DIFFERENCES

Although much of Roman life and law has been passed down to us in the western world, some of the following concepts are rather odd or even completely alien to our modern preconceptions, so Games Masters should spend time to completely familiarise themselves with them. All Roman social interaction was based on these ideas and they should be enforced to give a true Roman flavour to their campaigns.

For those who are having problems understanding Roman social conventions or portraying them to their players should try watching the HBO TV series 'Rome', which is a reasonable introduction to Roman family structure and the dictatorial authority of the father. Another good insight is the introductory sequence in the movie 'The Godfather', which gives an entertaining illustration of the Client-Patron system.

---

as a free man. Even employers had to declare the freedmen who work for them. The results of a census enabled the city to count its number of citizens, thereby predicting potential tax revenues and the manpower available for military service.

Each census was coordinated by two censors of senatorial class – ex-consuls deemed incorruptible. Much status relied on the opinion of the censors and those of higher rank had their moral behaviour in both private and public life closely scrutinised. Anyone thought lacking could be demoted from the Senate for such things as perjury, having an adulterous wife, failing to father children, not cultivating his lands correctly or even for appearing on the stage.

GUILDS (COLLEGIA)

King Numa Pompilius was reputed to be the ruler who first instituted Rome's work-related guilds in order to reduce the discontent between competing craftsmen of differing ethnic origin.

"So, distinguishing the whole people by the several arts and trades, he formed companies of musicians, goldsmiths, carpenters, dyers, shoemakers, skinners, braziers, and potters; and all other handicraftsmen he composed and reduced into a single company, appointing everyone their proper courts, councils, and religious observances."

Plutarch - Life of Numa

These occupational guilds (collegiae opificum) became an important aspect of Roman life, giving craftsmen a chance to protect their members and further their livelihoods. Members would pay a contribution to the guild's communal fund, which went to pay for renting their headquarters, the occasional celebratory feast and possibly legal fees if a guild member, or the guild itself, suffered litigation.

Eventually the number of guilds grew to cover more professions, including cooks, doctors, teachers, engravers, painters, weavers and even poets. However, by the late Republic many guilds had devolved into political clubs (collegia sodalicia) which used their membership to influence the election of magistrates, often using violence or intimidation to affect changes. Eventually they were suppressed for six years, starting in 64 BC and later, in 56 BC, abolished altogether by Julius Caesar for being politically subversive.

THE POPULACE (POPULUS)

"Nothing is so unequal than equality"

Pliny the Younger

Class and status is all-important in Roman life. Not only were Romans vehemently status conscious but it defined who one could interact with socially, what protection they could claim from the law, personal freedom and even the type of punishment one can expect if they performed a criminal deed. Although changing rank was possible, it was a rare thing, requiring wealth or patronage to achieve.

The populace can be roughly categorised as citizens and non-citizens.

The citizens (cives) of Rome are divided between the patricians and the plebeians. Both eventually have equal rights under citizen's law (ius civile) but in practice the poor still depended upon the patronage of the rich or powerful for protection. Only males could be citizens and only a citizen may wear the toga, which characterised their status. Citizens also wore rings denoting their status, usually made of iron but sometimes of more valuable metals in the higher social classes.

ROMAN CITIZENSHIP

Roman citizenship evolved over a long period of time, and included many minute details. Its most important aspects were gathered under two categories. Political rights, including those of voting (ius suffragii) and holding office (ius honorum); and civil rights, those of appeal (ius provocationis), trade (ius commercii), intermarriage (ius connubii) and making a will (ius testamenti).

Non-citizens included all women, freedmen, slaves and foreigners. They were prohibited some, or all, of the rights of ius civile and forbidden the wearing of togas and holding of public office.

PATRICIANS (PATRICII)

A patrician was a descendent from one of the 100 founding fathers, the patriarchs, chosen to form the first Senate. Originally only a patrician could hold magisterial office or priesthood. However, by the mid-Republic, these privileges had been worn away so that only certain priesthoods necessitated patrician status.

Although Rome started with 100 patrician families, time, war, and the fates of childbirth eroded their numbers. By the end of the republic, only 14 patrician gens remain.

PLEBEIANS (PLEBEII)

Quite simply, a plebeian is a citizen who is not of patrician status. Although prevented from gaining the highest positions in Rome due to the lack of patrician blood, there were many offices which could only be held by those of plebeian status.

During antiquity, the plebeians were divided into three tribes (tribus) each of which are subdivided into 10 units called curiae. This early classification system was based upon which region the citizen resided in, and by the end of the Republic the number of tribes had

risen to 35, growing as Rome conquered more territories. Of these, only four were urban tribes actually based in the city of Rome (see The Hills and Districts page 49). The tribes and curiae were used for administration purposes and electoral voting (See Government and Politics page 13).

Plebeians had their own class subdivision based on wealth. During military service in the Monarchic and early Republican periods, those plebs wealthy enough to provide their own horses were permitted to join the cavalry (equites). However, as time passed the equestrians lost their military aspect, becoming a social class in their own right, and gained many civic privileges. By the end of the Republic, only those citizens whose wealth was at least 400,000 sesterces were permitted to be members of the equestrian class and if the family lost its fortune it could be expelled.

WOMEN (FEMINAE)

"Our ancestors, in their wisdom, considered that all women, because of their innate weakness, should be under the control of guardians."

Cicero

As previously mentioned, women were not considered Roman citizens and, until the end of the republic, Roman women were always under the authority of a male family member. This was usually either their father or husband according to marital status. If a woman was left with no male family members, then she was assigned a new guardian, according to the wishes left in her previous guardian's will. The only women free of such authority were the six Vestal Virgins.

Despite this apparent draconian authority, Roman women enjoyed the most liberal lifestyle of any Mediterranean culture of the time (even the Greeks kept their women as virtual prisoners at home). Girls of sufficiently wealthy families were granted a similar, if not equal education as boys but specialising in literature, music, and dance. Although young women remained closely chaperoned until wed to ensure fidelity, they were permitted freedom to visit friends, shop and even watch the religious games. Once married, a woman was expected to socialise and entertain in order to support her husband's career.

Despite being allowed to be present during banquets and parties, which was seen as scandalous by Hellenic nations, women until the very end of the Republic were forbidden to consume wine or even recline, forced instead to drink grape juice and sit upright on chairs.

"Egnatius Metennius beat his wife with a cudgel and killed her because she had drunk some wine, and not only did no one accuse him in court because of this act, but he was not even criticized, for all men of good character believed that she had deserved the punishment for violating temperance, and indeed any woman who has an excessive desire for the drinking of wine closes the door to all virtues and opens it to vices."

Valerius Maximus - Memorabilia

Roman women usually ran the slaves within the household and were free to leave home as they willed. As time went on, the hard working duties of cooking, shopping, housekeeping, spinning thread and weaving clothes were slowly assumed by slaves, leaving wealthier women with little to do with their free time other than socialise.

Alea iacta est – The die is cast (Julius Caesar)

Although women were forbidden from voting or holding public office, they could still possess property in their own right.

FREEDMEN (LIBERTINI)

A freedman is a person who has been released from slavery. Although loosed from his bondage, a freedman's social stigma was barely above that of slave and most continued an obligatory client-patron relationship with their former masters, taking their master's name as their own.

Freedmen were forbidden from holding magisterial office but other than that limitation, they were deemed to have the full rights of citizens. Only those slaves granted a full formal manumission could pass on citizenship to their children. During the late Republic, those granted their freedom via manumissio inter amicos and manumissio per epistula lived free but died as slaves, preventing their children from being granted full citizen status and allowing their patron to claim any property belonging to the freedman.

SLAVES (SERVI)

Slavery was common throughout the ancient world as a method of using those vanquished by conquest as cheap labour. In fact the Latin word for slave – servi – literally means 'spared person', i.e. prisoners of war.

At the birth of Rome, the numbers of slaves were minimal but by the end of the Republic there are so many slaves that free citizens found it difficult to find employment. Indeed the undermining of Roman society by the late Republic was caused in part by its massive slave workforce, which put many smallholding farmers and craftsmen out of business, thus swelling the dispossessed populace of plebeians in Rome and leading to increased crime and unrest. However, many foreign slaves were actually better educated than the average citizen and the administration of the city was maintained by slave clerks and scribes.

A slave had no legal standing, could not get married (although male slaves could be rewarded with the right of contubernium – i.e. choose a female household slave to sleep with) and any children produced from sexual union would also be slaves, even if the other parent was a free citizen. Technically they could be killed at a whim, tortured or ill-treated with no right to defend themselves. However, masters who treated their slaves badly were ostracised or even censured for such behaviour.

> "He [Crassus] owned many silver mines, much valuable land and slaves to work it, yet one could think that this wealth counted for nothing compared to the value of his slaves; so many did he have, and of such quality, readers, secretaries, silversmiths, business managers, waiters. He used to be in charge of their education, and take part himself in teaching them, holding the general view that an owner should pay particular attention to the care of his slaves, as they were the living tools for household management. He was right about this..."
>
> Plutarch - Life of Crassus

The lot of a slave depended entirely on the master and type of work they were assigned to. The worst fate an uneducated slave could face was to be assigned to the mines or the galleys. Both professions faced a very short and hard life. Farm work was also hard, backbreaking labour and many farm slaves were chained together in the fields and placed in guarded barracks at night to prevent

SLAVERY

It should be stressed that several modern-day views of slavery do not apply to Roman society.

First and foremost slavery was simply a question of status. It was a social class for people technically regarded as 'dead, or should be dead'. A slave could quite legitimately achieve freedom and rise to greater things, whilst conversely a wealthy citizen brought to his knees by poverty or participating in rebellious acts could lose their class status and be demoted to slave-hood. Slave themselves had their own hierarchy of status.

Secondly, slavery is not based on ethnic background. A Roman did not judge a person's status by their colour or race. He makes a judgement by the type of clothing they wear. Many Latin, Italian and Greek slaves would be indistinguishable from their masters, if they wore the same clothing. Hence the legal restriction of wearing the toga to citizens.

Thirdly, slavery was not simply the mass exploitation of labour. Freeborn Romans worked side by side with slaves in many different types of work, even the most degrading manual labour. In fact many slaves were better skilled or educated than their free work companions.

Lastly, the concepts of equality and the liberation of all men were totally foreign to Roman (and indeed all Mediterranean) thought. Nobody, not even freed slaves themselves, ever considered such a thing. Citizens in the Republic who talk about universal suffrage are considered insane, since slavery is simply a question of status, and by changing the status of one class in society you are effectively threatening all the classes.

escapes. Conversely those slaves allocated to herding were granted a great deal of freedom necessary to guide ranging flocks of sheep and goats.

Household slaves had a somewhat more sheltered life; unlikely to face injury or death from their work, especially those in the homes of the rich. Yet being constantly under the eyes of their masters they had a greater chance of facing punishment from mistakes or experiencing sexual coercion.

Educated slaves who possessed great learning or valued skills were always in great demand and could bring fabulous prices in the market. In fact, some owners deliberately had their slaves educated to raise their value. An intelligent slave was valuable because they could work independently from their master and would not require constant supervision. Beauty was also highly prized and many slaves were specifically purchased for their appearance.

Although the common view of Rome is of cruelty and abuse towards slaves, few were maltreated, since slaves were property and had inherent value. Deliberate cruelty was frowned upon by Roman society in which slaves were still recognised as human beings. Slavery is considered more as a difference in status but despite this they were still looked down upon.

> "But let us remember that we must have regard for justice even towards the humblest. Now the humblest station and the poorest fortune are those of slaves; and they give us no bad rule who bid us treat our slaves as we should our employees: they must be required to work; they must be given their dues"
>
> Cicero - De Officiis

Conversely, treating slaves with overt kindness was considered a sign of weakness in Roman society, yet a good master who treated his slaves well was rewarded by greater loyalty and higher productivity.

Two hopes remained to a slave. Firstly that after many years of good, faithful service that their master would grant them freedom; and manumit them. Secondly, although slaves were forbidden to own property, they were allowed to save money to buy their freedom (peculium). Even though slaves were never paid wages, some managed to find additional employment to earn this money. This process was not granted out of kindness of their master but was an act of economic expediency. The money raised by a slave to buy freedom would go to purchase a younger, fitter replacement. In fact, some slaves used their savings to purchase their own slaves to act as substitutes for them.

FOREIGNERS (PEREGRINI)

Foreigners were not favoured in Rome. Romans tended to view foreigners as less cultured, or having strange and unwholesome habits. The most loathed were those of eastern civilisations such as Parthians, Selucids, and Egyptians. As such, whenever civil strife erupts, it was usually the foreigners who were first targeted for reprisals as a matter of course.

The majority of foreigners were merchants drawn to the metropolis by its wealth. Romans viewed commerce as vaguely disreputable, as decent wealth only came from land ownership, agriculture, and warfare.

A foreigner could not own property within Rome, and had to be sponsored by a citizen of good standing to set up a business. Foreigners were unable to vote during elections and lacked the legal rights of a citizen. They also had a separate series of laws to control their dealings with citizens, the law of nations (Ius Gentium). In a perverse way, a foreign slave was actually better regarded than a foreigner who was a freeman. A slave belonged, whereas a foreigner did not.

THE ROMAN WAY (VIA ROMANA)

The Romans had many well-defined morals which were regarded as vital for respectable members of society. A citizen's public image – and thus their place in the order of things – depended upon how well they demonstrated these ideals.

Because city life is by definition social, a person's worth was rated by how much they contributed to the well-being of the city (and the state) as a whole. Individualism was questionable, since it contributed little towards society; thus the cardinal virtues are social and political in nature, tending towards the very stern and austere.

The significance of these virtues is so great that many of them are worshipped as divinities in their own right (see Minor Roman Deities page 231). To reinforce their importance, many of the virtues were also minted on coins too, which not only educated the literate populace but also served as propaganda towards the other nations in the ancient world.

UNWANTED CHILDREN

Many infants were abandoned in Rome for a plethora of reasons. The family could be burdened by poverty, unable to feed an extra mouth. The child might have been born deformed or sickly. It may be the result of an illicit affair or even refused and cast out by the paterfamilias. Such abandoning was not illegal and carried no social stigma – since life was hard and caring for an extra babe could mean life or death for the rest of the family.

Whatever the reason, such babies were sometimes given to friends (since child mortality often left openings for a healthy child) or, if completely unwanted, simply abandoned to the elements in a public place. Some died from hypothermia or were even eaten by scavenging packs of wild dogs, which haunted the streets. But often such foundlings (expositi) were rescued by passers-by. Favourite places for abandoning infants were the Velabrum, a well-travelled street where oil and cheese merchants clustered, or the vegetable market in the Forum Romanum near the 'nursing column' (columna lactaria).

Foundlings could be legally claimed by anyone who desired them. Commonly they were raised as slaves, playmates for other children or even prostitutes. The hope of all parents who abandoned their child was that it would be discovered by a wealthy person and adopted into that family. Indeed, many comedies and farces of the period are based on the premise that the hero is an unwitting foundling from a wealthy family, who is eventually located by the remorseful father or grandfather seeking their long lost progeny.

ROMAN NOBILITY (NOBILITAS)

The ideal of nobility was based upon the concept of familial obligation to the city. Nobility was not awarded simply by birth. It had to be won (and maintained) with public duty, by serving as a senior magistrate. To be regarded as truly noble, one had to have three consecutive generations of fathers who have served in a curule magisterial position (see Magistrates page 16). Any interruption in this obligation caused the family to lose noble rank, dooming the next three generations to indignity.

Nobility is a burden of responsibilities, yet by following both legal and social duties, one could win respect from one's fellows. A Roman should display the correct virtues. Not only that, but the more distinguished one's ancestry, the greater their achievements should be in order to live up to expectations.

A young nobleman's career usually began with military service. As a teenager, a senatorial son usually served as a military tribune on the staff of a legionary commander, generally someone who was a relative or close friend of the family. During this time their conduct was tested for character flaws such as being tempted by foreign habits, cruelty or displaying cowardliness.

After the conclusion of their military path, a nobleman must then undertake a civilian career. As dangerous as army life might be, the web of feuds between noble families were far worse, promising to bring disaster on one's own family. Sons were expected to avenge disgrace or humiliation inflicted by political enemies, generally in the courtroom. After the age of 30 or thereabouts, a nobleman who had served in the lower offices then stood a chance at being elected to a high magisterial position (see Political Power Games page 18).

THE IMPORTANCE OF HONOUR

"Men no longer aspire to win praise for noble deeds, but think only of profit, profit, profit. Clutching their purses, always looking for more, too stingy to give away the tarnish that comes off their coins."

Theocritus

A Roman's honour (honos) was based upon his public reputation; an honourable man is one thought honourable by others. Thus a Roman sought confirmation of his ability and identity from the elders of their family, their patron, their clients, army comrades, or even – in an election – the general populace of Rome. No Roman could be his own judge but must see himself (and his virtues) only through the eyes of others.

Since the only use of glory and honour was to rise higher in society, any recognition gleaned from public opinion should immediately be used to further one's political fortunes, in the hope of achieving a seat in the Roman Senate. Therefore any success or achievement, whether in war or politics, was boasted widely to ensure that everyone knew about it. Ironically, since bragging was considered undignified, most found or paid other people to do it for them.

However, in a society in which so much depends on the light in which others see you, their opinion can not only elevate you but it can also destroy you. News and gossip were the lifeblood of Roman society. Public baths, inns, shop fronts and forums were all centres for conversation. Other media were available for those seeking to deride or extol, including composing ribald songs or scrawling graffiti on the nearest walls. Even actors at the theatres regularly praised or ridiculed public figures.

THE VIRTUES (GENERA BONITATIS)

There were a great many different virtues thought to be important by the citizens of Rome. Some were more dutifully followed than others but the following are those held in greatest regard:

"Marius said, 'I learned from my father and other righteous men that elegance is proper to women but toil to men, that all virtuous men and women ought to have more fame than riches, and that arms, not furniture, confer honour'"

Sallust - Jugurtha

Anguis in herba – A snake in the grass (Virgil)

HONOURABLE PROFESSIONS

In Roman eyes, the only truly honourable ways of making money were by farming, renting land or earning plunder during war. Highly educated professionals such as architects, teachers or large scale businessmen were considered acceptable. Labourers and entertainers were deemed to be barely better than selling themselves as slaves. However, the most despised careers were the tax collectors and money lenders.

"It is true that it might sometimes be better to try to gain wealth through trade, if it were not so risky, or again, to lend money at interest, if it were as honourable. But our ancestors took the view, and enacted it in a law, that while a thief was compelled to repay double, one who loaned at interest had to repay four times. From this one can judge how much worse than a common thief they considered the fellow citizen who lent at interest. And when they were trying to praise a good man they called him a good farmer and a good tiller of the soil, and the one who received this compliment was thought to have received the highest praise. The trader is an enterprising man, enthusiastic for making money, but, as I said above, the activity is risky and prone to disaster. Moreover, it is from the farmers that the bravest men and keenest soldiers come, and the wealth they make from agriculture is the most blameless of all, the most secure, and the least likely to incur envy, and the men engaged in this pursuit are least likely to be discontented."

Cato - De Re Rustica

Ω **Dignitas** – or dignity, is the idea of self-worth. A Roman should cultivate a sense of personal pride when performing their duties.

Ω **Fides** – faith in the family, the State, patrons, clients and mercantile dealings. It can be thought of as a sense of loyalty. A man with fides is worthy of the public trust.

Ω **Firmitas** – firmness of mind. To be decisive and stick to one's purpose once chosen.

Ω **Frugalitas** – frugality, the ability to be thrifty without appearing miserly; to live simply without ostentation or waste. Flagrant displays of wealth are publicly condemned and often restricted by law.

"The same, too, with the instance of Catus Aelius, who, when consul, after being found by the Aetolian ambassadors taking his morning meal off of common earthenware, refused to receive the silver vessels which they sent him; and, indeed, was never in possession, to the last day of his life, of any silver at all, with the exception of two drinking-cups, which had been presented to him as the reward of his valour, by L. Paulus, his father-in-law, on the conquest of King Perseus."

Pliny the Elder - Naturalis Historia

Ω **Gravitas** – denotes a seriousness of purpose and sense of responsibility. Romans with gravitas fail to be diverted by frivolous acts or trivial circumstances.

Ω **Honestas** – the image that one presents as a respectable member of society, or more specifically, the virtue of acting according to one's rank. To assume airs above one's station is pompous and to lower one's self by crassness is unseemly.

Ω **Industria** – industriousness, quite simply is the dedication towards any form of unremitting hard work, not necessarily just physical labour.

Ω **Patientia** – patience and endurance, to weather adversity and crisis.

Ω **Pietas** – piety is the sense of duty and devotion to one's family, the State and the gods. It demonstrates a willingness to perform an act for the greater good, at the expense of oneself. Family honour is inherently tied to ancestor worship, since the dead are always watching and judging their descendants.

Ω **Prudentia** – prudence, the maintenance of personal discretion.

Ω **Salubritas** – health, cleanliness and a wholesome way of life.

Ω **Severitas** – severity, or strictness, is the enforcement of personal judgement, even though it might pain you emotionally or financially.

Ω **Veritas** – truthfulness and honesty when dealing with others.

Ω **Virtus** – from which we gain the word virtue, possessed a slightly different meaning in Roman times. It basically means 'manliness' and combines strength, courage and self-control.

There were several other virtues that were regarded as double-edged, depending on popular views at the time. If exhorted by a man of great honour or status they can be seen as advantageous quirks. However, they were more often seen as a sign of social

PERSONALITY TRAITS

Since some ancient Roman values are somewhat different to modern day ones, using them as a guideline can be an invaluable aid to portray a character realistically.

As an optional rule, characters can choose one or more of these traits as some of their Passions (page 132). The following table lists each Roman virtue along with its opposite aspect. Games Masters can also use this table to randomly generate key personality traits for non-player characters, in which case roll a d20 the find the base virtue, then a d6 to determine whether the passion is positive (1-3) or negative (4-6).

d20	Virtue	Positive	Negative
1	*Clementia*	Clemens	Immitis
2	*Comitas*	Comis	Taetricus
3	*Dignitas*	Dignus	Indignus
4	*Fides*	Fidelis	Perfidus
5	*Firmitas*	Firmus	Infirmus
6	*Frugalitas*	Temperans	Prodigus
7	*Gravitas*	Gravis	Levis
8	*Honestas*	Honestus	Infamis
9	*Humanitas*	Urbanus	Infacetus
10	*Industria*	Industrius	Ignavus
11	*Misericordia*	Misericors	Durus
12	*Patientia*	Patiens	Impatiens
13	*Pietas*	Pious	Impius
14	*Prudentia*	Prudens	Imprudens
15	*Salubritas*	Sanus	Morbosus
16	*Severitas*	Severus	Remissus
17	*Veritas*	Verus	Falsus
18	*Virtus*	Fortis	Enervatus
19-20	Choose or Roll Again		

Aquila non captat muscas – The eagle doesn't capture flies

degeneracy, the antithesis of the originally harsh and stern Roman way of life.

Ω **Clementia** – clemency, the virtue of mercy and forgiveness. This was deemed a sign of weakness by the majority of republican Romans, who held that a proven enemy should be crushed or killed in order to prevent them from turning upon you again; a case proven in point by the eventual assassination of Caius Julius Caesar, who was famed for his clementia.

Ω **Comitas** – courtesy, openness, friendliness and good humour. Comitas could sometimes be seen as improper, undermining a person's Honestas and Gravitas, or making them vulnerable to those who would abuse their friendship. Many Romans in the early Republic are dour by nature.

Ω **Humanitas** – humanity, or more precisely, learning and culture. Although favoured as a virtue towards the end of the republican period, humanitas was originally regarded as an effeminate corruption introduced by the Greeks, a threat to the austere, simple life of the Roman gentiles. Over time however, the advantages of a broader education and imported foreign culture changed attitudes.

Ω **Misericordia** – is a combination of pity and compassion towards one's fellow human beings. This was also regarded as a moral weakness in the turbulent times leading up to the fall of republic. Compassion for your fellow men was an insidious danger in a society so heavily reliant upon slavery, and had no place in either the politics of the forum, or amongst the desperately poor of the streets.

"I have nothing more to write to you about, and I am actually rather disturbed as I write. The reason is that the handsome boy Sositheus, my lector, has died, and this has moved me more than the death of a slave seems to be supposed to do. I hope you will write to me often."

Cicero - Letters to Atticus

Many other virtues, albeit of lesser importance were also practiced.

SUICIDE (SUICIDIUM)

Roman citizens of high birth valued honour more than life itself. Not only was it the basis of their political careers and social circles, more importantly their acts also reflected upon their families. A disgraced Roman was left with few choices, namely exile or suicide.

Suicide was the socially accepted way of dealing with dishonour. Although it did little to cleanse the reputation of the discredited citizen, it did however redeem the damage done to the family's name, allowing other relations to continue their lives without ostracism.

Such was the value placed on personal honour that many high ranking Romans were destroyed by having false accusations placed against them; an event which occurred ever more regularly towards the end of the Republic. Many Romans would rather commit suicide than legally disprove such slander in court, which never totally obliterated the stains left by such allegations.

The best method for a Roman man to commit suicide was by falling upon his own sword, although slitting the wrists was an acceptable alternative for those lacking such weapons (or experience in their use). The latter was utilised more often by female Romans. Poisons were more often used by non-Romans and were considered effeminate in contrast.

GOVERNMENT AND POLITICS (RESPUBLICA)

Rome's form of government was subtly unique in the classical world. Starting from the traditional monarchy and progressing to an elected government, it grew and evolved from the constant political struggle between the oligarchic nobility and the common people. This in turn led to the development of the Roman passion for political affairs.

"For who is so worthless or indolent as not to wish to know by what means and under what system of polity the Romans in less than fifty-three years have succeeded in subjecting nearly the whole inhabited world to their sole government – a thing unique in history?"

Polybius - Histories

THE EVOLUTION OF ROMAN GOVERNMENT

Before the creation of the great city in 753 BC, the site of Rome was occupied by several independent villages that were either self-governed or under the authority of Alba Longa, the closest city state. Once Rome was founded, it was initially controlled by a succession of kings. With the first sovereign also came the first Senate, a 100 fathers chosen to offer their wisdom and advice to the king. The descendants of the 100 fathers became the patricians. The rest of the populace were divided up into three tribes, the Ramnes, Tities, and Luceres, each of which were further subdivided into 10 smaller units called Curiae. The Curiae formed the basis of an early form of assembly (Comitia Curiata) and were also used to raise men for military service.

Each king ruled autocratically but was himself chosen by popular support. The monarchy was not inherited and potential candidates selected by the Senate had to be vetted by the gods. This essential test was performed by priestly diviners (augures) who looked for favourable religious signs (auspices). Only then was a king inaugurated, after which his position was confirmed by the vote of the Comitia Curiata.

The king had power over all aspects of life; military, judicial, political and religious. This authority was called Imperium and was considered a divine right. Although the Senate could only advise the king, the fathers were considered to possess auctoritas, a religious prestige which was used to ratify issues raised by the Comitia Curiata.

When the king died, power was passed to the Senate, one of whom was raised to the position of Interrex (literally meaning 'between kings'). Each Interrex held the reins of power for only five days before passing on the office to the next senator. This continued until a new monarch could be found. It was the Senate who scrutinised the next king and nominated him via the current Interrex.

By the end of the regal period of Rome's history, the kings had subverted the power of the Senate and grasped power, ignoring the requirements of the auspices and the vote of the Comitia Curiata. The last king of Rome even went so far as to ignore the advice of the Senate and executed its more important members.

In 509 BC the final king was overthrown for his despotic acts, and was replaced by a Republican government. After this time the very idea of kingship (regnum) was vile and members of the ruling oligarchy were required to swear an oath to "Never allow any man to be king in Rome and to legislate against any who would aspire to it". These backlashes against monarchy led to a great deal of distrust between the ruling 'noble' families who disliked the thought that one of their peers would elevate themselves above the others, by currying support from the lower classes. Thus the nobility began not only to fear those who would be king but also the plebeians who could place one above them.

The new government took the form of a collegiate magistracy. Two men held the yearlong office of Consul (which was originally named Prætor) and were forbidden to be re-elected for consecutive terms. The candidate was required to be accepted by the Comitia Curiata as the kings had before them. In return the consuls held the power of Imperium, but were required to alternate the authority on a daily basis. If a dispute formed between the two, then the negative view should prevail. The Senate remained an advisory body but held great sway over the consuls, since most of the influential members had held the office themselves. Soon it was the Senate who governed Rome and the consuls were its executive officers.

In 500 BC a new office was formed, that of Dictatorship. This was instituted so that in times of emergency a dictator could be elected by the consuls and had absolute authority over the State. His wishes could not be appealed and it was forbidden to hamper his acts. However, a dictatorship had a duration of only six months, which was considered sufficient to handle any disaster.

After this, new magisterial positions were formed to assist the consuls with their work. All of the new offices required popular election. First came the Quæstors in 447 BC, closely followed by the Censors in 443 BC.

Despite the sophistication of the early republican government, its aim was not to rule efficiently but rather to prevent a return to autocracy. Indeed, the first 50 years of the Republic was rife with turmoil and chaos whilst powerful individuals, supported by small armies of clients, competed to fill the power vacuum that had been left behind with the fall of centralised authority.

Patrician senators controlled most aspects of the State and held a virtual monopoly over the magisterial offices. This disproportionate balance of power started the struggle between the order of the patricians and the plebeians. In 494 BC, the plebeians, who accounted for approximately 90% of the populace, threatened to leave Rome and start their own State, seeking protection from the capricious and unjust acts of the Senate and consuls. The Senate acquiesced, allowing the plebeians to form a political organisation of their own, the Assembly of Tribes (Concilium Plebis) and choose their own officials, the Tribunes.

Originally there were but two tribunes in mimicry of the consulships but in 450 BC this number increased to 10. The plebeians swore an oath to protect their tribunes, making them sacrosanct (sacrosanctitas) – any person who harmed a tribune faced being killed by the plebeians; a direct warning to the patricians to leave their representatives alone.

Although the tribunes had no right of Imperium, they possessed the power of potestas, which effectively enabled them to act as if they were magistrates and enforce their will by coercion (coercitio). Anybody interfering in the tribune's duties was subject to capital punishment, up to and including death. Later on they gained the power of intercession (ius intercessio) to veto magisterial acts or proposals, relying on their inviolate status to protect them against the State. The tribunes could only be elected by the Concilium Plebis and were required to be members of the plebeian class. Also their authority only existed within the city of Rome itself.

The tribunes won several important concessions from the Senate. Firstly in 450 BC, the civic laws of the Roman State were codified and published, granting the plebeians equal rights of citizenship. However it also introduced a new law forbidding marriage between patricians and plebeians. But in 445 BC, the tribunes repealed this law in the Lex Canuleia. This was important as it allowed for social mobility for those wealthy enough and also permitted plebeians to hold magisterial office.

The next political triumph won by the tribunes was in 365 BC which demanded that one consulship each year must be held by a plebeian. This act also created the new magisterial office of Prætor, a kind of assistant-consul, which initially could only be held by a patrician, to make up for the loss of one consulship.

Finally, in 287 BC, a law was passed that made the decisions of the Concilium Plebis binding on the whole state without action by any other body (the Lex Hortensia).

Towards the later days of the Republic after a series of successful conquests of foreign provinces, the freedom granted by the Lex Canuleia had the effect of expanding the senatorial class in numbers. The wars had brought vast wealth into Rome but at the same time the many thousands of men who fought in the legions (at that time only land owners could join the army) lost their farms to debt whilst they were forced to serve in years-long campaigns overseas.

This led to a crisis within the republic, the senatorial classes selfishly wishing to consolidate their position and power, leaving the plebeians who were now divorced from the land desperately selling their voting allegiance to the highest bidder.

By 133 BC the situation resulted in the establishment of two factions in the Senate, the Optimates 'the better people' whose primary interest lay in accumulating wealth and maintaining the status quo, and the Populares, the defenders of the depressed plebeians who wanted publicly owned land redistributed amongst the poor along with reforms of the magisterial voting system. These factions were not political parties but simply fluid groupings of individuals who shared the same opinion on a specific matter.

"There have always been in this state two classes of men who have worked hard to participate in public life, and to conduct themselves more successfully in it: one class wished to be held to be, and to be, populares, the other optimates. Those who wished their actions and words to be pleasing to the mass of people were the populares; those who conducted themselves so that their policies were approved by all the best people were the optimates."

Cicero - Pro Sestius

Although fewer in number, the Optimates maintained a stranglehold on political power; in the following decade two highly popular tribunes (the Gracchi brothers) were murdered by the Senate, which feared both the reforms that had been passed into law by these popular men and the threat of their planned future legislation.

The last century of the Republic maintained the oligarchic political structure but became increasing unstable, with many magistrates twisting the basic rules of appointment and re-election. Eventually a third political body came into being, in the form of the army who were inclined to offer their loyalties to their military leaders. The greed and personal ambition of both senators and plebeians resulted in a succession of civil wars, unconstitutional dictators and civic unrest. The aftermath was ironically a return to monarchic rule, under the first of the Roman Emperors, Imperator Caesar Augustus.

THE STRUCTURE OF REPUBLICAN GOVERNMENT

Roman political power is divided between the assemblies, the Senate and the magistrates. Each of these had a fundamental aspect to play in preserving a balance of power and preventing an autocracy from dominating the State.

POLITICAL PRESENCE

A critical aspect of Roman government is that anybody who wished to vote, present a decree for legislation or enforce their magisterial authority must be present in person. A Roman could not do anything by proxy. This fundamental requirement was abused in later years when magistrates were prevented from attending comitia, courts or the Senate by the simple expedient of physically blocking their progress to the meeting or intimidating them from leaving their own homes. Even if they did arrive at the place required for speaking, they could be shouted down or discommoded by crowds of partisans...

"As he finished his speech [which had been delivered with composure]... Clodius got up. There was such shouting at him from our side (it was nice to return the favor.) that he was able to keep neither wits nor speech nor countenance about him. This took place from noon, when Pompey had just stopped speaking, right until two, when all kinds of curses and in the end the most obscene ditties were being said about Clodius and his sister Clodia. He, furious and blanched, kept asking his supporters during the shouting who it was who were starving the plebeians... At about three o'clock, as though responding to a signal, Clodius' people began to spit at our side. Tempers flared. They started to try to shove us out of there. Our side charged, and his gang retreated Clodius was kicked off the podium, and at that point even I fled in case something were to happen in the crowd"

Cicero - Ad Quintum Fratrem

THE ASSEMBLIES (COMITIA)

In theory the assemblies were the source of authority in Rome. They elected the magistrates, accepted or rejected laws proposed by the magistrates and reviewed appeals against magisterial decisions. In reality however, their power was eventually undermined or abused by demagogic leaders. The following assemblies existed in Rome, each controlling a different aspect of government.

COMITIA CURIATA

The first assembly formed during the time of kings, it was presided over by the Pontifex Maximus. In its early days it would confer Imperium over military, civil and judicial matters by confirming the election of an inaugurated king and after the beginning of the Republic, the consuls. By the mid-Republic these civic duties were simply ceremonies performed pro forma.

COMITIA CENTURIATA

Formed from the 193 voting centuries derived from early military class structure, participation in the Comitia Centuriata depended on army service and land ownership. Membership to which class a citizen belonged was decided by personal wealth each census, that ultimately meant the richer citizens had more power over the assembly, thus biasing its vote. The Comitia Centuriata subsumed the duties of the Comitia Curiata, electing the major magistrates who held Imperium – consuls, prætors and censors; and it also had the power to declare an offensive war. Originally being a military comitia, it met outside the walls of Rome in the Saepta on the Campus Martius (the only area large enough to hold everyone) but was forbidden to convene on holidays (dies nefasti) or days set aside for court meetings (dies fasti).

GOVERNMENTAL PROCEDURE

To get a law passed in the Republic normally involved the following procedure:

1. *A proposed bill is placed before the Senate*
2. *After debate the Senate issues an advisory decree*
3. *The decree is presented to the Comitia Tributa by a tribune*
4. *A vote is taken, each tribe voting as a single block*
5. *If the proposed decree achieves a majority of 18 votes it is passed into law*

However, accepted procedural boundaries began to be undermined in the late Republic, as the tribunes and magistrates began abusing their powers: such as tribunes expelling other tribunes, excessive use of the veto, or circumnavigating the Senate entirely.

This famous example shows the legislative weakness of the Senate and the legal tools available to clever officials…

"[After the Senate, led by Cato, had refused to approve his land bill]. Caesar after this brought no further measures before the Senate in his year of office, but took everything he wanted directly to the people. Even then wishing to win the support of some of the leading men…. he began with his fellow-consul, and asked whether he disapproved of the law's provisions. Bibulus gave no answer except that he would not accept any innovations in his year of office, and Caesar supplicated him, and invited to people to join him in seeking to persuade Bibulus, saying: "You'll have the law, if he is willing". Bibulus shouted in reply that "You'll not have the law this year, even if you all want it", and then left. Bibulus did not give in even then, but after winning the support of three tribunes he kept obstructing the bill. Finally, when no further excuse for delay was open to him, he [as an augur] proclaimed a sacred period for each and every remaining day of the year, during which it would not be lawful for the people to meet in assembly."

Cassius Dio - Roman History

Military Class	No. of Centuries	Minimum Property Qualification
Equites	18	Cavalry horse
Infantry Class 1	80	100,000 asses
Infantry Class 2	20	75,000 asses
Infantry Class 3	20	50,000 asses
Infantry Class 4	20	25,000 asses
Infantry Class 5	30	11,000 asses
Army Engineers	2	11,000 asses
Musicians	2	11,000 asses
Proletarii (head count)	1	Ineligible for the legions

COMITIA TRIBUTA

An assembly that voted by tribes, it met in the Forum Romanum and elected curule ædiles, quæstors and all lower magistrates. It could legislate on all matters related to law and government.

CONCILIUM PLEBIS

Similar to the Comitia Tributa but differed in the fact that only plebeians could vote in it. This assembly elected plebeian ædiles and tribunes. It also could legislate upon anything except the declaration of an offensive war.

"He who orders to assemble not the whole of the people but a certain part, ought to call not a comitia but a concilium… When the voting is carried out according to families, this is the comitia curiata, when it is according to property and age it is the comitia centuriata, when according to regions and neighbourhoods it is the comitia tributa. However, it is forbidden for the comitia centuriata to meet within the city boundary (Pomerium) because the army must be assembled outside the city and it is not lawful for it to be assembled within the city."

Aulus Gellius - Attic Nights

THE SENATE (SENATUS)

The Senate was supposedly the advisory council of the State, which existed to advise and give counsel to the magistrates. In reality, it usurped authority and became the chief governing power of the Republic, despite the fact it actually possessed no power to actually pass legislation in its own right.

At the beginning of the Republic it roughly numbered about 300 men, normally ex-magistrates, who were appointed by the censors. However, during Sulla's reforms he increased membership to 600 and instituted the policy that all ex-magistrates automatically entered its ranks. This remained its de-facto size until a brief period when Julius Caesar increased its numbers to 900. Towards the end of the Republic, entry into the Senate was restricted to only those who'd held a major magistracy.

The powers of the Senate were:

Ω Discussion (and restriction) of new legislation before it was proposed as a decree to the assemblies
Ω Revision of the list of candidates for magisterial office
Ω Suspension of ordinary law in times of emergency (Senatus Consultum Ultimum), i.e. martial law
Ω Control of finances, taxation, and state religion
Ω Management of provinces and foreign affairs

As can be seen, these powers gave the Senate a huge degree of authority.

MAGISTRATES (MAGISTRATUS)

The Roman sense of duty, honour and the achievement of nobility was based on the concept of civic service. This was achieved by holding a magisterial position, a limited number of which were available each year.

Certain magisterial offices could only be achieved by progression through the ladder of previous lesser offices. This gave rise to the name Cursus Honorum (the course of honours), since by the late Republic, admittance to the Senate was restricted to those who had served in a major magistracy… and the ultimate objective of all Roman politicians was to become a senator.

Auri sacra fames - The accursed hunger for gold (Seneca)

No magistrate actually earned a wage. In fact most magisterial positions actually required the magistrate to pay for his own running costs and some were virtually guaranteed to bankrupt even the wealthiest patricians. A magistrate's family usually helped to fund their assignment. Indeed the costs were so high that few magistrates were beyond the temptation of accepting bribes to overlook law infractions or propose new policies in order to help pay for their term in office.

The general guidelines for political appointment ran as follows, however there were many exceptions and the precise regulations continuously changed throughout the span of the Republic.

Ω Each appointment was by popular election

Ω Each political office had a term of one year

Ω After completing an office, a candidate must wait for 2-3 years before attempting election to the next office in the Cursus Honorum

Ω A candidate seeking re-election to the same office must wait at least 10 years

Ω Appointment to the Senate was limited to ex-magistrates who had completed the first step of the Cursus Honorum as quæstor

The progression of the Cursus Honorum was from lowest to highest: quæstor, ædile (although strictly not needed, it was the best way to muster popular support for the next step), prætor and consul. Most senators only ever satisfied the position of quæstor.

The offices were also categorised as Major, Minor, Curule and Extraordinary magistrates.

The major magistracies were the offices of prætor, consul and censor. The minor magistracies were those of quæstor, ædile and tribune.

Curule magistracies were those offices ranked above quæstor, including curule ædiles but not plebeian ædiles. They were entitled to sit on ivory curule stools (sella curulis). The first man in a family to hold a curule magistracy was known as a novus homo ('new man'). Families which held curule offices for three successive generations were considered nobilitas.

Extraordinary magistracies were elected for a specific purpose and were therefore exempt from the normal fixed term of duration.

As a sign of their authority, all magistrates wore the toga prætexta, which possessed a purple stripe. The higher offices also granted the magistrate a small body of lictors – men who served as secretaries, messengers, heralds and personal bodyguards. They were identified by the fasces – a bundle of rods tied with red ribbons, which stood out as a symbol of strength through unity (one rod might break but many together will only bend). When outside the Pomerium (the ancient city boundary), the lictors would add an axe (securis) to the centre of the bundle, indicating the magistrate's authority over life and death. Only a dictator was permitted to bear the full fasces within the city proper.

"When, for the first time, a Dictator was created in Rome, a great fear fell on the people, after they saw the axes borne before him, and consequently they were more careful to obey his orders. For there was not, as in the case of the consuls, each of whom possessed the same authority, any chance of securing the aid of one against the other, nor was there any right of appeal, nor in short was there any safety anywhere except in punctilious obedience."

Livy - Ab Urbe Condita

In general, the higher the office, the greater number of lictors it granted. The prætors had six (only two within the city), consuls had 12 and a dictator had 24.

Unlike modern elections, the magistrates took office at differing times of the year, possibly to smooth any disruption caused by the handing over from old to new. Quæstors took office on December the 5th, tribunes on December the 10th and lastly consuls, prætors, and ædiles on January the 1st (the Roman year started in March – see Months & Dates page 120).

During their term of office, no magistrate could be legally prosecuted, no matter their crime. However, once they stepped down from office, those who had abused their position could be charged with malfeasance. Thus the temptation for abuse was effectively self-regulated, out of fear of reprisals by their peers. However, towards the end of the Republic, post-term legal charges brought by young up-and-coming men (who wished to make a name for themselves) became increasingly common, in part due to the greater excesses inflicted by corrupt governors on their provinces.

CONSULS

The commanders in chief of the Republic, called at first prætors ('leaders') during the very beginning of the Republic but soon after renamed as consuls ('colleagues'), two were elected each year by the Comitia Centuriata. Each had the power to veto any act performed by their colleague and for the majority of the Republic the consuls would also take the field, commanding the legions.

They held full Imperium allowing them to:

Ω Take the auspices

Ω Command the army and navy

Ω Control civil and criminal jurisdiction (eventually ceded to the prætors)

Ω Issue edicts and proclamations

Ω Summon and act as chairmen over the Senate or Assemblies

Their duties included presiding over the Centuriata during ballots. If the ultimate decree was passed by the Senate, then the consuls would grant dictatorial powers to a selected individual during emergencies.

Once Rome began to expand her borders, those who survived their term as consul would be made proconsuls and granted a governorship of a proconsular province, over which he would enjoy absolute authority. The normal trend would then be to milk the province for taxes in an attempt to recover monies spent climbing the Cursus Honorum and perhaps increase the size of their family fortune.

PRÆTORS

Prætors were judges who administered the courts of justice. They numbered six for most of the Republic but the number was eventually raised to eight by Sulla. They too could command armies and ex-prætors would be granted proprætorian provinces to govern just like consuls, which they too generally extorted.

The highest ranked was the Prætor Urbanus, who heard civil cases between citizens. By default he became the chief magistrate when the consuls left the city. The Prætor Peregrinus had jurisdiction over cases where one or both parties were foreigners. The remaining prætors presided over the permanent courts and heard criminal cases. The allocation of which prætorial assignments were received by the elected magistrates was made by drawn lot after their election.

During their terms in office, the prætors created forms of procedure and ruling, which was often included into Roman civil and criminal law.

ÆDILES

These magistrates supervised and maintained the public places of the city – managing streets, baths, sewers, market places, and temples. They were also in charge of the grain supply and the public games.

Each year four ædiles were elected: two Plebeian Ædiles by the Concilium Plebis and two Curule Ædiles by the Comitia Tributa (whom could be either plebeians or patricians). The plebeian ædiles could levy fines on people for infractions against (or in) public places, whereas the curule ædiles could sit in judgement over civil cases involving markets and currency.

Since the stipend from the Senate to complete all of these tasks was laughably small, it cost the ædile a great deal of personal wealth just to complete their basic duties. If however they wished to muster popularity for future election to prætor, they would normally borrow huge amounts of money to put on a spectacular series of games.

QUÆSTORS

The lowest elective office, quæstors were the administrators, bookkeepers and paymasters for the treasury, grain office, and provincial governors.

Of the 20 elected each year, only two remained in Rome, attached to the aerarium – the state treasury in the Temple of Saturn.

TRIBUNES

Although not strictly magistrates themselves, the original purpose of the tribunes was the protection of plebeian political rights against arbitrary magisterial autocracy. 10 were elected each year by the Concilium Plebis and only plebeians could hold the office.

They had the right of intercession over all magistrates by vetoing any of their decisions. Those who refused to obey the veto could be sentenced to capital punishment. Tribunes were considered sacrosanct and could not be harmed for fear of excessively violent reprisals by the plebs.

The tribunes were permitted access to the meetings of the Senate, in order to ensure no laws were made which harmed their wards. As the chief representatives of the Roman plebeians, during their term of office they were forbidden to travel more than a mile from the city walls and the doors to a tribune's house were required to be open to all at all times, day or night, so that supplicants could come to them.

During the late Republic, the office of tribune became gradually more corrupt as they accepted bribes from senators to derail the political manoeuvres of their opponents, till they effectively reduced themselves to merely tools in the hands of wealthy politicians.

MILITARY TRIBUNES

Military tribunes were elected from the young men of senatorial or equestrian rank as assistants to generals. Although they were not true magistrates either, the election to military tribune was usually

---

POLITICAL POWER GAMES

At first glance, the Roman magistracies are a bewildering number of ranks with odd titles and associated responsibilities. However, if a Games Master spends a little time clarifying the politics to their players, a sense of its possibilities becomes apparent.

The Romans were fiercely competitive for political power, initially more for the respect and status it provided than any indirect financial gain it could be milked for. As such, the Cursus Honorum is perfect for political campaigns, since striving for the ultimate honour of being elected censor can be a powerful motive for players.

In politically orientated campaigns, the character skills of 'Status' and 'Politics' are paramount and should be limited by the highest position the character has held on the social ladder of class and office. The following tables represent the maximum value that particular skill can be raised to, according to familial and political rank. These skills reflect not only contacts within society but the influence they user can bring to bear upon others.

Status Value	Social Class	Av. Wealth Rating	Wealth Cap
01-10	Foreigner	Any	Wealthy
11-25	Slave	Destitute	Poor
26-40	Freedman	Poor	Affluent
41-75	Plebeian	Average	Affluent
76-90	Equestrian	Affluent	Wealthy
91-00	Patrician	Wealthy	Wealthy

*Women use the Social Class of their family until married, whereupon they use the Class of their husband

Politics Value	Highest Previously Held Office
01-15	Lesser Official
16-35	Military Tribune
36-55	Quæstor
56-65	Plebeian Ædile
66-75	Curule Ædile
76-85	Prætor / Tribune
86-90	Consul
91-95	Censor
96-00	Dictator

As can be inferred from the tables, once a character initially achieves a particular class or office, their skill is automatically raised to the minimum possible value for that rank.

Since neither the Status nor Politics skill can be raised with normal Improvement Rolls, these skills can only be improved by performing some deed which brings victory or achieves a particular purpose relevant to Rome. Conversely, dishonour can lower the value of the skill to below the minimum value until the character can clear their name or wash away the disgrace by some further achievement. Penalties can also be applied for the source of the character's personal wealth (see Honourable Professions page 12) or bonuses added for the number and quality of the character's clients.

Those Games Masters who wish to allow starting characters freedom to select their own social class (or even hold office), may permit players to spend some of their starting points on purchasing these skills. However, care should be taken to limit or cap the highest possible values allowed.

Aut inveniam viam aut faciam – I will either find a way or I will make one

the first step of a Roman's political career (see The Army during the Mid-Republic page 95)

CENSORS

Censors were originally the magistrates responsible for civic morals and management of public finances. Unlike other magistracies, each pair of censors (usually ex-consuls) were elected by the Comitia Centuriata once every five years and remained in office for 18 months.

Their primary concern was the five-yearly censuses, which assessed the wealth and holdings of each citizen and assigned them to the correct tribes, classes and centuries for the purpose of military service and taxation. They also could expel members of the Senate for incorrect behaviour.

They also granted contracts for tax farming and the construction of public works such as paving streets, building aqueducts and the like. With their ability to elevate or reduce the social class of citizens, they were granted a great deal of respect and only those men deemed incorruptible were permitted to run for this office, which was considered to be the capstone of a political career. However, by the very end of the Republic, the office had lost most of its importance.

"The censors will record the ages, children, slaves, and property value of all citizens. They will undertake the building of temples, roads and aqueducts in the city, and will oversee the records of the public treasury. They will divide the citizens into tribes; they will also divide according to wealth, age, and status. They will enlist young men in the cavalry and infantry. They will control the morals of the people and will not allow anybody guilty of wicked deeds to remain in the Senate..."

Cicero

INTERREX

The interrex was a provisional chief magistrate appointed by the Senate to hold consular elections if one of the consuls died during his term or if civil unrest prevented the normal consular election. Just like their duty during the monarchic period, an interrex served only five days before passing on the responsibility to his appointed successor. This continued until the replacement consul had been elected.

DICTATOR

The Romans understood that their government, although designed to prevent any single man from usurping power over the State, made it vulnerable in times of emergency when decisive action could not be agreed upon. Their solution was the extraordinary office of dictator, a supreme commander appointed by the consuls in times of extreme crisis. He was granted total authority over the entire Republic and not even the tribunes could intercede against his decisions.

Each dictator chose a subordinate called the magister equitum (master of horse) who was his second in command should he perish during the catastrophe. Normally the rank was limited for the period of the crisis or a maximum of six months.

"[After defeating the Aequi and averting a military disaster] Quinctius Cincinnatus resigned on the sixteenth day the dictatorship which had been conferred upon him for six months."

Livy - Ab Urbe Condita

Unlike all other officials, the dictator was unaccountable for his acts during the term of office. He could not be prosecuted in hindsight for performing extreme deeds considered necessary at the time.

LESSER OFFICIALS

A number of lesser officials existed in Rome, overseeing important duties. They were collectively known as the Viginti Sex Viri – the college of 26.

Ω Decemviri Stlitbus Iudicandis – 10 men who debated and passed on questions concerning citizenship to the Senate.

Ω Quattuor Praefecti Capuam Cumas – four judges who served the prætor in Campania, the favourite summer holiday location for Rome's rich.

Ω Triumviri Capitales – a body of three men who served as police magistrates. They were under the authority of the ædiles and charged with maintaining order in the city, arresting criminals and securing evidence against those under indictment.

Ω Triumviri Monetales – three officials who ran the mint, the place where coinage was struck.

Ω Quattuorviri Viis in Urbe Purgandis – four officials who supervised the cleaning of the city streets within Rome's walls.

Ω Duumviri Viis extra Urbem Purgandis – two more officials who administered the cleaning of the streets outside the city.

LAW AND ORDER (IUS)

"There always will be homicides, tyrants, thieves, adulterers, ravishers, sacrilegious, traitors: worse than all these is the ungrateful man, except we consider that all these crimes flow from ingratitude, without which hardly any great wickedness has ever grown to full stature"

Seneca - De Beneficiis

One of the most difficult concepts to grasp about ancient Republican Rome is its lack of any official police force. Civic order was simply maintained by mutual consent and enforced by application of the client-patron relationship. It is somewhat ironic that the modern day evolution of this system has led to the development of families oriented towards crime (i.e. the mafia), rather than the original suppression of it.

With no organised force to prevent felonies, it was effectively up to the man on the street to protect himself. Hired gladiators or slaves were used as bodyguards and sentries over homes and property, and local communities organised themselves into neighbourhood watches to keep out known miscreants. This eventually led to the formation of street gangs, each guarding their own ward and, in time, often charging residents for the protection.

If a Roman fell victim to a crime, he had little recourse, other than taking matters into his own hands, petitioning the gods (see Curse Tablets page 143) or asking his patron for aid. A patron could use his contacts to try to find the person responsible or, if known, politely request recompense from the criminal's own patron. At the street level, such justice was swift, brutal and unofficial. However, if the perpetrator was a wealthier citizen using legal methods to extort or obfuscate, then they would be countered at the law courts.

Thus justice is only available to those who can muster the correct contacts.

LAW ENFORCEMENT (COMPREHENSIO)

Since armed soldiers were forbidden within the city walls, and neither the Praetorian Guard nor the Vigiles existed until their instigation by the first Emperor Augustus, the arrest of criminals was fraught with difficulty. In reality, criminals were only caught by either a throng of civic minded citizens mobbing or besieging the accused in their home, borrowing a gang of tough slaves or clients from a patron to aid a seizure or sending lictors to intimidate the criminal into submission... The respect given to the bearers of the fasces was indoctrinated into all Romans.

"It was a common expression among the Romans, for a person, "to be dragged to the prætor with his neck wrenched"; and we meet with it repeatedly in the writings of Plautus. It would appear that it was customary for the lictors or officers of justice to seize criminals in a peculiar manner, perhaps with a rope, and with the exercise of great violence, whatever their rank."

Pliny the Elder - Naturalis Historia

However, once caught (and possibly restrained), the accused could be brought before a prætor and charged by his accuser. Since legal procedure was in effect a spectator sport for the average Roman, there were always plenty of people willing to help drag an accused man to the courts.

Depending on the social class of the accused and if the case did not require summarily sentencing, then the indicted man was placed under house arrest in the home of a friend who guaranteed his custody or was put in prison to await trial.

Rome possessed only one prison, known as the Tullianum. Normally only the very worst criminals and foreign enemies of the State were incarcerated there. It was reputedly connected to the main sewer, Cloaca Maxima, by a door for the disposal of dead inmates. In Rome, imprisoning was only used to hold people awaiting trial or execution – imprisonment was never used as a punishment in itself.

Bene diagnoscitur, bene curatur – Something diagnosed well can be cured well

"There is a place called the Tullianum, about twelve feet below the surface of the ground. It is enclosed on all sides by walls, and above it is a chamber with a vaulted roof of stone. Neglect, darkness, and stench make it hideous and fearsome to behold."

Sallust - War with Catiline

Roman Laws (Leges)

In the monarchic period, the kings of Rome ruled by ancient codes called the Leges Regiae, a collection of religious ordinances, fashioned and subjectively applied by each king who technically acted as the chief priest of the gods. These rulings continued to be used in the early Republic, guiding the legal decisions of the consuls.

However, plebeian discontent of this arbitrary and often capricious system forced the Senate to codify the laws and a commission was sent to Athens and various Hellenic city states in order to gain inspiration in the matter. The original religious laws (fas) were combined with secular laws (ius) and eventually published as the Twelve Tables in the middle of the 5th Century BC. They contained ordinances on all the three branches of legal rights; civil, criminal and constitutional.

"It is not easy to resist a powerful people, if you allow them no rights, or next to none."

Cicero - The Commonwealth

Roman law was strict and originally orientated towards the protection of property and class privileges. Over the period of the Republic, it oscillated between granting more rights to the plebeian class and protecting the benefits of the patricians and Senate.

Slaves and Trials

A terrible legal precedent existed in the Republic, which declared that evidence given by a slave was not legitimate unless they had been tortured first. Although to the Romans it was obvious that the word of a slave was inherently untrustworthy, such examinations were mandatory and often led to the dreadful injuries, crippling hitherto valuable slaves.

Thus slaves were rarely called upon as material witnesses unless the crime was particularly serious. Indeed, in cases where the defendant was guilty, they ensured the silence of their slaves by having them sent off to be hidden in distant holdings or more ruthless masters could sell them to the galleys or mines where they would probably die before being located.

Note that the necessity of torture only applied to witnesses. If the legal case had been brought forwards by the slave themselves, then they were not tortured but could face a dreadful punishment if the case went against them. In fact many plots against Rome were brought forwards by slaves, who were often rewarded with freedom and sometimes even a little wealth, for their loyalty to the city.

The following chronological list indicates some of the most interesting and important statutes; and gives a rough overview of their purpose.

- Ω 451-448 BC Law of the Twelve Tables
- Ω 449 BC Leges Valeriae Horatiae, granted inviolability to serving tribunes and resolutions (plebiscita) of the Concilium Plebis to be entered into law
- Ω 445 BC Lex Canuleia, legalised marriages between Patricians and Plebeians and permitted plebeians to hold the new office of military tribune, which temporarily replaced the consuls
- Ω 367 BC Lex Liciniae Sextiae, restored the Consulship, reserving one of the two seats for plebeians; and also limited the amount of public land any man might farm
- Ω 313 BC Lex Poetelia, prevented indebted citizens from being sold as slaves to pay off their indentured bond
- Ω 300 BC Lex Ogulnia, admitted Plebeians to the priestly colleges. Lex Valeria, granted the legal right to appeal against any capital sentence passed on a Roman citizen
- Ω 287 BC Lex Hortensia, enforced decisions of the Concilium Plebis to be binding on the whole state, not just the plebeians
- Ω 286 BC Lex Aquilia, provided compensation to the owners of property, including slaves and herd animals, injured as a result of someone's fault
- Ω 218 BC Lex Claudia, prohibited senators from engaging in commerce and owning vessels with the ability to be launched at sea
- Ω 215 BC Lex Oppia, restricted both women's wealth and the display of it
- Ω • 204 BC Lex Cincia, prohibited (magistrates) accepting gifts above a certain amount
- Ω pre 186 BC Lex Plætoria protected young men (minores) from fraud (dolus) by money-lenders, transgressors being subject to criminal prosecution
- Ω 170-150 BC Lex Aebutia, revised legal procedure in court cases
- Ω 169 BC Lex Voconia, prohibited woman from inheriting property to the value of more than 100,000 sesterces
- Ω 146 BC Leges Provinciae, set the constitution and laws for each province
- Ω 131 BC Leges Tabellariae, allowed secret balloting in Rome for the first time
- Ω 90 BC Lex Julia de Civitate Latinus, gave the citizenship to Italians who had not taken up arms against Rome
- Ω 89 BC Leges Corneliae, returned power to the Senate by forcing all new laws to pass through them first
- Ω 70 BC Lex Aurelia, divided jury service between senators and equestrians
- Ω 67 BC Lex Acilia, imposed a fine on those guilty of bribery or corruption, with the additional penalty of exclusion from the Senate and all public offices. Lex Roscia Theatralis, gave the equestrians a special place at the spectacles, namely, the 14 rows of seats behind those of the senators
- Ω 45 BC Lex Julia Municipalis, instituted rules concerning city maintenance and the responsibility of property owners
- Ω 40 BC Lex Falcidia, by which heirs to inheritances could, if burdened by excessive debt, secure a fourth of the property bequeathed them by surrendering the rest

---

Referenda enacted by the popular assemblies (comitiae) were originally called Plebiscites but, after the Lex Hortensia in 287 BC, they became known as Leges and named after the tribunes by whom they were carried – just like those carried by magistrates. For example the Lex Canuleia, Lex Valeria, Lex Aquilia and Lex Oppia were plebiscites named after tribunes, while the Lex Valeria Horatia was named after two consuls, the Lex Publilia and Lex Hortensia were named after dictators and the Lex Aurelia after a prætor.

Another strange form of Roman law was a privilege (privilegium), which gave a temporary command or honour to a single recipient. These did not extend in perpetuity but instead lasted for a specified period of time, such as the Lex Curiata de Imperio, which conferred the right of commanding an army to a dictator, magister equitum, consul or prætor.

Some examples of interesting Roman Laws are:

Ω If one admitted to stealing or killing an animal or slave, he must pay the rightful owner the value of the property. If he denied the action and was found guilty, he would then be required to pay double the value.

Ω If a master of a household is killed by one of his slaves, then ALL the slaves belonging to that family shall be put to death.

Ω A thief caught in the night could be killed, provided the thief had been forewarned by a shout.

Ω One might legally kill to defend oneself.

Ω A father might recover the amount of his loss of prospective profit from his son's services should the son be maimed.

Ω Excessive brutality on the part of a teacher is culpable.

Ω Should one slip while carrying a heavy burden and that burden do harm to another, the 1st party is culpable since he should not have over-burdened himself nor been so negligent as to walk on a slippery surface.

Ω If one dies from a drug administered by another, the administering person is culpable. If the drug is given to the victim to take himself and he dies, he himself is at fault.

Ω If anyone mutilates another's limb, he should suffer the same unless he comes to a friendly understanding with the wounded one.

Ω Arsonists should be killed by fire.

Ω It is illegal for a freedman to claim to be freeborn.

Ω Paterfamilias could put his children and his slaves to death for any act of disobedience or disloyalty.

By the end of the Republic, Roman law was both fascinating and complex. Unfortunately it is not possible to cover it in any great depth but the reconstructed remnants of the Twelve Tables (as known to modern scholars) is reproduced in Appendix III. It is an excellent source for odd laws and plot ideas with which Games Masters can confound their players.

TRIALS (IUDICIA)

"In trials it is always a juror's duty to pursue the truth; the defence advocate's is sometimes to protect his client by means of the plausible, even if it is less true."

Cicero - De Officiis

Only reputable Roman citizens claiming innocence could request a trial. If they admitted guilt or were caught red-handed, then they could be summarily punished.

An odd feature of Roman court cases was the method with which the accused was defended. With the absence of forensic science, the majority of evidence was either questionable documents or eye witness recounts. Of course, both of these could often be less than reliable, which explains why forgery and false witness were considered heinous crimes.

"Our laws of the Twelve Tables, on the contrary – so careful to attach capital punishment to a very few crimes only – have included in this class of capital offences, the offence of composing or publicly reciting verses of libel, slander, and defamation, in order to cast dishonour and infamy on a fellow citizen. And they have decided wisely; for our life and character should, if suspected, be submitted to the sentence of judicial tribunals, and the legal investigations of our magistrates, and not to the whims and fancies of poets."

Cicero - The Commonwealth

Thus the majority of a trial was based on simply waxing lyrical upon the public reputation of those involved. Indeed, most trials turned into mud flinging exercises slandering the opposition with everything from witchcraft to paedophilia, whilst puffing up the honour and standing of their own client; which was why such spectacles were a primary source of public entertainment.

Of course, some cases were sometimes won by sheer overwhelming quantities of first-hand witnesses and noticeable changes in the personal wealth and possessions of the accused. However in the end, many trials were simply won by whoever hired the best orator to defend them, or just bribing the jury – thereby undermining justice by the application of wealth.

The actual procedure of a court case changed greatly from the founding of Rome. Originally all legal judgements resided with the king but, with the advent of the Republic, the responsibility transferred to the consuls. In turn, the increasing burden of their duties (along with the growing population) eventually forced the adoption of prætors to take over the consul's legal obligations.

Initially those cases brought before a court were first judged by the magistrate, who would decide if the plaintiff had a valid case. If so, the magistrate would issue a bill to enact a valid punishment against the defendant, who in turn was be given notice of their forthcoming trial; i.e. the punishment was declared before the trial.

If the case was a capital one (concerning the life or status of a citizen), the defendant could invoke his right of appeal and have the trial held before the Comitia Centuriata (summoned specifically for the hearing) who decided the final outcome and either passed or rejected the bill. If the case only involved a fine, it was tried instead before the Comitia Tributa.

"It is the people, then, who in many cases give verdicts in trials where the offence is punishable by a heavy fine, and especially when the accused have held the highest offices; only they can impose a capital sentence. In relation to such trials, they have a practice which is worthy of praise and record. This allows those on trial on capital charges, when they are in the process of being condemned, the freedom to leave openly, thus imposing voluntary exile upon themselves, if even just one of the tribes that pronounce the verdict has not yet voted."

Polybius

By the time of Sulla, these time consuming methods of trial (for the citizens of the comitia) were superseded by the establishment of standing courts (quaestiones perpetuae), although the archaic system was sometimes revived for special occasions. These were bodies of men who instead of being informally summoned to hear extraordinary cases, were on permanent duty judging cases.

Each of these courts handled specific types of cases and the criminal ones were presided over by those prætors other than the Prætor Urbanus and Prætor Peregrinus who dealt with civil and foreign cases respectively. The criminal courts were:

Ω Extortion (Repetundae)
Ω Bribery (Ambitus)
Ω Embezzlement (Peculatus)
Ω Treason (Maiestas)
Ω Murder and Poisoning (de Sicariis et Veneficis)
Ω Counterfeiting and Fraud (Falsi)

Each court consisted of the presiding magistrate who called for a jury (iudices) to be sworn in to judge the case. The juries were drawn by lot from a standing body (iudices selecti) that were originally mustered from the senatorial class. The precise number of jurors varied from court to court (and over time) but, for example, in extortion cases the number was 50, drawn from a standing body of 450. Both the prosecution and defence had the right to refuse a certain number of proposed jurors for lack of impartiality.

Unfortunately there was inherent bias in the system, since a senatorial jury were likely to find in favour of members of their own class. A law passed by C. Gracchus in 123 BC forced the jurors to be selected from the equestrian order instead. However, this was overturned by Sulla in 80 BC, who returned the privilege of jury service to the senators. Ten years later the Lex Aurelia found a balance between the two, declaring that one third of jurors should be senators and two thirds equestrians.

The magistrate of the trial had no say in the final verdict, he merely controlled proceedings. It was the jury who decided the outcome by writing in a ballot either 'A' (absolvo) for acquittal or 'C' (condemno) for conviction. The majority vote decided the trial.

PUNISHMENT (POENA)

"Then, when the concealed swords were produced from every corner of his lodgings, the matter appeared only too certain and Turnus was thrown into chains. Amidst great excitement a council of the people was at once summoned. The sight of the swords, placed in the midst, aroused such furious resentment that he was condemned, without being heard in his defence, to an unprecedented mode of death. He was thrown into the fountain of Ferentina and drowned by a hurdle weighted with stones being placed over him."

Livy - Ab Urbe Condita

Punishment for crimes in Rome was extremely harsh. It was designed to prevent repetition of serious misdemeanours and strongly followed the concept of 'an eye for an eye', sometimes literally. For example, in the case of a slave who killed their master, all of their fellow slaves in the household were put to death for their act.

However, favouritism was shown in the severity of the punishment according to the class of the guilty party. Whereas a poor plebeian might receive the death penalty, someone from the equestrian or senatorial class might be sentenced to exile instead for the same

crime, or in more extreme cases given a less horrific manner of death (see The Legality of Magic page 139).

One benefit held by Roman citizens was they could not be put to death, flogged, tortured or put in chains by verdict of a court in the provinces. Instead they could petition to be sent to Rome for their trial. Even if found guilty of a capital crime, Roman citizens were immune from death by crucifixion… although considering the other horrific forms of death sentence in existence at the time, suicide was often the best way out.

"Then Tullus said: "Mettius Fufetius. if you could have learnt to keep your word and respect treaties, I would have given you that instruction in your lifetime, but now, since your character is past cure, do at least teach mankind by your punishment to hold those things as sacred which have been outraged by you. As yesterday your interest was divided between the Fidenates and the Romans, so now you shall give up your body to be divided and dismembered." Thereupon two four-horse chariots were brought up, and Mettius was bound at full length to each, the horses were driven in opposite directions, carrying off parts of the body in each chariot, where the limbs had been secured by the cords."

Livy - Ab Urbe Condita

There were few set methods of punishment specific to a particular crime in the history of the Republic; traditions constantly changed. However, a few of the more notable ones were unchaste Vestal Virgins being buried alive, parricides being sewn into a leather sack and thrown into the River Tiber or the sea (sometimes with a dog, a cock, a viper and an ape sharing the sack) or being thrown from the Tarpeian Rock for a multitude of different sins from treason to disloyalty…

"When this affair became known, Marcus was thrust between two hides sewn together and drowned, in order that neither earth nor water nor sun might be defiled by his death; and beginning with him, this punishment has ever since prevailed in the case of parricides."

Cassius Dio - Roman History

The death sentence was given for a large number of crimes – false witness; adultery; forgery; murder; inciting riot; sorcery; arson; carrying weapons (within the Pomerium) with criminal intent; possession, purchase or sale of poison and many others. Most capital punishments normally involved scourging, decapitation, stoning, being beaten to death with sticks, burning alive, thrown to the beasts or in the case of slaves, crucifixion.

Civil punishments were primarily settled with compensatory fines or exile. Conviction of theft or damage inflicted by negligence required damages of double the original value lost. Money-lending (usury) at excessive interest required reimbursement of four times the original amount.

However, some fines could be as large as half, or all, of the guilty man's wealth depending on the extent of the crime. For example, Quintus Servilius Caepio was famously convicted for the negligent loss of his army against the Cimbrians.

"Caepio, who had caused the defeat by his rashness, was convicted; his possessions were confiscated (for the first time since king Tarquinius) and his powers abrogated."

Livy - Periochae

EDUCATION (ERUDITIO)

Up until Rome began involving herself with the policing (and eventual conquest) of the Hellenic nations, Roman children were taught by their parents and extended families; boys by fathers and girls by mothers.

The skills learned were rudimentary. Boys for instance were given a primarily physical education in preparation for military service, learning how to ride, swim and fight. However upon reaching maturity (after puberty), they would receive their toga virilis and also accompany their father on his daily business. In effect they would undertake an apprenticeship, gaining the morals, contacts and social skills necessary for their future profession. The adoption of reading, writing and counting was basic, and only mastered by those who required such skills.

"With regard, then, to the senators and the knights, this is the advice I have to give you, yes, and this also, that while they are still children they should attend the schools, and when they come out of childhood into youth they should turn their minds to horses and arms, and have paid public teachers in each of these departments. In this way from their very boyhood they will have had both instruction and practice in all that they will themselves be required to do on reaching manhood, and will thus prove more serviceable to you for every undertaking."

Cassius Dio – Roman History

Yet the slowly growing numbers of Greek slaves imported, at first from occupation of the city states in southern Italy and then in ever growing numbers from the subjugation of the Hellenic world, had a profound effect on Roman learning.

"For the first time at this period, Rome appears to have become studious of foreign literature. It was no longer a little rivulet, flowing from Greece towards the walls of our city; but an overflowing river of Grecian sciences and arts."

Cicero - The Commonwealth

Many Greek slaves were educated to a far higher degree than their masters and in consideration of this were utilised as teachers of children. Eventually schools opened, at first these were run by Greek freedmen in imitation of Hellenic schools but in time educated

---

KISSING IN ROMAN SOCIETY

It appears in the writings of authors of the period, that public kissing (osculatio) in Roman society was far more common between men, than between the sexes. A kiss to the cheek was a sign of salutation – an indication of equality between friends, companions or respect to an elder; whereas a kiss to the hand placed the kisser in an inferior position, something Romans of the Republic were loath to do. Kissing on the lips was only socially permitted between males and females of the same family.

Roman citizens lacking any trade took up the profession of school-teacher too. Such schools were simply hired shops (tabernae) open to the street where the teacher would hold his classes and the children sit on benches.

"It was a long time before they began to teach for pay, and the first to open an elementary school was Spurius Carvilius, a freedman of the Carvilius"

Plutarch - Roman Questions

Elementary schools (ludi) simply taught reading, writing and basic arithmetic, presumably to a higher standard than that offered by normal parenting but with a bias towards literature. Such schools were often divided by sex but only wealthier families tended to spend money to educate daughters – who tended not to continue their education much beyond puberty, since they were often married off at that age. The richest avoided the necessity of attending school entirely and merely hired private tutors.

Since lessons at schools required money, many of the poorer families in Rome could not afford to educate their children beyond the age of puberty (if at all), whereas in the agrarian regions of the countryside, and less densely populated suburbia, life could be a little easier. Indeed many of the most famous Roman authors were born and raised outside of Rome, gaining their fundamental education in provincial schools.

*"I owe it to my father, who, though poor,
Passed by the village school at his own door,
The school where great tall urchins in a row,
Sons of great tall centurions, used to go,
With slate and satchel on their backs, to pay
Their monthly quota punctual to the day,
And took his boy to Rome, to learn the arts
Which knight or senator to his imparts."*

Horace - Satires

After the age of maturity, schools focussed on teaching Latin and Greek literature and most importantly, rhetoric – the art of public speaking and influence. However, they did not stop there but introduced lessons on music, dance and eventually others which were considered frivolous subjects by more traditional Romans of the mid and late Republic.

"For that there are to this day schools for rhetoricians and, as I have said, for mathematicians and musicians, or, what is more to be wondered at, training schools for the most contemptible vices – the seasoning of food to promote gluttony and the more extravagant serving of courses, and dressers of the head and hair – I have not only heard but have even seen with my own eyes; but of agriculture I know neither self-professed teachers nor pupils."

Columella - De Re Rustica

Most families who could afford to educate their children possessed a paedagogus, a slave whose duty it was to guard his master's children, escort them to school and perhaps give some elementary instruction at home.

During the late Republic a liberal education began to include a period of further learning by sending young men to Hellenic cities to enrol themselves into various schools of philosophy. Such philosophic

---

Boni pastoris est tondere pecus, non deglubere – A good shepherd shears his sheep, he doesn't flay them (Tiberius)

training was considered the epitome of education, although still held lesser status than the more practical arts of rhetoric.

"At Rome I had my schooling, and was taught
Achilles' wrath, and all the woes it brought;
At classic Athens, where I went erelong,
I learnt to draw the line 'twixt right and wrong,
And search for truth, if so she might be seen,
In academic groves of blissful green"

Horace - Satires

MARRIAGE AND WEDDINGS (CONIUGIUM)

Roman marriage was essentially a contractual affair used to link two families more closely together for economic or political advantage. Such marriages were usually arranged when girls were still young, leading to long betrothals (sponsus) lasting many years.

Due to these customs, most young ladies were forced to lead somewhat retiring lives or always be accompanied by a matron who chaperoned their wards to ensure no untoward contact was made with members of the opposite sex. A betrothed girl who engaged in flirtatious behaviour could invalidate long-standing marriage promises, potentially causing the paterfamilias to lose face, pay out a compensatory fine for breaking the contract and perhaps even cause a rift between the two families. Only those who had completed puberty were legally able to marry. Once married however, the wife gained a considerable amount of personal freedom.

There were two forms of marriage. The first was marriage 'by the hand' (in manu), in which the father literally placed control of his daughter into her husband's hand at the time of the wedding. This transferred the father's rights and power to the husband, severing all kinship and transferring her completely into the authority of the new family. Although this prevented the return of the woman to her original family if she was divorced, it conversely allowed her to inherit part of her husband's estate on his death. In manu marriage could be performed as Confarreatio, an elaborate religious ceremony with 10 witnesses, the Flamen Dialis and Pontifex Maximus in attendance; Coemptio, where the wife carried a dowry into the marriage but was ceremoniously bought by her husband in front of at least five witnesses; or Usus which after a year's cohabitation, the woman by default came under her husband's hand.

The second, far less common form was sine manu, meaning that the women retained her connection with her family, remaining under the authority of her original paterfamilias. This prevented the husband from excessive punishment without gaining permission from the head of her family first (which was not necessarily withheld depending on the crime performed by the wife).

Marriages always involved a dowry, normally in the form of income earning farmland, property or businesses, which was negotiated as part of the contract and sized to attract a prospective spouse of the correct social standing. The husband gained full control over the dowry and could do what he liked with it. However, if the marriage ever failed, then the dowry, or its equivalent financial value, was legally required to be returned.

The duties of a wife were to procreate and support her husband's career. Children were all-important to Roman men, not only as a sign of their manliness but also to ensure the family survived so that the ancestors (and they themselves after death) would continue to be provided for in the afterlife. In fact in the designation of wedlock under Roman law was 'marriage concluded for the obtaining of lawful children'.

"Since you know your husband's life and fidelity belong to you, [my wife,] and no other woman presses or threatens your marriage bed, why do you torture yourself foolishly because of servants as though they were mistresses? Love with them is both brief and fleeting."

Martial - Epigrams

Children produced by marriage inherited the social class of the father. However, a father would first have to accept the child, which he did by picking up the baby. Failure to recognise the child in this way condemned it to illegitimacy or to being abandoned as a foundling.

Since most marriages were arranged by the paterfamilias, love was rarely part of the relationship. In fact, overt public displays of affection between husband and wife during the Republic was frowned upon, since it gave the appearance of weakness – something which even famous generals like Pompey and Marc Antony were accused of.

"Cato tells us that it was the usage for the male relatives to give the females a kiss, in order to ascertain whether they smelt of 'temetum'; for it was by that name that wine was then known"

Pliny the Elder - Naturalis Historia

Fidelity in marriage was one sided. Men could openly seek sexual gratification outside the relationship, whereas women were forbidden to do so, presumably since it called into question the patrimony of any children produced.

"If you should catch your wife in adultery, you may with impunity put her to death without a trial; but if you should commit adultery or indecency, she must not presume to lay a finger on you, nor does the law allow it."

Cato - On the Dowry

Despite the dangers however, the pursuit of adulterous affairs (stuprum) became ever more frequent with the erosion of Roman morals towards the end of the Republic.

Divorce was normally initiated by the husband and could only be legitimately claimed on the grounds of adultery, poisoning the husband's children or counterfeiting his keys. However, divorce necessitated the return of the dowry, less some small deductions for the education of any children produced, which without exception remained with the father.

"Friend, I have not much to stay, stop and read it. This tomb, which is not fair, is for a fair woman. Her parents gave her the name Claudia. She loved her husband in her heart. She bore two sons, one of whom she left on earth, the other beneath it. She was pleasant to talk with. She walked with grace. She kept the house. She worked in wool. That is all. You may go."

Anonymous Epitaph

Wedding Ceremonies (Nuptiae)

Weddings were usually held at the home of the bride's father. Other than the witnesses and priest necessary for the ceremony, members of both families, friends, patrons, clients and even business or political associates would be invited. Days not suitable for entering matrimony were the Calends, Nones and Ides of every month, all dies atri and the whole months of May and February (see Months & Dates page 120).

If her family could afford it, the bride would be dressed in yellow slippers (socci), a white tunic with a purple fringe (tunica recta), bound with a belt (cingulum) tied in a ceremonial protective knot (nodus Herculaneus), a yellow dyed hairnet (reticulum) and most importantly a saffron dyed bridal veil (flammeum) (see Dyeing and Cleaning page 39).

"Why do they part the hair of brides with the point of a spear? Does this symbolize the marriage of the first Roman wives by violence with attendant war, or do the wives thus learn, now that they are mated to brave and warlike men, to welcome an unaffected, unfeminine, and simple mode of beautification? …Or does this procedure hint at the manner of their separation, that with steel alone can their marriage be dissolved?"

Plutarch - Roman Questions

She would be accompanied by a matron of honour (pronuba) who had only married once. The ceremony began with a sacrifice of a pig or spelt wheat cakes to Jupiter and the auspices being taken by a priest. The bride consented to the marriage with the formulaic chant of "where you are Gaius, I then am Gaia", then the matron of honour took the right hands of the couple and placed them in each other, indicating the handing over of authority. After which the marriage contract (tabulae nuptiales) was signed by the requisite number of witnesses.

After congratulations from friends and family, and the presentation of gifts, a wedding banquet was given for the guests; that ended with the two families enacting a mock kidnapping in memory of the Rape of the Sabine Women, by stealing the bride away from her mother's arms. She was escorted to her husband's house in a procession, accompanied by three boys, one of whom would lead the way carrying a lighted torch, lit from the bride's hearth. The escorting guests would throw walnuts, along with obscene jokes to aid fertility in the marriage. She herself carried a distaff and spindle which represented her role to weave as a faithful wife and the whole procession would dance and sing on the way, often with musical accompaniment.

The husband ventured ahead in his own procession to reach his home first, singing rude songs (versus fescennini). When the bride reached the house she would smear oil and fat on the door and wind wool around the door posts. Then the groom helped his bride across the threshold (sometimes by carrying) to prevent any ill-fortune if she tripped on entering. Once inside, she would light the hearth with her torch, the charred remnants of which was thrown to the guests for good luck.

"Why do they not allow the bride to cross the threshold of her home herself, but those who are escorting her lift her over? Is it because they carried off by force also the first Roman brides and bore them in, in this manner, and the women did not enter of their own accord? Or do they wish it to appear that it is under constraint and not of their own desire that they enter a dwelling where they are about to lose their virginity?"

Plutarch - Roman Questions

Finally the bride was escorted to the marriage bed set up in the atrium, where the matron of honour helped her disrobe and prepare for the nuptials. In the morning she would dress as a matron in her own right and make sacrifices to the lares and penates of the household (the spirits of the family and of the larder).

It should be noted that it was not actually necessary for the husband to be present at the wedding at all. He could simply send a letter with his part of any verbal exchange.

Death and Funerals (Funus)

Death, as in life, was a family affair. A Roman known to be dying was attended by their relations for exchanges of last wishes and farewells. At the point of death a close family member would catch the final breath with their mouth, before closing the deceased's eyes and taking their ring. Then those others present would loudly call out the person's name (conclamatio) in an expression of sorrow.

After the initial grieving, the dead body would be washed by the women of the household, then anointed with perfumes or oils, embalmed and finally dressed in the deceased's best clothes. A coin was placed under the tongue to pay Charon to ferry their soul across the River Styx to the underworld. The body was then placed in state in the atrium of the house, so that extended family, friends, clients and patrons could pay their respects. The more popular and important the person, the longer the corpse remained on display. However, the oppressive heat of summer often curtailed this period of mourning due to rapid decomposition.

Subsequent to this was the funeral procession (pompa funebris), which in the cases of the poor and children were traditionally performed at night. Conversely, funerals of important persons could be elaborate ceremonial events held during the day and were often announced publicly in advance by heralds.

Wealthy processions were preceded by musicians, followed by torch bearers and professional female mourners (praeficae) who screamed and wailed in grief for the departed. The procession might even include dancers or clowns depending on the impression the family wished to make.

The most important participants were mimes who would wear the wax masks of previously deceased family members and imitate the physical mannerisms of those honoured ancestors (see Ancestor Worship page 108). Each accompanying 'predecessor' wore the clothing and insignia due their rank and awards they had won during their careers, and were borne along on carried couches, or in later days, chariots.

After this came men who bore the figurines of the household gods, in advance of the corpse carried aloft on a bier. At the rear would follow the family, friends and clients of the departed, which could accumulate to a significant crowd. All would wear black or dark clothing, men would cease to shave or cut their hair and covered their heads with their togas, whereas women would leave their hair uncovered and unbound.

If the deceased was a public figure, the funeral procession would stop in the Forum Romanum, where the son, or father, would make a speech lauding the departed. Normally this aspect only applied to dead males of magisterial achievement but a few women were similarly recognised during the Republic.

"He even delivered a funeral oration in his honour, which was so admired by the Romans and won such favour that from that time on, when their great and good men died, encomiums were pronounced upon them by the most distinguished citizens."

Plutarch - Life of Publicola

After this public display, which served to promote the reputation and importance of the deceased's family and ancestors, the procession would travel beyond the city walls where the body would either be buried or cremated; funerals being forbidden within the city. Cremation was the more popular form of disposal in the later Republic.

"The burning of the body after death, among the Romans, is not a very ancient usage; for formerly, they interred it. After it had been ascertained, however, in the foreign wars, that bodies which had been buried were sometimes disinterred, the custom of burning them was adopted. Many families, however, still observed the ancient rites, as, for example, the Cornelian family, no member of which had his body burnt before Sulla, the Dictator; who directed this to be done, because, having previously disinterred the dead body of Caius Marius, he was afraid that others might retaliate on his own."

Pliny the Elder - Naturalis Historia

The poor were generally buried in the great pits on the Esquiline Hill, sometimes after being cremated on a small pyre filling the grave. Wealthier cremations involved larger pyres of sweet smelling woods, onto which was cast incense and oils to honour the departed. Often included were objects the dead person valued in life which would be taken with the soul to the underworld.

"Aviola, a man of consular rank, came to life again when on the funeral pile; but, by reason of the violence of the flames, no assistance could be rendered him, in consequence of which he was burnt alive"

Pliny the Elder - Naturalis Historia

It normally fell to a close family member or friend to light the fire. Attendees would remain at the pyre until it burned down, whereupon it was doused with wine and a relative would collect the remaining bones and place them in an urn; which in turn was inhumed into a monument or family mausoleum in one of the necropolises. After this the attendees were free to depart, or even seek solace in the arms of one of the mourners or busturiae who frequented funerals (see Prostitution page 31).

In later times, most funerals, even those of the poor, were entrusted to undertakers who performed most of the duties whilst the family grieved. The differing employees were the pollinctores who washed, anointed and embalmed the body, vespillones who placed the corpse on the bier and carried it to the grave or pyre and the dissignatores who arranged and directed the funeral procession.

The dead were paid great respect by the remaining family, who would visit the mausoleums during Parentalia each year (see Roman Festivals page 115). Those who violated a sepulchre or dared to remove the bodies or bones were punished by death or condemnation to the mines.

CULTURE

As the city of Rome grew in size and prosperity, the wealthier populace found it less necessary to work so hard, the majority of their labours being taken over by the rising numbers of slaves and impoverished plebians. Of course, it was the higher classes who led the development of, and gave patronage to, many pursuits; but even the plebeians had time on their hands and often money to spend.

LEISURE (OTIUM)

Leisure was helped by the ever increasing number of festival days (dies festi) the Romans introduced into their calendar, each one showing devotion a particular god or celebrating an historical event (see Roman Festivals page 115). The majority of these festivals were holidays (holy days) upon which legal or political business was technically forbidden. Eventually the number of festival days surpassed the number of working days, giving the average Roman a large amount of spare time, once religious observances had been completed.

On top of this, the Roman citizen's workday, although beginning at sunrise, ended very shortly after midday, leaving them the entire afternoon for their own pursuits.

So how did Romans spend their free time?

PERFORMANCE ARTS (ARTES)

Although most Romans loved the performance arts, their actual practice is considered beneath their dignity. A 'proper' Roman would never sing, dance or play a musical instrument in public and, indeed, the learning of such skills was frowned upon. A brief renaissance occurred half way through the Republic when the hiring of Greek dancing and singing masters came into vogue; however, a famed general spoke out in indignation against the social iniquity of such pastimes.

"Hence the picture which Scipio Aemilianus, sane Hellenist and stout Roman, gazed at with astonished eyes and described in the vigorous and uncompromising language suited to a former censor." I was told," he said, "that free-born boys and girls went to a dancing school and moved amidst disreputable professors of the art. I could not bring my mind to believe it; but I was taken to such a school myself, and Good Heavens. What did I see there.

More than fifty boys and girls, one of them, I am ashamed to say, the son of a candidate for office, a boy wearing the golden boss, a lad not less than twelve years of age. He was jingling a pair of castanets and dancing a step which an immodest slave could not dance with decency."

Macrobius – The Saturnalia

After Scipio Aemilianus's denunciation, the Republic experienced a backlash against the perceived effeminacy of Greek culture and the training of such performance arts was abandoned, being replaced by a return to stoic asceticism. Thereafter the profession of musician, actor or dancer were considered despicable jobs. Usually only slaves or foreigners took up the role of performers and, despite occasional famous actors gaining wealth, the majority found it a subsistence form of employment.

"And now let me speak at once of the race which is most dear to our rich men, and which I avoid above all others; no shyness shall stand in my way. I cannot abide, Quirites, a Rome of Greeks; and yet what fraction of our dregs comes from Greece? The Syrian Orontes has long since poured into the Tiber, bringing with it its lingo and its manners, its flutes and its slanting harpstrings; bringing too the timbrels of the breed, and the trulls who are bidden ply their trade at the Circus."

Juvenal – Saturae

Within Rome most public entertainment was free to the masses with no concept of a theatre with paid admittance. Public performances were supervised by state magistrates (the ædiles) but actually sponsored by private individuals. By the end of the republic the two positions were often combined.

Owing to the rather poor quality of Roman light-sources, most public entertainments were presented during the daytime, just after noon during the early Republic but moving to just before noon by the middle Republic.

MUSIC (MUSICA)

Music in republican Rome was prevalent amongst all aspects of everyday life. Musical education was regarded by the elite as decadent and amateur performances were discouraged. Yet public music was performed as part of religious ceremonies, funerals, stage productions, festivals and the games.

"In processions, tightly stretched drums thunder out as they are struck by the hands of her attendants. Curved cymbals clash, and horns threaten with their harsh wailing. And the hollow flute stirs the heart with Phrygian Tune."
Lucretius – description of a procession in honour of Cybele

Music was also enjoyed in homes or taverns, the richest families providing private performances during meals for example. Ambient music was not only accompaniment for the meal itself but also whilst the food was prepared and afterwards during the cordial drinking sessions. Such music was called a symposium.

"We were about halfway through some very elegant hors d'oeuvres when Trimalchio himself was carried in to the sound of orchestra music and placed on a pile of pillows. This spectacle surprised us and made us laugh."
Petronius – The Satyricon

Romans did not place any great artistic value on music but inherited its development, as with most other things, from Greek and Etruscan culture. Although knowledge of music was considered a sign of learning, in reality the profession of all but the most accomplished musician was looked down upon and generally only provided by slaves or plebeians.

Many mosaics show small groups of musicians playing together with combinations of pipes, strings and percussion instruments. At the games or during large festivals, hundreds of musicians sometimes combined to provide lavish musical entertainment. Roman music has a very steady beat and listeners often accompanied the rhythm by stamping or clapping. The melodies were simple and involved following an elaborate series of modes which lended the music different emotional qualities.

"The musical modes differ essentially from one another, and those who hear them are differently affected by each. Some of them make men sad and grave, like the so called Mixolydian; others enfeeble the mind, like the relaxed modes; another, again, produces a moderate or settled temper, which appears to be the peculiar effect of the Dorian; and the Phrygian inspires enthusiasm."
Aristotle – Politics

Roman musical instruments are categorised as either wind, plucked or percussion. Some examples follow.

WIND INSTRUMENTS

Ω Tuba (trumpet) – A long, straight trumpet-like instrument made of bronze. Inherited from the Etruscans, the tuba is primarily used for military signalling but is also used during interludes at gladiatorial contests or large festivals.

Ω Cornu (horn) – A bronze Etruscan instrument, similar to a tuba except that it is curved and sometimes possesses a fancifully decorated flared bell in monstrous or animal shapes. Buccinae are larger versions of Cornu.

Ω Lituus (trumpet) – An Etruscan J-shaped instrument. Its inspiration, visible in its earliest examples, was a simple hollow cane with a cow horn for a bell.

Ω Fistula Obliqua (flute) – A wooden instrument very similar to the modern flute.

Ω Tibia (pipes) – Usually a simple single-reed pipe akin to a clarinet but smaller. Several versions of this instrument exist, including the Phrygian Tibia which has an animal horn mounted on the end to amplify its sound.

Ω Aulos (double oboe) – Another wooden instrument, unusual in the fact that there are two separate double-reed pipes attached together near the mouthpieces. Each hand plays a separate melody on the two halves.

Ω Ascaules (bagpipe) – In all probability the ascaules is in fact an aulos connected to a leather wind bag, allowing the player to sing in accompaniment with the music if desired.

Ω Fistula Panis (pan pipes) – A Greek instrument constructed from multiple hollow reed tubes of increasing lengths, strapped or glued together.

Ω Hydraulus (water powered organ) – Although the Organum was first designed and built by the Greeks in the third century BC, and is mentioned by Cicero in 50 BC, it is not definitively found in Rome until the Imperial period, where its volume was used during games or processions at the amphitheatres. However some Games Masters might wish to include it into their late republic period campaigns.

"If a dear friend is overcome with grief, would you offer him a sturgeon rather than a treatise by Socrates? Would you urge him to listen to a hydraulus playing rather than to Plato discoursing?"
Cicero – Tusculan Orations

PLUCKED INSTRUMENTS

Ω Lyra (lyre) – Another Greek instrument, originally formed from a tortoise shell and possessing seven strings attached to a crossbar. It is plucked using a plectrum. A folk instrument, the lyra was eventually superseded by the kithara.

Ω Kithara (zither) – A larger and heavier version of the lyra, it was formed from a deep wooden sounding box with two extended arms ending in a crossbar, between which ran the strings. The kithara is the most popular instrument of ancient Rome used by later professional musicians.

Ω Trigonum (harp) – A three sided lap harp, which originated from Egypt and the Middle East.

PERCUSSION INSTRUMENTS

Ω Drums – A versatile instrument, drums are used by the military, during hunts to drive prey and even by bee keepers to sooth the inhabitants of their apiaries. Drums come in a multitude of shapes and sizes.

Ω Tympanum (tambourine) – Part drum and part cymbals, a tympanum is played by beating and shaking.

Ω Sistra (rattle) – Made by stringing metal rings across the crossbars of a wooden or bronze frame and attached to a handle.

Ω Crotalum (castanets)

Ω Cymbalum (small bronze cymbals)

Ω Tintinnabulum (bell)

SINGING (CANTUS)

From the time of kings it was common that ballads praising famous men were sung at banquets, each guest singing in turn accompanied by a piper. This tradition was replaced in the early Republic by young boys singing ancient ballads celebrating heroes of former times instead. However, this too fell from favour when singing boys gained an immoral reputation.

"Would that we still had the old ballads of which Cato (the Censor) speaks."

Cicero

By the mid-Republic, just as with the playing of musical instruments, Romans appreciated singing yet did not often practice it themselves. The higher classes never publicly sang, save where it was a necessary part of religious duties, the only situation where it reinforced decorum. Choral singing was rare, occurring only during religious celebrations or as a part of theatrical performances.

"…Flutes and pipes and piccolos sounded a very soothing harmony. An attractive choir of carefully chosen boys, radiant in their white Vestments, followed, singing a hymn which had been composed by a skilful poet, inspired by the Muses, and which explained the processional rites of this important ceremony. Then came the pipe players dedicated to the cult of mighty Serapis. Holding their pipes out to the side, toward their right ears, they played a tune usually heard in a temple, by the god."

Apuleius – The Golden Ass

However singing was often a common pastime amongst foreigners or slaves during manual labour. It also occured in wine bars where inebriation and song seemed to live hand in hand, much to the despair of those living along the streets where groups of drunks passed on the way home.

DANCING (SALTATIO)

Dancing was originally introduced from the Etruscans, its first recorded example being in 364 B.C.E. when Rome was struck by a devastating plague. The inhabitants paid for professional Etruscan dancers to come and placate the gods, whose anger they believed they were suffering. Yet, despite their neighbouring culture's love of dancing, within Rome dance was scrupulously avoided by the higher classes or those imitating polite society, being considered uncouth and undermining gravitas. Indeed, dancing by women was regarded as the first step towards prostitution.

"Generally nobody sane dances, unless very mad."

Cicero

Professional dancers did not seem to exist before the late Republic, save as part of pantomime and other theatre performances. Dancing girls were sometimes used as entertainments at private parties but these dancers were always foreign slaves and usually performed as prostitutes too. Although most citizens forswore dance there were certain situations where dancing was permitted, for example during festivals, at funerals or simply when inebriated.

Religion and dance are irrevocably entwined in Roman culture with many cults performing dance as part of their worship. The Salii were young patrician males who, carrying spears and sacred shields (the ancilia, one of which is said to have fallen from the heavens during King Numa's reign), sang and danced their way through the city.

Other faiths encouraged their worshippers to participate in dance. The lupercalia, was a fertility festival which involved dancing to honour Faunus and dance was a prime part of worshiping other gods such as the Cybele or Bacchus.

"To the Phrygian home of Cybele, to the forest of the goddess, where the Phrygian player sounds a low note on his curving horn, where voice of cymbals clash, where the drums resound, where women wearing ivy wreath toss their heads in ecstasy, with sharp screams performing the holy rites of Our Lady. There the wandering band of Our Lady is forever fleeting"

Catullus – Attis

THEATRE (THEATRUM)

Roman theatre can be divided into several categories, comedies (comoediae), tragedies (tragoediae), farces (mimi) and pantomimes (pantomimi). Both comedies and tragedies were usually transcribed from Greek works by writers such as Livius Andronicus and Gnaeus Naevius, using the native stories, settings, costumes (fabulae palliatae) and masks but performed in Latin. These performances took the form of musical drama and included dance too.

Tragic drama never received much popularity in Rome and by the middle Republican period, only the more effusive comedies, such as those written by Plautus and Terence, gained any favour. However farces and pantomimes, originally short skits used as interludes during breaks between other performances, quickly grew in popularity and by the end of the late Republic had surpassed the traditional comedies. The two most famous actors in the late Republic were Roscius and Aesopus who came to epitomise comedy and tragedy respectively.

Farces (also known as mimes) and pantomimes were beloved by the lower classes since their mimicry, dance and acrobatics required little education to understand. Either form could be serious or satirical. If serious, the performance usually leaned towards historical stories or mythology. Satires (saturæ) usually depicted tales of depravity and buffoonery, often insulting those politicians, statesmen and women who were the centre of gossip at the time. Its crass humour eventually grew so indecent that it became offensive to polite society.

Mimes involved several actors, were spoken in nature, foreswore the use of masks and often depicted literal enactments of sex and violence. Pantomimes on the other hand were performed by a masked solo dancer who did not speak and was accompanied only by music and occasionally, a chorus.

Most plays were free public entertainments, usually held as part of religious games (ludi). The actors were exclusively men, either slaves or foreigners, since the Roman sense of propriety forbade public performance in such a demeaning environment. Indeed, one member of the equestrian order was demoted to plebeian status for indecency after performing on the stage at the request of Julius Caesar. Although reinstated to equestrian rank, he never recovered his status in the eyes of his fellow citizens.

The number of performers (histriones) in an acting troop (grex) was kept to a minimum, primarily due to cost. The actors used wigs and robes to differentiate between their various roles. This led to a convention of assigning explicit colours to specific characters. For example, black wigs for young men, purple robes for rich men, grey wigs or white robes for old men and red wigs for slaves. Men playing the part of women wore yellow robes and used cosmetics to disguise their faces. This colour coding had the added benefit of aiding comprehension since audiences were excessively noisy, a rough confusion of pushing, booing and shouted insults. They became so rowdy that members of the aristocracy withdrew their attendance, which helped lead to a general over-simplification of plays for the uncouth crowds.

Up to the end of the middle Republic, plays were performed in the open, on a specially built wooden platform set at the foot of a hillside or in one of the forums. The audience would lay, sit or stand as desired and often caused overcrowding near the stage, contributing to arguments and tussles in the already noisy environment.

By the 2nd Century BC, the aristocracy benefited from purpose-built, segregated seating closest to the stage, so that they could view the plays without being disturbed by the lower classes. These theatres were dismantled on the orders of the Senate once the scheduled performances were over, probably to recover the cost of the timber involved in its construction, and thereafter it became custom to construct a new theatre for each set of public games.

It was not until 55 BC that the first permanent theatre was built from stone by Gnaeus Pompeius Magnus in the Campus Martius. Able to seat 40,000 spectators, it was still dwarfed by the 100,000 capacity which could fit into the Circus Maximus (see Theatres and Amphitheatres page 54).

POETRY (POETICE)

Of all the performance arts, poetry was held in the highest esteem. Many Romans of high status wrote poetry and it was common to have poetry performed at dinner parties or feasts, usually by one of the guests. Poetry came in several different forms, differentiated by the metre with which they were pronounced. They can be split into the following general definitions.

Epics are narratives concerning heroes and mythology, such as Virgil's Aeneid. They are long and performed with a heavy, serious metre.

Epigrams are short witty poems originally created for funerals and as inscriptions on tombs or shrines. Often satirical, they were also scrawled as part of the ubiquitous graffiti that covered the walls of the city. By the late Republic they became so popular that a well-crafted epigram could be given as a gift for a respected patron or used as published verse for entertainment. Domitius Marsus, Lucan and Martial were considered masters of the style.

Lyrics take their name from being accompanied by a lyre. This form of poetry is performed in the first person, portraying the poet's own feelings and perceptions. Horace wrote much of his works in lyrical form.

Elegies are epigrams specifically concerning love and eroticism. Catullus, Propertius, Tibullus and Ovid were especially known for their elegies.

"I hate and I love. Perhaps you're asking why I do this? I don't know, but I feel it happening, and its torture."

Catullus

Prose lacks a rhythmic metrical structure and is strictly not a form of poetry. However, Roman prose does contain subtle arrhythmic patterns, which tailored it for public oratory and the retelling of history. Thus it is closely associated with more classical poetry and many authors specialised in writing in both styles. Over time the subtleties of such rhetoric eventually displaced poetry as the leading form of entertainment.

THE GAMES (LUDI CIRCENSES)

The Romans' love of chariot racing and gladiatorial combat is covered in The Games chapter, starting on page 75.

PROSTITUTION (MERETRICIA)

"we have courtesans for pleasure, and concubines for the daily service of our bodies, but wives for the production of legitimate offspring and to have reliable guardians of our household property"

Apollodoros – Against Neaira

Prostitution was an inherent part of every Mediterranean culture and Rome was no exception. Indeed, the legendary twin founders of the city, Romulus and Remus were supposedly suckled by the 'she-wolf' (lupa), which at the time was a euphemism for a female prostitute. A brothel (lupanar) is literally translated as 'wolf den'. Prostitution was an accepted part of life, and so commonplace that based upon the 22 establishments located in Pompeii, there was probably at least one official brothel for every 1,000 inhabitants.

Prostitution also occurred under the arches (fornix) of public buildings, the baths (balneae), inns (stabulae), lodging houses (diversoria), the crude huts of slum areas (tuguria), temples (templa) and, perhaps most strange of all, bakery shops (tabernae).

"As time went on, the owners of these turned the public corn mills into pernicious frauds. For, as the mill stones were fixed in places under ground, they set up booths on either side of these chambers and caused harlots to stand for hire in them, so that by these means they deceived very many, -- some that

came for bread, others that hastened thither for the base gratification of their wantonness."

Paulus Diaconus

Lupanaria for soliciting males were often called dove cotes (turturillae) from 'turtur' a euphemism for penis.

Prostitutes were both males and females, with many raised into the trade from abandoned infants (expositi) or being purchased as slaves. Prostitutes were required to register themselves with the ædile responsible for their trade, whereupon they gave their name, age, place of birth, the pseudonym they intended to work under and the price they would charge. They were then entered into the official lists and issued with a licence (licentia stupri).

"for Visitilia, born of a family of prætorian rank, had publicly notified before the ædiles, a permit for fornication..."

Tacitus

Registered prostitutes were called 'meretrices' while the unregistered ones 'prostibulae'. Once registered, a prostitute could never remove their name from the official lists and were forbidden from marrying into respectable families. If an unlicensed prostitute was caught practicing the trade, then they were sometimes fined but most often scourged and, at worst, exiled. However, unregistered courtesans servicing the higher classes often used the influence of their customers to avoid prosecution.

Female prostitutes were forbidden by law from wearing the stola (see Women's Clothing page 40), the normal dress of a free woman, thus emphasising their lack of decency. Nor were they permitted shoes, jewellery, cloth of purple or hair ties (vittae). Instead they were supposed to wear rough togas and sandals, which although respectable for men, had the opposite effect when donned by a woman. Female courtesans ought to have dyed their hair too but the regulations were often ignored. Instead many prostitutes flaunted such rules and wore vividly coloured or patterned togas, or licentious robes of gauze or silk. Sometimes a prostitute might eschew clothing entirely, simply sitting naked outside their place of work.

"You stood with the harlots, you stood decked out to please the public, wearing the costume the pimp had furnished you"

Seneca the Elder – Controversiae

Most prostitution was organised and run from brothels. Lupanaria came in two types, those which were staffed with slaves as the prostitutes and those which rented rooms out to independent whores. The owners of such establishments were known as lupanars and hired male pimps (adductores or leno) and female procurers (conciliatrices or lenae). The profession of pandering (lenocinium) was used to attract and negotiate with potential customers.

Most brothels advertised their location by displaying images of Priapus (a fertility god) or more often his symbol, a phallus carved in wood or stone, above their doors. The size of the carving was often of epic proportions, frequently painted to be more lifelike and accompanied by the inscription 'here dwells happiness' (hic habitat felicita). Such establishments sometimes paraded their courtesans upon balconies (pergulae) overlooking the street.

The better brothels generally comprised of an open courtyard with small cells leading from it. The clientele would wait in the portico with their heads covered (probably to disguise their identity),

THE DANGERS OF PROSTITUTION

Prostitution has many associated hazards. First and foremost is the chance that the prostitute is simply a lure for a waiting gang of ruffians or perhaps that the prostitutes are thieves themselves.

Second is the social stigma associated with visiting a prostitute. Whilst young men are given some leeway for disrespectful conduct in their youth, a politician or person of high status can lose much of their dignitas from being caught in purchased company. A common form of election slander is to be accused of consorting with prostitutes.

Third is the risk of venereal disease (morbus indecens). Roman doctors refused treatment for such infections, considering it an indecency. Women suffering from venereal disease could only pray to Juno and other goddesses for help or visit wise women for herbal medications, despite the fact that they may have legitimately caught such poxes from their husbands.

whilst waiting for their chosen consort to become available. The doorway to each cell would bear a tablet (titulus) advertising the name and price charged by the occupant. Its reverse bore the word 'occupata' and would be turned when the prostitute was engaged within.

Although prostitution was an everyday fact of life, it did attach some degree of social stigma, not only to the courtesan themselves but also to those who utilised their services.

"If there is anyone who holds the opinion that young men should be interdicted from intrigues with the women of the town, he is indeed austere. That, ethically, he is in the right, I cannot deny: but nevertheless, he is at loggerheads not only with the licence of the present age, but even with the habits of our ancestors and what they permitted themselves. For when was this NOT done? When was it rebuked? When found fault with?"

Cicero – Pro Coelio

Prostitution garnered some degree of respectability from the annual flower festival of Floralia, annually celebrated from the time of the monarchy. It was supposedly funded by a famous and successful courtesan, known either as Acca Lorentia or Flora, who bequeathed her immense wealth back to the people in the form of an endowment, the income of which was used to celebrate her birthday and the goddess each year. These festivals primarily involved erotic dancing and were incredibly popular with the populace. Although the more conservative members of the senate occasionally banned such exhibitions, they were always brought back.

"Now how great must that immortality be thought which is attained even by harlots. Flora, having obtained great wealth by this practice, made the people her heir, and left a fixed sum of money, from the annual proceeds of which her birthday might be celebrated by public celebrations, which they called Floralia."

Lactantius – Divinae Institutiones

However, the free availability of courtesans was seen to threaten the very lineage of citizenship, prompting one of the laws of the Twelve Tables (see page 228), the 'Coelebes Prohibito'. This compelled citizens of manly vigour to satisfy their sexual desire in the arms of a lawful wife, thus ensuring the continuance of his family line.

VIVRE SA VIE

There are many different types of prostitutes, categorised according to expense or location of business.

Ω *Aelicariae* – *Bakers' girls, whom entertain those waiting for their grain to be milled or bread to be baked.*

Ω *Amasia* – *A female lover.*

Ω *Amatrix* – *A female lover who takes the part of a male.*

Ω *Ambubiae* – *Singing girls, who were commonly prostitutes.*

Ω *Amica* – *A tribade lover.*

Ω *Blitidae* – *Low class women named for a cheap drink sold in the taverns they frequented.*

Ω *Busturiae* – *'Grave watchers'. Frequenters of cemeteries who cater to the emotionally distraught, sometimes within the tombs themselves. They often hired themselves out as mourners at funerals.*

Ω *Citharistriae* – *Harpists. Like ambubiae, they were almost invariably prostitutes.*

Ω *Copae* – *Bar maids. A bar maid could not be convicted for unlicensed prostitution, since they were by default considered prostitutes.*

Ω *Cymbalistriae* – *Cymbal players. Like most other female musicians and dancers, they were usually prostitutes.*

Ω *Delicatae* – *Kept mistresses of high class, normally unlicensed and expensive. They were considered courtesans rather than prostitutes.*

Ω *Diobolares* – *Two obol girls, named for the price of their services.*

Ω *Dores* – *Prostitutes of great beauty who wore no clothing.*

Ω *Famosae* – *Courtesans who were fallen women from respectable families, usually selling themselves for extra money or using their sex to influence powerful men. Expensive and high classed.*

Ω *Forariae* – *Countryside girls who frequented roadsides to solicit travellers.*

Ω *Gallinae* – *Thieving prostitutes who rob their customers.*

Ω *Lupae* – *She wolves, believed to be so named because they solicited by use of a peculiar wolflike cry to attract custom or from their bestial rapacity during the act.*

Ω *Mimae* – *Mime players. As with other artistic performers, they also acted as prostitutes.*

Ω *Noctiluae* – *Night walkers.*

Ω *Quadrantariae* – *Harlots who from age or disease no longer possessed beauty or charm… the lowest class of prostitute.*

Ω *Saltatrix tonsa* – *Shaved dancing girl.*

Ω *Scorta erratica* – *'Wandering sluts'. Clandestine prostitutes who walked the streets, possibly due to the lack of legitimate registration or a place of business.*

Ω *Scortum* – *As Scorta erratica above.*

SPORTS AND EXERCISE (LUSUS ET EXERCITATIO)

Although the Romans inherited the practice of athletics from the Greeks and Etruscans, their attitude towards sport and training was markedly different. Whereas the Greeks were ferociously competitive, the Romans instead sought the 'recreational, health-promoting and military usefulness' of such activities. While a Greek would throw a javelin for distance, a Roman would instead throw at a target.

"A healthy mind in a healthy body"

Juvenal

Health and physical fitness were an important part of daily life. Whilst most Romans gained plenty of exercise simply walking up and down the hills of the city, it was considered important for both men and women to keep one's body strong and vigorous. Those who failed to maintain their personal fitness were considered to lack self discipline and Romans knew that many disorders of the body and mind were the result of slovenly living.

"A person should put aside some part of the day for the care of his body. He should always make sure that he gets enough exercise especially before a meal."

Celsus

There were several places to exercise oneself in Rome. The most important was the Campus Martius, a flat open area which lay to the west of the city, outside its walls. This was originally the place where the militia trained but over time was used for other entertainments. It was here that the city's young men came to play sports or practice their martial skills (the Campus was originally off-limits to women). Activities included foot racing, jumping, throwing, wrestling, boxing, swimming, riding and sword fighting. After a hard training session, men swam in the Tiber, or relaxed at the baths back in the city.

"No hand-ball, no bladder-ball, no feather-stuffed ball makes you ready for the warm bath, nor the blunted sword-stroke upon the unarmed stump; nor do you stretch forth squared arms besmeared with oil, nor, darting to and fro, snatch the dusty scrimmage-ball, but you run only by the clear Virgin water [Acqua Virgo aqueduct]"

Martial

The gymnasium (palaestra) of the public baths was the other popular option, where all kinds of callisthenics were available, including training with weights and ball games. The palaestra were popular both with more mature men, who could ill afford to spend time at the Campus Martius to train, and women who were forbidden to do so.

"I am living near a bath: sounds are heard on all sides. Just imagine for yourself every conceivable kind of noise that can offend the ear. The men of more sturdy muscle go through their exercises, and swing their hands heavily

weighted with lead; I hear their groans when they strain themselves, or the whistling of laboured breath when they breathe out after having held in... If a ballplayer begins to play and to count his throws, it's all up for the time being."

Seneca

Romans also loved to play ball games (pilares lusiones). Some of these required special fields (palaestrae) or ball-courts (sphaeristae), which were sometimes provided at the baths.

"Over the undressing room is built the ball-court, which is large enough to admit of several different kinds of games being played at once, each with its own circle of spectators."

Pliny

Other ball games simply needed an open space. One record from Roman law implies an incident where a man being shaved outside was killed when a ball struck the barber – suggesting that ball games were played in the very streets of the city, probably much to the irritation of pedestrians and those plying their trades on the narrow avenues.

Other than the ubiquitous games of catch and football (which allowed the ball to be carried and goals were scored by kicking the ball into a barrel), there were other ball games, which included:

Expulsim Ludere

A form of handball akin to the modern game of squash, where the ball is bounced off one wall and struck with the hand (often protected with a glove) when rebounding from the ground. Although handball courts existed at many baths and private villas, the game could be played against any usable wall.

"If a small (pila), they drove it with the hand, armed with a kind of gauntlet, hence called the follis pugillatorius"

Plautus

Trigon

A three player game, Trigon requires each participant to stand at the corner of a triangle. The object of the game is to throw a small, hard ball (also known as a trigon and sometimes made of coloured glass) at another player so that they fail to catch it. Using feints to confuse your opponents was a major part of play and sometimes two balls were used simultaneously. Players could catch the ball in either hand – necessary when playing with two balls and batting the ball back without catching it first was considered skilful. Missing a catch or being struck by the ball was a score for the opponent. A score-keeper (pilicrepus) was used to keep count and ensure that scoring throws were possible of being caught.

"...the person who had the ball seemed to aim at one, but struck another"

Plautus

Harpastum

An ancient version of rugby, harpastum is a team game played on a rectangular field divided in half by a single line. The objective is to keep the ball in your own team's half, preventing the opposing team from seizing it. The actual method of scoring has been lost but the most obvious method would be gaining a point when the ball

had been recaptured from the opponents and successfully carried or passed back into your own half. The ball is not allowed to touch the ground but can be passed or thrown. Physical tackling is allowed but only on the bearer of the ball. If the ball touches the ground or is carried out of bounds then ownership of the ball passes to the team opposite to that which last touched it.

"Harpastum, which used to be called Phaininda, is the game I like most of all. Great are the exertion and fatigue attendant upon contests of ball-playing, and violent twisting and turning of the neck. Hence Antiphanes, 'Damn it, what a pain in the neck I've got.' He describes the game thus: 'He seized the ball and passed it to a team-mate while dodging another and laughing. He pushed it out of the way of another. Another fellow player he raised to his feet. All the while the crowd resounded with shouts of Out of bounds, Too far, Right beside him, Over his head, On the ground, Up in the air, Too short, Pass it back in the scrum.'"

Atheneaus

Pila

The general term Pila (ball game) is often used to describe this specific game. It is played by a number of participants standing in a circle, within which is a single runner. The objective is for the runner to intercept or capture the ball from the surrounding players who toss the ball to one another, somewhat like the English game of 'piggy in the middle'. There are a few rules to make it slightly more interesting: the ball may not be thrown to an immediately adjacent player in the circle and the runner in the middle may physically tackle (catastropha) the recipient of the ball. However, if the ball is passed before the tackle is made, then the runner has to twist away sometimes resulting in a bad fall (ruinosus flexus). If the ball is dropped or dislodged, then the player who loses it replaces the runner in the middle. If the ball is intercepted during mid throw, then the thrower instead must go into the circle.

"Here the illustrious Philomathius resolutely plunged into the ranks of the ball-players. He had been a fine player, but that was when still quite young. Now he was repeatedly pushed by the inside runner from his place in the standing circle, then again, being brought to inside the ring, he failed alike to cut across or to dodge the path of the ball on its course, as it flew close to his face or was flung over his head; and he would often bend low in a flying tackle and then scarcely manage to recover from his staggering swerve. So he was the first to retire from the stress and strain of the game, puffing and blowing in a state of internal inflammation"

Sidonius

Board Games (Aleae)

The Romans played a variety of board games and games of chance. Since most involved wagering, they were called Alea, which means 'gambling'. Playing such games was considered disreputable in Rome and by the late Republic, gambling on board games became so rife that it was banned by law save for during the festival of Saturnalia.

The fine for gambling is four times the amount wagered, so most players attempt to avoid the law by avoiding coins, instead using chips or roundels made from bone, carved with a numeral indicating its potential value, such as I, V, or X. Often these had the name of the owner inscribed on the reverse so that they could be used as a marker for future reimbursement.

TALI (ROLLED KNUCKLEBONES)

Played with actual knucklebones, or elongated dice (tali) which mimic the elongated shape of the bones, which give one of four possible results. The sides were marked with the numerals 1, 3, 4, or 6. Dice could be made from bone, wood, glass, ivory, marble, brass, silver, gold or even gemstones. Played with four bones, the objective of the game is to roll the highest possible value. There are several combinations which gave a better result, listed below in descending superiority;

Ω Venus (6, 4, 3, 1)
Ω Senio (6, X, X, X) A single 6 and any other combination
Ω Vultures (6, 6, 6, 6)
Ω Vultures (4, 4, 4, 4)
Ω Vultures (3, 3, 3, 3)
Ω Dogs (1, 1, 1, 1)
Ω Highest Total

TROPA (THROWN KNUCKLEBONES)

Similar in all ways to the game of Tali but adds an element of skill as the dice must be cast at a distance into the narrow neck of a transparent glass bottle or jar.

TESSERAE (DICE)

Similar to Tali, this game was played with cubic six sided dice. Only two dice were used and presumably the highest roll wins, although many Romans had their own conventions about which rolls mean what.

CALCULI (FIVE IN A ROW)

Called 'Stones' or 'Pebbles' in Latin, this game is similar to Noughts and Crosses but played on an 8x8 board. The objective is to get five pieces in an orthogonal (i.e. vertical or horizontal) or diagonal row. If the board is filled without this happening then the game is a draw.

LATRUNCULI (DRAUGHTS)

Known as 'Robber-Soldiers' or 'Mercenaries', Latrunculi was a very popular game in Rome. The boards are usually 8x8 or 8x12 and each player has a single row of counters along the longest edge. Pieces can only be moved in an orthogonal manner, akin to a rook in modern chess, and the game is won when all the opponent's pieces are captured, or if all his pieces are immobilised by being trapped against the edge of the board or within a ring of enemy counters.

> "The game played with many pieces is a board with spaces disposed among lines: the board is called the 'city' and each piece is called a 'dog'; the pieces are of two colours, and the art of the game consists in taking a piece of one colour by enclosing it between two of the other colour."
>
> Pollux – Onomasticon

DUODECIM SCRIPTA (EARLY BACKGAMMON)

The game of 'Twelve Lines' is an obvious predecessor to backgammon. The board was laid out in two rows of 12 squares and

---

SENTIS SANCTUS, PUNK?

Games Masters who want to add board games into their adventures have two choices. For fun they can play out games for real, using the rules given above. However some players may find this tedious and boring, and so the result of a board game can simply be abstracted to a simple opposed roll between the Gambling skills of the two characters.

Gambling with dice is simply a question of luck, unless the character wishes to cheat. To resolve an honest dice game, every participant simply makes a d100 roll and the highest result wins, although characters may influence the result using Luck Points as normal.

Attempting to cheat requires the player to roll against their Sleight skill to substitute dice or bones.

Ω **Critical** – *As a Success but the switch is undetectable.*
Ω **Success** – *The character may make two rolls in the game and chose the better result.*
Ω **Failure** – *No effect.*
Ω **Fumble** – *The character openly drops the substitute dice, automatically revealing his perfidy.*

Trying to spot cheating requires the observer to make an opposed test of his Perception skill against the cheater's Sleight roll.

---

the objective was to move your 15 counters from the first square on your side, around the board to the opposite (and final) square. Three knucklebones (see Tali, previous) are rolled from a cup and a counter moved a number of spaces according to the face value of each bone. Landing in a square occupied by a single counter belonging to the opponent returned that piece back to his first square. Winning occurred when you had moved all your counters to the final square.

TABULA (BACKGAMMON)

Just like Duodecim Scripta but it used six sided dice instead and added a few more the rules. The widespread popularity of Tabula was the direct reason that several laws against gambling were passed in the late Republic.

FELIX SEX (ADVANCED BACKGAMMON)

Although historically this game was also called Tabula or Duodecim Scripta, it has since been renamed 'Lucky Sixes' for the purpose of distinguishing it from its earlier counterparts. It was similar to Tabula, save that the playing board was three rows of 12 squares.

BATHING (LAVATIO)

Public baths were the centre of social life and Rome had hundreds. They were the place to go to clean, to shave, exercise, relax, exchange gossip, arrange business deals, practice politics, attend the lectures of philosophers – and even to pick up a prostitute.

In the early days of the Republic, Romans were recommended to bathe infrequently on holidays, cleaning themselves otherwise by washing their limbs from bowls of water. By the end of the Republic bathing had become a daily ritual.

"…it is important also that there be such places in which the household may bathe – but only on holidays; for the frequent use of baths is not conducive to physical vigour."

Columella – De Re Rustica

As the influence and wealth of women grew, many baths (balneae) became segregated. Later as baths grew in size and to keep the rooms more spacious, bathhouse owners (balnatores) kept the rooms communal but segregated use on a basis of time, the women getting the less desirable morning slot and men having the afternoon one. Baths were normally only ever open in the hours of daylight, since travelling in Rome after dark was dangerous. Occasionally a bath could be kept open after dark for some special event but it was expensive to illuminate such buildings after dark, requiring hundreds of lamps and pints of oil.

Bathing cost money. The cheapest charged a fee of 1 Quadrans (the smallest possible coin) to enter but most averaged ½ an As (2 Quadrans). Unusually, despite having to attend the baths at a less desirable time, women were also forced to pay double the rate for men. More exclusive baths with luxurious facilities were the preserve of richer patrons and could be prohibitively expensive for any plebeian to regularly enter. Despite the temptation of exclusivity, higher rank Romans preferred to been seen by the plebeian masses and shared baths specifically to raise their public profile and meet clients.

Occasionally, wealthy individuals would purchase sole use of a bathhouse for a period of time (an hour at midday, a day, a week and so forth) and throw it open for anyone to use free of charge. More often than not, this was a method of 'influencing' popular support for future elections, rather than simple philanthropy.

The average Roman spent at least a couple of hours at the baths, generally arriving from the eighth or ninth hour (see Hours of the Day page 120) and leaving before sunset.

First, after paying the entrance fee, you woul go to the changing rooms (apodyteria) and place your clothes in a cubby-hole or niche. If rich, you would leave a slave here to guard your belongings (theft is rife) or, if poor, you could pay an attendant to look after them for you. Since it was uncouth to exercise naked, those intending to visit the exercise ground (palaestra) would strip down to their shorts

or loincloth (subligaculum), if female a breastcloth (strophium or mamillare) too and be rubbed with oil.

"In our ancient laws, young men were prohibited from appearing naked in the public baths – so highly were the principles of modesty esteemed by our ancestors."

Cicero – Commonwealth

Once on the exercise ground you could indulge in some physical training, compete in a sport, play a board game in the shade of the portico, or simply watch other people working up a sweat. Following that you could then swim in the outdoor pool (natatio).

After completing your workout, you would return inside and collect your body slave (capsarius) who was carrying your scraper (strigil), perfumed oils (unguenta) and towel (linteum). You then had him scrape off the post-exercise sweat, oil and dead skin with the strigil and, once relatively clean, head off to the various chambers, each one having a pool of water at a different temperature, which you could move between at your own leisure.

"We see the more prudent among those who are given to this habit have themselves parboiled in hot-baths, from whence they are carried away half dead. Others there are, again, who cannot wait till they have got to the banqueting couch, no, not so much as till they have got their shirt on, but all naked and panting as they are, the instant they leave the bath they seize hold of large vessels filled with wine, to show of, as it were, their mighty powers, and so gulp down the whole of the contents only to vomit them up again the very next moment."

Pliny the Elder – Naturalis Historia

Once nicely relaxed you could seek the services of a masseur (iatralipta), using your perfumed oils to knead your body and then be strigilled clean again.

"Many persons quite pride themselves on enduring the heat of mineral waters for many hours together; a most pernicious practice, however, as they should be used but very little longer than the ordinary bath, after which the bather should be shampooed with cold water, and not leave the bath without being rubbed with oil."

Pliny the Elder – Naturalis Historia

Finally, after several pleasant hours of socialising in the pools with neighbours, friends and business acquaintances, you would be towelled dry, dress in (hopefully fresh) clothes and return home in time for the evening meal. 'Bene lava.'... 'Have a good bath.' was a familiar greeting.

ART (ARS)

Roman art was originally influenced by Etruscan and then Greek culture. But as time passed it slowly developed its own styles and media. Possessing fine art in Rome was both a sign of status and an indication of refinement,but also demonstrated the slow erosion of the austere values of the original Republic.

"As the fortune of the Republic grows better and more blessed every day – now we have already crossed into Greece and Asia and dragged back the treasures of kings stuffed with all the enticements of desire – so I fear all the

Contra vim mortis non est medicamen in hortis – There's no herb against the power of death

more lest those things have taken us captive rather than we them. Trust me; those statues brought from Syracuse are perilous to the city. Already I have heard too many men praising and wondering at the ornaments of Corinth and Athens and laughing at the terra-cotta antefixes of the Roman gods. I prefer the latter, the propitious gods, and so I hope they will be if we leave them in their places."

Cato the Elder

Romans prized many forms of artwork, the primary being sculpture, painting, architecture, mosaics, poetry and literature.

SCULPTURE (STATUARIA)

Sculpture in Republican Rome was initially absorbed from their Etruscan neighbours. Etruscan statuary was heavily biased towards funerary art, temple decoration and votive offerings. Most were crafted from terra-cotta, bronze or alabaster.

The sack of Syracuse in the second Punic War brought into Rome a vast amount of beautiful Hellenic sculpture and a taste for marble. The magnificent artworks soon displaced Etruscan statuary and became in such demand that workshops were created to copy the most popular pieces. This led to the disreputable pillaging of the Greek provinces once they became absorbed into the burgeoning empire.

Rome took the Etruscan and Hellenic skills and developed their own style, slowly changing idealistic classical proportions for down-to-earth ones. Indeed, many busts and statues are quite unflattering in their realism.

Whereas Greek sculpture focussed mainly on mythological subjects, Romans used it for self-aggrandisement. Statues were erected celebrating leaders, victories and the ideas of the state. Eventually this developed into portraiture, i.e. models of the head and features.

Note that all statuary was painted with vibrant colours to make it look realistic and was an inherent part of its artistic value. Statues which were displayed in the open often needed repainting to repair the damage caused by weathering or the droppings of birds.

PAINTING (PICTURA)

Roman painting first rose to prominence in the early Republic, with the decoration of the Temple of Salus by the founder of the patrician Fabii family, from which they gained the cognomen 'Pictor'.

Two primary media used during the Republic stand out. The first are frescoes, where paint is applied to wet wall plaster, leaving it effectively imperishable once the plaster dries. The second is wood (the first documented painting on canvas did not occur until the time of Nero). Wooden paintings looked just like modern ones and were hung on the walls of homes and public buildings. For example, the senate house was hung with many paintings, as were the temples. However, wooden painting diminished in popularity by the end of the Republic.

It is thought that the concept of painting on wood may have come from the decoration of war shields (clypei) and led to the art of painted, rather than sculpted, portraiture.

"So far as I can learn, Appius Claudius, who was consul with P. Servilius, in the Year of the City 259, was the first to dedicate shields in honour of his own family in a sacred or public place. For he placed representations of his ancestors in the Temple of Bellona, and desired that they might be erected in an elevated spot, so as to be seen, and the inscriptions reciting their honours read."

Pliny the Elder – Naturalis Historia

Other types of painting included statues to make them appear lifelike and wax funerary masks for the same purpose. Yet although paintings were highly regarded as art, by the start of the late Republic, the profession of painter was not.

"Next in celebrity were the paintings of the poet Pacuvius, in the Temple of Hercules, situated in the Cattle Market: he was a son of the sister of Ennius, and the fame of the art was enhanced at Rome by the success of the artist on the stage. After this period, the art was no longer practised by men of rank…"

Pliny the Elder – Naturalis Historia

Despite this, the price of individual paintings could reach astronomical proportions. Even foreign paintings were highly regarded.

"For upon the sale of the spoil on that occasion, King Attalus having purchased, at the price of six thousand denarii, a painting of Father Liber by Aristides, Mummius, feeling surprised at the price, and suspecting that there might be some merit in it of which he himself was unaware, in spite of the complaints of Attalus, broke off the bargain, and had the picture placed in the Temple of Ceres; the first instance, I conceive, of a foreign painting being publicly exhibited at Rome."

Pliny the Elder – Naturalis Historia

Roman painting during the Republic comprised of two styles. The earliest portrayed the subject matter, often mythological characters, as if it was composed from marble or masonry. The second, later style was the Roman application of perspective (originally developed by the Greeks in the 5th C.); realistically depicting three dimensional buildings and landscapes. The style was an understandable development when considering the lack of both views and external windows in many Roman homes.

ARCHITECTURE (ARCHITECTURA)

For the majority of the Republican period, Roman architecture matched that of the Etruscans and Greeks; small buildings with only a couple of floors and the column as the primary support of ceilings in larger public buildings. In the late Republic, as the population density of Rome grew to levels previously unseen, the Romans were forced to discover new architectural solutions to their residential problems. Their greatest innovations were those of the arch, the vault and concrete, which led to the construction of buildings and structures previously inconceivable.

The distinctive arch replaced Hellenistic columns and architraves, although colonnades continued to be used for decorative purposes. Brick and concrete rapidly rendered construction using cut stone uneconomic; save for ostentatious public buildings, which continued to use marble for its varied colouring and its ability to be decoratively carved. Roman architecture was not only idiosyncratic due to the prevalence of the arch, but also from the size and colouring of its buildings. (See The City page 47 onwards.)

MOSAICS (EMBLEMATA)

A mosaic is a type of decoration formed from the setting of small coloured pieces of stone or ceramic (tesserae) into the concrete of the floor or walls, to provide an overall image or pattern. Mosaics were brought back from Greece by Sulla during the late Republic, where they had been used to embellish buildings for centuries. They became increasingly popular and thereafter Romans rich enough to afford them installed mosaics almost everywhere.

Different colours could be produced from the materials used to make the tesserae. Reds and browns from ironstone, yellows and lighter browns from limestone and sandstone, blues and blacks from slate and whites from chalk.

By the end of the Republic, mosaics could be purchased at shops where the customer selected his desire from scrolls of standard designs, usually depicting geometric patterns or mythological scenes. Some craftsmen offered their services to design and lay unique patterns but this was a far more costly prospect than the already expensive prices of laying even a basic mosaic.

LITERATURE (LITTERAE)

Within Rome, the written word was an important medium for the exchange of ideas and ideals. It not only was a method of recording knowledge but also a source of artistic entertainment.

Literacy was widespread in Republican Rome, as can be inferred by the vast number of monument and funerary inscriptions, electoral posters and the inescapable amount of graffiti scrawled on walls – inscribed by prostitutes, common labourers and even gladiators. The widespread ability to read eventually led to the establishment of public libraries.

> *"This practice of grouping portraits was first introduced at Rome by Asinius Pollio, who was also the first to establish a public library, and so make the works of genius the property of the public."*
>
> Pliny the Elder – Naturalis Historia

The large number of literate Romans supported a massive publishing industry, utilising slaves to transcribe popular works onto scrolls (scapi) by hand. Scrolls could be made from either papyrus (charta) or parchment (membrana). The trade was so lucrative that Rome sported dedicated booksellers (librarii or bibliopolae), at whose shops one could purchase a scroll off the shelf or request a copy to be made of an existing work. Eventually it became a sign of conspicuous wealth to possess a private library of scrolls… even if you did not actually read them.

The literature of the Republic is notable for its style. Elegant use of language was highly regarded, especially when it came to pronunciation and metre, since during this period all Romans read aloud (written Latin lacks punctuation, which makes it very difficult to comprehend without verbal intonation).

> *"Having obtained ten assistants from the senate, he compelled each knight to render an account of his life, punishing some of those whose conduct was scandalous and degrading others; but the greater part he reprimanded with varying degrees of severity. The mildest form of reprimand was to hand them a pair of tablets publicly, which they were to read in silence on the spot."*
>
> Suetonius – The Life of Augustus

Poetry was the favoured literary form, which was read as much as it was performed. It was the equivalent of the paperback novel, encompassing a huge range of topics, from daily life to mythological tales and from political satire to love. Tragedy and comedy survive mostly in the form of plays. These too were certainly read as well as watched and became widely popular. Histories, including annals, biographies and works on natural history, were less common. Often biased to frame the ancestors of the author's patron in a better light, they were often criticised for their inaccuracies and political leanings. Many authors became rich from sales of their poetry and plays. Although some lost their fortunes, or were exiled due to the public commentary their work contained.

Towards the end of the Republic, the art of rhetoric became increasingly fashionable as entertainment. Eventually it grew to such popularity that speeches and debates were recorded and published as prose. Even the private papers of dead writers were collected to be sold due to the elegance, wit and passion of the author's words.

It is interesting to note that whilst women were barred from other arts, they could still find equality in writing literature. In fact, as the Republic progressed and education was granted to both sexes, it was the women who pursued literature to a greater depth, being barred from studying other subjects which were considered masculine. A Roman man's education did not normally stretch to covering literature beyond that required for rhetoric and military theory. Indeed, most of the greatest Roman male authors were originally citizens of other cities or manumitted foreign slaves.

FASHION (HABITUS)

What you wear in ancient Rome is in effect the public advertisement of your social status. Clothing differentiates your class and the degree of its ostentation designates your standing in that class.

Fashion can be roughly divided into several categories: fabrics, clothing, hair styles, cosmetics and jewellery. Like many other aspects of Roman life, fashion was continuously at war between the principle of asceticism and the desire to demonstrate success via wealth.

> *"You have often heard me complain of the expensive habits of women and often, too, of those of men, not only private citizens but even magistrates, and I have often said that the community suffers from two opposite vices – avarice and luxury – pestilential diseases which have proved the ruin of all great empires."*
>
> Cato the Elder – Speech in defence of the Lex Oppia

FABRICS (TEXTA)

Fabric in the Roman world was an expensive commodity. Fibres must be spun by hand and cloth woven on looms. Originally, all fabric was woven by the women of the household and this tradition continued right up until the end of the Republic. Yet as time passed, women of upper class families passed these tasks to domestic slaves or even began purchasing fabric commercially.

Four types of material were available as thread or cloth.

WOOL (LANA)

At the beginning of the Republic, almost all garments were made of wool. The best wools came from southern Italy, from Calabria,

Apulia and the finest from Tarentum. Wool dyes easily and it is available in a variety of different natural colours; red tinged brown from Canusium, pale yellow from Baetica in Spain, light grey from Mutina and dark grey or black from Pollentia in Liguria.

LINEN (LINUM)

A durable fabric, linen is often coarse and textured like wool. Although flax was grown in Italy, the best linens were imported. Spanish linen (saetabis) has a fine texture; Égyptian linen (byssus) has the highest regard due to its softness and gossamer weave.

"The flax of Egypt, though the least strong of all as a tissue, is that from which the greatest profits are derived… There is no tissue known, that is superior to those made from this thread, either for whiteness, softness, or dressing: the most esteemed vestments worn by the priests of Egypt are made of it."

Pliny the Elder – Naturalis Historia

COTTON (CARBASUS)

Imported from Mesopotamia, it is often woven with linen to form a slightly softer and less expensive fabric (carbasus lina), more suitable for clothing.

SILK (COA VESTIS)

True Asian silk (sericum) was unknown in Rome until the close of the Republic. Instead, 'silk' was imported from the Greek island of Cos. The material was so shear as to be almost transparent, giving rise to the opinion that women who wore it were dissolute. The material was so expensive, that Cos silk cost more than gold.

"Let her be clad in silk some woman of Cos has woven, diaphanous, shot through with golden rays.
Let swarthy slaves attend her, seared by India's heat, stained by the fires of the Sun's low-flying steeds.
Let Earth's far reaches vie to give her splendid hues: Afric crimson, royal-blue of Tyre."

Tibullus – Elegies

Two other types of cloth were known to Republican Rome, that being hair cloth (cilicium) made from goat or camel hair, sometimes used for cloaks and shoes due to its resistance to water and ramie, a nettle fibre, which sometimes substituted for fine linen.

DYEING AND CLEANING (TINCTUS ET FULLONICA)

Romans had access to a very wide range of colours for their fabrics, practically the entire range of the rainbow. However, men normally wore undyed clothing, decorated only with bands of purple if they were entitled. It was the women who wore brightly coloured fabrics.

Unfortunately it was very difficult to fix dyes permanently to textiles, so dye tended to run when it became wet; whether from washing, rain or perspiration. Because of this, garments could normally only be dyed a single hue. Most dyes also faded in sunlight.

"I care not for those golden flounces, or wool twice dipped in Tyrian purple. There are so many other colours that cost less money. Why carry all your fortune on your back? Look at this azure blue like a clear sky when the wind has ceased to herd the rain clouds from the South. Now look, too, at this

golden yellow; 'tis the colour of the ram which once on a time saved Phryxus and Helle from the snares of Ino. That green is called water-green from the colour that it imitates; I could easily imagine that the Nymphs were clothed in such apparel. This hue resembles saffron; it is the colour wherein. Aurora arrays herself when, moist with dew, she yokes her shining coursers to her car. There you will recognise the colour of the myrtle of Paphos; here the purple amethyst, the whitening rose, or the Thracian stork; and here again the colour of thy chestnuts, Amaryllis, or thy almonds, or the colour of that stuff to which wax has given its name. As numerous as the flowers which blow when sluggish Winter hath departed, and when beneath the Spring's soft breath, the vine puts forth its buds, so many and more are the hues that wool receives from all its many dyes."

Ovid – Artis Amatoriae

The most valuable dyes were saffron (crocum) and purple (purpura), both of which were worth many times their weight in gold.

Saffron, came from crocus flowers and was imported from the Greek island of Thera. Yellow Saffron dyed garments (vestes crocatae) were so expensive that it was normally reserved for wedding dresses and the clothing of the Vestal Virgins. Some infamous high-class courtesans also wore saffron robes as a matter of luxurious taste.

"And there are the dealers in flounces and underclothes and bridal veils, in violet dyes and yellow dyes, or muffs, or balsam scented foot-gear; and then the lingerie people drop in on you, along with shoemakers and squatting cobblers and slipper and sandal merchants and dealers in mallow dyes; and the belt makers flock around, and the girdle makers along with 'em. And now you may think you've them all paid off. Then up come weavers and lace men and cabinet-makers – hundreds of 'em – who plant themselves like jailers in your halls and want you to settle up. You bring 'em in and square accounts. "All paid off now, anyway," you may be thinking, when in march the fellows who do the saffron dyeing…"

Plautus – Aulularia

Tyrian Purple (purpura) was the most precious dye, which uniquely did not fade or wash out. It came from two different species of sea snail (Purpura pelagia and Purpura lapillus), the former producing a purple red colour, the latter a purple blue. Thousands of snails were rendered down in lead cauldrons to produce a few pounds of dye.

Purple came in a number of different hues. According to Pliny, these are amethyst (mauve), tyrian (deep purple), hysginian (royal blue) and crimson. Lighter shades were made by using less dye. The exact tint of purple that was in vogue changed throughout the history of the Republic. Because Tyrian purple was indelible, it was the only colour which could be combined with another less permanent dye, allowing cloth to be woven with stripes, or clothes to be decorated with borders.

Dyeing was a lucrative trade but required the use of noxious substances to act as mordants to fix colours into raw fibres. The smell of these compounds was so obscene that dyers were usually exiled to the edge of towns and cities along with tanners. Two of the most effective mordants were alum (alumen) and stale urine.

"…the white liquid alumen being employed for dyeing wool of bright colours"

Pliny the Elder – Naturalis Historia

Laundries (fullonicae) were common throughout Rome since nobody washed their own garments at home. Fullers (fullones) cleaned clothes in tubs of water and urine – which acted as a solvent for dirt, and scrubbed with fuller's earth to scour grease from the fabric.

The value of urine was so great, being used by both laundries and dyers, that it was collected in clay pots at home, in the lavatories (latrinae) of the public baths and even in pots at the fullers' premises. Professional collectors walked up and down the streets crying out and paying for urine. This was not only beneficial for the seller but for their neighbours too since it prevented such fluids from simply being thrown out into the road.

After washing, clothes were hung in the streets outside the doors of the laundry to dry. Undyed clothes would then be draped over pots of sulphur to whiten the fabric. Once dried woollen clothes would be brushed and carded to restore the nap of the fabric.

CLOTHING (VESTIS)

Roman clothing can be separated into two classes; undergarments (indutus) and outer garments (amictus). A Roman wearing only undergarments is considered naked (nudus). Whilst this is fine for bathing or labouring, a citizen or matron should, depending on their sex, wear a chlamys, pallium, laena or toga if presenting themselves in a formal setting.

MEN'S CLOTHING

Men's garb is comprised of the loincloth (subligar), tunic (tunica) and if a citizen, the toga.

Loincloths were either pieces of cotton or linen, wrapped about the loins, or sewn underpants made from soft leather. Not all Roman men wore a loincloth since it was difficult to extract oneself to urinate, if also trying to support a toga at the same time. Of course, this was only acceptable if the lack was disguised by wearing a tunic.

Tunics are made from wool, linen, or cotton. They extend to just above the knee and were sleeveless for the majority of the Republic. Tunics which reached the ankles, or those with sleeves, were known by the late Republic but considered effeminate. Usually two were worn, a figure-fitting under-tunic and a looser over-tunic, but when it was cold, multiple layers were worn. Whilst relaxing at home, tunics were worn without a belt (cingulum).

Male tunics are undyed. However, the tunic of an equestrian (tunica angusticlavia) and that of a senator (tunica laticlavia) are decorated with two narrow bands or stripes (clavi) of purple running from the bottom of the tunic over the shoulder and back down again. The senatorial stripes are distinguished by their greater width.

Togas were large, oval or semicircular pieces of cloth always made of wool. They were worn by being draped about the body, and held in place with the left arm. It usually requires a slave to help don the garment correctly. Because of their size and potential decoration, togas were very expensive.

The toga was forbidden to anyone but citizens. As such, its lack can be used to differentiate slaves and foreigners. It was a badge of respect for a man but the mark of disgrace for a woman, with prostitutes and women convicted of adultery forced to wear it in public (see Prostitution, page 31).

As with tunics, the decoration and colour of a toga was used to determine the social status of the wearer.

- Ω Toga Virilis – An unadorned toga the natural cream colour of undyed wool. Also known as a Toga Pura.
- Ω Toga Praetexta – An off-white toga with a broad purple stripe along its outer edge. Only curule magistrates could wear it.
- Ω Toga Pulla – A dark grey or black toga worn during periods of mourning.
- Ω Toga Candida – A white toga, bleached and artificially whitened by the application of chalk dust. Worn by candidates seeking political office.
- Ω Toga Picta – The fully purple toga embroidered with gold thread, worn by a general celebrating a triumph.
- Ω Trabea – A type of toga which was coloured either wholly purple, it was sacred to the gods and worn by their statues; with purple and white stripes, worn by the early kings of Rome; or with purple and saffron stripes, which was worn by augurs.

A dirty toga was called a sordida and its wearer sordidatus. This was sometimes done deliberately by accused persons at court to elicit sympathy.

WOMEN'S CLOTHING

Women's garb comprises the tunic (tunica interior), the girdle (strophium) or bra (mamillare), an overdress (stola), and shawl (palla).

The tunic (tunica), or chemise, was the first layer worn next to the skin. It had three quarter or full length sleeves and extended down to the knees. Tunics were commonly made of fine linen and sometimes embroidered. If the woman was wealthy enough, it could be of Coan silk. A chemise can be any colour but unless new its brightness was usually faded.

> *"If you want to keep your mistress's love, you must make her think you're dazzled with her charms. If she wears a dress of Tyrian purple, tell her there's nothing like Tyrian purple. If she's wearing a gown of Coan stuff, tell her that there's nothing becomes her so enchantingly."*
>
> *Ovid – Artis Amatoriae*

Made from linen or leather, a girdle was normally worn over the chemise, tied under the breasts to support them; whereas bras were worn under the chemise fastened across the bust to constrain the breasts. A bra was always worn when exercising at the baths.

> *"If you have too full a bust, contain it with a brassière."*
>
> *Ovid – Artis Amatoriae*

The stola is an overdress which denotes the status of matron or married woman. It is worn full length and fastened over the shoulders with broaches. The length of the garment is usually longer than the woman is tall and bloused up over the belt (zona) to form a small pouch overhanging the waist. It is open at the sides above the belt and has sleeves if the chemise is sleeveless. Stolae are coloured too and when worn they are normally a different hue than the chemise to emphasise the contrast of colours.

A palla is a shawl which wraps about the body, in a similar manner to a toga. It is a rectangular section of fabric, usually of wool, although flax or cotton can also be used when it is warm. Outside

the home, it is considered unseemly for a Roman woman not to wear a palla. Palla are sometimes decorated with embroidered, coloured or tasselled borders.

FOOTWEAR (CALCEAMENTA)

Romans wore a variety of different footwear. Shoes and boots were only worn outside and changed for sandals and slippers within the home. Slaves and poorer plebeians often went barefoot instead.

Women's footwear tended to be more colourful and decorated than men's, the level of ornamentation increasing with the wealth of the individual.

Calcei are shoes for wearing outside. They completely encompass the foot and are fastened by straps wrapped about the lower leg. They are considered de rigueur for wearing with the toga. Calceus Senatorius are special shoes reserved for members of the senatorial class and often have built up soles to elevate the wearer's height. Mullei are the same design but coloured red with crescent moon toggles at the ankles. Only patricians are allowed to wear them.

Caligae are the boots of soldiers and labourers. Made from a single-piece upper and a separate inner and outer sole, the latter is heavily hobnailed to increase their lifespan. The upper forms a web of open straps which allow the foot to breathe.

Crepidae are half-shoes with thick soles to which an upper of leather is attached, enclosing the heel and the sides of the foot and are fastened across the instep by straps or bands laced through holes set in the side pieces.

Carbatinae are worn by rustics such as farmers, herders and hunters. They are made from a single piece of untanned leather, unlike shoes which had a separate sole. They take the form of low shoes (gallicae) and calf length boots (cothurni).

Soleae are sandals comprising simply of a sole of leather attached to the foot by a thong between the toes or sometimes ankle thongs too. Sandals are only used for indoor wear. Baxae are slippers made from woven vegetable fibre, instead of leather.

Socci are indoor slippers.

Sculponaeae were wooden or cork soled clogs, used by slaves or the very poor.

HEAD-WEAR AND CLOAKS (TEGUMENTA ET AMICTUS)

Hats were used to ward off the sun from those exposed to it all day, thus they were not used much within the city. Protection from rain could be gained instead by pulling up the hood of a cloak or toga.

Hats were made of felt and come in two types: the conical skull cap (pilleus) worn by farmers and labourers and the broad brimmed hat (causea or petasus) worn by shepherds, travellers or people sitting in the theatre.

Only men wore hats. Women were expected to shield themselves using parasols (umbraculum) instead. As fashion accessories, women also wore veils (vela) and headbands (vittae).

Cloaks were normally made from wool and could be dyed for certain official positions.

Lacernae are short lightweight capes fastened at the shoulder with a broach or buckle. First used by soldiers and plebeians, they were eventually adopted by members of the equestrian and senatorial class towards the end of the Republic. If supplied with a hood, it was named a cucullus instead.

Trabeae and saga are heavy fabric cloaks, worn by soldiers which could double as bedrolls. When dyed purple they are called paludamentum which are worn by generals.

Culpam poena premit comes − Punishment closely follows crime as its companion (Horace)

Paenulae are travelling cloaks designed for harsh climates and resemble a hooded poncho. They are made from wool, leather or even fur.

Abollae are very loose cloaks worn by soldiers or philosophers.

JEWELLERY (ORNAMENTA)

The wearing of jewellery by Roman men was, for the majority of the Republic, considered overt and ostentatious. By law, only a citizen could wear a ring (annulus), originally made of iron. However, as time passed and wealth poured into Rome from her conquests, rings began to be made from more precious metals and included a setting, usually of coloured glass or a precious stone. Signet rings worn by the paterfamilias bore a unique design cut into the stone by a skilled gem-cutter (lapidarius).

> *"The Dictator Sylla, it is said, always made use of a seal which represented the surrender of Jugurtha. Authors inform us also, that the native of Intercatia, whose father challenged Scipio Æmilianus, and was slain by him, was in the habit of using a signet with a representation of this combat engraved upon it; a circumstance which gave rise to the well-known joke of Stilo Præconinus, who naively enquired, what he would have done if Scipio had been the person slain?"*
>
> Pliny the Elder – Naturalis Historia

Boys wore a neck chain that supported a circular shaped locket (bulla) which contained protective amulets. The higher the social class of the boy, the more valuable the materials the bulla and its chain would be made of – sometimes even gold. Boys could also wear small rings carved with the sign of a phallus for good luck.

Women had few restrictions on the jewellery they could wear, save for some sumptuary laws passed during the second Punic war (Lex Oppia), which restricted them to possessing no more than half an ounce of gold.

> *"The wealthy woman says, 'This levelling down is just what I do not tolerate. Why am I not to be admired and looked at for my gold and purple? Why is the poverty of others disguised under this appearance of law so that they may be thought to have possessed, had the law allowed it, what it was quite out of their power to possess?'"*
>
> Cato the Elder – Speech in defence of the Lex Oppia

The Oppian law was eventually repealed under the pressure of wives blocking the streets leading to the Forum Romanum and heckling both their husbands and the city's magistrates for the restoration of a matron's right to ornamentation.

> *"What kind of behaviour is this? Running around in public, blocking streets, and speaking to other women's husbands? Could you not have asked your own husbands the same thing at home? Are you more charming in public with others' husbands than at home with your own? And yet, it is not fitting even at home for you to concern yourselves with what laws are passed or repealed here."*
>
> Cato the Elder – Speech in defence of the Lex Oppia

After this, Roman women were free to vaunt their wealth with a plethora of different items of jewellery. Earrings (inaures), bracelets (armillae), chains (catenae), necklaces (monilia), hairnets, hair pins (acus) and broaches (fibulae)… all kept within her jewellery box (pyxis).

Gold was the most highly prized metal for jewellery, because of its immunity to tarnishing but silver was also very common. Poorer women had to put up with polished brass or copper. Often jewellery was emphasised with gems. Settings incorporated vibrantly coloured glass or stones, the most popular being garnets, cornelian, rock crystal, chalcedony and sardonyix. In lesser pieces, beads were frequently used, made from dyed bone, glass and painted pottery.

The most highly prized precious gems were pearls, emeralds (smaragdi) and adamas. The latter is an unknown crystal of incredible hardness from which we get the word adamant (they were not diamonds, which were actually unknown in the classical world).

> *"These stones are tested upon the anvil, and will resist the blow to such an extent, as to make the iron rebound and the very anvil split asunder. Indeed its hardness is beyond all expression, while at the same time it quite sets fire at defiance and is incapable of being heated; owing to which indomitable powers it is, that it has received the name which it derives from the Greek."*
>
> Pliny the Elder – Naturalis Historia

Female jewellery was often decorated by filigree and granulation, with such motifs as the knot of Herakles, the crown of Isis, Eros and various animal heads. These designs were believed to act as amulets to ward off evil.

Towards the end of the Republic, many matrons vied for status with ever more ostentatious ornaments and precious stones. Even men began collecting such jewels, to either court ladies who are desirous of such things, or simply as a method of showing off.

> *"A collection of precious stones bears the foreign name of "dactyliotheca." The first person who possessed one at Rome was Scaurus, the step-son of Sylla; and, for a long time, there was no other such collection there, until at length Pompeius Magnus consecrated in the Capitol, among other donations, one that had belonged to King Mithridates; and which, as M. Varro and other authors of that period assure us, was greatly superior to that of Scaurus. Following his example, the Dictator Cæsar consecrated six dactyliothecæ in the Temple of Venus Genetrix; and Marcellus, the son of Octavia, presented one to the Temple of the Palatine Apollo."*
>
> Pliny the Elder – Naturalis Historia

HAIR STYLES (COMAE)

Until the 3rd century BC, Roman men allowed their hair and beards to grow as they will. Even after the introduction of barbers, it was not until the start of the late Republic that it became fashionable to be clean shaven and with short-cut hair.

> *"…was the employment of barbers. The Romans, however, were more tardy in the adoption of their services. According to Varro, they were introduced into Italy from Sicily, in the year of Rome 454, having been brought over by P. Titinius Mena: before which time the Romans did not cut the hair. The younger Africanus was the first who adopted the custom of shaving every day."*
>
> Pliny the Elder – Naturalis Historia

Shaving (rasura) was a painful and potentially dangerous experience. Eventually at the end of the Republic shaving with a razor

Cum recte vivis, ne cures verba malorum – If you live properly, don't worry about what the evil ones say (Cato the younger)

(novacula) was briefly displaced by plucking, despite the fact it was considered effeminate.

"He was somewhat overnice in the care of his person, being not only carefully trimmed and shaved, but even having superfluous hair plucked out, as some have charged"

Suetonius – Divus Julius

Roman women also practiced plucking but from the body and eyebrows rather than the chin. Much more effort was invested in hairdressing; although for most of the Republic female hairstyles followed those of their Greek contemporaries. By the late Republic, Roman women began developing their own, increasingly complex fashions, using all manner of devices (pins, hairnets, egg-white gels and curling irons) to hold their locks in exotic coiffures.

"Long features demand that the hair should be simply parted on the forehead. Such was the style of Laodamia. Women with round faces should wear their hair lightly twisted into a knot on the top of the head, leaving the ears exposed. One woman will let her hair fall loose on either shoulder, like Apollo when he holds his dulcet lyre. Another must needs have her hair tied up behind, like Diana when she pursueth the wild beasts in the forests. One delights us with her loose flowing ringlets, another by wearing her hair closely patted down upon her temples. Some women like to adorn their hair with the shell of the Cyllenian tortoise, others to wear it in towering waves. But there are not more acorns on an oak tree, more bees on Hybla, or wild beasts on the mountains, than there are modes of doing a woman's hair, and new ones are invented every day."

Ovid – Artis Amatoriae

Fashions also included bleaching or dyeing hair in varying colours, which often resulted in the treated locks falling out, forcing the women to resort to wigs (capillamenta) to hide their shame.

"I told you to stop using that rinse, and now you've no hair left to tint. Why couldn't you let it be? You've only yourself to blame. You were asking for trouble applying that concoction. But thanks to our German triumph you're quite safe. One of the women prisoners can send you hers."

Ovid – Artis Amatoriae

Whereas men visited barbers, women employed dedicated wardrobe slaves (ornatrices) to dress their hair for them, washing, dyeing, plucking, combing, crimping and styling, and also decorating it with ribbons, false hair pieces,and hair nets.

COSMETICS (MEDICAMENTA)

During the latter half of the Republic, Roman women utilised cosmetics to emphasise, or regain, their beauty.

"Curls, makeup, cosmetics, greasepaint, and teeth you could buy, and with the same money you could have even purchased a new face."

Lucilius – Saturae

Cosmetics came in several varieties: face paints and powders (fuci), which included eye liner, eye shadow and lip stain; moisturising creams, toothpowder (dentifricium) and perfume (unguentum). Cosmetic makers (cosmetae and unguentarii) manufactured their wares by adding exotic materials, often poisonous, to lanolin and olive oils. These would be placed in small ceramic bottles (ampullae cosmianae) or alabaster jars (alabastron).

Ornatrices applied makeup to their mistresses. Traditional makeup used a white powder or paint to lighten the skin, rouge to redden the cheeks and lip gloss to redden the lips. Eyebrows and eyelashes were blackened and coloured eye shadow applied. The application would be examined in small polished metal mirrors (specula), those of pure silver being the best.

Roman cosmetics had the unfortunate property of running when the wearer perspired or got wet.

"The art that adorns you should be unsuspected. Who but would feel a sensation of disgust if the paint on your face were so thick that it oozed down on to your breasts? What words could describe the sickening smell of the æsypum although it comes from Athens; that oily juice which they extract from the fleece of sheep. I should also disapprove of your using stag's marrow, or of your cleaning your teeth when anyone is there to see. I know all that would enhance your charms, but the sight would be none the less disagreeable."

Ovid – Artis Amatoriae

Women often used perfumes to scent the water in which they washed. However, they were not only used for personal adornment but could also be rubbed on statues or used to retard inebriation at banquets. New perfumes were always becoming fashionable.

"The perfume of iris, from Corinth, was long held in the highest esteem, till that of Cyzicus came into fashion. It was the same, too, with the perfume of roses, from Phaselis, the repute of which was afterwards eclipsed by those of Neapolis, Capua, and Præneste. Oil of saffron, from Soli in Cilicia, was for a long time held in repute beyond any other, and then that from Rhodes; after which perfume of oenanthe, from Cyprus, came into fashion, and then that of Egypt was preferred. At a later period that of Adramytteum came into vogue, and then was supplanted by unguent of marjoram, from Cos, which in its turn was superseded by quince blossom unguent from the same place. As to perfume of Cyprus, that from the island of Cyprus was at first preferred, and then that of Egypt; when all on a sudden the unguents of Mendes and Metopium rose into esteem."

Pliny the Elder – Naturalis Historia

FOOD AND DRINK (ALIMENTA)

Nothing like the fabled excesses of Imperial Rome, food and drink during the Republic was basic and down to earth. The majority of the populace of Rome consumed a remarkably vegetarian diet, since meat was expensive and local fish stocks were low off the western shore of Italy. Not only were consumables expensive (see Food prices page 136) but difficult to purchase fresh. Most fruits and vegetables were seasonal and preserved by pickling or drying to extend their shelf life.

MEAL TIMES (MENSAE)

In Rome the meal times were roughly broken into breakfast, lunch and dinner.

Cum tacent, clamant – When they are silent, they cry out (Cicero)

Breakfast (ientaculum) when eaten, was consumed immediately after rising. It normally comprised of emmer bread, often dipped in wine or oil, with cheese, dried fruit or olives.

Luncheon (prandium) was eaten at midday. Like breakfast, it was a light meal, comprising of a slightly broader range of foods, usually leftovers from the day before; bread, cheese, cold meats, salad, fruits, nuts or olives. Romans who could afford it purchased warm food, fried or baked, from street vendors. After eating, most people retired for a quick nap.

Dinner (cena) started sometime between mid and late afternoon. This was the main meal of the day and the centre of social life, since friends and guests were often invited. For the lower classes, cena was comprised of a porridge (puls or pulenta) made from cold soaked cereals or beans, salt and fat, and also included olive oil and vegetables. If wealthy enough, the puls was eaten with eggs, cheese, honey or very rarely, meat or fish.

MEAL ETIQUETTE (ELEGANTIA MORUM)

Amongst the poor, cena was eaten whilst sitting upon benches or chairs about the table. The only cutlery was fingers and spoons (ligulae) and dinnerware was made from pottery or wood.

During the early Republic, the higher classes ate no differently from the lesser privileged. They continued to eat frugally and food was still prepared by the materfamilias. Even the wealthiest families had no specifically trained cooks, although experts could be hired for important occasions.

It was not until the last two centuries of the Republic that well-off Romans changed from sitting at the table to the Greek custom of reclining for meals. The cena became more formal and was split into initially two and then three different courses; starters (promulsis or gustatio), main course (cena or primae mensae) and dessert (bellaria or secunda mensae).

The first course was designed to stimulate appetite, serving only simple light dishes including such things as eggs, salads, molluscs, mushrooms and clams. The main course was comprised of meat or fish with vegetables. Dessert was usually fruits, nuts and sweet pastries.

Between the main course and dessert, a small offering of wine and cakes was made to the spirits of the home and hearth (lares).

Guests reclined on large, broad couches (lecti triclinares), which were arranged about the dining area, in a horseshoe shape about the central table (mensa). Three couches were the norm and a maximum of three people could sprawl on each, although for most of the Republican period, women were forbidden to recline and were forced by decorum to sit on chairs.

Before reclining, diners would remove their sandals and wash their hands and feet in bowls of water. Between courses, the fingers would be washed again and the mouth cleaned on napkins (mappae). Guests were welcome to take home any uneaten leftovers in their own personal napkins, which often ended up as treats for the household slaves.

Dinner conversation was the primary objective of a formal cena with guests. But if it was a special occasion, the courses might be interspersed or accompanied by other entertainments, for example poetry, musicians or acrobats. Such meals could last late into the night and be followed by a drinking session (comissatio) where

dining manners loosened, and to which dancers (i.e. prostitutes) were sometimes invited.

> *'Be friendly and don't quarrel. If you can't, go home.'*
> *Dining room graffiti, Pompeii*

VEGETABLES (HOLERA)

The bulk of foods eaten by Romans were vegetables. These were frequently pickled or dried to preserve them for winter months.

Pulses (legumina) – broad beans, chick peas, lentils, lupin beans and peas.

Salads – chicory leaves, cress, fennel, lettuces, mallow leaves and vine leaves. Also boiled and spiced elder, fenugreek, mallow, nettle, orache and sorrel leaves.

Vegetables – artichokes, asparagus, beets, broccoli, capers, carrots, cauliflower, courgettes, cucumbers, leeks, marrows, onions, parsnips, radishes and turnips.

Fungi – mushrooms and truffles.

GRAINS & BREAD (PANIS)

Grain was a staple foodstuff. In the early days of Rome it was the women of the house who milled their own grain and baked bread – tough backbreaking work. It was not until 173 BC that the trade of baker became common and people began taking their grain to commercial bakeries (pistrina) to be milled into flour (farina) and baked into bread. Most people lack their own bread ovens due to the risk of fires and the expense of charcoal.

By the late Republic, the milling operation and baking merged into a single occupation, using animals or water wheels for motive power.

FRUITS (FRUCTUS) & NUTS (NUCES)

Desserts were primarily comprised of fruit. Most fruits were cultivated and some were purposefully dried for preservation. Some Roman bakers specialised in tantalising varieties of breads, tarts, sweet buns and cakes blended with fruits and nuts.

Fruits – apples, apricots, blackberries, cherries, currants, dates, figs, grapes, hawthorn berries, melons, olives, peaches, pears, plums, pomegranates and quinces.

Nuts – almonds, chestnuts, hazelnuts, pine nuts and walnuts.

CHEESES (CASEA)

Roman cheese was made from sheep or goat milk and was generally sour and crumbly in texture. Cheeses came in two forms. Soft cheese was very fresh and had to be eaten soon after manufacture. Hard cheese was salted for preservation, desiccating it and adding to the taste. Cheeses were further flavoured with herbs or by smoking.

Milk was not drunk by Romans – save as a medicinal treatment. Nor did they eat butter, preferring to dip bread in olive oil.

MEATS (CARNES)

Meat was a very small part of the Roman diet, even in the upper echelons of society. It was both expensive and difficult to keep fresh in a world lacking refrigeration. Most meats were preserved by salting, smoking or desiccating in air. Sausages (farcimina) were very well-liked, made from combinations of meats and herbs. Countryside-made pork sausages (lucanicae) and blood sausages (botuli) were the favourite.

"Pound pepper, cumin, savory, rue, parsley, mixed herbs, laurel berries, and liquamen, and mix with this well-beaten meat, pounding it again with the ground spice mixture. Work in liquanum, peppercorns, plenty of pate and pine-kernels, insert into an intestine, drawn out very thickly, and hang in the smoke."

A recipe for Roman Lucanica sausage

Pork was the most popular commonly available meat, coming both from wild boars and farm raised pigs. Whole roasted pigs, stuffed with fruit, sausages and other meats, were reserved for large feasts or public festivals and only started appearing at the end of the Republic.

The most expensive meats came from fowl, generally geese and ducks, which were often force-fed to fatten them. Chickens were more expensive than ducks. Since they provided a regular supply of eggs, they were another luxury food in the city, although less so in the countryside. Pigeons were raised for food also. Less common were game birds which had to be hunted, such as pheasants, grouse, peacocks and swans.

Whereas pigs and birds were raised specifically for meat, goats and sheep were eaten after the animal had lived out its productive life; goats producing milk for cheese and sheep providing wool. The meat of these creatures was cheaper than pork and decidedly tougher.

Beef was not appreciated by Republican Romans. Cattle were raised only as work animals pulling carts and ploughs, or as temple offerings. Their milk was not drunk or even used for cheese. When a beast died, its meat is not wasted, although it could be tougher even than mutton if not specifically bred as a sacrifice.

Hare meat was considered a delicacy and dedicated preserves were kept by the rich for hunting them.

FISH (PISCES)

The regular consumption of fish in Rome did not begin until the late Republic. Fish was expensive – far more so than meat and was difficult to get to the city in fresh condition. Once the higher classes developed a taste for fish, they began excavating ponds on their estates to breed them.

"In the same age, also, Licinius Murena was the first to form preserves for other fish; and his example was soon followed by the noble families of the Philippi and the Hortensii. Lucullus had a mountain pierced near Naples, at a greater outlay even, than that which had been expended on his villa; and here he formed a channel, and admitted the sea to his preserves; it was for this reason that Pompeius Magnus gave him the name of " Xerxes in a toga." After his death, the fish in his preserves was sold for the sum of four million sesterces."

Pliny the Elder – Naturalis Historia

More important than fish was garum, a type of salty sauce used as a condiment to flavour food. Made from the salted innards of small fish allowed to ferment for several weeks under the sun, the sauce was often mixed with other ingredients such as spices to generate unique and subtle flavours.

"Another liquid, too, of a very exquisite nature, is that known as 'garum' it is prepared from the intestines of fish and various parts which would otherwise be thrown away, macerated in salt; so that it is, in fact, the result of their putrefaction."

Pliny the Elder – Naturalis Historia

Purchased in small one handled amphorae (congii), a jar of garum could be very expensive. The best kind was made from mackerel. Muria, a sauce of lesser quality, came from tuna.

SNAILS & SHELLFISH (COCHLEA ET CRUSTATA)

Romans had a great love for snails, mussels and oysters. By the end of the Republic, many farms were established to commercially breed them. The earliest reference to eating snails was in the form of a tasty medicine.

"Take a pot and pour into it six sextarii of water and add the hock of a ham, or, if you have no hock, a half-pound of ham-scraps with as little fat as possible. Just as it comes to a boil, add two cabbage leaves, two beet plants with the roots, a shoot of fern, a bit of the mercury-plant, two pounds of mussels, a capito fish and one scorpion, six snails, and a handful of lentils… it is an excellent purgative, and, besides, it is agreeable."

Cato, Recipe for a purgative – De Agricultura

A native edible snail lived on vine leaves, so collecting them was not only vital for vintners but was a welcome source of protein. The best snails were imported from overseas…

"The white ones were those that are produced in the district of Reate; those of Illyria were remarkable for the largeness of their size; while those from Africa were the most prolific;"

Pliny the Elder – Naturalis Historia

With the establishment of Rome's major port at Ostia, shellfish were regularly brought up the Tiber for consumption. Rising demand eventually exhausted local beds in the late Republic, so enterprising businessmen started purposely farming shellfish.

"The first person who formed artificial oyster-beds was Sergius Orata, who established them at Baiæ, in the time of L. Crassus, the orator, just before the Marsic War. This was done by him, not for the gratification of gluttony, but of avarice, as he contrived to make a large income by this exercise of his ingenuity."

Pliny the Elder – Naturalis Historia

WINE (VINUM)

The universal drink of the Romans was wine. Wine was normally drunk diluted with water to help stave off immediate drunkenness.

Not large my cups, nor rich my cheer,
This Sabine wine, which erst I sealed,
That day the applauding theatre
Your welcome pealed,
Dear knight Maecenas. as 'twere fain
That your paternal river's banks,
And Vatican, in sportive strain,
Should echo thanks.
For you Calenian grapes are pressed,
And Caecuban; these cups of mine
Falernum's bounty ne'er has blessed,
Nor Formian vine.
Horace – Vile Potabis, Odes

Since wine was made throughout all the lands bordering the Mediterranean sea, it was often imported into Rome, albeit at high expense. Amongst those held in highest regard were Coan (from Cos), Corinthian, Lesbian (from Lesbos), Cretan, Judean and Mamertine (from Messana in Sicily).

By the late Republic, Italian wine had come into its own and claimed a superior quality. The most lauded were the Caecuban, Fundanian, Setinian, Falernian, Alban and Statinian. Of these Falernian was considered king but vintages could vary in quality from year to year depending on the weather and climate.

Drunkenness was looked down upon by polite society and could cause the loss of dignitas if improper behaviour is witnessed. Unfortunately the increase of wealth as the Republic neared its end contributed towards public inebriation amongst the increasingly vulgar plebeian, equestrian and patrician classes.

"Thus we see wines quaffed out of impurities, and inebriety invited even by the hope of a reward – invited, did I say? – may the gods forgive me for saying so, purchased outright. We find one person induced to drink upon the condition that he shall have as much to eat as he has previously drunk, while another has to quaff as many cups as he has thrown points on the dice. Then it is that the roving, insatiate eyes are setting a price upon the matron's chastity; and yet, heavy as they are with wine, they do not fail to betray their designs to her husband. Then it is that all the secrets of the mind are revealed; one man is heard to disclose the provisions of his will, another lets fall some expression of fatal import, and so fails to keep to himself words which will be sure to come home to him with a cut throat. And how many a man has met his death in this fashion. Indeed, it has become quite a common proverb, that 'in wine there is truth.'"

Pliny the Elder – Naturalis Historia

The comissatio, or drinking bout, was an example of such behaviour. Participants wearing garlands of flowers (coronae convivales) as crowns would roll dice. Whoever threw the highest roll was declared magister and determined what proportions of wine to water would be mixed in the wine bowl (crater) for the evening and what entertainments each guest should perform. If the rules were broken, then the magister also determined the forfeits imposed. Such banquets often ended with the celebrants walking the

dangerous streets at night, revelling loudly and drunkenly, much to the irritation of their neighbours.

Whereas the Greeks added pine tree resin to their wines to prevent bacteria turning it into vinegar, by the mid-Republic the Romans began to use a preservative syrup called sapa, which was a boiled down concentrate of grape juice (also known as 'must').

"To coat the brim of wine jars, so as to give a good odour and to keep any blemish from the wine: Put 6 congii of the best boiled must in a copper or lead vessel... Boil the whole over a slow fire of faggots, stirring constantly to prevent scorching; continue the boiling, until you have boiled off a half."

Cato the Elder – De Agricultura

Sapa produced in lead kettles tasted very sweet due to the high acidity of the boiling grape juice dissolving large quantities of the metal from the vessel. This produced lead acetate, which had the unusual effect of increasing the sweetness of the syrup's flavour. Thus sapa was popular as both a preservative and a condiment but became the major source of lead poisoning in Roman society.

Mulled wine (calida) was drunk when the weather was cold. It was a mixture of wine, water and spices, which was warmed in a metal urn (authepsa), some of which possessed taps. It was also sold at taverns called thermopola.

Honeyed wine (mulsum) was made from mixing four parts wine to one part honey. It was normally the first drink of a dinner, served just after the appetisers (hence the name promulsis).

"There is a wine also made solely of honey and water. For this purpose it is recommended that rain-water should be kept for a period of five years. Those who eschew greater skill, content themselves with taking the water just after it has fallen, and boiling it down to one third, to which they then add one third in quantity of old honey, and keep the mixture exposed to the rays of a hot sun for forty days after the rising of the Dog-star; others, however, rack it off in the course of ten days, and tightly cork the vessels in which it is kept. This beverage is known as hydromeli, and with age acquires the flavour of wine. It is nowhere more highly esteemed than Phrygia"

Pliny the Elder – Naturalis Historia

Although beer (cervesa) was known to the Romans, they did not normally partake of it.

"Vita vinum est – Wine is life"

Petronius

THE FABLE OF FALERNIAN

Falernian wine became so popular that legends grew from its success. One concerns a farmer, Falernus, who ploughed the earth of Mt. Massicus. One day the god Bacchus paid the impoverished farmer a visit and the man gave the best of his humble fare to his guest. Bacchus rewarded the man's hospitality by causing the farmer's wooden cups to fill with wine. Soon the old man passed out from potent elixir but when he awoke the next morning he discovered that all his fields had been planted with vines from which grew grapes of outstanding perfection. From that point on, the fame of Falerus' wine spread far and wide.

De minimis non curat lex – The law does not concern itself with trifles

THE CITY

Once there was a river ford overlooked by a group of low hills, interspersed and surrounded by marshy swamps. It was here in this unlikely spot, that the dispossessed came to live; herders, thieves, exiles, slaves, the poor and their like, huddled in small huts with mud walls and thatched roofs. From their humble origin came the mightiest city of its age…

THE CITY DURING THE MONARCHY

The hills of Rome were first settled in the 8-9th Century BC. The legends from the Time of Kings record that Rome began upon the Palatine Hill, when Romulus marked out the ancient boundary, the pomerium, with a plough, fortified the hilltop settlement (during which time his brother Remus was slain after he had mocked the construction) and invited the poor and exiled to come and inhabit it. For his efforts the settlement was named after its founder. To venerate the gods, the first temple was built upon the neighbouring Capitoline Hill.

After battling with the Sabines, Romulus formed an alliance and a colony of them settled on the Quirinal Hill, doubling the size of the city. The second king, Numa, built many temples and the city spread to the Aventine Hill.

Tullus, the third king of Rome, built temples to Pallor and Pavor, and conquered the Albans, destroying their city. He welcomed all the refugees into Rome, doubling again the population. The Caelian hill was included in the city and that it might become more populated, Tullus chose it for the site of his palace lived there.

Fourth to be crowned was Ancus Martius. Forced to war, he continued to expand Rome's influence to the point where residential space was starting to become scarce.

Now Rome owned the majority of the territory surrounding it, including the Mesian Forest and the river Tiber, all the way to the sea. Ancus began the building of Ostia, Rome's port and the temple of Jupiter Feretrius was enlarged in consequence of the brilliant successes in the war.

Tarquin was the fifth king and, after a successful war against the Latins, divided up the land below the Capitoline Hill for building development.

> "Then for the first time a space was marked for what is now the "Circus Maximus." Spots were allotted to the patricians and knights where they could each build for themselves stands called "fori" from which to view the Games."
>
> Livy - Ab Urbe Condita

He also laid aside land around the Forum for arcades and shops.

> "He made preparations for completing the work, which had been interrupted by the Sabine war, of enclosing the City in those parts where no fortification yet existed with a stone wall. The low-lying parts of the City round the Forum, and the other valleys between the hills, where the water could not escape, were drained by conduits which emptied into the Tiber. He built up with masonry a level space on the Capitol as a site for the temple of Jupiter which he had vowed during the Sabine war, and the magnitude of the work revealed his prophetic anticipation of the future greatness of the place."
>
> Livy - Ab Urbe Condita

The sixth to reign in Rome was Servius Tullius. During his time the size of the populace had grown so big that he incorporated the final three hills, the Quirinal, Viminal, and Esquiline, and to give the last more importance he lived there himself. He surrounded the city with an embankment, ditches, and a wall, and expanded the ancient promerium to just within these new fortifications.

> "he at length induced the Latin tribes to join with the people of Rome in building a temple to Diana in Rome"
>
> Livy - Ab Urbe Condita

The last king of Rome, Tarquinius Superbus, did the least to expand his city. Foremost were his plans for the construction of a new temple to Jupiter on the Tarpeian Mount and supervising its foundations.

> "He then sketched out the design of a temple to Jupiter, which in its extent should be worthy of the king of gods and men, worthy of the Roman empire, worthy of the majesty of the City itself."
>
> Livy - Ab Urbe Condita

He also improved living conditions by the construction of the first sewer in the city.

> "[he] also compelled the plebeians to take their share of the work. This was in addition to their military service, and was anything but a light burden. Still they felt it less of a hardship to build the temples of the gods with their own hands, than they did afterwards when they were transferred to other tasks less imposing, but involving greater toil - the construction of the "fori" in the Circus and that of the Cloaca Maxima, a subterranean tunnel to receive all the sewage of the City."
>
> Livy - Ab Urbe Condita

After a period of 240 years of almost constant wars and conquests, the city had achieved its fundamental boundaries. It sprawled across seven hills, surrounded by strong walls, installed with rudimentary sanitation and filled with temples to the gods.

THE CITY DURING THE REPUBLIC

With the city and its walls established, Rome did not change its boundaries greatly over the next few hundred years. Although many of the original temples had been constructed from stone, the houses were still made of wood or mud brick topped with thatched roofs and even the Servian walls were only stone-fronted earthen embankments topped by palisades.

During the early Republic, very few public works were done to improve or beautify the city. Most of Rome's efforts were consumed in its continuous struggle for pre-eminence. In fits and starts, the walls were repeatedly patched up, dismantled and eventually replaced with more substantial masonry. The open ditches of the Cloaca Maxima were floored and walled with stone. Houses remained simplistic.

This started to change during the Samnite Wars. The conflict drained the populace severely but started to bring in tithes, taxes and new immigrants from subjugated towns. With these resources, new civic plans were commissioned, founded by consuls and censors. It was the individual who paid for these grand schemes, not the state. In 312 BC the censor Appius Claudius built the first aqueduct which improved the city's water supply. He also built the first road, the Appian Way, which connected Rome to the Greek cities of Campania.

This generated a renewed trend of financing public works, despite their purpose being generally done for self-aggrandisement rather than civic interest. By far the most common were the construction of temples, which were offered as supplications to the gods for bringing victory in Rome's never ending succession of battles. Over 40 of them were built during the Republic alone. They were usually modest in size, since all such public works were privately funded by the general who had lead the victory and as such paid out from their personal share of the loot.

More practical civil projects such as aqueducts, fountains, baths and roads also improved the city. These schemes were often helped by the succession of devastating fires which plagued Rome, which cleared land for new development. Maintenance of public buildings, roads, aqueducts and sewers fell within the ædiles' mandate.

Towards the late Republic, the round huts of plebeian lifestyle began to be replaced with apartment blocks, in order to more efficiently utilise the space within the walls for the swelling populace. Brick and concrete superseded wood and tile replaced thatch. However, it was not until 146 BC that marble was first used to build a temple in the Campus Martius.

A building renaissance favouring Hellenic styles began during the late Republic. This trend, mixed with Roman architectural improvements, began the wholesale importation of Greek columns and coloured marble for more aesthetic construction. Eventually more social monuments began to be constructed, such as covered colonnades, courts and meeting halls, theatres, public gardens and forums.

Deliriant isti Romani – These Romans are mad! (Asterix and Obelix)

THE HILLS AND DISTRICTS (COLLES ET REGIONES)

Rome proper was contained within the Servian walls, which originally only encompassed six hills: the Palatine (Collis Palatinus), Capitoline (Collis Capitolinus), Quirinal (Collis Quirinalis), Viminal (Collis Viminalis), Esquiline (Collis Esquilinus) and the Caelian (Collis Caelius). It was only during the early 4th Century BC when the fortifications were rebuilt and strengthened, that the walls were extended to contain the Aventine hill (Collis Aventinus) and Circus Maximus.

The city was divided up into four regions (regiones romae), the Suburana, Esquilina, Collina and Palatina. These were civil divisions which for the purposes of administration and voting. The tribe (tribus) one belonged to was determined by place of birth, not where one lived.

Ω Region 1, the Suburana, was roughly the southeast quarter of Rome, comprising the Sucusa, Ceroliensis, and Caelius hills (this is distinct from the Subura, the slum district, which lies elsewhere).

Ω Region 2, the Esquilina, was the northeast quarter, containing the Oppius and Cispius.

Ω Region 3, the Collina, was the northwest quarter, covering the Quirinal and the Viminal.

Ω Region 4, the Palatina, was the southwest quarter comprising of the Palatium, Velia, and Cermalus.

The Capitoline hill was not considered part of the Regiones Quattuor, since it was a separate religious fortification. Neither was the Aventine which was included later when the Servian walls were extended.

Each region was further divided into neighbourhoods which encompassed a street and its adjoining houses, tenements, businesses and temples. The social centre of each neighbourhood was a crossroads (compitum) where the residents (usually those of lowest social rank, i.e. slaves, freedmen and the poorest plebeians) maintained a small shrine for the area's guardian spirits (lares). Although not necessarily liked, everyone who lived within the boundary was considered a neighbour (vicanus) and generally stood up for one another during times of celebration or trouble. Each neighbourhood also elected an officer (magister vici) who liaised with the city administration and participated in civic religion.

THE TIBER RIVER (TIBERIS)

The Tiber was originally called the Albula due to the milky yellow white sediment which it washed down from the hills. According to legend, it was renamed when the Alban king Tiberinus Silvius drowned in the river and Jupiter raised him to become its guardian spirit.

The Tiber is famed and honoured as the river into which Romulus and Remus were thrown before they were washed up onto its bank at the spot where they later decided to found Rome. The city is built on the eastern shore, near an island which was once a fording point across the river. It frequently floods, inundating the lower parts of Rome, the Campus Martius, and the properties foolishly built upon it.

The greatest importance of the Tiber is both as a defensive barrier and the main thoroughfare for trade imported upstream from the port of Ostia.

> "And yet there is no river more circumscribed than it, so close are its banks shut in on either side; but still, no resistance does it offer, although its waters frequently rise with great suddenness, and no part is more liable to be swollen than that which runs through the City itself. In such case, however, the Tiber is rather to be looked upon as pregnant with prophetic warnings to us, and in its increase to be considered more as a promoter of religion than a source of devastation."
>
> *Pliny the Elder - Naturalis Historia*

BRIDGES (PONTES)

Since passage across the Tiber by fording or ferries was inconvenient, if not impossible when the river was in spate, the Romans built several bridges to ease the crossing. The original ones were made of wood which were constantly damaged by seasonal flooding. The earliest recorded bridge, the Pons Sublicius, spanned the Tiber River near the Forum Boarium downstream from Tiber Island. It was constructed around 642 BC by king Ancus and was famously defended singlehandedly by Horatius Cocles whilst facing the forces of Lars Porsenna, king of Clusium.

> "They say, moreover, that the custody and maintenance of the bridge, like all the other inviolable and ancestral rites, attached to the priesthood, for the Romans held the demolition of the wooden bridge to be not only unlawful, but actually sacrilegious. It is also said that it was built entirely without iron and fastened together with wooden pins in obedience to an oracle."
>
> *Plutarch – Life of Numa*

The Pons Mulvius was originally built in 206 BC and spanned the Tiber north of the city as part of the Via Flaminia. The first recorded stone arched bridge was the Pons Aemilius built in 142 BC. This was followed by the rebuilding of the Pons Mulvius with stone in 115 BC. Thereafter the Pons Fabricius was constructed in 62 BC, which spanned the river between the east bank and the island, and was soon followed by the Pons Cestius in 46 BC, which bridged the island and the west bank.

THE STREETS (VIAE)

Roman streets can be categorised into several types. The wider, better paved roads are named Viae. A lesser street (and the neighbourhood it services) is called a Vicus. The streets which lead up and down the hills are named Clivi meaning 'slope'. Steps (gradus or scalae) were used in places where a road would be too steep.

During the early Republic, none of Rome's streets were paved, either inside or outside the city, which meant that all roads turned to mud when it rained. Thus during the winter months, it was near impossible to travel long distances beyond the city walls. By the end of the Republic, most of Rome's streets were paved and the widest possess pavements for pedestrians, including stepping stones to cross what conceivably may have been roadways covered with animal dung and the filth conveniently thrown out of doorways and windows.

The default width of a street, according to the laws of the Twelve Tables in 450 BC, was only 8 ft., and up to double this where it curved. Although this is technically the width of the most important thoroughfares, most streets widen once they depart outside the city walls. With continual urban renovation and bribery of the ædiles to claim more building space, the majority of side streets and alleyways were much narrower, to the point wherein some alleys a man had to turn sideways to squeeze along it.

To the inhabitants, viae are known as 'two cart' streets since they are wide enough for two carts to pass each other. However, only the Via Sacra and the Via Nova were this wide. Acta or 'one cart' streets are self-explanatory, allowing only one-way wheeled traffic and itinera were streets so narrow that only pedestrians could fit. In a like manner, only the viae ran straight, while other roads were forced to bend and kink according to the buildings which lie on their path.

With most roads being overshadowed by high insulae, constricted in width, and forced to twist and turn by the sprawling buildings, the back streets of Rome were a confusing labyrinth. Unless a resident of the neighbourhood, most visitors rapidly become lost and disorientated.

The claustrophobic nature of the streets, combined with the difficulty of their passageway limits wheeled traffic to the major roads. The streets are also packed with pedestrians and are frequently so crowded that elbows are used to force passage. During riots when crowds surge, people are often trampled to death in the crush.

"When the rich man has a call of social duty, the mob makes way for him as he is borne swiftly over their heads in a huge Liburnian car. He writes or reads or sleeps inside as he goes along, for the closed window of the litter induces slumber. Yet he will arrive before us; hurry as we may, we are blocked by a surging crowd in front, and by a dense mass of people pressing in on us from behind: one man digs an elbow into me, another a hard sedan-pole; one bangs a beam, another a wine-cask, against my head. My legs are beplastered with mud; soon huge feet trample on me from every side, and a soldier plants his hobnails firmly on my toe."

Juvenal - Saturae

Government officials and married women could ride on two wheeled chariots, a two horse (or mule) chariot being called a biga and a four horse one a quadriga. Farmers and tradesmen were permitted to bring produce into the city by cart, which were normally drawn by oxen.

Yet, as the population density continued to rise during the Republic, forcing a path through the myriad walkers became increasingly difficult. Litters were used instead, as they could utilise the lesser streets and avoid blockages caused by innumerable carts. Traffic rolled through the streets at all times of the day.

"Most sick people here in Rome perish for want of sleep, the illness itself having been produced by food lying undigested on a fevered stomach. For what sleep is possible in a lodging? Who but the wealthy get sleep in Rome? There lies the root of the disorder. The crossing of wagons in the narrow winding streets, the slanging of drovers when brought to a stand, would make sleep impossible for a Drusus - or a sea-calf.

Juvenal - Saturae

In 174 BC, the censors began the task of paving the streets. Outside the city, roadbeds were deeply excavated then filled with layers of crushed rubble, gravel and sand mixed with lime, which turned the whole lot into a solid mass of concrete. The top layer

was paved with stone slabs and cantered to shed water. Within the city, the lesser streets were simply paved or cobbled with round flint stones without constructing major foundations. Paved roads enabled travel at all times of the year and benefited commercial as well as military traffic.

Street paving continued over time but the duty for paving roads was eventually given to the city ædiles. Towards the end of the Republic, maintenance of the streets was placed upon the owners of those properties which bordered them. Those who failed to keep their sections of the street clean were forced to pay for contractors appointed by the ædile in charge to do it for them.

"Each owner of property fronting on the streets of Rome or on streets within a mile of Rome, on which there is continuous settlement now or in the future, shall keep such portion of the street in repair at the discretion of that ædile who has jurisdiction in this quarter of the city by this law. The aforesaid ædile, at his discretion, shall provide that each owner of property fronting on the street shall keep in repair that portion of the street which by this law it is proper for him to maintain and he shall provide that no water shall stand there to prevent the public from convenient passage."

Julius Caesar - Lex Iulia Municipalis

Eventually in about 45 BC, the Lex Iulia Municipalis restricted commercial carts to night-time access to the city and within a mile outside the walls.

"no one shall drive a wagon along the streets of Rome or along those streets in the suburbs where there is continuous housing after sunrise or before the tenth hour of the day, except whatever will be 'proper' for the transportation and the importation of material for building temples of the immortal gods, or for public works, or for removing from the city rubbish from those buildings for whose demolition public contracts have been let."

Julius Caesar - Lex Iulia Municipalis

Vestal Virgins, the Rex Sacrorum and the Flamens were still allowed to ride chariots in the city for the purpose of official sacrifices, as were those celebrating Triumphs. Ox or donkey wagons that had been driven into the city by night were also excluded from the daytime ban as long as they carried dung from within the city or departed empty.

Since the use of most mounted animals or drawn vehicles was restricted within the city, many livery stables were set up at the edge of the suburbs. If a Roman wished to travel overland, it was usual for them to call at such a business and hire out a mount or vehicle, which would be returned to the same stable and paying a suitable deposit to protect against theft or damage. For those rich enough to afford and feed them, private mounts could be kept and exercised at these stables for an annual fee.

TEMPLES (AEDES)

During the early period, Rome had few temples. The early Roman divinities lacked form, being spiritual beings or concepts, and their worship was instead tied to natural objects or locations. Buildings dedicated to the gods were expensive to build, so many started out as simple wooden huts, rather than monumental stone edifices.

"Or one may come upon an entire temple, unimaginably ancient, so old it is made not of bricks and marble but of worm-eaten wood, its dim interior long ago stripped of all clues of the divinity that once resided there, but still held sacred for reasons no one living can remember."

Steven Saylor - Roman Blood

However, Rome possessed many altars (sacella) placed haphazardly on the sides of streets or in plazas. Many which had been originally constructed in open spaces to view the skies were swallowed by the encroaching city.

"One may step down a narrow winding street in a neighbourhood known since childhood and suddenly come upon a landmark never noticed before – a tiny, crude statue of some forgotten Etruscan god set in a niche and concealed behind a wild fennel bush, a secret known only to the children who play in the alley and the inhabitants of the house, who worship the forsaken and impotent god as a household deity."

Steven Saylor - Roman Blood

Temples served several purposes. Firstly they were places which allowed the populace to offer sacrifices and worship to the gods. Secondly they were used to store treasures, artworks and libraries for the state, or could be used by individuals as a place to deposit valuable documents… such as wills and testaments at the shrine of Vesta. Thirdly, they were places where the senate could meet and discuss state business.

Beyond these major responsibilities, temples were often used as places to leave messages or send letters to if the recipient had no permanent residence within the city (or wished to keep it secret).

Under the influence of the Etruscan kings, most early temples were Greek in design, although modest in scale. The Hellenic influence continued until the late Republic, whereupon the architectural style become more Roman – using columns only to decorate the front and building the temples on many layered podiums, presumably to raise them above the level of flood waters.

Most temples were state supported, although they usually kept their doors open for supplicants to enter and make individual donations for sacrifices.

FORUMS (FORA)

A forum is technically an open space given over to the people of Rome, for use as a place for athletics, gatherings or trade. The forums of Rome can be defined according to their use; judicial courts (fora civilia) and commercial plazas (fora venalia).

Up until the end of the Republic there was only one civil forum, the Forum Romanum, although it initially served as a market place also. This is the place where court cases were heard, politics were debated, assemblies summoned, and news displayed daily. The Forum Julium was built in 54-46 BC to relieve overcrowding in the older forum.

THE DAILY ACTS

Started in 131 BC, the Daily Acts (Acta Diurna) were message boards first erected in the Forum Romanum on which were originally posted the results of trials and other legal proceedings. The content gradually expanded to include important public notices, births, deaths and marriages. These news boards were the ones used by Sulla when he posted his lists of proscriptions and executions. Those reading the news were closely watched for signs of dissent or guilt. Famously, some senators openly expressed amazement at being included on the lists, only to be murdered by those standing around them for the reward.

In 59 BC Julius Caesar expanded the content to include more popular information such as news about the games, gladiatorial contests, gossip and astrological omens, the first horoscopes. Higher status readers who wished to be kept abreast of the news would assign literate slaves to watch the boards and either memorise or inscribe the contents on wax tablets, which the slave then related to their master on their return. Illiterate news seekers could always find someone in the crowds that surrounded the acta diurna to read the texts aloud for them.

The mercantile fora Venalia specialised in different types of product, mainly foods and originally followed the banks of the Tiber, where goods were more easily transported to the city.

Ω Forum Boarium – The cattle market of Rome, near the Pons Sublicius. Other types of livestock and meat were available here.

Ω Forum Cuppedinis – The delicatessen market, which lay between the Sacra Via and the Argiletum and was later absorbed along with the Forum Piscarum into the Macellum.

Ω Forum Holitorium – The vegetable and herb market lying outside the Servian wall, between the Porta Carmentalis and the Pons Fabricius.

Ω Forum Piscarium – The fish-market north of the forum, between the Sacra Via and the Argiletum, which was later absorbed into the Macellum.

Ω Forum Vinarium – The wine and garum market, situated near the Emporium, between the Aventine Hill and the Tiber.

Ω Macellum – A huge food market built in 179 BC which absorbed some of the other fora.

BASILICA (BASILICAE)

Whereas fora were open spaces for public business, basilicae were roofed buildings used for similar purposes, i.e. courtrooms, businesses or assembly places. They usually comprised of a rectangular hall, of considerable height, surrounded by one or two colonnaded porticoes, sometimes with galleries, and lit by openings in the upper part of the side walls.

The following basilicae exist during the Republic.

Ω Basilica Porcia – The first basilica in Rome, built for judicial and business purposes by Cato in 184 BC. It stood a little west of the curia, and in it the tribunes held court. It was destroyed by fire in 52 BC during the riots accompanying the funeral of Clodius.

Ω Basilica Sempronia – Built in 170 BC by the censor Gracchus, it stood where the Vicus Tuscus entered the Forum Romanum. It was knocked down when the Basilica Julia was built.

Ω Basilica Aemilia – Erected in 179 BC. 20 years later it was installed with a water clock (clepsydra). In 78 B.C., the consul M. Aemilius Lepidus decorated the basilica with engraved shields or portraits of his ancestors.

Ω Basilica Opimia – Constructed by the consul L. Opimius in 121 BC, at the same time that he restored the temple of Concord. It stood just north of the temple and was 'much frequented but not magnificent'.

Ω Basilica Julia – Built between 54-46 BC on the south side of the forum, between the Vicus Tuscus and the Vicus Iugarius.

Ω The Emporium, the huge dockyard and marketplace, originally built in 193 BC. It consisted of dozens of shops (tabernae), offices (officinae), wharfs (portus) and warehouses (horrea). Although it lay outside the city walls, in 174 BC it was provided with its own barriers to prevent thieves and paved to facilitate access by carts.

"The hours, however, still remained a matter of uncertainty, whenever the weather happened to be cloudy, until the ensuing lustrum; at which time Scipio Nasica, the colleague of Laenas, by means of a clepsydra, was the first to divide the hours of the day and the night into equal parts: and this time-piece he placed under cover and dedicated, in the year of Rome 595."

Pliny the Elder - Naturalis Historia

CURIA (CURIAE)

Curia were the places in which the senate held its meetings. A curia had to be a consecrated area (templum), since important political decisions could only be taken with the consent of the gods. Such templa were defined as areas where the augurs could perform the auguries, i.e. a divination based on the flights of birds. When the main curiae were unavailable, the senate would instead meet at a temple (aedes), which by default were sanctified.

Ω Curia Hostilia – The original senate house of Rome, situated atop a flight of steps on the north side of the Comitium, which lay on the eastern side of the Forum Romanum. It was erected by King Tullus Hostilius and was decorated with paintings, the most famous of which celebrated Rome's victory over the Carthaginians. In 52 BC it was burnt down when the followers of Clodius cremated his body inside.

Ω Curia Iulia – The new senate house begun by Julius Caesar in 44 BC just before his assassination. Completed and dedicated in 29 BC.

Ω Curia Pompeii – A hall in the Porticus Pompeius where the senate sometimes met. It was also the place where Julius Caesar was murdered.

"More than sixty joined the conspiracy against him, led by Gaius Cassius and Marcus and Decimus Brutus. At first they hesitated whether to form two divisions at the elections in the Campus Martius, so that while some hurled him from the bridge as he summoned the tribes to vote, the rest might wait below and slay him; or to set upon him in the Sacred Way or at the entrance to the theatre. When, however, a meeting of the Senate was called for the Ides of March in the Hall of Pompey, they readily gave that time and place the preference."

Suetonius - The Life of Julius Caesar

THE CIRCUS (CIRCUS MAXIMUS)

Roman circuses were structures devoted to the spectacle of sport. They were originally basic wooden structures built simply to provide seating and a better view for those behind the front rows. The first and only circus in Republican Rome was the Circus Maximus, a large plot of ground which lay between the Palatine and Aventine hills. This relatively flat area was divided by a natural brook and races were originally held on either side of the stream.

The Etruscan influence of Rome's early rulers led to the prizing of chariot racing above all other forms of equine sport. Under the guidance of king Tarquinius Priscus, the stream's course was straightened and bridged, forming a channel (euripus) which served as a central barrier (spina) for the now oval track. (This stream was later used as part of the sewage system and was the main channel of the Cloaca Circus Maximus – see Sewers page 63).

Despite the euripus, the circus was occasionally inundated when the Tiber's seasonal floods were higher than usual. A not infrequent occurrence…

"Owing to an inundation of the Tiber, the Circus was flooded in the middle of the Games, and this produced an unspeakable dread; it seemed as though the gods had turned their faces from men and despised all that was done to propitiate their wrath."

Livy - Ab Urbe Condita

Eventually the spina became a low wall completely covering the brook, mounted with monuments and shrines, including temples to Consus, Juventas, and one for Murcia (believed to be the divinity of the stream beneath).

Over the following centuries the Circus Maximus continued to be upgraded. In 329 BC permanent starting gates (carceres) were built, at the flat end of the track, where it led to the Forum Boarium. They were arranged in a slightly curving line so as to give no advantage to the team starting on the inside of the track. In 196 BC a triumphal arch was built in the circus.

> "L. Stertinius, who made no effort to obtain a triumph, brought away from Further Spain 50,000 pounds of silver for the public treasury, and with the proceeds from the sale of the spoil he erected two gateways in the Forum Boarium in front of the temples of Fortuna and Mater Matuta, and one in the Circus Maximus. On these three structures he placed gilded statues."
>
> Livy - Ab Urbe Condita

In 174 BC seven columns were constructed along the spina, each one topped with a large wooden egg (ovum). As each lap of a race was completed, one of the eggs would be removed, thus indicating how many laps remained. In 46 BC the circus was lengthened by Julius Caesar and a moat 10 feet wide and 10 feet deep added to separate the arena from the seating. This provided protection for spectators when the circus was otherwise used for animal hunts and gladiatorial combats. Finally in 33 BC, Agrippa (during his extensive rebuilding of the city) further supplemented the lap counting eggs

with a system of seven tilting bronze dolphins to aid the charioteers keep track of how many laps they had to go.

By the end of the Republic the circus possessed three tiers of seating; the first story was of stone and the two upper levels wood. It could seat at least 150,000 spectators and was surrounded by an arcade of arches (fornices). Those which did not contain access stairs into the circus were used as shops (tabernae) by fast food cooks, betting agents, prostitutes and diviners who provided both race predictions and curse tablets to hinder opposing teams.

The Circus Flaminius, which was named for its location on the Flaminian fields, the southern part of the Campus Martius, was in reality a public square used for markets and meetings, and not a permanent circus. The open field was sectioned off in 221 BC from encroaching buildings, which by then had gradually spread outside of the city walls.

The Ludi Plebii, and the Ludi Taurii, special games held to honour the Gods of the Underworld were held here. The Circus Flaminius was also the location of many temples which bordered its rectangular area. These included shrines to Hercules Custos, Vulcan, Neptune, Hercules, Pietas, Juno Regina, Diana, Jupiter Stator, Mars and Castor and Pollux.

Diligentia maximum etiam mediocris ingeni subsidium - Diligence is a very great help even to a mediocre intelligence (Seneca)

53

"One of the censors, M. Aemilius, asked the senate for a sum of money to be decreed for the Games on the occasion of the dedication of Queen Juno and Diana, which he had vowed eight years previously, during the Ligurian war. A sum of 20,000 asses was granted. He dedicated the temples which both stood in the Circus Flaminius, and exhibited scenic Games for three days after the dedication of the temple of Juno, and for two days after the dedication of the temple of Diana."

Livy - Ab Urbe Condita

THEATRES AND AMPHITHEATRES (THEATRA ET AMPHIHEATRA)

Theatres were semicircular buildings comprising of tiers of auditorium seating (cavea) surrounding a space (orchestra) where the chorus performed. This lay between the seating and the raised stage (podium) and a large wall acted as a backdrop (scaenae frons) for scenery. The semicircular design, originally conceived by the Greeks, acted as a natural amplifier for a performer's voice, thus permitting a larger audience to hear what was being said or played.

Amphitheatres were oval or circular buildings which also comprised of rising tiers of seating. Instead of a podium for performances, they instead had a sand filled area (arena) that was used for sporting or gladiatorial events. The design was conceptualised by the Romans who realised that oval seating allowed a larger audience at events where audibility was not required.

Both types of buildings possessed vomitoria, which converse to popular thought are the entrances and exits for audiences – not a place where one goes to regurgitate.

For the majority of the Republic, the city of Rome lacked any formal theatre for public performance. Displays, whether theatrical or gladiatorial in nature, were instead hosted in the fora upon temporary wooden stages (podia) or performed in the Circus Maximus. In 384 BC censor Gaius Maenius had wooden balconies built on top of the shops around the Forum Romanum, and thereafter the word 'maenianum' indicated the stalls of a theatre or amphitheatre. The luxury of seating was frowned upon by the Senate at this time which forbade sitting at theatrical performances…

"so that the manly behaviour of standing might be known as proper to the Roman people for the relaxation of their spirits"

Valerius Maximus - Memorable Words and Deeds

The first attempt to build a permanent wooden theatre was in 179 BC. It was never finished because it was thought that a permanent theatre would encourage citizens to attend plays so frequently that they would ignore day-to-day business matters.

Shortly before 155 BC the first stone theatre was started, sanctioned by the censors. However, before it could be completed, the consul Scipio Aemilianus in his backlash against Hellenic culture, appealed to the senate to pull the building down, since it would be "injurious to public morality"; thus precipitating a moratorium which prevented future construction of permanent theatres.

Following this edict, temporary wooden theatres continued to be built, each successive one constructed with more flamboyance than the last, as politicians strived to woo the populace. In 99 BC the scaenae frons of one theatre was elaborately painted and in 70

BC awnings (vela) were erected above a theatre's cavea to shade the audience from the sun. The next mention of a wooden theatre was in 60 BC, although it only describes its collapse during a storm.

"For of a sudden such a storm descended upon the whole city and all the country that quantities of trees were torn up by the roots, many houses were shattered, the boats moored in the Tiber both near the city and at its mouth were sunk, and the wooden bridge destroyed, and a theatre built of timbers for some festival collapsed, and in the midst of all this great numbers of human beings perished."

Cassius Dio - Roman History

Infamously in 58 BC the Theatrum Scauri outdid previous theatres in wasteful magnificence…

"During his ædileship, and only for the temporary purposes of a few days, Scaurus executed the greatest work that has ever been made by the hands of man, even when intended to be of everlasting duration; his Theatre, I mean. The stage of this building consisted of three storeys, supported upon three hundred and sixty columns; and this, too, in a city which had not allowed without some censure one of its greatest citizens to erect six pillars of Hymettian marble. The ground-storey was of marble, the second of glass, a species of luxury which ever since that time has been quite unheard of, and the highest of gilded wood."

Pliny the Elder - Naturalis Historia

Eventually the rule against permanent theatres was sidestepped in 55 BC when Pompey built a stone theatre (Theatrum Pompeii) in the Campus Martius, justifying the structure's cavea as an ornamental staircase to the Temple of Venus Victrix built atop it.

However, Pompey's theatre caused great consternation in the senate and narrowly avoided being torn down. Thus wooden structures continued to be built, used for a specific series of festivals and games, and thereafter were torn down again; with much of the often substandard materials being sold to property developers (for use in building insulae) whilst the richer items, such as marble columns being taken away to grace the sponsors' own homes.

In 53 BC, Scribonius Curio hosted funeral games in memory of his father and had erected a pair of theatres (Theatra Curionis) which could be rotated and joined together to form an amphitheatre. This was so novel, that the audiences refused to move from their seats whilst the theatres revolved, despite the danger of the movement and the chance of the structures collapsing.

"He caused to be erected, close together, two theatres of very large dimensions, and built of wood, each of them nicely poised, and turning on a pivot. Before mid-day, a spectacle of games was exhibited in each; the theatres being turned back to back, in order that the noise of neither of them might interfere with what was going on in the other. Then, in the latter part of the day, all on a sudden, the two theatres were swung round, and, the corners uniting, brought face to face; the outer frames, too, were removed, and thus an amphitheatre was formed, in which combats of gladiators were presented to the view; men whose safety was almost less compromised than was that of the Roman people, in allowing itself to be thus whirled round from side to side."

Pliny the Elder - Naturalis Historia

The first and only permanent amphitheatre built in Rome during the Republic was by Julius Caesar in 46 BC. This too was made of

PHYSICAL GRAFFITI

Ubiquitous with city life is the covering of most walls with graffiti (inscriptiones). The range of purposes which graffiti was used for is astounding… Magical curses, political slogans, boasts, personal insults, declarations of love, advertisements for the games or prostitutes, literary quotes, rewards for stolen property, jokes, and even secret messages. Sometimes they were simple warnings such as "Beware of the dog" (cave canem).

Graffiti was normally scrawled on any available wall, most commonly using chalk or charcoal. It could also be scratched into plaster using a sharp implement. Painted graffiti was not common, since paint was an expensive commodity due to its rare and difficult to extract pigments. The homes of more wealthy home owners were sometimes washed or repainted to remove the often offensive scribbles but, just as in modern times, this simply invited more graffiti to be drawn on the fresh surface.

Some graffiti was benevolent, such as the price lists of a shop, or free advertising of the goods available inside. One example is the illustration of a phallus with the text "Handle with Care" (mansueta tene) scrawled outside a brothel.

Not only does graffiti indicate that quite a large percentage of the populace was literate (although spelling and grammatical mistakes are common) but that people on the streets actually pay attention to what is written on the walls. For a realistic idea of the type and amount of graffiti in the city, the reader is encouraged to watch the HBO series 'Rome', in particular the introduction. For a more fun take on the whole issue, watch the "Romans go home" sketch from 'Monty Python's Life of Brian'…

Some examples of Graffiti;

"Cornelius made me pregnant."
"The petty thieves support Vatia for the ædileship."
"Helen is loved by Rufus"
"Io Saturnalia."
"I ask you to elect Gaius Julius Polybius ædile. He gets good bread."
"You're a big prick"
"Weep, you girls. My penis has given you up. Now it penetrates men's behinds. Goodbye, wondrous femininity."
"Burglar, watch out. "
"This is no place for idlers. On your way-lazy"
"An intellectual was on a sea voyage when a big storm blew up, causing his slaves to weep in terror. 'Don't cry,' he consoled them, 'I have freed you all in my will'"
"Lucius painted this"
"We have pissed in our beds. Host, I admit that we shouldn't have done this. If you ask: Why? There was no potty."
"Watch it, you that shits in this place. May you have Jove's anger if you ignore this"
"Myrtis, you do great blow jobs"
"I ask you to elect Marcus Cerrinius Vatia the ædileship. All the late drinkers support him. Florus and Fructus wrote this."
"Hedone says, "You can get a drink here for only one coin. You can drink better wine for two coins. You can drink Falernian for four coins."
"Chie, I hope your hemorrhoids rub together so much that they hurt worse than when they ever have before."
"Pyrrhus to his colleague Chius: I grieve because I hear you have died; and so farewell."
"A copper pot is missing from this shop. 65 sesterces reward if anybody brings it back, 20 sesterces if he reveals the thief so we can get our property back."
"His neighbors urge you to elect Lucius Statius Receptus duovir with judicial power; he is worthy. Aemilius Celer, a neighbour, wrote this. May you take sick if you maliciously erase this."
"I detest beggars. If somebody asks for something for free, he is an idiot; let him pay his cash and get what he wants."
"A hunt and 20 pairs of gladiators belonging to Marcus Tullius will fight a Pompeii on November 4-7"
"Guest House. Dining room to let, with three couches and furnishings."
"Perarius, you're a thief."
"Celadus the Thracian gladiator is the delight of all the girls"
"What a lot of tricks you use to deceive, innkeeper. You sell water but drink unmixed wine"
"I wonder, O, wall, that you have not fallen in ruins from supporting the stupidities of so many scribblers."

wood; although plans were drawn up to build one of stone, they never saw completion before the death of the dictator.

"He built a kind of hunting-theatre of wood, which was called an amphitheatre from the fact that it had seats all around without any stage. In honour of this and of his daughter he exhibited combats of wild beasts and gladiators."

Cassius Dio - Roman History

Seating in theatres was regulated by law and custom. The honorary seats set closest to the performance were reserved for use by Patricians, senators and serving magistrates, thus separating them from offensive behaviour or disturbances caused by the lower classes. Eventually the area called the orchestra was used for their stools instead, since the use of choruses eventually faded. However a law passed in 68 BC declared the next closest 14 rows of benches should be reserved for the equestrians, indicating the growing status of that class and providing a greater buffer for the patricians from the increasingly crass conduct of the plebeians.

From prologues of plays from the time, it appears that slaves and women were also allowed to attend public theatrical performances during the Republic, although they had no dedicated area assigned to them, the rest of the seating being 'first come, first served'.

HOUSES (DOMI)

From the time of kings until the end of the early Republic, most Romans lived in crude huts, built of unbaked brick or wood, with a pounded floor (pavimentum) of crushed brick or pottery and roofed with thatch or shingles. All houses were originally only a single story high but as the price of land within the city began to rise, so housing began adding extra floors so as to maximise living space on each plot. Only wealthier people could afford to build a sprawling domus, whereas the poor were gradually forced into living in multi-story tenement buildings.

"What is there more holy, what is there more carefully fortified with every degree of religious respect, than the house of each individual citizen?"

Cicero - On his house

It was not until the late Republic that magnificent houses began to be constructed, paid for by the wealth procured by Rome's overseas conquests. In its last 50 years, the Republic displayed a very rapid evolution of grandeur, with the addition of marble to decorate walls, furnish lintels and build columns. Such squandering of wealth was looked down upon in public by patricians and equestrians but increasingly imitated by them in private. Meanwhile, the living conditions of the plebeians grew ever more crowded and worse.

"M. Lepidus, who was consul with Q. Catulus, was the first to have the lintels of his house made of Numidian marble, a thing for which he was greatly censured."

Pliny the Elder - Naturalis Historia

A late Republican domus consisted of a formal arrangement of rooms, although the precise layout could vary according the size and shape of the plot it was built upon. It normally possessed two floors, a tiled roof and lacked any external windows, save perhaps on the upper floor, to improve security. In addition the domus would have a single main door accessing the building, although some might have a second portal leading to a back street for covert access and these would possess mechanical locks with supplemental bars and bolts.

In severe winter weather, heating was provided by portable braziers which held hot coals. Other than that, a traditional Roman had to wrap up warm and endure, or pay a visit to the baths and take advantage of their hypocaust heated hot rooms.

The example floorplan overleaf is based on a domus excavated in Pompeii. Note that most internal doorways (ostia) are closed off using curtains which allow better airflow but lack much in the way of privacy from sounds.

Atrium. The most important part of the house, this was the formal entrance hall and social centre of the home. It had an open hole in the roof (compluvium) above a pool (impluvium) into which rainwater drained. The pool in turn fed an underground cistern to supply the home with water. The roof was supported by columns and the opening allowed sunlight to illuminate the rooms adjoining the atrium, aided by reflections from the water. Because of the available light, the atrium was where the womenfolk worked during the day. In addition the pool acted as a cooling system when the temperature was hot. The atrium also contained the lararium, a small shrine to the household gods, the Lares.

Alae. Wings which improve the space available to the atrium and tablinum. Noble families also place the wax masks (imagines) of their illustrious ancestors on display here.

Cubicula or **Cellae**. Small rooms adjoining the atrium. They are normally dark due to a lack of windows but this is not considered as a hindrance since most of the time the family spends its time in the atrium. Those on the ground floor were normally used as storage rooms (cellae), libraries (bibliotheca) and so forth; those on the upper floor were used as bedrooms (cubicula). Those cubicula connected to the peristylium were probably used as slave quarters.

Culina. The kitchen, which normally contained ovens and stoves for cooking. In earlier times cooking would have been performed in the atrium.

Exedra. The garden room used for formal entertainments and lavish dinner parties. The walls were often painted with garden or rural themes.

Peristylium. A colonnaded courtyard which contains a garden. Like the atrium, the peristylium is open to the sky. The garden primarily provides both decoration and pleasant scents but is also used to grow fruits and herbs. The walls of the portico are normally painted with frescoes and the garden often contains statues, fountains, or even fish ponds.

Tabernae. If the domus fronts a busy street, it normally rents out the two roadside rooms as shops. These do not connect through to the house however. In more salubrious areas these rooms do not

---

LOCKS

Although originally developed in ancient Egypt, it took the Romans till the late Republic before they began to use door locks (clausurae). Property was originally guarded by family members or slaves, who would bar the door behind those who went out. This meant that homes or shops were never left unattended.

The first locks were intricate 'latch lifting' affairs, using keys with prongs which inserted into locks with an exactly matching series of holes – each one containing a locking pin. Only when all the pins were lifted clear, could the key move the lock bar sideward. Cheap door locks were made of wood; expensive ones of bronze or iron. This simple design did not evolve much beyond the basic concept and specialised thieves with mechanical knowledge could pick them with the right tools. This led to the disguising of door locks behind or within ornate metalwork facings. Eventually more complex designs introducing a 'quarter turn' of the key were developed, which made direct access to the pins more difficult.

Romans also used padlocks to secure chests. These worked on a similar principle but used springs instead of gravity assisted pins. These locks were always made of bronze or iron and could be extremely strong; in particular those locking the iron bound coffers, which contained a family's wealth. The Pater Familias normally carried the key to the strongbox, sometimes wearing it on a finger ring if the key was reasonably small. It was the duty of Roman Matrons to carry the keys to the doors of the home, which were usually large and carried as a bunch on the belt. It was considered wise to have locks on the doors of certain storage rooms, those containing valuable equipment or materials, such as wine for example.

Divina natura dedit agros, ars humana aedificavit urbes – The divine nature produced the fields, human skill has built cities (Tibullus)

open on the street, rather they are utilised for more internal space. One is generally given to the porter who answers the door.

Tablinum. In earlier times this was the master bedroom. Towards the late Republic it was instead used as an office or study and is the place where a patron meets his clients. It is also the room where the family records and strongbox (arca) are stored. Arcae are used to store money and valuables, so they are chained or pinned to the floor to prevent the entire box being carried off. The tablinum could be closed off from the rest of the home with curtains or folding panel doors.

Triclinium. The dining room. This was normally furnished with three large couches (triclinia) designed to hold up to three people each, surrounding a low table. Sometimes there are backed chairs in the room too for the use of women and old men. There were often two such dining rooms, the one in the peristylium being favoured for meals in the summer. Like most of the communal spaces in the domus, the walls were usually painted.

Vestibulum. The entrance hall which passed between the rented spaces used as shops. The length of the passageway helped to insulate the home from street noise. It was normally decorated and had welcoming messages inscribed on the walls such as salve (good heath), nihil intret mali (may no evil enter) or cave canem (beware of dog).

By the end of the Republic, further decoration for the home was provided by mosaics which had superseded the usual paved floor.

TENEMENTS (INSULAE)

Rome was the first city to use flats for residence. Tenement buildings were high-rise apartment blocks, into which families were increasingly shoehorned. Such insulae could be between three and nine stories high but most averaged about six or seven.

The majority of insulae were built cheaply from substandard materials (the poorest being made totally from second-hand wood) and were prone to collapse. Unlike today where the topmost penthouses are the most sought after, the upper floors in a Roman tenement were the cheapest since there were more flights of steps to climb (a concern if you must collect water daily) and they were the most difficult to escape from if the building caught fire.

"But here we inhabit a city supported for the most part by slender props: for that is how the bailiff holds up the tottering house, patches up gaping cracks in the old wall, bidding the inmates sleep at ease under a roof ready to tumble about their ears. No, no, I must live where there are no fires, no nightly alarms. Ucalegon below is already shouting for water and shifting his chattels; smoke is pouring out of your third-floor attic, but you know nothing of it; for if the alarm begins in the ground-floor, the last man to burn will be he who has nothing to shelter him from the rain but the tiles, where the gentle doves lay their eggs."

Juvenal - Saturae

The ground floor of any insula was used commercially for shops, businesses or taverns. The upper floors were for accommodation. Unlike domi, each upper floor of the building had windows for illumination, which could be sealed by shutters and were often covered by a wickerwork or iron grill to prevent access of birds or reptiles (no glass was used until after the Republic). Despite this, the level of illumination on the lower floors remained poor due to the overshadowing of neighbouring insulae.

LOST PROPERTIES

Attempting to find a particular address, let alone a specific person in the city of Rome is a serious problem. In the city, only the major streets have names; the other minor streets, lanes and alleyways do not – unless given colloquial nicknames by the local residents. In part this is due to the constant rebuilding of areas after collapsing insulae or fires. Thus finding your way requires a detailed description of routes to and from certain landmarks, such as statues, fountains, temples, baths, or even the homes of famous men. Even nameless streets were described as 'the road which leads to…'

In reality, the best a visitor could do is get to the approximate area and then ask around to see if anybody knows the particular person (or place) they were trying to find. The lack of official addresses and property numbers illustrates the fascinating chaos which city life entailed.

The lowest floors were the luxury apartments, which were larger in size, with wood supported concrete floors and ceilings. Sometimes the insulae had piped water to the ground and first floor.

The higher up you went, the smaller the apartments became, until they were just a single room. The floors, ceilings and internal walls switched from brick and concrete to wood in order to save weight. This meant that there was little sound insulation from your neighbours. These higher rooms could be little more than draughty rooms with leaking roofs. In essence, slums placed atop a vertical stack.

"I live in a little cell, with one window which doesn't even fit properly. Boreas himself would not want to live here."

Marshal - Epigrams

Security in an insulae was very important. Lower floors generally had metal grills to prevent theft via windows accessible to ladders. Poorer insulae relied on the watchfulness of nosy neighbours to help reduce burglary. The better apartment blocks had a door slave (janitor or ostiarius) who guarded access to the building. Often the man was chained in place to ensure continuous attendance.

The dangers posed by insulae did not just threaten the inhabitants. Passersby on the streets and alleyways bordering such buildings were constantly at risk from falling roof tiles (as famously portrayed in the film Ben Hur), night soil from tenants too lazy to carry it down to a collection jar, or even accidentally dropped chamber pots themselves. There were so many court cases concerning injury or death from such incidents, that after the Republic a law was passed to prosecute such events. A wise Roman always keeps an eye open on what is above.

Overall, most insulae are dangerous, noisy, ill-maintained and cost a large proportion of a Roman's wage to inhabit. Even so, most tenements were filled to the brim with residents; even space under the stairs was sold on a nightly basis. Thus they made a lot of rent money for their owners.

"The city block of the Arrii Pollii in the possession of Gnaeus Alleius Nigidius Maius is available to rent from July 1st. There are shops on the first floor, upper stories, high-class rooms and a house. A person interested in renting this property should contact Primus, the slave of Gnaeus Alleius Nigidius Maius."

Anonymous Graffiti

Villas (Villae)

Villas come in two kinds. A rural farm estate (villa rustica) and a luxurious home (villa urbana). Only the wealthiest people can afford to possess a villa in the suburbs of Rome. Most villas are situated in large grounds or estates, which in the case of villa urbana are planted with formal gardens, rather than turned over for agriculture. They usually take the same architectural form as domi except that they contain far more rooms and sometimes extra wings to house the additional serving staff such mansions require.

Those that can afford it leave Rome during the height of summer, fleeing the annual heat and diseases which afflict the city. Most nearby villas are therefore used as summer residences, unless the paterfamilias has retired from politics and no longer desires to be in immediate proximity to the city centre.

Since they are normally homes to the rich, most villas are located in positions which take advantage of the local scenery to not only display the home's magnificence but also provide it with spectacular views. Built with sometimes vulgar (and illegal) opulence, often on a monumental scale, they may include luxuries such as private bath houses.

> "But still, why did the laws maintain their silence when the largest of these columns, pillars of Lucullan marble, as much as eight-and-thirty feet in height, were erected in the atrium of Scaurus? a thing, too, that was not done privately or in secret; for the contractor for the public sewers compelled him to give security for the possible damage that might be done in the carriage of them to the Palatium. When so bad an example as this was set, would it not have been advisable to take some precautions for the preservation of the public morals? And yet the laws still preserved their silence, when such enormous masses as these were being carried past the earthenware pediments of the temples of the gods, to the house of a private individual."
>
> Pliny the Elder - Naturalis Historia

Families who own villas in the surrounding countryside often use them to display the treasures and artworks looted from the provinces, since a villa is generally safer from burglary or riots than a property in the city.

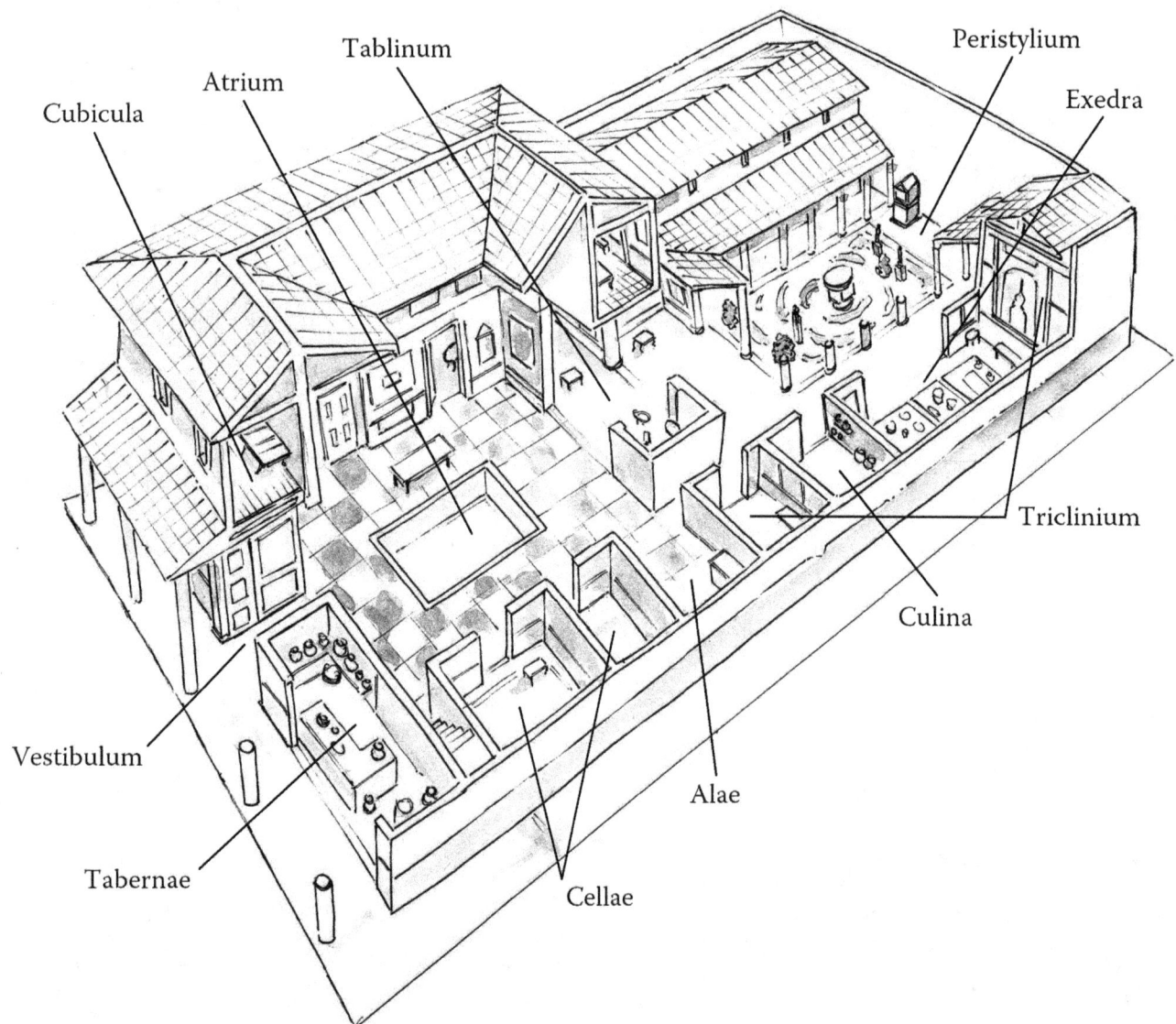

INTERIOR DECORATION (EXORNATIO)

Although early Roman homes were small and simple, the last century of the Republic brought a new era of style and taste, generating an outlet for the increasing wealth of the higher classes.

Walls which originally were simply plastered and painted a single colour now became covered in frescoes. Floors once pounded earth or plainly tiled, now sported mosaics of ever increasing complexity (see Art on page 36).

Romans had little furniture and most homes were quite Spartan, lacking anything beyond the necessities for life. Even wealthy households had limited amounts of furniture and utensils, although what they owned was more ostentatious, often ornately carved, painted, enamelled or gilded. It usually took the form of tables, chairs, couches, beds, carpets, chests and the occasional cabinet.

Tables were either circular with one or three legs (monopodium, or cilliba) or rectangular with four legs (mensa). Poorer Romans used plain tables made of unadorned wood with straight legs. The most expensive tables had surfaces of richly decorated wood or stone polished to bring out the grain of the material and often inlaid with other woods, tortoiseshell, enamels or metals. The legs (fulcra) were sometimes formed of ivory or precious metals and could be carved in the shapes of animal legs, graceful curves or lathed into exotic spindles. Some tables even had adjustable legs to modify the height of the surface.

Circular tables were normally used to support lamps or toiletries, whereas rectangular ones were for working on, whether that be scribing or cooking. A further type of table called an abacus was a sideboard with a top of marble for the display of gold or silver dinner services. It held partitions beneath the surface for storing the plate.

> "Gneius Manlius was the first who introduced brazen banqueting-couches, buffets, and tables with single feet, when he entered the City in triumph, in the year 567 AUC, after his conquests in Asia."
>
> Pliny the Elder - Naturalis Historia

Poor Romans used stools (sellae) or benches (subsellia) in the home, although benches were also used in public locations such as courtrooms or theatres. Folding stools with ivory legs (sellae curules) were a sign of high magisterial authority and only dictators, censors, consuls, prætors, curule ædiles and the Flamen Dialis were permitted to sit upon them.

High backed chairs with arms (solia) were normally used by the head of a household to conduct business, since the height of the chair's seat (which required a step to mount) lent the occupant an air of authority. Armless chairs with slightly more comfortable curving backs (cathedrae) were popular with lecturers and women. Although neither type of chair was upholstered, most Romans used stuffed pillows to pad the hardness of the wood.

The couch (lectus) was a multipurpose piece of furniture. It was used for sitting, reclining, reading, eating and sleeping, but was generally beyond the reach of poorer people to afford. Like chairs, couches were not upholstered, instead using thin mattresses, supported over a frame criss-crossed with leather or rope. Couches could have one or two arms, and sometimes also a back, depending on its purpose. Those designed for sleeping were generally larger than those used as a general sofa. Since they were articles of furniture used primarily by the wealthy, they were often richly decorated with inlays or precious metals and like tables possessed ornamental legs.

Beds (lecti cubiculares) were introduced with the spoils imported from Asia in the late Republic and eventually superseded couches for sleeping. They had the appearance of modern bedsteads with a headboard to retain pillows and four pillars to support a canopy (aulaea) which kept dust off, and might even have sported curtains for repelling insects whilst sleeping. Like couches they were sprung with a lattice of leather or rope straps, atop which a mattress was placed.

Common Romans continued to sleep on stuffed mattresses (tori) on the floor. These were originally filled with straw and dried herbs, but later the stuffing comprised of wool or even feather down for those who could afford it.

> "as a mattress having lost its Leuconian wool…"
>
> Martial - Epigrams

Carpets (tapetes) were another versatile piece of furniture, thicker ones used as wall hangings or floor coverings and thinner ones as throws spread over chairs, benches, couches or beds. They were as expensive as the dyes and designs woven into them and most were luxury items.

Chests (arcae) are used for storing clothing and items not used on a daily basis. They could be as decorated as the owner wished and of any size. Strongboxes were large, heavy chests devised to hold money, jewels and important documents in safety, usually being bound with bronze or iron and chained to the floor. Capsae were special circular boxes designed to hold and transport scrolls.

Cabinets (armaria) were upright items of furniture mounted against walls, with doors to keep out pests or thieves. They were originally used to store arms (weapons and armour) but soon held other semi-valuable articles such as scrolls, ornaments and even the wax masks of dead ancestors (imagines). They often included locks to prevent those without permission from opening the doors.

Since storage furniture was relatively expensive and took up considerable amounts of often limited living space, the walls of some domus and insulae were fitted with shelves, or incorporated cubby holes. In poorer residences, nails hammered into walls and hooks suspended from beams offered further storage for clothing and food.

Other important articles of a Roman household were those which provided light and heat.

Candles (candelae) were used by the poor and were made either of wax (cera) or tallow (sebum). Oil lamps (lucernae) could be made from either pottery or bronze. They burned olive oil, an expensive commodity but provided a brighter light than a candle. Roman candelabrum originally held candles but eventually evolved so that they supported multiple oil lamps, concentrating the illumination provided. Torches (faces) were never used for internal lighting since they produced large quantities of smoke and were inherently dangerous fire sources.

Many poor Romans lacked lights at night, forcing them to retire early or visit other establishments such as caupona or lupanaria, which provided (very) basic lighting for their customers.

Heating during the Republic was provided by braziers filled with slow burning charcoal. Being made from metal they were very expensive and could be as ostentatious as the purchaser desired.

Curtains (vela) were commonly used in households in place of internal doors or to divide rooms. Since even rudimentary fabric was costly, in poorer homes such curtains would probably be made from very rough cloth, rags beyond repair or even strings of beads.

Those who could afford such extravagance could further clutter their homes with statues, pools, fountains, and wall hung paintings.

Such artwork was considerably more expensive than furniture, and well beyond the reach of most plebeians.

Finally, no home save the worst slums lacked crockery, drinking vessels, water jugs and the ubiquitous chamber pot.

Shops (Tabernae)

Tabernae are places where items or services can be purchased. Within Rome, shops are generally found in two locations. Either

Shop Owners and Tradesmen (Tabernarii)

Although the ancient Latin nomenclature for many shops has been lost, the names of their proprietors can still be found in the surviving texts of the time. The following list is a brief overview of the diversity of differing occupations which could operate out of tabernae, officinae and pergulae towards the end of the Republic.

Accountants (calculatores)
Architects (architecti)
Artists (artifices)
Bakers (panifices)
Bankers (argentarii)
Barbers (barbitonsores)
Belt makers (baltearii)
Blacksmiths (ferrarii)
Book sellers (bibliopolae or librariae)
Bottle/Flask/Jar dealer (ampullarii)
Bronze/Coppersmith (aerarii)
Bronze vessel dealers (corinthii)
Builders (aedifices or fabricatores)
Butchers (lanii or carnarii)
Cake sellers (crustularii)
Candelabra maker (candelabrarii)
Carpenters (fabri)
Carpet/Rug maker (cilicarii)
Cart wrights (carpentarii)
Chest/Casket/Box makers (arcularii)
Cloak/Mantle makers (paenularii)
Cobblers (sutores)
Confectionary sellers (cuppedenarii)
Cooper (cuparii)
Copyists (bibliographi)
Cushion makers (culcitarii)
Embroiderers (plumarii)
Engravers (caelatores)
Fishmongers (bolonae)
Florists (rosarii)
Fruiterers (pomarii)
Fullers (fullones)
Furniture dealers (archiacae)
Girdle makers (zonarii)
Goldsmiths (aurarii)
Hairdressers (tonsores)
Helmet maker (cassidarii)
Ivory dealers (eborarii)

Jewelers (anularii)
Lamp makers (lucernarii)
Leather sack sellers (cullearii)
Lingerie delaers (strophiarii)
Locksmiths (clavicarii or claustrarii)
Mason (caementarii)
Metal vessel and tableware makers (vascularii)
Money dealers (monetarii)
Mosaic layers (tessellarii)
Needle sellers (acuarii)
Oil sellers (olearii)
Fresco Painters (pictores)
Paints and unguent sellers (pigmentarii)
Papyrus dealer (chartarii)
Perfume/Ointment sellers (unguentarii)
Pharmacists (pharmacopolae)
Pipe/Flute makers (aulopoii)
Plummers (plumbarii)
Pork sellers (porcinarii)
Potters (figuli)
Preserved food dealer (conditarii)
Rope makers (restiones)
Salt fish dealer (cybiarii)
Sandal makers (baxearii)
Sausage sellers (botularii)
Scribes (librarii)
Sculptors (plastae)
Second hand junk dealers (scrutarii)
Shield makers (scutarii)
Shoe sellers (calcearii)
Silk dealers (sericarii)
Silversmiths (fabri argentarii)
Slave dealers (venalicii)
Spice dealers (aromatarii)
Tailors (vestiarii)
Taper sellers (ceriolarii)
Tavern keeper (caupones)
Trouser makers (bracarii)
Trumpet/Horn maker (cornuarii)
Tunic makers (manulearii)
Undertaker (libitinarii)
Wine sellers (vinarii)
Wax dealer (cerarii)
Weaver (textores)
Wreath/Garland sellers (coronarii)

Dulce et decorum est pro patria mori – It is sweet and proper to die for one's country (Horace)

built into the front of houses and ground floors of insulae or situated around the sides of fora and basilicae. Most tabernae are simple, single room chambers open to the road, where passersby can purchase whatever is on display. They usually possess shutters to keep thieves out at night when the shop keeper either returns home or retires to the loft above their shop (which also acts as further storage for stock).

> *"Nor are these your only terrors. When your house is shut, when bar and chain have made fast your shop, and all is silent, you will be robbed by a burglar; or perhaps a cut-throat will do for you quickly with cold steel."*
> *Juvenal - Saturae*

Many shops also double as the workshop that produces the final product being sold, although by the late Republic the number of shops simply selling goods imported from the countryside or overseas increases dramatically with the growing wealth of the city.

Tabernae often utilise wall paintings (or even pavement mosaics for those wealthy enough) as advertisements indicating the type of product available within, and to identify particular shops amongst the multitude of other competing businesses.

Certain classes of shops posses their own specific names; Popinae are bistros, Cauponae sell wine, Thermopolia hot drinks and fast food, Pistrina are bakeries which specialise in either bread, pastries or confectionary, Lanienae are butchers shops, Librarii are booksellers, Fullonicae laundrettes, Calceariae shoe shops, Fabricae workshops, Ferraria black smithies, Figilinae potteries and Barbae (or Tonstrinae) are barbers/hairdressers.

Some tabernae were offices (officinae), where a service rather than a product could be purchased, for example accountants; and stalls (pergulae) which were temporarily erected tents or tables set up in the streets or fora, from which sellers would hawk their wares during the day and would then be collapsed and taken away at night. Stalls were presumably cheaper to operate since they paid less rent but required more effort.

Not all tabernae operated out of a small street facing room. Some required much larger premises such as fullers shops, which needed many large tubs to soak and bleach the clothing and space to dry it afterwards. Other professions, for example slave traders, needed a different type of location to expose their wares to a larger audience. Thus they would more usually set up in one of the fora. Antisocial businesses like dyers, armourers or garum manufacturers, would be by law restricted within the city limits, in order to save the local populace from the smell or noise.

Whilst most food, drink and service providers would be liberally scattered across the city, those shops specialising in more luxurious items, usually cluster together in more exclusive districts where they communally pay for better protection against theft and extortion.

TOMBS AND NECROPOLISES (SEPULCRA)

Following a tradition inherited from the Etruscans, wealthy Romans preserved and honoured the memory and ideals of dead ancestors by building tombs or monuments to them. However, since the bodies or ashes of the dead could not be interred within the city walls, these mausoleums were instead erected along the sides of the main roads leading from Rome, where their glory could be viewed by others. After many centuries streets such as the Via Appia were so thickly clustered with sepulchres for several miles along their length that they became known as necropolises and were notorious lurking places for bandits seeking to ambush travellers.

Tombs used to hold the bones and ashes of those cremated were called Sepulcra and those containing unburned bodies were known as Conditoria. The burial chambers of the latter were placed underground to help preserve the flesh and hide the smell of decomposition from passersby. The Romans originally disposed of their dead by burial but over the course of the Republic cremation superseded it as the fashionable form of hygienic disposal.

Tombs could be built in a range of architectural styles. Normally they took the form of altars or temples, but occasionally arches or

small edifices with niches were constructed as an alternative. They could be round, rectangular, pyramidal, possess porticos, multiple stories, statues, busts and so on and so forth. As long as there was a place for the body or funeral urn (urna) an architect could let his imagination run riot.

Smaller tombs that did not contain an internal chamber, but had the body or ashes buried directly under the monument instead, possessed small receptacles on the surface which were connected via a lead pipe to the remains below. These were used to make offerings of milk and wine to the spirits (manes) of the dead.

Most tombs were placed in a small plot of land surrounded by a low wall. The size of the plot was in part enforced by another law of the Twelve Tables, and limited only by the finances of the family. This space was used to plant funerary gardens of roses, violets and trees, often with a backdrop of shrubbery to enhance the tomb itself, and always incorporated a bench or seat for visiting relatives.

> *"No one, without the knowledge or consent of the owner, shall erect a funeral pyre, or a tomb, nearer than sixty feet to the building of another."*
> *Table X - Sacred Law*

The largest tombs incorporated other structures into their formal gardens. Since there were several festivals held throughout the year to honour the dead, most families journeyed out to their ancestor's tombs to give the spirits of the departed votive offerings. On more extensive grounds there were places of shelter, arbours and dining-rooms too, in which were celebrated the anniversary feasts. They also had private places for the burning of bodies (ustrinae). Furthermore, extensive funerary gardens could be decorated with pools (piscinae), fountains (fontes), or terraces (solaria) planted with grape vines.

The poor of Rome who could not afford a tomb were buried or burned on the eastern part of the Esquiline Hill. Their remains thrown into small pits (puticulae) along with the carcasses of dead animals and the night soil, rubbish and muck collected from the roads of the city. The resulting smell of decomposition was so bad, that the Esquiline was considered unfit for residence, meaning that only the worst slums subsisted there.

AQUEDUCTS (AQUAE DUCTUS)

Apart from the natural springs and wells on the hills, the only source of fresh, clean water comes from aqueducts which carry it from sources many miles away from the city. Marvels of engineering, the aqueducts follow lines of natural terrain and mainly run underground or in covered canals, which prevent the water from temperature variations and being polluted. Inverted siphons and viaducts were only built when the line of the aqueduct was forced to span open spaces such as valleys. Likewise tunnels (specus) and their associated inspection shafts were only dug through solid rock when no other option was available.

During the Republic the following aqueducts were constructed.

Ω Aqua Appia – Constructed in 312 BC by the censor Appius Claudius Caecus and terminated in the Forum Boarium, near the Porta Trigemina.

Ω Aqua Anio Vetus – Built from 272-269 BC, the Anio Vetus redirected river water to its terminus on the Viminal Hill. Between it and the Aqua Appia, every part of Rome was supplied with water, except for the Palatine Hill.

Ω Aqua Marcia – The longest aqueduct built in Rome, it was built from 144-140 BC by the prætor Quintus Marcius Rex. It followed the route of the Via Tiburtina into the city and supplied the Capitoline Hill. The aqueduct was well known for its cold, pure waters. It also supplied the Palatine Hill, filling the gap left by the previous two aqueducts.

"The most celebrated water throughout the whole world, and the one to which our city gives the palm for coolness and salubrity, is that of the Marcian Spring, accorded to Rome among the other bounties of the gods:"

Pliny the Elder - Naturalis Historia

Ω Aqua Tepula – Constructed in 126 BC by the censors G. Servilius Caepio and L. Cassius Longinus, the aqueduct was named for the tepid, lukewarm it delivered to the Aventine Hill, and was not considered fit for human consumption.

Ω Aqua Julia – built in 33 BC by Agrippa during his ædileship, the aqua Julia helped supply the Caelian and Aventine hills.

Once the aqueduct reached Rome, the water was diverted into vast covered reservoirs (castella) to deposit sediment and build up

sufficient pressure to feed the network of stone lined canals (canales structiles) and terracotta conduits (tubuli fictiles) which filled smaller storage reservoirs. Lead pipes (fistulae plumbeae) were used to connect the secondary cisterns to the buildings of the city. The majority of these pipes fed public fountains and basins – from which most Romans gained their water. Excess overflow from these was diverted to bath houses, latrines, and fullers shops, but the establishment had to pay for the privilege.

"'No private person shall conduct other water than that which flows from the basins to the ground' (for these are the words of the law); that is, water which overflows from the troughs; we call it "lapsed" water; and even this was not granted for any other use than for baths or fulling establishments; and it was subject to a tax, for a fee was fixed, to be paid into the public treasury."

Frontinus - De Aquis

A few wealthy individuals could purchase the right to have water piped directly into their homes but most illegally tapped the mains water and simply bribed the officials (aquarii) who were supposed to prevent such activity to look the other way.

"The cause of this is the dishonesty of the water-men, whom we have detected diverting water from the public conduits for private use. But a large number of landed proprietors also, past whose fields the aqueducts run, tap the conduits; whence it comes that the public water-courses are actually brought to a standstill by private citizens, just to water their gardens."

Frontinus - De Aquis

By the late Republic the amount of water flowing into the city had increased so much that further improvements were made to divert any surplus overflow of the public cisterns into tertiary reservoirs which were used to supply water for decorative ponds and gardens.

The water pressure from storage cisterns was normally so low that water could not be piped above the ground floor of most buildings. Those living in insulae had to send slaves to fetch water from the nearest fountain or carry it themselves up to the floor they lived on. Most Romans kept a small amount of water in their rooms, reserved in case of fire.

The ubiquitous lead pipes that fed water throughout the city were thought by the Romans themselves to cause poisoning. However, despite their clever observations, the high calcium content of Rome's water actually prevented the take-up of lead; elevated concentrations of which were far more likely to have come from the sweet sapa syrup used as both a preservative and condiment (see Wine page 46).

"Water conducted through earthen pipes is more wholesome than that through lead; indeed that conveyed in lead must be injurious, because from it white lead is obtained, and this is said to be injurious to the human system. Hence, if what is generated from it is pernicious, there can be no doubt that itself cannot be a wholesome body. This may be verified by observing the workers in lead, who are of a pallid colour; for in casting lead, the fumes from it fixing on the different members, and daily burning them, destroy the vigour of the blood; water should therefore on no account be conducted in leaden pipes if we are desirous that it should be wholesome."

Vitruvius - De Architectura

FOUNTAINS (FONTES)

During the early days of Rome, water was collected from the natural springs and streams which fed the marshes that lay between the hills. Notable ones were named the Fons Lupercalis, Fons Apollinaris, Fons Pici, and Fons Mercurii.

These were often walled to form pools or ponds (lacus) to contain the water so that it could be easily gathered without getting wet or muddy in the process. One example was the 'Public Pool' (Piscina Publica), a small lake in the southern part of the city. However, due to improved drainage and the ever increasing need for land development, this pool had nearly disappeared by the time of Augustus.

Other famous pools were the Lacus Iuturnae in the Forum Romanum where the mythological Dioscuri, Castor and Pollux (the sons of Jupiter and Leda), were said to have stopped to water their horses after aiding the Romans to victory at the battle of Lake Regillus in 499 BC. A temple to them was later built on the spot.

Another pool, also located in the Forum, was called the Lacus Curtius. This pool had three separate stories explaining its origin. The first was that this was the place where Metius Curtius, the leader of the Sabines, fell into a boggy hole when in the midst of a battle against the Romans under the command of Romulus. The second story said that a spring originated there after a divine thunderbolt had struck the ground in 445 BC. The third and more entertaining legend records that in 362 BC a bottomless hole opened up in the ground in the forum and an oracle foresaw that it could only be closed by throwing in the most valuable thing in Rome. A young man named Marcus Curtius, dressed himself in armour and on horseback, cast himself into the chasm; whereupon the abyss closed, leaving only a spring behind.

Yet despite the number of springs tapped in the early Republic, there was still insufficient water for the people of the city. Water had to be drawn from wells, carried from the River Tiber, or collected from rainfall stored in underground cisterns.

With the building of the aqueducts came the first public fountains. These came in two forms; water basins fed from beneath (castellum divisorium) and fountains with water spouts (salientes). Water basins were far more common than the ornamental fountains, and were designed for public use as sources of drinking and washing water.

"…how much is used for water basins, how much for fountains, how much for public structures, how much on account of the State, how much by private consumers."

Frontinus - De Aquis

Most fountains came in the shape of large flat bowls cut out of a single piece of stone, and supported by a central leg, somewhat like a shallow drinking vessel. More ostentatious fountains sported bronze statues, such as boys, tritons, nereids, and other mythological subjects, often with the water spouting from their features.

SEWERS (CLOACAE)

Rome was the first city to make extensive use of sewers and even had its own patron goddess Cloacina, whose shrine was built in the forum. Its main and most famous sewer, the Cloaca Maxima, was built during the time of the late Kings but in reality was simply a ditch which controlled the path of the streams which descended from the hills, and drained off the water which stagnated in the marshes between them. By the end of the Monarchy, the ditch was lined with stone and had effectively become an open topped canal (canalis).

The partial draining of the marsh allowed it to be developed into a communal area, eventually evolving into the Forum Romanum. Minor cloacae branched off from the main canal, taking strangely kinked routes to pass round buildings, rather than pass beneath them. In fact, the main channel of the Cloaca Maxima did not begin to be covered over with vaults until the 2nd century BC. Until that time, they remained open and had to be crossed by bridges. As such, they remained dangerous obstacles for the clumsy or unwary. A famous Stoic philosopher, Crates of Mallos, in 168 BC apparently broke his leg by falling in the Cloaca Maxima.

Unfortunately, the running waters of the cloacae were used by the populace to dispose of rubbish as well as night soil and almost from its original construction it became a sewer. However, such dumping created blockages.

"[In 184 BC] The censors cut off from the public aqueducts all supplies of water for private houses or land, and wherever private owners had built up against public buildings or on public ground, they demolished these structures within thirty days. They next made contracts for lining the reservoirs with stone and, where it was necessary, cleaning out the sewers, money having been set apart for the purpose, and also for the construction of sewers in the Aventine quarter and in other places where as yet there were none."

Livy - Ab Urbe Condita

The idea of using the running water to 'flush' away body wastes quickly caught on, and in the 2nd century BC the first public latrines were built and soon became very popular. Roman toilets were literally communal affairs with no partitions to hide your 'movements', which allowed people to socialise during their ablutions. Since paper did not exist at the time, you wiped your bottom using a sponge on a stick… What is worse is that the next person would rinse the same sponge in water before using it themselves.

Most public latrines cost money to use, although in return you would get clean marble seats to sit upon and they were heated in winter too. Despite this apparent cleanliness and luxury, Roman public latrines were probably rather unhygienic.

The baths (balneae) were also plumbed into the sewer system, so that their daily drained waste water could add to the general flow and help carry away effluent. Other urban runoff such as overflow from fountains and water basins also contributed to cleanse the sewer system. Despite the growth of the sewer network along and under the roads, few private residences during the Republic were directly connected to it, save those which were built directly after the Gallic sack of Rome by Brennus in 387 BC.

"In their haste, they took no trouble to plan out straight streets; as all distinctions of ownership in the soil were lost, they built on any ground that happened to be vacant. That is the reason why the old sewers, which originally were carried under public ground, now run everywhere under private houses, and why the conformation of the City resembles one casually built upon by settlers rather than one regularly planned out."

Livy - Ab Urbe Condita

Most private houses still used cess pits for disposal but these had to be dug out and emptied on a regular basis. Those people living in tenements used chamber pots instead. These were emptied in to vats stored under the building's stairwell, or if these were not provided, at a sewer access point in the street. Many citizens could not be bothered and simply cast the contents out of the nearest window.

"From every towering roof the rubbish falls, Striking the head, and injuries grow rank. See how pots strike and dint the study pavement there's death from every window where you move. You'd be a fool to venture out to dine, oblivious of what goes on above, without you having penned the dotted line Of your last testament, You can but hope they spill a chamber pot."

Juvenal - Saturae

During the late Republic there were three major sewer systems running into the Tiber.

Ω Cloaca Maxima – Runs from the Argiletum (the main street of the Subura) through the Forum Romanum, zigzags across the Velabrum, passes the Forum Boarium and empties into the Tiber downstream of the Pons Sublicius.

Ω Cloaca Circus Maximus – Built in the 6th century BC, this sewer flows down the centre of (and under) the Circus Maximus, and was bridged in at least two places to allow the chariot course to cross over it.

Ω Cloaca Magna (Great Drain) – Drained the Swamp of the Goats (Palus Caprae) on the Campus Martius. It started to be covered in 221 BC when the Circus Flaminius was constructed over it.

By the end of the Republic, the majority of the sewers had been covered over, allowing safer movement along the streets and probably helping to contain the smell too.

"The sewers, covered with a vault of tightly fitted stones, have room in some places for hay wagons to drive through them. And the quantity of water brought into the city by aqueducts is so great that rivers, as it were, flow through the city and the sewers; almost every house has water tanks, and service pipes, and plentiful streams of water..."

Strabo - Geography

Once vaulted however, the sewers took on a more sinister aspect, since they were often used for the disposal of dead bodies. In later times under cover of darkness Nero was reputed to have 'catch up a cap or a wig and go to the taverns or range about the streets playing pranks, which however were very far from harmless; for he used to beat men as they came home from dinner, stabbing any who resisted him and throwing them into the sewers', a trend which was probably inherited from the violence of the late Republic. Unfortunately, during times of pestilence the sewers were also used to dispose of the dead, which sometimes spread the disease.

"Not the least of the evils the city suffered, and the reason why the pestilence did not quickly abate, was the way in which they cast out the dead bodies. For though at first, both from a sense of shame and because of the plenty they had of everything necessary for burials, they burned the bodies and committed them to earth, at the last, either through a disregard of decency or from a lack of the necessary equipment, they threw many of the dead into the sewers under the streets and cast far more of them into the river; and from these

they received the most harm. For when the bodies were cast up by the waves upon the banks and beaches, a grievous and terrible stench, carried by the wind, smote those also who were still in health and produced a quick change in their bodies; and the water brought from the river was no longer fit to drink, partly because of its vile odour and partly by causing indigestion."

Dionysius of Halicarnassus - Roman Antiquities

Right at the end of the Republic in 33 BC, Marcus Vipsanius Agrippa during his term as ædile undertook to clean out and refurbish the entire sewer system of Rome. After this he founded a permanent group of 250 slaves that were to maintain the sewers and aqueducts.

"But it was in those days, too, that old men still spoke in admiration of the vast proportions of the Agger, and of the enormous foundations of the Capitol; of the public sewers, too, a work more stupendous than any; as mountains had to be pierced for their construction, and, like the hanging city which we recently mentioned, navigation had to be carried on beneath Rome; an event which happened in the ædileship of M. Agrippa, after he had filled the office of consul."

Pliny the Elder - Naturalis Historia

BATHS (BALNEAE)

The first record of balneae in Rome occurs in the 2nd century BC. By the end of the Republic there were hundreds of privately owned, yet publicly accessible balneae in the city, most serving the local residents of the district where it is built. The larger state owned thermae, which could cover an area the size of several apartment blocks, did not exist during the Republic.

Most baths are modest sized buildings, which can only service a few hundred people at any time. Acting as sports clubs as much as places of personal hygiene, some early baths maintain a degree of exclusivity by charging higher entry fees. Yet most are extremely cheap earning their profits by high turnover, rather than catering to richer patrons. By the end of the Republic, the baths had become a place where members of any social class can mingle and rub shoulders together.

Once the hypocaust was invented just before the Social War in 91 BC, Roman baths began to be heated. Before this, the waters would have remained cold, which in a warm, mild climate was not necessarily a bad thing, save in winter when it might have taken a Stoic to utilise them fully.

Later baths are built around a similar plan. They possess a warm room (tepidarium), a hot room (caldarium) and a cold room (frigidarium). The hypocaust funnels hot air from fires under the floor and up the walls, keeping the warmer rooms, as well as the water heated. In more comprehensive baths there might also be a wet steam room (sudatorium) and a hot, dry sauna (laconicum).

"In other cases, again, it is by their vapours that waters are so beneficial to man, being so intensely hot as to heat our baths even, and to make cold water boil in our sitting-baths;"

Pliny the Elder - Naturalis Historia

Bath houses have a changing room (apodyterium) which lies beyond the main entrance, where the charging booth is. They also have a gymnasium (palaestra) which lies either in the centre or behind the building.

Since during the Republic very few homes have a central heating system using hypocausts, when it is very cold many people go to the baths in order to warm themselves up.

"First of all that harsh and old-fashioned man inveighed against those persons who, in the month of April, were spending their time at Baiæ, and using the warm baths. What have we to do with this morose and severe man? The manners of our day cannot endure so austere and rigorous a magistrate, who, as far as he can help it, will not allow men older than himself to stay at their own estates and attend to their health with impunity, even at a time when nothing is doing at Rome."

Cicero – Speech against Publius Clodius

HAZARDS OF CITY LIFE (PERICULA URBIS)

A Roman citizen's life is always under threat from a multitude of different dangers. Apart from the earlier mentions of shoddy construction causing entire buildings to collapse, there was threat of crime, riots, fire, flood and pestilence. Even accidents could be fatal from being run down by a cart to having a flower pot dropped on one's head. In a time where medicine was still rather experimental, even a simple broken bone could cost you your life.

STREET CRIME (FACINUS)

Crime is synonymous with Roman city life. After the Punic wars, the number of dispossessed citizens dramatically increased. With no jobs available and no land to farm, many plebeians were forced to a life of crime to survive. Added to this were an ever growing number of freedmen, released from slavery by masters too mean to continue supporting them after injury or old age. Crime, particularly violent crime (vis) continued to grow until by the end of the Republic it had reached endemic proportions.

The streets of Rome were hazardous to those unfamiliar to the city. It was easy to become lost amongst the torturous alleyways and be ambushed by muggers or local gangsters. Travelling at night was particularly perilous. Since Rome lacked any form of street lighting (lamp oil being very expensive and torches being easy to steal), only fools, criminals, or those accompanied by slaves or clients would venture out after dark. In streets sheltered by high tenements, the darkness must have been near total, even on moonlit evenings.

Night was the time of muggers, vindictive drunks, and roaming groups of young noblemen looking for a good time. Encountering one of these could quickly lead to violence and possibly death…

"Your drunken bully who has by chance not slain his man passes a night of torture like that of Achilles when he bemoaned his friend, lying now upon his face, and now upon his back; he will get no rest in any other way, since some men can only sleep after a brawl. Yet however reckless the fellow may be, however hot with wine and young blood, he gives a wide berth to one whose scarlet cloak and long retinue of attendants, with torches and brass lamps in their hands, bid him keep his distance. But to me, who am wont to be escorted home by the moon, or by the scant light of a candle whose wick I husband with due care, he pays no respect. Hear how the wretched fray begins - if fray it can be called when you do all the thrashing and I get all the blows. The fellow stands up against me, and bids me halt; obey I must. What else can you do when attacked by a madman stronger than yourself?

Juvenal - Saturae

THIEVES

Roman thieves (Fures) come in several different kinds.

Ω *Burglars (effractarii) – rob houses and tenements, using stealth to enter buildings either by picking door locks or entering via the windows, which is why many lower floors in insulae have metal grills to prevent entry.*

Ω *Pickpockets (cleptae) – lift the money pouches from pedestrians, even though Romans did not have pockets. Most purses (sacculi) are carried round the waist in the form of a money belt or tucked up under the tunic and held in place by the belt. Some cutpurses use sharp knives to slit belts, allowing pouches stuffed under the tunic to drop to the ground. Cleptae could also be thieves who steal bathers' clothes at the baths... a lucrative and profitable item of trade.*

Ω *Muggers (raptores or insidiatores) – are the bane of the streets but did not only limit their activities to the night. Some side streets were famous for deadly robbers who often had no compunction about killing those they mugged. Most muggers operate in teams of at least two, one to distract the target whilst the other waylays them from behind.*

Ω *A bandit (latro) – is a robber who stakes out the roads outside the city, often using the necropolises as hiding places for ambushes. They normally operate as small gangs in order to overwhelm mounted victims. Sometimes however, these gangs comprise of nothing but desperate beggars seeking food or clothing.*

Ω *Gangsters (grassatores) – occupy each district and neighbourhood of the city. These hoodlums extract protection money from local businesses, run organised crime and are eternally warring with other gangs for control over territory. An enforcer (interfector) would be used to permanently settle more difficult problems…*

Ω *Assassins (sicarii) – are paid murderers. They can be located with the right criminal contacts. Since assassination is infrequent even in Rome, contracts are few and far between, forcing most professional killers to hold employment in a second, often nefarious, career.*

Ω *Forgers (falsarii) and swindlers (deceptores) – are rarely inherently dangerous. However they can separate a citizen from his money and place him in debt, a precarious situation in Rome, since both food and lodging are difficult for most people to afford. To be fleeced in Latin is to suffer a 'plucking' (depilatum).*

RIOTS (SEDITIONES)

Riots are one of the more frightening dangers of the city. Since Rome lacks any sort of police force and by tradition armed soldiers are forbidden within the walls, it is almost impossible to restore order once a riot erupts. The city is repeatedly stricken from civic uprisings during the late Republic.

Et tu, Brute! – You too, Brutus! (Shakespeare)

RULES FOR RIOTS

Riots are one of the few times that the average citizen gets to openly wield weapons within the city. Although 'technically' illegal, nobody is going to declaim or arrest somebody for carrying a knife or even a sword during a riot. People caught unprepared will grab anything to use as an impromptu weapon. Sticks and stones are easily improvised and there are period reports of the stools of magistrates or the separated rods of fasces being used during mob violence; and even some victims being stoned to death with tiles or paving slabs.

Considering most Romans lack any form of armour, becoming involved in a fight using knives or swords is usually lethal and the best advice for player characters is follow in the footsteps of some senators of the time and play dead.

Although violence is inherently dangerous, the most deadly aspect of a riot is actually being trampled by the rush of people fleeing the area. No matter how tough the individual, their strength is useless against a crowd of desperate people, especially when the throng is funnelled in the narrow streets of the city. All that can be done is try to remain upright whilst being pushed along in the flow.

Games Masters should use an Athletics or Brawn roll to see if a character caught up in the crowd surge retains their balance and escapes the scene. If a character fails the balance check then they fall over and must make an Evade roll applying the result on the table below…

Ω **Critical** – *the character miraculously finds some form of cover under a street stall or next to a wall and suffers no damage. They may regain their feet automatically.*

Ω **Success** – *the character suffers 1d6 damage to a single Hit Location but remains conscious and can extract themselves from the bodies, which pin them down once the riot has moved on.*

Ω **Failure** – *the character suffers 2d6 damage to either the Head, Chest or Abdomen, and is rendered unconscious from crushing or being repeatedly kicked.*

Ω **Fumble** – *the character is trampled to death. A Perception roll must be made to recognise the pulped remains once the riot clears.*

For further fun, a Games Master might also require a Status roll for those characters owning property near the epicentre of the riot to see if nearby buildings are looted. A failure means that the contents of the house, shop or apartment were stolen or wrecked. A fumble indicates that the property was raised to the ground by arson.

Rioters often devolve into mindless mob violence against both people and property, and looting is commonplace. When the threat of urban unrest is in the air, most Romans nail up boards across windows, pile up furniture against their doors and arm their slaves to prevent their homes and shops from being attacked.

"And just as often occurs when a riot has broken out in a large gathering of people, and the emotions of the lowly crowd rage, and torches and rocks fly: their fury provides the weapons".

Vergil - The Aeneid

Although a few of the most famous riots were spontaneous reactions from poverty stricken people suffering famine or moral outrage against an unfair judgement, the majority are instigated by ambitious or ruthless officials, who organise mobs to enforce their political will by threat of violence.

The dangers of such insurrections come primarily from factious rioters attacking one another, the trampling of people fleeing the rioters, and the threat of major conflagrations breaking out from looters. Since rioting causes so much death and destruction, and destabilises the city for days afterwards, the act of inciting a riot often results in a death penalty.

"The bystanders rescued him, and as he fled he implored "the protection of the Roman plebs," and said that he was the victim of a conspiracy amongst the patricians, because he had acted generously towards the plebs. He entreated them to come to his help in this terrible crisis, and not suffer him to be butchered before their eyes. Whilst he was making these appeals, Servilius overtook him and slew him. Besprinkled with the dead man's blood, and surrounded by a troop of young patricians, he returned to the Dictator and reported that Maelius after being summoned to appear before him had driven away his officer and incited the populace to riot, and had now met with the punishment he deserved. "Well done." said the Dictator, "C. Servilius, you have delivered the republic.""

Livy - Ab Urbe Condita

A list of the most famous riots follows:

Ω 133 BC – Tiberius Gracchus and 300 of his followers are assassinated by a group of senators fearing his political reformations.

"Now, the attendants of the senators carried clubs and staves which they had brought from home; but the senators themselves seized the fragments and legs of the benches that were shattered by the crowd in its flight, and went up against Tiberius, at the same time smiting those who were drawn up to protect him. Of these there was a rout and a slaughter, and as Tiberius himself turned to fly, someone laid hold of his garments. So he let his toga go and fled in his tunic. But he stumbled and fell to the ground among some bodies that lay in front of him. As he strove to rise to his feet, he received his first blow, as everybody admits, from Publius Satyreius, one of his colleagues, who smote him on the head with the leg of a bench; to the second blow claim was made by Lucius Rufus, who plumed himself upon it as upon some noble deed. And of the rest more than three hundred were slain by blows from sticks and stones, but not one by the sword."

Plutarch - Life of Tiberius Gracchus

Ω 121 BC – Gaius Gracchus, the brother of Tiberius, and Marcus Fulvius Flaccus attempt to protect their law reforms by raising a plebeian mob. The senate declares him an enemy of the state and they along with 3,000 suspected supporters are killed in the ensuing violence.

Ω 103 BC – Riots instigated by Gaius Norbanus, a tribune of the Plebs.

Ω 100 BC – Partisans of the seditious tribune Lucius Appuleius Saturninus murder a candidate running for consul and follow up by seizing the Capitoline hill. A battle erupts in the Forum Romanum between Saturninus' mob and the armed forces of Marius. Despite surrendering, Saturninus and his followers are then murdered by indignant renegade senators.

"Marius shut them up in the senate-house as though he intended to deal with them in a more legal manner. The crowd considered this a mere pretext,

Eventus stultorum magister – Events are the teacher of stupid persons

tore the tiles off the roof, and stoned them to death, including a quæstor, a tribune, and a prætor, who were still wearing their insignia of office."

Appian - The Civil Wars

Ω 98 BC – Publius Furius is brought to trial for his acts whilst tribune and is literally torn to pieces in the assembly.

Ω 87 BC – A riot breaks out between the followers of the two consuls Gnaeus Octavius and Lucius Cornelius Cinna over land redistributions proposed by Marius. Over 10,000 die in the resulting insurgence.

"While Octavius was still at home awaiting the result, the news was brought to him that the majority of the tribunes had vetoed the proposed action, but that the new citizens had started a riot, drawn their daggers on the street, and assaulted the opposing tribunes on the rostra. When Octavius heard this he ran down through the Via Sacra with a very dense mass of men, burst into the forum like a torrent, pushed through the midst of the crowd, and separated them. He struck terror into them, went on to the temple of Castor and Pollux, and drove Cinna away; while his companions fell upon the new citizens without orders, killed many of them, put the rest to flight, and pursued them to the city gates."

Appian - The Civil Wars

Ω 87 BC – Marius returns to Rome and orders the deaths of the leading supporters of Sulla. However things spread out of control and after five days of rioting, 4,000 rampaging soldiers are rounded up and killed, leaving 100 senators and equestrians dead, along with countless other citizens.

Ω 75 BC – Civil discord erupts over a shortage of grain, prompting the consul Gaius Aurelius Cotta to make a speech to the assembly of the people to calm the plebeians.

Ω 67 BC – Following a law reserving the front 14 rows of seats at the theatre for the exclusive use of the equites (whereas previously they had been available to those of any rank) the plebeians start a riot, requiring a public address from the prætor Marcus Tullius Cicero to suppress.

"Marcus Otho was the first to separate in point of honour the equites from the rest of the citizens, which he did when he was prætor, and gave them a particular place of their own at the spectacles, which they still retain. The people took this as a mark of dishonour to themselves, and when Otho appeared in the theatre they hissed him insultingly, while the equestrians received him with loud applause. The people renewed and increased their hisses, and then the equites their applause. After this they turned upon one another with reviling words, and disorder reigned in the theatre."

Plutarch - The Life of Cicero

Ω 66 BC – Rioting occurs at the trial of Caius Cornelius when he is accused of sedition (maiestas) by the brothers Cominii. The trial is abandoned after the brothers are forced to flee the city.

Ω 57 BC – Publius Claudius Pulcher purposely incites his partisans to violence to prevent the passing of a bill to recall

Marcus Tullius Cicero to Rome. Many people die as the assembly flees the pre-planned bloodshed.

"You recollect, O judges, that on that day the Tiber was filled with the corpses of the citizens, that the sewers were choked up; that blood was wiped up out of the forum with sponges; so that all men thought that such a vast number and such a magnificent show of gladiators could not have been provided by any private individual, or plebeian, but must be the exhibition of some patrician and man of prætorian rank."

Cicero - Orations

Ω 57 BC – After a succession of murders, the tribune Titus Annius Milo raises his own force to oppose the autocratic reign of terror the unrestricted violence of Clodius' armed gang has given him. This act condemns the city to another four years of intermittent, uncontrolled violence.

Ω 53 BC – The tribune P. Licinius Crassus Dives causes panicked riots after he proposes that Gnaeus Pompeius be appointed dictator to restore public order.

Ω 52 BC – Rioting runs rampant when the news of Clodius' death reaches Rome, and also takes place at his funeral when the mob builds a pyre for his body in the Curia Hostilia…

"As tribunes they conveyed the body into the Forum just before dawn, placed it on the rostra, exhibited it to all, and spoke appropriate words over it with lamentations. So the populace, as a result of what it both saw and heard, was deeply stirred and no longer showed any regard for things sacred or profane, but overthrew all the customs of burial and burned down nearly the whole city. They took up the body of Clodius and carried it into the senate-house, laid it out properly, and then after heaping up a pyre out of the benches burned both the corpse and the building."

Cassius Dio - Roman History

Ω 44 BC – The last major riot of the Republic follows oration of Marcus Antonius at Julius Caesar's funeral, where he reads Caesar's will and displays the bloody toga, naming the perpetrator of each stab wound. The crowd assault the property of the conspirators who flee the city in fear of their lives.

"And when he saw that the people were mightily swayed and charmed by his words, he mingled with his praises sorrow and indignation over the dreadful deed, and at the close of his speech shook on high the garments of the dead, all bloody and tattered by the swords as they were, called those who had wrought such work villains and murderers, and inspired his hearers with such rage that they heaped together benches and tables and burned Caesar's body in the forum, and then, snatching the blazing faggots from the pyre, ran to the houses of the assassins and assaulted them."

Plutarch - The Life of Antony

FIRES (INCENDIA)

Probably the most regular occurring disasters in Rome are fires. Blazes frequently start in the tenement buildings of the poor, when unsupervised cooking fires or lamps set fire to the (upper) wooden parts of the building. The most frightening thing to the average Roman living in an insulae was that if the fire started below them they could not escape and were faced with either burning to death, asphyxiation or dying by jumping from an upper story window.

Since during the Republic there are no professional firemen, it is up to both the inhabitants and neighbours of an enflamed building to extinguish the blaze themselves. A dangerous task they willingly undertake, since once a large fire starts in the densely packed buildings of the narrow streets, everyone else is threatened.

If a fire spreads out of control it is impossible to extinguish the flames and entire buildings have to be collapsed in order to stop the spread to other neighbourhoods. The loss of life and property from fires is severe. However, those who survive are generally taken care of by the local community in order to help them re-establish their lives after such a disaster. Such charity is freely given since the next time it might be the benefactor themselves who may suffer misfortune. This generosity even extended to the senatorial level.

"But if the grand house of Asturicus be destroyed, the matrons go dishevelled, your great men put on mourning, the prætor adjourns his court: then indeed do we deplore the calamities of the city, and bewail its fires. Before the house has ceased to burn, up comes one with a gift of marble or of building materials, another offers nude and glistening statues, a third some notable work of Euphranor or Polyclitus, or bronzes that had been the glory of old Asian shrines. Others will offer books and bookcases, or a bust of Minerva, or a hundredweight of silver-plate. Thus does Persicus, that most sumptuous of childless men, replace what he has lost with more and better things, and with good reason incurs the suspicion of having set his own house on fire."

Juvenal - Saturae

In the late Republic, the senator Crassus was famed for maintaining his own personal fire-fighting team of slaves. He would wander the streets waiting for a serious fire to occur, and then approach the distraught owner of the building and offer to purchase it at a ridiculously cheap price. If the owner sold, then Crassus would send his small army of slaves into the building to put out the fire, thereby picking up prime property for cut throat prices.

"Crassus missed no chance to accept or buy any properties. Further, seeing how constant and frequent were the problems at Rome of fires and collapses of buildings, because of their size and number, he bought slaves who were architects and builders. When he had five hundred of them, he bought the

properties which were burning down, and those next to them, as their owners would sell them for a very small price through fear and uncertainty, and in this way most of Rome came to be owned by him."

Plutarch - The Life of Crassus

During Rome's Republican history there were a number of catastrophic conflagrations:

Ω 390 BC – The first and greatest conflagration was the sacking of Rome by the Gauls. Since nearly all the buildings at the time were constructed of wood, with thatch or shingle roofs, the fire laid waste to huge swathes of the city, including the Forum Romanum, the Comitium, and all the pontifical records (including those recorded on bronze or stone) were also destroyed. After this the city underwent a significant period of rapid rebuilding, unfortunately without planning or forethought for the future.

"After all the arrangements that circumstances permitted had been made for the defence of the Capitol, the old men returned to their respective homes and, fully prepared to die, awaited the coming of the enemy… They [the Gauls] gazed with feelings of real veneration upon the men who were seated in the porticoes of their mansions, not only because of the superhuman magnificence of their apparel and their whole bearing and demeanour, but also because of the majestic expression of their countenances, wearing the very aspect of gods. So they stood, gazing at them as if they were statues, till, as it is asserted, one of the patricians, M. Papirius, roused the passion of a Gaul, who began to stroke his beard – which in those days was universally worn long – by smiting him on the head with his ivory staff. He was the first to be killed; the others were butchered in their chairs. After this slaughter of the magnates, no living being was thenceforth spared; the houses were rifled, and then set on fire."

Livy - Ab Urbe Condita

Ω 241 BC – The Temple of Vesta (rebuilt after the Gallic conflagration) burned down again. The Pontifex Maximus Caecilius Metellus entered the burning temple and rescued the holy Palladium, which was reputed to have been brought by the hero Aeneas from Troy. Although lauded for his selfless bravery, he was blinded for his impiety, since no male could gaze upon the sacred artefact.

Ω 213 BC – An inferno raged for two days, consuming everything between the Salinae (the salt warehouses on the Tiber next to the Aventine) to the southwest corner of the Capitoline, and extending as far north as the Forum Romanum. In its path it destroyed the Forum Boarium, the Forum Holitorium, and the temples of Spes, Mater Matuta and Fortuna.

Ω 210 BC – Another great fire broke out in the Forum Romanum burning the private houses and shops surrounding the forum, the Forum Piscarium, the Lautumiae (stone quarry district) on the eastern slope of the Capitoline, and once again the temple of Vesta. This time the temple of Vesta was saved by the bravery of 13 slaves who were all manumitted as a reward.

Ex vito alterius sapiens emendat suum – From the other man's mistake, the wise man corrects his own (Publilius Syrus)

"All this talk was suddenly interrupted by a fire which broke out in the night in several places round the Forum on the eve of the Quinquatrus. Seven shops which were afterwards replaced by five were burning at the same time, as well as the offices where the New Banks now stand. Soon after, private buildings, the Lautumiae, the Fish Market and the Hall of Vesta were alight. It was with the utmost difficulty that the Temple of Vesta was saved, mainly through the exertions of thirteen slaves, who were afterwards manumitted at the public cost. The fire raged all through the next day and there was not the smallest doubt that it was the work of incendiaries, for fires started simultaneously in several different places."

Livy - Ab Urbe Condita

Ω 203 BC – A conflagration erupted in the densely built tenements of the Clivus Publicius, a street leading south from the Circus Maximus over the Aventine. All the buildings were burned to the ground.

Ω 192 BC – The seemingly cursed Forum Boarium was again consumed in a fire which lasted a day and a night. It spread along the warehouses bordering the Tiber causing a great loss of life and reduced vast amounts of valuable merchandise to 'smouldering ruins'.

Ω 178 BC – A temple to Venus near the Forum Romanum was burned down.

Ω 148 BC – The Regia (house of the Pontifex Maximus) also burned down.

Ω 111 BC – The temple of Magna Mater on the Palatine suffered the same fate.

Ω 83 BC – During the civil war between Marius and Sulla the temple of Jupiter Capitolinus, as well as much of the city, was burned to its foundations.

Ω 52 BC – Partisans of Clodius carried his murdered body to the Comitium and built a pyre with the benches of senators and magistrates which set fire to the Curia Hostilia and Basilica Porcia, totally destroying both.

Ω 49 BC – Obviously upset by the civil unrest, the gods strike the Temple of Quirinus with lightning, burning the temple and its surroundings.

Ω 36 BC – The Regia once again fell prey to a small blaze.

Ω 31 BC – A fire started by a freedman during a riot in protest against his tax assessment, consumes a large proportion of the Circus Maximus. It spreads up the Aventine hill, destroying the temple of Ceres, the temple of Spes and numerous other residential buildings; continues between the Aventine and Palatine hills burning everything in its path till it reaches the Tiber, in the process destroying the Forum Holitorium and the temple to Janus located there. A vast amount of precious artworks which adorned the temples (the gods' icons, marble and bronze statues, and many paintings) are lost to the flames.

Because the deadly danger, the deliberate setting of fires (arson) is a capital offence. Punishment was death, even if the perpetrators were citizens of high status. For example, after the major conflagration of 210 BC, the perpetrators were sought and eventually punished.

"The senate accordingly authorised the consul to give public notice that whoever disclosed the names of those through whose agency the conflagration had been started should, if he were a freeman, receive a reward, if a slave, his liberty. Tempted by the offer of a reward, a slave belonging to the Capuan family of the Calavii, called Manus, gave information to the effect that his masters, together with five young Capuan nobles, whose fathers had been beheaded by Q. Fulvius, had caused the fire and were prepared to commit every description of crime if they were not arrested. They and their slaves were at once apprehended. At first they endeavoured to throw suspicion upon the informer and his statement. It was asserted that after being beaten by his master, the day before he gave information, he had run away and had made out of an occurrence which was really accidental the foundation of a false charge. When, however, the accused and accuser were brought face to face and the slaves were examined under torture, they all confessed. The masters as well as the slaves who had been their accessories were all executed. The informer was rewarded with his liberty and 20,000 asses."

Livy - Ab Urbe Condita

FLOODS (DILUVIA)

Built on the floodplain of the river Tiber, Rome regularly suffered from seasonal inundation. Normally this would be little more than the river rising a metre or two, which posed small threat to the early hill-top communities. However, as the city expanded and the hills were taken for the building of temples and houses, the majority of the populace were forced to live, work, exercise and shop in the valleys between.

However, the Tiber occasionally experienced severe flooding, which reached into the heart of the city. The most important buildings such as temples were built upon podiums to protect them from such occurrences. Although the buildings situated in the lower lying areas of the Campus Martius, Forum Romanum, and the Circus Maximus would be awash, sometimes to a depth where only boats could pass along the streets.

Whilst few people were in direct danger of being drowned during floods, the rising waters presented other dangers. Since floods would last for days, they had a tendency of weakening the foundations of buildings, and it was not uncommon for poorly built insulae to collapse, sometimes months later due to waterlogged brickwork and rotting timbers.

"Meantime the Tiber, either because excessive rains had occurred somewhere up the stream above the city, or because a violent wind from the sea had driven back its outgoing tide, or still more probably, as was surmised, by the act of some divinity, suddenly rose so high as to inundate all the lower levels in the city and to overwhelm many even of the higher portions. The houses, therefore, being constructed of brick, became soaked through and collapsed, while all the animals perished in the flood. And of the people all who did not take refuge in time on the highest points were caught, either in their dwellings, or in the streets, and lost their lives. The remaining houses, too, became weakened, since the mischief lasted for many days, and they caused injuries to many, either at the time or later."

Cassius Dio - Roman History

During unusually violent floods even the bridges crossing the river could also be swept away.

"The flooded Tiber made a more serious attack upon the city than in the previous year and destroyed two bridges and numerous buildings, most of them in the neighbourhood of the Porta Flumentana. A huge mass of rock, undermined either by the heavy rains or by an earthquake not felt at the time, fell from the Capitol into the Vicus Jugarius and crushed a number of people. In the country districts cattle and sheep were carried off by the floods in all directions and many farmhouses were laid in ruins."

Livy - Ab Urbe Condita

The second threat presented by flooding was perhaps the more dangerous, since the river water would flow up through the sewers, flushing effluent back into the streets or even inside buildings directly connected to the system. This combined with the residue of muddy deposits and water saturated ground inevitably led to disease.

"However, the first introduction of plays, though intended as a means of religious expiation, did not relieve the mind from religious terrors nor the body from the inroads of disease. Owing to an inundation of the Tiber, the Circus was flooded in the middle of the Games, and this produced an unspeakable dread; it seemed as though the gods had turned their faces from men and despised all that was done to propitiate their wrath."

Livy - Ab Urbe Condita

Although the Tiber inundated regularly, the greatest and most destructive floods of the Republic occurred during the years 414, 363, 214, 202, 193, 192, 189, 55, and 27 BC.

DISEASE (MORBUS)

Despite their more spectacular effects, fires, floods and civil disorder are insignificant in comparison to the death rate inflicted from pestilence. Throughout its history Rome suffered constantly from disease. The frequency of these outbreaks peaked during the middle Republic and then diminished as the city built aqueducts and expanded the sewer system. Social changes such as the taking of regular baths and passing laws to ensure streets were kept clean, also helped to reduce outbreaks of disease.

Despite improvements in hygiene, pestilences still plagued the city. The escalating population density of the city shoehorned into smaller and smaller insulae apartments, combined with a gradual lowering of nutrition due to the increasing poverty of the lower classes aided the spread of disease.

The location of Rome itself, built upon boggy quagmires and surrounded by marshlands, were breeding grounds of mosquitoes and other insects. That such terrain bred disease was well known by the late Republic, and was almost certainly part of the reason the drainage ditch of the Cloaca Maxima was originally dug.

"When building a house or farm especial care should be taken to place it at the foot of a wooded hill where it is exposed to health-giving winds. Care should be taken where there are swamps in the neighbourhood, because certain tiny creatures which cannot be seen by the eyes breed there. These float through the air and enter the body by the mouth and nose and cause serious disease."

Marcus Varro - Rerum Rusticarum de Agri Cultura

Another vector for disease was the lack of central heating in Roman homes. Private hypocausts did not become widespread even in the domus of the wealthy until the time of the Caesars.

DOCTOR WHO?

In 219 BC the Senate invited the first professional Greek doctor to Rome, one Archagathos the Peloponnesian, providing him with both citizenship and a salary provided by the state. However, due to his fondness for using the knife and cauterising, his brutal treatments earned him the nickname of 'The Executioner (carnifex)'! He left Rome, presumably once fear of his reputation reduced the number of patients willing to risk his sadistic cures.

After this, all physicians became "objects of loathing" according to Pliny, which did not change until the arrival of Asclepiades of Bithynia sometime towards the end of the 2nd Century BC. His skill was based on preventative measures against illness, such as exercise, diet and bathing, and these treatments were so popular that he became the most famous doctor of the period.

The inherent dampness of the city, being built upon many natural springs and streams, combined with cold weather of Rome's winter was detrimental to the aged and sick.

The three main diseases of the Republic were malaria, spread by summer mosquitoes; typhoid, caught from drinking polluted water; and tuberculosis, which was inflamed by substandard living conditions and cold weather. Plague and smallpox, the two great killers of later times were unknown in Republican Rome.

Once ill, there was very little any doctors of the time could do to treat such infections. Although in the majority of cases the disease was not immediately fatal, they left the body weakened so that secondary infections from other illnesses could cause death. Since malaria and tuberculosis could not be cured, their effects returned seasonally, eventually ending the life of their host prematurely.

Since it was known that certain diseases flourished at particular times of the year, many Romans tended to depart the city during its most pestilent months. It eventually became fashionable (for those who could afford it) to vacation in the country or seaside during the summer when fevers and mosquitoes were at their height.

Given that the medicine of the Republic was useless for treating the effects of pestilence, the normal treatments were dogged with superstition and devotion to the gods; sometimes with unfortunate consequences…

"There was a general desire to recall the condition of things which existed under Numa, for men felt that the only help that was left against sickness was to obtain the forgiveness of the gods and be at peace with heaven. Tradition records that the king [Tullus Hostilius], whilst examining the commentaries of Numa, found there a description of certain secret sacrificial rites paid to Jupiter Elicius: he withdrew into privacy whilst occupied with these rites, but their performance was marred by omissions or mistakes. Not only was no sign from heaven vouchsafed to him, but the anger of Jupiter was roused by the false worship rendered to him, and he burnt up the king and his house by a stroke of lightning."

Livy - Ab Urbe Condita

Many Romans prayed at the shrines of the gods responsible for such miseries, to appease and ward misfortune. Within the city there were multiple altars to the goddess of fever (Febris), the goddess of purification and foul odours (Mephitis), and the god of microbes (Verminus). The majority were clustered about the Esquiline hill, suggesting it was an unhealthy place to live (unsurprising considering the burial grounds of the poor lay just outside the city walls atop

DISEASE RULES

Considering the prevalence of the three major diseases of the period, it is assumed that most player characters possess some degree of partial immunity to them. Most people susceptible to such illness usually die in childhood and many wealthier Romans who avoided a violent death often survived to their 70s or 80s.

However, the fear of disease is a powerful motivation of the time. Games Masters who wish an extra degree of realism may introduce the following, which reflect the dangerous debilitation of such infections.

MALARIA

Spread by mosquitoes, which flourish during warm months, the symptoms of malaria include fever, shivering, joint pain, vomiting, anaemia and convulsions, which reoccur on a diurnal cyclic basis. The milder form of malaria is chronic and the infection remains for many years. Characters that remain in Rome during the summer will be exposed to malaria, above all those living in the lower districts near the Tiber.

Application: Injected (mosquito bite)
Potency: 65
Resistance: Endurance
Onset time: 1d8+6 days
Duration: 2 weeks or more
Conditions: Fever with possible Unconsciousness and Death. Failing the opposed Endurance roll indicates that the character is infected with a milder strain of malaria, which causes a succession of feverish paroxysms every 3 days, each bout of fever lasting about 6 hours. During this time the character treats all skills as Hard. This continues until the third week, when the character can make another opposed roll each week to see if the disease goes into remission.

Fumbling the original Stamina roll means the character has instead contracted a deadlier form of malaria. This induces paroxysms every 2 days but each bout of fever renders the victim unconscious for 24-36 hours. In addition the character must make an unopposed Stamina roll with each attack. If failed the victim dies.

Once infected with the milder form of malaria, characters must make a further Endurance roll each summer to see if they suffer a relapse. If so, then they suffer the same effects as their first bout of the disease. Yet, if they roll a critical success, then their body purges the infection and they no longer suffer from the disease.

TYPHOID

This disease is transmitted from the consumption of water or food contaminated by faecal waste. Its symptoms commonly include a sustained high fever, headaches, diarrhoea, stomach pains and sometimes a rash of pink spots. It is often fatal, particularly to those weakened by other infections.

Characters that drink river water downstream from any of the cloacae outlets or anyone remaining in the city after a major flood of the Tiber, should make an opposed Endurance roll. Losing indicates that they have been infected. The disease progresses in three stages, each one typically lasting a week.

Application: Ingestion (drinking tainted water)
Potency: 50
Resistance: Endurance
Onset time: 1d4 weeks
Duration: 3 weeks
Conditions: Exhaustion, Fever & Hallucinations, Death. During the first week, the character suffers a slowly rising temperature, a general feeling of weakness, headaches and a cough. During this time the character suffers an extra level of Fatigue, atop any they are currently suffering from.

In the second week the character becomes prostrate from the high fever and experiences frequent (green coloured) diarrhoea. If this was not bad enough, they also suffer from delirium, which can become violent. The third week is the most dangerous point, where the patient suffers intestinal bleeding and potential heart failure. They are rendered helpless and must succeed an unopposed Endurance roll or die at the end of the week.

Those Games Masters who wish to add a further touch of macabre realism can add the following rule. If a character manages to roll a fumble when initially resisting Typhoid, they are naturally immune carriers of it. This becomes a horrifying affliction, since the character will be a living plague source, infecting all those in their presence if they prepare meals, share drinking vessels or have aural contact...

TUBERCULOSIS

The majority of Rome's inhabitants are infected with tuberculosis. Congested streets and overcrowded insulae facilitate the spread of the disease. Anyone in proximity to an actively coughing sufferer must pass an opposed Endurance roll to avoid catching it themselves. For the majority of healthy people this infection remains latent, never developing into full blown active tuberculosis.

Unfortunately, many of the poorer plebeians and slaves of the city are not at their full health, often suffering from malnutrition and poor housing. Each winter, characters that are living at the subsistence level should make unopposed Endurance rolls. On a fumble, they progress to active tuberculosis. Once activated, the character must succeed in an Endurance roll each month, otherwise the disease flares up.

Application: Inhalation (in proximity to an active sufferer)
Potency: 60
Resistance: Endurance
Onset time: Only activates if the annual winter Endurance roll is a fumble
Duration: Monthly
Conditions: Exhaustion. Once the tuberculosis becomes active, each month the character fails an unopposed Endurance roll they spend that month coughing and feeling weak. After a while the sufferer will begin to note traces of blood in their phlegm. Due to lung scarring the Fatigue loss is permanent, eventually leading to death from accumulating weight loss, pulmonary bleeding and respiratory failure.

the hill). Even in the Forum Romanum was a shrine to the goddess of the sewers (Venus Cloaca) who presumably protected the city by carrying away filth and dirt.

It was generally the slaves and poorest classes who suffered worst in any pestilence, presumably due to a lower level of nutrition and inferior housing.

> *"The work of enrolment was all the more difficult for the consuls, because the pestilence which the year before had attacked the cattle had now turned into an epidemic, and those who fell victims to it seldom survived the seventh day; those who did survive were subject to a long and tedious illness, which generally took the form of a quartidian ague. The deaths occurred chiefly amongst the slaves and their unburied bodies lay scattered in all the streets, and not even in the case of the free population could the funeral rites be carried out decently. The corpses lay untouched by dog and vulture and slowly rotted away, and it was generally observed that neither in this nor in the previous year had a vulture been anywhere seen."*
>
> *Livy - Ab Urbe Condita*

Some epidemics were so deadly that the city became severely depopulated. In such cases even the wealthiest died due to the inability to clear the dead from homes and streets. Many historical records of the time specifically list the fatalities of serving magistrates.

> *"[in 451 BC] Rome was afflicted with a pestilence more severe than any of those recorded from past time. Almost all the slaves were carried off by it and about one half of the citizens, as neither the physicians were able any longer to alleviate their sufferings, nor did their servants and friends supply them with the necessaries. For those who were willing to relieve the calamities of others, by touching the bodies of the diseased and continuing with them, contracted the same diseases, with the result that many entire households perished for want of people to attend the sick."*
>
> *Dionysius of Halicarnassus - Roman Antiquities*

Eventually, during one epidemic in 293 BC the senate ordered the Sibylline Books to be consulted, and these advised that the cult of Aesculapius be brought to the city.

> *"When the people suffered from a plague, envoys were sent to bring a statue of Aesculapius from Epidaurus to Rome. They brought with them a snake that had joined them in the ship, and which no doubt was a manifestation of the god; from the ship, it went to the island in the Tiber, to the place where the temple of Aesculapius has been erected."*
>
> *Livy - Periochae*

The temple of Aesculapius became the centre of healing in the city and it was the place that the poor came to beg help for their ailments. Despite this faith, the priests of the god used psychology rather than science to treat their supplicants. Patients were placed into a narcotic induced sleep so that the god might send a dream revealing the proper treatment for their affliction. The priests interpreted these dreams and, if the therapy was successful, a votive totem (in the shape of the part of the body afflicted) was suspended in the temple, along with a tablet describing the treatment.

Wealthier or more sceptical patients often took a different approach to a cure. They would be carried out into the streets and left under porticoes, so that passers-by could give them advice on cures based on their personal experience. Doctors in general were regarded with suspicion, and were expensive to hire. Not until the late Republic did the advances in Greek medicine start to gain Roman trust.

> *"Until recently, Diaulus was a doctor; now he is an undertaker. He is still doing as an undertaker, what he used to do as a doctor"*
>
> *Marshal - Epigrams*

REPUBLICAN
ROME

Cloaca
Anio Aquaduct
Tapula-Julia Aquaduct
Appia Aquaduct
Marcia Aquaduct
Servian Wall
River
Road

Four Regions of Servius Tulius

1. Temple of Flora
2. Temple of Quirinus
3. Temple of Simo Sancus
4. Altar of Mars
5. Saepta (Voting Ground)
6. Navalia (Shipyards)
7. Theatre of Pompey
8. Portico
9. Villa Publica
10. Flaminian Circus

11. Temple of Bellona
12. Temple of Juno Moneta
13. Senate House and Comitium
14. Prison
15. Asylum
16. Temple of Apollo
17. Temple of Jupiter Capitolinus
18. Tarpeian Rock
19. Tabularium (Records Office)
20. Temple of Saturn, Aerarium (State Treasury)
21. Temple of Vesta
22. Temple of Jupiter Stator
23. Temple of Jupiter Victor
24. Forum Holitorium
25. Fabrician Bridge
26. Temple of Aesculapius
27. Cestian Bridge
28. Aemilian Bridge
29. Sublician Bridge
30. Temple of Portunus
31. Forum Boarium
32. Hut of Romulus
33. Circus Maximus
34. Temple of the Moon
35. Temple of Minerva
36. Temple of Diana
37. Temple of Juno Regina
38. Emporium
39. Temple of Bona Dea
40. Temple of Honour and Virtue
41. Tomb of the Scipios
42. Temple of Juno Lucira
43. Necropolises

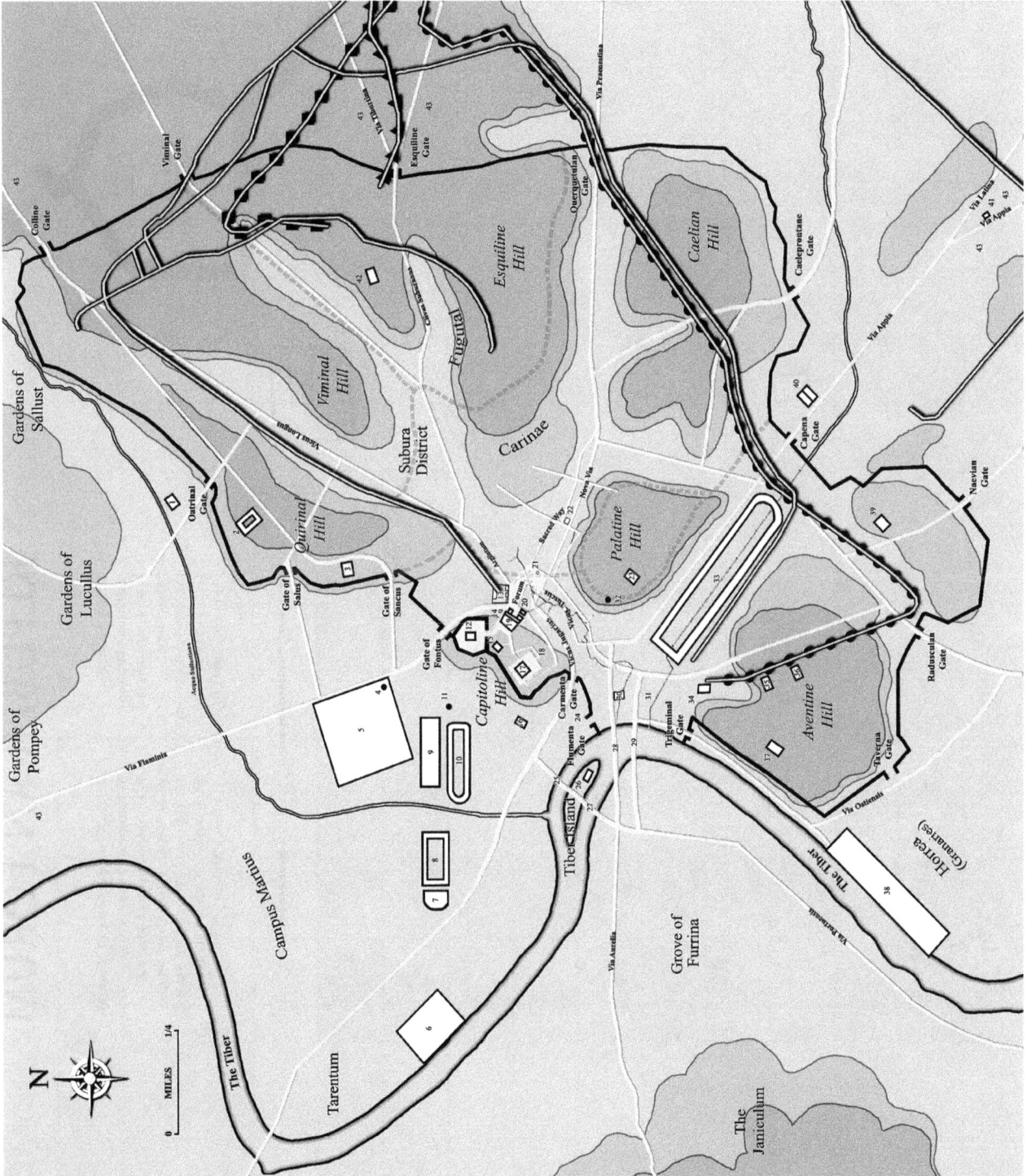

REPUBLICAN FORUM

Villa Publica

Flaminian Circus

Temple of Bellona

Temple of Apollo

Capitoline Hill

Temple of Jupiter Capitolinus

Tarpeian Rock

Gradus Monetae

Asylum

Temple of Juno Moneta

Arx (Citadel)

Clivus Capitolinus

Aequimelium

Tullianum (Special Oracle)

Clivus Argentarius (Laumiae)

Gate of Janus

Curia Hostilia (Senate House)

Comitium

Forum

Basilica Sempronia

Temple of Castor

Temple of Vesta

Grove of Vesta

Temple of Happiness

Velabrum

Regia

House of the Vestals

Sepulcretum

House of the Pontifex Maximus

Macellum (Provision Market)

Argiletum

Porta Fabianus

Vicus Tuscus (Tuscan Street)

Vicus Jugarius (Team Street)

Clivus Victoriae

Carmenta Gate

Temple of Hope

Forum Holitorium
(Vegetable Market)

Flumenia Gate

Forum Boarium

Temple of Portunus

(Cattle Market)

Temple of Hercules

Ara Maxima

Armilian Bridge

River Tiber

Sublician Bridge

Scalae Caci

Hut of Romulus

Temple of Magna Mater

Palatine Hill

Temple of Jupiter Victor

Romulae Gate

Mugonian Gate

Nova Via (New Street)

Temple of Jupiter Stator

Sacred Way

Velia

Carinae

N

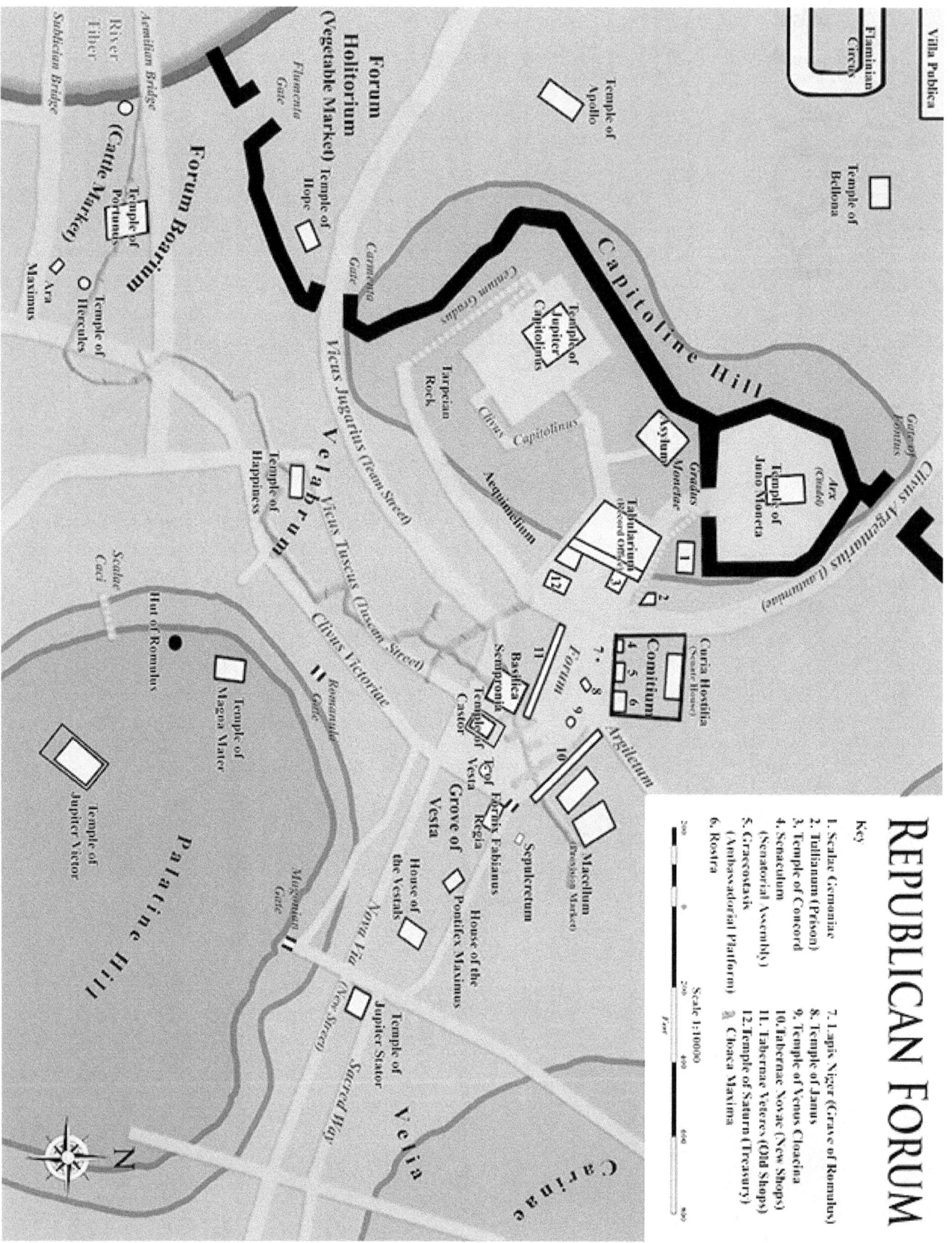

THE GAMES

"He gave entertainments of diverse kinds: a combat of gladiators and also stage-plays in every ward all over the city, performed too by actors of all languages, as well as races in the circus, athletic contests, and a sham sea-fight. In the gladiatorial contest in the Forum Furius Leptinus, a man of praetorian stock, and Quintus Calpenus, a former senator and pleader at the bar, fought to a finish. A Pyrrhic dance was performed by the sons of the princes of Asia and Bithynia. During the plays Decimus Laberius, a Roman knight, acted a farce of his own composition, and having been presented with five hundred thousand sestertii and a gold ring, passed from the stage through the orchestra and took his place in the fourteen rows. For the races the circus was lengthened at either end and a broad canal was dug all about it; then young men of the highest rank drove four-horse and two-horse chariots and rode pairs of horses, vaulting from one to the other. The game called Troy was performed by two troops, of younger and of older boys. Combats with wild beasts were presented on five successive days, and last of all there was a battle between two opposing armies, in which five hundred foot-soldiers, twenty elephants, and thirty horsemen engaged on each side. To make room for this, the goals were taken down and in their place two camps were pitched over against each other. The athletic competitions lasted for three days in a temporary stadium built for the purpose in the region of the Campus Martius. For the naval battle a pool was dug in the lesser Codeta and there was a contest of ships of two, three, and four banks of oars, belonging to the Tyrian and Egyptian fleets, manned by a large force of fighting men. Such a throng flocked to all these shows from every quarter, that many strangers had to lodge in tents pitched in streets or along the roads, and the press was often such that many were crushed to death, including two senators."

Suetonius – Life of Julius Caesar

The games began originally as religious festivals to please and placate the gods. Given the lack of public entertainments at the time, these festivals became increasingly popular – not least because they were free. Despite popular misconceptions the games did not simply comprise of gladiatorial combats (munera); those came later and were separate religious observances to the spirits of the dead. Instead the amusements the games provided were a mélange of differing entertainments, classed as sports (ludi circenses), or theatrical performances (ludi scaenici).

Ludi circenses were originally a mixture of athletic contests and equestrian races. Over the course of time the athletics displays were sidelined, and chariot racing grew to overwhelming popularity.

Ludi scaenici were a combination of other forms of spectacle. Primary amongst these were plays, which helped to spread the popularity of comedy and mime. There were also processions (pompae), public feasts and animal displays. The latter involved the importation of unknown creatures from the ends of the world, which were shown to the populace as novelties. It was not until the late Republic that they decided to kill the creatures for entertainment instead.

Although initially staged for religious observance, additional games were introduced to celebrate military victories (ludi votivi) or simply to boost public morale. Eventually the entire concept was corrupted as politicians used the games as means to raise public support from voters. By the end of the Republic, gladiatorial combats were merged with the games to provide greater spectacles, which birthed an appetite for blood and cruelty which had previously been unknown.

Ludi were managed by the magistrates of the city. The Ludi Apollinares and Ludi Victoriae Sullae were supervised by the urban prætor. The Ludi Plebeii was presided over by the plebeian ædiles and the remainder were run by the curule ædiles. All these were originally funded by taxes on allied (or subjugated) cities but during the late Republic, ædiles began to supplement the costs of bigger and better games out of their own pockets in order to influence their electoral chances of higher office. Eventually the senate attempted to limit the expense of the games, but to no avail.

The first games were the Roman Games (Ludi Romani), originally held as a votive offering in honour of Jupiter Optimus Maximus in 509 BC. They comprised of a triumphal procession from his temple atop the Capitoline hill to the Circus Maximus, followed by a series of contests.

"The contests were horse-racing and boxing, the horses and boxers mostly brought from Etruria. They were at first celebrated on occasions of especial solemnity; subsequently they became an annual fixture, and were called indifferently the "Roman" or the "Great Games.""

Livy – Ab Urbe Condita

These games were repeated infrequently during times of great portent, until almost a century and a half later, when they finally became an annual event. Additional celebrations were added throughout the remainder of the Republic.

The following list describes the names and dates of the annual games celebrated.

LUDI MEGALENSES (4-10 APRIL)

First held in honour of the Cybele, whose statue was brought to Rome in 204 BC by order of an oracle found in the Sibylline Books. Once her temple was finally completed in 191 BC, the games were hosted annually. The majority of the celebrations were ludi scaenici, with feasts and processions. Only the final day was there a ludi circenses.

LUDI CEREALES (12-19 APRIL)

The games of Ceres, dedicated to the goddess of the harvest began by 202 BC. A particular spectacle of these celebrations was the release of foxes which had lit torches tied to their tails.

"In a valley, he caught, in the depths of a willow copse, a vixen, who'd stolen many birds from the yard. He wrapped his captive in straw and hay, and set fire to it all: she fled the hands that were out to burn her: In fleeing she set the crops that covered the fields, ablaze: And a breeze lent strength to the devouring flames. The thing's forgotten, but a relic remains: since now there's a certain law of Carseoli, that bans foxes: And they burn a fox at the Cerialia to punish the species, destroyed in the same way as it destroyed the crops."

Ovid – Fasti

Like the Ludi Megalenses, only the last day was a ludi circenses, featuring chariot races. The rest were all ludi scaenici. Another tradition of these games was the wearing of white clothes in respect of the goddess of grain, which meant that anyone in mourning could not attend.

"White is fitting for Ceres: dress in white clothes for Ceres. Festival: on this day no one wears dark-coloured thread."

Ovid – Fasti

LUDI FLORALES (28 APRIL – 3 MAY)

Although originally celebrations to the goddess Flora, the Floralia were superseded by the Ludi Florales, when a new temple to her was built in 238 BC on the Aventine hill overlooking the Circus Maximus. By 173 BC the games were an annual occurrence. It comprised of four days of ludi scaenici performances involving naked actresses and prostitutes, with the final day being used for ludi circenses.

"Those games, therefore, are celebrated with all wantonness, as is suitable to the memory of a harlot. For besides licentiousness of words, in which all lewdness is poured forth, women are also stripped of their garments at the demand of the people, and then perform the office of mime players, and are detained in the sight of the people with indecent gestures, even to the satiating of unchaste eyes."

Lactantius – Divinae Institutiones

LUDI APOLLINARES (6-13 JULY)

These games were first held in 212 BC in propitiation of Apollo, to avert the fears generated by Hannibal's invasion of northern Italy. They were made permanent four years later to forestall the ravages of a pestilence, since Apollo was a god of healing. Only the final two days of the games were ludi circenses, the rest were given to theatrical productions.

LUDI VICTORIAE CAESARIS (20-30 JULY)

Originally named the Ludi Veneris Genetricis and held by Julius Caesar in 46 BC to celebrate the completion of the temple to Venus Genetrix. However, after his assassination the following year, the games were moved to July to mark the month of Caesar's birth and commemorate his victories. They comprised of seven days of ludi scaenici followed by four days of ludi circenses.

LUDI ROMANI (5-19 SEPTEMBER)

The original public games held in deference to the deity Jupiter Optimus Maximus. Yearly games started in 366 BC.

LUDI VICTORIAE SULLAE (26 OCTOBER – 1 NOVEMBER)

Commenced in 82 BC to celebrate Sulla's victory at the Colline Gate. They comprised of six days of ludi scaenici followed by a single day of ludi circenses.

LUDI PLEBEII (4-17 NOVEMBER)

The second eldest public games, established in 216 BC in tribute of the reconciliation between the patricians and plebeians after the plebeians moved to either the mons sacer or, according to other sources, the Aventine Hill. There were nine days of ludi scaenici performances, followed by a great feast held in honour of Jupiter, the Senators eating at public expense upon the Capitoline, while the Roman public dined in the Forum. This was continued with a grand procession led by statues of the Capitoline Triad, which would proceed to the Circus Maximus, and begin a further four days of ludi circenses.

PROCESSIONS (POMPAE)

Formal processions were a large part of public entertainments. They were given as part of triumphs – victory celebrations of wars, appeals for divine intercessions in times of disaster and, of course, part of the annual ludi. Descriptions written by Dionysius of Halicarnassus record an example of such a parade during the Ludi Romani, which followed a traditional format.

At the head of the procession led the consuls and other magistrates as befitting their place as leaders of the city. These were followed by a groups of young men sometimes mounted, who were either wastrel fans of the circus entertainments, or had political intentions. After them came the chariot drivers in their vehicles, followed by the athletes dressed only in loincloths to display their physiques.

Dancers came next, usually youths or boys, dressed in red tunics, bronze belts and crested helmets, carrying swords and spears… accompanied by various musicians. They were followed by men dressed as mythological satyrs and silenoi, with wineskins and huge phalluses, who comically impersonated the military dancers who preceded them. These too were escorted by musicians.

Finally, after the comic section of the procession passed, came the sacred objects of the gods (or their anthropomorphic images in the later Republic); on litters (fercula) bourn upon the shoulders of the priests. At the end of the procession were wisely led the sacrificial animals, presumably so their dung would not sully the steps of those before them.

Add flower wreaths, thrown petals, street hawkers and excited throngs of spectators jammed into the streets or looking down from open windows, and one can begin to understand the true spectacle…

ANIMAL SHOWS (VENATIONES)

In Republican Rome, animal shows were a mixture of displaying rare creatures, shows of performing beasts and most notoriously, the hunts. These venationes were normally held at the Circus Maximus.

The first recorded display of wild animals at the games was in 250 BC, when 142 Carthaginian elephants captured in Sicily were shipped back to Rome. There were many other notable displays of strange or frightening animals, such as the loosing of lions in the Forum Romanum by Sulla in 93 BC, the showing of a hippopotamus and five crocodiles in 58 BC, and in 46 BC even the parade of a giraffe by Julius Caesar.

The first record of animals being hunted at the games was in 186 BC. After the display, which outraged some senators, animal hunts were banned for 20 years, but eventually they returned with a vengeance.

"The hunting of lions and panthers formed a novel feature, and the whole spectacle presented almost as much splendour and variety as those of the present day."

Livy – Ab Urbe Condita

Some animal hunts were infamous. In 55 BC Pompey had 500 lions and 410 leopards killed in the Circus Maximus, which he followed by the slaughter of 18 elephants. Unfortunately for him, the last scene evoked the sympathies of the audience, which publicly cursed him for his cruelty.

"Indeed, five hundred lions were used up in five days, and eighteen elephants fought against men in heavy armour. Some of these beasts were killed at the time and others a little later. For some of them, contrary to Pompey's wish, were pitied by the people when, after being wounded and ceasing to fight, they walked about with their trunks raised toward heaven, lamenting so bitterly as to give rise to the report that they did so not by mere chance, but were crying out against the oaths in which they had trusted when they crossed over from Africa, and were calling upon Heaven to avenge them.

Cassius Dio – Roman History

Those who participated in these hunts were known either as hunters (venatores) or beast handlers (bestiarii). Venatores were professional hunters trained to kill wild animals, whereas bestiarii were of inferior status, used to care for and drive the animals into combat using whips or burning torches – although sometimes they could be attacked by the beasts instead. Most venatores and bestiarii were recruited from condemned criminals or prisoners of war – or those desperate enough to volunteer – and were regarded less highly than gladiators.

Normally venatores were armed only with hunting spears (venabula) and wore no armour save knee length leather wrappings (fasciae crurales). At the end of the Republic, hunters placed against dangerous predators began to be armed like gladiators instead, with sword and shield.

The hunt was not the only form of animal combat however. Many shows displayed clashes between different types of animals, which were chained together to ensure they would fight. Popular matches were leopards versus lions and bears versus bulls. However, the Romans experimented with all sorts of combinations to provide novelty in the arena, using elephants, rhinoceroses, bulls, bears, boars, lions, leopards, pythons and even crocodiles… although hunts involving the use of dogs against stags or boars, were probably more usual.

"While the trainers were gingerly provoking a rhinoceros, and the anger of the great wild beast was taking a long time to build up, the anticipated battle looked as if it would not take place. But finally the rage of the beast previously much in evidence returned, for he thus lifted up a heavy bear with his twin horns…"

Marshal – Liber Spectaculorum

Horseback bull wrestlers (taurocentae) were a specialist form of combatant. They rode beside a bull, leapt onto its back and tried to wrestle it to the ground by twisting its head. The more familiar bull fighters (taurarii) faced their beasts in single combat, as in their modern day successors but the contest was more even, with the bulls winning far more frequently.

In fact, those animals who won their combats were frequently discharged from the arena alive and some made great names for themselves as man killers.

"But what pleasure can it possibly be to a man of culture, when either a puny human being is mangled by a most powerful beast, or a splendid beast is transfixed with a hunting-spear?"

Cicero – Letters

Not all displays were necessarily lethal. There were snake charmers, crocodile wrestlers and bull leapers too.

Venationes usually ended with a show of performing animals. These extravaganzas could range from tamed lions, to apes driving chariots, and even elephants walking on tightropes.

"It is recorded that Hanno, one of the most distinguished of the Carthaginians, was the first human being who dared to handle a lion and exhibit it as tamed, and that this supplied a reason for his impeachment, because it was felt that a man of such an artful character might persuade the public to anything, and that their liberty was ill entrusted to one whom even ferocity had so completely submitted."

Pliny the Elder – Naturalis Historia

ATHLETICS (CERTAMINA ATHLETARUM)

Athletics were first introduced into Rome from their Etruscan neighbours. These sports were divided into two categories: the severe, which were combat orientated and the light, which were 'individual' tests of running, jumping or throwing.

Romans originally only practiced the sports of running (cursus), wrestling (lucta) and most popularly, boxing (pugilatus). The pentathlon (quinquertium) was eventually introduced from Greece and expanded the athletic disciplines to include long jumping, the discus and javelin throwing.

The games were normally only attended by professional athletes (athletae), although amateur competitors (agonistae) – who normally only practiced the discipline for health and fitness – could also participate if they desired. They competed for monetary reward, and champions won palm branches (palmae), ribbons and wreaths – the traditional Roman signs of victory.

Roman athletics were an established feature of the ludi circenses, continuing to remain popular throughout the Republic. Greek athletics, however, first performed in 186 BC and repeated infrequently for the next century and a half, were not particularly popular, reputedly due to the Greek tradition of completing completely nude.

Of course, the Romans preferred the severe disciplines of Boxing, Wrestling and Pancratium.

Boxing was the prince of the sports and took a slightly different format to its modern version. Roman boxing lacked the concept of 'rounds' and there were no weight divisions either, the basic rules being that only the fists could be used to strike and no holding was allowed. There were no rules against striking prone opponents, and neither was there a limit against what might be targeted. Once started, a fight continued without rest until the knockout or submission of the opponent.

Most boxers were only loincloths, and gloves (caestus) which left the fingertips and thumb free, and had straps which extended down the entire forearm. Across the knuckles was a wide strap of reinforced leather (padded on the inside with fur) which connected to a stuffed cylinder held in the hand. Despite its fearsome reputation, the caestus was primarily designed to protect the bones in the hand, rather than inflict additional damage to the opponent. Metal caestus did not occur until after the Republic.

Yet armed with only basic leather gloves, Roman boxers still dispensed terrific injuries upon each other; fractured bones, broken jaws and noses, lost teeth, and concussions were common. Deaths, although unintentional, also occasionally occurred from untreatable cerebral contusions.

FOR A FISTFUL OF CAESTUS
Roman boxing gloves of the Republic were not the brutal devices of the later Imperial games. Caestus grant no additional damage when used to box. However, they do provide a degree of protection to the hands and forearms, which allows them to block damage from both armed and unarmed attackers. Treat caestus as 2 points of Armour.

Wrestling was the least dangerous of the athletic sports, requiring the opponent to be thrown or tripped to the ground three times to win. The pancratium however was a brutal, no holds barred form of fighting which did not gain popularity until the close of the Republic. No protection of any sort was worn and the only rules were that biting and eye gauging were forbidden. Anything else was allowed. The winner was the man who knocked out, killed or otherwise caused his opponent to surrender. Historical records remain of a pancratium champion who won an Olympic competition by default, due to his intimidating reputation of deliberately breaking the fingers of his opponents.

CHARIOT RACES (CURRICULA)

"Now let me describe the mass of people, unemployed and with too much time on their hands. For them the Circus Maximus is a temple, home, community centre and the fulfilment of all their hopes. All over the city you can see them quarrelling fiercely about the races… They declare that the country will be ruined if at the next meeting their own particular champion does not come first out of the starting-gate and keep his horses in line as he brings them round the post. Before dawn on a race day they all rush headlong for a place on the terraces at such a speed that they could almost beat the chariots themselves."

Ammianus Marcellinus – Res Gestae

Of all the public entertainments, the chariot races were by far the most popular. The straining horses, the skill of the drivers and the not-infrequent accidents, all combined with legal gambling on the race results made it a heady spectacle.

Chariot races existed in Rome from the period of the monarchy, and were inherited from the Etruscans. They were always held in the Circus Maximus which could seat the majority of the city's populace. There were no restrictions on seating at the races. Men and women, slaves and citizens all rubbed shoulders and as one of Ovid's poems relates, it was the perfect place to meet or secretly fraternise with members of the opposite sex.

Fames est optimus coquus – Hunger is the best cook

During the Republic, chariot races usually comprised of two horse (bigae) or four horse (quadrigae) chariots, although other numbers of horses and even other animals were occasionally used for novelty. Yet, the latter were not common and four horse chariots remained the favourite type of vehicle, probably due to the increased skill needed to control them.

Races involved starting from the 12 stalls (carceres) built along the straight end of the circus (it was actually slightly curved to equalise the starting distances to the beginning of the central barricade), completing seven laps (spatia) around the central barrier (spina) and then a breakneck sprint to the finishing line (calx), which was placed halfway back between the end of the spina and the starting gates. The total length of this course was about five and a half kilometres, depending on how tightly one could drive the chariot around the turning posts (metae) at either end of the central barrier. This made the duration of a race between eight and nine minutes.

Between 10 and 12 races were held per day; each one involving either four, eight or 12 chariots and interspersed with displays of acrobatic riders (hortatores). Traditionally, from the time before the starting gates had been built in 329 BC, each race was begun by the dropping of a white starting flag (mappa) by the presiding magistrate.

"the second day of the Roman Games, whilst the consul was mounting the stand to start the chariots, a despatch-bearer who said that he had come from Macedonia handed him a despatch wreathed in laurel. After the chariots were started he mounted his own and, riding across the course to the raised benches where the spectators were seated, held up the laurelled despatch [declaring the defeat of the Macedonian king] for the people to see."

Livy – Ab Urbe Condita

All charioteers (aurigae) belonged to one of four circus factions (factiones) which were named after colours – the Reds (russati), Whites (albati), Blues (veneti), and Greens (prasini).

"Chariots very properly have their drivers clad in the colours of idolatry. For at first there were only two colours: white and red. White is sacred to winter, for the gleaming white of the snow, red to the summer because of the Sun's redness. Later, as pleasure and superstition gained ground together, some dedicated the red to Mars, others the white to the Zephyrs, the green to Mother Earth, the blue to Sky and Sea."

Tertullian – De Spectaculis

Although individual prizes were given to the winning charioteer, chariot races were actually team sports. Each faction was granted an equal number of places per race for their own drivers and these team-mates cooperated tactically to try to ensure their own side won. The factions would be paid handsomely for submitting racing teams and part of that wealth went towards supporting the staff, accommodations and stabling each faction maintained on the Campus Martius, with the excess going towards raising and training new horses on the stud farms in the countryside or simply lining the pockets of the private owners and investors in the sport.

Chariot racing was dangerous, and many drivers lost their lives from collisions (naufragia). In order to protect themselves from such an end, most drivers wore a crash helmet (pilleus) made from felt or leather, leg wrappings (fasciae) and a corset made of leather straps, worn over the coloured tunic identifying which faction they raced for. Since the reins controlling the horses were wrapped and tied about one of the driver's arms, they also carried a curved knife in order to cut themselves free if the chariot crashed and they found themselves being dragged across the sand.

Not only were the charioteers at risk. Men were needed to clear wreckage and bodies from the track whilst the race continued. There were also young track boys (sparsores) who splashed water on the passing horses and the chariot wheels to reduce friction and they were often run down by the chariots.

Despite the dangers of racing, there was no end of freedmen or slaves willing to enrol as charioteers. By the end of the Republic the financial rewards for winning were phenomenal, being in the order of thousands of sesterces per race at a time when the annual salary of a legionary barely amounted to 225 sesterces a year.

From 292 BC palm fronds were given to race winners and this remained the sign of victory from then on. By the late second century BC, gold wreaths (coronae) rather than ones of simple foliage started to be presented too. Winners would also earn tips when taking a victory lap, receiving flowers, garlands and small coins thrown from the crowd.

To be a successful charioteer meant fame and fortune and many died as extremely wealthy men. Fans idolised their champions as with professional sportsmen today and some were so popular that their deaths were considered tragedies…

"We find it stated in our Annals, that Felix, a charioteer of the red party, being placed on the funeral pile, some one of the number of his admirers threw himself upon the pile; a most silly piece of conduct. Lest, however, this circumstance might be attributed to the great excellence of the dead man in his art, and so redound to his glory, the other factions all declared that he had instead been overpowered by the fumes of the incense."

Pliny the Elder – Naturalis Historia

Although technically forbidden, dirty tricks were a part of every race. Deliberate blocking of opposing faction drivers was considered normal tactics; and forcing chariots to swerve at critical moments, by cutting across them or crowding the opponent's horses into the spina, simply a fact of life.

The more underhanded ploys involved 'accidental' whipping of an opponent's horses or the driver themselves, if they passed close enough to your own horses to get away with it. Records remain of veterinary remedies for such injuries to the eyes and heads of chariot horses.

The spoke breaking hubs seen in the movie Ben Hur would not have worked in real life since the teams of horses were much wider than the small one man chariots and therefore one would never be able to drive two chariots wheel to wheel. However, a chariot slightly in advance of an opponent's team could catch the legs of the outside horse in its wheel spokes, usually leading to the inevitable mangling of the horse and loss of control as the beast went down, dragging its team with it.

"His horses were brought down, a multitude of intruding legs entered the wheels and the twelve spokes were crowded, until a crackle came from those crammed spaces and the revolving rim shattered the entangled hooves. Then he, the fifth victim, was flung from his chariot which fell upon him, caused a mountain of manifold havoc and blood disfigured his prostrate brow…"

Sidonius Apollinaris – Letter to Consentius

Running a Chariot Race

The following section will hopefully allow Games Masters to recreate the excitement of chariot races. Bear in mind that in history this sport was dangerous and often fatal, which has been reflected in these rules.

For the sake of simplicity, a chariot race is broken down into the following stages:

Stage 1 – Leaving the starting gates (carceres)
Stage 2 – First lap
Stage 3 – Second lap
Stage 4 – Third lap
Stage 5 – Fourth lap
Stage 6 – Fifth lap
Stage 7 – Sixth lap
Stage 8 – Seventh lap
Stage 9 – Sprint for the finishing line (calx)

During each stage the participants roll against their Drive skill. Games Masters who are running races with 8 or 12 vehicles are recommended to divide up the NPC chariots amongst the other players, to make the race more competitive.

The result of the Drive roll indicates how quickly the chariot has moved each lap and a running total should be kept throughout the race to keep track of relative positions.

Ω **Critical** *– 3 movement points. The driver takes the perfect line around the turning posts (metae).*

Ω **Success** *– 2 movement points. The chariot moves without hindrance.*

Ω **Failure** *– 1 movement point. The driver is forced to reign back in order to avoid an obstacle on the track.*

Ω **Fumble** *– Roll on the crash table. The chariot hits a piece of wreckage on the track, takes a bend too fast or the horses stumble whilst trampling a water boy, causing a smash-up.*

The actual distance represented by these movements is purely abstract. Running totals merely indicate the current race order as each stage is completed. I.e. the highest value is the race leader; the second highest total is in second place and so on. If two or more chariots share the same value, then they are considered running neck and neck.

The eventual winner is the driver with the highest total at the end of race. Draws are permissible.

Of course, Roman chariot racing is not necessarily a challenge of gentlemanly conduct. Tactics and dirty tricks abound. Those Games Masters who desire a grittier race are encouraged to let their players use the following options…

Chariot Manoeuvres

After the chariots have left the starting gates, drivers may begin to use special manoeuvres to impede the progress of their opponents. Each manoeuvre costs a number of movement points to perform, because a driver must sacrifice straight line distance to either jockey for position or perform some other nefarious deed. These points are taken off the running total and are not limited to the roll for that particular stage in the race.

Each lap, every driver must select one of the following manoeuvres. These are declared in advance, in order of Initiative. Only after every driver has decided which tactic they will use, are rolls made; and the results are all calculated simultaneously.

Manoeuvres are sometimes limited in their application according to the position the chariots are to one another. Normally, drivers may only affect the chariots directly ahead, beside or behind them in the race order. Relative positions are easily calculated from the running total of movement points.

When running chariot races it should be remembered that drivers of the same faction act as a team. Thus some chariots will be used for blocking so that one can break free of the pack and head for the finishing line.

Ω *Block Opponent – Cost 1. Can only be used on chariots behind the driver in the race order. The driver swerves to prevent one opponent from overtaking. The blocked chariot loses 2 from their movement total.*

Ω *Crowding – Cost 2. Can only be used on chariots that are neck and neck or behind in the race order. The driver deliberately squeezes the opponent into another chariot or the central barrier of the track. This takes more manoeuvring but has the potential of causing a crash. The crowded opponent reduces the success level of his Drive skill roll that lap by one step. If this results in a fumble, he crashes.*

Ω *Evade Trouble – Cost 2. The driver keeps his head down and does his best to keep out of trouble. During that stage of the race he is immune to any other dirty tricks. Although this slows him down, it potentially saves him from suffering crashes.*

Ω *Sideswipe – Cost 3. Can only be used on chariots neck to neck in the race order. A malicious trick, the driver manoeuvres his chariot to catch his opponent's horse's legs. Not only does the opponent reduce the success level of his Drive skill that lap by one step but he must roll against the skill twice and take the lower result. If this results in a fumble, he crashes.*

Ω *Sprint Ahead – Cost 0. Usually left to the final stages of the race, this tactic allows the driver to make an extra Drive roll and add the results to his movement total. However this comes at a penalty. From the following stage onwards, each time the driver makes a Drive roll, his level of success is automatically reduced by one step, due to the exhaustion of the horses.*

Ω *Trample – Cost 1. Can only be used on drivers who have suffered a crash and still remain on the track. If not already dead, the target of the trampling attack must make a successful Evade roll to escape, else suffer 2d6 damage to every Hit Location.*

Ω *Whipping – Cost 1. Can only be used on chariots neck to neck or just ahead in the race order. Technically illegal, a driver can whip the horses or driver of another chariot. Although whipping does not cause any serious injury, it does distract a driver or upset his horses. The opponent is forced that lap to make two Drive rolls and take the lowest result.*

Crashes

Unlike the portrayal of the chariot that leaps (or rather bounces) over the wreckage of a previous crash in the movie Ben Hur, Roman racing chariots are actually very fragile. If a chariot hits an obstacle – the result is a smash-up which will immediately shatter or overturn the vehicle. Whether or not the driver survives is calculated by the driver making an Athletics roll and consulting the following results.

Critical *– A miraculous escape. You roll clear of the crash suffering no damage but lie prone and winded until the next lap. The gods obviously favour you.*

Success *– You take 1d6 damage to a single lower body Hit Location (roll 1d10) as you are dragged clear of the wreckage by the horses, who continue to race around the track. Each lap you take a further 1d6 damage to a randomly determined location from abrasion until you can cut yourself free. Skill rolls (such as cutting yourself free using a Combat Style) are halved due to the difficulty of the situation.*

Failure *– You fail to leap free of the chariot and are crushed by its weight or pinned beneath the bodies of your horses. Take 3d6 damage to a single Hit Location.*

Fumble *– A gruesome and spectacular death. Your body is thrown through the air to land like a rag doll on the consul's podium; or lands head first through the spokes of an opponent's chariot wheel, where it obscenely flops about until the mangled mess finally decapitates. Your ghastly death is talked about for months afterwards and immortalised in graffiti.*

It is unknown if drivers who fell from their chariots were deliberately trampled down or run over. It is unlikely that such things were frequent, as a charioteer who performed such an act would probably be hunted down by fans of the maligned faction and murdered in revenge.

Since gambling on chariot races was legal (gambling in the city was normally forbidden), the passion of winning and losing races was intensified. After particularly important races, it was not uncommon for a small riot to break out between opposing fans. Indeed, it was wise for supporters of the same faction to sit together for protection, in case tempers became carried away.

Spectators even went as far as purchasing 'curse tablets' to bring misfortune to the opposing teams. The use of such seems to have been rife, despite proscriptions against magic and sorcery.

"I adjure you, demon whoever you are, and I demand of you from this hour, from this day, from this moment, that you torture and kill the horses of the Greens and Whites and that you kill in a crash their drivers...and leave not a breath in their bodies.""I conjure you up, holy beings and holy names, join in aiding this spell, and bind, enchant, thwart, strike, overturn, conspire against, destroy, kill, break Eucherius, the charioteer, and all his horses tomorrow in the circus at Rome. May he not leave the barriers well; may he not be quick in contest; may he not outstrip anyone; may he not make the turns well; may he not win any prizes..."

Curse mentioned by Ammianus Marcellinus – Res Gestae

The chariot horses themselves were regarded as much heroes as the drivers. Many mosaics were laid depicting the names and images of famous equines. Some even won praise for completing races without their drivers…

"When the charioteer Corax, who belonged to the white party, was thrown from his place at the starting-post, his horses took the lead and kept it, opposing the other chariots, overturning them, and doing every thing against the other competitors that could have been done, had they been guided by the most skilful charioteer; and while we quite blushed to behold the skill of man excelled by that of the horse, they arrived at the goal, after going over the whole of the prescribed course."

Pliny the Elder – Naturalis Historia

GLADIATORIAL COMBATS (MUNERA)

At the beginning of the Republic, funeral rites involving blood sacrifice did not exist in Rome. Roman sacrifices were originally of bread and salt. The concept of using blood to feed the spirits of the dead (manes) was originally Greek, and slowly spread across the Mediterranean via their city states.

The Roman adoption of gladiatorial combats as funeral rites came from the region of Campania; which not only decorated its tombs with images of such fights, but was where the first stone amphitheatres were built too.

"Whilst the Romans made use of this armour [captured during a battle in 310 BC] to honour the gods, the Campanians, out of contempt and hatred towards the Samnites, made the gladiators who performed at their banquets wear it, and they then called them 'Samnites'."

Livy – Ab Urbe Condita

Although gladiatorial contests were held in Campania during the 4th Century BC, it was not until 264 BC that the first funeral rites were held in Rome. Somewhat modestly, only three pairs of gladiators fought in Forum Boarium. These ceremonies continued to be held for the most important citizens of the city but moved to the Forum Romanum where they were observed from tiers of temporary wooden seating.

The numbers of gladiators 'shown' at these munera, continued to increase until the next record of a gladiatorial contest – nearly half a century later in 216 BC. This time the funeral ceremonies included 22 pairs of fighters. After that, depending on the wealth of the man hosting the rites, these numbers grew unrelentingly.

Unlike the public games, these munera were privately funded events which actually charged entrance fees for seating. A small number of tickets were given away free to the upper classes, as was expected by those who would honour the spirit of one of their peers. Other blocks of seating were purchased by groups (guilds and such), which distributed or sold them to their members. The remaining seats were then sold to the general public.

Just as with popular concerts and sports events of today, ticket touts were part of Republican Rome. These touts (locarii) bought up large numbers of seats in advance and then sold them on at an inflated price.

As these gladiatorial celebrations grew in reputation and spectacle – the poorer classes, unable to afford entry, became resentful of these private shows. Eventually, in 122 BC the tribune Caius Gracchus ordered the removal of the temporary wooden seating to allow the poor to see without charge. However, this act furthered his downfall and munera continued in the main to be pay-for-entry for the rest of the Republic.

"The people were going to enjoy an exhibition of gladiators in the forum, and most of the magistrates had constructed seats for the show round about, and were offering them for hire. Caius ordered them to take down these seats, in order that the poor might be able to enjoy the spectacle from those places without paying hire. But since no one paid any attention to his command, he waited till the night before the spectacle, and then, taking all the workmen whom he had under his orders in public contracts, he pulled down the seats, and when day came he had the place all clear for the people."

Plutarch – Life of Caius Gracchus

By the last century BC, the munera had lost their ritualistic significance, instead devolving into crass displays of conspicuous wealth and opportunities to raise political support from the plebeians.

GLADIATORS (GLADIATORES)

The gladiators used in funerary rites came from several sources. The majority were either criminals condemned to death (noxii), prisoners of war, or disobedient slaves. During the mid-Republic there was a constant source of war captives but as Rome conquered all the lands in its vicinity, criminals and fractious slaves by necessity took a greater share. Those convicts condemned to the sword (ad gladium) were obliged to be killed within a year; others condemned to gladiator school (ad ludum), could obtain their discharge at the end of three years if they survived.

Occasionally, volunteers (auctorati) of freedman or even citizen status would be driven to gamble their lives, agreeing to bind themselves to the owner (lanista) of a gladiatorial troop (familia gladiatoria) with a solemn oath (sacramentum)… "I will endure to be burned, to be bound, to be beaten, and to be killed by the sword." In return they gained regular meals, the best health care available, and the chance to earn prize money. Since gladiators were often seen as sex symbols, additional 'physical' rewards might also have tempted those desperate enough to enrol.

"Scipio returned to New Carthage to discharge his vows and to exhibit the gladiatorial spectacle which he had prepared in honour of the memory of his father and his uncle. The gladiators on this occasion were not drawn from the class from which the trainers usually take them – slaves and men who sell their blood – but were all volunteers and gave their services gratuitously."

Livy – Ab Urbe Condita

Gladiators were trained in the owner's school (ludus), by expert teachers (doctores). Their training included repeatedly striking at a wooden post (palus) which extended six Roman feet above the ground, sparring with fellow students and in formulaic pattern exercises akin to modern martial arts kata. Since gladiators normally tended to fight other members of their own troupe, they were sometimes criticised for fighting in too choreographed a manner, instead of putting on a show of real combat.

The fighting record of gladiators was an important part of their individual reputation, just as in modern boxing today. Such information was often inscribed on their tombstones, listing the number of bouts in the arena and their victories. Occasionally even their tied combats and losses were also recorded, such as one inscription from Sicily where Flammius a 30-year-old had fought 34 times, scoring 21 victories (victoriae), 9 draws (stantes) and had been pardoned four times after being defeated (missio). They definitively reveal that professional gladiators, although beaten, were often spared.

TRAINING SCHOOLS (LUDI GLADIATORII)

Training schools for gladiators existed across the territories controlled by Rome. The most renowned ones were located in Capua and Praeneste. There were also a number within Rome itself. Soon after the beginning of the 1st Century BC, a ludus belonging to a man named Scaurus had its gladiators subpoenaed by the consul Rutilius, in order to train newly recruited soldiers how to use their weapons. Another, the Ludus Aemilius, was mentioned by Horace in a book on poetry of all things.

Despite the uprising of Spartacus in 73 BC (incidentally starting at a ludus in Capua), gladiatorial schools still remained in the city, although probably limited in size in order to prevent a slave revolt from occurring again. Eventually a law was passed in 65 BC to prevent individuals from owning too many gladiators, in case they were used as a private army to overthrow the senate.

"Caesar gave a gladiatorial show besides, but with somewhat fewer pairs of combatants than he had purposed; for the huge band which he assembled from all quarters so terrified his opponents, that a bill was passed limiting the number of gladiators which anyone was to be allowed to keep in the city."

Suetonius – Life of Julius Caesar

Most schools were effectively prison encampments, where gladiators could be secured and trained under close guard. Much of their space was devoted to a central training arena, surrounded by small cells for sleeping. Other areas were included such as a refectory, a kitchen and a holding pen for the more rebellious trainees. The ludus was a self-contained world, from which only the most trusted gladiators would be allowed to leave. Life was not all discipline and brutality however. Feasts were often given for fighters who would appear in the next munera and prostitutes were also made available.

Within the schools, new recruits (novicii) were normally chained until they conformed to the rules and discipline of the ludus and learned to fight with a wooden sword (rudis). Once their tuition was completed the unproven trainees (tirones) would be ready for their first fight. If they survived, they would be regarded as gladiators proper and rise through a hierarchy of grades (paloi), which reflected their experience and skill. Being labelled as Primus Paloi meant you were amongst the best fighters in your style.

Owners of these schools earned money by renting or selling members of their troupe. The profits could be lucrative but came at the price of becoming a social pariah, since lanistae were regarded as being lower than pimps due to their profiteering of men's potential deaths. However, some members of equestrian and patrician class managed to avoid becoming sullied by their 'investments' as long as it was clear that they were strictly dabbling amateurs whose gladiatorial profits were merely a sideline and not the basis of their fortunes.

Towards the end of the Republic, even Julius Caesar himself owned a school in Capua stocked with hundreds of gladiators. Ironically confirming the fears of the senate decades earlier, the gladiators were eventually used as a counter insurgency force during the civil war.

"At Capua they first began to take courage and to rally, and determined to raise levies in the colonies, which had been sent thither by the Julian law: and Lentulus brought into the public market place the gladiators which Caesar maintained there for the entertainment of the people, and confirmed them in their liberty, and gave them horses and ordered them to attend him."

Julius Caesar – The Civil Wars

A DAY AT THE MUNERA

Funerary celebrations were widely advertised to encourage a full attendance. Not only did this attract more attention to the memory of the departed but it also had the benefit of driving up the price of seats, thus defraying part of the costs of the spectacle. Programs (edicta munerum) describing the featured entertainments were scrawled as graffiti on building walls, and pamphlets (libelli munerarii) were sold on the day of the combats.

These ads not only promoted the name of the gladiatorial troop (which could draw in more interest if its reputation was good), but sometimes also listed the names of the more famous gladiators, the

Fide, sed qui, vide – Trust but take care whom

proposed matches to be fought, which schools they had trained in and their previous wins and losses. Some adverts also promised additional comforts such as awnings to keep the sun off the spectators or the watering of the fighting area to keep the dust down.

Most munera started with a procession of all the competitors around the arena in which they would battle and recognition of the sponsor of the games (editor muneris) who had paid for the event. This was followed by a display of fighting using wooden weapons. This undoubtedly gave the participants a chance to warm up in preparation for the real match, thus avoiding the chance of pulled muscles or torn ligaments, which could not only ruin their fitness for future fights but might also cost them their lives.

Once warmed up, the combatants would be given real weapons previously checked by the editor for adequate sharpness. Then the fight would begin under the supervision of two referees, the summa rudis and secunda rudis. Each match was introduced and sometimes accompanied by music to either give the fight a tempo or match it, incidentally increasing the excitement of the audience.

Spectators participated as modern fans do today with cheering and shouted insults. Common cries were "Habet, hoc habet" – he's had it, "Iugula." – cut his throat and "Missum" – release him.

The bout continued until one or both gladiators submitted, died or were injured so badly that they were unable to carry on. At that moment the referees would stop the fight, preventing the disadvantaged (or submissive) gladiator from being further wounded.

Defeated gladiators raised a finger of their left hand in supplication to be granted permission to be dismissed alive (missio). Although it was the editor who decided whether the loser was released, the opinion of the audience could heavily influence his choice, especially if the sponsor was seeking popular support.

> *"Now they give munera and, with a turn of the thumb, win favour by slaughtering in accordance with the whims of the mob"*
> *Juvenal – Satires*

The visual signal of the crowd's disapproval was the turned thumb (pollex versus) although nobody is sure exactly what that means today. The sign for release was supposedly the waving of a handkerchief. The Roman audience during the Republic was not as bloodthirsty as those of the later Empire; yet they showed contempt for those who exhibited cowardice, and rewarded courage and skill.

> *"...we despise gladiators if they are willing to do anything to preserve their life; we favour them, if they give evidence of their contempt for it."*
> *Seneca – De Tranquillitate Animi*

Normally the loser was allowed to live, since a trained gladiator was an expensive commodity. Compensation of up to a 100 times the worth of the gladiator had to be paid to the lanista for those which died during the munera. For famous gladiators this could be ruinously expensive.

If the loser was seriously wounded, then they were loaded onto wheeled carts looking rather like stretchers and carried off to be treated immediately by medical staff. Those who had received an injury which would become mortal were put out of their misery, out of sight of the audience. Survivors who were maimed were dismissed from the school and the lanista claimed compensation from the editor of the munera.

Few fights were declared as 'bouts to the death' (sine missione) but these became more popular towards the end of the Republic. It is probable, considering the expense of compensation, that the gladiators assigned to these matches were actually untrained criminals or slaves who had been condemned ad gladium.

In the unlikely event that the loser was refused honourable dismissal from the arena, they were expected to face death bravely by kneeling, grasping their opponent's leg and holding still whilst they were given the coup de grâce. The bodies of dead gladiators were buried but those of condemned noxii were thrown into the Tiber instead.

The winner was presented with a victory palm leaf (palma) and prize money (praemium) from the editor. The higher their rank, the more money they would win. If they had fought exceptionally well, a laurel wreath (corona) was added as well. Then the victor would run around the perimeter of the arena to the applause of the crowd.

> *"It does the people good to see that even slaves can fight bravely. If a mere slave can show such courage, what then can a Roman do? Besides, the games harden a warrior people to sights of carnage and prepares them for battle."*
> *Cicero*

During the Republic the emphasis of gladiatorial combat was on the display of bravery and skilful combat, not killing. An analysis of gladiator gravestones from just after the end of the Republic revealed that the chances of a trained gladiator dying during a match were low – less than 10%. These were probably more likely due to accidents rather than deliberate murderous intent, since most fights would be between compatriots from the same troupe. Although combat was dangerous, honourable dismissal and even draws were the norm.

AVE IMPERATOR, MORITURI TE SALUTAMUS.

The famous quote "Hail emperor, we who are about to die salute thee." was, according to the writings of Suetonius, used only once in history, by the noxii sentenced to death at a great mock naval battle hosted by the emperor Claudius.

> *"But when the combatants cried out: "Hail, emperor, they who are about to die salute thee," he [Claudius] replied, "Or maybe not," and after that all of them refused to fight, maintaining that they had been pardoned. Upon this he hesitated for some time about destroying them all with fire and sword, but at last leaping from his throne and running along the edge of the lake with his ridiculous tottering gait, he induced them to fight, partly by threats and partly by promises. At this performance a Sicilian and a Rhodian fleet engaged, each numbering twelve triremes, and the signal was sounded on a horn by a silver Triton, which was raised from the middle of the lake by a mechanical device."*
> *Suetonius – Life of Claudius*

In reality, such a pessimistic salute would never be used by superstitious gladiators who realistically faced good odds of survival. However, it would probably be a sensible idea for any player character gladiator to pay their respects to the editor hosting the munera with some sort of salute. A dramatic or bravely proclaimed salutation could swing the balance between life and death.

Those gladiators who had been sentenced ad ludum and reached the end of their term could, if proven popular champions, be granted their freedom. This was ritually symbolised by the presentation of a wooden sword (rudis). A retired gladiator (rudiarius) then faced the decision of what to do with their life, since they would no longer be supported by the familia. Often they hired themselves out as bodyguards and those with the greatest reputations could find employment teaching other gladiators how to fight. Some, finding independent life too difficult or boring without the adoring fans and women 'groupies' (ludiae), simply sold themselves back into a school.

Types of Gladiators

The earliest gladiatorial combats held by Rome's neighbours appear to have used men dressed in tunics or loincloths and equipped with spears, circular shields and bronze helmets. But by the late Republic styles within Rome had changed.

Gladiators from this period were dressed as traditional Roman enemies (and initially were actually captives), equipped from the spoils of Rome's many battles. There was the Samnite, the Gaul and the Thracian. All three were similar in arms and armour, the more exotic gladiators not appearing until the Imperial period. The only other type of gladiator was the horseman (eques) based on Rome's own cavalry troops, who started combat on horseback, armed with lances but finished it on foot.

To provide more tactically interesting fights, different types of gladiator (save for the equites) were paired together. The arms and armour of each was designed to be minimalist, yet still provided effective protection.

The reasons for this were simple. Gladiatorial combat provided no rest breaks, the contestants continuing until submission, injury or death. Considering a gladiator might be fighting under the blazing sun, exhaustion and overheating was a significant problem. Since it is much easier to strike at the limbs and head of an opponent, it made sense to leave the torso exposed, allowing it to act as a radiator. The weight of armour was also a contributing factor and metal pieces were kept to a minimum except on those locations more frequently struck.

Republican gladiatorial armour comes in two forms. The first are leather wrappings about the lower leg (fasciae) or forearm (manicae). In later periods, these seem to have been replaced by quilted sleeves and leggings extending over the entire limb. The second type is made from metal which was formed into greaves (ocreae), rectangular breastplates (cardiophylaces) and helmets (galeae). Unlike those of later periods, these helmets had cheek guards and sometimes a brim, but left the face open. Helmets were decorated with either crests or feather holders and padded with felt to help cushion blows.

Samnite (Samnis)

Dressed in a loincloth held in place with a broad, decorated leather belt (2 AP), Samnites wear a short greave on the leading leg (4 AP), a square breastplate (4 AP) and a brimmed helmet with feathers (5 AP). Their weapon hand and lower arm are wrapped with leather straps (2 AP). One of the heaviest and well-armed gladiator types, they tend to favour brute force in bouts, wielding a Gladius (short sword) and a shortened Scutum (treat as a rectangular Hoplite shield).

Samnite Combat Style: Gladius, Short Scutum; and either 'Batter Aside' or 'Solid Stance' (resist Knockback, Leaping Attacks and Bash as if using the brace action), depending on the ludus.

Gaul (Gallus)

Based on conjecture, these gladiators are dressed only in trousers, padded or embroidered for protection (1 AP) and a brimless helm with cheek guards (5 AP). They use a large oval shaped Scutum reinforced with a vertical rib and the longer Spatha (treat as a broadsword). The further reach of this weapon combined with the extra coverage of his shield make up for the lack of armour, often giving them initiative in combat; whether first strike due to superior reach or being less hindered by unnecessary weight.

Gaul Combat Style: Spatha, Scutum; and either 'Daredevil' or 'Intimidating Scream' depending on the ludus.

Thracian (Thraex)

Dressed in the same loincloth and belt combination as the Samnite (2 AP) they also have the padded sleeve or wrapped leather protector for their weapon arm (2 AP). However they wear two greaves instead, which extend further up the leg to mid calf (6 AP), making up for their smaller shields. Thracian helmets are crested, brimmed and possess full face protection with grills over the eyes (8 AP). They are armed with a large forward-curved slashing knife called a Sica (dagger) and a small square shield called a Parma (treat as a Heater).

Thracian Combat Style: Sica, Parma; and either 'Defensive Minded' or 'Hooker' (allows use of Pin Weapon special effect on a normal success) depending on the ludus.

Horseman (Eques)

Unlike the previous gladiators the equites wore mail on their torso (6 AP), probably to provide greater protection from the spears they used on horseback. The fact that for at least the first part of the fight they were mounted also prevented the gladiator from becoming winded by its weight. In addition the horseman had leather strapped arms (2 AP) and a brimmed but crestless helmet (7 AP). However, they possessed no leg protection, implying that they were forbidden to strike below the waist in fear of injuring the horses they rode… which were another expensive commodity. They were also armed with a Gladius and small target shield called a Palma Equestris; the traditional armament of Republican cavalry.

Equites Combat Style: Spear, Gladius, Parma Equestris; and either 'Beast-back Lancer' or 'Mounted Combat' depending on the ludus.

The Thirteenth Gladiator… Anachronistic Combats

Republican gladiators are rather limited in scope when compared with the later styles of combat in the Imperial age. Games Masters who desire a more anachronistic variety to their munera can add other types as one-off spectacles. During the Republic there were few conventions to break and the traditional armaturae had yet to be developed and formalised. Editores like Julius Caesar introduced many innovations to woo the jaded plebeian factions, such as the time when he staged a munus where all the gladiators wore silvered armour.

An example of a gladiator from the later period is the retiarius:

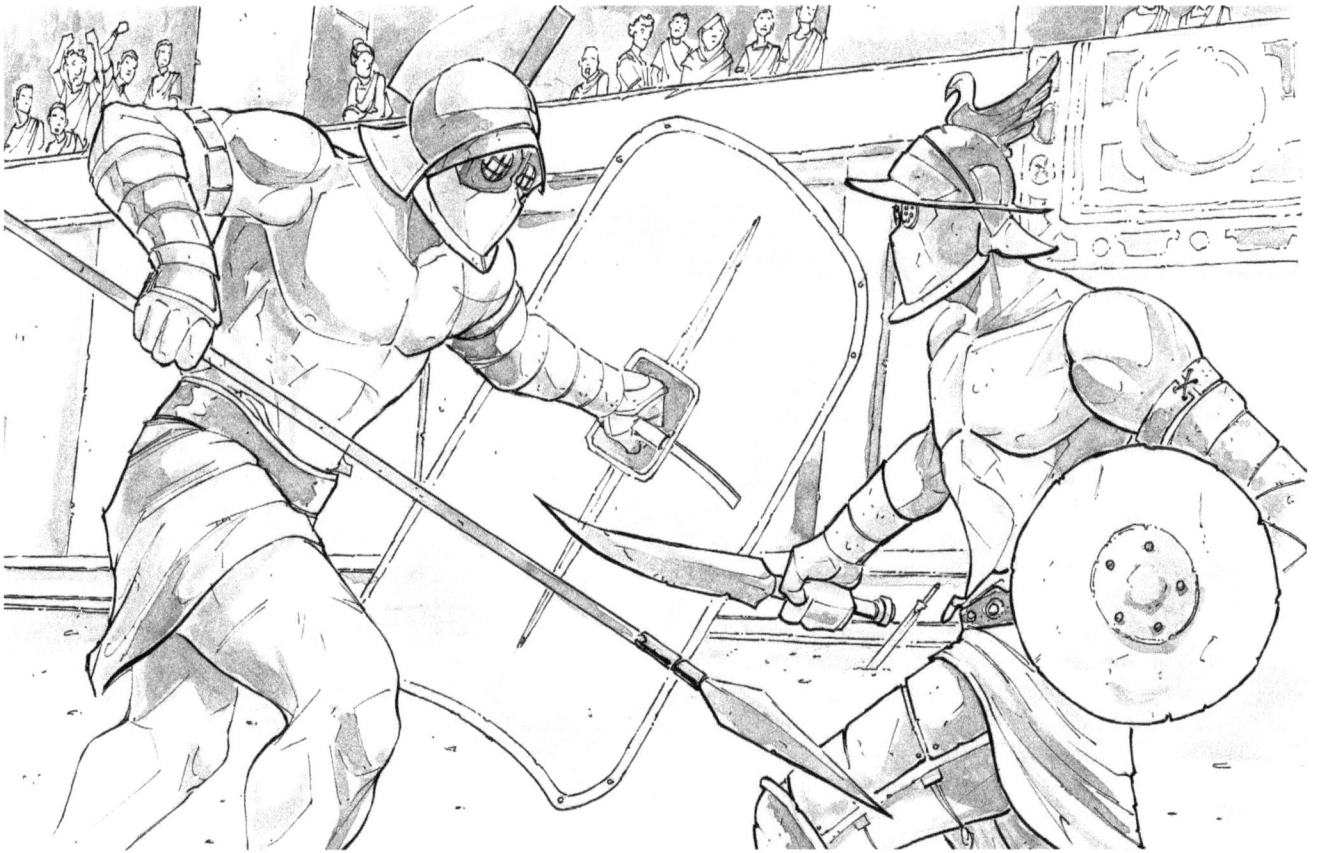

NETMAN (RETIARIUS)

Sporting the same loincloth and belt combination (2 AP), a retiarius also has a padded sleeve up to the shoulder of their left arm, supplemented with a metal shoulder plate (4 AP). Other than that they wear no other armour whatsoever, making them faster and more manoeuvrable than their opponents. The retiarius is armed with a Fuscina (trident) in the right hand and a Rete (net) in the left, which can be used to throw or parry as desired. They also have a backup Pugio once the net has been cast. To survive, a retiarius must utilise the length of their trident to keep foes such as Secutores at bay, preventing them from attacking until their opponent manages to close.

Retiarius Combat Style: Fuscina, Rete, Pugio; and either 'Cautious Fighter' or 'Mancatcher' depending on the ludus.

Later classes such as the Provocator, Hoplomachus, Murmillo and Secutor were simply refined versions of the earliest gladiators. Other more exotic categories included the Dimachaerus (two swords), Crupellarius (heavily armoured), Laquerarius (lasso using versions of a Retiarius) and Sagittarius (bowmen).

NAVAL BATTLES (NAUMACHIAE)

The most spectacular of all gladiatorial combats were the mock naval battles which used full sized ships crewed by thousands of oarsmen and warriors. The earliest (and biggest) were held in Rome on natural or artificial lakes (stagna) excavated for the spectacle. Unfortunately for Games Masters who desire historical accuracy, only one of the great naumachiae was ever hosted during the time of the Republic, by Julius Caesar in 46 BC.

> *"Finally he produced a naval battle, not on the sea nor on a lake, but on land; for he hollowed out a certain tract on the Campus Martius and after flooding it introduced ships into it. In all the contests the captives and those condemned to death took part."*
>
> Cassius Dio – Roman History

These battles were populated with either condemned men or prisoners of war. Enlisted gladiators were not used due to the high levels of slaughter in what was effectively an un-martialled battle.

Each naumachia reflected a historical conflict, Egyptians vs. the Tyrians for Caesar's and the combatants which could number in the thousands were split into two sides. Survivors of the ensuing carnage were occasionally granted a reprieve of their death sentence in reward for their efforts.

> *"There was a combat of elephants, twenty against twenty, and a naval engagement of 4,000 oarsmen, where 1,000 fighting men contended on each side."*
>
> Appian – The Civil Wars

PLOT HOOKS

Ω The characters are approached by the magistrate in charge of the games, who asks them to investigate a matter of some delicacy. It appears that the star of the next venatio – the famous man-eating lion named Audacius (fearless) – has been stolen from his cage. The magistrate is desperate to recover the animal, which is a key part of his games, and is offering a small fortune for the lion's return. A little later, gossip on the streets reveals that a senator has been killed in a mysterious accident. Suspiciously his body is not laid in open state at his home, due to the horrific injuries he suffered. The house slaves are tight lipped and forbidden to leave the house but bribing the undertaker reveals that the senator was mauled by some big animal. Was he murdered by being thrown to Audacius? Did the senator have a dark secret of desiring to be a venator, a pastime forbidden to his rank? Or was this 'accident' the result of something far more nefarious...

Ω A gang of thugs approach one of the player characters who is about to participate in an important boxing match or is the patron of an up and coming boxer of considerable talent. The thugs suggest in no uncertain terms that in the next fight – which will be against a champion of great reputation but fading skill – the character (or his client) should take a fall. A considerable amount of prize money and reputation are at stake. Should the PC back down and forfeit the fight, or should they begin a feud with the criminal underworld?

Ω After winning his last few fights, a player character gladiator is approached by a lady of patrician rank and great beauty. An illicit affair ensues, with the gladiator gaining valuable gifts and a degree of freedom from the ludus to visit the patroness. After a period of time the character is informed by the lady that her husband has discovered the affair and has threatened to have him killed. The gladiator is faced with a tough decision. Should he kill the husband himself or steadfastly face the increasingly murderous combats in the arena against opponents bribed to slay him. Whatever he chooses, the husband ends up dead, stabbed in a side street on the way home. The gladiator has no reliable alibi and it becomes apparent that the entire situation has been a machination devised by the lady for her own advancement, and if truly despicable, her pleasure too...

Ω Although no sane Roman citizen would ever participate in naumachiae unless becoming a condemned criminal first, a cunning Gamemaster could use the following ideas to get their player characters involved in the horrific massacre.

Revenge – At a critical point in an ongoing campaign, an old enemy captures the characters by drugging their wine or ambushing them on the way home. When they awake, they find themselves bound and gagged in the hold of a ship. Any assumptions they might have had about kidnapping or transportation are crushed when they emerge into the beginnings of the battle. The characters will need to put all of their skills together to forge the criminal crew into a coordinated unit. If successful they might escape certain death, and be able to seek who it was that placed them the ship for his, or her, sadistic pleasure.

Youthful Bravado – Younger, inexperienced characters from the equestrian or patrician class may be challenged to prove their bravery, by participating in the naumachia. Using stealth, wits or bribery they can attempt to stowaway on one of the ships the night before the battle begins. Only once the merciless fighting starts should the characters realise that they are out of their depth, surrounded by vengeful prisoners of war who care nothing about the character's status or wealth. Alternatively, the characters could be hired to find a group of foolish young

patrician sons who have vanished on the eve of the naval battle and get caught up in the brutal bloodshed in order to save them.

Welcome To Rome – A campaign could begin with the player characters all starting as Gallic prisoners of war. Placed aboard one of the ships, they must fight for survival against condemned men turned psychotic with bloodlust and fear. If they manage to live they are part of a pitiful handful of survivors granted their freedom. Such a massacre would be instrumental in setting the adventurer's attitudes towards the city. They could use their newfound camaraderie with the other survivors to join the criminal underworld; or the characters might be regarded as celebrities for their toughness and approached by gladiator troupes, rich patrician women, or deceitful politicians for their… err, services.

Ω On the eve of an extremely important race, a team of very successful and very expensive chariot horses belonging to one of the player characters is brutally killed. Somebody did not want the team to win but why and who? The number of suspects is countless. Was it one of the gambling syndicates run by a shady figure rumoured to be a senator in financial difficulty? Was it one of the rival factions, fed up with the popularity of the winning team and lost revenue? Or was it a rival driver in the same team who was jealous of the continuously victorious driver? Once the investigation starts, the characters are led beyond the disreputable world of professional racing and uncover a more sinister plot. The horses were sacrificed to a dark and deadly cult, which is secretly plotting to control the city using religion and magic. However, the horses did not bring the desired result, and now the cultists are seeking the blood of the charioteer himself...

Ω The characters start as foreign captives, rebellious slaves or criminals. Due to their deeds they are condemned to be gladiators. Life inside the school is brutal, the doctores are sadists and several friends die during training. Eventually two of the player characters are forced to fight each other to the death for the personal perverse pleasure of the lanista. Faced with death and armed with proper weapons, the characters could attempt a breakout. If successful they then face the decision of whether to simply slip back into the underworld of the city; or enraged by the cruelty of gladiatorial life, begin a slave uprising. Perhaps one of their fellow escapees is named Spartacus...

Ω One of the player characters is caught carrying a deadly weapon inside Rome (an almost certain event in the case of most adventurers). If the character is a citizen of high standing, the judgement of the magistrate is that he be taught a lesson, and learn that a Roman of courage and wit requires no armament inside the walls of his own city. He is sentenced to appear at the next games and participate in the boxing competition. The populace think this is a marvellous idea and betting runs rampant. The PC is approached by a senator who offers an ex-champion to give the character a crash course over the next few weeks. Should they accept the help? Are there strings attached? Will the character be tempted to cheat if the opportunity is presented?

Ω One of the player characters is caught carrying a deadly weapon inside Rome (an almost certain event in the case of most adventurers). If the character is a citizen of high standing, the judgement of the magistrate is that he be taught a lesson, and learn that a Roman of courage and wit requires no armament inside the walls of his own city. He is sentenced to appear at the next games and participate in the boxing competition. The populace think this is a marvellous idea and betting runs rampant. The PC is approached by a senator who offers an ex-champion to give the character a crash course over the next few weeks. Should they accept the help? Are there strings attached? Will the character be tempted to cheat if the opportunity is presented?

THE ARMY

"After Quintus Sertorius had learned by experience that he was by no means a match for the whole Roman army, and wished to prove this to the barbarians also, who were rashly demanding battle, he brought into their presence two horses, one very strong, the other very feeble. Then he brought up two youths of corresponding physique, one robust, the other slight. The stronger youth was commanded to pull out the entire tail of the feeble horse, while the slight youth was commanded to pull out the hairs of the strong horse, one by one. Then, when the slight youth had succeeded in his task, while the strong one was still struggling vainly with the tail of the weak horse, Sertorius observed: "By this illustration I have exhibited to you, my men, the nature of the Roman cohorts. They are invincible to him who attacks them in a body; yet he who assails them by groups will tear and rend them."

Frontinus - Stratagems

Although this campaign supplement focuses upon adventuring specifically within Rome, it does not prohibit the inclusion of war and glory. In fact, during the monarchy and early Republic, the city was almost continuously at war with its surrounding territories. Hannibal came knocking at the gates of Rome in the mid-Republic during the Punic wars and the late Republic was a period of successive slave uprisings, civic disorder and civil war. Indeed there are very few periods before Imperial rule when Rome was not facing armed conflict on its own doorstep.

Games Masters who desire military adventure can easily set their campaigns during the early and mid-periods; when Rome's army comprised only of a levy of its own citizen population during the summer campaigning season, to conquer or defend against her neighbouring city states. This allows an easy shift from battlefield to city, taking advantage of both role-playing situations.

Setting military campaigns in the late Republic offers some difficulties due to the change in the length of time a levy was conscripted for, thus committing player characters to a minimum of six years' service, unless they play officers of high social rank. Of course a legionary citizen may be prematurely retired due to crippling wounds or could desert the army all together.

It took Rome the best part of five and a half centuries to conquer the whole of Italy, before they expanded outwards and conquered an empire. Despite its reputation of unstoppable progress, the Roman army suffered many terrible defeats but eventually overcame all adversity out of sheer stubbornness more than anything else.

This chapter gives a superficial overview of Rome's toughest enemies, illustrating many aspects of army life from the annals of the period. The Historical Timeline (pages 195-224) gives more information about when certain battles occurred but for greater detail Games Masters are encouraged to undertake their own research and read Livy and Polybius for descriptions of the wars up until the end of the mid-Republic, or Gaius Julius Caesar and Sallust for the wars of the late Republic. They make fascinating reading and provide a wealth of NPC's and events for scenarios.

It should be noted that the arms and armour presented in this chapter are but rough guidelines. Up until the Marian Reforms in the late Republic, there was no consistency in the manufacture of any culture's military equipment; thus even within the same unit, each man's armament could be very different in terms of looks, quality and protective value. Because a soldier had to arm themselves from their own resources, personal wealth or breakage and scavenging during a campaign could radically change their panoply.

THE NAMING OF WEAPONS

Even amongst the Roman authors, the names of weapons described in the annals are varied and erratically applied. In describing some of the armaments of Rome and her enemies, the most applicable that could be found were used. However, their accuracy cannot be guaranteed, as this extract shows...

"Once upon a time, when I was riding in a carriage, to keep my mind from being dull and unoccupied and a prey to worthless trifles, it chanced to occur to me to try to recall the names of weapons, darts and swords which are found in the early histories... Those, then, of the former that came to mind at the time are the following: spear (Hasta), pike (pilum), fire-pike (phalarica), half-pike (semiphalarica), iron bolt (soliferrea), Gallic spear (gaesa), lance (lancea), hunting-darts (spari), javelins (rumices), long bolts (trifaces), barbed-javelins (tragulae), German spears (frameae), thonged-javelins (mesanculae), Gallic bolts (cateiae), broadswords (rumpiae), poisoned arrows (scorpii), Illyrian hunting-spears (sibones), cimeters (siciles), darts (veruta), swords (enses), daggers (sicae), broadswords (machaerae), double-edged swords (Spathae), small-swords (lingulae), poniards (pugiones), cleavers (clunacula)."

Gellius - Noctes Atticae

Gladiator in arena consilium capit – The gladiator is making his plan in the arena (Seneca)

The armament examples in the following sections only give a generic guideline based on the few archaeological finds thus far discovered and ancient authors' reports, which themselves could be written centuries after the period.

COMBAT STYLE & TRAITS

An often overlooked aspect of ancient militaries is that they were usually levies of common citizens, with little or irregular training in formations or tactics. To represent this state of affairs, most of the Combat Styles describing Romans and their enemies possess only a single combat style trait. Only the later mercenary and professional armies are granted access to two or more traits. The following are new or modified traits to help reinforce the fighting styles as described by ancient authors at the time.

Batter Down trait *– If the fighter's Damage Modifier is one or more steps greater than his opponent's, his Damage Modifier roll is counted as double solely for the purposes of calculating Knockback.*

Intimidating Scream *– As well as its normal effect, this trait allows the formation to utilise the Intimidate creature ability (MYTHRAS page 216) but only before combat starts or when they have their opponents at a severe disadvantage.*

Press Home *– Allows the formation to engage and keep an enemy unit at Short reach, penalising foes using longer weapons.*

THE ARMY DURING THE MONARCHY

Up until the reforms of Marius in 104 BC, the army of Rome was made up entirely of conscripted citizens who had to provide and maintain their own arms and armour.

The majority of these citizens were land owning farmers who had return to their fields once the campaigning season was over. The men of the levy (legio – from whence the word Legion evolved) were not paid at this time, because it was considered your civic responsibility to participate in defence of the city. However, a successful conclusion to a military campaign, such as capturing a city or defeating an army, resulted in plunder which would be shared out amongst the troops. It was this which made the yearly levy worthwhile... that and not being conquered by foreigners and sold into slavery.

The first mention of the Roman army's organisation was the military restructuring which took place under the rule of king Servius Tullius. The 'classes' he formed were social ones based on wealth, and from each citizen class was drafted a certain number men to form the army.

"Those whose property amounted to, or exceeded 100,000 lbs. weight of copper were formed into eighty centuries, forty of juniors and forty of seniors. These were called the First Class. The seniors were to defend the City, the juniors to serve in the field. The armour which they were to provide themselves with comprised helmet, round shield, greaves, and cuirass, all of bronze; these were to protect the person. Their offensive weapons were spear and sword. To this class were joined two centuries of carpenters whose duty it was to work the engines of war; they were without arms. The Second Class consisted of those whose property amounted to between 75,000 and 100,000 lbs. weight of copper; they were formed, seniors and juniors together, into twenty centuries. Their regulation arms were the same as those of the First Class, except that they had an oblong wooden shield instead of the round brazen one and no

cuirass. The Third Class he formed of those whose property fell as low as 50,000 lbs.; these also consisted of twenty centuries, similarly divided into seniors and juniors. The only difference in the armour was that they did not wear greaves. In the Fourth Class were those whose property did not fall below 25,000 lbs. They also formed twenty centuries; their only arms were a spear and a javelin. The Fifth Class was larger it formed thirty centuries. They carried slings and stones, and they included the supernumeraries, the horn-blowers, and the trumpeters, who formed three centuries. This Fifth Class was assessed at 11,000 lbs. The rest of the population whose property fell below this were formed into one century and were exempt from military service."

Livy - Ab Urbe Condita

Since Rome was then under the influence of Etruscan kings and much of Etruscan culture was descended from Hellenic sources, the Roman army was effectively mustered and armed in the Greek tradition. It fought as a phalanx supported by wings (alae) of lighter armed troops. Interestingly, it was the most prosperous citizens who bore the duty of either paying the upkeep of their horses or standing in the front of the phalanx; forcing those who had most to lose to make the greatest commitment both financially and physically.

"After thus regulating the equipment and distribution of the infantry, he re-arranged the cavalry. He enrolled from amongst the principal men of the State twelve centuries. In the same way he made six other centuries (though only three had been formed by Romulus) under the same names under which the first had been inaugurated. For the purchase of the horse, 10,000 lbs. were assigned them from the public treasury; whilst for its keep certain widows were assessed to pay 2000 lbs. each, annually. The burden of all these expenses was shifted from the poor on to the rich."

Livy - Ab Urbe Condita

Another fascinating aspect of this structure was the division of each class into two parts, the senior men who were held as the Home Guard and the younger, fitter junior men who engaged in campaigns against other towns. Thus Rome technically possessed two armies, each of 8,500 men. However, depending on the number of recent battles, famines and pestilences, the total strength of the army could be considerably less than this. As Rome's population was not so large in its early days, such losses could take years to replace. It is not surprising to find gaps of up to 20 years between active campaigns in the early Republic, indicating that some enemies required an entire generation of boys to grow up before starting their conflicts again.

THE ARMAMENT OF THE PRE 4TH CENTURY ROMAN ARMY

The weapons (arma) and armour (panoplia) of each class of men are listed here. Each unit (as with following army descriptions) is listed with its combat style trait, along with the weapons used. Note that Roman Chalcidian or Attic style helmets are decorated with a horsehair or feather crest which runs along the centre ridge from front to back. Rome's neighbouring Latin and Etruscan opponents were all armed in similar manner.

CAVALRY (EQUITES) - MOUNTED COMBAT trait
1H Spear (Hasta) M, L, 1d8+1+db, Impaling
Sword (Xiphos) M, S, 1d6+db, Bleeding

FIRST CLASS (LOCHOI) - FORMATION FIGHTING trait
Etruscan Bronze Hoplite Armour

At the end of the monarchy, Rome's army was supplemented with troops levied from allied Latin towns. Facing a command and control problem, king Lucius Tarquinius Superbus formed units comprised half of Romans and half of Latins, thus placing them under the direct authority of the Roman commander and ensuring discipline. From this arose the concept of the maniple.

> *"In compliance with the order contingents assembled from all the thirty towns, and with a view to depriving them of their own general or a separate command, or distinctive standards, he formed one Latin and one Roman century into a maniple, thereby making one unit out of the two, whilst he doubled the strength of the maniples, and placed a centurion over each half."*
>
> Livy - Ab Urbe Condita

THE ARMY DURING THE EARLY REPUBLIC

With the start of the Republic the army was no longer commanded by a king, but was led by two generals instead – the chief magistrates of the city. These were originally known as prætors but by the 4th century BC they were renamed consuls and the title of prætor was used to denote the second rank of civil magistrates.

During the 5th century BC, the most significant enemies of Rome were the Volsci and Aequi hill tribes, who proved to be a thorn in the city's side for more than 60 years. An unending series of battles occurred between them but neither tribe was completely conquered until the end of the Second Samnite War.

The hill tribes were equipped differently to the Romans, probably because of the difficulty of crossing and fighting in mountainous terrain whilst encumbered. Thus they wore lighter armour and used skirmishing tactics which placed the slower moving Roman phalanx at a severe disadvantage.

THE ARMAMENT OF THE 5TH CENTURY HILL TRIBES

The distinctive armour of these tribesmen was a circular pectoral breast and back plate worn instead of the cuirass, and supplemented with a sword harness consisting of broad bronze shoulder straps and belt. Their helmets were distinctive too, crested pot helms possessing a very broad brim.

AEQUI OR VOLSCI WARRIOR - SKIRMISHING TRAIT

Volsci Bronze Armour
Pectoral with cross straps (Lorica), 4 AP (Chest)
Brimmed Helmet (Cassis) plus Throat Guard, 5AP, (Head)
2H Spear (Hasta), L, VL, 1d10+1+db, Impaling
Javelins (Veruta), L, –, 1d6+db, Impaling
Sword (Kopis), M, S, 1d4+2+db, Bleeding

Although the formations, arms and armour of the Roman army remained fundamentally unchanged from the beginning of the Republic, in the 4th century BC it began to adjust its tactics in reaction to the different style of warfare used by their newest enemies… the Gallic tribes migrating into the north of Italy. Around 387 BC the Romans were defeated in the battle of Allia, and Rome itself was sacked.

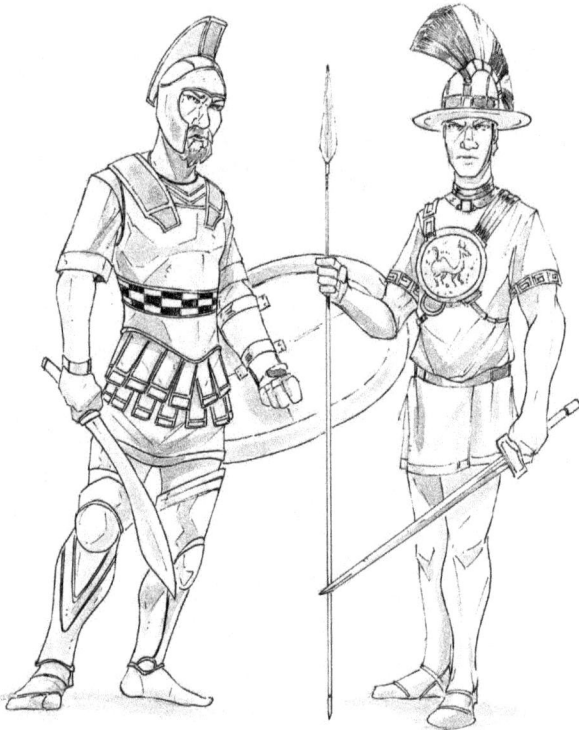

Cuirass (Lorica Musculata), 5 AP (Chest and Abdomen)
Greaves (Ocreae), 5 AP (Legs)
Full Helmet (Cassis), 6 AP (Head)
Bronze Faced Hoplite Shield (Hoplon), H, S, 6 AP/15 HP
Passive Blocks 4 Locations
1H Spear (Hasta), M, L, 1d8+1+db, Impaling
Sword (Xiphos), M, S, 1d6+db, Bleeding

SECOND CLASS - FORMATION FIGHTING TRAIT

Partial Bronze Hoplite Armour
Greaves (Ocreae), 5 AP (Legs)
Full Helmet (Cassis), 6 AP (Head)
Wooden Hoplite Shield (Aspis), L, S 4 AP/15 HP
Passive Blocks 4 Locations
1H Spear (Hasta), M, L, 1d8+1+db, Impaling
Sword (Xiphos) , M, S, 1d6+db, Bleeding

THIRD CLASS - FORMATION FIGHTING TRAIT

Pot Helmet (Cassis), 4 AP
Wooden Hoplite Shield (Aspis), L, S, 4 AP/15 HP
Passive Blocks 4 Locations
1H Spear (Hasta), M, L, 1d8+1+db, Impaling
Sword (Xiphos), M, S, 1d6+db, Bleeding

FOURTH CLASS - SKIRMISHING TRAIT

Wooden Hoplite Shield (Aspis), L, S, 4 AP/15 HP
Passive Blocks 4 Locations
1H Spear (Hasta), M, L, 1d8+1+db, Impaling
Javelins (Veruta) L, –, 1d6+db, Impaling

FIFTH CLASS (FUNDITOR) - CAUTIOUS FIGHTER TRAIT

Sling (Funda), S, –, 1d8, Crushing

Gutta cavat lapidem, non vi sed saepe cadendo – The drop hollows the stone, not by force but by falling on it often (Ovid)

Similar to the Romans, only the wealthier Gauls engaged in warfare. The majority lacked body armour but wore pot helms and used large shields, generally oval shaped and decorated with individual ensigns. Although most wore trousers and cloaks, some Gauls were reputed to go into battle naked.

"In their journeying and when they go into battle the Gauls use chariots drawn by two horses, which carry the charioteer and the warrior; and when they encounter cavalry in the fighting they first hurl their javelins at the enemy and then step down from their chariots and join battle with their swords. Certain of them despise death to such a degree that they enter the perils of battle without protective armour and with no more than a girdle about their loins. They bring along to war also their free men to serve them, choosing them from among the poor, and these attendants they use in battle as charioteers and as shield-bearers"

Diodorus Siculus - Bibliotheca Historica

They were armed with javelins and spears but their fearsome reputation came from using long (for the period) swords in close combat, since the size and reach of the Gauls using slashing swords were difficult to ward with circular hoplite shields.

"For stature they are tall, but of a sweaty and pale complexion, red-haired, not only naturally, but they endeavour all they can to make it redder by art. They often wash their hair in water boiled with lime, and turn it backward from the forehead to the crown of the head, and thence to their very necks, that their faces may be more fully seen, so that they look like satyrs and hobgoblins."

Diodorus Siculus - Bibliotheca Historica

The Gallic method of war was indelibly linked to personal status. Battles started with challenges to single combat and the taking of heads as trophies.

"It is also their custom, when they are formed for battle, to step out in front of the line and to challenge the most valiant men from among their opponents in single combat, brandishing their weapons in front of them to terrify their adversaries. And when any man accepts the challenge to battle, they then break forth into a song in praise of the valiant deeds of their ancestors and in boast of their own high achievements, reviling all the while and belittling their opponent, and trying, in a word, by such talk to strip him of his bold spirit before the combat."

Diodorus Siculus - Bibliotheca Historica

Due to their lighter armaments and use of chariots to manoeuvre about the field of battle quickly, Gallic tactics focused on the use of intimidating charges, using their height in close combat to overreach circular shields, and flanking to break the discipline of their foes – turning the ponderous defensive strength of the phalanx into a weakness.

THE ARMAMENT OF THE 4TH CENTURY GAULS

GALLIC INFANTRY - BATTER DOWN trait
Bronze Pot Helmet (Cassis), 4 AP (Head)
Large Wooden Oval Shield (Thureos), L, S, 4 AP/15 HP
Passive Blocks 4 Locations
Sword (Spatha), M, M, 1d8+db, Bleeding
Light Javelin (Lancia), L, –, 1d6+1+db, Impaling

CHAMPIONS AND CHALLENGES
Not all wars were decided by battle. During the monarchy and early Republic, many were settled by the individual combat of champions. Often the generals would agree to abide by the result in order to save lives. At other times the blow to the morale of the losing side caused them to retreat from the field in superstitious fear. The following account describes such an event in 364 BC, demonstrating the wonderful opportunities available to heroically inclined players characters.

"A Gaul of extraordinary stature strode forward on to the unoccupied bridge, and shouting as loudly as he could, cried: "Let the bravest man that Rome possesses come out and fight me, that we two may decide which people is the superior in war." A long silence followed. The best and bravest of the Romans made no sign; they felt ashamed of appearing to decline the challenge, and yet they were reluctant to expose themselves to such terrible danger. Thereupon T. Manlius, the youth who had protected his father from the persecution of the tribune, left his post and went to the Dictator. "Without your orders, General," he said, "I will never leave my post to fight, no, not even if I saw that victory was certain; but if you give me permission I want to show that monster as he stalks so proudly in front of their lines that I am a scion of that family which hurled the troop of Gauls from the Tarpeian rock." Then the Dictator: "Success to your courage, T. Manlius, and to your affection for your father and your fatherland. Go, and with the help of the gods show that the name of Rome is invincible." Then his comrades fastened on his armour; he took an infantry shield and a Spanish sword as better adapted for close fighting; thus armed and equipped they led him forward against the Gaul, who was exulting in his brute strength, and - even the ancients thought this worth recording - putting his tongue out in derision. They retired to their posts and the two armed champions were left alone in the midst, more after the manner of a scene on the stage than under the conditions of serious war, and to those who judged by appearances, by no means equally matched. The one was a creature of enormous bulk, resplendent in a many-coloured coat and wearing painted and gilded armour; the other a man of average height, and his arms, useful rather than ornamental, gave him quite an ordinary appearance. There was no singing of war-songs, no prancing about, no silly brandishing of weapons. With a breast full of courage and silent wrath Manlius reserved all his ferocity for the actual moment of conflict. When they had taken their stand between the two armies, while so many hearts around them were in suspense between hope and fear, the Gaul, like a great overhanging mass, held out his shield on his left arm to meet his adversary's blows and aimed a tremendous cut downwards with his sword. The Roman evaded the blow, and pushing aside the bottom of the Gaul's shield with his own, he slipped under it close up to the Gaul, too near for him to get at him with his sword. Then turning the point of his blade upwards, he gave two rapid thrusts in succession and stabbed the Gaul in the belly and the groin, laying his enemy prostrate over a large extent of ground. He left the body of his fallen foe un-despoiled with the exception of his chain, which though smeared with blood he placed round his own neck. Astonishment and fear kept the Gauls motionless; the Romans ran eagerly forward from their lines to meet their warrior, and amidst cheers and congratulations they conducted him to the Dictator. In the doggerel verses which they extemporised in his honour they called him Torquatus ("adorned with a chain"), and this soubriquet became for his posterity a proud family name. The Dictator gave him a golden crown, and before the whole army alluded to his victory in terms of the highest praise."

Livy - Ab Urbe Condita

Gallic Fanatics - Intimidating Scream trait
Large Wooden Oval Shield (Thureos), L, S, 4 AP/15 HP
Passive Blocks 4 Locations
1H Spear (Hasta), M, L, 1d8+1+db, Impaling
Light Javelin (Lancia), L, –, 1d6+1+db, Impaling

Gallic Charioteer - Chariot Fighting trait
Bronze Pot Helmet (Cassis), 4 AP (Head)
Large Wooden Oval Shield (Thureos), L, S, 4 AP/15 HP
Passive Blocks 4 Locations
Sword (Spatha), M, M, 1d8+db, Bleeding
Light Javelin (Lancia), L, –, 1d6+1+db, Impaling

Gallic Cavalry - Mounted Combat trait
Bronze Pot Helmet (Cassis), 4 AP (Head)
Passive Blocks 4 Locations
Sword (Spatha), M, M, 1d8+db, Bleeding
Light Javelin (Lancia), L, –, 1d6+1+db, Impaling

The Roman army, placed at a disadvantage by the revolutionary new tactics of close fighting, was forced to evolve countermeasures. They began arming their heavier troops with larger shields (scuta) that had reinforced iron edges for better protection against slashing swords and the heavy javelin (pilum) to break up charges. The structure of the army was also revised. The phalanx was abandoned, replaced with a formation formed of three lines.

The front line comprised of 15 units (manipuli) of 60 heavy infantry (Hastati), formed from the most youthful soldiers. Each maniple had an additional 20 lightly armed skirmishers (Leves) assigned to it. The middle line consisted of 15 maniples of 60 heavy infantry (Principes) who were in their maturity and considered the best soldiers in the army. The much larger rear line was formed from 15 companies (Ordines) of 180 soldiers. However, each ordo was further subdivided into three parts or vexillae of 60 men; old veterans (Triarii) in the front, the younger skirmishers (Rorarii) in the middle and the reserves (Accensi) in the rear. Each vexilla and

maniple was commanded by two centurions and possessed a standard bearer (vexillarius).

"When the battle formation of the army was completed, the Hastati were the first to engage. If they failed to repulse the enemy, they slowly retired through the intervals between the companies of the Principes who then took up the fight, the Hastati following in their rear. The Triarii, meantime, were resting on one knee under their standards, their shields over their shoulders and their spears planted on the ground with the points upwards, giving them the appearance of a bristling palisade. If the Principes were also unsuccessful, they slowly retired to the Triarii, which has given rise to the proverbial saying, when people are in great difficulty "matters have come down to the Triarii." When the Triarii had admitted the Hastati and Principes through the intervals separating their companies they rose from their kneeling posture and instantly closing their companies up they blocked all passage through them and in one compact mass fell on the enemy as the last hope of the army. The enemy who had followed up the others as though they had defeated them, saw with dread a now and larger army rising apparently out of the earth."

Livy - Ab Urbe Condita

The tactics of this new Roman army revolved around the use of missile weapons and swords. Firstly the skirmishers would attempt to break up an enemy formation with thrown javelins and then disperse to guard the flanks. Then the Hastati would cast their pila and charge in with swords. If the enemy failed to break, the Hastati would retreat between gaps left between the Principes who would in turn repeat the manoeuvre. If the second line was also beaten, the Principes too would retreat through the spear armed Triarii who would close ranks and the entire army withdraw from the field under the protection of their hedgehog.

The Armament of the 4th Century Roman Army

The manipular armour of this period had evolved away from that of earlier phalanxes. Firstly was the adoption of the pectoral first used by the hill tribes, to replace the heavier cuirass. The Roman pectoral however was square and covered a larger amount of the chest. Secondly, only the leading leg was armoured, again in an attempt to save weight and expense.

Hastati and Principes - Cautious Fighter trait
Bronze Half Hoplite Armour
Large Pectoral (Lorica), 4 AP (Chest)
Single Greave (Ocrea), 5 AP (Left Leg)
Helm with Cheek Flaps (Cassis), 5 AP (Head)
Iron Rimed Oval Shield (Scutum), L, S, 5 AP/15 HP
Passive Blocks 5 Locations
Sword (Falcata), M, S, 1d4+2+db, Bleeding
Heavy Javelin (Pilum), H, –, 1d8+1+db, Impaling

Triarii - Formation Fighting trait
As Hastati, but armed with a spear instead of Javelins
1H Spear (Hasta), M, L, 1d8+1+db, Impaling

Rorarii and Accensi - Skirmishing trait
Open Helmet (Cassis), 4 AP
Iron Rimed Oval Shield (Scutum), L, S, 5 AP/15 HP
Passive Blocks 5 Locations
1H Spear (Hasta), M, L, 1d8+1+db, Impaling

LEVES - SKIRMISHING TRAIT
  Wooden Hoplite Shield (Aspis), L, S, 4 AP/15 HP,
  Passive Blocks 4 Locations
  Light Javelin (Veruta), L, −,1d6+1+db, Impaling

Since the Roman army was spending more and more time in the field, at the start of the 4th century BC soldiers began to be paid compensation for their military service. The amount was basic and barely covered the expenses of paying for their own food and replacing damaged weapons. However, soldiers could still expect to claim a share of any spoils gained during the campaign.

During the latter half of the 4th century, the Romans as head of the Latin League, entered a new war against the Samnites. Hostilities lasted for over 50 years and these new enemies proved to be amongst the most difficult Rome had ever faced.

The Samnites were originally a collective of hill tribes which occupied the region of the south central Apennines. Following the collapse of the Etruscan nation (due to Rome's rise) they flowed down from their mountains and by military conquest formed a federation of allied tribes, eventually occupying the entirety of Italy south and east of Campania. Since the region under their control was primarily a collection of Greek settled coastal cities, the arms and armour of the Samnite Federation was heavily influenced by Greek tradition.

The fighting style of the Samnites lent itself to rapid manoeuvrability in loose formations. They did not carry swords, so their primary attacks were missile fire from javelins and spear work, presumably using the speed of their lighter armed troops to outflank and break up heavier formations. Atop this, the Samnite cavalry was at the time reputed to be the best in Italy.

THE ARMAMENT OF THE 4TH – 3RD CENTURY SAMNITES

Samnite armour is generally well decorated. Helmets extend lower in the back to help guard the neck, have cheek guards (adopted from the Gauls) and display feather holders as well as the horsehair crest. They sometimes even sport bronze wings. Body armour varies in style between the square plate muscled cuirass and a version decorated with or formed from three discs. Below the cuirass is worn a broad bronze belt for further protection. If possessed, greaves are worn as pairs.

HEAVY INFANTRY - CAUTIOUS FIGHTER TRAIT
  Samnite Bronze Hoplite Armour
  Square or Triple Circle Pectoral (Lorica), 5 AP (Chest)
  Broad Bronze Belt (Balteus), 4 AP (Abdomen)
  Greaves, (Ocreae), 5 AP (Legs)
  Helm with Neck Guard & Cheek Flaps (Cassis), 6 AP (Head)
  Large Wooden Oval Shield (Thureos), L, S, 4 AP/18 HP
  Passive Blocks 4 Locations
  1H Spear (Hasta), M, L, 1d8+1+db, Impaling
  Light Javelin (Veruta), L, −, 1d6+1+db, Impaling

LIGHT INFANTRY - SKIRMISHING TRAIT
  Samnite Light Armour
  Broad Bronze Belt (Balteus), 4 AP (Abdomen)
  Helm with Neck Guard & Cheek Flaps (Cassis), 6 AP (Head)
  Large Wooden Oval Shield (Thureos), L, S, 4 AP/18 HP
  Passive Blocks 4 Locations

  1H Spear (Hasta), M, L, 1d8+1+db, Impaling
  Light Javelin (Veruta), L, −, 1d6+1+db, Impaling

CAVALRY - BEAST-BACK LANCER TRAIT
  Samnite Light Armour
  Broad Bronze Belt (Balteus), 4 AP (Abdomen)
  Helm with Neck Guard & Cheek Flaps (Cassis), 6 AP (Head)
  2H Spear (Hasta), L, VL, 1d10+1+db, Impaling
  Light Javelin (Veruta), L, −, 1d6+1+db, Impaling
  Horse Armour, Peytral, 4 AP (Chest)
  Chamfron, 4 AP (Head)

By the 3rd century BC the metal working skills of the Gauls had led them to the development of iron mail armour, iron helmets with extended neck protection and hinged face plates and longer, more resilient, swords. These breakthroughs were so successful that over the following centuries they were adopted by the Roman army.

> *"For swords, they use a long and broad weapon called Spatha, which they hang across their right thigh by iron or brazen chains. Some gird themselves over their (mail) coats with belts gilt with gold or silver. For darts they cast those they call Lancia, whose iron shafts are a cubit or more in length, and almost two hands in breadth. For their swords are as big as the javelins of other people, but the points of their javelins are larger than those of their swords; some of them are strait, others bowed and bending backwards, so that they not only cut, but break the flesh; and when the dart is drawn out, it tears and rents the wound most miserably."*
>
> Diodorus Siculus - Bibliotheca Historica

Eventually though, the Gallic tribes were defeated and the most warlike forced from northern Italy. Those which remained were − like the other conquered peoples of the peninsula − granted ally status (socii), whereupon they were permitted self-rule in exchange for supplying troops for the army, and placing their foreign policy in Rome's hands.

THE ARMAMENT OF THE 3RD – 1ST CENTURY GAULS

The majority of Gallic warriors still lacked any form of body armour. Only chieftains could afford mail shirts or gift it to their champions. Thus the term 'Heavy Gallic Infantry' should be interpreted as individual leaders and their personal warbands scattered though out the battle line.

HEAVY GALLIC INFANTRY - BATTER DOWN TRAIT
  Gallic Iron Armour
  Mail Vest (Lorica Hamata), 6 AP (Chest and Abdomen)
  Montefortino Helm (Galea), 6 AP (Head)
  Large Iron Rimed Oval Shield (Thureos), L, S, 5 AP/18 HP
  Passive Blocks 4 Locations
  Long Sword (Spatha), M, M, 1d8+db, Bleeding
  Light Javelins (Lancia), L, −, 1d6+1+db, Impaling

LIGHT GALLIC INFANTRY - CAUTIOUS FIGHTER TRAIT
  Pot Helmet (Cassis), 4 AP
  Large Wooden Oval Shield (Thureos), L, S, 4 AP/18 HP
  Passive Blocks 4 Locations
  1H Spear (Hasta), M, L, 1d8+1+db, Impaling
  Light Javelins (Lancia), L, −, 1d6+1+db, Impaling

Hoc natura est insitum, ut quem timueris, hunc semper oderis − It's an innate thing to always hate the one we've learnt to fear

93

GALLIC CHARIOTEER - CHARIOT FIGHTING TRAIT
Pot Helmet (Cassis), 4 AP
Large Iron Rimed Oval Shield (Thureos), L, S, 5 AP/18 HP
Passive Blocks 4 Locations
Long Sword (Spatha), M, M, 1d8+db, Bleeding
Light Javelins (Lancia), L, −, 1d6+1+db, Impaling

GALLIC CAVALRY - MOUNTED COMBAT TRAIT
Gallic Iron Armour
Mail Shirt (Lorica Hamata), 6 AP (Chest and Abdomen)
Montefortino Helm (Galea), 6 AP (Head)
Long Sword (Spatha), M, M, 1d8+db, Bleeding
1H Spear (Hasta), M, L, 1d8+1+db, Impaling
Light Javelins (Lancia), L, −, 1d6+1+db, Impaling

The final enemy of Rome during the early Republic was Pyrrhus, king of Epirus, who landed in Italy with an army organised into a Macedonian-style phalanx and supported with heavy shock cavalry and elephants.

> *"With this point in our minds, it will not be difficult to imagine what the appearance and strength of the whole phalanx is likely to be, when, with lowered sarissae, it advances to the charge sixteen deep. Of these sixteen ranks, all above the fifth are unable to reach with their sarissae far enough to take actual part in the fighting. They, therefore, do not lower them, but hold them with the points inclined upwards over the shoulders of the ranks in front of them, to shield the heads of the whole phalanx; for the sarissae are so closely serried, that they repel missiles which have carried over the front ranks and might fall upon the heads of those in the rear. These rear ranks, however, during an advance, press forward those in front by the weight of their bodies; and thus make the charge very forcible, and at the same time render it impossible for the front ranks to face about."*
>
> *Polybius - Histories*

Pyrrhus defeated the Roman army time after time, but ultimately lost the war due to an inability to replace his wounded and dead. From this costly campaign we get the phrase 'Pyrrhic Victory'.

> *"The two armies separated; and we are told that Pyrrhus said to one who was congratulating him on his victory, "If we are victorious in one more battle with the Romans, I shall be utterly ruined." For he had lost a great part of the forces with which he came, and all his friends and generals except a few; moreover, he had no others whom he could summon from home, and he saw that his allies in Italy were becoming indifferent, while the army of the Romans, as if from a fountain gushing forth indoors, was easily and speedily filled up again, and they did not lose courage in defeat, nay, their wrath gave them all the more vigour and determination for the war."*
>
> *Plutarch - Life of Pyrrhus*

It was from Pyrrhus that the Romans learned the value of erecting a fortified camp at the end of each day; a skill which saved them many times in the future.

> *"In ancient times the Romans and other peoples used to make their camps like groups of Punic huts, distributing the troops here and there by cohorts, since the men of old were not acquainted with walls except in the case of cities. Pyrrhus, king of the Epirotes, was the first to inaugurate the custom of concentrating an entire army within the precincts of the same entrenchments. Later the Romans, after defeating Pyrrhus on the Arusian Plains near the city of Maleventum, captured his camp, and, noting its plan, gradually came to the arrangement which is in vogue today."*
>
> *Frontinus - Stratagems*

THE ARMAMENT OF THE 3RD C MACEDONIAN PHALANX

HEAVY PHALANGITE -

FORMATION FIGHTING, SIEGE WARFARE TRAITS
Heavy Macedonian Armour
Scaled Cuirass (Kataphraktes), 5 AP (Chest and Abdomen)
Greaves, (Knimis), 5 AP (Legs)
Full Helm (Kranos), 6 AP (Head)
Bronze Phalangite Shield (Aspis), L, S, 6 AP/12 HP
Passive Blocks 3 Locations
2H Pike (Sarissa), L, VL, 1d10+2+db, Impaling
Sword (Kopis), M, S, 1d4+2+db, Bleeding

LIGHT PHALANGITE -

FORMATION FIGHTING, SIEGE WARFARE TRAITS
Light Macedonian Armour
Quilted Linen Cuirass (Linothorax), 3 AP (Chest and Abdomen)
Open Helm (Kranos), 4 AP (Head)
Bronze Phalangite Shield (Aspis), L, S, 6 AP/12 HP
Passive Blocks 3 Locations
2H Pike (Sarissa), L, VL, 1d10+2+db, Impaling
Sword (Kopis), M, S, 1d4+2+db, Bleeding

MACEDONIAN CAVALRY -

BEAST-BACK LANCER, MOUNTED COMBAT TRAITS
Macedonian Cavalry Armour
Scaled Cuirass (Kataphraktes), 5 AP (Chest and Abdomen)

Plated Leather Skirt (Pteryges), 4 AP (Legs)
Open Helm (Kranos), 4 AP (Head)
2H Pike (Sarissa), L, VL, 1d10+2+db, Impaling
Sword (Kopis), M, S, 1d4+2+db, Bleeding

With the eventual defeat of Pyrrhus, the whole of Italy ostensibly fell under Roman dominance, although some regions still simmered with dissent and even outright rebellion, over the next few centuries.

THE ARMY DURING THE MID-REPUBLIC

Driven by their needs to expand their territory, the next series of conflicts Rome faced were the Punic wars with Carthage, interspersed by a Gallic invasion from the north. During this time the structure of the Roman army was refined – it maintained its structure around the Hastati, Principes, and Triarii but the Rorarii and Accensi were dropped or absorbed into the rest of the army.

During this time Rome mustered a mere four legions (legiones), placing two each under the authority of the consuls. In times of emergency, the entire army could be commanded by a dictator and his second in command, the Master of Horse (magister equitum) for a period of six months.

The consuls appointed 24 military tribunes (tribuni militum) from the senatorial class, who were assigned six apiece between the legions. Half of the tribunes (comitiati) were elected by the popular assembly and the other half (rufuli) being selected by the commanders-in-chief. Tribunes could either be former magistrates such as prætors, consuls, or young inexperienced men starting their public career.

Only half of the troops in each legion were Romans, the other half assembled from the population of allied cities. These men were still divided according to age and personal wealth into different classes. The youngest and poorest formed the lightly armed Velites (formally known as the Leves). The remaining youths were placed in the Hastati, those in the prime of life in the Principes, and the oldest in the Triarii.

The legion comprised of about 4,200 men, broken down into the following units:

Ω 10 maniples of Hastati, each maniple containing 120 heavy infantry and 40 Velites.

Ω 10 maniples of Principes, each maniple containing 120 heavy infantry and 40 Velites.

Ω 10 maniples of Triarii, each maniple containing 60 heavy infantry and 40 Velites.

Each maniple had two centurions, the prior and posterior and each centurion had his own rear-guard officer called an optio. With this command structure a maniple could be further subdivided into two centuries, each one under the direct leadership of a single centurion, aided by his optio. The centurions rewarded the two best and bravest men of each maniple with the duty of standard bearer (signiferi). Every maniple also had at least one trumpeter (tubicen) and hornblower (cornicen) for signalling purposes. The most senior centurion (primus pilus) of the legion was permitted to attend meetings of the high command.

The cavalry were organised into squadrons of 300 Equites, which could be broken down into 10 turmae of 30 men. Each turma comprised of three files (decuriae) of 10 men, led by a decurion and assisted by a 'rear ranker' optio.

As Rome became embroiled in campaigns overseas and faced conflict on several different fronts, the number of legions required grew beyond the previously sufficient four urban legions. During the 2nd Punic war there were upwards of 20. The right to raise new legions was voted on by the Senate, which carefully restricted the numbers of troops which any single commander was permitted to enlist.

THE ARMAMENT OF THE 3RD CENTURY ROMAN ARMY

Similarly equipped to the troops of the previous century, the major differences are in weaponry rather than armour. The Hastati and Principes now carry two pila, one thick and one thin, presumably to use at short and long range respectively. Contact with Spanish mercenaries in the first and second Punic wars led to the addition of a dagger (pugio) and the replacement of the single edged, hacking falcata with the shorter, stabbing gladius. In the last quarter of the 3rd century BC after the final Gallic invasion, those legionaries who could afford it began to adopt Gallic style sleeveless mail shirts (loricae hamatae) and Montefortino style helmets (galeae) with better neck protection and cheek guards.

"The common soldiers wear in addition a breastplate of brass a span square, which they place in front of the heart and call the heart-protector, this completing their accoutrements; but those who are rated above ten thousand drachmas wear instead of this a coat of chain-mail. Finally they wear as an ornament a circle of feathers with three upright purple or black feathers about a cubit in height, the addition of which on the head surmounting their other arms is to make every man look twice his real height, and to give him a fine appearance, such as will strike terror into the enemy."

Polybius - Histories

HASTATI AND PRINCIPES - SHIELD WALL TRAIT
Armoured either as in the 4th Century or upgraded to...
Mail Shirt (Lorica Hamata), 6 AP (Chest and Abdomen)
Brimmed Montefortino Helm (Galea), 6 AP (Head)
Iron Rimed Oval Shield (Scutum), H, S, 5 AP/18 HP
Passive Blocks 5 Locations
Sword (Gladius), M, S, 1d6+db, Impaling
Heavy Javelin (Pilum), H, –, 1d8+1+db, Impaling

TRIARII - SHIELD WALL TRAIT
Armoured as Hastati
Iron Rimed Oval Shield (Scutum), H, S, 5 AP/18 HP
Passive Blocks 5 Locations
Sword (Gladius), M, S, 1d6+db, Impaling
1H Spear (Hasta), M, L, 1d8+1+db, Impaling

VELITES - SKIRMISHING TRAIT
Small Wooden Round Shield (Parma), M, S, 4 AP/12 HP
Passive Blocks 3 Locations
Sword (Gladius), M, S, 1d6+db, Impaling
Light Javelin (Veruta), L, –, 1d6+1+db, Impaling

Cavalry (Equites) - Mounted Combat Trait

Cavalry Armour
Mail Shirt (Lorica Hamata), 6 AP (Chest and Abdomen)
Open, Crested Helm (Cassis), 4 AP (Head)
Small Wooden Round Shield (Parma), M, S, 4 AP/12 HP
Passive Blocks 3 Locations
Sword (Gladius), M, S, 1d6+db, Impaling
1H Spear (Hasta), M, L, 1d8+1+db, Impaling

The Carthaginians were Rome's greatest enemies of the mid-Republic, hostilities starting with the 1st Punic war being fought over control of Sicily; the Republic's first foreign campaign overseas. Although several legions fought on mainland Sicily (Sicilia) itself, the campaign soon bogged down into a succession of sieges. The major conflicts occurred at sea and Rome found herself at a loss, not possessing a navy (classis) of her own. Ships were built and sailors initially recruited from the 5th class of citizens but the Romans suffered for their lack of seamanship and over the period of the war lost 700 warships, thousands of supply vessels and hundreds of thousands of men (of which at least 50,000 were Roman citizens). The majority of ships foundered due to inexperienced commanders, poor construction and bad weather rather than actual combat and eventually the wealth qualifications were lowered so that sailors could be recruited from the un-propertied poor.

Roman sailors were expected to fight just as the regular legionaries who acted as marines. Rome's naval tactics involved mass boarding actions rather than ramming, using a type of drop down bridge (corvus) with a spike at the end which 'nailed' it to the enemy ship, with low walls to help prevent the marines from falling off.

"When the Carthaginians thought they had drawn off the first and second squadrons far enough from the others, they all, on receiving a signal from Hamilcar's ship, turned simultaneously and attacked their pursuers. The engagement that followed was a very hot one, the superior speed of the Carthaginians enabling them to move round the enemy's flank as well as to approach easily and retire rapidly, while the Romans, relying on their sheer strength when they closed with the enemy, grappling with the corvi every ship as soon as it approached, fighting also, as they were, under the very eyes of both the consuls, who were personally taking part in the combat, had no less high hopes of success."

Polybius - Histories

Being based in Africa, the Carthaginians used many mercenary troops recruited from the neighbouring nations of Libya and Numidia, as well as the colonies it had established in Sardinia, Corsica and other islands in the western Mediterranean. These mercenaries were used for the land battles in Sicily and in defence of Carthage itself when Rome attempted its ultimately doomed first invasion of Africa…

"Acting on this authority, he sent the elephants forward and drew them up in a single line in front of the whole force, placing the Carthaginian phalanx at a suitable distance behind them. Some of the mercenaries he stationed on the right wing, while the most active he placed together with the cavalry in front of both wings. The Romans, seeing the enemy drawn up to offer battle, issued forth to meet them with alacrity. Alarmed at the prospect of the elephants' charge, they stationed the Velites in the van and behind them the legions many maniples deep, dividing the cavalry between the two wings... But the first

---

MARINES IN THE ROMAN ARMY

Since most sailors were recruited from the poorest classes of citizens, few could afford any form of armour, which would have just hindered ship-board duties anyway. Although expected to fight, sailors were only equipped with a single side arm, such as a knife or some other impromptu weapon. They could also be issued with javelins or bows to provide missile support.

Roman marines were simply legionaries placed aboard ship, with no differences in armament. After the Punic wars, Rome gave up on maintaining its own navy, recruiting fleets from Greek allies instead.

---

ranks of those [Romans] who were stationed opposite the elephants, pushed back when they encountered them and trodden under foot by the strength of the animals, fell in heaps in the mêlée, while the formation of the main body, owing to the depths of the ranks behind, remained for a time unbroken. At length, however, those in the rear were surrounded on all sides by the [mercenary] cavalry and obliged to face round and fight them, while those who had managed to force a passage through the elephants and collect in the rear of those beasts, encountered the Carthaginian phalanx quite fresh and in good order and were cut to pieces."

Polybius - Histories

A decade and a half after the 1st Punic war, the Gauls, seeing their lands in the Po valley under threat from the Roman's inexorable advances northwards, invaded for the final time. They crossed the Apennines and were defeated at the Battle of Telamon. Over the following few years the Po valley was completely subjugated.

During the 2nd Punic war, the range of mercenaries became more diverse, including Iberian swordsmen from Hispania and Gauls urged to revolt against Roman rule.

"At the same time Hannibal brought his Balearic slingers and spearmen across the river, and stationed them in advance of his main body; which he led out of their camp, and, getting them across the river at two spots, drew them up opposite the enemy. On his left wing, close to the river, he stationed the Iberian and Celtic horse opposite the Roman cavalry; and next to them half the Libyan heavy-armed foot; and next to them the Iberian and Celtic foot; next, the other half of the Libyans, and, on the right wing, the Numidian horse."

Polybius - Histories

Several of the mercenary types used in the Punic wars stood out from the norm. The Numidians were regarded as the best light cavalry in the world. Unable to directly charge opponents, they were used for scouting, skirmishing with thrown javelins, breaking formations by flanking manoeuvres, and pursuing routed enemies. The Balearic slingers were famed for their skill in slinging heavy stones with great accuracy.

"The armour of the Libyans was Roman, for Hannibal had armed them with a selection of the spoils taken in previous battles. The shield of the Iberians and Celts was about the same size, but their swords were quite different. For that of the Iberians can thrust with as deadly effects as it can cut, while the Gallic sword can only cut, and that requires some room. And the companies coming alternately - the naked Celts, and the Iberians with their short linen tunics bordered with purple stripes, the whole appearance of the line was strange and terrifying."

Polybius - Histories

Homines quod volunt credunt – Men believe what they want to (Julius Caesar)

THE ARMAMENT OF THE CARTHAGINIAN ARMY

The Carthaginians primarily used mercenaries to fight its battles and maintain garrisons, paid for by the wealth of its trading fleets. The majority of its own people were employed as merchants or sailors. These troops cover a range of different types used during the three separate Punic wars.

LIBYAN PHALANGITE - FORMATION FIGHTING TRAIT
Looted Heavy Roman Armour (See Armament of the 3rd Century Roman Army previously)
Medium Bronze Shield (Aspis), L, S, 6 AP/15 HP
Passive Blocks 4 Locations
2H Pike (Sarissa), L, VL, 1d10+2+db, Impaling
Sword (Kopis), M, S, 1d4+2+db, Bleeding

IBERIAN SWORDSMEN (SCUTARII) -
CAUTIOUS FIGHTER, SHIELD WALL TRAITS
Quilted Linen Cuirass (Linothorax), 3 AP
Sinew Cap/Hood (Pilos), 3 AP
Iron Rimed Oval Shield (Scutum), L, S, 5 AP/15 HP
Passive Blocks 4 Locations
Sword (Espasa), M, S, 1d6+db, Impaling
Dagger (Pugio), S, S, 1d4+1+db, Impaling
Heavy Barbed Javelin (Saunion), H, -, 1d8+1+db, Impaling
1H Spear (Hasta), M, L, 1d8+1+db, Impaling

IBERIAN SKIRMISHERS (CAETRATI) - SKIRMISHER TRAIT
Sinew Cap or Hood (Pilos), 3 AP
Small Round Shield (Caetra), M, S, 4 AP/12 HP
Passive Blocks 3 Locations
Dagger (Pugio), S, S, 1d4+1+db, Impaling
Heavy Javelins (Pila), H, −, 1d8+1+db, Impaling

IBERIAN CAVALRY -
BEAST-BACK LANCER, MOUNTED COMBAT TRAITS
Sinew Cap or Hood (Pilos), 3 AP
Small Round Shield (Caetra), M, S, 4 AP/12 HP
Passive Blocks 3 Locations
1H Spear (Hasta), M, L, 1d8+1+db, Impaling
Sword (Espasa), M, S, 1d6+1+db, Impaling

NUMIDIAN CAVALRY -
MOUNTED COMBAT, RANGED MARKSMAN TRAITS
Small Round Shield (Caetra), M, S, 4 AP/12 HP
Passive Blocks 3 Locations
Javelins (Veruta), L, −, 1d6+1+db, Impaling

ELEPHANTS - MOUNTED COMBAT, TRAINED BEAST TRAITS
See Creatures on page 150. War elephants are heavily armoured on the head and chest (6 AP atop their already thick skin) and carry on their backs a howdah with a crew of two or three men armed with bows and pikes. The elephant also carried a driver, called a mahout.

For details of the Carthaginian's Gallic allies, please use The Armament of the 3rd − 1st c Gauls page 93.

After the 2nd Punic war, Rome began to engage full scale in foreign wars, expanding the territory of her blossoming empire. During this time she fought again against the Gauls of the Po Valley and engaged in a series of wars with Macedonia, before finally

destroying Carthage in the 3rd Punic war. The final conflict of the mid-Republic was against the Iberians, concluding with the Numantine war.

For examples of troops used in these later conflicts, use those described under The Armament of the 3rd c Macedonian Phalanx for the Macedonians, The Armament of the 3rd − 1st c Gauls for the Gauls and The Armament of the Carthaginian Army for the Iberians. Remember that by this time the Romans were universally using mail armour, Montefortino helmets and gladii.

THE ARMY DURING THE LATE REPUBLIC

Rome continued her expansion across the Mediterranean world and up into northern Europe. However, since the focus of this book is on the local environs of Rome itself, the foreign campaigns which often lasted many years are not examined in any detail. Other than the migrating German tribes, the greatest foe Rome faced during the late Republic was herself. This was the time of civil wars where Romans fought Romans.

Games Masters who wish to run foreign battles can use the armament guidelines mentioned in the previous section, for example − using the Gallic troop descriptions for Germans). There were few new developments in personal arms and armour during this period.

At the end of the 2nd century BC, Rome faced its final serious challenge. Due to incompetent leadership the Romans lost five successive battles against the migrating Germanic tribes of the Cimbri, Teutones and Tigurines. This disastrously wiped out the available manpower of the middle classes of Rome and her allies... The total numbers of casualties estimated between 150–180,000 men in a period of only seven years.

Fearing annihilation, Rome's only successful general at the time, Gaius Marius, was elected consul for an unprecedented five years in a row, starting in 104 BC. Using his authority he, or his contemporary generals, completely reorganised the Roman army. From his experiences fighting the Numidians of North Africa, Marius had learned the value of flexible troop deployment and the need for both a professional army and experienced commanders to lead it.

His tactical reorganisation regrouped the soldiers of a legion into 10 cohorts, rather than the older system of 30 maniples. Each cohort comprised of a maniple each of the Hastate, Principes, and Triarii (raised to equal strength) along with their associated Velites. Thus a cohort numbered about 480 men and was capable of independent action. However, the distinction between the armaments and function of the maniples was lost with the issue of standardised armour and weapons. All legionaries now wore chain armour and were armed with gladius, scutum and pilum. Each cohort could be subdivided into six 'centuries' of 80 men, and these were divided again into 8 man units called contubernia that tented and messed together in camp.

Other important changes was a return to regular training and strict discipline (which had lapsed in the mid-Republic) and the requirement that each soldier carry his own baggage (weapons, armour, an entrenching tool, up to 15 days dried rations, one day's water and several stakes for the camp defences). These reforms allowed the army to move faster and further each day and insulated it against the possible loss of the (now reduced) baggage train.

"Setting out on the expedition, he [Marius] laboured to perfect his army as it went along, practising the men in all kinds of running and in long marches, and compelling them to carry their own baggage and to prepare their own food. Hence, in after times, men who were fond of toil and did whatever was enjoined upon them contentedly and without a murmur, were called Marian mules."

Plutarch - Life of Marius

Socially, Marius devolved the unpopular conscription, which with overseas campaigns sometimes forced a propertied man to serve with no appreciable remuneration for up to six years at a time if the legion was not disbanded at the end of its campaign first. Instead of protecting their own farms and livelihood, enforced service was causing many small holder farmers to become bankrupt as their lands went to seed.

Instead, the property requirements were lowered to the point where the only qualification a volunteer needed was citizenship. Weapons, armour and even clothing were supplied by the state. These changes allowed recruitment from the largest part of Rome's population, the poor. Indeed, since the army offered regular meals and some chance of earning a fortune from plunder, there was no lack of volunteers.

The reorganisation of the legions also resulted in the abolishment of Roman cavalry, once the unit into which only the richest class could join. Foreign cavalry were instead raised or hired from provinces noted for their superior horsemen (Numidian, Gallic and German in particular) and led by their own chieftains.

Each general also recruited a personal bodyguard from their legions, named the Prætorian Cohort after the prætorium, the area of the camp where the commander's tent was pitched. Other special units were the scouts (exploratores) and the elite troops (antesignani), formed from the bravest legionaries, used for spearheading assaults or rapid manoeuvres. Capable individuals could also be handpicked as spies (speculatores).

Eventually, the casualties lost to constant wars forced Roman generals to recruit primarily from their allies or even foreign provinces. Such men were promised the additional benefit of receiving citizenship for distinguished military service. With the possibility of additional wages (donativa) paid by the general from his own pocket, citizenship and the promise of land being provided after disbandment or retirement, these new professional soldiers became fiercely loyal to their commander, viewing him as their patron, rather than the state whom they were supposed to protect.

Such changes in loyalty ultimately led to the majority of the 1st century BC becoming a succession of unending civil strife both on Italian soil and in the provinces. Despite this, throughout the same period Rome continued to expand overseas, fighting a series of wars with Mithridates of Pontus, the Armenians, the Gauls, the Germans, the Belgae, the Britons, the Egyptians and the Parthians.

The command structure of legions was gradually reformed, finally being legalised under Sulla's new constitution. Consuls (whose inexperience or incompetence had often led to defeats) no longer directly led the legions, instead proconsuls and elected commanders now became the generals (duces). Also the limit to the number of legions one general could command was no longer restricted to that issued by senatorial decree. However after 80 BC, a general who led their soldiers out of their assigned provinces into Italian territory, except for the purpose of celebrating a triumph, was guilty of treason.

Although military tribunes were still assigned to each legion, they become increasingly younger men starting their magisterial careers, often with little military experience or ability. Thus overall command over a legion was sometimes shifted from the senior tribune (tribunus) to a legate (legatus), a more seasoned officer attached to the general's staff, although still of senatorial rank. Foreign troops (auxilia) or marines were, towards the end of the period, commanded by prefects (praefecti). Officers wore Greek style armour of either bronze or moulded leather and donned purple cloaks to denote their rank.

The command rank of the centurions remained unchanged but they received a pay rise in recognition of their importance. Centurions at this time wore transverse crests on their helmets and greaves on their legs. They also carried a vinewood staff to enforce discipline.

An additional rank of tesserarius was created for the man who was in charge of sentry duty, placing him 3rd in command of the century after the centurion and his optio. Each century had a standard bearer (signifer), who was now also in charge of the men's pay and savings and a hornblower (cornicen) for signalling.

Lastly, a new position was made called the aquilifer – the bearer of the legion's eagle. This solitary rank was a step towards promotion to centurion.

THE ARMAMENT OF THE 1ST C ROMAN ARMY

This is the advent of the true heavy infantry, fully armoured for close quarter battlefield fighting. As part of his reforms, Marius had the top and bottom curved edges removed from scutum, giving them their distinctive rectangular shape.

LEGIONARY (LEGIONARIUS) -

PRESS HOME, SHIELD WALL, SIEGE WARFARE TRAITS
    Mail Shirt (Lorica Hamata), 6 AP (Chest and Abdomen)
    Brimmed Montefortino/Coolus Helm (Galea), 6 AP (Head)
    Iron Rimed Rectangular Shield (Scutum), H, S, 5 AP/18 HP
    Passive Blocks 5 Locations
    Stabbing Sword (Gladius), M, S, 1d6+db, Impaling
    Heavy Javelin (Pilum), H, -, 1d8+1+db, Impaling
    Dagger (Pugio), S, S, 1d4+1+db, Impaling

CENTURION (CENTURIO)
    As a Legionary, but with the addition of leg protection
    Greaves, (Ocreae), 5 AP (Legs)

OFFICER (DUX, LEGATUS, TRIBUNUS) - NO TRAIT
    Bronze Cuirass (Lorica Musculata), 5 AP (Chest and Abdomen)
    Greaves and Skirt (Ocreae and Pteryges), 5 AP (Legs)
    Extravagant Attic Helm (Galea), 6 AP (Head)
    Small Wooden Round Shield (Parma), M, S, 4 AP/12 HP
    Passive Blocks 3 Locations
    Stabbing Sword (Gladius), M, S, 1d6+db, Impaling

AUXILIA GALLIC & GERMANIC CAVALRY
(EQUES) - MOUNTED COMBAT TRAIT
    Mail Shirt (Lorica Hamata), 6 AP (Chest and Abdomen)
    Brimmed Montefortino/Coolus Helm (Galea), 6 AP (Head)
    Small Wooden Round Shield (Parma), M, S, 4 AP/12 HP
    Passive Blocks 3 Locations
    1H Spear (Hasta), M, L, 1d8+1+db, Impaling
    Sword (Spartha), M, M, 1d8+db, Bleeding

AUXILIA MERCENARY ARCHERS
(SAGITTARIUS) - SKIRMISHING TRAIT
    Small Buckler (Aspidiotas), M, S, 4 AP/9 HP
    Passive Blocks 2 Locations
    Recurve Bow (Arcus), H, -, 1d8+db, Impaling
    Sword (Xiphidion), M, S, 1d6+db, Bleeding

AUXILIA BALEARIC MERCENARY SLINGERS (FUNDITOR)
- CAUTIOUS FIGHTER, RANGED MARKSMAN TRAIT
    Sling (Funda), S, –, 1d8

'And their training in the use of slings used to be such, from childhood up, that they would not so much as give bread to their children unless they first hit it with the sling. This is why Metellus, when he was approaching the islands from the sea, stretched hides above the decks as a protection against the slings.'
Strabo - Geographica

ROMAN MILITARY DISCIPLINE (DISCIPLINA MILITARIS)

The austere lifestyle and greater civic virtue of the early Republic gave the part-time civilian legionary a high reputation for discipline and training. However, these traits slowly eroded over the centuries and after military disasters such as those during the 2nd Punic War, Germanic invasions and terrors of Spartacus' uprising, the skills and honour of the legions were often lost with their massacre.

The rapid formation of newly levied legions, comprised of inexperienced troops, with few veteran centurions to train them and poor generals, led to lazy, useless soldiers and sometimes outright rebellion.

"When the Roman army before Numantia had become demoralized by the slackness of previous commanders, Publius Scipio reformed it by dismissing an enormous number of camp-followers and by bringing the soldiers to a sense of responsibility through regular daily routine. On the occasion of the frequent marches which he enjoined upon them, he commanded them to carry several days' rations, under such conditions that they became accustomed to enduring cold and rain, and to the fording of streams. Often the general reproached them for timidity and indolence; often he broke utensils which served only the purpose of self-indulgence and were quite unnecessary for campaigning"
Frontinus - Stratagems

Iron discipline was restored by frequent exercises and harsh punishments for lax duty. Training commonly involved route marches with full packs, formation drills, swimming, practicing with double weight weapons and shields and frequent building of encampments. During the late Republic when not on active campaign, the legions would not be allowed to sit idle and run to seed; rather they were sometimes used to provide skilled labour for civil engineering projects such as building roads, aqueducts, or city walls.

Whenever a Roman citizen enrolled as a soldier, whether part of a conscripted levy or willing enlistment, he swore a military oath (sacramentum) to the Senate and Roman People; and later directly to the general himself. The oath forced the soldier to 'voluntarily' give up his citizen's right of appeal for any death sentence and agree to fulfil the conditions of military service.

> *"Up to that day there had only been the military oath binding the men to assemble at the bidding of the consuls and not to disband until they received orders to do so. It had also been the custom among the soldiers, when the infantry were formed into companies of 100, and the cavalry into troops of 10, for all the men in each company or troop to take a voluntary oath to each other that they would not leave their comrades for fear or for flight, and that they would not quit the ranks save to fetch or pick up a weapon, to strike an enemy, or to save a comrade. This voluntary covenant was now changed into a formal oath taken before the tribunes."*
>
> Livy - Ab Urbe Condita

Military discipline was extremely rigorous, even for the times and the general had the power to summarily execute any soldier under his command. This level of obedience was necessary to ensure the health and safety of a legion as a whole, and built an esprit de corps which helped to maintain morale in the midst of battle.

> *"The Roman army put their soldiers through basic training. They did running exercises, obstacle courses while wearing all their armour and weapons, and marched eighteen miles three times a month. On these marches the soldiers had to carry all their equipment. They drilled in flanking and column movements used in battles and ceremonies. The Roman army was very strict about being perfect in drilling. But most important they trained in the usage of their weapons."*
>
> Flavius Josephus

Punishments came under two classes: those for crimes which broke laws and those for dishonourable, shameful acts. Convictions of 'unmanly acts' were in some ways more serious than normal crimes, since they were accompanied with a mark of shame which could ruin a man's standing in the legion, or his posthumous reputation.

> *"...the following [crimes] being treated as unmanly acts and disgraceful in a soldier - when a man boasts falsely to the tribune of his valour in the field in order to gain distinction; when any men who have been placed in a covering force leave the station assigned to them from fear; likewise when anyone throws away from fear any of his arms in the actual battle. Therefore the men in covering forces often face certain death, refusing to leave their ranks even when vastly outnumbered, owing to dread of the punishment they would meet with; and again in the battle men who have lost a shield or sword or any other arm often throw themselves into the midst of the enemy, hoping either to recover the lost object or to escape by death from inevitable disgrace and the taunts of their relations."*
>
> Polybius - Histories

Minor punishments could be meted out by any centurion, optio or tesserarius for ignominious activities such as slovenly appearance, poorly maintained equipment, shirking jobs and other minor misconducts. More serious crimes were refusing an order, embezzlement, theft, murder, cowardliness and, ultimately, rebellion. These were normally tried by court-martial. The more common or infamous punishments, in ascending order of seriousness, are as follows;

Munerum indictio – additional duties. These could take quite strange forms, such as standing to attention for the entire day; and

as a further display of public shame, be refused the right to dress in a soldierly manner.

> *"Because Gaius Titius, commander of a cohort, had given way before some runaway slaves, Lucius Piso ordered him to stand daily in the headquarters of the camp, barefooted, with the belt of his toga cut and his tunic ungirt, and wait till the night-watchmen came. He also commanded that the culprit should forgo banquets and baths."*
>
> Frontinus - Stratagems

Pecunaria multa – fines or deductions from the pay allowance for minor infractions.

> *"When the consul Quintus Petilius had been killed in battle by the Ligurians, the Senate decreed that that legion in whose ranks the consul had been slain should, as a whole, be reported "deficient"; that its year's pay should be withheld, and its wages reduced."*
>
> Frontinus - Stratagems

Castigatio – corporal punishment. More specifically, animadversio fustium was the punishment of being struck by a centurion's staff.

> *"and they killed a centurion, Lucilius, to whom, with soldiers' humour, they had given the name "Bring another," because when he had broken one vine-stick on a man's back, he would call in a loud voice for another and another."*
>
> Tacitus - Annals

Verberatio – a flogging, given for more severe violations. It could also be a prelude to a worse punishment too…

> *"In the consulship of Publius Cornelius Nasica and Decimus Junius those who had deserted from the army were condemned to be scourged publicly with rods and then to be sold into slavery."*
>
> Frontinus - Stratagems

Gradus deiectio – a reduction in rank.

> *"On motion of Appius Claudius the Senate degraded to the status of foot-soldiers those knights who had been captured and afterwards sent back by Pyrrhus, king of the Epirotes, while the foot-soldiers were degraded to the status of light-armed troops, all being commanded to tent outside the fortifications of the camp until each man should bring in the spoils of two foemen."*
>
> Frontinus, Stratagems

Missio ignominiosa – dishonourable discharge. This could be applied to an entire legion simultaneously.

> *"When sedition broke out in the tumult of the Civil War, and feeling ran especially high, Gaius Caesar dismissed from service an entire legion, and beheaded the leaders of the mutiny. Later, when the very men he had dismissed entreated him to remove their disgrace, he restored them and had in them the very best soldiers."*
>
> Frontinus - Stratagems

Fustuarium – death from being stoned or beaten with cudgels by his fellow soldiers. This punishment was given to those court-martialled for desertion, falling asleep on sentry duty, theft (from the camp or their companions), giving false witness or sexually abusing of a fellow soldier. It could also be given to persistent re-offenders of lesser crimes. The sentence would be performed by the assembled troops of the camp. Those who managed to escape the camp's boundaries were not pursued, but eternally banished from Rome.

> *"The man who advocates sedition will be put to death on the spot, and no one will be allowed to say the things which are uttered amongst you with impunity. With us the man who deserts his standard or abandons his post is liable to be cudgelled to death, but those who urge the men to abandon the standards and desert from the camp are listened to, not by one or two only; they have the whole army for an audience."*
>
> Livy - Ab Urbe Condita

Decimatio – the penultimate (and rarely meted out) military discipline used to punish mutinous or cowardly soldiers. A cohort selected for punishment by decimation was divided into groups of ten; each group cast lots and the soldier on whom the lot fell was executed by his nine comrades, by stoning or clubbing. The remaining soldiers were given rations of barley instead of wheat and forced to sleep outside of the Roman encampment until they had remitted their shame.

> *"At this Antony was enraged, and visited those who had played the coward with what is called decimation. That is, he divided the whole number of them into tens, and put to death that one from each ten upon whom the lot fell. For the rest he ordered rations of barley instead of wheat."*
>
> Plutarch - Life of Antony

More extreme than decimation was the total annihilation of an entire cohort or legion. This was ordered when the men involved in a rebellion were beyond redemption, or had committed an atrocity.

Military court-martials were held in the camp's tribunal and were reserved for more serious crimes. Legionaries were tried by the tribunes, and the tribunes tried by their commander. They were held as traditional Roman trials with witnesses brought forwards to give character references or evidence. The final decision was solely in the hands of the tribune or commander in charge. Even the tribunes were not exempt from corporal or even capital punishment.

> *"Caius Lusius, a nephew of his [Marius], had a command under him in the army. In other respects he was a man of good reputation, but he had a weakness for beautiful youths. This officer was enamoured of one of the young men who served under him, by name Trebonius, and had on made unsuccessful attempts to seduce him. But finally, at night, he sent a servant with a summons for Trebonius. The young man came, since he could not refuse to obey a summons, but when he had been introduced into the tent and Caius attempted violence upon him, he drew his sword and slew him. Marius was not with the army when this happened; but on his return he brought Trebonius to trial. Here there were many accusers, but not a single advocate, wherefore Trebonius himself courageously took the stand and told all about the matter, bringing witnesses to show that he had often refused the solicitations of Lusius and that in spite of large offers he had never prostituted himself to anyone. Then Marius, filled with delight and admiration, ordered the customary crown for brave exploits to be brought, and with his own hands placed it on the head of Trebonius, declaring that at a time which called for noble examples he had displayed the most noble conduct."*
>
> Plutarch - Life of Marius

WAGES, EXPENSES & PLUNDER (STIPENDIA, DISPENDIA ET PRAEDA)

Until 405 BC, the Roman levied soldier actually received no pay (stipendium) for active military service. Since all members of the army were citizens of a minimum wealth, they were considered self-supporting. It was only sometime between the 2nd and 3rd Punic Wars that legionaries began to be compensated 100 asses per month and the Centurions and Equites double that. However, soldiers' pay was effectively lost in charges made for the food, clothing, replacement armaments and fodder (if cavalry) they used. Thus the money was only a sustenance payment.

With gradual inflation any chances for actually earning an income from this stipend was lost. Eventually pay was doubled by Julius Caesar during his Gallic campaigns and he gave them other bonuses (donativa) as he was able.

> *"He doubled the pay of the legions for all time. Whenever grain was plentiful, he distributed it to them without stint or measure, and now and then gave each man a slave from among the captives."*
>
> Suetonius - Life of Julius Caesar

Save for looting and the slim opportunity to be granted a pension comprising of a plot of land at the end of their service, no honest legionary could ever make any significant money during their enlistment.

Booty won on campaign came in four forms. General plunder (praeda), money from plundered objects when sold (manubia), personal objects stripped from an enemy (exuviae) and more specifically armour and weapons (spolia). Examples of such spoils were trophies including chariots, army standards, the rams of ships, ornate armour, statues, metal ingots, slaves and other artworks, as well as the normal treasures of coinage and jewellery. Spolia Opima were the armaments of an enemy commander which could only be won by a Roman Commander defeating him in single combat and were regarded as a very great sign of honour.

"Claudius Marcellus, having unexpectedly come upon some Gallic troops, turned his horse about in a circle, looking around for a way of escape. Seeing danger on every hand, with a prayer to the gods, he broke into the midst of the enemy. By his amazing audacity he threw them into consternation, slew their leader, and actually carried away the spolia opima in a situation where there had scarcely remained a hope of saving his life."

Frontinus - Stratagems

Plunder won by an army was divided up according to rank; the more senior the officer, the larger the share. The greater part would always be assigned to the general however, but they were free to donate all or part of their share to the adorning or building of temples or as a bonus to their men to repay, or maintain, their loyalty. Division of spoils was usually performed at the end of a campaign so that the accumulated wealth could be displayed as part of a Triumph and prevent erosion of discipline or even the premature disbanding of the legion.

"Marcus Salinator, when ex-consul, was condemned by the people because he had not divided the booty equally among his soldiers."

Frontinus - Stratagems

Pensions (emerita) did not become an official perk of military service until after the Republic had ended. Before this, legionaries were reliant upon their general to intercede with the Senate in order to be granted lands or monies to support them after retirement.

"When, in honour of his defeat of the Sabines, the Senate offered Manius Curius a larger amount of ground than the discharged troops were receiving, he was content with the allotment of ordinary soldiers, declaring that that man was a bad citizen who was not satisfied with what the rest received."

Frontinus - Stratagems

By the late Republic the Senate were hesitant to make such land grants, since it meant dispossessing a former owner to make room for an ex-soldier and, save for newly conquered regions overseas, most of the lands were owned by the patrician and equestrian families who populated the Senate. The naked greed behind such refusals to grant legionaries their own lands helped fuel the civil wars of the late Republic.

DECORATIONS AND REWARDS (PRAEMIA)

Faithful duty in the military could be rewarded in other ways than pure financial gain. Honours (beneficia) could be requested by generals from the state to reward those who had demonstrated good service. The reward could take the form of promotion, decorations, material gifts (such as land), favours, citizenship or even the reduction of more laborious duties.

"Not the least conspicuous feature of the spectacle was the sight of Sosis the Syracusan and Moericus the Spaniard who marched in front wearing golden crowns. The former had guided the nocturnal entry into Syracuse, the latter had been the agent in the surrender of Nasos and its garrison. Each of these men received the full Roman citizenship and 500 jugera of land."

Livy - Ab Urbe Condita

Military decorations were the equivalent of modern-day medals. Rewards granted for demonstrating bravery or commendable conduct were often commonplace objects of superior value – probably looted from defeated enemies – such as torques (named after Titus Manlius Torquatus, who first looted a golden neck ring from a Gallic chieftain he defeated in single combat) and bracelets (armillae). Embossed precious metal discs (phalerae) were particularly prized, being worn on straps over armour during parades.

The highest accolades were only granted for extreme acts of note and took the form of crowns (coronae), an article normally banned from being worn due to its associations with monarchy.

"In the presence of the two armies rewards and decorations were bestowed by both Carvilius and Papirius. Papirius had seen his men through many different actions in the open field, around their camp, under city walls, and the rewards he bestowed were well merited. Spurius Nautius, Spurius Papirius, his nephew, four centurions, and a maniple of Hastati all received golden bracelets and crowns. Sp. Nautius won his for his success in the manoeuvre by which he frightened the enemy with the appearance of a large army; the young Papirius owed his reward to the work he did with his cavalry in the battle and in the following night, when he harassed the retreat of the Samnites from Aquilonia; the centurions and men of the maniple were rewarded for having been the first to seize the gate and wall of the city."

Livy - Ab Urbe Condita

Corona Obsidionalis (Corona Graminea) – The highest military award in the Roman army. They were given to those who broke the siege of a beleaguered Roman army. The crown is a wreath made of grass gathered from the site of the lifted siege and presented by the army so relieved.

"...but up to the present time it [the Corona Graminea] has been given to a single centurion only, Cneius Petreius Atinas, during the war with the Cimbri. This soldier, while acting as primus pilus under Catullus, on finding all retreat for his legion cut off by the enemy, harangued the troops, and after slaying his tribune who hesitated to cut a way through the encampment of the enemy, brought away the legion in safety."

Pliny the Elder - Naturalis Historia

Corona Civica – The second highest regarded military award, primarily due to its epitome of Roman civic virtues. Awarded to a soldier who saved the life of another in battle, it took the form of a crown of oak leaves and acorns. The rescued soldier could only make the recommendation himself (something most were loath to do) and would present the crown to his saviour. The honours accorded to the soldier awarded this crown included the right to be seated next to the Senate at public spectacles, freedom to himself, his father and grandfather from 'public burdens' and the eternal respect from the person who owed their life – as if they were a son to a father.

"But this is a thing which even common soldiers do against their will, and they are reluctant to give a civic crown to a citizen, and to confess that they have been saved by any one; not because it is discreditable to have been protected in battle, or to be saved out of the hands of the enemy (for in truth

In alio pediculum, in te ricinum non vides – You see a louse on someone else, but not a tick on yourself (Petronius)

that is a thing which can only happen to a brave man, and to one fighting hand to hand with the enemy), but they dread the burden of the obligation, because it is an enormous thing to be under the same obligation to a stranger that one is to a parent."

Cicero - Pro Plancio

Corona Muralis – A crenulated gold crown decorated with towers, which is awarded to the first soldier or Centurion over the walls into a besieged city.

"Then he praised the courage of his troops, whom, he said, nothing had daunted, neither the sortie of the enemy, nor the height of the walls, nor the untried depth of the lagoon, nor the fort on the hill, nor the unusual strength of the citadel. Nothing had prevented them from surmounting every obstacle and forcing their way everywhere. Though every man amongst them deserved all the rewards he could give, the glory of the mural crown belonged especially to him who was the first to scale the wall, and the man who considered that he deserved it should claim it. Two men came forward, Q. Tiberilius, a centurion of the fourth legion, and Sextus Digitius, one of the marines. The contention between them was not so heated as the excitement with which each body advocated the claim of its own representative... ...He [Scipio] then announced that he had definitely ascertained that Q. Tiberilius and Sextius Digitius had both surmounted the wall at the same moment, and he should honour their bravery by presenting them each with a mural crown."

Livy - Ab Urbe Condita

Corona Vallaris – A golden crown decorated with the uprights of a palisade. It is awarded to the first soldier or centurion to force their way over the entrenchments and walls of an enemy camp.

Corona Rostrata – Awarded for the destruction of an enemy fleet. It was a golden crown surmounted with the beaks (rostra) of ships and historically only granted once to Agrippa for his defeat of Antony at the Battle of Actium.

Corona Navalis – A gold crown awarded to the first man who boarded an enemy ship during a naval engagement.

Corona Triumphalis – A crown made of laurel, given to commanders who are awarded a triumph.

Corona Ovalis – A crown made from myrtle, given only to commanders who are awarded an ovation for successful military campaigns against 'inferior' foes, such as Crassus received for defeating Spartacus, despite the fact that this 'mere slave' had defeated legion after legion in open battle and had thrown the entirety of Italy into terror.

All these decorations were of vital importance to the average Roman, for they demonstrated his manly courage (virtus), self-sacrifice (devotio),and helped spread his fame (gloria). Scars too were a sign of virtus and there were incidents in Roman law where court cases were dismissed when the battle scars of a defendant were shown to be all on the front of their body.

"I cannot, to justify your confidence, display family portraits [wax effigies of renowned ancestors] or the triumphs and consulships of my forefathers; but if occasion requires, I can show spears, a banner, horse trappings and other military prizes, as well as scars on my chest. These are my portraits, my patent of nobility, not left to me by inheritance as theirs were, but won by my own innumerable efforts and perils."

Sallust - War with Jugurtha

TRIUMPHS AND OVATIONS (TRIUMPHI ET OVATIONES)

Triumphs and ovations were massive celebrations given to successful military commanders upon their return to Rome. They were jealously awarded by the Senate, who also donated a sum of money to defray against the expenses of hosting the festivity.

Only a victorious general, lauded as 'Imperator' by his troops, who had held the office of dictator, consul or prætor, was permitted a triumph and only then in legitimate wars against enemies of Rome. The campaign should also have brought a new province under the control of Rome and the territory reduced to a state of peace.

Ovations were a lesser form of triumph, awarded when the enemies were of inferior numbers or status (such as fighting against slaves) or when the war had not been fully concluded.

Considering the number of requirements for eligibility, it is hardly surprising that the celebration of a triumph was a rare event.

In the early days of Rome, a triumph consisted simply of a procession led by the captured men and leaders of the enemy, behind whom rode the victorious general upon a chariot and followed by the standards and troops of his army laden with plunder. After them came the celebrating populace, singing victory songs and jeering at the defeated captives. When the procession arrived at the Capitoline hill, certain members of the captive leaders would be put to death and the general would ascend to the Temple of Jupiter to offer a sacrifice of a bull. After this, a public banquet was thrown for the people of the city.

In the later years of the Republic, the spectacle became far more pompous. The procession was led by the Senate headed by the magistrates, followed by a mass of trumpeters, who in turn were trailed by exotically decorated carts which were loaded with the most spectacular of the booty captured during the campaign – such as gold and silver coins, jewellery and plate, embroidered cloth, brightly woven carpets, armour and weapons, and other beautiful artworks.

After this, flute players proceeded before the priests, accompanying flawless white oxen with gilded horns, which were destined for sacrifice. Then came a menagerie of strange unforeseen animals native to the province conquered. Following this was a display of the spolia opima of the captured enemy leaders and then the captives themselves.

Next was a display of crowns and tributes granted to the imperator by allied rulers and states, followed by his lictors bearing their fasces bound with laurel. Then came the imperator himself, riding in a four horse chariot and wearing a gold embroidered purple robe (toga picta) and flowered tunic (tunica palmata), bearing in his right hand a laurel bough and in his left a sceptre, his brows were encircled with a laurel wreath (corona triumphalis). In addition his body was painted bright red.

In the chariot with him would be young children in order to avert envy and ill-will (invidia). To further encourage humility, a little magic charm (fascinum) and a whip (flagellum) were attached to the vehicle as symbols that the occupant could still suffer the misfortune of death or scourging. Also present was a slave standing behind the general, whose purpose was to whisper in the ear of the Imperator the warning words "respice post te, hominem memento te" – "look behind you, remember that you are mortal".

In cauda venenum – In the tail (of the scorpion) is the poison

"And he would not be alone in the chariot, but if he had children or relatives, he would make the girls and the infant male children get up besides him in it and place the older ones upon the horses - outriggers as well as the yoke-pair; if there were many of them, they would accompany the procession on chargers, riding along beside the victor."

Cassius Dio - Roman History

Behind the chariot would be the adult sons of the imperator, his legates, military tribunes and equites of his army. The rear was brought up by the legionaries in marching order, bearing spears wreathed with laurel and shouting either complements or sarcastic insults about their commander. Both were allowed and actively encouraged.

"[As said by Caesar's troops during his Triumph] Romans, watch your wives, the bald adulterer's back home. You fucked away in Gaul the gold you borrowed here in Rome".

Suetonius - Life of Julius Caesar

After such magnificence the imperator would as tradition commanded, oversee the execution of the enemy leader and then mount to the Temple of Jupiter to perform the sacrifice. A tithe of the plunder (usually a tenth), was donated to the temple and the laurel wreath was left in lap of the god. This was followed by a public speech and the rewarding of the troops, the most notable being mentioned by name and presented with gifts.

The ceremonies were concluded by lavish public banquet to which the imperator's friends and the city magistrates were invited, although the consuls were politely asked not to attend so that the recipient of the triumph would not be overshadowed by their presence. When the feast finally ended, the imperator was escorted home by torchlight, accompanied by grateful citizens and musicians.

Of course there were occasions when certain generals tried to outdo previous triumphs, such as when Pompey arranged to have his chariot drawn by elephants instead of horses, but was stymied when it was discovered that the city gates were too narrow to permit entry.

Caesar displayed some of the greatest triumphs and showed extemporary generosity to the men of his legions.

"Having ended the wars, he celebrated five triumphs, four in a single month, but at intervals of a few days, after vanquishing Scipio; and another on defeating Pompey's sons. The first and most splendid was the Gallic triumph, after that the African, and finally the Spanish, each differing from the rest in its equipment and display of spoils. As he rode through the Velabrum on the day of his Gallic triumph, the axle of his chariot broke, and he was all but thrown out; and he mounted the Capitol by torchlight, with forty elephants bearing lamps on his right and his left. In his Pontic triumph he displayed among the show-pieces of the procession an inscription of but three words, "I came, I saw, I conquered," not indicating the events of the war, as the others did, but the speed with which it was finished. To each and every foot-soldier of his veteran legions he gave twenty-four thousand sesterces by way of booty, over and above the two thousand apiece which he had paid them at the beginning of the civil strife. He also assigned them lands, but not side by side, to avoid dispossessing any of the former owners."

Suetonius - Life of Julius Caesar

An ovation differed from a full triumph, being a lesser spectacle. The general entered the city on foot instead of riding in a chariot and wore the simple toga praetexta of a magistrate. His wreath was made of myrtle, not laurel, and he bore no sceptre. Also missing were the trumpets, senatorial procession and accompanying legionaries, so that the imperator was attended only by the equites and any plebeians who wished to join in. The final sacrifice was only a sheep rather than a bull.

LEGIONARY STANDARDS (SIGNA)

At the beginning of Rome, the legions possessed a number of different standards based upon creatures noted for their strength, virility or ferocity. These provided a rallying point easily identifiable during battle or march and inspired the troops which bore it.

However, during his reforms in 104 BC, Marius made the eagle emblem supreme because of its close associations with Jupiter, replacing all the other animal totems. Each legion was assigned a silver eagle standard (aquila) and was charged with dire punishments and disgrace if it were lost in battle. Thus the senior standard bearer became known as an aquilifer.

"And while our men were hesitating [whether they should advance to the shore], chiefly on account of the depth of the sea, he who carried the eagle of the tenth legion, after supplicating the gods that the matter might turn out

In dubio pro reo − When in doubt, favour the accused (Corpus Juris Civilis)

favourably to the legion, exclaimed, "Leap, fellow soldiers, unless you wish to betray your eagle to the enemy. I, for my part, will perform my duty to the commonwealth and my general." When he had said this with a loud voice, he leaped from the ship and proceeded to bear the eagle toward the enemy. Then our men, exhorting one another that so great a disgrace should not be incurred, all leaped from the ship."

Julius Caesar - The Gallic Wars

Prior to Marius, every legion was a temporary levy authorised solely by the Senate, which was disbanded after it had completed the campaign it was assigned to. This prevented the legions from building any long term traditions. However, after the reforms, a large part of the army became standing legions, which were retained continuously unless destroyed or dishonoured in battle. These new professional legions slowly evolved a sense of identity and by the end of the Republic had begun to claim individual names based upon origin, region of service or victories; in addition, they selected emblems (often zodiacal) to further distinguish themselves. Julius Caesar normally appointed his legions with a bull and Octavian the sign of a Capricorn. Eventually, the legionaries began to venerate their standards and treated them as sacred religious items.

PLOT HOOKS

Ω During the 2nd Punic War, the Romans lost a vast number of both its allies and own troops. The squander became so desperate that the dictator Marcus Junius Pera was forced to draft several legions comprised of slaves and criminals.

"After duly discharging his religious duties and obtaining the necessary permission to mount his horse, he published an edict that all who had been guilty of capital offences or who were enslaved for debt and were willing to serve under him would by his orders be released from punishment and have their debts cancelled. 6,000 men were raised in this way, and he armed them with the spoils taken from the Gauls and which had been carried in the triumphal procession of C. Flaminius."

Livy - Ab Urbe Condita

This could be the perfect occasion for a Games Master to turn the tables on a group of player characters convicted for profiteering in Rome and send them out to face Hannibal on his approach to the city. Slave characters could volunteer for the army and be granted their freedom in reward for faithful service towards the State... assuming they survive.

Ω In 105 BC, Quintus Servilius Caepio the proconsul of Southern Gaul, travelled to Tolosa distracted from his military orders by rumours of an ancient treasure hidden within the city, reputedly looted from Delphi by the infamous chieftain Brennus.

Ω On capturing Tolosa, Caepio confiscated an immense horde of 15,000 talents of gold and silver hidden within the shrines and sacred lakes of the city. However, during its transport back to Rome, the majority of this treasure mysteriously disappeared. Apparently cursed by the gods for his impiety, Caepio then suffered a disastrous defeat at the Battle

of Arausio where his army of 80,000 men was annihilated.

He was prosecuted for losing his army (although the gold probably biased the outcome), stripped of citizenship and spent the remainder of his life in exile in Smyrna. The theft of the gold by Caepio was never proven, although rumours abounded of the suspiciously weak guard escort he had placed on the treasure and the fact he displayed previously unseen levels of wealth after.

An adventure could be based around discovering who exactly did steal the gold. Was it taken back by the vengeful Celts, Caepio's own bodyguard, the worshippers of Apollo or possibly the ghost of Brennus? Conversely, the characters could be part of the escort provided for the treasure, offering them the chance to save the gold or perhaps steal it themselves...

Ω One of the characters has won the vaunted position of signifer in the maniple or the party is assigned as guards for the legion's eagle. To their horror, during the night the standard goes missing. The characters know that they will take the blame, despite the fact that the standard might have vanished during the previous watch, or could have been stolen by the maniple's senior centurion who left the tent as they came on duty.

The players have several options. Investigate the disappearance, whereupon they uncover a tale of political corruption and blackmailing (with the innocent centurion desperately trying to hide the fact that his is chronically short sighted); or alternately try to steal a standard from another maniple and hope to cover up the original crime.

If the disappearance is discovered before the original is found or substituted, then the characters are going to lose status and reputation, before being sentenced to some sort of capital punishment...

Ω The characters are either facing bankruptcy or currently suffering abject poverty. With no other choice, they have accepted loans from a notorious banker in order to pay for food and rent. However, the bailiffs of the banker will be calling round on the next market day for repayment... and they are ex-gladiators with a mean streak. The bodies of defaulters end up being found dead in the sewers.

However, the following day a Triumph is being celebrated and the characters see vast quantities of precious metals and artworks rolling past in carts, literally just out of arms reach. Will they be tempted to perform a desperate act? Not only do they need to perform the theft under the eyes of the veteran soldiers guarding the treasure but they will also need to escape the crowds of spectators who will see the theft as an impious act.

If they fail to be tempted, then the banker could approach them in the crowd and offer to clear their debts (and perhaps add a small bonus) in return for humiliating the triumphant general; pelting him with rotten fruit or upsetting his chariot for example. This option might save them from the murderous ex-gladiators but would gain the characters an enemy of high status and unceasing wrath…

Ω During an attack on the encampment of an enemy army, the players are placed in the situation of being first over the walls. Survivors of the beachhead are awarded a Corona Vallaris for bravery in the face of great danger. However, during the award ceremony, an old nemesis of the party steps forwards and claims the honour for himself, backed up by the lies of half a cohort of sycophantic 'eye witnesses'.

Since the nemesis is a person of high social rank, or an immediate superior in the legion (e.g. a sadistic centurion), the commander is placed in a difficult position and several different results could occur.

If the players stubbornly defend their honour, an investigation is held into the backgrounds and reputations of both the party and their nemesis. This could lead to the case going either way and unsubstantiated accusations by the players could actually cause them further problems in the future.

If the players lose their case, then they might be approached by sympathetic troops within the legion who see this as an unjust act and wish to use it as the cause for starting a rebellion; which the players are free to join if they wish…

If on the other hand, the players sense the factious tension within the legion and decide to back down in order to prevent the arguments from breaking down into outright violence, then the commander will award the crown to the nemesis but reward the players in a different way. Perhaps allowing the honourable characters a chance to show up the impostor's bravery and let them win even greater glory.

RELIGION

Rome and religion are inseparable entities. Like most peoples of the time, religion is a fundamental part of everyday life. Offerings are made to the protective gods of the household, prayers made to divinities to help grant aid in war, enterprise, or love, and the temples become crowded in times of adversity.

The Romans believed in supernatural beings and were intensely superstitious. It was only with the introduction of certain Hellenistic philosophical ideas (such as Epicureanism) that atheism was planted in the minds of well-educated Romans of the late Republic.

Despite these new ideas, Rome continued to sacrifice to the gods, welcoming new cults and forcibly bringing icons of foreign, captured enemy faiths to the eternal city. Freedom of belief and religious tolerance was very important; very few faiths were ever censured during the Republic. Religion, whether or not its priests were truly pious, was a powerful tool for civic control.

"To those who look at a city and see not humanity but stone, Rome
is overwhelmingly a city of worship. Rome has always been a pious place,
sacrificing abundantly (if not always sincerely) to any and every god and
hero who might become an ally in the dream of empire. Rome worships the
gods; Rome gives adoration to the dead. Temples, altars, shrines, and statues
abound. Incense may abruptly waft from any corner."

Steven Saylor – Roman Blood

RELIGION (RELIGIO)

The gods of the Romans were originally animistic in origin, spirits of rivers, soil and sky, combined with ancestor worship. As time passed they evolved to embrace more sophisticated concepts, specific to human activity and values. Eventually these undefined deities took on anthropomorphic shapes in mimicry of Hellenic tradition.

All Romans are polytheists, that is to say, they freely worship all the gods in their pantheon. One morning they might give a bowl of milk to the 'lares' of the household, then pay for the sacrifice of a dove to Venus and in the evening spill a libation to Jupiter in thanks for not being struck by lightning during the storm that day.

Worship is generally proactive to beg for help in a certain deed or reactive so as to ward the worshipper from the harm which that deity represents. Games Masters interested in rules for such divine interventions should refer to Calling upon the Gods page 140.

The divinities of Rome can be broken down into four rough categories: spirits of the home, ancestor worship, animistic deities and deified concepts.

SPIRITS OF THE HOME

There are several spirits which ward the home from harm. The gods of the store cupboard (Di Penates), the god of the hearth fire (Vesta) and the spirits of protection (Lares). These minor divinities had their own images and altar (aedicula) within the dwelling,

whether it was an apartment in an insula or a villa. They were appeased with garlands on the calends, nones and ides of each month, offers of food from each evening meal placed on the hearth and the monthly burning of incense.

> *"Divine Penates of our ancestors, to you I commend the good fortune of my parents, and to you, Spiritual Father of our family, that you safeguard them well"*
>
> Plautus – Mercator

Shrines to the Lares could also be found at every crossroads (compitum) in the city, where some spirits looked after whole districts. These were worshiped during the compitalicia festival held in early January and offerings made to them of cakes by both slaves and citizens.

The final household spirit was the Genius, the guardian of the family. This was represented as a (sometimes bearded) snake in art- but was thought to actually reside within the head of the household – the paterfamilias. Respect was shown to the genius by a libation of wine.

ANCESTOR WORSHIP

The Romans believed that the afterlife was a shadowy reflection of the living world and that the souls of the dead required nourishment to survive. Thus it was considered vital that dead ancestors (di parentes) be provided with libations, offerings and gifts (inferiae) to show them respect and ensure their continuance. These rites were normally performed in the home and, during certain festivals (Parentalia, Feralia and Lemuria), at the family necropolis outside the city walls.

Wealthy Romans traditionally took wax facial masks (imagines) of newly dead ancestors, which would be placed on display in the atrium of the house. During family funerals, actors would wear the masks and act out the physical mannerisms of the dead person, so as to be a receptacle for the spirit of the ancestor. To help actors in their portrayal, the masks were often stored with a papyrus describing the ancestor's traits, as well as listing their deeds and magisterial positions.

> *"Next after the interment and the performance of the usual ceremonies, they place the image of the departed in the most conspicuous position in the house, enclosed in a wooden shrine. This image is a mask reproducing with remarkable fidelity both the features and complexion of the deceased. On the occasion of public sacrifices they display these images, and decorate them with much care, and when any distinguished member of the family dies they take them to the funeral, putting them on men who seem to them to bear the closest resemblance to the original in stature and carriage."*
>
> Polybius – Histories

Such processions of respected ancestors would provide an inspiration and guide to younger members of the family, since as stated by Polybius, "who would not be inspired by the sight of the images of men renowned for their excellence, all together and as if alive and breathing?"

ANIMISTIC DEITIES (NUMINA)

Originally, the Roman gods were simple supernatural representations of either places (genii locorum) or natural processes – such as the weather, growing of crops or death. They were at first depicted only with symbols but with the influx of Hellenism the gods were granted anthropomorphic images and their unique Roman aspects gradually subsumed by the mythology of their Greek versions. The names of the greatest Roman gods survived the centuries and were used to identify the very planets themselves.

During the early and mid-Republic, Rome experienced repeated disasters. At these times, the senate would consult the Sibylline Books (page 111), whose prophesies often required the city to appease specific gods by the hosting of festival games, building of temples, ceremonial offerings of food or even the importation of foreign deities.

> *"In accordance with an oracle found in the Sibylline books, which stated that a foreign invader would be expelled if the Idaean Mother [Cybele] had been brought to Rome, the Idaean Mother was brought to Rome from the Phrygian town Pessinus. She was given to the Romans by king Attalus of Asia. Because the oracle had ordered that the deity had to be received and consecrated by the best man, she was received by Publius Scipio Nasica, who was judged by the Senate to be the best man, although he was young and had not even reached the quæstorship."*
>
> Livy – Periochae

The following gods were considered of the highest importance in Rome. They either possessed the largest temples or held major annual celebrations;

Apollo – god of the sun, poetry, music and oracles, originally an Olympian

Bona Dea – goddess of fertility, healing, virginity and women. Also known as Fauna

Bacchus – god of wine and sensual pleasures

Carmenta – goddess of childbirth and prophecy, and assigned a Flamen minor

Ceres – goddess of the harvest, mother of Proserpina and an Olympian, also assigned a Flamen minor

Cybele (Magna Mater) – earth mother

Diana – goddess of the hunt, the moon, virginity and childbirth; twin sister of Apollo and an Olympian originally served by a runaway slave who had act as her priest

Falacer – obscure god, he was assigned a Flamen minor

Flora – goddess of flower, and assigned a Flamen minor

Fortuna – goddess of fortune

Furrina – obscure goddess the waters, one source claims she was a goddess of robbers and thieves, she was assigned a Flamen minor

Janus – two-headed god of beginnings and endings and of doors

Juno – Queen of the Gods, goddess of matrimony and an Olympian

Jupiter – King of the Gods and the storm, air and sky god, and an Olympian, also assigned a Flamen maior.

Mars – god of war and father of Romulus, an Olympian and assigned a Flamen maior

Mercury – messenger of the gods and bearer of souls to the underworld, also an Olympian

Minerva – goddess of wisdom and war, and an Olympian

Neptune – god of the sea, earthquakes and horses, and an Olympian

Ops – goddess of plenty

Palatua – obscure goddess who guarded the Palatine Hill, she was assigned a Flamen minor

Pluto – King of the Dead, also known as Orcus

Pomona – goddess of fruit trees and assigned a Flamen minor

Portunes – god of keys, doors and livestock, he was assigned a Flamen minor

Proserpina – Queen of the Dead and a grain-goddess

Quirinus – Romulus, the founder of Rome, was deified as Quirinus after his death. Quirinus was a war god and a god of the Roman people and state, and was assigned a Flamen maior

Saturn – a titan, god of harvest and agriculture, the father of Jupiter, Neptune, Juno and Pluto

Venus – goddess of love, beauty, sex and prostitution, mother of the hero Aeneas and an Olympian

Vesta – goddess of the hearth and the Roman state and an Olympian

Volcanus – god of the forge, fire and blacksmiths, and an Olympian, assigned a Flamen minor

Volturnus – a god of water assigned a Flamen minor

"Olympus is the name which the Greeks give to the sky, and all peoples give to the mountain in Macedonia; it is from the latter, I am inclined to think, that the Muses are spoken of as Olympiads..."

Varro – On the Latin Language

Many of these gods were originally Etruscan or Latin in origin and brought to Rome during its gradual conquests of neighbouring territory. Diana was originally from Aricia and Juno was an Etruscan goddess from Veii, introduced via the ritual of evocation – a sacred rite for inviting the patron deities of captured or besieged towns to abandon their homes and migrate to Rome.

"Juno Regina, who in Veii now dwells, I pray, that after our victory You will follow us to our City, soon to become Your City as well, where a holy precinct worthy of Your dignity will be built to receive You"

Livy – Ab Urbe Condita

DEIFIED ABSTRACT CONCEPTS

With Hellenism were introduced hundreds of other lesser religions, many of which encompassed a single philosophical idea, such as peace (Pax), freedom (Libertas) or justice (Iustitia). These 'higher' concepts gained widespread worship during the late Republic. Although never granted as great a status as the original numina, countless shrines and temples to these minor deities proliferated.

Since these lesser gods are so numerous, it is impossible to describe each one individually. However an abridged list of their names and attributes is included in Appendix IV.

THE PRIESTHOOD (SACERDOTIUM)

During the period of the Monarchy, there were three distinct colleges of priests, who gave sage advice and conducted religious rites. At the foundation of the Republic, only patricians were eligible for election into the collegium of priests but to sooth the feelings of the plebeians, at about 367 BC half the positions in the Sacris Faciundis were opened to those of lower class and later in 300 BC the same occurred for the pontifices and augurs too. Once elected, the office of priesthood was retained for life and the holder exempted from all civil and military duties.

First ranked in importance was the Collegium Pontificum, the college of Pontiffs. They followed the following hierarchy in order of precedence…

Ω Rex Sacrorum ('King of Rites') – introduced after the fall of the monarchy to replace the religious duties held by the king.

Ω 3 Flamines Maiores ('Major Flamines') – the leading priests of Jupiter (Flamen Dialis), Mars (Flamen Martialis) and Quirinus (Flamen Quirinalis). Only patricians could be flamines maiores.

Ω Pontifex Maximus ('Principle Pontif') – by the late Republic the Pontifex Maximus had risen in authority to the head of the religious hierarchy.

Ω Subordinate Pontifices – four in 509 BC, nine in 300 BC and 14 in 81 BC. These officials gradually took over the administration of newer gods introduced during the Republic.

Ω 12 Flamines Minores (Minor Flamines) – priests of Carmenta, Ceres, Falacer, Flora, Furrina, Palatua, Pomona, Portunus, Volcanus and Volturnus. These priests were elected from the plebeians. By the late Republic the functions of some of these gods, as well as the names of the last two divinities had been forgotten.

The college of Pontiffs were in charge of maintaining religious tradition and recorded all omens and prodigies (lightning strikes, births of two headed animals, rains of stones or blood and so on) in their sacred books (libri pontificales).

Second in importance were the Augurs. Experts on the auguries (auguria), which indicated whether a proposed action was favourable (fas) or unfavourable (nefas) to divine will. This involved the watching of the heavens for the movements of birds (auspicia). Originally formed by King Numa, the second king of Rome, in 509 BC they numbered only three, one for each tribe. But this increased to nine in 300 BC and they eventually totalled 15 in 81 BC.

The lowest ranked priesthood were the Sacris Faciundis. Created by the final kings of Rome, the Etruscan Tarquins, they originally assisted in the rites and sacrifices to the gods. Eventually they were placed in charge of consulting the Sibylline Books and implementing the prophesies contained within. They numbered only two in 509 BC but expanded to 10 in 367 BC and 15 in 81 BC. Instead of their official title, the priests were referred to as the 'Two Men' (duumviri), 'Ten Men' (decemviri) or 'Fifteen Men' (quindecemviri) according to how many they numbered at the time.

The final college of priests, the Epulones was created during the mid-Republic in 196 BC. The lowest ranking of the priesthoods, their task was to assist the Pontifices with organising the growing number of feasts associated with sacrifices, hence the name of 'Banqueters'. They originally numbered three but this had increased to seven in 81 BC.

The only group of women priestesses that held any status in Rome were the Vestal Virgins who tended the sacred flame of Vesta, goddess of the hearth and home. Their temple was founded in the reign of King Numa and initially only two priestesses served. However this number was soon raised to six.

The Vestals were important political entities in their own right, being the few women allowed to own property and vote. They had places reserved for them at all public ceremonies, festivals and feasts, and were permitted to travel in a wheeled cart, proceeded by a lictor bearing the fasces. Being incorruptible of character, they were entrusted with wills, contracts and state documents. They were even granted the power to free condemned prisoners or slaves by merely touching them.

Despite a rigorous service of 30 years, during which time the priestess was sworn to chastity, the life of a Vestal was greatly sought after due to the elevation of status and freedom from control of men. If however, the Vestal ever broke her oaths, the punishments could be terrible…

"The Virgins' minor offences are punished by beating, which is administered by the Pontifex [Maximus], with the offender naked, and in a dark place with a curtain set up between them. A Virgin who is seduced is buried alive near what is known as the Colline gate. At this place in the city there is a little ridge of land that extends for some distance, which is called a 'mound' in the Latin language. Here they prepare a small room, with an entrance from above. In it there is a bed with a cover, a lighted lamp, and some of the basic necessities of life, such as bread, water in a bucket, milk, oil, because they consider it impious to allow a body that is consecrated to the most holy rites to die of starvation."

Plutarch – Life of Numa Pompilius

Etruscan Priests

With a reputation for a deeper knowledge of divination and the supernatural, Etruscan priests became a class apart from their fellow members of the sacred colleges. Whereas Roman priests were in effect merely citizens who held a public office assumed via politics, Etruscans priests were specifically trained for the position.

Their education took place in special institutes and took years of laborious study. Much like an ancient university, they learned an eclectic curriculum of both divine and secular knowledge. Particular subjects included religious law, theology, astronomy, meteorology, zoology, ornithology, botany and geology. In effect they were studying many of the life sciences, save that it was inclined towards an application to divination.

They even learned the art of hydrology so as to be able to divine for water, dig wells, excavate irrigation or drainage ditches, and even bore through hillsides to channel fresh water. Experts in such matters were called aquivices. Other specialities were engineering and surveying.

"Romulus made a beginning with the foundation of the city. He had sent for men from Etruria to direct every action within the founding with certain sacred offerings and rules and to teach how it was prescribed in the Sacred Law."

Plutarch – Life of Romulus

Thus not only were Etruscan priests interpreters of divine will but they were also able to apply that will in practical ways, useful to society. In many ways the Etruscan priesthood was not unlike the Celtic druids of the same period.

The Ceremonies & Restrictions of Priests

Although the honour of becoming a priest is very great, the responsibilities (Mores Sacerdotales) attached to it are burdensome. Indeed, some ceremonies are so onerous that few men desired the position of a flamines majores or minores. A list of restrictions applicable to the Flamen Dialis is quoted below and Games Masters are encouraged to create their own obscure superstitious guidelines for other priesthoods.

"Only a free man may cut the hair of the Dialis. It is not customary for the Dialis to touch, or even name, a she-goat, raw flesh, ivy, and beans. The priest of Jupiter must not pass under an arbour of vines. The feet of the couch on which he sleeps must be smeared with a thin coating of clay, and he must not sleep away from this bed for three nights in succession, and no other person must sleep in that bed. At the foot of this bed there should be a box with sacrificial cakes. The cuttings of the nails and hair of the Dialis must be buried in the earth under a fruitful tree. Every day is a holy day for the Dialis. He must not be in the open air without his cap; that he might go without it in the house has only recently been decided by the Pontiffs, so Masurius Sabinus wrote, and it is said that some other ceremonies have been remitted and he has been excused from observing them. The priest of Jupiter must not and touch any bread fermented with yeast. He does not lay off his inner tunic except under cover, in order that he may not be naked in the open air, as it were under the eye of Jupiter. No other has a place at table above the Flamen Dialis, except the Rex Sacrificulus. If the Dialis has lost his wife he abdicates his office. The marriage of the priest cannot be dissolved except by death. He never enters a place of burial, he never touches a dead body; but he is not forbidden to attend a funeral."

Gellius – Noctes Atticae

A humorous scenario idea would be to allow a player character the opportunity to be elected to the position of flamen, only then to lay upon them the full horror of the sacred oaths and duties during their elevation ceremony. Of course, the character could always refuse to swear, perhaps fast talking their way out of the 'honour' with some long forgotten family vow or publicly shaming themselves by revealing a hidden impropriety which makes them invalid for the post…

Subsidiary fraternities called sodalitates preserved archaic rites but were not strictly priests. These were the:

Ω Luperci – two young patrician men who performed the Lupercalia

Ω Arval Brethren – 12 men who enacted the rites of Dea Dia

Ω The Salii – the 12 dancers of Mars

Ω Fetiales – 20 men learned in the sacred declarations of war or peace treaties

Last, but by no means least, was a group of soothsayers called haruspices. They came from Etruria and practiced haruspicy, which is the examination of the entrails of sacrificed animals and birds, and could interpret lightning too.

"We receive many further warnings from prodigies, from entrails, and a number of other phenomena, of which a long experience has been so observant as to have produced an art of divination."

Cicero – De Divinatione

However, the haruspices were regarded as individual specialists and their Etruscan origins prevented harmonious integration into the official hierarchy of Roman religion. Although they were first introduced during Rome's founding as a natural part of the influx of conquered and conquering peoples, haruspices never achieved independent political authority during the Republic, remaining primarily as consultants for animal sacrifices.

> "Furthermore, Romulus ordered one soothsayer out of each tribe to be present at the sacrifices. This soothsayer we call hieroskopos or "inspector of the vitals," and the Romans, preserving something of the ancient name, haruspex. He also made a law that all the priests and ministers of the gods should be chosen by the curiae and that their election should be confirmed by those who interpret the will of the gods by the art of divination."
>
> Dionysios of Halikarnassos – Roman Antiquites

As time passed and religious law was superseded by secular law, the authority of the priesthood slowly diminished. Since the responsibilities of the priesthood were heavy and some of the positions required restrictive taboos, which forced the holders to lead tedious, withdrawn lives, it was often difficult to find novices willing to fill positions left open by the death of the previous holder.

By the end of the Republic, the priesthood had become little more than a political office and many priests became lax in performing their ritualistic duties.

SUPERSTITION (SUPERSTITIO)

The Romans believed in many things… divine blessings and infernal curses, good fortune and bad. The influx of foreign ideas with immigrants, over hundreds of years built up a huge eclectic body of superstitious law.

Leading amongst these, the interpretation of extraordinary natural phenomena (prodigia) was introduced by the Etruscans, who read omens (omina) in such things as lightning strikes, thunder claps or rumblings of earthquakes. Certain days of the year – the dies atri – were considered unlucky. During them fires would not be lit, no sacrifices made at altars and public worship was forbidden.

There were two particular forms of the dies atri. The dies postriduani (the days after the Kalendae, Nonae and Ides of each month) were regarded as bad omens for beginning private activities, business or journeys. The dies vitiosi were specific dates decreed by the Senate to be unlucky, due to some historical disaster. Sometimes these became regular additions to the annual calendar.

Ω The 18th day of Quintilis (July) (after 477 BC), commemorating the defeat on the Allia River and the following sack of Rome by the Gauls.

Ω The 2nd day of Sextilis (August) (after 216 BC), when the Romans were massacred by Hannibal at the Battle of Cannae.

Ω The 6th of October (after 105 BC), the battle of Arausio where 80,000 Romans were annihilated by the combined tribes of the Cimbri and Teutoni.

Almost any unusual event was considered a portent or omen by the Roman people. Extraordinary ones would be recorded in the libri pontificales. It was the responsibility of the priesthood to

---

THE SIBYLLINE BOOKS

According to legend these sacred books (Fata Sibyllina) were originally written by the Cumaean Sibyl, who sold them to Tarquinius Priscus, the fifth King of Rome.

> "they say that she [the Sibyl] brought nine books to the king Tarquinius Priscus, and asked for them three hundred pieces of gold, and that the king refused so great a price, and derided the madness of the woman; that she, in the sight of the king, burnt three of the books, and demanded the same price for those which were left; that Tarquinius much more considered the woman to be mad; and that when she again, having burnt three other books, persisted in asking the same price, the king was moved, and bought the remaining books for the three hundred pieces of gold:"
>
> Lactantius quoting Varro – Institutiones Divinae

During the very worst crises of the Republic, the senate would order the consultation of the Sibylline Books by the priests of the Sacris Faciundis and act upon their recommendation. The books were considered so important that their contents were held as secret and hidden within the sanctuary of the Temple of Jupiter atop the Capitoline Hill. Tragically when the temple burned down in 83 BC, the books were also lost. Six years later, at the Senate's order, envoys were sent across the empire to compile a new collection of sibylline quotations.

The terrible authority of the books was such that they were responsible for the introduction of new religious faiths, festivals and even human sacrifices. Thus they would only be consulted during the very worst times, to limit their proclivity for instituting cultural change.

> "…the severe winter was followed by a pestilential summer, which proved fatal to man and beast. As neither a cause nor a cure could be found for its fatal ravages, the senate ordered the Sibylline Books to be consulted. The priests who had charge of them appointed for the first time in Rome a lectisternium. Apollo and Latona, Diana and Hercules, Mercury and Neptune were for eight days propitiated on three couches decked with the most magnificent coverlets that could be obtained. Solemnities were conducted also in private houses. It is stated that throughout the City the front gates of the houses were thrown open and all sorts of things placed for general use in the open courts, all comers, whether acquaintances or strangers, being brought in to share the hospitality. Men who had been enemies held friendly and sociable conversations with each other and abstained from all litigation, the manacles even were removed from prisoners during this period, and afterwards it seemed an act of impiety that men to whom the gods had brought such relief should be put in chains again."
>
> Livy – Ab Urbe Condita

---

interpret these occurrences and if considered harmful, decide on a method of placating the gods. In later times, some priests were not above using them to make political gestures.

> "Numerous stories of portents filled men's minds with superstitious terrors. It was said that crows picked with their beaks some of the gold on the Capitol and actually ate it, and rats gnawed a golden crown at Antium. The whole of the country round Capua was covered by an immense flight of locusts, and no one knew whence they had come. At Reate a foal was born with five feet; at Anagnia fiery meteors were seen in different parts of the sky and these were followed by a huge blazing torch; at Frusino a thin

bow encircled the sun, which afterwards grew to such a size that it extended beyond the bow; at Arpinum there was a subsidence of the ground and a vast chasm was formed. Whilst one of the consuls was sacrificing, the liver of the first victim was found to be without a head. These portents were expiated by sacrifices of full-grown animals, the college of Pontiffs intimated the deities to whom they were to be offered."

Livy – Ab Urbe Condita

Crossing the threshold of a house right foot first, a snake dropping from roof into your atrium, meeting a mule bearing the herb hipposelinum (used to decorate tombs), hearing a cock crow during a dinner party, attending a banquet with an even number of people, tripping over your own doorstep, or even spilling wine, water, or oil were all considered premonitions of bad luck.

Some portents were somewhat more obvious, such as the cracking of a roof beam foretelling disaster, since even if the roof did not immediately collapse, you would still have to pay for an expensive repair.

Certain animals had associations with fortune. Black cats that entered your home, images of snakes and scorpions, and catching sight of an owl (believed to be transformed witches), were all signs of impending calamity… whereas bees and eagles were the opposite. Poultry were often used to predict the outcome of battles and each legion had a position called the 'Keeper of the Sacred Chickens'.

"…will not even the instances in our own history teach us to acknowledge the power of the gods? Shall we remain unimpressed by the tale of the presumptuous conduct of Publius Claudius in the first Punic war, who, when the sacred chickens, on being let out of the coop, refused to feed, ordered them to be plunged into the water, that they might, as he said, drink, since they would not eat? He only ridiculed the gods in jest, but the mockery cost him many a tear (for his fleet was utterly routed), and brought a great disaster upon the Roman people."

Cicero – De Natura Deorum

Even food was regarded with superstition. Garlic was consumed in large quantities by soldiers and gladiators, since it was believed to bring strength. Cabbage was thought to prevent drunkenness and even protect against pestilence.

PRAYERS, SACRIFICES AND THANKSGIVING (VOTA, SUPPLICATIO ET SACRIFICIA)

Romans were constantly praying to their gods. Requests for good luck, the return of stolen goods, favour in love, success in business or battle or even calling curses upon others. In some cases prayers were given in thanks for the perceived fortune that a god might have already granted… the survival of a sea crossing for example. There were few things for which a prayer would not be offered.

Prayers were almost always accompanied by a sacrifice or the future promise of a greater donation, worthy of the deity's generous intervention. In most cases this was either an offering of sustenance – wine, milk, fruit, cakes and so forth – or a blood sacrifice of an animal (victima). The larger the request or more important the god, the bigger the sacrifice required.

Certain deities had specific types of animals they particularly favoured for explicit celebrations, such as rams for Janus. Even the sex and colour of the animal was important. However, in times of want or poverty, symbolic sacrifices of lesser animals, or even cakes shaped as cult specific animals could be made without fear of censure from the deity.

"Priapus, a large cup of milk and this libum bread is all you can expect each year, guardian of a pauper's garden"

Virgil – Eclogues

Most sacrifices were either domestic rituals held in the home, with the paterfamilias acting as the priest, or public sacrifices held in the temples during festivals. A private sacrifice could be made at a temple too but this required attendance in the more serious attire of the toga, as well as a probable donation to the priests beyond the cost of the animal to be offered.

The ritual of a formal sacrifice took place at the god's altar, next to which was positioned a brazier or fireplace (focus). The fire was used as the receptacle for consumable offerings, i.e. incense, wine or food stuffs. Cleanliness was important. At the start of the ritual the proprietor would cover their head in the folds of their toga (to display their piety) and wash their hands, before touching the altar and uttering their prayer. This was accompanied by a libation or burning of incense or cakes in the fire.

After these preparations, the main sacrifice would be made. The cleaned and decorated animal sacrifice (in ribbons or sometimes partially gilded) would be consecrated to the god with either a sprinkling of salt and splash of wine (ritus Romanus), or similarly with grain and water instead (ritus Graecus).

"Of old the means to win the goodwill of gods for man were spelt and the sparkling grains of pure salt. As yet no foreign ship had brought across the ocean waves the black-distilled myrrh; the Eufrates had sent no incense, India no balm, and the red saffron's filaments were still unknown. The altar was content to smoke with savine, and the laurel burned with crackling loud. To garlands woven of meadow flowers he who could violets add was rich indeed. The knife that now lays bare the bowels of the slaughtered bull had in sacred rites no work to do."

Ovid – Fasti

Once completed, the animal was then killed by a special butcher (victimarius) by being bled (larger animals often necessitated a blow from a mallet to stun them first). If the animal showed panic then it was considered a bad omen, requiring a new sacrifice to be done. The carcass of the sacrifice was then opened and its entrails (exta) examined for abnormalities by an assistant haruspex. If no anomalies were found, then the ritual was considered acceptable to the gods (litatio) and could proceed.

The entrails of the beast would then be cooked (grilled or boiled) and offered to the god being honoured. Chthonic deities had the offerings cast upon the ground or buried. Water deities had theirs cast into an appropriate water source (sea, spring and so on). Otherwise the offering was burned in the focus of the fire.

The remaining meat would then be served at the banquet (epulum) after the sacrifice. This would be eaten by the priests and attendees as guests of the god, unless the ritual was held for a deity of the underworld – in which case it was forbidden (or simply unwise) to share a feast dedicated to a god connected with death.

Although this was the general method of making sacrifices, other deities often had their own idiosyncrasies. Flowers for the goddess Flora for example would not be burned but used as decorations for her temple instead. Sometimes musical instruments would be played as part of the ceremony, often to cover the secret words uttered during the ritual.

Any sacrifice which had failed due to the distress of the animal or the pollution of its entrails required an additional sacrifice to ward off the anger of the god. Only if this was successful could the original sacrifice be repeated.

Greater sacrifices than cult animals were rare, reserved to show proper reverence for gods which had brought about some great intercession on behalf of the worshipper. These material offerings were called donaria and could take the form of a statue, a work of art, or in some cases a new altar or entire new temple.

Generals often made mighty oaths to deities which brought them victory on the battlefield. Such declarations – if made publicly – could strengthen the failing morale of an army. The donaria usually took the form of a new temple, or the presentation of a large share of the spolia won on the battlefield.

> *"In the middle of it all the consul, raising his hands towards heaven and speaking in a loud voice so that he might be well heard, vowed a temple to Jupiter Stator if the Roman army stayed its flight and renewed the battle and defeated and slew the Samnites. All officers and men, infantry and cavalry alike, exerted themselves to the utmost to restore the battle. Even the divine providence seemed to have looked with favour on the Romans, so easily did matters take a favourable turn."*
>
> Livy – Ab Urbe Condita

Divine blessings took a slightly different form than normal prayers. The ritual of lustration was given by sprinkling pure water over the objects or persons to be protected, accompanied by the display of foliage and burning of herbs. Lustrations were commonly used for purifying fields of crops or flocks of livestock – warding them from disease and evil magic. Even the Roman army was blessed in such a manner each time they took the field against an enemy.

Beyond traditional offerings, there were a number of extraordinary sacrifices made at times of apparent divine anger, when Rome was facing destruction.

The lectisternium and sellisternium were peculiar banquets held specifically for the gods. Male gods had couches and food provided for them throughout the city, whereas female deities were provided with chairs instead; hence the two different names for the same ritual.

The penultimate sacrifice was the ver sacrum, a common custom amongst the early city-states, where everything born the following spring is promised as a sacrifice to the gods. This was only done in the direst of circumstances. Although this vow included baby children too, the custom was eventually changed so that any infants were allowed to grow up but were then driven out of the city upon reaching their 20th or 21st year to found a new colony. Rome however was more merciful; both recorded times the Romans vowed a ver sacrum, the oath was confined to the sacrifice of only animals.

> *"The Sabini, since they had long been at war with the Ombrici, vowed (just as some of the Greeks do) to dedicate everything that was produced that year; and, on winning the victory, they partly sacrificed and partly dedicated all that was produced; then a dearth ensued, and some one said that they ought to have dedicated the babies too; this they did, and devoted to Mars all the children born that year; and these children, when grown to manhood, they sent away as colonists, and a bull led the way;"*
>
> Strabo – Geography

Everything the Romans did as part of religious rituals was intensely formulaic. The slightest mistake would force the entire ritual to be performed again from the start. Eventually even some of the language used became obscure, so that the participants were no longer sure exactly what they were intoning.

HUMAN SACRIFICE (HUMANA HOSTIA)

Despite Rome's later reputation for civilised behaviour, it was in many ways no different than the cultures which surrounded it. The city had a long history of ritual human sacrifice. Indeed, Rome can be viewed as somewhat hypocritical in its justification of the final annihilation of Carthage, based in part on the Carthaginians practice of human sacrifice, since it was not until 97 BC that the practice was officially banned by law in Rome; although this did not completely stop the act from continuing to occur, even up to the end of the Republic.

A human sacrifice was the ultimate offering that could be made to the gods but only to those of the underworld (dii inferni) rather than the celestial deities (dii consentes).

The earliest Roman laws from the Twelve Tablets had a form of punishment where a man who had broken his oaths, defrauded his clients or moved boundary markers was considered to have broken the sacrosanct rules of society and would be declared sacer; that is, "given to the gods". Rather than a blessing, this was in fact a terrible curse, which removed the man from the protection of society. In effect, his life was now dedicated to the deities of the underworld and he could be abused or even killed by any person with no fear of reprisal or censure. With such chastisements, it is unsurprising that the Romans of the early Republic placed so much importance in honesty and personal integrity.

Further hints of early human sacrifice were entwined with two annual festivals. The first was the Feriae Latinatae held at the end of April, where puppets were hung in trees in exchange for the previous practice of sacrificing young boys. The second was a processional ceremony held on the ides of May (See Festivals page 115), when the Vestal Virgins would cast rush puppets (argei) into the River Tiber from the Pons Sublicius (the first bridge in Rome) in substitution for the original practice of throwing in old men.

> "...he [Hercules] taught them to appease the anger of the god by making effigies resembling the men they had been wont to bind hand and foot and throw into the stream of the Tiber, and dressing these in the same manner, to throw them into the river instead of the men..."
>
> *Dionysios of Halikarnassos – Roman Antiquites*

The first record of people being directly sacrificed to the gods began in the monarchy. When King Servius expanded the city walls, four human sacrifices were buried beneath the old pomerium, which encircled the Palatine Hill, to placate the gods over the enlargement of the sacred boundaries of the city.

Most human sacrifices were authorised by the state. In times of dire portents a Vestal Virgin was sometimes accused of breaking her vow of chastity (being used as a scapegoat), whereupon they would be buried alive not only as a punishment but more importantly as propitiation to the manes, the spirits of the dead.

On several occasions (228 BC, 216 BC and 113 BC) the Sibylline Books demanded human sacrifices to the dii inferni. Each time, a pair of Gauls and a pair of Greeks were buried alive under the Forum Boarium.

> "Thereupon a barbarian slave of a certain equestrian gave information against three Vestal Virgins, Aemilia, Licinia, and Marcia, that they had all been corrupted at about the same time, and that they had long entertained lovers, one of whom was Vetutius Barrus, the informer's master. The Vestals, accordingly, were convicted and punished; but, since the deed was plainly atrocious, it was resolved that the priests should consult the Sibylline books. They say that oracles were found foretelling that these events would come to pass for the bane of the Romans, and enjoining on them that, to avert the impending disaster, they should offer as a sacrifice to certain strange and alien spirits two Greeks and two Gauls, buried alive on the spot."
>
> *Plutarch – Roman Questions*

Such sacrifices did not stop even in the late Republic. When rebellious soldiers of Julius Caesar attempted an insurrection in Rome, the dictator, acting as the Pontifex Maximus, ordered their sacrifice in the Campus Martius at the hands of the Pontifices and Flamen Martialis.

> "In fact they did not cease their rioting until Caesar suddenly came upon them, and seizing one man with his own hands, delivered him up to punishment. So this man was executed for the reason given, and two others were slain

> as a sort of ritual observance. The true cause I am unable to state, inasmuch as the Sibyl made no utterance and there was no other similar oracle, but at any rate they were sacrificed in the Campus Martius by the Pontifices and the priest of Mars, and their heads were set up near the Regia."
>
> *Cassius Dio – Roman History*

Not all sacrifices were instigated by the senate. The rite of devotio was the dedication of oneself to the manes. It was most famously performed by Roman generals, who had offer themselves to the gods and then charge headlong into the enemy. This courageous death would then ensure victory.

> "In like manner as I have uttered this prayer so do I now on behalf of the commonwealth of the Quirites, on behalf of the army, the legions, the auxiliaries of the Roman People, the Quirites, devote the legions and auxiliaries of the enemy, together with myself to the Divine Manes and to Earth." After this prayer he ordered the lictors to go to T. Manlius and at once announce to his colleague that he had devoted himself on behalf of the army. He then girded himself with the Gabinian cincture, and in full armour leaped upon his horse and dashed into the middle of the enemy. To those who watched him in both armies, he appeared something awful and superhuman, as though sent from heaven to expiate and appease all the anger of the gods and to avert destruction from his people and bring it on their enemies. All the dread and terror which he carried with him threw the front ranks of the Latins into confusion which soon spread throughout the entire army. This was most evident, for wherever his horse carried him they were paralysed as though struck by some death-dealing star; but when he fell, overwhelmed with darts, the Latin cohorts, in a state of perfect consternation, fled from the spot and left a large space clear. The Romans, on the other hand, freed from all religious fears, pressed forward as though the signal was then first given and commenced a great battle."
>
> *Livy – Ab Urbe Condita*

A devotio offering was akin to the Greek idea of the scapegoat; a single man volunteering to absorb all misfortunes and then willingly sacrificing himself so that he carries the calamities away with him. The act of offering oneself in this way brought great honour and reward to the family of the dead man. Sometimes however, the willing volunteer was blessed by the gods and failed to actually die. In such circumstances an alternative sacrifice was made, in the same manner as the argei puppets mentioned previously.

> "I ought to add here that a consul or dictator or prætor, when he devotes the legions of the enemy, need not necessarily devote himself but may select any one he chooses out of a legion that has been regularly enrolled. If the man who has been so devoted is killed, all is considered to have been duly performed. If he is not killed, an image of the man, seven feet high at least, must be buried in the earth and a victim slain as an expiatory sacrifice"
>
> *Livy – Ab Urbe Condita*

Last, but by no means least, were the gladiatorial combats. Although these eventually devolved into mere entertainment, they began as a serious religious observance, with volunteer participants shedding blood to the spirits of the dead. Even though the original intention of these fights was not death, fatalities were an accepted part of the ceremonies.

THE DISCIPLINA ETRUSCA

The origins of Etruscan religious and divinatory knowledge were supposedly a gift from a genius loci, which appeared whilst a founding father of the Etruscan nation was ploughing near Tarquini.

"One day in a field near the river Marta in Teruria, from a newly ploughed furrow rose up a divine being with the appearance of a child, but with the wisdom of an old man. The startled cry of the ploughman brought the priest-kings hurrying to the spot. To them the wise child, Tages, chanted the sacred doctrine, which they reverently wrote down so that this most precious possession could be passed on to their successors. Immediately after the revelation, the miraculous being fell dead and disappeared into the ploughed field."

Cicero – De Divinatione

The compiled religious and divinatory law was written in a number of collected books known to the Romans as the Disciplina Etrusca. Each text was a separate body of sacred information, written on its own set of scrolls. The entire collection must have been the equivalent of a small library in itself.

Ω *The Libri Haruspicini dwelt upon methods of divination using the entrails of sacrificed animals.*

Ω *The Libri Fulgurates concerned the portents revealed by thunder and lightning.*

Ω *The Libri Rituales dealt with ritual knowledge such as consecration of altars, shrines and temples, the founding of cities, blessing of defensive walls, divisions of the people and organisation of festivals.*

Ω *The Libri Fatales explained the measuring of time and the lifespan of individuals and peoples.*

Ω *The Libri Acherontici illustrated the underworld and rituals needed to guide the soul to the proper afterlife.*

Ω *The Libri Ostentaria defined the rules for interpreting portents (including prognostication from trees) and described the propitiatory and expiatory acts needed to placate the gods.*

Ω *The Libri Tagetici further prophesies of Tages, the source of Etruscan knowledge.*

Ω *The Libri Vegoritici contained cosmic prophesies made by the nymph Vegoia.*

Ω *The Liber Linteus described the calendar rituals of the year.*

ROMAN FESTIVALS (FERIAE)

During the Republic special holy days (the dies feriae), were assigned as religious festivals to show devotion to the gods of the state (cultus civiles). On many of these days no legal business could be performed, only religious rites. Thus they slowly transformed into holidays where those who could afford to performed pious rituals and took a day of rest.

Since the religious beliefs of the early Romans centred on the concepts of death and purification, war and agriculture – their original festivals reflected these important aspects of their lives. As time passed however, more deities were given sacred dates in the calendar and the primary purpose was lost amid a clutter of contesting faiths.

Eventually, almost every day of the year was sacred to one god or another and some days held significance for two or more deities simultaneously. In consideration of space, a foreshortened list of the most important festivals of the monarchy and early Republic follow. The dates of the religious games, the ludi, are separately listed on page 76.

THE CYCLE OF THE DEAD

Lemuria – 9th, 11th and 13th May. Propitiations made to the lemurs, the 'hungry ghosts' of dead family members who were considered dangerous and harboured ill-intent. During the nights of the Lemuria, the paterfamilias would rise at midnight, wash himself clean and then barefoot and loose robed, walk through the house spitting black beans from his mouth. Then chanting "with these beans I redeem me and mine" he would wash his hands a second time whilst the lemures supposedly collected the beans in preference to the souls of the living. Once cleansed a second time he would clang bronze household instruments together and walk through the house chanting "Paternal ghosts, get out."

Rite of the Argei – 15th May. The purification ceremony when the Vestal Virgins, led by Pontifex Maximus, threw rush puppets into the Tiber.

Mundus Patet – 24th August, 5th October, and 8th November. Three times a year, the mundus (a vaulted ritual pit located in the Comitium on the Palatine Hill) was opened by removing its stone slab cover (lapis) and an offering of fresh fruits lowered within. During these days the gates of the underworld were considered to be opened and ghosts were free to walk the streets of Rome. No military or public matters were permitted when the 'gates of Orcus' (ostia Orci) were open.

"When the mundus is open, it is as if a door stands open for the sorrowful gods of the underworld."

Macrobius quoting Varro

Parentalia – 13th to 21st February. A privately celebrated festival when families honoured their ancestral dead, processing to the tombs of relatives bringing gifts of wine, water, milk, honey, oil, salt, black coloured cakes (shaped as sacrificial victims) to nourish the dead souls, and also flowers with which to decorate their mausoleums. During Parentalia all temples were closed, no fires burned on the altars, marriages were forbidden and the magistrates laid aside their insignia.

Feralia – 21st February. A public festival which marked the end of Parentalia. It involved the placating sacrifice of sheep to the manes in general.

THE CYCLE OF WAR

Feriae Marti – 1st March. The beginning of the new year. Festival in honour of Mars, where the Salii dressed in ancient armour, processed around Rome dancing, leaping and chanting ancient hymns.

Equiria – 14th March. Dedication of cavalry horses to Mars, followed by horse races held on the Campus Martius.

Quinquatrus – 19th to 23rd March. The purification of the sacred shields (ancilae) by the Salii, followed by a sacrifice to Mars and an accompanying feast. Also celebrated was the Minervalia in

THE SALII

The Salii were a lesser priesthood (sodalitas) comprised of two groups of 12 men, the Palatini (devoted to Mars) and the Collini (devoted to Quirinus). Only patricians with both parents living were permitted to join the order. The religious garb of the Salii was a very old style of military dress: a colourfully painted or dyed tunic (tunica picta), a bronze breast plate and a short military cloak with scarlet stripes and a purple border. On their heads they wore a conical helmet (apex) and carried spears. The most important part of their gear however was the shield (ancile) shaped roughly like a figure-8.

According to myth, Jupiter dropped a shield from heaven as a gift to Numa, the second king of Rome. Afraid that it would be stolen, Numa had a smith forge 11 identical copies (so no one would know the divine one) and stored them in the Regia. With them were also stored the spears of Mars, which were said to foretell disaster when they shook spontaneously. Legendarily, the spears were said to have shaken the night before Julius Caesar was assassinated.

The Salii were a vital component of most of the ancient festivals dedicated to Mars and Quirinus. Their task was to perform war dances in honour of their gods, whilst chanting hymns. The spectacle of fully armed, leaping dancers demonstrated the vitality and splendour of Rome's military prowess but must have been a terrible test of the priest's endurance, where failure to perform the dance correctly (or energetically enough) could have been publicly viewed as a failure to invoke the blessings of the gods…

honour of the dedications of the temples to Minerva, another war goddess.

Tubilustrium – 23rd March. The lustration of the war trumpets (tubae) calling upon Mars to sanctify them before the start of the campaigning season.

Equus Octobris – 15th October. The sacrifice of the October horse to Mars, followed by a traditional fight over possession of the decapitated head. The tail of the horse was soaked in its blood and carried to the temple of Vesta, where it was preserved by the Virgins for use in the festival of Parilia.

"It was called the October Horse, the one harnessed on the right of the winning chariot, because it is burned in sacrifice to Mars in October every year in the Campus Martius; over this horse's head there is no small contest between the Suburans and the people on the Sacra Via, so that the latter can affix it on the wall of the Regia, and the former on the Mamilian tower."

Festus – De Uerborum Significatu

Armilustrium – 19th October. The purification by the Salii of the armaments of the mustered legions before they were placed back into storage. This festival marked the end of the campaigning season for the year.

THE AGRARIAN CYCLE

The fecundity festivals were primarily grouped around three periods of the year: March/April, the months of birthing, sprouting, and flowering, August, the month of harvesting and December, the month of planting/sowing.

Liberalia – 17th March. Festival of Liber and Libera the god and goddess of generative functions. Old women wearing wreaths of ivy upon their heads sat at all parts of the city with cakes, which they burned in sacrifice on braziers for anyone who purchased them.

Cerialia – 12th to 19th April. Festival in honour of Ceres. Women wore white and carried lit torches on the streets to represent the goddess's search for her lost daughter Proserpina. Offerings of salt, flour, incense, pine branches, milk, honey or wine were made on the private alters (lararium) of the home. For the entire duration of the festival it was forbidden to engage in sexual relations.

Fordicidia – 15th April. The sacrifice of pregnant cows in honour of Tellus, goddess of Earth. The unborn calves are taken from the womb, burned on the sacred flame of Vesta and the ashes saved by the Virgins for the following festival of Parilia.

Parilia – 21st April. A purification festival held in honour of Pales, goddess of the herds. A public ceremony was held by the Vestal Virgins who built a sacred fire into which were thrown bean husks and the October horse blood and calf ashes previously saved. In the countryside the pens of herd animals were cleaned and ritually purified with the smoke of burning sulphur, rosemary and fir wood, after which the animals were blessed with a lustration. The ceremonies finished with a bonfire through which the flocks and their shepherds were then driven three times, accompanied by the music of flutes and cymbals, to protect them from predators, sickness and starvation. This date was also the anniversary of the birth of Rome (Roma condita).

Vinalia – 23rd April. Libations of the first wines of the year offered to Jupiter and a lamb offered by Flamen Dialis in order to ward off the frosts that kill new vine shoots.

Robigalia – 25th April. Propitiation to Robigus, god of blight and rust to protect the crops. It involved the sacrifice of a red coloured dog and a sheep by the Flamen Quirinalis at the fifth mile on the Via Claudia, where there was a sacred grove.

"Spare Ceres' grain, O scabby Robigo, let the tips of new shoots sway gently above the earth, let growing crops be nourished… keep your scaly hands from the harvest… Grip harsh iron rather than the tender wheat, Destroy whatever can destroy others first. Better to gnaw at swords and harmful spears"

Ovid – Fasti

Floralia – 28th April to 3rd May. A festival honouring Flora, who brought crops into flower. Animals blessed with great fertility, such as rabbits or deer, were released into the Forum Romanum. During the festivities people would wear flower garlands and women dressed in their brightest coloured clothes.

Consualia – 21st August. Celebrated the completed harvest and the granary deity Consus. The Pontifex Maximus and Vestal Virgins would remove the soil covering his temple in the Circus Maximus and sacrifice fruits upon his altar prior to refilling the city's grain storage vaults located there. All animals which laboured were rested on this day and decorated with garlands.

Opiconsivia – 25th August. Festival honouring the wife of Consus. The Vestal Virgins and the Pontifex Maximus (also dressed in the vestments and veil like the priestesses) held rites in her shrine in the Regia to give thanks for the fertility of the soil. Originally the rites were performed in the main granary.

Consualia – 15th December. A fertility festival started by Romulus, commemorating the rape and insemination of the Sabine women.

Malum est consilium quod mutari non potest – A plan that cannot be changed is bad (Publilius Syrus)

Saturnalia – 17th December. The festival of Saturn was celebrated after the vintage and harvesting was complete but before the onset of full winter. It started with a sacrifice of young pigs to Saturn and then continued with feasting and unrestrained merrymaking. It also included exchanging presents and offering sacrifices. Masters served their slaves as a token of the equality of rank. By the end of the Republic the festival had been extended to three days in length.

Opalia – 19th December. Festival in honour of Ops, the goddess of plenty and wife of Saturn.

Lupercalia – 15th February. A fertility and purification ritual sacred to Faunus. It began with a sacrifice of goats and a dog in the Lupercal cave on the Palentine Hill, the blood was daubed onto the faces of two young boys of patrician families dressed only in goat-skin aprons (the luperci). Carrying strips of leather in their hands, the boys would then run around the city and whip young women waiting along the way to increase their fertility.

FORBIDDEN RELIGIONS AND RITES (CULTUS ILLICITI)

Despite being a conservative society, Rome was surprisingly open-minded about the introduction of new deities. Religious tolerance was a fundamental keystone of Roman life. Yet, even the Romans had their limits when religion began to threaten social order.

At least three religions were officially suppressed during the Republic.

Foremost amongst these were the proscriptions passed by the Senate in 186 BC against the worshippers of Bacchus, the Roman god of wine. The bacchanals of the cult had grown into excesses of pleasure, involving uninhibited inebriation, dancing, and perverse sexual acts. Not only were these celebrations morally abhorrent to the majority of Roman citizens but leaders of the cult had organised their worshippers (bacchanales) into a syndicate of crime.

> *"Nor was the mischief confined to the promiscuous intercourse of men and women; false witness, the forging of seals and testaments, and false information, all proceeded from the same source, as also poisonings and murders of families where the bodies could not even be found for burial. Many crimes were committed by treachery; most by violence, which was kept secret, because the cries of those who were being violated or murdered could not be heard owing to the noise of drums and cymbals."*
>
> *Livy – Ab Urbe Condita*

The outrages of the cult became so great that the Senate was forced to act. They issued orders that anyone initiated into the cult was to be imprisoned, whereas those who had performed criminal or murderous acts were to be put to death. They then published an edict forbidding any one to sell or buy anything for the purpose of flight or to receive, harbour, or in any way assist those who fled. Ultimately, over 7,000 people were implicated in the plot, the majority of whom were executed or committed suicide, after which all the bacchanalian shrines in Italy were destroyed.

The Bacchanalia were the first of a series of mystery cults that gradually infiltrated Roman society. They were generally regarded with suspicion due to their secretive nature and initiation rites. Such closed cults were considered gathering points for the seditious by the Senate and genuinely feared as sources of rebellion or social corruption.

The next religion which faced censure was that of Cybele, the great mother. Although the rites were not secretive like those of Bacchus, they still embraced what was considered improper behaviour in Roman society.

> *"The rites of the Idaean goddess are a case in point; for the prætors perform sacrifices and celebrated games in her honour every year according to the Roman customs, but the priest and priestess of the goddess are Phrygians, and it is they who carry her image in procession through the city, begging alms in her name according to their custom, and wearing figures upon their breasts and striking their timbrels while their followers play tunes upon their flutes in honour of the Mother of the Gods. But by a law and decree of the senate no native Roman walks in procession through the city arrayed in a parti-coloured robe, begging alms or escorted by flute-players, or worships the god with the Phrygian ceremonies."*
>
> *Dionysios of Halikarnassos – Roman Antiquites*

Although these displays were thought of as lacking decorum, worse still were the extremes of religious enthusiasm inspired by Cybele's worship, which included voluntary self-mutilation. Indeed, to become a priest of her faith (Galli) required the advocate to castrate himself with a flint knife.

> *"He tore at his body too with a sharp stone, And dragged his long hair in the filthy dust, Shouting: 'I deserved this. I pay the due penalty In blood. Ah. Let the parts that harmed me, perish. Let them perish.' Cutting away the burden of his groin, and suddenly bereft of every mark of manhood. His*

madness set a precedent, and his unmanly servants toss their hair, and cut off their members as if worthless…"

Ovid – Fasti

Such acts were severely dealt with. Slaves who mutilated themselves in this manner were transported overseas away from the city. Citizens who did the same were no longer considered men and were unable to benefit from the law in the courts.

The third restricted religion was the Egyptian cult of Isis and Serapis. These gods were introduced to Rome around the time of the consulship of Lucius Cornelius Sulla and soon became popular amongst the plebeians and slaves – especially women. Eventually the city possessed dozens of shrines dedicated to them. Thus it was fear that the cult could be used for political ends, religiously unifying the under-classes, which caused its persecution.

Claiming the cult of Isis and Serapis was causing a loss of piety towards the traditional Roman deities, the Senate initially ordered Isis's cult statue to be removed from the Capitoline hill in 58 BC. Then in 53 BC the Senate forbade private worship of the goddess and ordered her shrines be destroyed. In retaliation, new sanctuaries

were built outside the pomerium (i.e. outside the sacred area within the city walls).

The Senate continued their suppression of the cult, placing accusations of licentiousness and orgies against it. Eventually, in 50 BC the consul L. Aemilius Paulus was forced to doff his toga and begin the destruction of her temples himself when the plebeian workforce refused to follow his orders.

Again the temples were rebuilt and, in 48 BC, the Senate decreed that they be destroyed again. This time, an adjoining temple to Bellona (a female god of war) was accidentally pulled down during the demolition, leading to a rather grisly discovery…

"Among other things that happened toward the end of that year [48 BC] bees settled on the Capitol beside the statue of Hercules. Sacrifices to Isis chanced to be going on there at the time, and the soothsayers gave their opinion to the effect that all precincts of that goddess and of Serapis should be razed to the ground once more. In the course of their demolition a shrine of Bellona was unwittingly destroyed and in it were found jars full of human flesh…"

Cassius Dio – Roman History

Eventually acknowledging defeat, the second Triumvirate granted the cult official sanction and ordered a temple to be built at the state's expense.

PHILOSOPHY (PHILOSOPHIA)

Roman philosophy was based upon ideas imported from the Greeks, following Rome's imperialistic meddling in their constant wars. Several schools of philosophy were introduced during the later half of the second century BC; most notably those of Pythagoreanism, Stoicism, Epicureanism and Scepticism.

To the Roman mind, religion was concerned with the relationships between man and the Gods, whilst philosophy was primarily concerned with the relationships between men. It provided a guide to how one should live one's life and even though philosophy usually encouraged rationalistic thinking, they also allowed for the supernatural and were therefore compatible with the rituals and practices of the Roman religion.

"This is the difference between us [philosophers] and the Etruscans, who have consummate skill in interpreting lightning: we think that because clouds collide, lightning is emitted; but they think the clouds collide in order that lightning may be emitted."

Seneca – Quaestiones naturales

Eventually it was the rival philosophies of Stoicism and Epicureanism that grew in popularity and provided the foundation of correct Roman behaviour.

STOICISM (STOICA RATIO)

Perhaps the most important philosophy of Republican Rome was Stoicism, which seemed to embrace the traditional Roman virtue of virtus meaning 'manliness' or 'toughness'.

The central concept of Stoicism was logos – the rational order of the universe. The Stoics argued that nature was a system designed

THE BACHANALIA

The rites of Bacchus were initially benign celebrations held only by women, led by a matron of respected character three times a year. The religion was supposedly debased by the teachings of a low born Greek in Etruria who was "a hedge-priest and wizard, not one of those who imbue men's minds with error by professing to teach their superstitions openly for money, but a hierophant of secret nocturnal mysteries." These mysteries became so popular that the cult and their shrines spread across the length and breadth of Italy.

By the second century BC the religion had become completely corrupted and performed many depravities, up to and including human sacrifice.

"At the same time she made the rite a nocturnal one, and instead of three days in the year celebrated it five times a month. When once the mysteries had assumed this promiscuous character, and men were mingled with women with all the licence of nocturnal orgies, there was no crime, no deed of shame, wanting. More uncleanness was wrought by men with men than with women. Whoever would not submit to defilement, or shrank from violating others, was sacrificed as a victim. To regard nothing as impious or criminal was the very sum of their religion. The men, as though seized with madness and with frenzied distortions of their bodies, shrieked out prophecies; the matrons, dressed as Bacchae, their hair dishevelled, rushed down to the Tiber with burning torches, plunged them into the water, and drew them out again, the flame undiminished, as they were made of sulphur mixed with lime. Men were fastened to a machine and hurried off to hidden caves, and they were said to have been rapt away by the gods; these were the men who refused to join their conspiracy or take a part in their crimes or submit to pollution. They [the bacchanales] formed an immense multitude, almost equal to the population of Rome; amongst them were members of noble families both men and women. It had been made a rule for the last two years that no one more than twenty years old should be initiated; they captured those to be deceived and polluted."

Livy – Ab Urbe Condita

by the divinities and believed that humans should strive to live in accordance with nature. Thus they taught that one can achieve freedom and tranquillity only by becoming insensitive to material comforts and external fortune and by dedicating oneself to a life of virtue and wisdom.

In practical terms, Stoicism led to the embracing of an austere lifestyle, upholding the law and not to complain about adversity. During the mid-Republic such things were already a natural part of society and required no external philosophies to reinforce. As Rome grew in wealth and started to embrace indolent lifestyles, Stoicism grew increasingly important as a method of resisting corrupting influences from foreign territories. Vergil's epic poem the Aeneid concerning the founding of Rome epitomises the qualities of Stoicism, reflecting its popularity at the time.

EPICUREANISM (SCHOLA EPICUREA)

"Harvest the day, trusting as little as possible in tomorrow."
Horace – Odes

Unlike its rival Stoicism, Epicureanism advocated the existence of 'free will'. Its objective was to promote happiness by removing the fear of death. Its founder Epicurus, maintained that natural science was important only when applied in making practical decisions that helped people achieve the maximum amount of pleasure, which he identified with gentle motion and the absence of pain.

Epicureanism also embraced the idea that the gods were neutral and did not involve themselves in human affairs. This radical concept planted the seeds which eventually developed into atheism.

"If God is willing to prevent evil, but is not able to, then He is not omnipotent. If He is able, but not willing then He is malevolent. If He is both able and willing then whence cometh evil? If He is neither able nor willing then why call Him God?"
Riddle of Epicurus

In time, the teachings of Epicureanism began to undermine several keystones of Roman society. Firstly that one should live an ascetic life and secondly the public belief in the gods. Both these trends became extremely worrying to the more traditional members of the Senate, who imposed various sumptuary laws to prevent what they saw as the moral decline of the Republic.

The popularity of Epicureanism reached a new high with the publication of De Rerum Natura (On the Nature of Things) written by the Roman poet Lucretius in the 1st century BC.

SKEPTICISM (SCEPTICA RATIO)

The school of Skepticism embraced the questioning of objective knowledge, using logic as a powerful critical device, to skilfully undermine any positive philosophical view.

Sceptics insisted that wisdom consisted in awareness of the extent of one's own ignorance. They believed that the way to tranquillity and fulfilment lies in a complete suspension of judgment of things which one has no true knowledge of.

Carneades, a Skeptic in the mid-2nd century BC was famous for his ability to oppose Stoic arguments and is said to have demonstrated his ability to construct opposing arguments on a famous trip to Rome, as part of an Athenian embassy.

"This Carneades, when he had been sent by the Athenians as ambassador to Rome, disputed copiously on the subject of justice, in the hearing of Galba and Cato, who had been censor, who were at that time the greatest of orators. But on the next day the same man overthrew his own argument by a disputation to the contrary effect, and took away the justice which he had praised on the preceding day"
Lactantius – Divine Institutes

Unfortunately, this scientific display of rhetoric shocked the Roman sense of 'sincerity' and, as a result of that, Cato banned all Greek philosophers (albeit temporarily) from the city.

Somewhat more esoteric than Stoicism or Epicureanism, the school of Scepticism never really flourished as its own school during the Republic but its philosophical concepts were gradually incorporated into rhetoric schooling and thereby wormed itself into Roman society.

PYTHAGOREANISM (SCHOLA PYTHAGOREA)

Pythagoreanism combined ethical, supernatural and mathematical beliefs with many ascetic rules, such as obedience, silence, refraining from sensual pleasures and simplicity of dress and possessions.

They believed in the transmigration of the soul, which when released by death would reincarnate into a succession of animal bodies before regaining the form of a human. Because of this Pythagoreans were vegetarian, eating no meat and somewhat strangely refused to consume beans also. A pure and simplistic life would allow this cycle to be broken, freeing the soul to reside with the gods.

Pythagoreans viewed the world from the perspective of mathematics, musical theory, and astronomy – and thus tried to live in harmony with the insights brought by these sciences. In the 1st century BC Publius Nigidius Figulus famed as both a philosopher and magus, revived the doctrines of Pythagoras in Rome, leading to the start of Neo-Pythagoreanism.

PHILOSOPHIES AS PASSIONS

Roman characters are permitted to take a philosophy as a Passion, as part of character creation, page 133. They may use their philosophy to subvert the normal mores of Roman customs or to resist the influence of others.

For example a Skeptic may substitute their Skepticism passion for Insight when seeing through the lies of another or a stoic could use their Stoicism passion to augment Willpower or Endurance when overcoming physical privation.

As always the Games Master has final say on whether the Passion has relevance in that situation and it should be remembered that the same passion will restrict the behaviour of characters so as not to act outside the bounds of their philosophy.

Mater artium necessitas – Necessity is the mother of invention (Apuleius)

TIME (TEMPUS)

Romans, like all ancient peoples, had great difficulties with keeping track of time, whether the hours of the day or the number of days in the year. The whole problem of seasonal slippage was originally dealt with by the kings during the monarchy. With the advent of the Republic, the problem was passed onto the priests instead, making it a religious duty, which often caused difficulties when the serving Pontiffs and Flamens were lax in performing their tasks.

Roman timekeeping is rather unusual and very confusing. From a modern perspective they lacked accurate clocks (horologia), originally kept a lunar calendar, did not use numbers for dates in a month, and noted years by the names of the reigning consuls.

"We have two measures of time, one annual which the sun bounds by its circuit, the other monthly which the moon embraces as it circles."

Varro – De Re Rustica

Using authentic times and dates can emphasise the atmosphere of a campaign, so the concepts of Roman timekeeping are carefully explained below.

HOURS OF THE DAY (HORAE)

The hour (hora) of the day was calculated using sun dials (solarium). The day was broken into 12 equal parts and the same for the night. This had the interesting effect that the duration of an hour varied between summer and winter. A midsummer daylight hour lasted 75½ minutes, and a midwinter one 44½ minutes.

Of course determining the time when it was cloudy or dark became pretty much a matter of guesswork. Because of this, the first water clock (clepsydra) was installed by the censor P. Scipio Nasica in 159 BC. These soon spread to other public locations in the city.

Romans refer to a particular time by saying the number of the relevant hour, i.e. the first, second, third hour etc. The working day starts with the first hour, beginning at daybreak. Since they have no consideration of minutes, arranging appointments can be quite vague.

Prima hora – first hour
Altera hora – second hour
Tertia hora – third hour
Quarta hora – fourth hour
Quinta hora – fifth hour
Sexta hora – sixth hour
Septima hora – seventh hour
Octava hora – eighth hour
Nona hora – ninth hour
Decima hora – tenth hour
Undecima hora – eleventh hour
Duodecima hora – twelfth hour

The Roman day was broken into two parts: morning (antemeridianum) and afternoon (pomeridianum), with midday being meridies.

LENGTH OF THE WEEK

Republican Romans did not have days of the week. However, on every eighth day a market was held. This was called the nundinae which technically means 'ninth day', because Romans count inclusively; i.e. you start counting by saying the current day as day 1, rather than assigning tomorrow as the first as we do in modern times.

Market days are considered dies fasti (see Calendars page 121).

MONTHS & DATES (MENSES ET DIES)

Originally at its foundation under Romulus, the Roman year possessed only 10 lunar months, each one starting at the new moon. However, this lunar calendar became badly out of synch with the solar year. Thus the second king of Rome, Numa Pompilius, added two further months, Ianuarius and Februarius.

"When Rome's founder established the calendar. He determined there'd be ten months in every year. You knew more about swords than stars, Romulus, surely, since conquering neighbours was your chief concern."

Ovid – Fasti

Despite the two extra months, the year was still 10¼ days too short. Therefore an intercalary period (intercalans) of 22 or 23 days was introduced. This was known as Mercedonius and was inserted after the 23rd of February on alternate years. This somewhat complex system was under the jurisdiction of the Pontiffs and was frequently mishandled until the calendar eventually fell three months out of synch with the seasons.

ROMAN MONTHS

Month Number	Name	Meaning	Number of Days
1	Martius	Mars, God of War	31
2	Aprilis	Venus (Aphrilis), Goddess of Love	29
3	Maius	Maia, Goddess of Spring	31
4	Iunius	Juno, Queen of the Gods	29
5	Quintilis	Fifth Month	31
6	Sextilis	Sixth Month	29
7	September	Seventh Month	29
8	October	Eighth Month	31
9	November	Ninth Month	29
10	December	Tenth Month	29
11	Ianuarius	Janus, God of Doors	29
12	Februarius	Februa, Feast of Purification	28

"That the Romans, at first, comprehended the whole year within ten, and not twelve months, plainly appears by the name of the last, December, meaning the tenth month; and that Martius was the first is likewise evident, for the fifth month after it was called Quintilis, and the sixth Sextilis, and so the rest; whereas, if Januarius and Februarius had, in this account, preceded Martius, Quintilis would have been fifth in name and seventh in reckoning."

Plutarch – Numa Pompilius

It was not until 153 BC that the order of months was officially changed to make December the last month of the year, although it took a while to catch on.

To identify a particular date in a month, the Romans referred to one of three temporal points. The Kalends was the first day of the month (when rent and interest on debts was paid), the Nones the fifth or seventh day and the Ides the 13th or 15th day, the Nones and Ides coming on the later date in the months of March, May, July and October.

All dates were expressed as the number of days before the next temporal point, thus any day after the Ides is counted back from the Kalends of the following month.

Once again the Romans' habit of counting inclusively bewilders matters. Thus for example the 23rd October would be known as 'X Kalends November' (the first day is the Kalends itself, the second day before is the 31st of October, the third day before is the 30th, and so on until the 23rd which is the 10th day before.). To add to the confusion, instead of saying 'two days before' the Romans use the word pridie for the day before.

MARKING THE YEARS

There were two methods of noting the year in Roman society. The first used the names of the ruling consuls of that specific year to identify it, which caused problems if the person you were speaking to had not memorised the long tedious lists of politician's names.

The second method was used by Roman historians of the period when writing their annals. They counted the number of years since the mythical founding of the city of Rome, AUC – ab urbe condita.

"In the 551st year from the foundation of the City, during the consulship of P. Sulpicius Galba and C. Aurelius and within a few months of the conclusion of peace with Carthage, the war with King Philip began."
Livy – Ab Urbe Condita

For the purposes of clarity in this book, most dates are referred to using the modern nomenclature of BC – before Christ. To convert BC to AUC, is a simple matter of subtracting the year from the value of 753 and add one (inclusive counting again), since the first year of the city 1 AUC, is the same year as 753 BC. For example, the assumption of Augustus to the position of the first Emperor of Rome was in year 727 AUC.

CALENDARS (FASTI)

Roman calendars marked each day with a row of letters and abbreviations.

The first letter identified the Nundinae. Since the length of the year was not a multiple of eight, the position of the nundinae would shift each year. To indicate this, a designated letter between A and H would represent the market day for the whole of that year.

If the day was one of the kalends, nones, or ides of that month, it would be marked with the following abbreviations:

K. – Kalends followed by the month; K.IAN for the kalends of January, K.FEB for the kalends of February, etc.

NON – Nones

EIDVS – Ides

The second part of the sequence indicated the type of day it was, which in turn controlled what work was permitted:

C – dies comitalis. Days when Romans could meet in assemblies (comitia) but not if the day was also a nundinae.

N – dies nefasti. Days when no legal transactions or public voting could take place.

F – dies fasti. Days when legal actions were permitted.

EN – endotercissus. 'Cut or split' days which were nefasti in the morning or the evening but fasti otherwise.

LOST IN TIME

Working out the days using Roman nomination is guaranteed to bend the mind of the most able Games Master. So to help out, here are two formulae to calculate dates…

A date after the Ides but before the Kalends of the following month can be calculated by subtracting the modern date from the total number of days in the month plus two. Thus October 29th would be… 31 (days in October) +2 and minus 29; which equals 4. Thus Oct 29th is 'IV Kalends November'.

A date before the Nones or Ides can be calculated by subtracting the modern date from the total number of days in the month plus one. Thus May 3rd is… 7 (Nones) +1 -3; or the 'V Nonas Maius'. Or May 10th is… 15 (Ides) +1 -10; being the 'VI Idus Maius'.

For those of you still helplessly confused, here's a table.

1st	Kalendis	Kalendis	Kalendis
2nd	VI Nonas	IV Nonas	IV Nonas
3rd	V Nonas	III Nonas	III Nonas
4th	IV Nonas	Pridie Nonas	Pridie Nonas
5th	III Nonas	Nonis	Nonis
6th	Pridie Nonas	VIII Idus	VIII Idus
7th	Nonis	VII Idus	VII Idus
8th	VIII Idus	VI Idus	VI Idus
9th	VII Idus	V Idus	V Idus
10th	VI Idus	IV Idus	IV Idus
11th	V Idus	III Idus	III Idus
12th	IV Idus	Pridie Idus	Pridie Idus
13th	III Idus	Idibus	Idibus
14th	Pridie Idus	XVII Kalends	XVI Kalends
15th	Idibus	XVI Kalends	XV Kalends
16th	XVII Kalends	XV Kalends	XIV Kalends
17th	XVI Kalends	XIV Kalends	XIII Kalends
18th	XV Kalends	XIII Kalends	XII Kalends
19th	XIV Kalends	XII Kalends	XI Kalends
20th	XIII Kalends	XI Kalends	X Kalends
21st	XII Kalends	X Kalends	IX Kalends
22nd	XI Kalends	IX Kalends	VIII Kalends
23rd	X Kalends	VIII Kalends	VII Kalends
24th	IX Kalends	VII Kalends	VI Kalends
25th	VIII Kalends	VI Kalends	V Kalends
26th	VII Kalends	V Kalends	IV Kalends
27th	VI Kalends	IV Kalends	III Kalends
28th	V Kalends	III Kalends	Pridie Kalendis
29th	IV Kalends	Pridie Kalendis	-
30th	III Kalends	-	-
31st	Pridie Kalendis	-	-

NP – indicated public holidays (feriae) and were considered dies nefasti.

FP – were another kind of religious holiday but the specific meaning has been lost.

FESTIVALS (FERIAE)

There were a great number of festivals and holidays (holy days) celebrated in Rome. At these times, citizens suspended politics and law suits and slaves were freed from labour. Originally 'feast days', these originated back to the early days of the Republic when the aristocracy would give banquets to feed the poor.

There are three types of feriae. Feriae stativae, annual festivals which occur on fixed days, feriae conceptivae, festivals whose dates are determined yearly by priests or magistrates and feriae imperativae, one-off holidays proclaimed by consuls, prætors or dictators to celebrate military victories.

PLOT HOOKS

Ω The idea of being sacrificed to the gods by the rite of ver sacrum is an excellent way of starting a campaign during the early period of Rome. The characters could all be exiled from their home city and led to Rome by a divinely inspired beast, which accompanies them. There they could be driven by the desire for just retribution to take vengeance on their families who cast them out. Conversely, the characters could be expelled from Rome instead and forced to create their own city. This would give them a chance to rise to the top of the hierarchy of the newly founded state and possibly grow to become a rival of Rome herself.

Ω Early Rome had several purification rites which utilised the concept of the scapegoat, a volunteer who took upon themselves the ills of the city and then was ritually exiled or sacrificed. In later years these victims were usually replaced with ceremonial replicas. However, many cults may have simply performed their true rites in secret and this idea could be incorporated into a scenario in several different ways.

During a disaster affecting the city (e.g. a pestilence), the senate could request a scapegoat for the people of Rome. If a player character volunteers for the position, his family will be raised in honour (perhaps being promoted to the equestrian class) and receive a large donation of money. The character would either have to leave the city forever, or be actually killed. However, in return, the Games Master could reward the brave, self-sacrificial act by granting the player bonus characteristics, skill points or divine blessings to his next character, especially if from the same family.

On the other hand, the scapegoat maybe an unwilling victim; a patron, friend or family member of one of the player characters. The adventure would be a hunt for the cult that has kidnapped the victim; a slow unveiling of growing horror, ultimately leading to a direct confrontation on the night of the ceremony. Of course if the scapegoat is freed in time, certain dire disasters could then affect the city, forcing the characters to feel guilty for their interruption of the sacred rites, or maybe even performing a reversal of their original intentions.

Ω The excesses of the Bacchanalia are an excellent thread to weave into adventures. Although the Senate banned the cult in the early second century BC, it does not mean that it did not continue in a more secretive nature. Initiation into the Bacchic rites can be used in a variety of different ways to intrigue or hamper player characters.

Subversive Secret Societies – These could be groups dedicated to the overthrow of the Republic and the Bacchic rites proof of the member's dedication to the cause and a way of blackmailing them if they suffer hesitation in following orders. Something like the situation which Cataline was accused of when he organised his rebellion from amongst the young men of the city.

Mythic Horror – The Bacchanals could be used as a source of otherworldly power in ostensibly magic-free campaigns. The perverse rites and human sacrifices a source of horror for the player characters, in particular if their own family members or trusted friends are victims. In such campaigns the bacchanales can be reoccurring enemies.

Seductive Power – For mature groups, the player characters could be seduced into the rites of Bacchus; offering tantalising rises in social and political rank, in exchange for initiating themselves ever deeper into the cult. Sadistic Games Masters could inflict serious anxiety on the characters, by carefully describing the perversity, degradation or horror required at each level. These need not be sexually orientated… instead involving such acts as giving their sister to the cult, publicly betraying a long respected patron, stealing items dedicated to a god from his temple and so on. Each test should increasingly strain the character's morals to the limit, until they eventually cannot perform what is required of them and must try to break free of the cult's hooks.

Mens sana in corpore sano – A sound mind in a sound body (Juvenal)

CHARACTERS

To generate Mythic Rome characters, follow the Character Creation rules as laid out in MYTHRAS but using the alternate Characteristics, Cultures and Professions described here.

ROMAN CHARACTERISTICS

Roman characters are generated as per the standard MYTHRAS rules, except for when rolling the SIZ characteristic. It is often stated in the annals of the time that Romans were distinctly shorter than the northern barbarians they frequently encountered. For that reason, Roman PCs should roll 2d6+3 for their SIZ and reserve the normal 2d6+6 for Celtic and Germanic slaves or enemies.

NAMES

To a Roman, his name was everything. It represented his family, his clan and gave him the dignity and gravitas earned by his ancestors. Names were so important that they were passed from father to first son with little or no change, which made identification of a particular male family member sometimes difficult without using the epithet of 'the elder' (maior) for the father and 'younger' (minor) for the son.

Patrician and Equestrian names are usually made up of three parts. First was the forename (praenomen), used by relations or close friends. Strangely, only 18 different forenames were used during the later Republic. Next was the clan name (nomen), which denoted the common ancestor of the gens. Lastly was the name of the family branch (cognomen) within the clan.

Often the cognomen was based on some physical or personality trait of the founder of the family line and since it was initially awarded by his fellows (and not by the founder himself), they were often derogatory. With this in mind, Games Masters are encouraged to choose cognomina for his players, or award them in play for their actions.

A few individuals who performed outstanding service or virtue were granted an additional honorific (agnomen) in recognition of their deeds. Such accolades could only be granted by others, generally by approbation of the Senate.

Most, but not all, plebeians lack a cognomen. Slaves are normally given a single nickname, usually something descriptive based on nationality or physical appearance. Unmarried females also only have a single name, the feminine form of their father's nomen. To generate female nomen, you simply replace the final letters 'us' with an 'a'. Thus the female version of Flavius would be Flavia. Multiple daughters also required epithets to distinguish between them, such as 'greater' (Maxima), 'lesser' (Minima), 'the first' (Prima), the second (Secunda) and so on. By the late Republic, wedded women would adopt the feminine form of their husband's cognomen as a second name.

Of course, depending on the tone of the campaign, character names can simply be linguistically humorous – following in the tradition of 'Bigus Dickus' in Monty Python's Life of Brian. A comprehensive list of names appears on the following pages.

SOCIAL CLASS

Characters may roll on the Social Class table to determine their place in Roman society. However, the Games Master is at liberty to restrict certain classes or pre-define what class the characters will be in order to fit the intended campaign. If desired, the Wealth rating of the character's class can be used to limit which professions are available to them.

SOCIAL CLASS

d100	Social Class	Av. Wealth Rating	Wealth Cap
01-02	Foreigner	Any	Wealthy
03-20	Slave	Destitute	Poor
21-70	Freedman	Poor	Affluent
71-95	Plebeian	Average	Affluent
96-99	Equestrian	Affluent	Wealthy
100	Patrician	Wealthy	Wealthy

ROMAN CULTURE

All native Roman characters start with the Civilised culture (MYTHRAS page 14). Foreigners and slaves use either Civilised (Etruscan, Carthaginian, Greek, Macedonian, Parthian, Egyptian and Cappadocian), Barbarian (Gallic, Germanic, Hispanic, Numidian), or Nomadic (Scythian) as defined by their nationality.

NAMES

P*raenomen (First Names):* Appius, Aulus, Decimus, Gaius, Gnaeus, Kaeso, Lucius, Mamercus, Manius, Marcus, Numerius, Oppius, Publius, Quintus, Servius, Sextus, Tiberius, and Titus

Nomen (Clan Names): Abudius, Aeternius, Afranius, Albinius, Albius, Antius, Appuleius, Aquilius, Atrius, Caecilius, Caedicius, Caelius, Calidius, Calpurnius, Calvisius, Caninius, Cassius, Catilius, Cicereius, Claudius, Cloelius, Cocceius, Comicius, Cominius, Cornelius, Cornuficius, Curius, Curtius, Decius, Dexius, Didius, Domitius, Duilius, Equitius, Fabius, Fabricius, Flaminius, Flavius, Folius, Fulvius, Furius, Gabinius, Geganius, Gellius, Genucius, Helvius, Herennius, Hermenius, Hirtius, Horatius, Hortensius, Iulius, Iunius, Iuventius, Labienus, Laelius, Larcius, Laronius, Licinius, Livius, Lucilius, Lucretius, Lutatius, Manlius, Marcius, Marius, Memmius, Menenius, Minicius, Modius, Mucius, Munatius, Naevius, Nautius, Nerius, Nigidius, Nonius, Norbanus, Numicius, Octavius, Ogulnius, Opimius, Oppius, Otacilius, Ovidius, Ovinius, Ovius, Papirius, Pedius, Peducaeus, Perpenna, Pinarius, Plautius, Pleminius, Poetelius, Pompeius, Pomponius, Pontius, Popillius, Porcius, Postumius, Publilius, Pupius, Quintilius, Quintius, Rabuleius, Romilius, Roscius, Rutilius, Salonius, Sallustius, Salvius, Scribonius, Sellius, Sempronius, Sentius, Sergius, Sertorius, Servilius, Sestius, Sicinius, Sosius, Statilius, Suetonius, Sulpicius, Tarpeius, Tarquinius, Tarquitius, Terentius, Tetrilius, Titinius, Titurius, Titurnius, Trebellius, Trebius, Trebonius, Tuccius, Tullius, Valerius, Vatinius, Ventidius, Vergilius, Veturius, Villius, Vipsanius, Virginius, Vitellius, Vibius, Vitruvius, Volcatius, and Volumnius

Cognomen (Family Name/Nickname):

Adjutor – the helper
Adventor – the visitor
Agelastus – he who doesn't laugh
Agricola – the farmer
Agrippa – he who was born feet first
Ahala – cognomen of gens Servilia
Albinus – cognomen of gens Postumia
Amandus – loveable
Ancus – crooked/bent
Aper – the boar
Aquila – the eagle
Aquilinus – eagle-like
Aquilius – brown
Arcarius – he who deals with money/cash
Armiger – he who bear arms
Arvina – the fat one
Asellio – the keeper of donkeys
Asina – the female donkey
Asprenas – rough/hard
Audens – the daring
Auspex – the diviner
Avitus – he who takes after his grandfather
Balbillus – Probably diminutive of Balbus
Balbus – he who stutters
Barbatus – the bearded one
Baro – the dunce
Bassus – the plump (i.e. fat) one
Bellator – the fighter / the warmonger

Bellicus – warlike
Bellus – good-looking
Bestius – the animal
Bibaculus – heavy drinker
Bibulus – he who doesn't refuse a drink.
Blandus – flattering
Bonifatus – he on whom fate smiles
Brocchus – toothy
Brutus – the stupid, foolish one
Burrus – the red haired one
Buteo – the buzzard
Caecina – cognomen of gens Licinia
Caecus – the blind
Caelestis – the heavenly one
Caepio – the onion vendor
Caesar – with the fine head of hair
Caldus – hot tempered
Calvinus – cognomen of gentes Domitia & Veturia
Calvus – the bald
Camillus – a child who helped during sacrifices
Candidus – the bright, the white
Capito – he who has a big head
Caprarius – the goat keeper
Carbo – charcoal
Carinus – (nut) brown
Carnifex – the executioner
Cascus – the archaic
Castus – the pure, chaste one
Catilina – cognomen of gens Sergia
Cato – cognomen of gens Porcia
Catulus – calf, cognomen of gens Lutatia
Catus – the shrewd
Celatus – the hidden
Celeris – the quick
Celsus – high, tall
Cerinthus – waxy
Cethegus – cognomen of gens Cornelia
Cicero – chick pea
Cimber – the Cimbrian
Cinna – cognomen of gens Cornelia
Citus – the swift
Clarus – the famous
Clemens – the forgiving
Collatinus – cognomen of gens Tarquinia
Columella – little column
Commodus – favourable
Concessus – the gift; granted
Constans – the reliable
Corbulo – little basket
Cordus – late-born
Cornutus – horned
Corvinus – like a crow
Corvus – the crow, cognomen of gens Valeria
Cotta – cognomen of Gens Aurelia
Crassus – the fat
Crispinus – the curled
Crispus – he who has curly hair
Culleolus – leather sack
Curio – priest of a Curia
Cursor – the swift
Damasippus – cognomen of gens Licinia
Disertus – the eloquent
Dolabella – the pick-axe
Drusus – cognomen of gens Livia
Durus – the hard

Eugenius – born from a good family
Fabillus – little Fabius, from the gens Fabia
Facilis – the easy
Falco – the falcon
Familiaris – the householder
Felix – the lucky
Festus – the merry
Fidelis – the faithful
Figulus – the potter
Fimbria – the fringe
Firmus – the firm
Flaccus – the floppy, with floppy ears
Florens – blossoming
Florus – the flowery
Fortunatus – the fortunate
Fronto – he who has a prominent forehead
Frugi – the fruit
Frugius – the fruitful
Fuscus – the dark, the dark-haired
Gemellus – the twin
Germanus – blood-relative
Geta – the Getan (a Thracian tribe), cognomen of gens Licinia
Glabrio – the hairless, cognomen of gens Acilia
Glaucia – the bleater
Gracchus – cognomen of gens Sempronia
Gracilis – the slender
Gratus – welcome
Hilarus – the cheerful
Homullus – the midget
Humilis – the low-born
Ingenuus – born of free (respectable) parents
Iustus – the just
Laeca – cognomen of gens Portia
Laenas – cognomen of gens Popillia
Laevinus – from the Laevi, an Italian tribe
Lateranus – cognomen of gentes Claudia & Sextia
Lentulus – the slow, cognomen of gens Cornelia
Lepidus – the charming
Libo – cognomen of gentes Marcia & Scribonia
Ligur – the Ligurian, a celtic tribe, cognomen of gentes Aelia & Octavia
Longus – the tall
Longinus – cognomen of gens Cassia
Lucullus – small grove, cognomen of gens Licinia
Lupus – the wolf, cognomen of gens Rutilia
Lurco – the glutton
Macro – the big
Maius – born in May
Maior – born first
Mancinus – cognomen of gens Mucia
Mansuetus – the mild
Marcellinus – little Marcellus
Marcellus – little Marcus
Marinus – the sailor
Maritimus – of the sea
Maro – cognomen of Vergilia
Maternus – related to mater
Mercator – the merchant
Merula – the blackbird
Messala – cognomen of gens Valeria
Messor – the reaper
Metellus – the army follower
Moderatus – the temperate
Montanus – of the mountains

Murena – the moray (eel), cognomen of gens Licinia

Mus – the mouse, the rat

Musa – the muse or a poet

Musicus – musical

Nasica – having a thin, long nose

Naso – the nose, cognomen of gens Ovidia

Natalis – on the birthday

Nepos – grandchild

Nero – cognomen of gens Claudia

Nerva – cognomen of gentes Cocceia & Silia

Nigellus – diminutive of Niger, black/dark

Niger – black/dark

Nigrinus – related to Niger, black/dark

Oceanus – he who lives by the ocean

Optatus – chosen, desired

Otho – cognomen of gens Roscia

Paenula – wearing a hooded travelling cloak

Paetus – blinking

Pansa – he who walks with his legs spread

Pappus – old man

Pastor – shepherd

Paterculus – daddy

Paternus – fatherly

Patiens – the patient

Paulinus – a little, a small quantity

Paulus – a little, a small quantity, a small thing

Pavo – the peacock

Pennus – sharp

Peregrinus – the foreigner

Pertinax – stubborn

Pictor – the painter

Pilatus – dense, armed with a pilum

Piso – the mortar, cognomen of gens Calpurnia

Placidus – the peaceful

Plautus – flat footed

Pollio – the strong

Poplicola / Publicola – of the people

Postumus – the last born

Primus – the first one, the first born

Priscus – very ancient, old-fashioned

Probus – the upright

Proculus – born while the father was away

Pudens – the sensible

Pulcher – the handsome

Quietus – the calm

Ravilla – grey eyed

Reburrus – he with hair tied back

Regillus – little king, cognomen of gens Aemilia

Regulus – the child king

Rufinus – of red hair

Rufus – reddish, ginger haired

Rullus – the rude

Ruso – cognomen of the gens Abudia

Rusticus – from the countryside

Sacerdos – the priest, cognomen of gens Licinia

Salinator – he who harvests salt

Scaeva – left handed

Scaevola – cognomen of gens Mucia

Scapula – with large shoulders

Scaurus – the lame

Scipio – triumphal wand, cognomen of gens Cornelia

Scrofa – the sow

Secundus – the second one; blessed

Seneca – probably related to senex, the old man

Senecio – probably related to senex, the old man

Seronatus – he who was born after term

Severus – the strict

Silanus – from the forest, cognomen of gens Iunia

Silo – snub-nosed

Silus – cognomen of gens Sergia

Silvanus – from the forest

Similis – the same, he who bears a resemblance

Simplex – simple, straight forward

Sisenna – cognomen of gens Cornelia

Speratus – hoped for

Strabo – cross-eyed

Sulla – cognomen of gens Cornelia

Superbus – the proud

Superstes – the survivor

Sura – having large calves

Tacitus – the quiet

Tertius – the third one

Tranquillus – the calm

Triarius – the rear guard

Tuditanus – cognomen in gens Sempronia

Tutor – protector

Urbicus – from the city, city dweller

Ursinus – related to Ursus, the bear

Ursus – the bear

Valens – strong, in good health

Valgus – knock-kneed

Varro – cognomen of gens Terentia

Varus – bow-legged

Vatius – bow-legged

Venator – the hunter

Verecundus – the shy

Verres – cognomen of gens Cornelia

Verrucosus – having warts

Verus – the truthful

Vespillo – the undertaker

Viator – the traveller

Victor – the conqueror

Vindex – the avenger

Virilis – the manly

Vitalis – the vigorous

Vocula – the soft-spoken

Vopiscus – the surviving twin

Vulso – he who has regular spasms

Agnomina (Honorific Titles)

Achaicus – conqueror of Achaea

Africanus – victor in Africa

Britannicus – victor over the Britons

Magnus – great

Maximus – very great

Numantius – conqueror of Numania

Pius – dutiful

Sapiens – prudent

The cultural Combat Style depends entirely on the region and period the game is set. It is important to remember that from the founding of Rome up until the Marian Reforms, every Roman citizen (see The Populace page 8) was expected to serve in the legions, as part of his civic duties – the army was formed from mandatory annual conscription and professional soldiers did not appear until the start of the 1st century BC. To reflect this, citizen characters prior to this date are permitted access to the Roman Legion combat style, comprising of the military arms and traits of that period – which are described in The Army chapter (Monarchy page 89, Early Republic page 92 and mid-Republic page 95).

Conversely, most citizens of the Late Republic have little or no military training and a reduced chance to purchase weaponry, leaving those who are not professional legionaries or gladiators access only to the default Roman Citizen combat style.

Roman Citizen Combat Style: Sica, Pugio, Club, Thrown Stone; Street Mob trait (Permits a group of three or more fellow citizens to utilise the Intimidate creature ability (MYTHRAS page 216), but only before combat starts or when they have their opponents at a severe disadvantage).

In a similar fashion, foreign characters would be expected to learn the military combat style of their nation, at least before the period when they were conquered by Rome.

PROFESSIONS (DISCIPLINAE)

Not everyone in Rome works or has a strict career. Some of the following professions simply reflect lifestyles, enabling the character to learn the skills necessary to survive or maintain their social class. All are based on the format presented in the MYTHRAS rules, with an additional line which grants a bonus or penalty to a character's Status skill according to how the profession was viewed in Roman society.

Most of the following professions are exclusively male, save for those of Dancer, Musician, Prostitute and Slave, for which alternative feminine Latin titles are given.

ACTOR (HISTRIO)

Actors are held with contempt in Roman society, primarily because they are viewed as prostituting themselves for public entertainment. In fact, some are indeed prostitutes on the side. Actors work on a per commission basis, usually hired to perform at particular festivals and games, or travelling as a troupe and performing one or two days at each town before moving on. Most actors are slaves or foreigners and it would be a social scandal if a plebeian would lower himself to act. In fact senators have been removed from the Senate for engaging in public performance.

Ω Wealth: Poor to Average
Ω Status: Characters who are, or have been actors, have their Status reduced by 10%
Ω Standard Skills: Athletics, Dance, Deceit, Influence, Insight, Native Tongue, Sing
Ω Professional Skills: Acting, Language (Greek), Literacy, Musicianship, Rhetoric, Seduction, Streetwise

ARTIST (ARTIFEX)

See Craftsman.

ROMAN SNOBBERY

Most professions greatly affected the social status of the family which depended upon it. As can be seen by the following quote, Romans are extremely social conscious.

"Now in regard to trades and other means of livelihood, which ones are to be considered becoming to a gentleman and which ones are vulgar, we have been taught, in general, as follows: First, those means of livelihood are rejected as undesirable which incur people's ill-will, as those of tax-gatherers and usurers. Unbecoming to a gentleman, too, and vulgar are the means of livelihood of all hired workmen whom we pay for mere manual labour, not for artistic skill; for in their case the very wage they receive is a pledge of their slavery. Vulgar we must consider those also who buy from wholesale merchants to retail immediately; for they would get no profits without a great deal of downright lying; and indeed, there is no action that is meaner than lying. And all craftsmen are engaged in vulgar trades; for no workshop can have anything liberal about it. Least respectable of all are those trades which cater for sensual pleasures: 'fishmongers, butchers, cooks, and poulterers, and fishermen', as Terence says. Add to these, if you please, the perfumers, dancers, and all performers of the ludus talarius. But the professions in which either a higher degree of intelligence is required or from which no small benefit to society is derived – medicine and architecture, for example, and teaching – these are proper for those whose social position they become. Trade, if it is on a small scale, is to be considered vulgar; but if wholesale and on a large scale, importing large quantities from all parts of the world and distributing to many without misrepresentation, it is not to be greatly disparaged. Nay, it even seems to deserve the highest respect, if those who are engaged in it, satiated, or rather, I should say, satisfied with the fortunes they have made, make their way from the port to a country estate, as they have often made it from the sea into port. But of all the occupations by which gain is secured, none is better than agriculture, none more profitable, none more delightful, none more becoming to a freeman."

Cicero – De Officiis

ATHLETE (ATHLETA)

Although strictly speaking there were not any professional athletes in Rome, a character could be a Greek athlete who has been brought to the city by a wealthy patron in order to put on a performance at the games or an ex-champion who offers his skills as a personal fitness trainer. Most are skilled in the classic sporting disciplines of the Pentathlon and spend most of their time at the gymnasiums in the baths or the Campus Martius. Only Olympic champions are particularly well regarded but their fame soon fades along with patronage. Otherwise, most are looked down upon for either making life hell at the gymnasium or for following what is in reality a Greek rather than a Roman tradition.

Ω Wealth: Poor or Average
Ω Status: Athletes suffer a 10% penalty to their Status However, Olympic champions gain a temporary 25% bonus to their Status for several years, after which their normal Status penalty is cleared
Ω Standard Skills: Athletics, Brawn, Endurance, Evade, Pugilism, Swim, Willpower
Ω Professional Skills: Acrobatics, Culture (Other), Gambling, Language (Other), Lore (Any), Streetwise and the Pentathlete Combat Style (Wrestling, Discus, Javelin; no trait)

BANKER (ARGENTARIUS)

Bankers and usurers are the most despised people in Rome. They charge a steep annual rate to keep your money safe or to issue credit notes against it when your travel. Worse still, they impose extortionate rates of interest if you are foolish enough to borrow their money. Most bankers have to hire bodyguards for personal protection, to keep their strongboxes safe and act as enforcers to extract payment from late payers. Although bankers often come from the equestrian class, they are usually ostracised by polite society.

Ω Wealth: Affluent to Wealthy
Ω Status: Bankers are barely tolerated and suffer a 15% penalty to their Status
Ω Standard Skills: Brawn, Conceal, Deceit, Influence, Insight, Locale, Willpower
Ω Professional Skills: Bureaucracy, Commerce, Gambling, Language (Other), Literacy, Lore (Any), Streetwise

BARBER (BARBITONSOR)

Barbers perform several vital services. As well as haircutting, hairdressing, shaving and plucking; barbers performed extraction of teeth. Barbers are also sources of daily news and gossip. Most work on the streets, where the light is better and they avoid paying rent. Barbers do not arrive in Rome until the mid-Republic, since men preferred beards up to this time.

Ω Wealth: Poor to Average
Ω Status: Barbers are regarded with neutrality and suffer no penalty to their Status
Ω Standard Skills: Customs, Deceit, First Aid, Influence, Insight, Locale, Perception
Ω Professional Skills: Commerce, Courtesy, Craft (Barber), Healing, Language (Other), Lore (Any), Streetwise

BEAST HUNTER (VENATORES)

Hunters who work in the amphitheatre killing unusual animals. Use the Gladiator profession.

BEGGAR (MENDICUS)

Usually beggars are freed-men or foreigners. No citizen would lower himself to such work without losing their Status first. Beggars generally sport (or fake) terrible scars or injuries that help them evoke pity from potential donators. Most beggars belong to a gang for mutual protection and hang about the bridges and main streets of the city where the most people pass.

- Ω Wealth: Destitute or sometimes Poor
- Ω Status: Beggars are not well thought of in Roman society and suffer a 10% penalty to their Status
- Ω Standard Skills: Customs, Deceit, Evade, Influence, Insight, Locale, Perception
- Ω Professional Skills: Acting, Commerce, Language (Other), Streetwise, plus three other professional skills reflecting their previous life before they were reduced to destitution.

BODYGUARD (STIPATOR)

These were usually ex-gladiators. See the Gladiator profession for details.

BUREAUCRAT (ADMINISTRATOR)

Bureaucrats are members of the Roman civil service and were the real power behind the magistrates and Senate. They fulfil the tasks of administrators, scribes, customs officials, trade supervisors and judicial secretaries. Normally only State owned slaves and a few freedmen work in the bureaucracy, and most magistrates find the internal workings unfathomable.

- Ω Wealth: Most are secretly Average to Affluent, perhaps due to corruption or extortion
- Ω Status: Bureaucrats are the heart of the Republic and suffer no penalty to their Status
- Ω Standard Skills: Customs, Deceit, Influence, Insight, Locale, Perception, Willpower
- Ω Professional Skills: Bureaucracy, Commerce, Courtesy, Language (Other), Literacy, Lore (Any), Streetwise

CHARIOTEER (AURIGA)

Reckless, sporting heroes of the Roman world, they are both famous and short-lived. Racing in the Circus Maximus is dangerous, since both on and off the track there are few rules save to win at any cost. Successful charioteers or even their horses are frequently cursed, and sometimes poisoned prior to important races.

- Ω Wealth: Average, although successful charioteers can achieve Affluent, or even Wealthy.
- Ω Status: Famous charioteers gain a 10% bonus to their Status
- Ω Standard Skills: Brawn, Conceal, Deceit, Drive, Endurance, Evade, Perception
- Ω Professional Skills: Acrobatics, Commerce, Gambling, Language (Other), Mechanisms, Seduction, Streetwise

CRAFTSMAN (FABER)

Craftsmen are the artists and manufacturers of the Roman world. All are plebeians or freedmen, since no member of the equestrian or patrician class would openly lower themselves to such work. Most craftsmen sell their goods from the front of their workshop, which normally opens out directly onto the street. Artists work on a commission basis, to decorate homes, paint or carve statues and so forth. Most lack the funds to simply create art for art's sake

- Ω Wealth: Poor to Average
- Ω Status: Trades with a social stigma such as fishermen, undertakers, dyers, launderers etc., suffer a 10% penalty to Status
- Ω Standard Skills: Brawn, Drive, Endurance, Influence, Insight, Locale, Perception
- Ω Professional Skills: Art (Any), Commerce, Craft (Any), Engineering, Language (Other), Mechanisms, Streetwise

DANCER (SALTATOR OR SALTATRIX)

Dancers are effectively the same as Actors in terms of skills, their use as prostitutes and public attitude towards them.

DILETTANTE (ARDELIO)

Dilettantes represent those members of the wealthy classes who neither work for a living, nor actively seek magisterial office to support the Republic. Many live in indolent luxury, waited on hand and foot by slaves and providing patronage for artists and poets. Some dilettantes are young, dissatisfied sons of high rank blocked from a political career, who waste their time (and father's money) on unceasing entertainment and dubious intrigues.

- Ω Wealth: Affluent to Wealthy
- Ω Status: Dilettantes gain no adjustment to their Status
- Ω Standard Skills: Athletics, Dance, Deceit, Influence, Insight, Locale, Sing
- Ω Professional Skills: Courtesy, Gambling, Literacy, Lore (Any), Rhetoric, Seduction, Streetwise

DIVINER (HARUSPEX)

Most diviners are foreign soothsayers who pander to Roman superstitions. They live a borderline legal existence usually paying bribes to city magistrates to be overlooked during their frequent expulsions from Rome. Many people, even those of the highest classes, seek the advice of diviners before undertaking decisions. Diviners use many strange and exotic methods to see the future, some are frauds or self-deluded, but others show an uncanny ability for precognition (see Divination on page 141). Practitioners of divination are often sought out to perform other, darker, magical rites...

- Ω Wealth: Poor to Affluent
- Ω Status: Most are simply treated as foreigners but those who display reliable accuracy or otherworldly powers receive a 10% bonus to Status
- Ω Standard Skills: Customs, Dance, Deceit, Influence, Insight, Locale, Willpower
- Ω Professional Skills: Bureaucracy, Divination, Language (Other), Literacy, Lore (Any), Rhetoric, Streetwise

DOCTOR (MEDICUS)

Doctors must decide whether to be either Physicians or Surgeons. Somewhat surprisingly of the two, the surgeon was considered inferior, because most surgery was limited to battlefield treatments and usually failed to preserve life despite rudimentary knowledge of disinfectants. Physicians on the other hand specialise in treating illness using physical exercises, sanitary lifestyle, diet and medicines. They cannot perform surgery since they are specifically forbidden by the Hippocratic oath to cause harm to a patient. Most doctors of either speciality possessed questionable knowledge of medicine or anatomy and even less about their dubious cures. In many situations the doctor was only called in as the last resort. Doctors are usually fluent in Greek, as most medical texts are written in that language.

Ω Wealth: Average to Affluent

Ω Status: Doctors are an honourable profession and suffer no penalties to Status

Ω Standard Skills: Customs, First Aid, Influence, Insight, Locale, Perception, Willpower

Ω Professional Skills: Commerce, Healing, Language (Other), Literacy, Lore (Any), Rhetoric, Streetwise

---

"All the more if they send their [Greek] doctors here. They have sworn to kill all barbarians with medicine – and they charge a fee for doing it, in order to be trusted and to work more easily. They call us barbarians, too, of course, and opici, a dirtier name than the rest. I have forbidden you to deal with doctors"

Pliny quoting Cato the Elder

FARMER (AGRICOLA)

Farmers in early Rome are the backbone of its economic and military strength. Most are smallholders, working the land themselves to feed their family and barter excess produce for other necessities. However over time, with the drain of manpower in the ceaseless wars, many small farms go to seed and the families are forced to sell to cover their debts. In later years the yeoman farmer still exists but now as either a tenant farmer, or the manager of larger, conglomerated farms (latifundia), which are worked by slaves. For landlords of huge estates, use the Dilettante profession instead.

Ω Wealth: Poor to Average

Ω Status: Farmers are traditionally well thought of and those who own their own land gain a 10% bonus to Status

Ω Standard Skills: Athletics, Brawn, Drive, Endurance, Locale, Perception, Ride

Ω Professional Skills: Commerce, Craft (Any), Language (Other), Lore (Farming or Herding), Navigation, Survival, Track

GLADIATOR (GLADIATOR)

Usually, but not always, freedmen or slaves, gladiators fight men or beasts for public entertainment. There are many specialities of gladiator, each one trained to fight in different weapon and armour combinations. Combatants who put on a spirited or entertaining show usually survive defeat, assuming their injuries can be treated. Popular gladiators are granted the rudis (wooden training sword) that earns their freedom from the amphitheatre. Gladiators can also earn extra money or gifts by acting as sex-slaves or bodyguards during or after their careers.

Ω Wealth: Poor to Average

Ω Status: Gladiators start with a penalty of 10% to their Status, but each victory adds 1% up to a maximum of +10%. Losing reduces it likewise. Retired champions retain their final bonus/penalty for the remainder of their lives

Ω Standard Skills: Athletics, Brawn, Customs, Endurance, Evade, First Aid, Pugilism

Ω Professional Skills: Acting, Commerce, Gambling, Language (Other), Seduction, Streetwise, and one gladiatorial Combat Style chosen from those described on page 84

LABOURER (OPERARIUS)

Labourers are slaves, freedmen or plebeians who perform the backbreaking work of construction, engineering or farming. They are usually poorly educated and poorly skilled but some are men who have fallen from high station either via poverty or criminal activity.

Ω Wealth: Destitute to Average

Ω Status: Labourers are disparaged and suffer a 10% penalty to Status

Ω Standard Skills: Athletics, Brawn, Drive, Endurance, Locale, Perception, Willpower

Ω Professional Skills: Commerce, Craft (Any), Engineering, Gambling, Language (Other), Streetwise, Survival

LAWYER (JURISCONSULTUS)

Strictly speaking there were no professional lawyers in Republican Rome. Young men of high social class took up litigation in the law courts as a prequel to serving in the magistracies of the Curses Honorum. Use Senator instead.

LEGIONARY (LEGIONARIUS)

This career is for those professional legionaries raised in the first century BC. They are given months of hard training in diverse skills. Tough, disciplined and (usually) loyal to their generals, ex-legionaries are sometimes granted land to farm after extended campaigns. Legionaries often learn other languages in their postings around the empire and are experienced with several different weapons. Roman marines are basically land troops placed aboard ship.

Ω Wealth: Destitute to Average

Ω Status: Although military service is the epitome of a true Roman, professional legionaries are usually recruited from the dispossessed. Only centurions or professional legates gain a 10% bonus to Status

Ω Standard Skills: Athletics, Brawn, Conceal, Endurance, Perception, Pugilism, Swim. Auxiliary cavalry replace Swim with Ride

Ω Professional Skills: Command (Centurions or Officers only), Craft (Carpentry, Leatherworking, Masonry or Smithing), Engineering, Gambling, Language (Other), Ride (Auxilia only), Survival, and the relevant Late Republican military Combat Style as described on page 99

MAGISTRATE (MAGISTRATUS)

A magistracy is a short term appointment. Use Senator instead.

MERCHANT (MERCATOR)

Whereas craftsmen manufacture and sell their own goods, merchants are experts in buying and selling goods in bulk. Generally this involves moving merchandise to and from the city, or acting as an auctioneer for others. Merchants have less Status than craftsmen, save those who run (or rather own) huge import/export enterprises where they cease to be the negotiating middleman. Most merchants have a Lore skill appropriate to the goods they trade or business procedures, such as Geography or Accounting.

- Ω Wealth: Average to Wealthy
- Ω Status: Merchants other than large scale wholesalers suffer a 10% penalty to their Status
- Ω Standard Skills: Boating, Drive, Deceit, Insight, Influence, Locale, Ride
- Ω Professional Skills: Commerce, Courtesy, Culture (Any), Language (Other), Lore (Any), Navigation, Streetwise

MUSICIAN (MUSICUS OR MUSICA)

Although decried by some snobbish Romans as a sign of decadence, musical performances are common and skilled musicians highly valued. Music has great importance in certain religious contexts and is popular at feasts or celebrations. Most musicians have a range of performance skills to satisfy their patrons.

- Ω Wealth: Poor to Average
- Ω Status: By the late Republic as the arts become more valued, musicians suffer no penalty to their Status
- Ω Standard Skills: Customs, Dance, Deceit, Influence, Insight, Sing, Willpower
- Ω Professional Skills: Art (Composition), Commerce, Courtesy, Language (Other), Musicianship, Seduction, Streetwise

PHILOSOPHER (PHILOSOPHUS)

Scholars who dedicate themselves to the understanding of the universe, philosophers study both sciences and society. They are a highly regarded profession, usually Greek or Greek speaking and most belong to a specific school of philosophy. In general philosophers are skilled in several areas of knowledge but also teach and hold open debate about the truth of the world.

- Ω Wealth: Poor to Affluent
- Ω Status: As intellectuals, philosophers are generally well regarded and suffer no penalty to their Status
- Ω Standard Skills: Customs, Influence, Insight, Locale, Native Tongue, Perception, Willpower
- Ω Professional Skills: Culture (Any), Language (Other), Literacy, Lore (Primary), Lore (Secondary), Rhetoric, Teach

POET (POETA)

Those poets who are not wealthy dilettantes live a marginal life in Rome. They rely on patronage to support themselves whilst creating new works and in return perform their compositions at banquets and dinner parties. Most poets come into vogue for a brief period of time before eventually their popularity fades. Towards the end of the

Republic, many poets begin to directly satirise leading politicians, often at great danger to themselves.

- Ω Wealth: Poor to Average
- Ω Status: Respectable poets apply no penalty to their Status
- Ω Standard Skills: Customs, Deceit, Influence, Insight, Locale, Native Tongue, Willpower
- Ω Professional Skills: Art (Poetry), Courtesy, Language (Other), Literacy, Lore (Any), Musicianship, Rhetoric

PRIEST (SACERDOS)

In general, priesthood was an appointed honour rather than a career in itself. Most people perform their own rituals and sacrifices to their household gods and ancestors. Even the priests of the major State gods were elected positions (often influenced by political motivations), whose duties were performed as an adjunct to their normal lives and responsibilities. State priests are normally Senators who gain a 10% bonus to their Status for the honour. However, the following profession is available for temple slaves or priests of foreign sects which insinuate themselves into the city and maintain themselves on the contributions of their worshippers.

- Ω Wealth: Poor to Affluent
- Ω Status: Since Romans are very religious, most priests receive no penalty to their Status
- Ω Standard Skills: Customs, Deceit, Influence, Insight, Locale, Native Tongue, Willpower
- Ω Professional Skills: Bureaucracy, Courtesy, Cursing, Divination, Language (Other), Literacy, Theology

PROSTITUTE (EXOLETUS OR MERETRIX)

Roman prostitutes come in many types from the lowliest streetwalkers to the highest paid courtesans and can be either men or women (see Prostitutes page 31). Those who do not work in an official brothel are sometimes also thieves. Whilst prostitution is an accepted fact of life, it does hold a degree of social stigma and many prostitutes lose some legal rights in terms of marriage.

- Ω Wealth: Destitute to Affluent
- Ω Status: Prostitutes suffer a 10% penalty to their Status
- Ω Standard Skills: Dance, Deceit, Influence, Insight, Native Tongue, Perception, Sing
- Ω Professional Skills: Acting, Commerce, Language (Any), Musicianship, Seduction, Sleight, Streetwise

SCHOLAR (DOCTUS)

Scholars are an affectation rather than a viable profession in ancient Rome, being those people who study or even write about particular subjects in their spare time. Most are either independently wealthy enough not to need to work or have retired.

SHOPKEEPER (TABERNARIUS)

Most shopkeepers are either Craftsmen or small scale Merchants. For more examples of Latin names for specific types of shopkeeper, see Shop Owners and Tradesmen page 60.

SENATOR (SENATOR)

Leaders of the Republic, senators are the commanders of the army, priests of the Roman pantheon and politicians who guide the

State. They normally come from the patrician and eventually equestrian class and take the lion's share of the annual magisterial offices. Although senators are technically only those who have served as a magistrate, for the purposes of simplicity this profession should be used for up and coming sons of the nobility too, as they are groomed for future office.

- Ω Wealth: Affluent to Wealthy
- Ω Status: A senator gains a 10% bonus to their Status
- Ω Standard Skills: Customs, Deceit, Influence, Insight, Native Tongue, Perception, Willpower
- Ω Professional Skills: Bureaucracy, Command, Courtesy, Law, Literacy, Politics, Rhetoric

SLAVE (SERVUS OR SERVA)

This profession is for household slaves who lack the skills for a different profession, such as craftsmen, gladiators, labourers, priests or teachers. The majority of urban slaves are granted some freedom of movement to accompany their masters, maintain their education or even earn money for themselves. Since most are foreigners, or the children of foreign slaves, they usually speak another language.

- Ω Wealth: Destitute to Poor
- Ω Status: Slaves, already at the bottom of the social ladder, suffer no other penalty to their Status
- Ω Standard Skills: Brawn, Conceal, Endurance, Insight, Locale, Perception, Stealth
- Ω Professional Skills: Commerce, Courtesy, Craft (Any), Language (Other), Literacy, Lore (Any), Streetwise

SORCERER (MALEFICI OR STRIGAE)

Sorcerers and witches live under great suspicion in Rome, at risk of being denounced and potentially put to death. Their reputation concerning the dark arts draws the discontented who seek retribution or revenge. Most pose as diviners. However, to continue practicing their arts requires secrecy and maintaining a few choice customers in the upper classes to convince the authorities to turn a blind eye.

- Ω Wealth: Poor to Affluent
- Ω Status: Despite their negative connotation, sorcerers gain a +10% bonus to Status from the fear they instil
- Ω Standard Skills: Customs, Deceit, Influence, Insight, Locale, Native Tongue, Willpower
- Ω Professional Skills: Cursing, Divination, Necromancy, Language (Other), Literacy, Pharmacy, Shape-Shifting

TAVERN KEEPER (CAUPONES)

Rome is full of taverns, inns, wine bars and even small stalls on the streets. Most tavern keepers offer wines and cheap food and bar maids act as informal prostitutes. Tavern keepers are viewed with neutrality, since they are a centre-piece of Roman life.

- Ω Wealth: Poor to Average
- Ω Status: Tavern keepers suffer no penalty to their Status
- Ω Standard Skills: Brawn, Conceal, Deceit, Endurance, Locale, Perception, Pugilism
- Ω Professional Skills: Commerce, Craft (Brewing, Cooking or Vintner), Gambling, Language (Other), Lore (Any), Sleight, Streetwise

TEACHER (MAGISTER)

Teachers only came into existence for the last couple of centuries of the Republic. Before that children were taught by members of their own family. Teachers can be slaves, freedmen or plebeians and teach everything from basic literacy and numeracy to artistic skills. They are normally fluent in Greek since most ancient literature available at the time was written in that language.

- Ω Wealth: Poor to Average
- Ω Status: Teachers suffer no other penalty to their Status
- Ω Standard Skills: Customs, Influence, Insight, Locale, Native Tongue, Perception, Willpower
- Ω Professional Skills: Courtesy, Culture (Any), Language (Other), Literacy, Lore (Primary), Lore (Secondary), Teach

THIEF (FUR)

Roman criminals range between burglars, confidence men, muggers, forgers, pick pockets or even street thugs. Life is hard and short for a thief, since punishment if captured, is brutal. Many criminals form gangs for mutual protection, which often clash when rival gangs invade each other's territory. Members treat their gang leader as their patron.

- Ω Wealth: Poor to Affluent
- Ω Status: Thieves suffer a 10% penalty to their Status
- Ω Standard Skills: Athletics, Deceit, Evade, Insight, Perception, Pugilism, Stealth
- Ω Professional Skills: Acting, Commerce, Disguise, Lockpicking, Mechanisms, Sleight, Streetwise

SKILLS (ARTES)

The following are skills that have either been renamed or have been tweaked to suit the setting. A few are unique and are further described elsewhere in the book.

The **Status** and **Politics** skills are not actually skills per se but rather ratings granted by the character's family prominence and personal achievements. Neither skill has a Base Chance but their initial value depends on the character's social class, profession and whether they have held a political office. See Political Power Games page 18.

Those skills which differ in either name or application from the core MYTHRAS Rules are described as follows.

Nemo ante mortem beatus − Nobody is blessed before his death

ART (ARS) [SPECIFY] POW+CHA

The arts practised in ancient Rome are:

Ω Compose – Creation of music and songs
Ω Mosaics – Setting of tiled floors and walls
Ω Painting – Decorating statues, ceramics or frescoes
Ω Poetry – Composing of poems and epics
Ω Sculpture – Carving of statues from stone
Ω Writing – Authoring of histories, biographies, and novels

COMMAND (IMPERIUM) INT+CHA

The ability to lead others primarily but not exclusively, in a military context. It replaces the usual skill of Lore (Strategy and Tactics). Until the Late Republic the position of a military commander (Consul, Tribune and Dictator) was a political appointment, thus those elected to the position often lacked significant knowledge of warfare, which led to many of Rome's military disasters. In game terms some commanders lack the Command skill entirely, substituting Rhetoric at a penalty of one or more difficulty grades; representing strength of their raw leadership rather than a grasp of military knowledge.

COMMERCE (PACTIO) INT+CHA

Most Romans use this skill on a daily basis when shopping for food, haggling over purchases, negotiating wages or contracts and even arranging a suitable bribe. Those lacking this skill will be gouged 10-30% more on the price of everything (1d3x10%).

CRAFT (FABRICA) [SPECIFY] DEX+INT

There are a huge number of different crafting specialities applicable in Rome. Some examples include Apothecary, Baking, Barbering, Brewing, Carpentry, Cooking, Dyeing, Glassblowing, Laundering, Leatherworking, Locksmithing, Masonry, Metalworking, Mining, Pottery, Sandal making, Scribing, Slaving, Tailoring, Undertaking, Vintner and Weaving.

CURSING (EXSECRATIO) POW+CHA

See Magic page 143.

DIVINATION (DIVINATIO) INT+POW

See Magic page 141.

DRIVE (AGENDUM) DEX+POW

Covers the ability to drive a wagon or chariot. Most city-based Romans have little practical knowledge of driving, as wheeled vehicles are generally too wide to fit any except the main streets and such transport is expensive to maintain. If the animals used to pull the vehicle are different from those the driver is normally used to, they suffer a difficulty grade of Hard or worse.

LAW (LEX) INT+CHA

This is the familiarity with and understanding of Rome's legal system and how to use it to one's advantage. Most Romans have a basic knowledge of their legal rights, since Roman society is driven by politics and watching legal cases at the basilicae is a main form of entertainment. The Law skill can be used in an opposed/abstract way when resolving litigation in the courts.

LANGUAGE (LINGUAE) INT+CHA

All characters start off knowing their Native Tongue at INT+CHA+30%. Foreigners (as many slaves are), must learn Latin as an extra language to be able to function within Rome. This skill acts as a cap to other communication skills, indicating the importance of a wider vocabulary and better elocution.

LITERACY (LITTERAE) INT x2

Although Rome's population has one of the highest literacy rates in history, proficiency in reading is not learned by default. Characters must learn a new literacy skill for each language they wish to read, since at this time most languages have their own unique alphabet, grammar, and script. This automatically includes the ability to write.

LOCK PICKING (IRRUPTIO) DEX x2

This skill is intended for thieves and spies who wish to covertly bypass latches and padlocks. Since Roman locks are relatively simplistic, most people have a small chance of picking an average lock. A single attempt may be made by rolling their DEX or less on a d100, with failure resulting in the lock being irreparably damaged and making it obvious that someone tried to force it. Because of this fact, most households either leave family members at home or supplement their security with door slaves and gladiators.

LORE (SCIENTIA) [SPECIFY] INT x2

This skill represents those areas of knowledge normally unavailable to the common citizen. It has a number of specialities which should include: Accounting, Animal Training, Architecture, Art (for connoisseurs), Bureaucracy, Farming, Geography, Herding, History, Literature and so forth.

MEDICINE (MEDICINA) INT+POW

Replaces the normal Healing skill. Up until the end of the Republic, medical training was often next to useless. Physiology was poorly understood due to the superstitious (and religious) prohibition against dissecting human bodies; and pharmacy was based more upon the use of ingredients selected for sympathetic function, rather than empirically observed medicinal effect. Since most treatments

---

REALISTIC ROMAN MEDICINE

The Medicine skill works as noted in the MYTHRAS rulebook on page 46, save that a 'failed' roll is treated as a fumble on the table (i.e. it inflicts more damage, or makes diseases and poisons worse) and a 'fumbled' roll causes the rapid death of the patient. It is the very dangerousness of fledgling medicine which gives most doctors a justified reputation of being quacks or butchers.

Games Masters who like frequent combats in their campaigns should be at pains to understand that there are no rapid methods of healing at this time. No magic, no mystically potent herbs and no first aid kits. Wounds recover naturally as described under Healing from Injury (MYTHRAS page 80), unless characters wish to risk the attentions of someone using the medicine skill. Thus lethal combat should be constrained to such times as the annual legion conscription or part of a specific climax to a scenario. Otherwise the death rates of player characters will be high. Even professional gladiators fought only a handful of times each year, probably to give them time to fully recover from injuries.

Nemo saltat sobrius – Nobody dances sober (Cicero)

were no more than ritual spells combined with often noxious reme-dies or fumbling surgery on ill-understood body parts, the following option is suggested for Games Masters who prefer brutal reality over character survivability.

NAVIGATION (GUBERNATIO) INT+POW

This skill is not very useful for the average citizen in Rome, who uses the Streetwise skill to get around (see Lost Properties on page 57). Even those Romans who made journeys overland usually had a good road to follow and as such a good sense of navigation was not really needed. This sometimes caused difficulties during times of war however. Many of Rome's defeats in its early history were caused by consuls leading the army across unfamiliar terrain and either becoming lost or trapped.

NECROMANCY (NECROMANTIA) INT+CHA

This skill should be reserved for campaigns using supernatural magic, see Magic page 144.

PHARMACY (MEDICAMENTARIA) INT x2

See Magic page 145.

POLITICS (RESPUBLICA) *

Further described under Political Power Games (page 18), Poli-tics signifies the political standing of a character and the authority he can bring to bear in the political arena of the Senate or Assemblies.

PUGILISM (PUGILATIO) STR+DEX

This is the Unarmed skill renamed.

RHETORIC (DECLAMATIO) POW+CHA

This is the Roman name for the Oratory skill.

SHAPE-SHIFTING (ARS VERSIPELLIS) CON+POW

Like Necromancy, this skill should be reserved for campaigns using supernatural magic, see Magic page 147.

STATUS (STATUS) *

Status indicates the social standing of the character, which can be used to impress or intimidate others. It has a default value based on the social class of the character. Profession can further modify this. See Political Power Games page 18.

STREETWISE (SCITUS) POW+CHA

Within Rome, this skill represents the social contacts of a char-acter and, to a lesser degree, their knowledge of famous persons and social order. With this, the user can pick up on local gossip, find patrons, ask questions to navigate their way through unknown streets and so on.

THEOLOGY (THEOLOGIA) POW x2

See Magic page 140.

WEAPON STYLES (TELUM) [SPECIFY] STR+DEX

Unless playing professional gladiators, it is recommended that Games Masters limit characters to the pre-defined cultural combat styles described earlier in this chapter (page 125). Whilst some play-ers might rebel at the thought of being limited to such 'inferior' weapons, the reasons for this are very simple. Firstly, within the walls of Rome weapons and weapon training are strictly limited,

so it is historically correct. Secondly, unless off on a military cam-paign or taking part in a sanctioned suppression of civil uprising, nobody wears any armour – so allowing characters to run amuck with swords and axes will quickly result in mass slaughter, followed by the inevitable death of the instigators themselves.

UNCOMMON SKILLS

Whilst the professions provided are comprehensive for a city dwelling Roman, characters of foreign backgrounds or those with eccentric habits may wish to know other skills. Games Masters are encouraged to permit some leeway learning alternate skills, as long as the character's background provides a valid rational.

SEAMANSHIP (NAVIGATIO) INT+CON

This is a very rare skill for any Roman citizen to know. Save for a brief period before and during the Punic Wars, Rome did not main-tain its own navy. Those fleets it did build were repeatedly destroyed by inept consular admirals, knowing nothing of sailing and naviga-tion. After the final defeat of Carthage, the Republic simply hired their fleets from client states. This skill is primarily known by Greek or Egyptian sailors, who were employed to captain or crew Roman owned ships.

"The Carthaginian admiral, on seeing what Junius had done, decided not to incur the risk of approaching such a dangerous shore, but, gaining a certain cape and anchoring off it, remained on the alert between the two fleets, keeping his eye on both. When the weather now became stormy, and they were threatened with a heavy gale from the open sea, the Carthaginian captains who were acquainted with the locality and with the weather signs, and foresaw and prophesied what was about to happen, persuaded Carthalo to escape the tempest by rounding Cape Pachynus. He very wisely consented, and with great labour they just managed to get round the cape and anchor in a safe position. But the two Roman fleets, caught by the tempest, and the coast affording no shelter at all, were so completely destroyed that not even the wrecks were good for anything"

Polybius – Histories

TRACK (INDAGATIO) INT+CON

Another rare skill amongst urbanised citizens of the city, tracking was far more common in the early days when many of the popu-lace still comprised of shepherds and herders. In the later Republic, the skill is normally only known by foreigners or slaves, who either perform most of the work concerning animal husbandry or are captured barbarians who used the skill in everyday life. Tracking within the city is always considered a Formidable difficulty roll; since despite incidental filth on the streets, the sheer amount of foot traffic soon destroys any spoor.

PASSIONS

No game set in ancient Rome would be complete without Pas-sions to give the players a focus. Characters may start with between 1 and 3 Passions which they can work out with the help of the Games Master to suit their background. Common choices include:

Loyalty to Rome
Loyalty to Patron
Loyalty to Street Gang

Loyalty to Legion

Love Chariot Races

Love Gladiatorial Fights

Love Gambling

Love Family

Hate Family

Hate Social Rival (specific individual)

Hate Political Rival (specific individual)

Dislike Foreigners

Lust for Political Power

Lust after Money

Desire Freedom

Seek Vengeance (for specific event)

Overthrow the Senate

Fear Plebeians

Fear Doctors

Fear the Supernatural

Respect the Gods

All passions have a base value of POW x2, with an additional starting bonus of +30% for the first, +20% for the second and +10% for the third.

If desired, characters may substitute a school of philosophy for one of their Passions, representing their interest in its tenets. The following describes the common philosophies of the time and demonstrate how each could be used in a campaign. These should be treated as rough guidelines rather than hard and fast rules, subject to the Games Master's discretion. Only one specific school of philosophy may be chosen; since the Passion reflects adherence to that philosophical mindset, rather than just academic knowledge. The following schools each grant benefits in particular situations.

STOICISM

A follower of Stoicism can use his philosophy to augment any Willpower roll, in order to maintain self-control, hide their emotions or overcoming fear. Conversely stoic characters may not openly complain, disobey orders, or show signs of weakness without first failing a roll against their Stoicism passion.

EPICUREANISM

Devotees of Epicureanism can apply their positive perspective and pursuit of pleasure to influence social intercourse. They use their philosophy as an augment for the following skills: Art, Commerce, Courtesy and Influence, providing the attempt is to increase their personal gratification. On the other hand an Epicurean must fail tests against their philosophy to resist being diverted whenever such opportunities present themselves.

SKEPTICISM

Skeptics are skilled at using logic and observation to perceive the truth. They can apply their philosophy as an augment when utilising Rhetoric or the Perception skill. In return they cannot act in an intuitive or illogical manner without the Games Master requesting them to roll against (and fail) their Skepticism.

PYTHAGOREANISM

Followers of this school can employ their philosophy to resist any type of physical or mental temptation, in lieu of Endurance or Willpower. In addition, their devotion to the sciences means they can use it to augment any Lore skill. In return however, Pythagoreans must lead a miserable life of self-denial, being forced to refute rewards, promotions and even decent food (meat, fish and beans being banned).

MONEY AND POSSESSIONS (PECUNIA)

In the earliest period of Rome, most transactions were dealt with in terms of pure barter, often using livestock or personal service as payment. Precious metals, originally lumps of raw bronze (aes rude) then bronze ingots (aes signatum), were used as a form of proto currency – but only as a way of converting wealth into an accountable form. Every five years when the census was taken, every citizen in Rome was appraised in terms of how many asses of bronze his property and holdings was worth.

Eventually coins from other cultures (notably those from the Greek city states in the south of Italy) began to be used in the city but it was not until around 280 BC that the first Roman bronze coinage (aes grave) was cast and about 211 BC when they began to mint silver coins. By the end of the Republic a fairly stable and un-debased currency system was in circulation.

The coins (nummi) and their values are:

Ω Quadrans – the smallest value copper coin, two quadrantes equal a semis

Ω Semis – two copper semisses equal an as

Ω As – two copper asses equal a dupondius

Ω Dupondius – two copper dupondii equal a sestertius

Ω Sestertius – a small silver coin, four sesterces equal a denarius (its name originally meant 'two and a half asses' – the original value of the coin)

Ω Denarius – the largest silver coin, 25 denarii equal an aureus (in 211 BC the denarius was worth 10 asses, hence its name, but was revalued at 16 asses in 141 BC when the size of bronze coins were shrunk)

Ω Aureus – the only gold coin, these were used for transactions of the State and never entered common circulation

COINAGE

Coin	Value in asses pre 141 BC	Value in asses post 141 BC
Quadrans	¼	¼
Semis	½	½
As	1	1
Dupondius	2	2
Sestercius	2½	4
Denarius	10	16
Aureus	250	400

"when Hannibal was pressing hard upon Rome, in the dictatorship of Q. Fabius Maximus, asses of one ounce weight were struck, and it was ordained that the value of the denarius should be sixteen asses and that of the sestertius four asses"

Pliny the Elder – Naturalis Historia

A single quadrans would pay for admission to a public bath or latrine. During the Republic the value of goods and property was usually priced in sesterces, the smallest silver coinage.

Although Rome's treasury is kept in the Temple of Saturn, coins are actually minted in the Temple of Juno Moneta (from which we get the word money.). Roman coins were often struck with images of gods and ancestors, yet it was not until Julius Caesar that the first coins were made with a living Roman's image on them. Another interesting fact is that before 167 BC the tax rate in Rome was only 1% of a citizen's total wealth, which was only raised in times of severe war but only up to a maximum of 3%. After this date, taxes were waived since the newly conquered provinces were taxed instead.

THE VALUE OF GOODS AND SERVICES

The problem with assigning set prices to goods and services of ancient Rome is that all monetary values are subject to inflation, quality and availability. For instance, grain prices in the mid-Republic rose threefold by end of the late Republic. Availability was also a major factor; in a year when pirates or slave uprisings interrupted imports, then the price could double, triple or even more, potentially causing starvation for those families living at the sustenance level. During the 2nd Punic War when Hannibal ravaged central Italy, the price of grain rose to six times its normal price.

In the face of these difficulties and to avoid the impossibility of defining fluctuating values throughout each period of Rome's history, prices have been given as an aspect of Wealth Levels. Games Masters who normally run campaigns with specific monetary values are encouraged to use this more abstract system according to the following guidelines:

Ω To prevent abuse by characters who attempt to stockpile or trade various goods by repeated use of their Status skill and Wealth Level, each transaction should be vetted for the availability of the item requested, or by limiting the number of such 'purchases' per game week.

Ω Characters who desire items above their normal Wealth Level can only access them via their patron (who will require an equivalent service in return) or by taking a loan from a banker or usurer (which also leads to some interesting plot possibilities).

Ω When the city of Rome is under direct threat (for example during the 2nd Punic War or the later civil wars) the values of everything, including food, should be raised by one level.

Instead of simply doling out thousands of sesterces at the end of an adventure, financial rewards for characters can instead be items beyond their normal means, such as expensive clothing, luxury items, better accommodation, paying off a debt or loan, promotions, marriage and so on. No actual money needs to be defined and indeed this can encourage a better understanding of how both status and the client-patron relationship work in ancient Rome.

Bear in mind that the following 'value' lists reflect what is acceptable expenditure for a given Wealth Level. It does not directly represent the actual intrinsic cost of each item. For example, purchasing a pair of patrician's shoes is considered a Priceless expense; whereas a month's rent of a large room in an insula is merely Average.

Although in real terms the price of the patrician's footwear may be less than the rent, to a plebeian the rent is a necessary expenditure, whereas the shoes are a needless luxury. Thus values are inherently linked to personal wealth.

AVAILABILITY OF GOODS AND SERVICES

An interesting aspect of Roman commerce is that up until the mid-Republic there are very few craftsmen who actually maintain a stock of ready-to-sell products in their workshops. Most only make those items that have been commissioned in advance by a customer. Stalls displaying immediately available goods that can be browsed are the realm of merchants, who normally purchase their stock from either craftsmen or from captured war spoils and thus take upon themselves the risk that the goods will not sell.

Early Roman households only contain basic utensils and furniture, often items manufactured by the family itself. Not only is it deemed rather poor taste to live luxuriously but the opportunities to purchase even such basic items as clothing are nearly non-existent. Campaigns set in early Rome should emphasise the chance to loot luxuries and furniture from conquered cities as part of the annual military service.

Only towards the late Republic do shops become stocked with items which the average Roman used to make for themselves, or more exotic foreign goods imported from overseas.

"Friends share' – is this your 'sharing', Candidus, which you grandly bang on about by night and day? A toga washed in Lacedaemonian Galaesus swathes you, or one which Parma provided from a special flock; yet as for mine, the first dummy which has suffered the rage and horns of a bull wouldn't want to call it its own. Cadmus' country has sent you Agenorian cloaks; you won't be able to sell my scarlet clothes for three sesterces. You balance round Libyan tabletops on Indian ivory: my beechwood table is propped up with a fragment of pottery. Oversized mullets cover your yellow gold-inlay plates: lobster, you blush on my plate that shares your colour. Your 'flock' could compete with the Trojan catamite: but instead of a Ganymede it's my hand that comes to my aid. Out of so much wealth you give nothing to an old and faithful friend and you still say, Candidus, 'Friends share'?"

Martial – Epigrams

Tables for the goods and services follow at the end of this chapter, starting on page 136.

STARTING EQUIPMENT

All characters begin play with:

Ω One or more complete sets of clothing appropriate for their wealth level

Ω A personal family heirloom, usually a ring, sword, drinking cup or something similar

Ω Any trade tools or armaments applicable to their profession and class

Ω Living accommodation appropriate for their wealth level

Nil sine magno labore vita dedit mortalibus – life does not give mortals anything but hard labour (Horace)

SERVICES (MINISTERIA)

Many jobs were paid for on a per incidence basis. The following list illustrates the costs of such 'services'.

Service	Value
Having a bath	Cheap
Using the public toilet	Cheap
Getting a shave	Inexpensive
Laundry	Inexpensive
Prostitute Cheap[1]	Cheap
Prostitute Average	Inexpensive
Prostitute Good	Average
Scribe writing a legal document	Average
Scribe writing a letter	Inexpensive
Pleading a law case	Expensive

[1]Make an Endurance roll to avoid catching a venereal disease.

FOOD (CIBUS)

Romans purchase dried foods (such as grain or desiccated vegetables) by the Modius, a measurement of volume. Fresh food is bought by the pound weight. Liquids are bought by the Sextarius or Amphora. These measures translated into modern terms are:

1 sextarius = about a pint or half a litre in volume
16 sextarii = 1 modius
48 sextarii = 1 amphora
20 amphorae = 1 culleus

A modius of grain would provide an adult with 10 days of bread after being milled and baked. However, baking bread was expensive in terms of fuel, so many of the poor simply crushed their grain and left it to soak to make a porridge known as puls. The most basic dietary cost a Roman could live on (porridge, poor vegetables, a little olive oil and cheapest wine) was ½ a sestertius per day – the same price as two loaves of baked bread or a bowl of stew at an inn.

Meat and fresh vegetables are purchased by the libra, the ancient equivalent of the pound (lb). Most Romans rarely ate meat simply due to the cost.

Wine came from all over the fledgling empire but the most well regarded wines were local Italian ones (see Wine page 46). Poor quality wine was little more than sour flavoured vinegar but when mixed with hot water became a favourite drink of the legions. Where the price given has a range, the lower value is for 'second quality' whereas the upper value is for 'first quality'. By the end of the Republic, members of the higher classes are expected to offer foods and wine of good or exquisite quality to guests or suffer a lowering of their status.

CLOTHING AND FABRIC (VESTIS ET TEXTUM)

For much of the Republic, the women of most Roman households spent their time weaving cloth, from which the family's clothes were made. In fact many matrons of poorer class earned a supplementary income spinning and weaving for other people. Old clothes were often given by patrons to their clients. Once clothing reached a point it could not be repaired anymore, it was turned into patches for other garments.

SLAVES AND LIVESTOCK (SERVI ET PECUDES)

Slaves are normally sold on the auction block, stripped to reveal their physique. The price of a slave depends upon their skills and beauty. After successful wars, prices fall due to the glut of new slaves on the market. Otherwise most slaves are imported from the eastern Mediterranean, where most have been captured by pirates and sold into servitude.

Livestock is traded in the Forum Boarium where unblemished animals can also be purchased as sacrifices for those wishing to propitiate the gods.

TRANSPORT (VECTATIO)

Most Romans travel by foot or litter in the city but use donkeys, horses or wagons when travelling to or from the countryside. Renting is the preferred method since the upkeep of slaves or animals dedicated purely for transport is very high. Ships are horribly expensive to build and are usually funded by collectives of investors.

Purchasing the mode of transport outright, increases its Value by one step

GENERAL PARAPHERNALIA

As previously mentioned, most early period and poor Romans own few material possessions save the basic necessities of plates, cups, knives, workman tools (depending on profession) and buckets or amphorae (to carry water). Furniture too would be basic, often crafted by the family itself.

Over times, however, those who could afford luxuries began to find many objects to spend their money on. Jewellery, dinner services made of silver, statues, bronze oil lamps, upholstered couches, tables or cabinets made of exotic woods, iron bound chests with locks, marble vases, book scrolls, paintings; the list grew as the borders of Rome's empire expanded.

Where the values have a range, the lower value is for crude items made of wood or pottery, the mid values for those fashioned from exotic woods or bronze, and the upper value for premium quality objects crafted from (or inlaid with) silver, ivory, marble or glass. Artwork also ranges in value depending on its quality.

ARMS AND ARMOUR

Armaments are freely available for sale in the city up until the late Republic, whereupon they gradually become more restricted in availability until they are only sold as part of wholesale contracts to the legions, or to young gentlemen of the upper classes engaging in their military careers. Armour and weapons are expensive due to the difficulties (and costs) of smelting and forging bronze or ,later, iron; and most armaments are heirlooms, captured spoils, gifts from patrons, or a significant expenditure paid for by the extended family... and eventually the State. Variance in values represents the amount of ornamentation included on the armament.

ACCOMMODATION & PROPERTY (HABITATIO ET POSSESSIO)

Living in the eternal city is expensive. Most inhabitants can only afford to rent a single room in one of the ubiquitous insulae. Only prosperous characters live in houses and even then they are normally under the authority of their father (or grandfather) who owns the place and may still live there.

GENERAL EXPENSES (SUMPTUS)

Many Romans attempt to improve their social status by sponsoring entertainments or erecting monuments. However, most of these expenses are beyond the pocket of most common plebeians to provide. Even the richest men in Rome have to borrow heavily from friends or relations in order to pay for such spectacles.

PRICE AND VALUE LISTS

DRIED FOOD

Item	Av Value in Modius	Notes
Dried Vegetables	Cheap	Peas, beans
Cheap Grain	Cheap	Millet, oats, barley, rye
Good Grain	Inexpensive	Wheat
Salt	Average	Course crystalline or rock
Spices	Expensive to Priceless	Anything from sage to saffron

FRESH FOOD

Item	Av Value in Libra	Notes
Fresh Vegetables	Cheap	
Fresh Fruit	Inexpensive	
Beef	Inexpensive	Beef was not favoured for consumption
Fish (Freshwater)	Average to Expensive	Prices range from poor to best quality
Fish (Saltwater)	Average to Expensive	Prices range from poor to best quality
Goat	Average	
Lamb	Average	
Pork	Average	
Sausage	Average to Expensive	Prices range from poor to best quality
Chicken	Average	
Goose	Expensive	
Pheasant	Expensive	

FABRIC

Item	Av Value per Libra Weight
Wool	Inexpensive
Linen	Average
Cotton	Average
Undyed Coan silk	Expensive
Purple dyed Cloth	Priceless

CLOTHES

Clothing[1]	Av Value per Item
Mammillare/subligar	Inexpensive
Plain tunic	Average to Expensive
Stola	Average to Expensive
Hooded Cloak (Lacerna)	Average to Expensive
Soldier's Cloak (Sagum)	Average to Expensive
Toga plain	Expensive
Toga praetexta	Priceless
Soldiers boots	Average
Patrician's shoes	Priceless
Senatorial shoes	Expensive
Equestrian's shoes	Expensive
Normal Gallic sandals	Inexpensive

1 *Treat old clothes (-5% Status) as being one Value level lower, and rags (-20% Status) as two levels lower*

WINE AND OIL

Wine[1] or Oil	Av Value in Sextarius	Notes
Poor Wine	Cheap	Normally part, if not all, vinegar
Average Wine	Inexpensive	
Good Wine	Average	Coan, Corinthian, Lesbian, Cretan, Judean, and Mamertine
Fine Wine	Expensive	Caecuban, Fundanian, Setinian, Falernian, Alban, and Statinian
Olive Oil	Inexpensive to Expensive	Depending on quality
Liquamen	Inexpensive to Expensive	Depending on quality

1 *Spiced or heated wine adds one to its value*

LIVESTOCK

Types	Av Value
Dove	Inexpensive
Chicken	Inexpensive
Goat	Average
Sheep	Average
Pig	Average
Ox	Average
Donkey	Average
Horse	Expensive
Dog[1]	Expensive
Successful Chariot Team	Priceless
Leopard	Priceless
Lion	Priceless

1 *Assumes a dog specially bred and trained for hunting or guarding. Otherwise dogs can be found wild in the streets or necropolises for those brave enough to attempt to domesticate one*

Noli turbare circulos meos! – Do not upset my circles! (Archimedes)

SLAVES

Duties/Skills[1]	Av Value
Unskilled labourer	Average
Household slave	Average
Music or Dancing slave	Average
Educated slave	Expensive
Trained gladiator or charioteer	Expensive
Household manager	Priceless
Trained doctor	Priceless
Popular gladiator or charioteer	Priceless

[1] Particularly beautiful or handsome slaves raise their Value by one level

TRANSPORT

Type	Av Value
Rented slave-borne litter	Expensive
Rented donkey	Average
Rented horse	Expensive
Rented wagon	Average
Hire a merchant ship	Priceless

GENERAL GOODS

Type	Av Value
Pot	Cheap to Expensive
Dish	Cheap to Average
Matched Dinner Service	Inexpensive to Priceless
Vase	Average to Priceless
Oil lamp	Cheap to Average
Chandelier	Average to Priceless
Bucket	Cheap to Inexpensive
Knife	Inexpensive to Average
Labourers Tools	Cheap to Inexpensive
Craftsmen Tools	Inexpensive to Average
Artists Tools	Average to Expensive
Storage Box	Cheap to Priceless
Lockable Chest	Average to Priceless
Furniture	Inexpensive to Priceless
Artwork	Value
Book (Papyrus Scroll)	Average to Expensive
Jewellery	Average to Priceless
Hanging Paintings	Average to Priceless
Wall Frescos	Average to Priceless
Mosaics	Expensive to Priceless
Statues	Expensive to Priceless

PROPERTY

Type	Av Value
Modest house in Rome	Priceless
Large house in Rome	Beyond Priceless
Run down insula2	Priceless
Well maintained insula2	Beyond Priceless
Smallholding3	Average
Humble farm3	Expensive
Modest villa3	Priceless
Large estate with villa3	Beyond Priceless

[1] The new maximum value of 'Beyond Priceless' has been added to represent the difficulties of even the super rich being able to purchase the most precious commodity in Rome, that of land and property itself.

[2] The number of floors the insula possesses is the annual % chance the insula will collapse or burn each year. Well maintained insulae halve the chance of disaster. If the insula is the character's major source of income, their Wealth Level drops to the value of their next largest business or property until it is rebuilt.

[3] Each year the owner, depending on whether he is managing or farming the land, should roll against his Command or Craft (Farming) skill and look up the result on the following table:

Ω Critical – Excellent cultivation improves the quality of the land. Not only does the bountiful harvest increase the income by one step for the following year, but the Value of the land itself is permanently enhanced, raising its Value by a level

Ω Success – The land provides a normal income

Ω Failure – Wretched weather or bad management causes the harvest to fail. The income drops by one step for the following year

Ω Fumble – Disaster strikes. The land is poisoned or blighted. No income is produced and the land's Value permanently drops by one level

GENERAL EXPENSES

Type	Av Value
Maintain clients	Value equal to the Wealth Level of the client
Throwing an elaborate party[1]	One Value step higher than your Wealth Level
Hold a wedding or funeral	One Value step higher than your Wealth Level
Hold an elaborate wedding or funeral2	Two Value steps higher than your Wealth Level6
Sponsor a play[2]	Expensive
Host a private gladiator combat[2]	Expensive
Erect a public monument[3]	Priceless
Run in an election (bribery and counter-bribery)	Priceless
Build a major temple[4]	Beyond Priceless
Host munera or ludi games[5]	Beyond Priceless

[1] A successful party gives the host a brief 5% bonus to their Status when next negotiating a favour from a guest. Multiple parties do not stack bonuses

[2] Elaborate spectacles or entertainments grant a yearlong 10% bonus to Status with those who attend

[3] Public monuments grant a permanent 10% bonus to Status. Multiple monuments do not stack bonuses

[4] Erecting a major temple can bring favour from the gods (see Theology page 140)

[5] A spectacular set of games can bring a temporary 25% bonus to the Politics skill when the sponsor seeks their next magisterial office

[6] To a maximum of Beyond Priceless

ARMOUR

Type	AP	Av Value
MONARCHIC ROMAN ARMOUR		
Bronze Cuirass (Chest and Abdomen)	8	Priceless
Bronze Greaves (Legs)	4	Priceless
Bronze Chalcidian or Corinthian Helmet (Head)	8	Priceless
Bronze Pot Helm (Head)	4	Expensive
EARLY REPUBLICAN ROMAN ARMOUR		
Bronze Pectoral (Chest)	6	Priceless
Bronze Greaves (Legs)	4	Priceless
Bronze Helmet with Cheek Flaps (Head)	5	Priceless
Bronze Pot Helm (Head)	4	Expensive
MID-REPUBLICAN ROMAN ARMOUR		
Iron Mail Shirt (Chest and Abdomen)	7	Priceless
Iron Helmet with Neck and Cheek Guards (Head)	7	Priceless
Bronze Pectoral (Chest)	6	Expensive
Bronze Greaves (Legs)	4	Expensive
Bronze Helmet with Cheek Flaps (Head)	5	Expensive
LATE REPUBLICAN ROMAN ARMOUR		
Commander Armour (Chest, Abdomen, Legs and Head)	8	Priceless
Iron Mail Shirt (Chest and Abdomen)	7	Expensive
Iron Helmet with Neck and Cheek Guards (Head)	7	Expensive
Iron Greaves (Legs)	4	Expensive

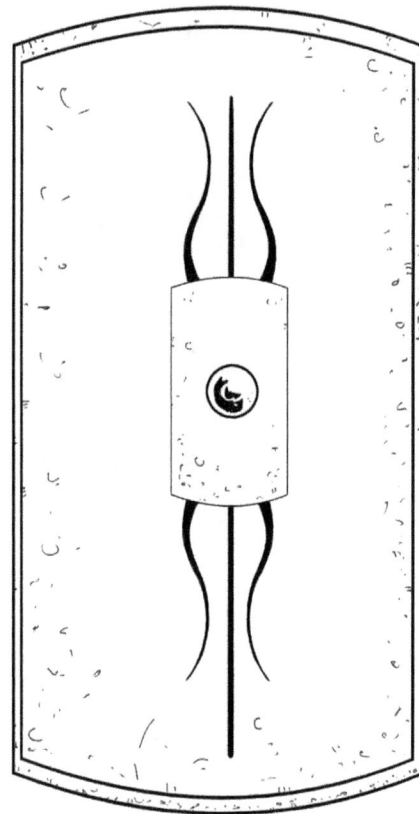

SHIELDS

Shield	Damage	Size	Reach	AP/HP	Notes	Period	Value
Bronze Hoplite Shield (Hoplon)	1d4	H	S	6/15	Passive Blocks 4 Locations	Monarchy	Priceless
Wooden Oval Shield (Aspis)	1d4	L	S	4/15	Passive Blocks 4 Locations	Monarchy	Average
Wooden Round Shield (Parma)	1d3	M	S	4/12	Passive Blocks 3 Locations	Monarchy - Mid Republic	Average
Iron Rimed Oval Shield (Scutum)	1d4	L	S	5/15	Passive Blocks 5 Locations	Early Republic	Expensive
Iron Rimed Oval Shield (Scutum)	1d4	H	S	5/18	Passive Blocks 5 Locations	Mid Republic	Average
Iron Rimed Rectangular Shield (Scutum)	1d4	H	S	5/18	Passive Blocks 5 Locations	Late Republic	Average

WEAPONS

Weapon	Damage	Size	Reach	AP/HP	Notes	Value
Dagger (Sica)	1d3+1	S	S	5/6	Bleeding	Inexpensive to Average
Dagger (Pugio)	1d4+1	S	S	5/8	Impaling	Average to Priceless
Short Sword (Xiphos)	1d6	M	S	6/6	Bleeding	Expensive
Hacking Sword (Falcata, Kopis)	1d4+2	M	S	6/7	Bleeding	Expensive
Stabbing Sword (Gladius)	1d6	M	S	5/8	Impaling	Expensive
Cavalry Sword (Spatha)	1d8	M	M	5/10	Bleeding	Expensive
Spear (Hasta)	1d8+1	M	L	4/5	Impaling	Average to Expensive

RANGED WEAPONS

Ranged Weapon	Damage	Damage Mod	Force	Range	Load	Impale Size	AP/HP	Combat Effects	Cost
Heavy Javelin (Pilum)	1d8+1	Y	H	10/20/50	—	M	3/8	Impale, Pin Weapon (Shield)	Average
Light Javelin (Veruta)	1d6+1	Y	H	10/20/50	—	M	3/8	Impale	Average
Sling (Funda)	1d8	N	L	10/150/300	3	—	1/2	Stun Location	Cheap

MAGIC & SUPERSTITION

Magic and superstition are rife in Rome. Ceremonies propitiate the gods, divinations are held before the Senate can begin business and in the darker alleyways curses are written on lead tablets. By necessity the city is repeatedly purged of the evils of foreign sorcerers, which threaten the morals and beliefs of the people.

Such a fundamental aspect of Roman life is impossible to separate from any accurate portrayal of the city. However, deciding how influential magic will be is an important consideration for a campaign, since it grants supernatural options to overcome problems to both players and their foes. Whether magic actually works is up to the Game Master, who has several choices regarding magical reality…

- Ω No Magic – sorcery does not work and is complete nonsense.
- Ω Psychological Magic – sorcery is merely applied psychology or pharmaceutical effects.
- Ω True Magic – sorcery is real and the gods and spirits have power over the world.

It should be noted that none of the following magical systems use the magic rules described in the MYTHRAS core book. Rather they have been designed to accurately model the magical arts as described by the Romans themselves. Such magic is neither potent nor flashy. It cannot reproduce the elemental powers and spells of Greek mythology, which cause rivers to flow backwards or summon weather. Instead it is far more subtle; controlling the minds and fears of men, the application of herbal concoctions, interpreting unusual events and foreseeing the future.

Roman magic can be broadly divided into the following categories. In game terms, each one is treated as a separate skill.

- Ω Theology (theologia)
- Ω Divination (divinatio)
- Ω Cursing (exsecratio)
- Ω Necromancy (necromantia)
- Ω Pharmacy (medicamentaria)
- Ω Shape-shifting (ars versipellis)

Strictly speaking there are no hindrances to who can learn magic, anyone of any class or standing can practice such things…. Yet some forms of magic are less socially acceptable than others. For example, praying to the gods is fine but summoning the dead is damning and eventually proscribed.

Characters wishing to learn the darker arts will find it difficult to find teachers without travelling overseas, purchasing (or capturing) foreign slaves already possessing such knowledge or seeking out the secretive professional practitioners in the city.

THE LEGALITY OF MAGIC

Some forms of magic are forbidden in Rome's history. In the original laws of the Twelve Tables written in 451 BC, two different types are actively forbidden. "Whoever has sung an evil incantation (malum carmen)…" and "It is illegal for anyone to charm away another man's crops". The penalty for the latter form of malefic sorcery was sacrifice to the goddess Ceres.

During the reprisals against the Bacchic rites, Roman magistrates ordered the execution of more than 5,000 worshippers accused of malign magic and poisoning (veneficium). By the late Republic the laws against certain types of magic and their practitioners had been formalised by Sulla, and continued to be exceedingly stringent in their punishments.

"Those who perform or direct the performance of impious or nocturnal rites, in order to bewitch, bind, or tie a person, are either crucified or thrown to the beasts. Those who sacrifice a human being, make offerings of human blood, or pollute a sanctuary or temple, are thrown to the beasts or, if they are of the upper classes, executed. It is resolved to subject those who know the craft of magic to the ultimate punishment, that is, to throw them to the beasts or crucify them. Actual mages, however, are burned alive. No one may have books on the craft of magic in his house. If they are found in someone's house, they are burned in public and their owner has his property confiscated; upper classes are deported to an island, lower classes are executed. Even the mere knowledge of this craft, let alone its pursuit as a trade, is forbidden."

Sulla – Lex Cornelia de Sicariis et Veneficis

Yet even after this proclamation, Rome remained full of scrolls concerning magic and prophesy, from which much lore was probably preserved. But in 31 BC Octavian finally ordered their destruction in one of the first mass book burnings in history.

"After he had at long last taken on the office of Pontifex Maximus on the death of Lepidus (for he had not had the heart to deprive him of it during his lifetime), he gathered together from all quarters over two thousand books of prophetic writings in Greek and Latin, commonly held to be anonymous or penned by insufficiently suitable authors, and burned them. He just preserved the Sibylline Books, but in the case of these too he chose some and rejected others. He buried them in two gilded boxes under the pedestal of Palatine Apollo."

Suetonius – Augustus

TYPES OF MAGICIANS

Magical practitioners are known by many different names, according to the powers they work with. Despite the rather disreputable reputation of the craft, magicians remain an inseparable part of society – fulfilling the needs of the populace, whether psychological or nefarious.

Astrologers (astrologi), diviners (vates) and foreign soothsayers (haruspices) use various different methods of divination to foretell fate and the future. Some are regarded as charlatans who prey on peoples' fears and insecurities to encourage repeated consultations.

Sorcerers (venefici and malefici) are male dabblers in the darker sides of magic: summoning the dead, inflicting curses and brewing poisons. They live a far more dangerous life, at risk of being reported to the authorities by unsatisfied clients.

Witches (sagae and strigae) are female sorcerers. Saga are wise women who brew traditional herbal remedies for disease, injury, or abortion. Striga are the more ominous casters of curses, brewers of poisons, and love potions; they could even shape shift themselves or their victims.

"…there's a certain old woman called Dipsas… I suspect she changes, at will, in the shadows of night and her old woman's body grows feathers. I suspect it, and that's the rumour. Her eyes shine too with double pupils, and twin lights come from the orbs. She calls up ancient ancestors, ghosts from the grave and with long-winded charms splits solid earth."

Ovid – The Procuress, Elergies

Priests of the state gods, augurs, and those haruspices warranted by the Senate are not considered magicians and remain above and, ostensibly beyond, censure.

THEOLOGY (THEOLOGIA)

The worship of the gods is universal amongst the inhabitants of the city of Rome, no matter their personal philosophy or the pantheon they propitiate. Everybody believes. Although respect is given by all Romans, calling for their aid requires specific knowledge of the ancient formats and formulae used.

Only those characters who cultivate the Theology skill know how to phrase prayers in the correct manner so that the gods to listen to their entreaties. Calling upon the gods to intervene in their lives is known as Divine Intervention but this requires that any help given is paid for, usually with an appropriate sacrifice.

The Theology skill not only represents the degree of favour with which the gods look upon their worshipper but also grants knowledge of the pantheon's deities and customs. Since the position of priest within Rome is a political one, characters striving for elevation into one of the collegia need not actually be particularly skilled in Theology but are expected to learn after election.

CALLING UPON THE GODS

Anybody possessing the Theology skill may make an appeal for divine aid. However, the contractual nature of such bargains is exact and the worshiper must not make any mistakes, else the gods ignore their request… Only if the prayer is invoked correctly will that character be briefly blessed with divine fortune.

A call for divine aid must be made before the character begins an endeavour; it cannot be performed retroactively. The invocation requires spending at least a minute uttering the entire invocation – first addressing the correct divinity, then framing the request and concluding with a promise of a sacrifice reciprocal to the divine assistance. The prayer can be shouted out for all to hear or merely muttered under one's breath.

"From the very outset I pray to You, Apollo, inventor of music and of all the healing arts, come to my aid and this undertaking, bless it with your laurel"

Ovid – Remedia Amoris

To determine whether or not the deity agrees to the contract, the player makes a roll against their Theology skill. If successful, then the god has accepted the prayer and will 'bless' the character in their forthcoming enterprise.

The blessing allows the character to 'bump' the success of a single skill check by one level. It will turn a fumble into a fail, a fail into a success or a success into a critical. The opportunity to utilise the blessing remains active for the remainder of that scene/encounter and if not used will be wasted.

"Venus, I offer you thanks, and I beg and entreat you that I may win the man I love and long for, and that he may be gracious to me, and not reject my desire for him"

Plautus – Miles Gloriosus

After the conclusion of the blessing, the god will refuse to grant further boons until the promised sacrifice has been made.

Non omne quod licet honestum est - Not everything that is permitted is honest (Corpus Iuris Civilis)

APPROPRIATE SACRIFICES

Since all promised sacrifices must ultimately be made at a shrine of the god called upon, repetitive requests for divine aid require close proximity to the pertinent temple or a priest of that deity who can temporarily consecrate altars. Atop this, the cost of an appropriate sacrifice can be prohibitively expensive to those of meagre finances.

The minimum sacrifice required for a personal blessing (i.e. something which only directly benefited the worshipper) is the donation of an animal suitable to that cult. In most cases this is something modest like a dove, goat or sheep. But for higher status gods it may involve more expensive and individualistic animals, such as flawless white bulls for example (see Prayer, Sacrifices and Thanksgiving on page 112).

Sacrifices for blessings which have a larger scale effect, such as rallying a losing army, preventing the loss of a fleet to bad weather, or diffusing a mob before it can riot, require a much larger bequest. This normally involves donating a tenth of the spoils of a battle or a promise to redecorate or renovate the god's temple.

> *"If You, Father of the Gods and of men, hold back our enemies, at least from this spot, delivering the Romans from their terror, and stay their shameful retreat, then this I vow to You, Jupiter Stator, that a holy precinct and shrine will be built in Your honour as a memorial to remind our descendents of how once the city of Rome was saved by Your aid"*
>
> *Livy – Ab Urbe Condita*

Those very few that can afford to make a massive commitment, can build a new temple to the god they deem as their patron. Such investments cost millions of sesterces and years of construction. However, at the conclusion of its building, after it has been dedicated, the founder is under a continuous blessing. Once each day they may call upon their patron god to aid them, and never have to make another sacrifice to restore that god's favour.

THE BLESSINGS OF THE GODS

Choosing the correct god to call upon is very important. Each deity has a specific domain over which they have authority and sometimes a god has several different aspects referring to many different areas of power. For example, a legionary will call upon Mars for divine protection in battle, whereas the commander of the legion might instead request aid from Jupiter Victor (bringer of victory).

It is the Game Master's responsibility to rule whether the deity being supplicated is applicable to the task being performed. For the

---

CHARIOTS OF THE GODS

Although the Theology skill grants a definite benefit, divine blessings could simply be the result of psychosomatic inspiration by those who are truly pious. Of course, some Game Masters might prefer that the gods really do exist, playing with their worshippers for their entertainment or even their own divine survival. In campaigns where the gods are real, it should be remembered that, unlike Greek mythology, the major Roman gods do not physically manifest themselves (although their legendary champions might). Instead they work through the medium of dreams and portents. Historical examples include lightning strikes from the sky, eagles landing on a shoulder or the toppling of statues. Like all aspects of the Roman supernatural, the gods are not brazen but subtle (well, as subtle as a being struck by lightning can be…).

---

major gods of Rome see Religion page 108. A list of the minor gods is included in Appendix IV.

DIVINATION (DIVINATIO)

The Romans have an odd attitude towards divination. On the one hand, State authorised augurs and haruspices do not actually foretell the future, they merely divine the 'will of the gods' at that moment; that is to say, they report if the gods approve of a particular course of action (omina).

On the other hand, the precise revelation of future events is considered illegal and subject to severe punishment; despite the fact that the State sometimes consults the Sibylline Books, which are full of such prophesy concerning the future of Rome. Yet in secret, many Romans seek just such divinations from seers and soothsayers to help guide them in their political, financial, and even gambling activities.

> *"Do we wait for the immortal gods to converse with us in the forum, on the street, and in our homes? While they do not, of course, present themselves in person, they do diffuse their power far and wide. The Stoics reason that, if there are gods and they do not make clear to man in advance what the future will be, then either they do not love man or they themselves do not know what the future will be."*
>
> *Cicero – De Divinatione*

There are a number of different schools of divination, each utilising unique means to read the future. Most are foreign in origin, which adds an element of exotic mystery to their reputation.

- Ω Astrology (astrologia) – Divination by charting the motion of the stars, planets, comets and other celestial phenomena in the night sky and comparing them to dates of birth.
- Ω Augury (auguratio) – The interpretation of the flights, numbers and species of birds to judge whether something was approved or disapproved of by the gods.
- Ω Cleromancy (sortilectio) – Divination by drawing lots, usually stones or beans from a jar or from a bag, rolling dice or knucklebones, or drawing straws.
- Ω Dendromancy (dendromanteia) – Divination by listening to the sounds of leaves in wind-blown trees, or by studying the rings in a freshly snapped branch.
- Ω Haruspication (haruspicina) – Divination by examining the entrails (especially the liver) of sacrificed animals.
- Ω Lycanomancy (lycanomanteia) – Oil is dripped onto water and the pattern it makes tells the diviner about events in the future.
- Ω Meteromancy (meteromanteia) – Divination by watching the weather, cloud formations, the direction of the wind, sun on the clouds and so forth.
- Ω Lychnomancy (lychnomanteia) – Lamp divination, through the flickering of a lamp, smoke of incense burning on a charcoal brazier, or of flower and laurel leaves smouldering on a fire. The flame or smoke reveals patterns of future events to the diviner.

"...that there are gods; that they rule the universe by their foresight; and that they direct the affairs of men... Then surely it must follow that the gods give to men signs of coming events... Flight patterns of birds; entrails of sacrificed animals; types of dreams"

Cicero – De Divinatione

Of course, true divination does not need to be present in campaigns with no real magic or a Game Master may wish to restrict its use to the province of NPC's.

HOW DIVINATION WORKS

In role-playing games, prophesying the future is somewhat impractical. After all, the Game Master is not omnipotent and the randomness of dice rolls (or capricious players) can invalidate the simplest prediction. Thus instead of divination being used to predict the future, a player character soothsayer can instead change events to create their own desired future.

Of course such modifications are usually minor affairs, which do not greatly disrupt reality. However, major events can be generated by soothsayers of significant skill or daring. In essence the soothsayer uses psychology to influence their clients or listeners into particular courses of action, or draws upon seemingly random coincidences to fulfil their predictions.

The presence of witnesses is vital to the divination, since the reactions of those listening is often the cause of many prophesies coming true.

MAKING A DIVINATION

The Divination skill is used in the following manner. The player performs a divination ritual, states his intended result as a suitably melodramatic prophesy, rolls the requisite number of dice to see how many Magic Points it costs, and then the Game Master rolls against the character's Divination skill.

The result of the roll should remain hidden from the soothsayer, since he has no idea if his attempt to predict the future has succeeded or not.

- Ω **Critical** – The prediction immediately occurs, precisely as the player desired.
- Ω **Success** – Will bring the desired result within a week, in a series of odd coincidences.
- Ω **Failure** – The prediction completely fails to occur, undermining the soothsayer's reputation.
- Ω **Fumble** – Causes the twisting or reverse of the original intention (which can be particularly bad if the prophesy concerns death). The more important or influential the failed prophesy, the greater the risk that the seer is killed for his temerity, inaccuracy or simply executed for maleficent sorcery.

The Magic Point cost of the divination varies according to the changes prophesied. Large scale prophesies are extremely dangerous to cast and must be performed before a large number of people in order to work.

1d6 – Prediction affects a single individual
2d6 – Prediction affects a family or college
3d6 – Prediction affects an entire city
+1d6 – Prediction brings disaster or fortune
+2d6 – Prediction causes death

The number of Magic Points spent generating the prediction is rolled at the conclusion of the ritual. If the total cost exceeds the available Magic Points of the soothsayer, then the strain of changing reality to such a great degree causes them to collapse and either die or go insane as the Game Master desires. However, even if the seer dies, their dying words can still come true if the Divination roll succeeds.

"Moreover, proof of the power of dying men to prophesy is also given by Posidonius in his well-known account of a certain Rhodian, who, when on his death-bed, named six men of equal age and foretold which of them would die first, which second, and so on."

Cicero – De Divinatione

LOOSE TALK COSTS LIVES

All prophesies should be phrased in the traditional 'loose' manner, allowing the success of the foretelling to occur from an infinite number of different possibilities. They should also be made in a public manner so that any psychological influence can affect the subjects of the divination.

For example, a seer attached to a legion proclaims that the city they are besieging "shall fall when the apples kiss the ground". The GM rolls the dice and the seer is successful in his divination. He can implement this prophesy in a number of different ways. A normal success might mean the campaign drags on several more weeks until the rains of an autumn storm collapse part of the city's fortifications, coincidentally at the time the apples drop in the orchards. On a critical success, a table supporting a bowl of apples near the seer overturns and several apples roll into a hitherto unnoticed hole, revealing a secret passage under the walls...

Once a prophesy has been made, it cannot be rescinded or replaced. The future has now been set. Another soothsayer who successfully divines future events will make exactly the same prediction. This can be extremely bad if a prediction is specifically made about a player character. Of course, the Seer may not have succeeded in his Divination roll but if he has, then the GM is duty bound to force the events to happen. Large scale events usually take a longer time to occur.

Note also that a soothsayer cannot make a divination concerning their own future. Those that try invariably cause the prophecy to twist against themselves.

CURSING (EXSECRATIO)

"There is no one, who does not dread being spell-bound by means of evil imprecations"

Pliny the Elder – Naturalis Historia

Perhaps unsurprisingly for a society so entrenched with the concepts of vengeance and retribution, curses are one of the most prolific forms of magic in Rome. Although most people know a few choice phrases invoking the gods of the underworld, dabbling in such arts is inherently dangerous and the majority go to a professional sorcerer or witch for really effective curses (dirae).

"And when the other tribunes would not permit this, the attendant released Crassus, but Ateius ran on ahead to the city gate, placed there a blazing brazier, and when Crassus came up, cast incense and libations upon it, and invoked curses which were dreadful and terrifying in themselves, and were reinforced by sundry strange and dreadful gods whom he summoned and called by name. The Romans say that these mysterious and ancient curses have such power that no one involved in them ever escapes, and misfortune falls also upon the one who utters them, wherefore they are not employed at random nor by many... yet had he involved the city in curses which awakened much superstitious terror.

Plutarch – Life of Crassus

Although curses can be performed by verbal invocation (fascinatio) or the 'evil eye' (invidentia), most curses are inscribed upon lead tablets and cast into pits, wells or buried in graves – where spirits of the dead carry the request to the infernal deities. In this way, even if the caster is 'dealt with' for their maledictions, the curse (inscribed as it is on permanent material) is believed to continue ad infinitum.

Cursing was a frequent part of law cases, either to affect the results of litigation, or sometimes to denounce the reputation of the accused.

"When I had rounded off the case for the defence on behalf of Cotta's Titinia in a very important private suit, he [Curio] was speaking against me on behalf of Servius Naevius. All of a sudden he forgot his entire case and said that this had been caused by Titinia's spells and incantations."

Cicero – Brutus

In most campaigns the effects of cursing can be readily explained by the simple application of psychology. Romans believe in curses, so when they themselves are accursed, their own minds play tricks on them, hindering everyday tasks. As there are no actual manifestations attached to curses, they do not need to have an actual supernatural explanation.

CURSE TABLETS (DEFIXIONES)

Although curse tablets are normally inscribed upon lead, they can be made with other materials such as carved stone, papyrus, wax and even occasionally gemstones. Since a large proportion of Rome's populace are illiterate, curse tablets are often written by professionals and sold to customers to invoke for themselves.

Other than litigation curses, maledictions are used to hinder opponents in competitions, blight the success of rival tradesmen, punish ex-lovers or would-be lovers and more interestingly, bring justice upon those who have wronged the writer and even return stolen goods (for specific examples of competition curses, see Chariot Races page 81).

"The one who has stolen my bronze bowl is accursed. I give the person to the temple of Sulis, whether woman or man, whether slave or free, whether boy or girl, and may the man who did this pour his own blood into the very bowl. I give you that thief who stole the item itself, for the god to find, whether woman or man, whether slave or free, whether boy or girl."

Anonymous Curse

After inscription, those defixiones placed upon flexible materials are rolled up and have a nail hammered through them, thus 'fixing' the curse. They are then ritually buried in graves of the untimely dead or thrown in chthonian sanctuaries or wells which are all thought to connect with the underworld. This also has the benefit of hiding the curse from the person so blighted, since its destruction will negate the magic. In many cases, the victim is informed of the malediction and can purchase the curse tablet back or rescind the act which caused them to be cursed in the first place.

CASTING A CURSE

Invoking a malediction requires the Cursing skill. A simple roll against the skill determines if the curse has been successfully cast. However, the victim of the curse may resist its effects by winning an opposed test of their Willpower against the caster's Cursing roll.

Targets of a curse, whether or not it takes effect, always feel such nefarious attacks with some form of physical or psychosomatic consequence – although the sensations might not be recognised for what they truly are... for example shivers down the spine, or overt thumping of the heart.

"He [Olympius] had a contemptuous attitude toward Plotinus because of his own desire to be the first. His attacks culminated in an attempt to use magic to sun-scorch him. But when he perceived that the assault was rebounding on himself, he told his friends that Plotinus's soul was so powerful that it could beat back attacks against him and turn them on those who were trying to harm him. However, Plotinus perceived Olympius's attack and said that at that moment his body felt drawn tight as if by purse strings, with his limbs being crushed together. After repeatedly exposing himself to harm as opposed to inflicting it on Plotinus, Olympius gave up."

Porphyry – Life of Plotinus

Failure to affect the target of a successfully invoked curse rebounds the detrimental effect back upon the caster, although this might not be immediately obvious. Thus cursing can be a foolish thing to attempt for the uninitiated.

The effects of a curse are many and varied. The caster may choose from the following options.

Ω Loss of fertility, preventing the production of children, livestock or crops

Ω Plagued by dreams (if attracting) or nightmares (if chastising), which begin to drive the victim to increasing levels of fatigue

Ω Reduction of competence in a single skill by continuously reducing the success levels of any rolls against it by one step (e.g. Failures downgrade to Fumbles, Successes to Failures and so on)

Invoking curses costs the caster 1d6 POW, which is temporarily removed from the characteristic until the curse is allowed to lapse. Thus curses can be maintained for years if necessary but at a detrimental effect to the caster since each malediction twists his personality, saps magical energy and can reduce Luck Points.

Once a curse is allowed to drop, the caster regains the POW expended. Those curses cast without a curse tablet (such as the Evil Eye), can be prematurely ended with the death of the caster.

CURSES, CURSES.

Those prone to being cursed on a regular basis, such as charioteers for example, often have dozens, if not hundreds of maledictions cast upon them. This would mean that eventually some curses would take hold. Although this perhaps explains the high mortality rate of the profession, it does open the gates of game abuse.

To counteract this wave of negativity, those skilled in cursing can also counter-curse, providing protection against defixiones. These are cast and cost exactly the same as a normal cursing but any curse attempting to affect the target must first overcome the Cursing skill of his guardian in an opposed test, before it may continue onto the victim. Such protection is expensive but in many cases worthwhile.

Since curses normally require time to prepare and enact, and have a detrimental effect on the caster, cursing should not cause undue game balance difficulties in most campaigns.

NECROMANCY (NECROMANTIA)

"The impious chief of an unspeakable religion, accustomed to learning the fates in advance through human entrails, laid the spasming guts of a free born breast in the flames and broke the ground with a magical incantation. He dared to draw Pompey from the Elysian Fields. For shame. That Magnus should look upon this rite. Stupid man, why do you seek Pompey among the shades of the underworld? His spirit could not be confined by the earth."

Annonymous Epigram

The art of summoning and controlling the dead is a potent force. Necromancy is intimately woven into the legends of Rome's founding, from the voyage of Aeneas in the Aeneid, to the placation of the vengeful ghost of Romulus' brother, Remus. The Romans thought that those who died premature deaths (for whatever reason) or could not pay for the ferry across the River Styx were trapped on the edge of the underworld, still able to return to haunt the living. Only once

the full extent of their allotted hundred years had passed could they then cross over to seek eternal peace.

The dead were believed capable of revealing knowledge held by the departed and even foretelling the future, (although such predictions were considered unreliable, ultimately turning against the questioner). Spirits could also be summoned to haunt, or even slay, the living. Thus sorcerers and witches were greatly feared and given respect by their neighbours.

"You [Vatinius], who are accustomed to call yourself a Pythagorean and to conceal behind the name of a most learned man your monstrous and barbarian customs, what crookedness of mind possessed you, what frenzy so great? You have undertaken unheard-of criminal rites. You are accustomed to call up the spirits of the dead. You are accustomed to make sacrifices to the ghosts of the dead with the entrails of boys."

Cicero – In Vatinium

PERFORMING NECROMANCY

Summoning, controlling or exorcising the dead requires the Necromancy skill. Its implementation by necessity involves the use of dead bodies or casting spells in places where the dead are buried. As such, the lengthy rituals required are usually held at night, in forgotten graveyards or remote necropolises.

Summoning a spirit for questioning requires a cadaver to inhabit, so that the eidolon can use the dead body's voice to communicate. This means the dubious obtainment of a fresh corpse. The summoner must expend 1d6 Magic Points and roll successfully against their Necromancy skill to correctly recall a spirit to the corpse. It is then bound to answer questions its summoner poses. Each question costs the summoner a further 1d6 Magic Points and another roll (performed by the Game Master) against their Necromancy skill to obtain the correct answer. The dead are cunning and pervert answers unless rigidly held to the will of the witch or sorcerer.

"As the blood struck them the organs beneath the chill breast quivered, and life, creeping anew into the innards that had forgotten it, mingled itself with the death. Then all the dead man's limbs shook, and his sinews flexed. The corpse did not raise itself from the ground gradually, one limb at a time. Rather, it shot up from the earth and was upright in an instant. The eyes were laid bare, the mouth an open grimace. His appearance was of one not yet fully alive, but of a man still in the phase of dying. He was still pallid and stiff,

---

THE REALITY OF THE RESTLESS DEAD

On the face of it, necromancy appears to have no place in campaigns that abjure real magic. However even if no true supernatural powers are used, practitioners could still falsely portray some frightening and convincing effects. Many of the historical witches and sorcerers were reputed to use mediums, usually young boys if not themselves, through which the spirits spoke – a device still used till modern times. The employment of reanimated corpses could also be mere trickery, using fine threads disguised by very dim lighting to make the corpse move, augmented with ventriloquism. Even the sending of ghosts to haunt or murder might simply be persons frighteningly disguised with ashes and makeup, or even delusions suffered from the viewer being subtly poisoned... Those Game Masters who want to use 'real' ghosts should refer to the Lemures on page 161.

Non vestimentum virum ornat, sed vir vestimentum – Not the raiment graces the man, but the man the raiment

and in consternation at being brought back into the world. But his tightened mouth made no mutter. Voice and tongue were granted him only for replying. "Tell me," said the Thessalian witch, "what I command you, and you shall be well rewarded."

Lucan – Pharsalia

Calling forth a lemur from the underworld to haunt a victim is a far more dangerous procedure. Without a body to confine its spirit, the ghost can potentially break free of the summoner's control. It costs 3d6 Magic Points and a successful roll against the Necromancy skill to summon a lemur; if the cost is more than the Magic Points the witch or sorcerer has available, then control over the ghost is lost, leaving them vulnerable to its predilections… normally meaning imminent possession or death.

"She [an unfaithful wife] asked for one of two results, either that her husband should be pacified, and that she should be reconciled with him, or, if she could not do that, that at any rate a ghost or some dreadful demon be sent to do violence to him and destroy him. Then the witch, able as she was to compel divine powers, opened a skirmish with just the basic weapons of her evil trade. She tried to redirect the husband's mind from its deep feelings of offence toward love. The plan did not work as she had intended. She became angry with the powers, and was impelled to her task now not only by the promised profit of her payment, but also by the contempt of the powers for her. Now she began to threaten the life itself of the unfortunate husband, and sent the ghost of a woman killed by violence to kill him."

Apuleius – Metamorphoses

Necromancy can also be used in a more benevolent manner to lay the dead to rest, or simply drive them off. Exorcising a ghost requires the necromancer to win an opposed test of their Necromancy skill against the spirit's Willpower.

"My son," he [the boy's father] said, "is not sufficiently dead. He still roams abroad when the stars shine in the night. When daylight is gone, he puts an end to his death, returns home, and terrorizes his mother in her sleep. Find something; find some bonds of words, pushing your craft and your energies to their limits. Great is your glory, if you can confine my son, who returns to his mother even from death." A deleterious spell is put around the tomb, and the urn is closed off with terrible words. Then for the first time the son becomes a corpse and shade."

Quintilian – Declamationes Maiores

PHARMACY (MEDICAMENTARIA)

The traditional province of witches, pharmacy is the concoction of potions from exotic, weird or downright toxic ingredients. Although the skill could be used for more innocent purposes – medicines for example – the most infamous uses of this skill were the production of poisons and love potions.

"By the spell of Thessalian women love flows into hard hearts, contrary to destiny, and austere old men burn with the flames of unlawful desire. Their powers are not restricted to harmful potions or the hippomanes, stolen from the mare, the succulent gland that grows on a foal's forehead, the pledge that its mother will love it. A mind, even when not corrupted by a poisonous drink, can be overcome with incantations. Couples who cannot be bound to each other by the contract of the marriage bed or the power of a lovely form are dragged together by the magical twisting of threads."

Lucan – Pharsalia

The components for pharmacy are gathered from a plethora of different sources. Most are animal or plant derived but some ingredients even come from exhumed human cadavers. These recipes

A ROMAN GHOST STORY

The Romans had many stories concerning the dead, some were brought from Greece but others such as the ghost of Remus were part of the legends of the city. These stories were treated seriously and recorded by historians of the period.

"Two Arcadian companions hit the road together and came to Megara. One of them went to stay with an innkeeper, the other with a friend. After a meal they took to their beds. Just after he had retired for the night the man who was staying with his friend saw a vision of the other companion in his dreams, in which he begged him to come help, because the innkeeper was plotting to murder him. His first reaction was to wake in terror at the dream, but then he gathered his wits, concluded that the vision was nugatory, and went back to sleep. As he slept on he saw another vision in which the same man begged him that he should not suffer his death to go unavenged, since he had not come to help him while still alive. After killing him, he said, the innkeeper had thrown his body on the back of a cart and covered it with dung. He asked him to bring himself to the town gate in the morning before the cart could leave the place. This dream disturbed him, and so he confronted the driver at the gate and asked him what was in the cart. He fled in terror, the dead man was pulled out of the dung, all was revealed, and the innkeeper paid the penalty."

Cicero – De Divinatione

THE LADYKILLERS

The following story was a historic event in the period of the mid Republic. It shocked the patriarchal society of the time and helped fuel later sanctions against magicians and poisoners, who were regarded as the same thing in Roman society, hence sharing the name of venefici.

"The foremost men in the state were being attacked by the same mysterious malady, which in almost every case proved fatal. A maid-servant went to the city magistrate, Quintus Fabius Maximus, and promised to reveal the cause of these suspicious deaths, provided the state would guarantee her safety. Fabius went at once to the consuls, who referred the matter to the senate, which authorized a promise of protection and immunity. The maid-servant then accused certain women of concocting poisons. If officers would follow her at once, she said, they could catch the poison makers in the act. The officers followed the informant and did indeed find the accused compounding poisonous substances, along with batches of poisons which were already made up. The evidence was seized and brought into the Forum. Twenty high-born matrons, at whose houses poisons were discovered, were brought before the magistrates. Two of the women, Cornelia and Sergia, both from ancient patrician families, contended that the concoctions were medicinal preparations. Accused of lying, the maid-servant suggested that the women should drink some the supposed medicine themselves; if they wishes to prove it was harmless. The court was cleared of spectators. The accused women consulted among themselves. All consented to drink the potions, whereupon they all died."

Livy – Ab Urbe Condita

sound disgusting but gave the final potion a great deal of authenticity to the average ill-educated Roman. For example the "Gall of the wild boar, smeared on" promoted copulation and similarly the fluids, described by Virgil "from a horse's copulation and a horse's testicles, dried so that they may be ground up and put in a potion, or the right testicle of an ass drunk in wine in a suitable dose" were common ingredients of love potions.

The normal place scoured to recover human ingredients was the Esquiline Hill outside of the city walls, where the burial pits were located.

"One can live on the salubrious Esquiline now and go for walks on the sunny rampart, whereas until recently one could only look gloomily on a field disfigured by white bones. It is not so much the thieves and the wild animals accustomed to disturb the place that concern and bother me, so much as the women who try to twist human minds about with spells and poisons. I just cannot put an end to these women or stop them collecting bones and destructive herbs, once the wandering moon brings out her comely face."

Horace – Satires

Of course such concoctions were often more poisonous than effective, despite the psychosomatic effects attributed by its imbiber. The punishments for producing potions were harsh, either being sent to the mines or marooned on an island, in an attempt to stop the needless deaths caused by malpractice.

CONCOCTING POTIONS

To brew a potion the character must possess the Pharmacy skill, allowing them to concoct a variety of potions, if they can locate the correct ingredients. Each dose takes at least several hours to concoct and must be invested with 1d6 Magic Points to activate it. These Magic Points do not regenerate until the potion is consumed, applied, or allowed to go stale.

The duration of a potion's effect is permanent, until countered by another potion. Some examples of Roman potions are…

Ω **Love potions (amatoria)** – These cause the imbibers to fall madly in love with the person the potion was made for (who supplies part of the potion's ingredients). It is resisted by winning an opposed roll of the drinker's Willpower against the Pharmacy skill of the concoctor.

"And yet no herb, no root lying hidden in rough places has escaped me. Does he lie on a drugged bed and forget all my rivals? Ah. He walks abroad, delivered by the spell of a more knowledgeable witch. I will not use the familiar potions. Varus, you will weep at length and run back to me. Your mind will not return to me summoned merely by Marsian spells. I am preparing something stronger."

Horace – Epodes

Ω **Warding potions (tutelae)** – Brewed to protect the drinker from the ill effects of other mentally affecting concoctions. The potency of any such potion later consumed is reduced by the Pharmacy skill of whomever brewed the warding infusion. If the imbiber is already under the domination of a mind-altering potion, they are allowed to make another opposed test to throw off the effect – this time using the Pharmacy skills of the respective concoctors.

Ω **Poisons (venena)** – Other than serpent bites, the poisons of witches are some of the most lethal substances known to Romans. The potency of any such poison is equal to the Pharmacy skill of the concoctor. See overleaf for a description of how particular types of poison work.

Ω **Medicines (medicamenta)** – Wise women (sagae) can sometimes brew medicines which aid against disease. The imbiber may use the Pharmacy skill used to create the medicine against the disease potency it was brewed for, instead of using their own Endurance. Obviously most of these herbal medicines are less effectual than a healthy constitution but they can still aid the young or elderly.

Pharmacy in non-magical campaigns can be easily explained as applied pharmacology. Narcotics and poisons can still be produced without supernatural powers. However, to preserve game balance the Game Master should limit the proliferation of such substances by making their ingredients rare and difficult to obtain.

WHAT'S YOUR POISON?

Although the Romans knew of many different poisonous substances, the majority were herbal in nature. Most mineral poisons were actually regarded as medicines at the time and animal poisons normally required the creature to inflict its own venom since it rapidly lost its effectiveness after it was killed.

The following poisons were the ones known to be potentially fatal to a man. None are given a strict potency, since the strength of a herbal poison depends on the skill of the pharmacist preparing it (see Concocting Potions above). However their medical effects are described for realism.

Nosce te ipsum! – Know thyself! (Cicero)

Victims of these poisons must match their Endurance against the Potency of the poison in an opposed test. Success means that the victim is only seriously ill and all skills suffer a difficulty grade of Formidable for a number of days equal to one tenth the Potency, until the character fully recovers. Failing the Resistance Roll means the character dies. Additional conditions may be applied as described by its symptoms.

Ω **Henbane** – Symptoms: Rapid onset within minutes of ingestion, dry mouth, abnormally rapid heartbeat and a progression of neurological symptoms varying from sedation to delirium, hallucination, mania, paralysis, coma and death.

Ω **Thorn Apple** – Symptoms: Similar to henbane. Seeds produce mainly maniacal symptoms, whilst leaves tend towards stupor and coma. Survivors have amnesia of the event.

Ω **Deadly Nightshade** – Symptoms: As for henbane. Known as strychnos, spears were sometimes coated with it.

Ω **Mandrake** – Symptoms: Dry mouth and rapid heartbeat but neurologically it causes sedation, motor depression and death via heart failure.

Ω **Aconite** – Symptoms: Rapid onset of numbness and tingling of the mouth and throat which spreads over the rest of the body; pain and twitching of the muscles, progressing to general weakness, cold and clammy extremities, irregular heart rhythm and abnormally low blood pressure, respiratory paralysis, drowsiness, convulsions, stupor and death. Extremely poisonous even in small doses.

Ω **Hemlock** – Symptoms: Rapid onset of nausea, salivation and vomiting, abdominal pain, headache and degrees of mental confusion. General weakness may be associated with convulsions, and death is caused by progressive paralysis and respiratory failure.

Ω **White Hellebore** – Symptoms: Rapid onset of tingling over the whole body, sneezing, vomiting, and diarrhoea, followed by abnormally low blood pressure, cardiovascular collapse and respiratory paralysis causing death.

Ω **Colchicum (autumn crocus)** – Symptoms: Tingling of the whole mouth and throat, after 2-6 hours it is followed by an impaired ability to swallow, nausea, vomiting and diarrhoea (often bloody). Circulation collapse may follow, with general paralysis, often convulsions and death due to respiratory failure.

Ω **Yew** – Symptoms: After approximately one hour there is onset of dizziness, vomiting, rapid heartbeat, dilation of the pupils, dilation of the blood vessels causing a reddish face and shallow breathing. Death results from respiratory paralysis. The Scythians were said to dip their arrows in yew-sap.

Ω **Opium** – Symptoms: Induces a somniferous state with euphoria and pinpoint pupils, progressing to stupor with muscular relaxation, slow respiration and ultimately death from respiratory failure. Pliny wrote that opium was sometimes used by elderly Romans to commit suicide.

Ω **Fly Agaric Mushrooms** – Symptoms: Within minutes to two hours, salivation, excessive production of tears, breathing problems and severe abdominal pain with diarrhoea. Vertigo and progressive mental symptoms like confusion, delirium, excitement (occasionally convulsions) may lead to coma and death within hours.

Ω **Panther Cap Mushrooms** – Symptoms: Like the Fly Agaric above but with slower onset and higher fatality.

Ω **Death Cap Mushrooms** – Symptoms: Latent period of 6-15 hours is followed by abdominal pain, vomiting and diarrhoea (often bloody). Renal failure then sets in with death 2-3 days later, usually in hepatic coma.

SHAPE-SHIFTING (ARS VERSIPELLIS)

Of all Roman magic, shape-shifting is by far the most fantastical. It intimates an actual physical change, unique amongst the normal Roman tradition of subtle sorcery; save for a few reports of werewolves (versipelles) from Greece, the only shape-shifters were recorded as entertaining stories rather than actual fact.

"Rather, as was clear to see, my hair thickened into bristles, and my tender skin hardened into leather. All the fingers on the ends of my hands reduced in number and coalesced into undivided hooves. A large tail was produced from the base of my spine. By now my face was huge, my mouth long, my nostrils gaped and my lips hung down. At the same time my ears shot up high and grew shaggy. There was not one good thing about this pitiful transformation, except that my genitals increased in size, although I was no longer in a position to embrace Photis. Without the means to help myself, I looked over all my body and saw that I was not a bird but an ass."

Apuleius – Metamorphoses

Less magically orientated campaigns might prefer to remove this form of enchantment completely. Conversely, it can be twisted so that its practitioners or victims believe than they have been changed into beasts, whilst they actually gallivant about either naked or dressed in the skins of the beasts they unwittingly imitate.

The province of shape-shifting was firmly under the control of witches. They could, like the famous Greek witch Circe, transform men into beasts. Or they themselves could switch into more useful forms. Traditionally, Romans believed that owls were shape-shifted witches…

"First Pamphile divested herself of all her clothes. She opened a casket and took a few little boxes from it. She took the top off one of these and scooped some lotion out of it. For a while she worked it between her palms and then she smeared herself all over with it, from the ends of her toenails to the hairs on the top of her head. She had a mysterious conversation with her lamp and set her limbs fluttering. As they gently flowed, soft down sprung from them, and strong feathers grew. Her nose grew hard and became hooked, and her toenails curved round into talons. An owl was made of Pamphile. With this she issued a mournful screech and, testing herself, jumped up from the ground, a little higher each time. Then she pulled herself aloft and flew out of the house, using the full power of her wings."

Apuleius – Metamorphoses

CHANGING FORMS

Most shape-shifting needs the application of an enchanted ointment or salve to achieve the desired transformation. To create these enchantments requires the Shape-Shifting skill. However, the final potion, once concocted, can be used by anyone.

Each enchantment takes at least several days to concoct and, assuming a successful Shape-Shifting skill roll is made, can then be invested with a number of Magic Points to activate it (see table below). These Magic Points do not regenerate until the enchantment is either used or allowed to go stale.

The animal, into which an enchantment transforms its user, must be decided in advance, since the material components used to formulate it are specific to the creature desired.

To employ a shape-shifting enchantment, all of the user's clothes must be first removed. Then the potion is smeared over the whole of their body. Once applied, the physical change is very rapid – taking only 1d3 rounds to complete. The duration of the shape-shifting effect is permanent until countered by a neutralising potion, normally produced in advance by sensible shape-shifters.

(COUNTER) ENCHANTMENT MAGIC POINT COST:

1d6 – Small animals: Mice, Frogs, Owls, etc.
2d6 – Medium animals: Wolves, Boars, Snakes, etc.
3d6 – Large animals: Lions, Panthers, Bears, etc.

Enchanted animal skins differ slightly from potions in that they can be removed at will by the wearer and do not lose their magic once doffed. However, the cost to create these priceless artefacts requires the permanent sacrifice of an amount of POW equivalent to the normal Magic Point expenditure.

THE PRICE OF POWER

As can be seen from the preceding sections, the darker arts of Roman magic are expensive both in terms of investing (tying up) Magic Points and in the lengthy durations required to prepare invocations.

Such hindrances are deliberate. In both the historical reports and entertaining plays of the period, magic was a difficult (and extremely dangerous) power to call upon. An invocation or concoction took hours of preparation before casting and each new enchantment required fresh components – rather than maintaining a stockpile of pre-prepared curse tablets or potions.

The reasons for this are manifold. But the primary one is that every spell must be specially crafted for its intended victim/recipient. Sympathetic superstition is a vital aspect of Roman magic, making it stronger, or at least increasing the witnesses' belief in it.

Practitioners of forbidden magic normally reserve their most powerful abilities for a single patron at a time and are expensive to support. These compounding difficulties should prevent the proliferation of magic in campaigns; turning its occurrence into singular, unique events, rather than a regular method to solve problems.

PLOT HOOK

The name of Rome's own patron god is a very closely guarded secret during the Republic. Known only to the highest priesthood, it is never uttered in public lest enemies can use the knowledge to steal or even curse the deity. An adventure could be set around the idea that an impious priest has sold or been blackmailed into revealing this sacred name and the characters must follow a grisly trail of dead priests and politicians to prevent the information being sold to the city's enemies…

"Verrius Flaccus cites authors whom he deems worthy of credit, to show that on the occasion of a siege, it was the usage, the first thing of all, for the Roman priests to summon forth the tutelary divinity of that particular town, and to promise him the same rites, or even a more extended worship, at Rome; and at the present day even, this ritual still forms part of the discipline of our pontiffs. Hence it is, no doubt, that the name – of the tutelary deity of Rome has been so strictly kept concealed, lest any of our enemies should act in a similar manner."

Pliny the Elder – Naturalis Historia

CREATURES

Most Romans have little direct contact with the animal world. Save for the early days of the city when nature was still allowed to roam the hills, the populace saw little but the birds of the air and the livestock in the Forum Boarium. Although hunters, farmers and shepherds could still encounter wild life, eventually the region surrounding Rome was settled and cultivated to such a degree that only vermin remained.

The majority of wild animals seen by the people of Rome were exotic creatures imported from overseas, usually places like Africa, which supplied an unending source of strange beasts. They were initially used for the simple purpose of display at festivals, somewhat like the travelling circuses of the 19th and 20th centuries. However, in 186 BC the novel entertainment of the beast hunts began, where ferocious animals were matched against hunters in the Circus Maximus. Eventually these animals were fought against each other and started a tradition of gambling, which still survives to the modern day.

The creatures described in this chapter are split into two sections. The first are the real animals, which can be used as encounters in the early days of the City or as opponents in the Circus. The second part concerns mythological creatures, which Games Masters can include if they desire more fantastic encounters.

ANIMALS (BESTIAE)

These animals are either native to Europe of the period or imported at great expense from the provinces. Where known, the date of the first appearance in the city is also included.

FIGHTING QUADRUPEDS

Remember that – as a rule – when four legged animals fight, the creature places its head towards its opponent. Given the size of most quadrupeds, it is difficult for a single human to strike any location other than the forequarters, front legs, or head of the beast. For this reason, it is suggested that when a character attacks such an animal, they roll a d10+10 for the Hit Location. Of course, if the animal is surrounded by multiple foes, then the full range of its target locations should be available.

BEARS (URSI)

A popular opponent for venators in the earliest beast hunts; bears were also used as part of paired beast matches – bears versus bulls or lions being a favourite. Bears were initially common in the alpine regions of Italy but as time passed they had to be imported from northern Europe. For statistics, see MYTHRAS page 230.

BULLS (TAURI)

Probably an evolution from the ancient Cretan traditions of Bull Dancing, bull fights were one of the earliest forms of beast hunt in the Circus. Initially widespread across Europe, wild aurochs (uri) became rare by the end of the Republic, the best coming from Germania and beyond. The statistics of a normal bull are presented here. For those of its giant brethren, the Aurochs, see MYTHRAS page 226.

Bull	Attributes
STR: 2d6+18 (25)	Action Points: 2
CON: 2d6+9 (16)	Damage Modifier: +1d12
SIZ: 2d6+21 (28)	Magic Points: 7
DEX: 2d6 (7)	Movement: 8m
INS: 2d6+4 (11)	Initiative Bonus: +9
POW: 2d6 (7)	Armour: Shaggy Hide
	Abilities: Trample

1d20	Location	AP/HP
1 – 3	Right Hind Leg	4/9
4 – 6	Left Hind Leg	4/9
7 – 9	Hindquarters	4/10
10 – 12	Forequarters	4/11
13 – 15	Right Front Leg	4/8
16 – 18	Left Front Leg	4/8
19 – 20	Head	4/9

Skills

Athletics 52%, Brawn 73%, Endurance 62%, Evade 34%, Perception 38%, Stealth 38%, Willpower 44%

Combat Style & Weapons				
Fearless Stampede 52%				

Weapon	Size/Force	Reach	Damage	AP/HP
Gore	L	M	1d8+1d12	As for Head
Trample	H	T	2d12	As for Leg

BOARS (APRI)

Seen more as a source of food rather than an animal for public spectacle, wild boars are common throughout all of Italy and Europe – many being escaped domestic stock. Hunting boars however, still remains a dangerous occupation. For statistics, see MYTHRAS page 230.

CROCODILES (CROCODILI)

The first crocodiles were exhibited at Rome by the ædile Scaurus in 58 BC. Eventually they became popular as opponents to lions in beast matches. For statistics, see MYTHRAS page 237.

DOGS (CANES)

Dogs are actually not very popular in Rome itself, especially after the sacking of the city by the Gauls, when the dogs were considered lax in their guard duties. Some people however still use dogs to deter thieves and scavenging packs of wild dogs which roam the streets can be dangerous to the unwary.

Normally dogs are only used by hunters and shepherds who reside in the countryside. Roman dogs are often given a spiked collar (melium) to protect them from being wounded by wild beasts (automatic 1d3 damage to the attacker if they bite at the head or neck). For statistics, see the notes for Wolf, MYTHRAS page 272.

> "…there are, then, two sorts of dogs – the hunting-dog suited to chase the beasts of the forest, and the other which is procured as a watch-dog and is of importance to the shepherd"
>
> *Varro – De Re Rustica*

ELEPHANTS (ELEPHANTI)

Most of the elephants of this period are African forest elephants, which are somewhat smaller than their plains cousins (and are now extinct). Initially seen by the Romans in their war with General Pyrrhus, they were frightening beasts, which repeatedly broke the lines and discipline of the legionaries. The first display of elephants in Rome was in 251 BC. It was not until the end of the Republic when the animals began to be used in beast hunts. For statistics refer to MYTHRAS page 256, but reduce STR and SIZ by another 4 points apiece.

> "Hannibal pitted a Roman prisoner against an elephant, and this man, having secured a promise of his freedom if he killed the animal, met it single-handed in the arena and much to the chagrin of the Carthaginians dispatched it. Hannibal realized that reports of this encounter would bring the animals into contempt, so he sent horsemen to kill the man as he was departing"
>
> *Pliny the Elder – Naturalis Historia*

HIPPOPOTAMI (HIPPOPOTAMI)

First seen in Rome in 58 BC in concert with the first crocodiles, hippos became popular creatures for private collections. Second only in weight to the elephant and a deadly beast in the water (its preferred environment), hippopotami share the same fierce and aggressive temper as their smaller relations, the boar.

Hippopotamus	Attributes
STR: 2d6+27 (34)	Action Points: 2
CON: 2d6+6 (13)	Damage Modifier: +2d8
SIZ: 2d6+40 (47)	Magic Points: 7
DEX: 1d6+3 (7)	Movement: 6m
INS: 2d6+4 (11)	Initiative Bonus: +9
POW: 2d6 (7)	Armour: Thick Hide
	Abilities: Trample

1d20	Location	AP/HP
1 – 3	Right Hind Leg	5/12
4 – 6	Left Hind Leg	5/12
7 – 9	Hindquarters	5/13
10 – 12	Forequarters	5/14
13 – 15	Right Front Leg	5/11
16 – 18	Left Front Leg	5/11
19 – 20	Head	5/12

Skills	

Athletics 41%, Brawn 81%, Endurance 66%, Evade 24%, Perception 38%, Stealth 28%, Swim 47%, Willpower 54%

Combat Style & Weapons	

Bellicose Beast 61%

Weapon	Size/Force	Reach	Damage	AP/HP
Bite	E	S	1d8+2d8	As for Head
Trample	C	T	4d8	As for Leg

HORSES (EQUI)

Normally forbidden within Rome, most horses are stabled away from the city walls, in locations where there is still grazing land to support them. Owning a horse is expensive in terms of daily care and feed, so most hire steeds as and when they need them. During the Roman period, horses were much smaller than modern breeds and specially trained warhorses, taught to attack, didno t exist. For statistics see MYTHRAS page 251, but reduce STR and SIZ by 4 points apiece.

Nullum magnum ingenium sine mixtura dementiae fuit – There has been no great genius without some madness (Seneca)

HYENAS (HYAENAE)

Imported from Africa, the hyena is a scavenger with extremely powerful jaws. Also known as the Crocotta, the Romans believed it to be an animal produced by the union of the wolf and the dog, "for it can break any thing with its teeth and instantly on swallowing it digest it with the stomach". It was also reputed to be able to change its colour or sex at will.

Hyena	Attributes
STR: 1d3+9 (11)	Action Points: 2
CON: 3d6 (11)	Damage Modifier: None
SIZ: 1d6+9 (13)	Magic Points: 7
DEX: 3d6 (11)	Movement: 8m
INS: 2d6+6 (13)	Initiative Bonus: +12
POW: 2d6 (7)	Armour: Fur
	Abilities: Night Sight, Savage

1d20	Location	AP/HP
1–2	Right Hind Leg	1/5
3–4	Left Hind Leg	1/5
5–7	Hindquarters	1/6
8–10	Forequarters	1/7
11–13	Right Front Leg	1/5
14–16	Left Front Leg	1/5
17–20	Head	1/5

Skills

Athletics 62%, Brawn 54%, Endurance 62%, Evade 52%, Perception 50%, Track 54%, Willpower 44%

Combat Style & Weapons

Pack Attack (Bite) 62%

Weapon	Size/Force	Reach	Damage	AP/HP
Bite	M	T	1d6	As for Head

SAVAGE

If the creature manages to attach itself to a victim, by biting and holding on with the Grip special effect, they continue to inflict damage, shaking their head (or their entire body) back and forth to tear the wound open. This ability allows the creature to spend an Action Point on its Turn to automatically roll damage without needing an attack roll, whilst also permitting it to ignore any negative Damage Modifier it might normally possess.

LIONS (LEONES)

Lions were sometimes privately owned and Marcus Antonius was reputed to have driven a chariot drawn by lions from Brindisi to Rome. The first lion hunt was held in 186 BC and they soon became a staple opponent in the matched beast fights. During 93 BC Sulla turned 100 lions loose in the Forum Romanum and in 55

BC Pompey had 500 killed as part of his theatre's inauguration. For statistics, see MYTHRAS page 253.

PANTHERS (PARDI)

In ancient Rome leopards are known as panthers. They were first shown in 186 BC along with lions. Panthers were also favourite opponents for the beast hunts, not only for their agile fierceness but also for their beauty. Their popularity continued to rise and by 168 BC, 63 panthers were shown in the games. Towards the end of the republic, some panthers were kept as exhibits in private menageries.

If a panther's claw or bite hits, it remains attached to prevent its prey from escaping and the panther uses an alternative attack. If it has two solid holds, then the panther can apply its Savage ability using its hind claws to rake.

Panther	Attributes
STR: 1d6+9 (13)	Action Points: 3
CON: 3d6 (11)	Damage Modifier: +1d2
SIZ: 1d6+9 (13)	Magic Points: 7
DEX: 1d6+12 (16)	Movement: 8m
INS: 2d6+6 (13)	Initiative Bonus: +15
POW: 2d6 (7)	Armour: Fur
	Abilities: Leaper, Night Sight, Savage

1d20	Location	AP/HP
1 – 3	Tail	1/4
4 – 5	Right Hind Leg	1/5
6 – 7	Left Hind Leg	1/5
8 – 10	Hindquarters	1/6
11 – 14	Forequarters	1/7
15 – 16	Right Front Leg	1/4
17 – 18	Left Front Leg	1/4
19 – 20	Head	1/5

Skills

Athletics 69%, Brawn 46%, Endurance 52%, Evade 72%, Perception 60%, Stealth 79%, Willpower 54%

Combat Style & Weapons

Stealthy Hunter 69%

Weapon	Size/Force	Reach	Damage	AP/HP
Claw	M	S	1d4+1d2	As for Leg
Bite	M	T	1d6+1d2	As for Head

"It so happened, that being one day at the Docks, where there were some wild beasts from Africa, while he (Pasiteles) was viewing through the bars of a cage a lion which he was engaged in drawing, a panther made its escape from another cage, to the no small danger of this most careful artist."

Pliny the Elder – Naturalis Historia

RHINOS (RHINOCEROTES)

Matched in aggressiveness with the Hippo but easier to transport, the Black Rhino was a terrifying foe in the beast hunts. Anything caught in the rhino's charge was doomed and stories tell of beast fights where rhinos tossed bulls and bears tumbling into the air, killing them outright.

Rhinoceros	Attributes
STR: 2d6+30 (37)	Action Points: 2
CON: 2d6+9 (16)	Damage Modifier: +2d8
SIZ: 2d6+39 (46)	Magic Points: 7
DEX: 1d6+6 (10)	Movement: 8m
INS: 2d6+4 (11)	Initiative Bonus: +11
POW: 2d6 (7)	Armour: Thick Hide
	Abilities: Intimidate, Trample

1d20	Location	AP/HP
1 – 3	Right Hind Leg	6/13
4 – 6	Left Hind Leg	6/13
7 – 9	Hindquarters	6/14
10 – 12	Forequarters	6/15
13 – 15	Right Front Leg	6/12
16 – 18	Left Front Leg	6/12
19 – 20	Head	6/13
19 – 20	Head	1/5

Skills

Athletics 47%, Brawn 83%, Endurance 72%, Evade 30%, Perception 38%, Stealth 31%, Willpower 54%

Combat Style & Weapons

Cantankerous Charge 67%

Weapon	Size/Force	Reach	Damage	AP/HP
Gore	E	M	1d12+2d8	As for Head
Trample	C	T	4d8	As for Leg

SCORPIONS (SCORPIONES)

There are a variety of scorpions available from foreign lands. Normally people that possess such creatures have no legitimate reason for ownership, save apothecaries or sorcerers who use them for concocting 'medicines' or to impress their customers. In Egypt there are even believed to be winged scorpions with double stings.

REALISTIC SCORPION AND SNAKE VENOM

Animal venoms work somewhat differently to ingested plant toxins, having a swifter onset time and principally affecting the body location struck. Although in this day and age few envenomisations are fatal, the reverse is true for the ancient world. Poor health and nutrition are factors, plus the lethal reputation of poisonous creatures cause victims to panic, precipitating severe shock and hastening venom absorption. In addition, medical treatments of the period would likely raise the morbidity or mortality of the wound. (see Realistic Roman Medicine page 131)

Games Masters who feel pity towards their players could allow characters to spend a Luck Point when struck by a venomous creature, resulting in a 'dry' bite or sting where the creature has not actually injected any toxin. Or they could instead say nothing, deciding in secret that the attack was merely a non-venomous warning and sadistically allow their players to sweat in anticipation of imminent death...

Few scorpions are lethal to humans but can make the victim of a sting very ill. Usually only children and elderly are at risk. Scorpions come in all colours and sizes (up to ten inches in length) and normally only sting those who mistakenly surprise them. Depending on species the venom can vary in Potency and effect but always causes the Agony condition in the location hit. The sting itself causes no other damage. Once stung the victim can easily withdraw to avoid further stings (unless the arachnid is inside the victim's clothing), or kill the scorpion with a successful attack.

SNAKES (ANGUES)

Although large constrictor snakes are mainly imported for display (snake dancing or wrestling acts), they are also infrequently used for beast fights. Poisonous asps or cobras can be imported too but their ownership is viewed with suspicion, since there is little one can do with a venomous snake save nefarious deeds.

Like scorpions, venomous snakes attack only in defence or when surprised. Once they strike, they generally retreat and can easily be avoided. Large constrictors however, can be quite persistent if they manage to entangle a lone victim in their coils.

VENOMOUS SNAKES

There are countless types of venomous snakes ranging from one to three metres in length. Although their mouths are universally too small to damage humanoids, their venom is not to be underestimated. Vipers should be treated more akin to one-shot traps or accidental encounters, biting out of self-defence before wriggling away or being hacked down by the victim. Whilst the native viper is indigenous to Italy, more venomous snakes must be imported from Arabia or Africa.

SCORPION VENOMS

Species	Potency	Resistance	Onset Time	Duration	Venom Effect
Yellow Tailed Scorpion	40%	Endurance	Instant	1d6 hours	Agony in the Hit Location stung
Fattail Scorpion	50%	Endurance	Instant for Agony, 1d3 hours for Exhaustion, and 1d10+5 hours for Asphyxiation	1d3 days if not fatal	Agony in the Hit Location followed by Exhaustion. Victim is permitted a second resistance roll to survive the Asphyxiation
Deathstalker Scorpion	60%	Endurance	Instant for Agony, 1d3 hours for Nausea, and 1d3+3 hours for Death	Nausea lasts 1d3 weeks if not fatal	Agony in the Hit Location followed by Nausea. Victim is permitted a second resistance roll to avoid Death

Nunc est bibendum – Now it's time to drink (Horace)

SNAKE VENOMS

Species	Potency	Resistance	Onset Time	Duration	Venom Effect
Native Viper	30%	Endurance	1d3 Turns	1d6 hours	Agony in the Hit Location bitten
Puff Adder	50%	Endurance	Instant for Agony, Maiming starts after 1 day	1d3 hours for Agony. 2d6 days for Maiming	Immediate Agony in the bite site followed by Maiming (1 Hit Point per full day), usually leading to death from necrosis
Egyptian Cobra	70%	Endurance	1d3x10 minutes	Permanent	Victim initially suffers Paralysis, followed 1d3 hours later by death via Asphyxiation
Black Mamba	90%	Endurance	1d6+4 minutes	Permanent	Exhaustion followed by Death 10 minutes later.

Venomous snakes have a Stealth skill of 70+1d10% and a Toxic Strike combat style of 60+1d10%. By default they possess the Cold-Blooded and Venomous abilities, and use Inject Venom if they win a special effect in combat. Each species has its own venom as defined in the above table.

CONSTRICTOR SNAKES

The only constrictor snakes that can be imported to Rome are African rock pythons, which can sometimes grow up to six metres in length. They are dangerous if they manage to grapple an opponent, being able to wrap the victim up in its coils and slowly crushing them If not actively crushing to inflict damage, a python may instead make an attack roll to engulf another Hit Location in its coils.

Constrictor	Attributes
STR: 1d6+12 (16)	Action Points: 3
CON: 2d6+6 (13)	Damage Modifier: +1d2
SIZ: 1d6+9 (13)	Magic Points: 10
DEX: 2d6+6 (13)	Movement: 4m
INS: 2d6+5 (12)	Initiative Bonus: +13
POW: 1d6+6 (10)	Armour: Scales
	Abilities: Cold-Blooded, Dark Sight (heat only), Grappler

1d20	Location	AP/HP
1 – 3	Tail Tip	2/6
4 – 5	Mid End-length	2/6
6 – 7	Fore End-length	2/6
8 – 9	Rear Mid-length	2/7
10 – 12	Mid Mid-length	2/7
13 – 14	Fore Mid-length	2/7
15 – 16	Rear Fore-length	2/6
17 – 18	Mid Fore-length	2/6
19 – 20	Head	2/6

Skills

Athletics 59%, Brawn 69%, Endurance 56%, Evade 56%, Perception 42%, Stealth 65%, Swim 59%, Willpower 50%

Combat Style & Weapons

Crushing Doom 69%

Weapon	Size/Force	Reach	Damage	AP/HP
Bite	M	S	1d4+1d2	As for Head
Constrict	H	T	1d6+1d2	As for Body

WOLVES (LUPI)

A significant animal in the Roma psyche, the wolf is treated with respect for its cunning and ability to hunt as a pack. Few humans are directly at risk of wolf attacks but they tend to prey upon free-ranging animals under the supervision of shepherds. Romans believe that wolves are able to steal the voice of a man.

Wolves are sometimes displayed in the Circus, perhaps due to their commonplace nature or maybe because they are part of Rome's sacred founding. However, wolves are also native to the mountainous regions of Italy, and both shepherds and travellers may encounter them. For statistics see MYTHRAS page 272.

MYTHOLOGICAL CREATURES (MONSTRA)

Most of Rome's mythological creatures were inherited from Greek legends or reports from the first explorers of Africa and Persia... very few were fundamentally Roman. The most important have been included for those Games Masters who desire a mythic or horror based campaign.

It should be noted that although these creatures were written about by academics and historians, the presence of such foreign creatures would be incongruous outside of the wild mountains of the Aegean nations or the arid wastes of North Africa. The few that are native to Italy are mentioned specifically for those campaigns which remain in the environs of Rome.

The inhabitants of the Eternal City are by nature very superstitious, and the sight of a supernatural creature in their own streets is an excellent time to apply the Terrifying ability (MYTHRAS page 217), as the sight of one of their feared nightmares or legends in the flesh is likely to turn most Romans mad with fear.

Some of the following monsters are measured in cubits, an ancient measurement. A cubit is technically the length of your forearm from fingertip to elbow, which in modern terms is about 45cm.

AITHIOPIAN BULLS (TAURI AETHIOPICI)

Monstrous bulls of gargantuan size, lumbering speed, a violent temperament and a carnivorous appetite, which drives them to attack other animals. They also possess a red coloured hide, which is reputedly impervious to iron weapons.

Aithiopian Bull

Aithiopian Bull	Attributes
STR: 2d6+24 (31)	Action Points: 2
CON: 1d6+12 (16)	Damage Modifier: +2d6
SIZ: 4d6+24 (38)	Magic Points: 7
DEX: 2d6 (7)	Movement: 10m
INS: 2d6+4 (11)	Initiative Bonus: +9
POW: 2d6 (7)	Armour: Bristly Hide
	Abilities: Immunity (Iron), Intimidate, Trample

1d20	Location	AP/HP
1 – 3	Right Hind Leg	6/11
4 – 6	Left Hind Leg	6/11
7 – 9	Hindquarters	6/12
10 – 12	Forequarters	6/13
13 – 15	Right Front Leg	6/10
16 – 18	Left Front Leg	6/10
19 – 20	Head	6/11

Skills

Athletics 48%, Brawn 69%, Endurance 62%, Evade 34%, Perception 58%, Stealth 38%, Willpower 54%

Combat Style & Weapons

Belligerent Bull 68%

Weapon	Size/Force	Reach	Damage	AP/HP
Gore	H	M	1d10+2d6	As for Head
Trample	E	T	4d6	As for Leg

"It seems that those Aithiopian Bulls which they call 'flesh-eaters' are the most savage of animals. They are twice the size of Bulls in Greece, and their speed is very great. Their hair is red, their eyes blue-grey, more so than the eyes of lions. In normal times they move their horns as they do their ears, but when fighting they raise them, making them stand strongly up, and so do battle; and once raised in passion owing to some truly wonderful natural cause their horns do not go aslant. No spear, no arrow can wound them: iron, you see, does not penetrate their hide, for the Bull raises its bristles and throws off the weapons showered upon it in vain. And it attacks herds of horses and also wild animals. Accordingly herdsmen who wish to protect their flocks dig deep concealed ditches and by these means ambush the Bulls. And when they fall into these ditches they are choked with rage. "

Aelian – On Animals

AMPHISBAENA

"The Amphisbaena has a twin head; that is one at its tail-end as well, as though it were not enough for poison to be poured out of one mouth."

Pliny the Elder – Naturalis Historia

This odd creature is a two headed serpent, one at either end of its body. It probably originated from the confused descriptions of real snakes, which are occasionally born with two heads. It was reputed to travel by grasping its mouths together and rolling along the ground.

The Amphisbaena attacks by either spitting venom at an opponent's eyes or leaping upon them and biting (safely within the victim's weapon reach), before wriggling off and waiting for them to die. If spat and the victim fails to Evade, a failed resistance roll causes immediate (but temporary) blindness. If instead the victim is bitten and fails the resistance roll, they suffer convulsions and respiratory failure after 15-30 minutes.

Amphisbaena	Attributes
STR: 2d6 (7)	Action Points: 3+1 (Multi-Headed)
CON: 2d6 (7)	Damage Modifier: -1d4
SIZ: 2d4 (5)	Magic Points: 7
DEX: 2d6+12 (19)	Movement: 4m wriggling, 10m rolling
INS: 2d6+5 (12)	Initiative Bonus: +16
POW: 2d6 (7)	Armour: Scales
	Abilities: Cold-Blooded, Multi-Headed, Venomous

1d20	Location	AP/HP
1 – 3	Rear Head	1/3
4 – 5	Mid End-length	1/3
6 – 7	Fore End-length	1/3
8 – 9	Rear Mid-length	1/4
10 – 12	Mid Mid-length	1/4
13 – 14	Fore Mid-length	1/4
15 – 16	Rear Fore-length	1/3
17 – 18	Mid Fore-length	1/3
19 – 20	Front Head	1/3

Occasio aegre offertur, facile amittitur – Opportunity is offered with difficulty, lost with ease (Publius Syrus)

Skills

Athletics 66%, Brawn 42%, Endurance 44%, Evade 78%, Perception 49%, Stealth 61%, Willpower 54%

Combat Style & Weapons

Rolling Doom 66%

Weapon	Size/Force	Reach	Damage	AP/HP
Bite	S	T	1d4-1d4+Venom	As for Head
Spit	-	VL	Blinding	-

AMPHISBAENA VENOM

Potency	Resistance	Onset Time	Duration	Venom Effect
60%	Endurance	Instant for Blindness, or 1d4+2 x 5 minutes for Asphyxiation	1d3+3 hours for Blindness	If spat the victim suffers temporary Blindness. If the victim is bitten instead, the victim dies from Asphyxiation

BASILISK (BASILISCUS)

Native to the African province of Cyrene, the basilisk was a serpent of small size, which possessed a white spot resembling a diadem upon its forehead. They are so venomous that their poison legendarily could travel up a weapon used to strike them and thus kill its wielder. These monsters were probably based upon rumours of spitting cobras, but a very deadly, mythological version is presented here.

The basilisk repels all serpents in its presence by hissing. Its exhaled breath also withers all plant life in the region of its hole. The basilisk's extremely potent venom instantly kills anyone bitten, the victim turning black and necrotic. Its breath is less powerful however, having only half the Potency. Anybody coming close enough to strike the serpent with a melee weapon must enter the invisible corona of its miasmic exhalation – which has a range equal to its STR in metres. Those who successfully resist the venom take no other effect but must make a new save at the start of each round they stay within the cloud.

It may seem that the only way to deal with a basilisk is to shoot it from afar but assuming characters can even spot it, the Games Master should remember the situational modifiers of a prone target, a tiny SIZ, and the easy availability of cover leaving it completely obscured most of the time.

> *"As to the basilisk, a creature which the very serpents fly from, which kills by its odour even, and which proves fatal to man by only looking upon him, its blood has been marvellously extolled by the magicians. This blood is thick and adhesive, like pitch, which it resembles also in colour: dissolved in water, they say, it becomes of a brighter red than that of cinnabar. They attribute to it also the property of ensuring success to petitions preferred to potentates, and to prayers even offered to the gods; and they regard it as a remedy for various diseases, and as an amulet preservative against all noxious spells."*
>
> Pliny the Elder – Naturalis Historia

Basilisk	Attributes
STR: 2d3 (4)	Action Points: 3
CON: 2d6+6 (13)	Damage Modifier: -1d6
SIZ: 1d3+1 (3)	Magic Points: 13
DEX: 3d6+6 (17)	Movement: 6m
INS: 2d6+5 (12)	Initiative Bonus: +15
POW: 2d6+6 (13)	Armour: Scales
	Abilities: Camouflaged, Cold-Blooded, Venomous

1d20	Location	AP/HP
1 – 3	Tail Tip	1/4
4 – 5	Mid End-length	1/4
6 – 7	Fore End-length	1/4
8 – 9	Rear Mid-length	1/5
10 – 12	Mid Mid-length	1/5
13 – 14	Fore Mid-length	1/5
15 – 16	Rear Fore-length	1/4
17 – 18	Mid Fore-length	1/4
19 – 20	Head	1/4

Skills

Athletics 51%, Brawn 17%, Endurance 46%, Evade 64%, Perception 65%, Stealth 69%, Willpower 56%

Combat Style & Weapons

Death Near or Far 61%

Weapon	Size/Force	Reach	Damage	AP/HP
Necotic Bite	S	T	1d3-1d6+Venom	As for Head
Miasma	-	VL	Venom	-

BASILISK VENOM

Potency	Resistance	Onset Time	Duration	Venom Effect
100%	Endurance	Instant	Inapplicable	Death whether bitten or coming into contact with the noxious fumes

CACUS

> *"Once a cavern there, deeply recessed in the hill-side, impervious to the sun's rays; its occupant was a half-human, horrible creature, Cacus; its floor was forever warm with new-spilt blood, and nailed to its insolent doors you could see men's heads hung up, their faces pallid, ghastly, decaying. This ogre was the son of Vulcanus; as he moved in titan bulk, he breathed out his father's deadly flame."*
>
> Virgil – Aeneid

Cacus was a fire-breathing, smoke-belching giant who lived in a cave on the Palatine Hill before the establishment of Rome. Cacus ate human flesh, nailing the heads of his victims to the doors of his cave. Being of divine descent from Vulcan, he was a formidable foe and was eventually destroyed by the hero Hercules. This legend was

Cacus		Attributes
STR: 30		Action Points: 3
CON: 21		Damage Modifier: +1d12
SIZ: 27		Magic Points: 31
DEX: 15		Movement: 8m
INT: 13		Initiative Bonus: +14
POW: 31		Armour: Divine Skin
CHA: 5		Abilities: Breathe Flame, Earth Sense, Intimidate

1d20	Location	AP/HP
1 – 3	Right Leg	7/10
4 – 6	Left Leg	7/10
7 – 9	Abdomen	7/11
10 – 12	Chest	7/12
13 – 15	Right Arm	7/9
16 – 18	Left Arm	7/9
19 – 20	Head	7/10

Skills

Athletics 45%, Brawn 67%, Craft (Cook Human) 68%, Craft (Smithing) 88%, Endurance 72%, Evade 30%, Perception 74%, Stealth 78%, Willpower 82%

Combat Style & Weapons

Ogre Appetites 85% (Unarmed, Club, Thrown Rock, Flaming Breath)

Weapon	Size/Force	Reach	Damage	AP/HP
Unarmed	L	M	1d6+1d12	As for Limb
Fiery Breath	-	-	2d6	Once per Round

the foundation for the worship of Hercules by the Romans and of the ancient cave of Cacus, which reputedly existed near the Porta Trigemina – the gate in the Servian wall at the north end of the Aventine Hill.

Treat the breath of Cacus like the Breathe Flame creature ability (see MYTHRAS page 215) at the cost of 1d6 Magic Points. If desired Cacus can instead exhale a cloud of thick choking smoke for the same cost; this blinds everyone (including himself) within a range equal to his POW in metres and lasts several minutes before dissipating. However, the ogre can then rely on his Earth Sense to perceive those about him.

CACUS: PLOT HOOK

One of the few truly Roman monsters, Cacus has the potential to appear within the Eternal City; either as a demigod raised from the abyss via some vile cult worship, or as a ghost during the times of the year when the dead walk the streets again. The epic nature of Cacus places him beyond the ability of most characters to defeat directly. However, an adventuring party of noble Romans might be able to summon the shade of Hercules from his temple in the Forum Boarium to save the city or sacrifice themselves in combat whilst the rest of the populace flees to safety of the temples.

CATOBLEPAS

The Aethiopian Catoblepas is a bull shaped beast whose heavy head, when raised, causes the death of those it looks at. The frightful gaze may only affect a single target each round and must be resisted using Willpower in an opposed test. Failure indicates instant gibbering death. It costs the Catoblepas one Magic Point each time it gazes at an opponent and after expending all its Magic Points the beast is helpless.

Catoblepas		Attributes
STR: 2d6+15 (22)		Action Points: 2
CON: 2d6+9 (16)		Damage Modifier: +1d10
SIZ: 2d6+21 (28)		Magic Points: 13
DEX: 2d6 (7)		Movement: 6m
INS: 2d6+4 (11)		Initiative Bonus: +9
POW: 2d6+6 (13)		Armour: Hide
		Abilities: Death Sense, Gaze Attack (Death)

1d20	Location	AP/HP
1 – 3	Right Hind Leg	4/9
4 – 6	Left Hind Leg	4/9
7 – 9	Hindquarters	4/10
10 – 12	Forequarters	4/11
13 – 15	Right Front Leg	4/8
16 – 18	Left Front Leg	4/8
19 – 20	Head	4/9

Oderint dum metuant – Let them hate, so long as they fear (Lucius Accius)

Skills
Athletics 59%, Brawn 60%, Endurance 52%, Evade 34%, Perception 54%, Stealth 48%, Willpower 66%

Combat Style & Weapons
Cranky Catoblepas 59%

Weapon	Size/Force	Reach	Damage	AP/HP
Deadly Gaze	-	-	Death, if not resisted	-

"In Western Aethiopia there is a spring, the Nigris, which most people have supposed to be the source of the Nile. In its neighbourhood there is an animal called the Catoblepas, in other respects of moderate size and inactive with the rest of its limbs, only with a very heavy head which it carries with difficulty--it is always hanging down to the ground; otherwise it is deadly to the human race, as all who see its eyes expire immediately."

Pliny the Elder – Naturalis Historia

CETOS

The Cetos is a gigantic sea-monster of undefined description. Whales are known and feared in the Iberian Sea in the west of the Mediterranean, whereas serpents were more popular amongst Greek legends. For the sake of simplicity, use the statistics for the Sea Serpent (MYTHRAS page 264) to represent both.

"The huge Ketea that are bred in the habitations of Poseidon are, I declare, no whit meaner than the ravening children of the land, but both in strength and size the dauntless terrors of the sea excel… The Ketea that are nurtured in the midst of the seas are very many in number and of exceeding size. And not often do they come up out of the brine, but by reason of their heaviness they keep the bottom of the sea below. And they rave for food with unceasing frenzy, being always hungered and never abating the gluttony of their terrible maw – for what food shall be sufficient to fill the void of their belly or enough to satisfy and give a respite to their insatiable jaws?"

Oppian – Halieutica

DRAGONS (DRACONES)

Large serpents destitute of venom were known as dragons. They were supposedly at least 20 cubits in length and were the avid foes of elephants. From this perspective dragons are not really mythological creatures save for their huge size. To calculate the dragon's statistics, use the characteristics of the giant snake (MYTHRAS page 266).

"…the dragon, which is perpetually at war with the elephant, and is itself of so enormous a size, as easily to envelope the elephants with its folds, and encircle them in its coils. The contest is equally fatal to both; the elephant, vanquished, falls to the earth, and by its weight, crushes the dragon which is entwined around it."

Pliny the Elder – Naturalis Historia

"It is a well-known fact, that during the Punic war, at the river Bagrada, a serpent one hundred and twenty feet in length was taken by the Roman army under Regulus, being besieged, like a fortress, by means of balistae and other engines of war. Its skin and jaws were preserved in a temple at Rome, down to the time of the Numantine war."

Pliny the Elder – Naturalis Historia

EALE

Yet another Aethiopian monstrosity, the Eale or Yale, was a creature the size of a hippopotamus, with an elephant's tail of a black or tawny colour, the jaws of a boar and movable horns more than a cubit in length, which in a fight are erected alternately and presented to the attack or sloped backward in turn as necessary.

In terms of characteristics, use the Hippopotami described earlier, reducing its Armour to 3AP, increasing its combat style by +10% and replacing the Bite with Gore (1d10+2d8).

ETRUSCAN DAEMONES

Represented in the art of Etruscan tombs, these Daemones of the underworld brought great fear to the Romans. Any place associated with Dis (the underworld), such as deep natural grottos or the mephitic springs at Cumae, is thought to be haunted by these fearful beings, as well as the spirits of the dead which they shepherd or punish.

The appearance of daemones can vary depending on whether they are masculine or feminine. Charun and Tuchulcha are represented as large winged beings with beards, beaks or beaked noses, pointed donkey-like ears, blue skin and hissing serpents wrapped around their head or arms. Daemones such as Vanth or Lasa are

DAEMONES: PLOT HOOK

Etruscan Daemones are perfect for Italian or Roman based adventures. They are a fundamental part of the Latin psyche, being represented in ruined Etruscan tombs and temples built in the early days of the city. They are never discussed or written about but always feared. The appearance of a blue-skinned daemon can be used to great effect if the initial sightings are brief glimpses from the corner of the adventurer's eye, momentarily writhing frescoes or haunting dark dreams. Whether the daemon awaits the death of the character or a major nemesis is up to the Games Master but the final appearance should only occur at the demise of the truly wicked, caused in part by the daemon itself. Seeing the victim being dragged off to Dis screaming in terror, should provide a memorable ending which will haunt the characters for the remainder of their lives, particularly for those guilty of questionable deeds…

Daemones		Attributes	
STR: 2d6+9 (16)		Action Points: 3	
CON: 2d6+9 (16)		Damage Modifier: +1d4	
SIZ: 1d6+12 (16)		Magic Points: 19	
DEX: 1d6+12 (16)		Movement: 6m Walking, 12m Flying	
INS: 2d6+6 (13)		Initiative Bonus: +15	
POW: 2d6+12 (19)		Armour: Divine Skin	
		Abilities: Flying, Terrifying	

1d20	Location	AP/HP
1 – 2	Right Leg	8/7
3 – 4	Left Leg	8/7
5 – 6	Abdomen	8/8
7 – 8	Chest	8/9
9 – 10	Right Wing	8/7
11 – 12	Left Wing	8/7
13 – 15	Right Arm	8/6
16 – 18	Left Arm	8/6
19 – 20	Head	8/7

Skills

Athletics 62%, Brawn 52%, Endurance 62%, Evade 52%, Perception 72%, Stealth 72%, Willpower 78%

Combat Style & Weapons

Reaping Souls 82%

Weapon	Size/Force	Reach	Damage	AP/HP
Iron-bound Great Club	H	L	2d6+1d4	6/10
Serpent Twisted Fist	M	S	1d4+1d4+Venom	As for Arm

somewhat less intimidating females with fair hair and light coloured or white wings and carrying objects suitable to the soul they have come to claim.

Since such beings only come forth to claim the souls of those who are dead, or about to die, and as immortals they are not expected to enter combat with characters. However, seeing a daemon (in particular the blue skinned ones) can be exceptionally frightening, even to those who are not the target of the manifestation.

GRYPES

The Latin version of the Gryphon comes directly from its Greek origins, as an eagle-headed and winged lion, which collects and lines its mountaintop nests with gold. They supposedly live in the Rhipaean Mountains (thought to be the Urals) near Scythia, from which the Boreas wind comes. For characteristics see Griffin (MYTHRAS page 248).

"I have heard that the Indian animal the Gryps is a quadruped like a lion; that it has claws of enormous strength and that they resemble those of a lion. Men commonly report that it is winged and that the feathers along its back are black, and those on its front are red, while the actual wings are neither but are white. And Ktesias records that its neck is variegated with feathers of a dark blue; that it has a beak like an eagle's, and a head too, just as artists portray it in pictures and sculpture. Its eyes, he says, are like fire. It builds its lair among the mountains, and although it is not possible to capture the full-grown animal, they do take the young ones."

Aelian − On Animals

HARPY (HARPYIA)

Another Greek monster introduced into Latin literature, the Harpies are described as bird-bodied, girl-faced things with faces haggard with insatiable hunger. They were spirits of the storm winds, sent to steal people away from the earth or castigate those who defy the gods. Their place of abode was the Strophades Islands in the Ionian Sea.

Although in the Aeneid they could not be harmed, the Greek legends said they were vulnerable to those swift (or foolish) enough to pursue them. Harpies either carry off people or possessions to the far corners of the world or they inflict starvation on a victim by fouling and stealing their food. Whoever eats food spoiled by a harpy or is wounded by one is exposed to Typhoid (see Disease page 71). For statistics, see Harpy (MYTHRAS page 250), but change their Armour Points to 6AP from divine protection.

"The Harpyiae are on us, horribly swooping down from the mountains. They tear the banquet to pieces, filthying all with their bestial touch. Hideous the sounds, nauseous the stench about us. We choose a secluded spot under an overhanging crag, enclosed by trees and their shifting shadows, to set up our tables again and light a fire on a new altar. Again from their hidden lairs, flying in from different angles, that noisy coven claws at the feast, hovering around it, their mouths tainting the meal. So then I order my friends, stand to arms, for we must fight this damnable brood. They did as they were ordered: they put their shields out of sight beside them. So when the creatures again came screeching round the bay, Misenus from an observation post above us, blew the alarum. My friends went into an unfamiliar combat, trying their steel on sinister birds of the sea. But blows did not make them turn a feather, their bodies would not be wounded − they simply flew off at high speed into the blue, leaving a half devoured feast and their own disgusting traces. "

Virgil − Aeneid

JACULUS

The Jaculus is a type of deadly snake, which kills by launching itself from trees with incredible force and piercing through the bodies of its victims − according to Pliny like a bolt from a siege engine. Being an ambusher by nature, once the Jaculus has landed it is effectively helpless until it can scale another position of height, so it tends to wriggle away into the nearest cover or flee. Since their body is in effect a living javelin, it is capable of inflicting an Impale special effect but instead of remaining in the wound, they pass straight through.

Jaculus	Attributes
STR: 2d4+9 (14)	Action Points: 3
CON: 2d6 (7)	Damage Modifier: None
SIZ: 1d6+3 (7)	Magic Points: 7
DEX: 2d6+12 (19)	Movement: 6m
INS: 2d6+5 (12)	Initiative Bonus: +16
POW: 2d6 (7)	Armour: Scales
	Abilities: Camouflaged, Cold-Blooded, Leaper

1d20	Location	AP/HP
1 – 3	Tail Tip	1/3
4 – 5	Mid End-length	1/3
6 – 7	Fore End-length	1/3
8 – 9	Rear Mid-length	1/4
10 – 12	Mid Mid-length	1/4
13 – 14	Fore Mid-length	1/4
15 – 16	Rear Fore-length	1/3
17 – 18	Mid Fore-length	1/3
19 – 20	Head	1/3

Skills

Athletics 73%, Brawn 21%, Endurance 34%, Evade 78%, Perception 49%, Stealth 71%, Willpower 34%

Combat Style & Weapons

Death from Above 63%

Weapon	Size/Force	Reach	Damage	AP/HP
Impaling Leap	S	-	1d10	As for Head

"Behold. afar, around the trunk of a barren tree, a fierce serpent − Africa calls it the jaculus -wreathes itself, and then darts forth, and through the head and pierced temples of Paulus it takes its flight: nothing does venom there affect, death seizes him through the wound. It was then understood how slowly fly the stones which the sling hurls, how sluggishly whizzes the flight of the Scythian arrow."

Lucan − Pharsalia

KYNOPROSOPOI

The dog-men of the desert, the Kynoprosopoi were probably exaggerated reports of baboons. However, for those who want the mythic version, the following statistics are provided. According to Latin authors, the dog-men were generally friendly towards travellers.

If provoked to combat, kynoprosopoi attack with a claw, maintaining contact and allowing the bite to be brought into play. If the bite hits, the dog-man uses its Savage ability each round thereafter until the Hit Location is rendered useless.

"After traversing the Egyptian oasis one is confronted for seven whole days with utter desert. Beyond this live the human Kynoprosopoi (Dog-Faces) along the road that leads to Aethiopia. It seems that these creatures live by hunting gazelles and antelopes; further, they are black in appearance, and they have the head and teeth of a dog… …They are however not endowed with speech,

Kynoprosopoi	Attributes
STR: 3d6+6 (17)	Action Points: 2
CON: 3d6 (11)	Damage Modifier: +1d2
SIZ: 3d6 (11)	Magic Points: 11
DEX: 3d6 (11)	Movement: 6 metres
INT: 2d6+6 (13)	Initiative Bonus: +12
POW: 2d6+6 (13)	Armour: Fur
CHA: 3d6 (11)	Abilities: Savage

1d20	Location	AP/HP
1 – 3	Right Leg	1/5
4 – 6	Left Leg	1/5
7 – 9	Abdomen	1/6
10 – 12	Chest	1/7
13 – 15	Right Arm	1/4
16 – 18	Left Arm	1/4
19 – 20	Head	1/5

Skills

Athletics 58%, Brawn 48%, Deceit 54%, Endurance 42%, Evade 52%, Insight 46%, Perception 56%, Stealth 44%, Willpower 36%

Combat Style & Weapons

Tribe Defender 58% (Spear, Sling), Unarmed 68% (Teeth & Claws)

Weapon	Size/Force	Reach	Damage	AP/HP
Bite	M	T	1d4+1d2	As for Head
Claw	S	S	1d3+1d2	As for Arm
Shortspear	M	L	1d8+1+1d2	4/5
Sling	L	-	1d8	1/2

but utter a shrill squeal. Beneath their chin hangs down a beard; we may compare it with the beards of Drakones, and strong and very sharp nails cover their hands. Their whole body is covered with hair – another respect in which they resemble dogs. They are very swift of foot and know the regions that are inaccessible: that is why they appear so hard to capture."

Aelian – On Animals

LAMIA

The Lamiae were beautiful women with serpentine tails in place of their legs. By using illusions to disguise their form, they would seduce young men, take them as lovers and slowly drain them of their vitality until death. Lamiae avoid direct confrontation where possible, preferring to subtly charm victims into falling in love with them. Their illusionary ability allows them to project the appearance of normal humanity at a cost of 1 Magic Point per hour but the illusion cannot be maintained if they are forced to use their constriction attack.

Magical seduction requires that the Lamia overcomes her victim in an opposed test of her Seduction skill verses his Willpower. If the victim succeeds, then he is immune to her charms for that day. Otherwise he will willingly be taken to bed and engaged in a night of delirious passion. The strength of his desire causes the victim to cease eating and spend his entire time desiring to return to his beloved. Each day of passion after the first causes the temporary loss of a level of Fatigue. These points recover at one each day of

Lamia	Attributes
STR: 3d6 (11)	Action Points: 3
CON: 3d6 (11)	Damage Modifier: +1d4
SIZ: 2d6+15 (22)	Magic Points: 16
DEX: 3d6+6 (17)	Movement: 6 metres
INT: 2d6+9 (16)	Initiative Bonus: +17
POW: 2d6+9 (16)	Armour: Scales on serpent parts
CHA: 2d6+6 (13)	Abilities: Illusion, Night Sight, Poison Immunity

1d20	Location	AP/HP
1 – 3	Tail End	3/7
4 – 6	Mid Tail	3/7
7 – 9	Upper Tail	3/8
10 – 12	Chest	0/9
13 – 15	Right Arm	0/6
16 – 18	Left Arm	0/6
19 – 20	Head	0/7

Skills

Athletics 58%, Brawn 73%, Deceit 69%, Endurance 62%, Evade 74%, Influence 56%, Insight 72%, Perception 62%, Seduction 79%, Stealth 63%, Willpower 72%

Combat Style & Weapons

Slithering Horror 68%

Weapon	Size/Force	Reach	Damage	AP/HP
Constrict	H	T	1d4	As for Tail
Tail Lash	L	L	1d8+1d4	As for Tail End

Omnia vincit amor – Love conquers all (Virgil)

enforced rest and eating. Unless this is imposed by helpers, the victim eventually dies.

THE TRAGEDY OF SCORPUS: PLOT HOOK

Gaius Antonius is more popularly known as Scorpus, a famed charioteer who is well on his way to winning his five hundredth race. Once a slave, he won his freedom a few years ago and has lived a life of relative luxury since.

In recent months Scorpus has been losing races. Of course, not every charioteer wins all the time but Scorpus has been losing contests he should have won easily. He seems tired; he is making mistakes. His patrons are worried and the characters are tasked with investigating. Scorpus has a big race coming up – his patrons are banking on him winning, and much money rides on the outcome. If he does not recover his form, he will surely lose.

By following and watching Scorpus, they find he has a new lover. She rarely leaves the fine villa the charioteer has bought but the two can be glimpsed in the gardens, deep in conversation and sometimes in other activities. Scorpus is clearly besotted but any attempts to either meet this new love or convince him to return to his previously strenuous training regime is met with outright hostility.

The new lover is Livia and she is a lamia. She has chosen Scorpus for his virility, which she is is slowly draining with each night of passion. Within a week he will be dead and the crucial race is in a little over that. The irony is, Livia genuinely loves Scorpus. Other men would be withered husks by now but Scorpus is intelligent, strong and is also in love with Livia. He suspects what she is but has fallen so deeply in love with her, he is blind to what is happening.

The characters must try to save Scorpus from his doom. He will resist – so will Livia. And if Scorpus is convinced to abandon his lover, Livia turns her attentions to one of the characters – the strongest, most passionate character, intending to find a new lover and a new source of sustenance.

THE LAMIA OF LYBIS

The Libyan Lamia is a legendary figure who is used by Roman mothers to frighten young children into obedience. She is a monster who roams the streets stealing and eating any children she can find, appearing as an old hag who has removed her own eyes. Of course there are many dangers in Rome, which might explain the frequent disappearance of young children, but the presence of the true Lamia in the Eternal City would make a very disturbing adventure.

"nor should it extract a living child from the stomach of the ogress, Lamia, after she has dined"

Horace – Ars Poetica

LEMURES

The spirits of the dead, Lemures are objects of particular dread to the average Roman. Many festivals are held annually to placate the hungry dead and show them proper respect. This is extremely important since three days each year the stones covering the gates to

the underworld were opened and ghosts were free to walk the streets of Rome.

"I scarcely believe it, but they say that ancestral spirits came moaning from their tombs in the still of night, and misshapen spirits, a bodiless throng, howled through the City streets, and through the broad fields. Afterwards neglected honour was paid to the tombs"

Ovid – Fasti

Most dead spirits only return to plague those who have wronged them. Families can be haunted for the failure to show proper respect to their ancestors or permitting the neglect of their tombs. Murderers or political enemies are often plagued for causing the death of the ghost until justice is served. Unwary fools who remain in the presence of necropolises after dark are prone to attack from insane lemures who only desire to taste blood from those who wander near their long forgotten sepulchres.

"Flitting phantoms appear midst the tombs and unburied bones, gibbering menace"

Petronius – The Satyricon

Roman spirits never manifest physically as wraiths, although some are able to move physical objects. Instead they drive their object of their haunting mad with repeated visitations. Malicious lemures return during the nights of festivals which honour the dead (see The Cycle of the Dead on page 115), in an attempt to possess their victims; if successful, will force them to commit suicide. Lacking physical form, these spirits cannot be harmed, save for the intercession of magic (see Necromancy on page 144). Lemures can be represented by using the characteristics of Haunts (see MYTHRAS page 150), but lack the Wither ability.

"Another variety of "daemon" consists of the human soul that abandons its body when it has finished its services in life. I note that in the old Latin language these used to be termed lemures. Now, to some of these lemures was allotted the care of their descendants. These occupy houses with a propitious and peaceful attitude, and they are called Lares of the family. But others, because of their misdeeds in life, are punished with a kind of exile, namely, with the denial of a home and with undirected wanderings. They can only be harmless terrors to good men, but they are dangerous to bad men. People usually call these larvae. When it is unclear what category of ghost one is dealing with, whether it is one of the Lares or the larvae, one uses the term Di Manes."

Apuleius – De Deo Socratis

LEUCROCOTA

" the Leucrocota, swiftest of wild beasts, about the size of an ass, with a stag's haunches, a lion's neck, tail and breast, badger's head, cloven hoof, mouth opening right back to the ears, and ridges of bone in place of rows of teeth – this animals is reported to imitate the voices of human beings."

Pliny the Elder – Naturalis Historia

A strange chimera from Aethiopia, formed from the combination of stag, lion and badger, the Leucrocota was feared for its ability to mimic human voices. It used this power to lure people away from their companions or campfires before tearing them to pieces.

The Leucrocota can attack with its horrific gaping mouth and kick with its hooves. Whilst a deadly man eater in its own right, the Leucrocota cannot stand up to a coordinated attack, hence its use of mimicry to entice lone victims into its reach, whereupon it springs upon the victim and consumes him alive.

Leucrocota	Attributes
STR: 2d6+9 (16)	Action Points: 3
CON: 2d6+6 (13)	Damage Modifier: +1d8
SIZ: 2d6+15 (22)	Magic Points: 13
DEX: 2d6+9 (16)	Movement: 8m
INS: 2d6+7 (14)	Initiative Bonus: +15
POW: 2d6+6 (13)	Armour: Fur
	Abilities: Leaper, Night Sight

1d20	Location	AP/HP
1 – 3	Tail	2/6
4 – 5	Right Hind Leg	2/7
6 – 7	Left Hind Leg	2/7
8 – 10	Hindquarters	2/8
11 – 14	Forequarters	2/9
15 – 16	Right Front Leg	2/6
17 – 18	Left Front Leg	2/6
19 – 20	Head	2/7

Skills	
Athletics 62%, Brawn 58%, Endurance 46%, Evade 62%, Imitate Voice 78%, Perception 67%, Stealth 70%, Willpower 56%	

Combat Style & Weapons	
Cunning Crocotta 72%	

Weapon	Size/Force	Reach	Damage	AP/HP
Bite	L	S	1d8+1d6	As for Head
Hoof	L	M	1d6+1d6	As for Leg

MANTICHORA

Originally from the Middle East, the Mantichora is a melange of a red coloured lion with a human head and a huge scorpion tail covered with barbs and a sting over a cubit in length. It is a man eater (hence its name) and can fire its barbs in any direction out to a range of 30 metres by flicking its tail. Worse still is that the barbs and sting are infused with a poison fatal to everything save elephants.

The Mantichora is fearless, attacking groups of men for the taste of their flesh. Use the statistics of a Manticore (MYTHRAS page 256) but change its tail venom to a Potency of 70%, and instead of Paralysis it causes internal haemorrhaging (Bleeding) at one level per hour until death.

"...which he calls the Mantichora; it has a triple row of teeth, which fit into each other like those of a comb, the face and ears of a man, and azure eyes, is of the colour of blood, has the body of the lion, and a tail ending in a sting, like that of the scorpion. Its voice resembles the union of the sound of the flute and the trumpet; it is of excessive swiftness, and is particularly fond of human flesh."

Pliny the Elder – Naturalis Historia

NEADES

There is very little known about the Neades save that they left their monstrous bones on the island of Samos. Modern theories suggest that these may even have been dinosaur or mammoth bones discovered by the Greek inhabitants. Bearing that in mind, Games Masters might wish to have an island of 'Fearfully Great Lizards' or slightly less fanciful prehistoric mammals from the Pliocene Epoch using suitable creatures from the MYTHRAS core rules.

"...in primeval times Samos was uninhabited, for there appeared in the island animals of gigantic size, which were savage and dangerous to man to approach, and they were called Neades. Now these animals with their mere roar split the ground. So there is a proverbial saying current in Samos, 'He roars louder than the Neades.' And the same writer asserts that huge bones are displayed even to this day"

Aelian – On Animals

For those desiring a more classical version, the following characteristics are for giant quadruped lizards whose roar can cause earthquakes. These monsters may either attack once per round or roar. Roaring costs the creature 1d6 Magic Points and causes a localised earth tremor. Everything within 100 metres must roll an opposed test of their Athletics skill against the monster's Thunderous Roar skill. Failure indicates that object or person has fallen over, suffering the prone penalty if the monster decides to trample over them.

Realistically such creatures should only be faced by a cohort armed with ballistae.

Neades	Attributes
STR: 2d6+18 (25)	Action Points: 2
CON: 2d6+15 (22)	Damage Modifier: +2d8
SIZ: 4d6+45 (59)	Magic Points: 11
DEX: 2d6 (7)	Movement: 6 metres
INS: 2d6+4 (11)	Initiative Bonus: +9
POW: 3d6 (11)	Armour: Tough Hide and Bony Spikes & Plates
	Abilities: Area Attack (Tail), Cold-Blooded, Intimidate, Trample

1d20	Location	AP/HP
1-3	Tail	8/17
4-5	Right Hind Leg	6/17
6-7	Left Hind Leg	6/17
8-10	Hindquarters	8/18
11-14	Forequarters	8/19
15-16	Right Front Leg	6/16
17-18	Left Front Leg	6/16
19-20	Head	8/17

Skills

Athletics 35%, Brawn 94%, Endurance 84%, Evade 24%, Perception 42%, Thunderous Roar 70%, Willpower 52%

Combat Style & Weapons

Unstoppable Juggernaut 52%

Weapon	Size/Force	Reach	Damage	AP/HP
Tail Bash	C	VL	2d6+2d8	As for Tail
Trample	C	T	4d8	As for Leg

OPHIES

Many coloured snakes with two pairs of wings, which emit acidic urine on those who disturb them. A particularly nasty beast, male Ophies are killed by the females after copulation, who in turn are consumed by their young, who eat their way out of her body. Ophies inhabit the frankincense trees of Arabia and are considered a terrible pest by those who desire to harvest the rare spice. The serpents can be driven briefly away with the smoke of burning Storax Resin, imported at great expense from the Phoenicians. Normal encounters are with flying flocks of Ophies, making them difficult opponents to face. For rules concerning Acid, see MYTHRAS page 68.

"Megasthenes states that in India there are snakes (ophies) with wings, and that their visitations occur not during the daytime but by night, and that they emit urine which at once produces a festering wound on anybody on which it may happen to drop."

Aelian – On Animals

Ophies	Attributes
STR: 2d4 (5)	Action Points: 3
CON: 2d6 (7)	Damage Modifier: -1d6
SIZ: 2d4 (5)	Magic Points: 7
DEX: 2d6+12 (19)	Movement: 4m Wriggling, 12m Flying
INS: 2d6+5 (12)	Initiative Bonus: +16
POW: 2d6 (7)	Armour: None
	Abilities: Cold-Blooded, Flying

1d20	Location	AP/HP
1 – 3	Tail	0/1
4 – 6	Rear Length	0/2
7 – 9	Mid Length	0/3
10 – 12	Fore Length	0/4
13 – 15	Right Wing	0/4
16 – 18	Left Wing	0/4
19 – 20	Head	0/3

Skills

Athletics 34%, Brawn 10%, Endurance 24%, Evade 38%, Fly 74%, Perception 59%, Stealth 61%, Willpower 34%

Combat Style & Weapons

Aerial Assault 64%

Weapon	Size/Force	Reach	Damage	AP/HP
Urine Squirt	S	-	1d2 Weak Acid	-

PEGASI

The Roman version of the classic winged horse differs slightly from the Greek in the fact that it has horns. Note that Pegasi are a species living in Africa, whereas the mythological Pegasus came from the slaying of Medusa by Perseus. Normally pegasi flee from combat, but if cornered or injured will strike back with wing buffets to knock foes down and kick with its hoofs.

"Aethiopia produces… many monstrosities… [including] winged horses armed with horns, called Pegasi."

Pliny the Elder – Naturalis Historia

Pegasi	Attributes
STR: 2d6+15 (22)	Action Points: 2
CON: 2d6+6 (13)	Damage Modifier: +1d10
SIZ: 2d6+21 (28)	Magic Points: 13
DEX: 2d6+6 (13)	Movement: 10m Walking, 15m Flying
INS: 2d6+4 (11)	Initiative Bonus: +12
POW: 2d6+6 (13)	Armour: Hide
	Abilities: Flying

1d20	Location	AP/HP
1 – 2	Right Hind Leg	1/9
3 – 4	Left Hind Leg	1/9
5 – 7	Hindquarters	1/10
8 – 10	Forequarters	1/11
11 – 12	Right Wing	1/10
13 – 14	Left Wing	1/10
15 – 16	Right Front Leg	1/8
17 – 18	Left Front Leg	1/8
19 – 20	Head	1/9

Skills

Athletics 55%, Brawn 60%, Endurance 56%, Evade 46%, Fly 75%, Perception 54%, Stealth 44%, Willpower 56%

Combat Style & Weapons

Equine Fury 55%

Weapon	Size/Force	Reach	Damage	AP/HP
Kick	L	M	1d6+1d10	As for Leg
Wing Buffet	M	VL	1d4+1d10	As for Wing

SPHINXES

Roman Sphinxes as described by Pliny were an Aethiopian species derived from the combination of a woman's head with the body of a lion, possessing "…brown hair and a pair of udders on the breast…". The Greek sphinx however was a unique creature with wings who questioned travellers in Thebes. Those who answered her riddles wrongly were eaten.

The following characteristics can be used for either beast, save that Aethiopian Sphinxes cannot fly or riddle and have INS instead of INT.

Sphinx	Attributes
STR: 2d6+12 (19)	Action Points: 3
CON: 2d6+6 (13)	Damage Modifier: +1d8
SIZ: 2d6+15 (22)	Magic Points: 13
DEX: 2d6+12 (19)	Movement: 8m
INS: 2d6+6 (13)	Initiative Bonus: +16
POW: 2d6+9 (16)	Armour: Fur on lion parts
	Abilities: (Flying), Leaper, Night Sight

1d20	Hit Location	1d20	Hit Location	AP/HP
1 – 3	Right Hind Leg	1 – 2	Right Hind Leg	1/7
4 – 6	Left Hind Leg	3 – 4	Left Hind Leg	1/7
7 – 9	Hindquarters	5 – 7	Hindquarters	1/8
10 – 12	Forequarters	8 – 10	Forequarters	1/9
*		11 – 12	Right Wing	1/8
*		13 – 14	Left Wing	1/8
13 – 15	Right Front Leg	15 – 16	Right Front Leg	1/6
16 – 18	Left Front Leg	17 – 18	Left Front Leg	1/6
19 – 20	Head	19 – 20	Head	0/7

Skills

Athletics 55%, Brawn 60%, Endurance 56%, Evade 46%, Fly 75%, Perception 54%, Stealth 44%, Willpower 56%

Combat Style & Weapons

Equine Fury 55%

Weapon	Size/Force	Reach	Damage	AP/HP
Kick	L	M	1d6+1d10	As for Leg
Wing Buffet	M	VL	1d4+1d10	As for Wing

"Here afore time she stood, fierce uplifting her pallid cheeks, her eyes tainted with corruption and her plumes all clotted with hideous gore; grasping human remains and clutching to her breast half-eaten bones she scanned the plains with awful gaze, should any stranger dare to join in the strife of riddling words, or any traveller confront her and parley with her terrible tongue; then, without more ado, sharpening forthwith the unsheathed talons of her livid hands and her teeth bared for wounding, she rose with dreadful beating of wings around the faces of the strangers"

Statius – Thebaid

STRIX

These strange creatures are nocturnal birds of ill-omen, which rend flesh and drink human blood. Strix generally only attack the young or helpless, even carrying off babies small enough to be borne. They are reputed to live at the outskirts of Tartarus but these 'owls of hell' can be warded off with the leaves of the Arbutus tree or be given the meat of pigs as a substitute for their normal appetites. Being an indelible part of Roman mythology, these creatures could easily be encountered in Rome.

"Their heads are large, their eyes stick out, their beaks fit for tearing, their feathers are grey, their claws hooked. They fly by night, attacking children with absent nurses, and defiling their bodies, snatched from the cradle. They're said to rend the flesh of infants with their beaks, and their throats are full of the blood they drink. They're called screech-owls, and the reason for the name is the horrible screeching they usually make at night. Whether they're born as birds, or whether they're made so by spells, old women transformed to birds by Marsian magic"

Ovid – Fasti

Strix	Attributes
STR: 1d3+6 (8)	Action Points: 3
CON: 1d6+6 (10)	Damage Modifier: −1d4
SIZ: 1d3+1 (3)	Magic Points: 7
DEX: 2d6+15 (22)	Movement: 15 metres flying
INS: 2d6+5 (12)	Initiative Bonus: +17
POW: 2d6 (7)	Armour: None
	Abilities: Diving Strike, Flying, Night Sight

1d20	Location	AP/HP
1 – 3	Right Leg	0/2
4 – 6	Left Leg	0/2
7 – 9	Body	0/4
10 – 13	Right Wing	0/3
14 – 17	Left Wing	0/3
18 – 20	Head	0/3

Skills

Brawn 21%, Endurance 40%, Evade 44%, Fly 70%, Perception 69%, Stealth 74%, Willpower 44%

Combat Style & Weapons

Night Hunter 60%

Weapon	Size/Force	Reach	Damage	AP/HP
Claw Rake	S	T	1d4-1d4	As for Leg
Peck	S	T	1d3-1d4	As for Head

STRIX PLOT HOOKS

The Strix is a fabulous creature to set upon unsuspecting characters in Rome. Superstitious Romans consider even the merest sight or sound of an owl to be terrible bad luck. Games Masters need not even introduce a true Strix into their games…. Simply including an owl into an adventure and making occasional hidden rolls can drive up the paranoia of the players.

For more supernatural adventures, the characters could fall foul of some sinister chthonian cult and have these creatures set upon them nightly, until they uncover the source of the attacks. Or perhaps they have been cursed by an enemy and the Striges are drawn to the stygian doom upon them.

A scenario could be designed so that the characters stumble upon the body of a drunk in the street, up from which flutters a dark shape. On inspection the man is discovered to be dead and drained of blood, the beginning of a murderous trail by a shape-shifted witch. Failure to solve the mystery could lead to a close family member ending up dead, or the characters being accused of the deed(s) themselves…

SYLVAN DAEMONES

The sylvan daemones are the untamed nature spirits of the woods and mountains, which included satyrs, fauns and other strange spirits such as nymphs. In Latin mythology they were the orgiastic, drunken entourage of Bacchus the god of wine and Faunus, the god of the woods and pastures.

Fauns (also known as panes) are bearded humans from the waist up, hoofed goats below, and have the pointed ears and horns of a goat. Satyrs however have human legs, but the ears and tails of asses.

"The countryfolk, the Sylvan Deities (Numina Silvarum), the Fauni and brother Satyri and the Nymphae."

Ovid – Metamorphoses

Both the fauns and satyrs were players of musical instruments and the fauni in particular were reputed to be able to cast illusions. They were also savage in battle and possess a malicious sense of humour. Due to their bestial nature, many areas about Rome were deliberately left as wilderness or sacred groves to propitiate them.

"The Panes (fauns) madly made battle skipping with light foot over the peaks. One of them gript an enemy's neck tight with encircling hands, and ript him with his goat's-hooves, tearing through the flank and strong corselet together. Another caught a fugitive and ran him through this middle where he stood, then lifting him on the curved points of his two long branching antlers, sent him flying high through the airy ways, rolling over himself like a tumbler. Another waved in his hand the straw-cutting sickle of sheaf-bearing Deo, and reaped the enemy crops with claw curved blade, like corn ears of conflict, like gavels of the battlefield. There was a revel for Ares, there was harvest-home for Dionysos, when the enemy's heads were cut. He offered the curved blade to watching Bacchus, dabbled with human dew, and so poured a blood-libation to Dionysos, and made the Moirai (Fates) drunken with the battle cup he filled for them. Another man was standing, when one goat-foot Pan twined both hands interlacing about his neck, and struck his well corseted enemy with his horn, tearing his flank with the double point. Another met a fellow rushing on him with a blow from his cudgel, and smashed his forehead right between the ends of his eyebrows."

Nonnus – Dionysiaca

Sylvan Daemones	Attributes
STR: 2d6+15 (22)	Action Points: 3
CON: 1d6+12 (16)	Damage Modifier: +1d4
SIZ: 2d6+6 (13)	Magic Points: 16
DEX: 2d6+9 (16)	Movement: 6 metres
INT: 2d6+6 (13)	Initiative Bonus: +15
POW: 2d6+9 (16)	Armour: Hide on legs and abdomen
CHA: 3d6 (11)	Abilities: Frenzy (Battle), Leaper
	Magic: Folk Magic

1d20	Location	AP/HP
1 – 3	Right Leg	1/6
4 – 6	Left Leg	1/6
7 – 9	Abdomen	1/7
10 – 12	Chest	0/8
13 – 15	Right Arm	0/5
16 – 18	Left Arm	0/5
19 – 20	Head	0/6

Skills

Athletics 68%, Brawn 55%, Dance 77%, Endurance 72%, Evade 62%, Insight 59%, Locale 56%, Musicianship 77%, Perception 59%, Willpower 52%

Combat Style & Weapons

Sylvan Savage (Sickle, Club) 68%, Unarmed (Fist, Head Butt, Hoof) 78%

Weapon	Size/Force	Reach	Damage	AP/HP
Club	M	M	2d6+1d4	4/4
Sickle	M	S	1d4+2+1d4	6/4
Hoof	M	T	1d4+1d4	As for Arm
Horns	M	S	1d6+1d4	As for Head

THE ORIGINAL BEASTMEN?

The fauns and satyrs were frequently represented in art, being popular subjects in paintings and statuary, particularly in gardens where they are thought to bless and protect the plants. They also became indispensable characters in many Greek and Latin plays, where they began to take on personalities of their own...

"*Twelve horned Panes (fauns) there were, with this changeling shape and horn bearing heads, who were begotten of the one ancestral Pan (Faunus) their mountain ranging father. One they named Kelaineus (Blackie) as his looks bore witness, and one Argennos (Whitey) after his colour; Aigikoros (Goatgluts) was well dubbed, because he glutted himself with goat's-milk which he pressed from nannies udders in the flock. Another masterly one was called Eugeneios (Longbeard), from a throat and chin which was a thick meadow of hair. Daphoineus (the Bloody) came along with Omester (Eat-em-raw); Phobos (the Frightaway) with shaggy-legged Philamnos (the Lamb's Friend). Glaukos with Xanthos, Glaukos glaring like the bright sea, with a complexion to match. Xanthos had a mane of hair like a bayard, which gave that name to the horned frequenter of the rocks. Then there was bold Argos with a shock of hair as white as snow . . . Along with these came Phorbas (Fear) to join their march, savage and insatiate.*"

Nonnus – Dionysiaca

Such stories show that these wilderness deities were an inescapable part of the Roman psyche, who even dressed the choruses in their theatres up as fauns and satyrs. The superstitious Romans truly fear the deep dark woodlands for the presence of these wild beings and thus they can be introduced even into ostensibly historical campaigns still set within Italy.

UNICORNIS

The Roman version of the Monoceros, it was a legend developed from Greek reports of the first rhinoceroses seen in ancient India. In some accounts they are as large as horses with a white body, a dark red head, their eyes bluish and they have a horn in their forehead about a cubit in length. The lower part of the horn, for about two palms distance from the forehead, is quite white, the middle is black, the upper part, which terminates in a point, is a very flaming red. Those who drink out of cups made from it are proof against convulsions, epilepsy and even poison.

"*But that the fiercest animal is the Monoceros (Unicorn), which in the rest of the body resembles a horse, but in the head a stag, in the feet an elephant, and in the tail a boar, and has a deep bellow, and a single black horn three feet long projecting from the middle of the forehead. They say that it is impossible to capture this animal alive.*"

Pliny the Elder – Naturalis Historia

Unicornis		Attributes
STR: 2d6+15 (22)		Action Points: 3
CON: 2d6+3 (10)		Damage Modifier: +1d10
SIZ: 2d6+18 (25)		Magic Points: 19
DEX: 2d6+9 (16)		Movement: 12 metres
INT: 2d6+6 (13)		Initiative Bonus: +15
POW: 2d6+12 (19)		Armour: Hide
CHA: 3d6 (11)		Abilities: Disease Immunity, Formidable Natural Weapons (Horn), Poison Immunity

1d20	Location	AP/HP
1 – 3	Right Hind Leg	1/7
4 – 6	Left Hind Leg	1/7
7 – 9	Hindquarters	1/8
10 – 12	Forequarters	1/9
13 – 14	Right Front Leg	1/6
15 – 16	Left Front Leg	1/6
17 – 20	Head	1/7

Skills

Athletics 58%, Brawn 57%, Endurance 50%, Evade 72%, Perception 62%, Stealth 69%, Willpower 78%

Combat Style & Weapons

Horned Lancer 77%

Weapon	Size/Force	Reach	Damage	AP/HP
Kick	L	M	1d6+1d10	As for Leg
Horn	L	L	1d8+1d10	6/12

WEREWOLF (VERSIPELLIS)

The Versipellis was the Roman werewolf. It differed from the modern version in that the wolf needed to reclaim its clothes in order to return to human form. It was also vulnerable to normal weapons, although somewhat tougher than a normal human. Indeed the werewolf described in the Satyricon is impaled through the neck but the following morning is seen alive in human shape, the wound being tended by a doctor.

Werewolves use the characteristics as described for Lycanthropy in the Wolf description (see MYTHRAS page 273).

"The moon was shining like the midday sun. We arrived among the tombs. My man went for a pee against a gravestone. I held back, singing and counting the stones. Then, when I looked back at my companion, he had taken all his clothes off and laid them beside the road. I almost died of fright, and I stood there like a dead man. He peed a circle around his clothes and suddenly became a wolf. Don't think I'm joking. No one's inheritance is so valuable as to make me lie. But, as I'd begun to say, after he had become a wolf, he began to howl and ran into the woods."

Petronius − The Satyricon

CAMPAIGNS

DESIGNING A ROMAN CAMPAIGN

As illustrated in the earlier chapters, ancient Rome is often an incomprehensible blend of tradition, superstition, honour and treachery. Its very strangeness is its attraction and the fluid hierarchy of family status, wealth and patronage present a fantastic opportunity for a Games Master to raise his beginning characters from obscurity to the leading magistrates of the city. Or even the other way around, falling from nobility to become criminal gang leaders, or even revenge driven slaves. Nothing is impossible because at the time, nothing was.

Republican Rome caters to every taste. It lauds heroism, self-sacrificing altruism, integrity and honour. Yet it breeds ruthless ambition, greed, corruption and hypocrisy. Only by wholeheartedly embracing both paths does Roman society function, where any man – hero or profligate – can briefly hold ultimate power and law enforcement is in the hands of your peers.

Role-playing games set in ancient Rome possess the potential for an incredibly diverse range of events. Scenarios can include such things as wars, criminal gangs, politics, corruption, slave uprisings, gladiatorial combat, chariot racing, subversive religious cults, floods, fires, pestilence, supernatural manifestations, noxious sewers, riots, fantastic beasts, looting and pillaging foreign cities – the scope is near limitless. A good campaign will mix these differing occurrences together; keeping a couple as the core thread which draws the characters along, whilst others can provide exciting diversions.

Before creating a Roman campaign, the Games Master should think carefully about the following issues. Each will have a significant bearing on how games are run, from cultural role-playing to character survivability and thus the enjoyment that players will gain from it.

FAMILY

Of the greatest importance to any Roman was their family. Venerating ancestors and obeying the Paterfamilias are two inviolate cornerstones of society, along with striving to raise the status of the family name. All three of these concepts have vital roles to play in a campaign.

Failing to propitiate your ancestors can bring trouble to any character, since not only does it lower reputation in the eyes of your family and friends but it could also attract supernatural reprisal. Slaves might leave the household in superstitious fear and enemies may be perfectly justified to slander those guilty of such impious behaviour.

A Paterfamilias is probably the best sadistic tool available to a Games Master. The querulous commands of old men can drive players to extremes of desperation. Since the word of a paterfamilias is law within his family, there is no recourse but to obey – unless the character wishes to be killed, be sold into slavery or take the most heinous of steps and commit patricide. This stick, often without a carrot, can be used to precipitate all kinds of ethical dilemmas and test the spirit of the character.

The reputation of a family's name is revered by its members. Fierce pride drives relations to defend their family honour against any who would besmirch it; and ambition to raise its honour and rank compels sons to climb the Cursus Honorum. The strength of these imperatives are a vital aspect of Roman psyche, causing disparate members of a family gens to gather together to perform great deeds, religious observances, or even fund a relative in his political career.

a man, and their fort taken. It is generally agreed that three hundred and six men perished, and that one only, an immature youth, was left as a stock for the Fabian house to be Rome's greatest helper in her hour of danger both at home and in the field"

Livy – Ab Urbe Condita

WEALTH

The wealth level of characters is another important consideration. A low wealth level gives the campaign a gritty feeling as characters scrabble to survive in the city, emphasising the need for patrons to aid them with their everyday problems. Starting with high wealth levels is the other side of the coin, allowing role-playing of a more luxurious lifestyle and the support of clients instead. The bias of such a campaign would be the retention of wealth and power, rather than the seeking of it.

"Speaking as an aristocrat myself, I can tell you that the advantages of high birth are greatly overrated. You get to hold high office, which can get you killed or prosecuted; you are qualified for the highest priesthoods, and I cannot imagine anything more boring than that. Worst of all, you have to spend a lot of time with your fellow aristocrats, most of whom are bores, insane, or congenital criminals. Be content with wealth and luxury. Those will get you all the respect and deference you could ask for, without all the other headaches."

John Maddox Roberts – Oracle of the Dead

A Games Master should think carefully about permitting characters to start out at wildly differing wealth levels, since social contact is limited between those of different classes. Although this could be handled in such a way that the other characters all play the servants and clients of the richest party member, it can lead to chaffing of the poorer characters to escape from the authority of their patron.

ASSASSINATION AND MURDER

An interesting aspect of a Roman setting is that the blatant murder of an enemy is utterly prohibited. Such an act would bring the censure of peers or patrons, along with a swift death sentence to prevent the social disintegration caused by vendettas. If a player wishes to eradicate a longstanding foe, they must do it subtly, or indirectly, so that they cannot be accused of a misdeed. Even killing thieves is only permitted at night and only after you have given a shouted warning of your intention.

Since the merest suspicion of unlawful killing can bring rebuke, most enemies of high Status must instead be defeated via the law courts; and except for the most heinous of crimes, a patrician or equestrian found guilty is normally fined or flees into exile, rather than be executed. Thus enemies can continue to return and plague the player characters in pursuit of revenge; or quite surprisingly may offer alliances in order to defeat the plans of a new threat. In politics especially, enmity is transient.

The social reproof of casual killing may take some players of traditional fantasy a while to take on board but the knife cuts both way, and this constraint can be used by player characters to save their own lives. After all, exile is not always a permanent sentence.

CIVIC ORDER

Rome at this time has no police force and soldiers are prohibited from mustering within the walls. This means that there is no official force which protects citizens from miscreants. This is both a blessing and curse for characters, since they are free to throw their weight around if they wish... but there is nobody official to defend them when the inevitable backlash comes.

To deal with the problems of crimes and violence, citizens use social bonds to protect each other. Neighbourhoods, whether they be just an insulae or an entire street, keep a wary watch for suspicious behaviour and band together when confronted by an external threat (think of Block Wars in Judge Dredd, except the populace are armed with roof tiles and paving slabs instead of guns). Citizens can also avoid trouble by invoking the name of a patron or by calling on him for direct help if the implied threat does not work. Richer citizens gain protection vice-versa by surrounding themselves with their clientele. A large crowd of clients not only demoralises most thieves and thugs, but can also be used to force a way through crowded streets or shout down hecklers.

Thus, the true strength behind social order is a communal sense of civic responsibility and the client-patron relationship... not the number of bodyguards you have.

Games Masters are encouraged to teach their players that the city will always meet force with greater force. If they bully a single citizen, then that man's family will come seeking redress. Intimidating the entire family will call attention from that family's patron. Bribing thugs to beat up the patron may bring the local gang down on the attackers and all too soon hired gladiators will start lurking outside the homes of the characters. Eventually the character's own patron will be leaned upon and told to keep his clients under control. If they continue to push, bloodshed will spiral out of control and eventually the Senate itself will proscribe the players as Enemies of

the State and they will be hunted down by the entire city. In the end, civic order will be maintained.

COMBAT

Combat in MYTHRAS is deadly. If using the more realistic version of the Medicine skill (as suggested on page 131), combat becomes even deadlier. In ancient Rome there are no curative spells, no magical potions to recover hit points, no unusual herbs which accelerate healing... a character usually heals damage at their natural rate. This has a profound effect on how violence should be handled in a Roman game.

Within the walls of Rome the wearing of armour and carrying of weapons is forbidden, proscribed by law. Of course many people, especially during the closing stages of the late Republic, ignore these rules but the expense of armour keeps it is beyond the reach of everyone but the richest. What this means is that without protection, the lowliest street thug armed with a sica can be extremely intimidating.

In general, fighting with weapons should be avoided at all costs. A bit of good natured street brawling (such as in the October Horse festival) or an occasional boxing match is all well and good. But as soon as a knife gets drawn, somebody is going to die and it may very well be one of the player characters. Games Masters should encourage the idea of fleeing combat, most people do. However, players with psychopathic tendencies can be educated by the loss of a limb or being forced to miss out on entire scenarios, immobilised in bed for several weeks whilst their wounds slowly knit back together.

Nevertheless, up until the late Republic almost all citizens are expected to muster for military service. Games Masters can improve the survivability of these – initially annual – expeditions by allowing the characters to own or loot decent armour for protection. In addition, intelligent tactics may allow them to bias battlefield odds in their favour, friends can jump in to save them if they fall in formation and just as in modern warfare, becoming a casualty means that you are retired from active service until healed, which generally means no more fighting till the following year... if the army manages to leave the field in good order.

> "Now, for the first time, the youth, as soon as they were able to bear the toils of war, acquired military skill by actual service in the camp, and took pleasure rather in splendid arms and military steeds than in the society of mistresses and convivial indulgence. To such men no toil was unusual, no place was difficult or inaccessible, no armed enemy was formidable; their valour had overcome everything. But among themselves the grand rivalry was for glory; each sought to be first to wound an enemy, to scale a wall, and to be noticed while performing such an exploit. Distinction such as this they regarded as wealth, honour, and true nobility. They were covetous of praise, but liberal of money; they desired competent riches, but boundless glory."
>
> Sallust – Conspiracy of Catiline

Battle is not the only (or indeed the most satisfying) option for defeating belligerent enemies. Since most players wish to overcome opponents in a competitive situation, the Games Master should offer alternatives to deadly combat. Historically, glory and reputation was also won in rhetorical argument in the law courts, challenges on the sports fields, artistic performances, political elections and even in philosophical debate.

POLITICS

Politics are the centre point of Roman life and should be an inescapable part of any campaign. As an ostensibly democratic city, citizens of whatever rank have the possibility (or responsibility) to vote in magisterial elections and sit in judgement on new laws. Both of which are wonderful opportunities for scenarios.

In the eternal battle over social rights between the patricians and plebeians, new legislation can be an excellent source of antipathy to player characters if the law encroaches on personal liberties or sources of wealth. Are they steadfast Optimates or Populares, or do they swap their political position depending on selfish (or fearful) self-interest?

> "I myself, however, when a young man, was at first led by inclination, like most others, to engage in political affairs; but in that pursuit many circumstances were unfavourable to me; for, instead of modesty, temperance, and integrity, there prevailed shamelessness, corruption, and rapacity. And although my mind, inexperienced in dishonest practice, detested these vices, yet, in the midst of so great corruption, my tender age was ensnared and infected by ambition; and though I shrunk from the vicious principles of those around me, yet the same eagerness for honours, the same obloquy and jealousy, which disquieted others, disquieted myself."
>
> Sallust – Conspiracy of Catiline

Great fun can be had trying to undermine the election of a hated adversary, particularly if the slur campaign fails and he decides to use the authority of his magistracy to seek revenge. Corruption and bribery become commonplace in politics as the Republic nears its end, granting a Games Master the chance to subvert character's morals with ever more tempting gifts or seeding adventures where they uncover and expose underhanded policies. Such activity is dangerous as the web of political relationships is complex and could lead to the accidental exposure of their own patron, or even the current consul... with predictable results if they ignore the increasingly dire threats.

It does not matter if the characters are mere plebeians or members of the senate. Politics has a daily effect on their lives, and they should ignore it at their own peril. At times in Rome, your political affiliation can get you exiled or killed and nobody is allowed to sit on the fence.

MAGIC

The Games Master may wish to decide whether magic really is magical or simply trickery and psychology. For most forms of magic (save Shape-shifting) the rules work essentially the same but the actual truth behind how it functions can be kept nebulous. Remember that everyone in this period is intensely superstitious. People believe in the paranormal, even if it is completely bogus.

Of course, the inherent nature of magic and the gods in everyday life can be completely ignored by those wishing to run a more secular game. But Games Masters are encouraged to squeeze as much prophecy, witchcraft, curses and divine worship as they can into their scenarios, since it builds up a vivid image of the everyday nature of irrational Roman belief.

SUPERNATURAL CREATURES

Since most legendary beasts in Roman knowledge are simply exaggerated reports of real animals from Africa or the Middle East, such creatures can be included into even those games lacking the paranormal. However, unless the campaign is planned to visit foreign provinces, it has little effect unless explorers or merchants bring back live exhibits or the stuffed bodies or bones of such monsters.

The only supernatural creatures likely to be stumbled upon within Rome or its local environs are ghosts, demons, fauns or strix. Such an encounter in a hitherto 'realistic' game will radically change the superstitions and fears of the characters, much to everyone's enjoyment.

DISASTERS

Misfortune abounds in Rome. Every few years the city suffers a major flood, fire or pestilence which can be both exciting and tragic at the same time. Games Masters can instil a tangible sense of fear in their players with a vividly described catastrophe, not only by threatening the survival of the characters directly — but also menacing their families, sources of wealth or even monuments they may have built.

A well timed disaster can be used to test character's stoicism, if it strikes when they are at a peak of career or riches. Yet how they respond to the adversity, with bravery or generosity, can grant them a greater reward in terms of fame and glory from grateful clients, neighbours and citizens.

Like all epic disaster movies, a little goes a long way. Catastrophes should be used sparingly but when they do occur, they should inflict personal loss and cull a few NPCs along the way.

PERIOD

The period in which a campaign is set is critical, providing a background storyline and potentially affecting character freedom. For example, up until the late Republic every citizen is expected to annually serve in the army, allowing these games to legitimately involve mass battles and regular combat. In the last century BC however, the legions slowly transform into professional armies, making the alternation between city life and war adventures more difficult, if not impossible, for most citizens. Example periods are:

Ω The Founding of Rome – Aiding Romulus and Remus to found and protect the fledgling city of Rome.

Ω The Monarchy – Military and social conflicts during the time of kings, including plenty of heroic single combats.

Ω The Creation of the Republic – Support or oppose the last king of Rome in his struggle against the neophyte Republic.

Ω The Etruscan and Latin Wars – A period full of battles as Rome slowly conquers her neighbouring city states one by one, with the high drama of Rome being sacked by the Gauls.

Ω The Pyrrhus Campaign – Fighting against the phalanxes and elephants of the famous king.

Ω The Punic Wars – Another classic period full of politics and war, with the first naval battles, slave armies, Hannibal laying waste to central Italy and several invasions of north Africa.

Ω The Bacchanalian Conspiracy – Dark cult worship, murder, and sacrifice, as Bacchantes corrupt the youth of the city.

Ω The Gracchi Reforms – A high political campaign as the Gracchi brothers in turn, break Roman convention; applying laws in hitherto unthinkable ways to achieve their objectives, being killed by the Senate for their threatening actions and opening the door for future mob violence.

Ω The Germanic Threat – A tough military campaign against the massed Germanic tribes pushing towards Roman territory, when several armies are massacred.

Ω The Civil War of Marius and Sulla – A combination of politics and warfare, including the horrors of proscriptions where thousands die for their political affiliation or wealth.

Ω The Spartacus Revolt – A group of gladiators break free of their school and begin to run riot across Italy, repeatedly defeating the Roman armies sent against them.

Ω The Catiline Conspiracy – The young and politically marginalised band together under Catiline, who plans to overthrow the Senate.

Ω The Rise of the First Triumvirate – A political campaign either supporting or undermining the triumvirate, with more mob violence on the streets of Rome.

Ω The Civil War of Caesar and Pompey – The division of Rome between the two leaders, with the possibility of hastening or perhaps preventing Caesar's assassination.

Ω The Second Triumvirate – Battles and politics between the second triumvirate and the murderers of Caesar, before open hostility between Octavian and Marc Antony descends into war for ultimate rule over the Republic.

"But when, by perseverance and integrity, the republic had increased its power; when mighty princes had been vanquished in war; when barbarous tribes and populous states had been reduced to subjection; when Carthage, the rival of Rome's dominion, had been utterly destroyed, and sea and land lay

everywhere open to her sway, Fortune then began to exercise her tyranny, and to introduce universal innovation. To those who had easily endured toils, dangers, and doubtful and difficult circumstances, ease and wealth, the objects of desire to others, became a burden and a trouble. At first the love of money, and then that of power, began to prevail, and these became, as it were, the sources of every evil. For avarice subverted honesty, integrity, and other honourable principles, and, in their stead, inculcated pride, inhumanity, contempt of religion, and general venality. Ambition prompted many to become deceitful; to keep one thing concealed in the breast, and another ready on the tongue; to estimate friendships and enmities, not by their worth, but according to interest; and to carry rather a specious countenance than an honest heart. These vices at first advanced but slowly, and were sometimes restrained by correction; but afterwards, when their infection had spread like a pestilence, the state was entirely changed, and the government, from being the most equitable and praiseworthy, became rapacious and insupportable."

Sallust – Conspiracy of Catiline

INVIOLATE HISTORY

The Games Master should decide in advance on whether they wish to stick to the official timeline of Roman History. If history is inviolate, it makes it difficult for player characters to achieve fame in their own right and forces the Games Master to keep key historical figures sacrosanct until certain events occur. Of course, characters can still work behind the scenes to cause history to turn out the way it does or alternately the players could unknowingly take the parts of real historic personages.

Without inviolate history, characters can derail the timeline completely by their actions. This allows players the freedom to act without unnecessary constraint. In some ways this can be a very enjoyable option since you can then generate the future as desired, and keep the more historically knowledgeable players guessing.

ALTERNATE CAMPAIGN STYLES

Although this book focuses on role-playing in ancient Rome as a Roman, a campaign need not limit itself to a traditional historic setting. A myriad of alternate fantasy or science fiction ideas exist where the city or its culture can be given a unique and unusual slant to the campaign.

PAX CTHULHU

Combining Rome with the Cthulhu Mythos is an easy way of creating a horror campaign of epic scope at a time where foreign cults are regularly introduced into the city. Carthage could worship the Elder gods, explaining why certain members of the Senate demand its total eradication. Blood sports in the Circus Maximus may be the tithe required to pacify Rome's own dark gods that sleep under its streets. Perhaps the cult of Bacchus is attempting to call Nyarlathotep into the world, or do Deep Ones live in the city sewers..?

USING HISTORICAL SOURCES

One of the best things a Games Master can do before running any Roman campaign is to dip into the plethora of histories (or annals) written during the period. To read one completely is both daunting and unnecessary but a brief glance at the text can immediately snag one's attention and inspire a plot idea. Indeed, many of the entertaining quotes in this book are derived from the following works.

Recommended authors for the Monarchic and Republican periods of Rome are:

Ω Livy – Ab Urbe Condita, from which most of our knowledge of early Rome comes from

Ω Polybius – The Histories, good coverage of the military campaigns about the time of the Punic Wars

Ω Sallust – Catiline's War, the political machinations which led to the ineffectual coup

Ω Caesar – The Gallic Wars and The Civil Wars, which both cover politics and military campaigns

Ω Plutarch – Parallel Lives, although not written during the Republic, it contains interesting biographies of famous Romans of the period

English translations of these works can be found for free on the internet (see the Bibliography page 225 for suggested web addresses).

The histories often give the names and personalities of dozens of protagonists, fascinating events (sometimes supernatural) and anecdotes, all of which can simply be copied wholesale as plot devices, complete with pre-generated NPC's.

Of course, these suggestions are not necessary to run a Roman campaign. But they can often provide scenario ideas more intriguing, and convoluted than anything a Games Master can normally come up with himself. Truth is stranger than fiction, and the Roman world is definitely best studied via their own words.

TEMPUS AMBULATUS

Time travel campaigns could stop off in Rome. A number of Republican battles are key focal points for changing history. What would happen to the future if Hannibal followed up after his victory at Cannae by assaulting Rome? Indeed why did he not? The characters could be recruited by godlike time travelling agents (or be agents themselves) in order to prevent such occurrences. Of course, if the timeline is inherently resilient to change, then Rome might instead be the perfect place where a time travelling criminal might hide or vacation, with its massive population and lack of any technology for tracking individuals. Another idea might be to have characters in an erstwhile Sci-Fi campaign, suffer the backlash of some wormhole experiment and be permanently stranded in the past. Unable to return, the characters themselves might themselves introduce the technical advances the fledgling Republic uses during its climb to Empire.

FANTASY ROME

A fantasy Roman campaign would place the city in world full of mythological creatures and real gods, the most obvious being those of Greek derivation. This would permit spectacular scenes of Minotaur gladiators in the Circus Maximus, Sea Serpent drawn war galleys, or Jupiter himself casting lightning bolts to obliterate enemy generals. The setting need not be classical of course; a group of Romans or even the entire city itself could be transported into an alternate world full of wizards and monsters, as in Harry Turtledove's Legion of Videssos series. Or perhaps the eternal city is actually ruled by an oligarchy of dead ancestors, who refuse to continue over the Styx to the underworld but remain instead to continue personal machinations with their still living descendants as game pieces.

HIGH SCIENCE FICTION

What if a Roman adventurer, whilst exploring a ploutonion, discovered that the underground tunnels suddenly transformed into metal corridors? Or an exiled explorer climbing the highest peaks of the Alps or Atlas mountains sees the edge of the world on the other side. Rome and its surroundings could be a replica built on a gargantuan scale on an artificial world. Maybe the joke or social experiment of an advanced civilisation such as those described in Iain M. Banks' Culture novels or Philip José Farmer's World of Tiers. The campaign could centre on exploring or escaping from the construct or even battling their hitherto undiscovered alien masters or neighbours. David Drake's stories 'Ranks of Bronze' and 'Lambs to the Slaughter' offer the idea of a Roman legion being sold into service as primitive mercenaries for an advanced alien race.

ALTERNATE TIMELINE

A campaign could be set where certain geopolitical events of Rome's history are significantly changed. For example Livy himself questioned what might have happened if Alexander the Great had expanded west towards Rome, instead of east. Much fun could be had trying to defeat one of the greatest generals of history. What if a central African civilisation rises to oppose the Republic? An army of pseudo Zulus invading Italy might be a very entertaining scenario.

"Had Alexander the Great, after subjugating Asia, turned his attention to Europe, there are many who maintain that he would have met his match in Papirius."

Livy – Ab Urbe Condita

CARRY ON UP THE TIBER

Comic adventures can be great fun considering how Latin lends itself to abuse in the English language. As mentioned previously in the chapter on Character Generation, humorous pseudo-Roman names are very easy to come up with and there are some plots that can be borrowed wholesale from movies and mercilessly parodied. Movies such as 'A Funny Thing Happened on the Way to the Forum' are of course already parodies of farces written by Plautus in the 3rd and 2nd centuries BC but imagine what could be done in a comic version of Ben Hur or Spartacus... Start the game with a few glasses of wine and calling your tough Centurion 'Limpus Dickus' and everything else will flow naturally.

A CENTURY OF PLOT SEEDS

Considering the huge variation of possible starting options on which to base a Roman campaign, the author has not included a detailed introductory adventure. Ultimately most Games Masters will wish to use a conflicting time period, social beginning, or adventure style.

Therefore in order to help Games Masters through their first few games, 100 different scenario ideas follow. Each can be used as either the introduction into a campaign or possible split off scenarios until the campaign gains its own momentum.

To flesh out these scenario seeds, a list of pre-generated non-player characters follow this section. Since Roman politics tend to be played at several subtle levels simultaneously, some of these plots should be tied into longer running campaign threads with powerful individuals ultimately pulling the strings.

GLADIATORIAL SCENARIOS

1. One or more of the characters start as slaves and must earn their freedom in the gladiatorial arena, during which time they can gradually interact with the darker side of the city, building underworld contacts and learning the social conventions of Rome.

2. The gladiator is hired as a bodyguard for a senator marked for assassination. Will he defend the senator, gaining a powerful future patron? Or should he accept a bribe large enough to purchase his freedom and step aside?

3. The gladiator is sought after by an elderly matron who wants him as a paramour. Enduring the caresses of the wrinkled grandmother will bring gifts and possible favours, whereas refusal will result in enmity.

4. The gladiator engages in a romantic relationship with a young woman, who turns out to be the daughter of someone very important. The gladiator is forced to face very desperate odds in the arena unless he ends the relationship or solves the problem another way.

5. Faced with daily abuse from a sadistic trainer, the other gladiators approach the player characters and ask them to join a revolt. Should they break free and gratuitously satisfy their thirst for vengeance or reveal the plan to their owner in the (possibly forlorn) hope of freedom?

6. One of the characters is forced to face his best friend (another player character) in an unusual combat to the death. Should they really try to kill each other, refuse and face terrible punishment or attempt a daring escape?

7. The gladiator is hired to perform an assassination but unfortunately he knows the target. Perhaps it is a now-freed gladiator who showed him kindness in the arena or the unsuspecting father of his current lover?

8. The gladiator is hired for a private show and is challenged to a fight by an inebriated senator, whom he then kills when the pompous oaf fumbles one of his parries. What should the gladiator do? Keep quiet and hope it is covered up, call in a favour from a patron or defend himself in the courts?

9. A sadistic fellow ex-gladiator makes death threats against a recently retired player character for imagined crimes.

Ceaseless hounding and derogatory graffiti ensure the issue must eventually be settled either publicly in the arena or down a dark alley. Of course a murder will cast suspicion on the players.

10. The gladiator is approached by a gambling syndicate who wish him to take a fall in the next fight. Despite the seriously large bribe, the loss will set back the character who is building the reputation of a champion. Failing to agree to the business arrangement will bring retributive murder attempts.

CHARIOTEERING SCENARIOS

1. One or more of the player characters are brought to Rome as a team of charioteers. They must face corruption, cheating and outright murder in order to win enough races to earn their freedom.

2. The charioteer character is the wastrel son of a senator (who disapproves of his sons' interest in the Circus Maximus) and secretly races wearing a golden mask to hide his features. However, his competitors now see it as a challenge to unmask the character during the races.

3. No matter how skilled the charioteer character he always comes second to a rival, who constantly rubs his nose in it. The bragging should eventually drive the character into doing something illegal and win at any cost.

4. Just before a major race the charioteer finds one of his team mates, a close friend, has been murdered. Who killed them? A fan of a rival faction or the financiers his own team? Seeking revenge may uncover deeper levels of corruption and match fixing, placing the character himself in serious danger.

5. The charioteer begins to find his performance on the track suffering. Ill fortune dogs every race and soon it becomes apparent that he is cursed. He must find protection against the malediction or find the source of this potent hex and terminate it.

6. The character has accepted bribes to 'lose' races but on the advent of a particularly important race he is instead blackmailed into poisoning the rest of his team. Should he betray his racing companions or attempt to silence the blackmailers?

7. After accidentally whipping a rival charioteer's horses during a race, the incensed adversary begins a lethal enmity on the track, where he deliberately attempts to kill the player character using increasingly suicidal manoeuvres. Can he be placated or bought off or will the rivalry continue until someone dies?

8. A challenge is made to race chariots from Rome to Capua (a la 'Montecarlo or Bust'). Dirty tricks abound to manipulate the race result, such as sabotaging chariot wheels, applying laxatives, hiring gangs of thugs to set ambushes, switching road signs and so forth.

9. A foolish senator drives a chariot drawn by lions into the Forum where he loses control, a player character must try to mount and control the chariot before too many people are killed. Success brings brief glory and possible new patrons but also earns the hostility of the embarrassed senator.

10. A seller of narcotics offers the charioteer a mysterious potion, which will allow him to win any race. If the PC turns it down, the seller offers it to another charioteer who then wins everything. However the substance is addictive and soon costs horrendous amounts of money to purchase (half skills during withdrawal).

RELIGIOUS SCENARIOS

1. The worshippers of Bacchus (under a pseudonym) attempt to lure the player characters into their cult, where they are slowly corrupted until they are given a test which pushes them to the limit of their morals. At this point they are cast out and hunted as enemies of the cult.

2. Late at night a lone player character is approached by a beautiful woman who begs him for sex. The next day at a public sacrifice, the character recognises the woman as one of the Vestal Virgins. The sentence for deflowering one of the priestesses is a horrible death for both parties but should he confess? If not, a series of seemingly divinely sent disasters begins to strike Rome...

3. An evil cult begins in the sewers of the city, grabbing people off the street and sacrificing them. The lower class inhabitants begin to leave the city in terror but the problem is not treated seriously by the characters' patrons or the Senate. Investigation reveals that the leading patron is in fact a priest of the cult.

4. Due to dire omens, the Senate consults the Sibylline Books and orders a lustrum for certain gods, in which the player characters must participate. Much pressure is placed on the characters, since if they fail to perform the ritual correctly, the entire lustrum must be repeated.

5. During a military campaign against a neighbouring city, the player characters are asked to infiltrate the temple of its patron god and steal the deity, by performing certain rituals. Considering that the ceremony requires animal sacrifices, performing the rite stealthily is a serious challenge.

6. By subtle dreams and omens, a player character is driven by one of the gods to recover a valuable artefact or substance from an enemy city and place it on his or her altar. Persuading others that the quest is real could be a problem considering the dangers involved.

7. During the rebuilding of a major temple, a passageway sealed under the cult statue is discovered and volunteers brave enough to explore the tunnel are called for. Will they discover an ancient shrine of an enemy cult, signs of human sacrifice, a long forgotten god craving worship or an entrance to hell?

8. Whilst sorting through the effects of a dead ancestor, a player character discovers an old pledge to build a temple to the now-fallen family's divine founder. Should the character squander the family's remaining fortune to fulfil the ancient pledge? If ignored, perhaps the ghost of the founder will plague him.

9. The ancestral gods of a character's household are stolen and must be recovered at all costs. Why were they stolen,

who has them, and what is suitable vengeance towards the perpetrators? Until their recovery, the character is placed under a curse and cannot call upon any gods for aid.

10. After the mysterious disappearances of some of the divine fowl, the player characters are ordered to guard the Sacred Geese. Is this the psychological or supernatural prequel to an attack on Rome? Or just the desperate acts of a starving, impious plebeian?

LEGION SCENARIOS

1. During a siege the brutality of a centurion causes his cohort to revolt. Do the player characters participate, decrying their conditions in the army, attempt to restore the loyalty of their fellow men, or flee to the enemy city for protection?

2. A hoard of valuable scrolls is discovered during the sack of a city and the characters are 'volunteered' to guard it during its transport to Rome. Their general asks them to be somewhat lax in their duties, offering a large bribe. Should they trust their general or will they be tempted to read or steal some them?

3. The characters save the life of a spoiled patrician's son serving as a military tribune, who promises them the Corona Civica but later recants his offer and denies it ever happened. Should they push their claim and cause dissention, or buckle under the intimidation and threat of their commanding officer?

4. An extended campaign against an enemy city has exhausted the troops of both sides, so the commanders mutually agree that the battle should be decided by a challenge of single combats. The player characters should volunteer or they will be selected for whatever reason.

5. The player characters are unfortunately members of a legion which flees from combat and as part of its punishment the legion is decimated – the characters (one of whom may draw the short straw) have to club some of their compatriots to death. Will they do it or will they desert instead?

6. During a civil war, the player characters are sent to assassinate the commander of the opposing army. However they discover the general is either a relation or patron of one of the characters, potentially placing their loyalties at odds. Should they switch sides?

7. After being massacred during a battle, the legion loses its eagle. It is up to the player characters to clear the shame of the disaster by recovering the standard themselves. If successful they gain considerable status within the legion and possible promotion.

8. After a battle where the Romans are badly defeated, a few hundred survivors find themselves surrounded in enemy territory, lost and without supplies. The player characters are the only remaining officers and must take charge, using guile and strategy to escape or reverse the situation.

9. As the legion retreats in the face of overwhelming odds, its commander asks for volunteers to form a rear-guard. If the player characters step forwards, they are set to defend a bridge or narrow gully against a force a hundred times their number. Success, even if they die, brings immense glory to their families.

10. A fighting competition is held between the cohorts in the legion. Betting is rife and dirty tricks abound, in order to bias the outcome of the tourney. The winner will be promoted, receive a torque in honour of their victory and a bonus to their Status in the legion.

CRIME SCENARIOS

1. During a visit to the baths, the character's clothes are stolen, including a very expensive new toga given to him by his patron. Tracking down the thief may require contacting local criminals, or should he embarrassingly ask his patron for help?

2. On the way home after a late party, the player characters are ambushed by a gang of muggers. Should they pay or fight? If conflict breaks out, neighbours may join in by pelting all the combatants with rubbish or more dangerously, roof tiles.

3. If a player character owns a shop then he is approached for protection money from the local street gang. Failure to pay up causes increasingly violent incidents to occur, until all the customers are frightened away. Should the character attempt to overthrow the gang or ingratiate himself instead?

4. If unemployed, a player character is propositioned by the local gang to see if he wishes to join. He must prove himself by beating up a member of a neighbouring gang, thus precipitating a gang war.

5. At a banquet the host, a senator of small standing, is poisoned. The player characters are assigned the task of researching his death and finding the culprit. Was it his adulterous wife, his cheating business partner, a vengeful political opponent, an insulted poet or did the head slave do it?

6. A recent purchase by one of the player characters turns out to be stolen property; the character must seek compensation in court and suffer the slanderous indignities of the legal process.

7. The father of a player character dies under mysterious circumstances. The character is accused of patricide in court and faces a horrific execution unless his name is cleared. Was the old man murdered or was he accidentally killed by his medication?

8. A literate player character is approached to write a forged will. The bribe is very, very impressive but the punishment if caught is death. If the character agrees, news arrives a few days after completion that the man whose will was been forged is now dead...

9. The mistress of a player character is being blackmailed over some love poetry she wrote and sent to an older paramour. She begs the character to break into the house of the blackmailer and steal the scroll back. However, the dogs and several ex-gladiator guards make a direct break-in somewhat tricky.

10. A boxed package is delivered to the home of a player character with a note from an old friend to keep it secure. Inside is a crude tarnished statuette of a lead eagle. All too soon

protagonists turn up wanting the bird, which under the thin lead layer is actually an exquisite silver legion eagle...

ANIMAL SCENARIOS

1. A leopard escapes from its cage on the docks and runs riot. The player characters can attempt to capture or kill it as desired; capturing grants a reward but killing earns the enmity of the out-of-pocket owner. Either way the characters gain the brief adoration of the local populace.

2. A number of children go missing in the Via Sacra area, which unknown to the PCs is the haunt of an immense python. Investigation around the temples results in the discovery of several huge scales by sharp eyed characters. Hunting the creature will be tricky since it normally hides in the Cloaca Maxima.

3. A player character is challenged to prove his manhood by fighting a lion single handed at the next beast show. Armour and weapons are permitted. Success improves the character's Status and the eternal respect of the challenger.

4. The characters are asked to help solve a succession of high profile jewellery thefts. Despite setting guards in the gardens and inside the houses, the thefts continue. Fur trapped in the oozing resin of a newly installed window grating gives a clue that the thief might be a specially trained monkey.

5. One of the characters belatedly discovers a scorpion in his shoe. Assuming he survives the malicious attempt on his life, he then finds one in his bed, his folded toga at the baths, the wine cup at the tavern... Has the character offended some ancient deity or sorcerer? Or is one of his slaves trying to assassinate him with the deadly insects?

6. During some beast hunts at the games, the elephants go berserk and break into the stands of the audience. The player characters can run, or bravely hold back the enraged beasts so that others may escape. Gifts, patronage and increases to Status are the rewards for saving important dignitaries.

7. The player characters see a young boy being chased down the street by a pack of rabid dogs. Interceding diverts the mad dogs to attack the characters instead and any successful dog bite may expose the injured character to the (POT 13) fatal disease. The grateful father is a gang boss who offers each rescuer a single favour or patronage if desired.

8. A dockside warehouse in Rome's port of Ostia is raided and vandalised night after night and a reward is offered to anyone who can help. If the PCs stake out the store, they will discover that the thief is a giant octopus seeking amphorae of pickled fish. It can be killed, driven off or perhaps captured as desired.

9. A number of mutilated dead bodies appear downstream of the sewers, all of which have odd bite marks on their bodies. Bravely entering the sewer, characters can eventually trace the bodies back to the crocodiles kept at the villa rented as the Egyptian embassy. Who is being thrown into the sacred pool and why?

10. Local shepherds flocks are being decimated by wolves and the player characters are asked by a patron to deal with the problem. However the wolves appear to be highly intelligent; are they really wolves or is it a group of shape-shifters?

DISASTER SCENARIOS

1. The River Tiber floods and submerges the lower city, stranding people in the upper floors of their insulae. As food rapidly runs out, life becomes a fight for survival with the inhabitants of each building using violence to protect their scraps and possessions against neighbours, looters and each other.

2. Whilst one of the player characters is entertaining guests in his apartment, a fire on the ground floor spreads rapidly out of control and grows into an inferno. The characters find themselves trapped on the upper floors and must figure out an escape before the flames reach the roof.

3. Whilst shopping in the Forum Romanum, an argument starts between two equestrians, one of whom splashed mud onto the pristine toga of another. Their clients begin a riot which soon spreads out of control. Will the characters try to intervene, flee the area or use the opportunity to loot a shop?

4. A pestilence hits the city, killing thousands of people each day. Lacking guidance from their sick patrons the player characters must independently find a pious priest and learn how to appease Apollo in order to divert the plague.

5. Within several weeks an unusual number of insulae collapse across the city. On investigation one of the characters discovers his apartment block was also built by the same consortium that has used substandard materials. If ignored, the character's insula will collapse with possibly them or their family in it.

6. Whilst watching the excavation of a collapsed or burned out building, a character notices that the work is undermining the nearby aqueduct. Direct appeal to the slaves or their supervisor has no effect and the characters must rapidly locate the absent Aedile in charge of the operation before it topples.

7. A player character hears rumour of a planned assassination of their patron at the next festival games. Trying to locate the vengeful assassin turns up the name of a distinguished ex-gladiator but it is not until zero hour that knowledge of his past as an architect comes to light. Intelligent deduction may infer that the wooden supports of the temporary theatre have been sabotaged.

8. A conflagration starts on the Aventine hill and spreads across the city. Heroic characters need to stand firm and create a fire break by collapsing some insulae, before the flames engulf them. Eventually the fire is traced back to the apartment of one of the characters, placing him under suspicion of negligence or arson.

9. A great and terrible storm engulfs Rome, with lightning repeatedly striking the city. The characters are asked by a terrified patron to ascend the Capitoline Hill and perform a successful sacrifice to appease the wrath of Jupiter. Failure risks being struck by lightning...

10. A famine hits the city and the PCs are given the critical duty of guarding one of the grain storehouses in the Circus Maximus. How will they react to being presented with the sight of starving babies, being offered huge bribes and eventually outright, desperate hostility?

SUPERNATURAL SCENARIOS

1. During the Lemuria festival, a character's household is petrified with fear by the spectral manifestation of an ancestor who threatens death if the family mausoleum is not rebuilt. But on its next appearance the character might notice the ghost bears an uncanny resemblance to one of his slaves. If chastised for his impious jape, the slave is found dead the following morning with a look of utter horror on his face.

2. The player characters are asked to locate a patron who has gone missing for several days. Retracing his last known steps, they discover his clothes neatly folded and hidden in a sepulchre. If they take the clothes the characters will notice each evening that they are shadowed by a very large and fierce wolf, the shape-shifted form of their patron who wishes to transform back to his human shape.

3. The characters are sent to Capua to ask a question of the Sibyl there and must journey into the underworld to locate her. During their terrifying descent through the pitch black caves, they see demons and multi-headed dogs. But are they real or merely hallucinations caused by volcanic gases?

4. The following morning after upsetting an old female beggar, a player character finds himself transformed into the shape of an animal. He must locate his compatriots and seek a way to be returned to his real shape, discovering in the process that the old beggar was really a witch in disguise.

5. After unwittingly consuming a love potion, one of the player characters falls madly in love with a middle aged widow of questionable beauty and overzealous lust. His companions need to discover the reason for this radical personality change and free him from his slavery with their own potion.

6. The characters are asked to investigate the authenticity of a soothsayer in the Campus Martius. The probe is inconclusive until they become threatening, at which point the seer kicks them out of his shack and makes a disastrous prediction about the characters which later that day comes true.

7. During one of the festivals of the dead, the vengeful ghost of a major enemy returns to haunt one of the characters and attempts to kill him. He returns each night until successful or is banished back to the underworld by a necromancer.

8. The player characters are asked by a busy patron to travel out of the city and perform a ceremony to placate the god of a woodland grove before it is thinned out for timber. If successful they receive a blessing but if they mess it up, the grove's faun savagely kills the woodsmen and leaves their torn apart bodies as a warning.

9. During a drunken dinner party, the characters are asked to prove their bravery and spend the night in the burial grounds on the Esquiline Hill. Whilst there they see some witches perform a necromantic ritual from afar. Whether or not they interfere is their decision but will have repercussions good or bad according to how courteously they act.

10. Whilst wandering through one of Rome's many outlying necropolises, a player character sees a demon, which leers at him. Although no trace of the being can be found, the natural paranoia of the character and his player should be encouraged by the Games Master. Later on, during a life or death critical moment such as combat, the demon reappears and saves the helpless character, by dragging his enemy screaming off to the underworld.

PATRON SCENARIOS

1. In return for bailing out a character from a disastrous financial investment, his patron later returns and asks for the character's most treasured possession (a family heirloom, military award, his wife or children...). If the character refuses then he must sever his client-patron bond and gains an enemy. If he resignedly fulfils his obligation, then he is rewarded tenfold for his loyalty.

2. The son of a patron is kidnapped and sold into slavery. The client character is asked to find and free the boy, leading the characters into the seedy criminal underworld and mounting a daring rescue on a gang run brothel.

3. The patron departs Rome for the summer, leaving his house unoccupied. The player characters are asked to protect the property from thieves and vandals. Of course, having possession of an expensive house may lead to temptations such as raiding the wine store, or hosting a wild party to gain Status.

4. After many years of service between their families, the current inheritor of the position of patron suddenly fails to be able to satisfy the next request the characters make of him. It become apparent that he has gone bankrupt via an illegal embezzlement, but will the characters sever a long-standing familial relationship or should they band together and find a way of restoring the patron's fortune?

5. The daughter of the patron is never seen due to being disfigured from birth, when an oil filled brazier was accidentally knocked over on her. Unhappy that she will never find love or marriage, she persuades her father to marry her to one of his clients... one of the player characters. Although terribly scarred, the daughter will make an excellent good wife for he who volunteers to the marriage (skilled in command, crafts and Greek & Roman literacy) and eventually inherits a fortune.

6. A client of a player character begs for protection in a forthcoming legal case. At first glance the client seems guilty as hell but will the PC fulfil his obligation to the client-patron relationship? As the case progresses, it appears that the purpose of the suspicious case is to drag the name of the player character into disrepute.

7. The client of a character claims that his family has been murdered by a certain wealthy patrician. The client seeks retribution and the player character must decide the best path. Should he call in some favours owed to him or deal with the problem personally in the courts?

8. A well-groomed young man offers his services as a client to a player character. He refuses to reveal his past but proves worthy of trust and capable of completing many challenging tasks. After some time an acquaintance recognises the man as the disgraced grandson of a recently deceased censor, making the youth as sole inheritor and fabulously

wealthy. If he was well treated the young man offers patronage and makes a powerful ally for his ex-patron.

9. A client gifts his player character patron a wagonload of the finest vintage falernian wine, asking for funding in return, in order to journey south and set up a wine importing business. In consideration of the wine's exquisite quality the answer should be yes and the client vanishes with a large quantity of cash. However, soon afterwards when a magistrate is invited to dinner, the official recounts that his wine cellars were cleared out by thieves, just as he is about to sample the unique vintage...

10. After giving a beggar an overly large donation by mistake, the tramp follows the player character loudly proclaiming his generosity. Each morning the beggar will turn up on the character's doorstep as a loyal client, expecting more handouts. If the character disparages the beggar and drives him off, the local ghetto where the PC lives will be full of graffiti lampooning his munificence and causing him a loss in Status. However if the character continues to give alms, then he discovers that the beggar has access to a large amount of gossip, superior to any information purchased by professional espionage.

POLITICAL SCENARIOS

1. The characters are asked by a patron to attend him as he canvasses for support in the Forum Romanum. An opposing group of supporters start heckling, leading to a full blown slanging match. The characters should reciprocate, until eventually somebody loses their temper and throws half a loaf of bread, starting an all-out brawl...

2. The craftsmen's guild to which one of the player characters belongs, agrees to vote for a particular aspirant in the consular elections. However, at the voting tables, the guild leader votes for a different candidate who eventually wins by a hair's breadth. Was the guild leader bribed or threatened, and can the characters prove that the election was rigged before the new consuls take office?

3. A character is visited by a slave claiming that some senators are planning to overthrow the senate. Soon afterwards, the character is invited to join the insurrection. Should he report this information to the Senate, after all, who can he trust? Or is the slave a test of the character's loyalty to the rebellion?

4. To repay a favour owed to one of the current tribunes of the Plebs, the characters are asked to stand guard outside the house of the praetor urbanis, and prevent him from reaching the Curia, so that he cannot propose a new law. The characters must foil several escape attempts, eventually culminating in the praetor dressing up as a woman and leaving his home with the household slaves on their daily shop.

5. The characters are asked to organise the production of propaganda cups and bowls for the election campaign of their patron (crockery with election slogans and their patron's name inscribed on them) and distribute them freely amongst the plebeians. However on the day of delivery all the vessels are found smashed but the still soft crockery of a political rival has been left unattended, ready to be fired...

6. Rome is engaged in a particularly critical war when a totally incompetent leader appears to be about to bribe his way to consulship. Should the characters prevent the election before such an inept general is given power over the legions? Or should they wait on the sidelines and hope their own patron is sent to clean up the resulting mess, and thus gain a potential triumph at the expense of thousands of dead?

7. The characters are asked to investigate the personal habits of a particular tribune of the plebs. Despite many rumours to the contrary, nothing worthy of blackmail can be found; instead they are ordered to engineer a shocking event in order to stain the man's spotless reputation.

8. A fellow client of a player character's patron, known for spreading bribes to the plebs, is found murdered. The characters are asked to investigate to prove the patron's suspicions that one of his enemies is responsible. But if the characters dig too deep they discover it was the patron himself who had the client killed. Why? And what will the characters do with the information?

9. The player characters are sent as ambassadors to negotiate a settlement treaty with an enemy city. However the residents are confrontational, making the task extremely difficult. Do they try to win over the city leaders with soft words and silver greased palms, or match belligerence with arrogance? Unknown to the others, a character will privately be offered a huge bribe to undermine his companion's efforts during negotiations and with the Senate back in Rome.

10. The characters are ordered by the current consul to subtly look into the mint in the Temple of Juno Moneta for signs of negligence, where they eventually discover a devious plot debasing the coinage. The trail of the embezzled silver leads back to the co-reigning consul, who abuses his authority to have them blocked, then terminated if they persist in their investigation.

A CAST OF CHARACTERS

Here are some pre-generated non-player characters, which can be used as the dramatis personae for any of the previously suggested plot seeds. Since most characters should be recurring (outright killing of foes being rare), they can be reused from scenario to scenario as the players slowly build up their social contacts and enmities.

THE PATRON – MANIUS SCRIBONIUS MUSA

STR 11, CON 12, SIZ 10, INT 14 , POW 14, DEX 10 CHA 11
HP: 5/7/6/4/5, Damage Modifier: None

Notable Skills: Art (Poetry) 78%, Courtesy 72%, Gambling 63%, Insight 71%, Language (Greek) 55%, Language (Latin) 74%, Literacy (Greek) 50%, Literacy (Latin) 63%, Lore (Art) 79%, Lore (Literature) 60%, Rhetoric 59%, Status 77%, Streetwise 71%

A happy member of the equestrian class with far too much money, he spends his free time reading literature, avidly collecting art, and performing (often quite tedious) epic poetry at the dinner parties he hosts.

THE OLD FRIEND – TITUS GABINIUS RUSTICUS

STR 11, CON 12, SIZ 10, INT 14 , POW 14, DEX 10 , CHA 13 HP: 5/7/6/4/5, Damage Modifier: None

Notable Skills: Athletics 63%, Commerce 60%, Craft (Vintner) 69%, Drive 61%, Gambling 50%, Influence 51%, Language (Latin) 72%, Lore (Farming) 67%, Ride 56%, Status 59%, Combat Style (Legionary) 68%

A farmer who once served in the legions, he is a faithful friend and promising wine producer, whose vineyards are maturing.

THE MILITARY OFFICER – AULUS FURIUS BELLATOR

STR 17, CON 13, SIZ 15, INT 14 , POW 07, DEX 15 , CHA 08 HP: 6/8/7/5/6, Damage Modifier: +1d4

Notable Skills: Athletics 69%, Command 71%, Evade 61%, Language (Latin) 70%, Language (Numidian) 64%, Perception 62%, Status 70%, Swim 60%, Theology 68%, Combat Style (Legionary) 89%

A grizzled centurion recently returned from campaigning in Africa, he is both pious and a firm disciplinarian who has been awarded a plethora of civic awards for bravery.

THE COURTESAN – FABIA VULSO

STR 06, CON 14, SIZ 09, INT 15 , POW 11, DEX 10 , CHA 17 HP: 5/7/6/4/5, Damage Modifier: -1d4

Notable Skills: Commerce 63%, Courtesy 52%, Dance 79%, Insight 72%, Language (Latin) 79%, Literacy (Latin) 75%, Perception 62%, Seduction 74%, Status 66%, Stealth 59%, Streetwise 66%

A widowed equestrian who has taken the drastic step of becoming a professional courtesan but in reality she uses the position to act as a spy, selling information about her paramours to their enemies.

THE SENATOR'S WIFE – TULLIA DOMITIA PENNA

STR 09, CON 07, SIZ 10, INT 13 , POW 10, DEX 12 , CHA 15 HP: 4/6/5/3/4, Damage Modifier: None

Notable Skills: Art (Composition) 64%, Craft (Weaving) 66%, Courtesy 68%, Influence 56%, Language (Greek) 74%, Language (Latin) 75%, Literacy (Greek) 63%, Literacy (Latin) 67%, Lore (Literature) 76%, Politics 54%, Status 92%, Streetwise 51%

A devoted wife who acts as the perfect hostess to support her husband's political career but in secret publishes satirical poetry about the Senate under a male name.

THE MERCHANT – DECIMUS VIBIUS GRACILIS

STR 14, CON 12, SIZ 16, INT 14 , POW 12, DEX 13 , CHA 06 HP: 6/8/7/5/6, Damage Modifier: +1d4

Notable Skills: Commerce 72%, Courtesy 78%, Deceit 58%, Influence 57%, Insight 57%, Language (Latin) 75%, Language (Syrian) 71%, Literacy (Latin) 69%, Lore (Trade Routes) 69%, Pharmacy 52%, Status 81%

An equestrian importer of fine linen from Syria, he has been corrupted by the luxurious lifestyle of the east and now sports a corpulent body. Ruthless in terms of business and protecting his interests, he will bribe his way out of difficult situations with those of superior rank or use a subtly administered poison to deal with those the lower classes.

THE GLADIATOR – MARCUS CARNIFEX

STR 15, CON 16, SIZ 14, INT 10 , POW 14, DEX 15 CHA 10, HP: 6/8/7/5/6, Damage Modifier: +1d4

Notable Skills: Acting (Choreographed Fighting) 72%, Athletics 89%, Evade 76%, Gambling 60%, Language (Latin) 55%, Language (Numidian) 70%, Necromancy 64%, Pugilism 87%, Status 47%, Combat Style (Thracian) 88%

The son of an African tribal shaman, captured and sold into slavery, he eventually won his freedom fighting as a gladiator. Now a freedman and ex-champion of the arena, he hires himself as a high profile bodyguard, using his necromantic skills in private to lay the ghosts of those he slays to rest.

THE CHARIOTEER – APPIUS PAVO

STR 13, CON 12, SIZ 09, INT 11 , POW 17, DEX 13 , CHA 14 HP: 5/7/6/4/5, Damage Modifier: None

Notable Skills: Athletics 64%, Drive 79%, Evade 64%, Gambling 54%, Language (Latin) 55%, Lore (Horse Training) 67%, Perception 54%, Pugilism 73%, Ride 62%, Status 24%, Streetwise 71%, Combat Style (Whip) 75%

Although still a slave, the up and coming charioteer soon hopes to purchase his freedom from the paltry share of the prize money he earns from races he manages to win. As a talented slave he is given a long leash, and frequently finds himself embroiled in some bar fight over which chariot faction is the best.

THE GANG LEADER – SEXTUS TAURINUS

STR 16, CON 11, SIZ 14, INT 17 , POW 09, DEX 16 , CHA 09 HP: 5/7/6/4/5, Damage Modifier: +1d4

Notable Skills: Commerce 66%, Deceit 76%, Evade 68%, Gambling 74%, Language (Latin) 85%, Perception 77%, Pugilism 80%, Status 63%, Stealth 80%, and Streetwise 72%

Starting life as a young boy running gambling games on the streets to support his mother, he now controls his own gang who run a reasonably benevolent protection racket. His headquarters is a gambling den in a tavern adjoining the Clivus Suburanus.

THE FAITHFUL SLAVE – SERVUS

STR 09, CON 10, SIZ 14, INT 18 , POW 15, DEX 08 , CHA 11 HP: 5/7/6/4/5, Damage Modifier: None

Notable Skills: Courtesy 62%, Influence 57%, Insight 65%, Language (Greek) 90%, Language (Latin) 68%, Lore (Geography) 52%, Lore (History) 77%, Perception 74%, Rhetoric 52%, Status 23%, Stealth 73%

A Greek slave well educated and faithful, he manages the other household slaves and keeps alert to any chicanery which may threaten his adoptive family.

THE WASTREL – QUINTUS TARQUINIUS BIBULUS

STR 11, CON 12, SIZ 13, INT 12 , POW 09, DEX 11 , CHA 14 HP: 5/7/6/4/5, Damage Modifier: None

Notable Skills: Courtesy 54%, Deceit 78%, Gambling 75%, Insight 55%, Language (Latin) 63%, Literacy (Latin) 59%, Lore (Dirty Songs) 73%, Lore (Wine) 69%, Sing 71%, Pugilism 74%, Seduction 52%, Status 74%, Streetwise 62%

A young man with no purpose to his life, he spends all his time gambling, drinking and partying with his friends. Lacking prospects until the death of his father grants him financial freedom, he is slowly descending into depravity and debt.

Quem di diligunt, adulescens moritur – Whom the gods love, dies young (Plautus)

THE BEGGAR – LUCIUS MUS

STR 09, CON 13, SIZ 12, INT 14 , POW 11, DEX 17 , CHA 05 HP: 5/7/6/4/5, Damage Modifier: None

Notable Skills: Acting (Exaggerate Disability) 62%, Commerce 67%, Cursing 79%, Deceit 63%, Insight 73%, Language (Latin) 70%, Perception 59%, Sleight 58%, Status 31%, Streetwise 65%, Combat Style (Roman Citizen) 62%

A freedman thug who has lost an ear, has an evil scar down one side of his face and a maimed left arm. Crippled, he has turned to begging for survival, supplying street gossip or surveillance for those who pay him regular stipends. He is left alone by those who know of the reputed potency of his curses.

THE MAGISTRATE – PUBLIUS HORTENSIUS CAECUS

STR 13, CON 08, SIZ 12, INT 15 , POW 15, DEX 11 , CHA 10 HP: 4/6/5/3/4, Damage Modifier: +1d4

Notable Skills: Command 79%, Courtesy 59%, Insight 56%, Language (Latin) 75%, Law 58%, Literacy (Latin) 68%, Lore (Architecture) 78%, Politics 73%, Rhetoric 76%, Ride 69%, Status 95%

An up and coming, though rather short-sighted, magistrate of middle years. One of the two curule ædiles of the year, his ultimate objective is to become a censor, so that he might use the city treasury to rebuild all the temples and forums in a new architectural style he himself has personally designed.

THE PRIEST – GAIUS OVIDIUS AGELASTUS

STR 09, CON 13, SIZ 10, INT 17 , POW 05, DEX 09 , CHA 12 HP: 5/7/6/4/5, Damage Modifier: None

Notable Skills: Acting (Religious Ritual) 61%, Commerce 60%, Divination 71%, Influence 56%, Insight 52%, Language (Latin) 85%, Sing 68%, Status 57%, Streetwise 70%, Theology 72%

An Etruscan trained haruspex of questionable personal habits, devoted to the gods and a diviner of skill. His life is corralled by religious observance which makes his presence at social events rather restrictive. Despite his lowly station, his life seems blessed by good fortune.

THE MUSICIAN – PHILOXENUS

STR 10, CON 11, SIZ 10, INT 14 , POW 16, DEX 14 , CHA 13 HP: 5/7/6/4/5, Damage Modifier: None

Notable Skills: Art (Composition) 69%, Commerce 60%, Courtesy 58%, Insight 66%, Language (Latin) 57%, Language (Greek) 80%, Musicianship (Fistula Panis) 71%, Musicianship (Tibia) 76%, Perception 72%, Status 35%, Streetwise 64%

An ex-slave brought from Greece, he performs at festivals or parties for small gratuities. With a reputation for innovative material, his popularity and status is growing, and the more youthful members of the equestrian class now seek to employ his services.

ROMANS

Romans details a few of Rome's most famous sons, daughters and enemies. It is by no means fully comprehensive but merely an introduction to some of the key personalities of the era. They include a brief resume of their achievements but lack any characteristics since it is impossible to cover their personal development over the courses of their lives. It is up to the Game Master to flesh them out with skills, if necessary, to match their campaigns.

The list is ordered by time to help locate the correct personalities for a particular period. Specifically for the kings the first year is the start of their rule and the second is that of their death. For all others the two years are for birth and death. These dates are only rough guidelines, subject to debate by historians.

ROMULUS (753-716 BC) AND REMUS (753-753 BC)

The sons of Mars and founders of Rome, abandoned to the River Tiber, they were suckled by a wolf (or prostitute) and raised by a local shepherd. Romulus and Remus founded the city of Rome with fugitives and slaves, and ruled it jointly. Resentment grew between them, after a dispute about where the city should be built and who would name it. The bitterness eventually led to Romulus killing his brother. Afterwards Romulus founded the Senate, created the first legion, instigated the kidnap of the Sabine Women and conquered much of the surrounding territory. After his death, Romulus was deified as Quirinus.

> *"Romulus, then, after making a vow that if he should conquer and overthrow his adversary, he would carry home the man's armour and dedicate it in person to Jupiter, not only conquered and overthrew him, but also routed his army in the battle which followed, and took his city as well"*
>
> Plutarch – Life of Romulus

NUMA POMPILIUS – 2ND KING OF ROME (715-673 BC)

A Sabine elected to kingship by the people of Rome. His was a rule of peace and justice, legendarily taught to him by the Nymph Egeria. His piety was rewarded by Jupiter who dropped a sacred shield from the sky, upon which was written a prophesy concerning the city. Numa had 11 copies made to disguise the real one and they were used by the Salii priests in religious processions. He also established the Pontifices, the earliest guilds and invited the first Vestal Virgins to the city. It was also by his order that the gods were given no images in their temples.

> *"By natural temperament he was inclined to the practice of every virtue, and he had subdued himself still more by discipline, endurance of hardships, and the study of wisdom. He had thus put away from himself not only the infamous passions of the soul, but also that violence and rapacity which are in such high repute among Barbarians, believing that true bravery consisted in the subjugation of one's passions by reason"*
>
> Plutarch – Life of Numa

TULLUS HOSTILIUS – 3RD KING OF ROME (673-641 BC)

The third king of Rome, his skill was the art of war. He battled against and subjugated the cities of Alba Longa, Fidenae and Veii. One battle was settled in a battle of champions, the three Horatii brothers fighting for Rome, against the Curiatii triplets who fought for Alba Longa. During the fight the triplets were all wounded but two of the Horatii were killed. The remaining brother fled, causing his injured pursuers to spread out, whereupon he turned about and slew them one by one. After the conquered Albans refused to honour their peace treaty, Tullus had their dictator ripped apart by two chariots and destroyed their city, resettling the populace in Rome. In fighting so much he neglected the gods, who sent a plague – so he performed a sacrifice to Jupiter to cure the people but fumbled the ceremony and was struck down by a thunderbolt.

ANCUS MARCIUS – 4TH KING OF ROME (641-616 BC)

Deciding that a peaceful, pious king was needed, the people of Rome elected the son of Numa as the fourth king of Rome. However, he was forced to defend Rome's territory from aggressive neighbours and eventually ended up conquering the league of Latin city states, resettling some of them on the Aventine Hill. He fortified the Janiculum west of the city, built the first wooden bridge across the Tiber – the Pons Sublicius and founded the port of Ostia.

LUCIUS TARQUINIUS PRISCUS – 5TH KING OF ROME (616-579 BC)

An Etruscan who had migrated to Rome where, upon his arrival, an eagle snatched up his cap, flew away and then returned dropping it back onto his head – a prophesy of future greatness. He was adopted as the son of Ancus for his generosity and was elected king over his deceased father's true sons. He defeated the Sabines in a battle within the very streets of Rome and then followed his success by conquering the Etruscan cities of Corniculum, Firulea, Cameria, Crustumerium, Americola, Medullia and Nomentum. With the plunder he expanded the public buildings of the city, began the Circus Maximus and drained the lowlands with a ditch called the Cloaca Maxima thus recovering the land to start the Forum Romanum. During his reign he eventually purchased the Sibylline Books from the Cumaean Sibyl after she had burned six of the nine volumes. He also began the Temple of Jupiter Capitolinus and was eventually assassinated by the disgruntled sons of his adoptive father.

SERVIUS TULLIUS – 6TH KING OF ROME (579-535 BC)

Originally an Etruscan and a slave, Servius married a daughter of Lucius Tarquinius Priscus and thus succeeded him with the blessing of his mother-in-law, rather than by an election consulting the people. After battling the rebellious city of Veii and other Etruscan cities, he reformed the army and Roman political administration and built several temples to goddesses, including Diana and his patroness Fortuna. He also established the first census and expanded the city walls to include all seven hills. Favouring the plebeians over the patricians, he was eventually assassinated by his son-in-law Lucius Tarquinius Superbus and daughter Tullia, who drove her chariot repeatedly over his body.

LUCIUS TARQUINIUS SUPERBUS – THE 7TH KING OF ROME (535-495 BC)

Tarquin the Proud was the last king of Rome, who seized the throne via assassination. He levelled the top of the Tarpeian Rock, removing the Sabine shrines built on it, completed the Temple of Jupiter Capitolinus. His son Sextus raped the noblewoman Lucretia – whose dramatic suicide to save her honour precipitated a revolt against the Tarquinii dynasty. Forced to flee into exile, Tarquinius drummed up support from neighbouring Etruscan and Latin kings and attempted to retake the city, but the fledgling Republic survived and he retired to Cumae.

LUCIUS JUNIUS BRUTUS (545-509 BC)

Brother to a senator who had been killed by Tarquinius, Brutus insinuated himself into the Tarquin family by feigning simple-mindedness. He accompanied the king's sons to the Oracle of Delphi, who prophesised that the next ruler of Rome would be the first person present to kiss his mother. Brutus pretended to trip and kissed the ground, whom he interpreted as the symbolic mother of all men. Later he witnessed the suicide of his sister Lucretia after her rape and grasping the dagger from her hand he led the overthrow of the Tarquins. He passed power to the hands of the senate who elected him as one of the first two prætors (proto consuls) and made the people swear an oath that they would never allow a king to rule Rome again. Eventually Brutus was forced to execute his own two sons for conspiring against the Republic. He died in single combat against the Etruscan leader Arruns, each stabbing the other with their spear.

"Brutus, like the tempered steel of swords, had a disposition which was hard by nature and not softened by education, so that his wrath against the tyrants drove him upon the dreadful act of slaying his sons"

Plutarch – Life of Brutus

PUBLIUS VALERIUS PUBLICOLA (560-503 BC)

The co-founding prætor of the Republic, after the battle against the Tarquins and their Etruscan allies, where his colleague Lucius Junius Brutus died, he celebrated the very first triumph by parading through Rome mounted on a four horse chariot, thus setting a tradition. He also passed many laws which shaped the Republic, some of which lasted down to the assassination of Julius Caesar, including such conventions such as removing the axe heads from the fasces whilst within Rome. His laws were so just he was named 'Publicola' meaning 'friend of the people'. After passing over the consulship in 503 BC he died a poor man but the populace all donated something towards his funeral and he was mourned by the women for an entire year. His memory was so honoured that ever after, eminent members of the family were allowed to be buried in the same spot within the walls of Rome, an accolade forbidden to other Romans.

"Valerius, as we are told, while Rome was still a kingdom, was conspicuous for his eloquence and wealth, always employing the one with integrity and boldness in the service of justice, while with the other he gave liberal and kindly aid to the poor and needy. It was therefore clear that, should Rome become a democracy, he would at once be one of its foremost men"

Plutarch – Life of Publicola

LARS PORSENA (6TH CENTURY BC)

The king of the Etruscan city of Clusium, who attacked Rome in 509 BC to overthrow the Republic at the request of the exiled king Tarquinius Superbus. After the failed assassination attempt by Mucius Scaevola, he instead made peace.

GAIUS MUCIUS SCAEVOLA (6TH - 5TH CENTURY BC)

A courageous Roman who sneaked into an Etruscan army camp besieging Rome in order to assassinate Lars Porsena. He killed the wrong man but when captured he defiantly declared to the king that he was the first of three hundred Romans ready to sacrifice themselves to kill him. To prove his dedication he thrust his right hand into the flames of a brazier, showing no pain as his hand burned. The Etruscan king was so impressed he let Mucius go and the assassin was forever after named Scaevola or 'lefty'.

HORATIUS COCLES (536-490 BC)

The one-eyed hero who (accompanied by Titus Herminius & Spurius Lartius) defended the Pons Sublicius against an invading Etruscan army in 506 BC. Asking his two companions to destroy the bridge behind him so that the enemy would not be able to enter Rome, he single handed fought off several champions till the bridge collapsed and he swam across the turbulent river. He was rewarded with as much land as he could plough around in a single day and a statue erected in the Temple of Vulcan.

Then out spake brave Horatius, the Captain of the Gate:
"To every man upon this earth death cometh soon or late.
And how can man die better than facing fearful odds,
For the ashes of his fathers, and the temples of his Gods"
Lord Macaulay – Lays of Ancient Rome
Lucius Quinctius Cincinnatus (519-438 BC)

Served as consul in 460 BC, and then dictator in 458 and 439 BC. Nicknamed Cincinnatus for his curly hair, he was an active opponent of equality between the plebeians and patricians, being

Qui pro innocente dicit, satis est eloquens – He who speaks for the innocent is eloquent enough (Publius Syrus)

firmly in the aristocratic faction. He fell in to antipathy with the tribunes of the plebs, after his son fled into exile charged with murder, forcing Cincinnatus to liquidate his estates to pay for the defaulted bail. Serving his term as consul, he refused an offered second consecutive term in protest against the (in his eyes) disgrace that plebeian tribunes could continuously be re-elected to office. Retiring to his small farm, all that was left of his estates, he was recalled by the Senate to help aid a Roman army fighting against the Aequi tribe, which had become besieged in the Alban hills. Nominated dictator by the consul remaining in Rome, he raised a new army from the remaining men of military age and destroyed the enemy Aequi in a two pronged attack. Forcing the enemy commanders to pass beneath the yoke (an act of submission), he resigned his dictatorship after only 16 days, and returned to his farm. This act of voluntarily surrendering and eschewing power was seen as a paragon of civic duty... despite that before he did, Cincinnatus took the vindictive opportunity to expel from Rome all those witnesses responsible for his son's exile. In like manner, he immediately gave up his second dictatorship after crushing a plebeian rebellion, the task for which he'd been appointed.

GAIUS MARCIUS CORIOLANUS (527-490 BC)

A patrician who won a corona civica at the Battle of Lake Regillus and further honour in the siege against the Volsci city of Corioli, from which he earned his name. Being an avid aristocrat he argued against surrendering legal rights to the exploited plebs, which caused him to lose an election for consul. During a famine he was further humiliated in the Senate after he demanded that the plebs be starved into renouncing their tribunes. In retaliation the tribunes charged him with treason, and he was exiled. In anger against his treatment, he defected to the Volscians and successfully led their army to the walls of Rome. Before the city was captured he was persuaded to stop by the intercession of his wife and mother. Withdrawing the army he retired to Antium, where he was assassinated for betraying his allies.

"Marcius bore witness for those who hold that a generous and noble nature, if it lacks discipline, is apt to produce much that is worthless along with its better fruits, like a rich soil deprived of the husbandman's culture. For while the force and vigour of his intelligence, which knew no limitations, led him into great undertakings, and such as were productive of the highest results, still, on the other hand, since he indulged a vehement temper and displayed an unswerving pertinacity, it made him a difficult and unsuitable associate for others."

Plutarch – Life of Coriolanus

BRENNUS (5TH-4TH CENTURY BC)

The Gallic chieftain of the Senones, Brenuus defeated the Romans at the Battle of the Allia and captured Rome, laying siege to the populace atop the Capitoline Hill. After an almost successful night attack, prevented only by the warning hisses of the Sacred Geese of Juno, the Romans were forced to pay a thousand pounds (weight) of gold as settlement. When they complained about the accuracy of the weights, Brennus threw his sword upon the scales and uttered "Woe to the vanquished".

MARCUS FURIUS CAMILLUS, THE 2ND FOUNDER OF ROME (447-365 BC)

A patrician soldier and statesman, he was dictator five times in 396, 390, 385, 368, and 367 BC; celebrated four triumphs and on his death was granted the title "Second Founder of Rome". His first great victory was the capture of long besieged Veii by infiltrating via tunnels dug into the sewage system; after which displayed shocking impiety by using white horses to draw his triumphal chariot – an act normally reserved for the gods. He also defeated the cities of Capena and Falerii, then later by an act of honourably returning children taken hostage by a defector. Because the city surrendered he forbade it from being looted, which alienated his soldiers who'd expected booty. He was exiled from Rome on charges of embezzling state plunder from his previous campaigns, but legendarily prayed to the gods that if his expulsion was unjust that Rome would suffer a great calamity, and beg for his return. Soon after he was recalled and appointed dictator in order to defeat Chieftain Brennus, whose tribe had sacked Rome. Several further military campaigns against the Aequi and Volsci followed, and he finally concluded his military career by defeating the Gauls at the Battle of the Anio River. During his political career he passed a law sharing the consulships between the patricians and the plebs, and started the construction of a Temple to Concord to celebrate this domestic settlement. He died during a pestilence which struck Rome.

VALERIUS MAXIMUS CORVUS (386-285 BC)

Starting his military career under M. Furius Camillus against the Gauls, Valerius famously accepted a challenge to single combat by a huge Gallic warrior. As the fight started, a raven flew down and clawed at the Gaul's face, enabling the Roman to win. In recognition he took the name Corvus, to show his ally respect. He was consul six times, in 348, 346 (when he finally crushed the Volscians), 343, 335, 300, and 299 BC; dictator three times in 342, 302, and 301 BC; and celebrated four triumphs. He was popular with the soldiers with whom he engaged in athletic competitions, and interceded when the army mutinied. His constant military activities continued up to the age of 70, and he died still fit at the age of 100.

APPIUS CLAUDIUS CAECUS (350-271 BC)

A patrician who, unusually, started his political career by serving as censor in 312 BC and went on to serve as consul twice in 307 and 296 BC, and dictator once. His term in office was contentious, being accused of placing his own clientele into the Senate over better qualified aristocrats, biasing the voting majorities in favour of his own political aims. He was struck blind (hence his cognomen), apparently as a punishment from the gods for sacrilegiously removing the custodianship of the Temple of Hercules from the Potitian family to State owned slaves. His major contributions to Rome were the building of the first aqueduct (Aqua Appia), and major road (Via Appia). During his military campaign against the Samnites he vowed to and built a Temple to Bellona.

LUCIUS PAPIRIUS CURSOR (4TH CENTURY BC)

Roman general, five times consul in 326, 320, 319, 315, and 313 BC, and twice dictator in 325 and 309 BC. When appointed dictator for the first time he famously sentenced his Master of Horse to death for disobeying orders, which was narrowly avoided by the intercession of the father of the subordinate, the Senate and people. His

---

cognomen Cursor (the swift) came from his ability to march 50 miles a day, and he was a firm disciplinarian. After defeating the Samnites at Longula he was awarded a triumph.

PUBLIUS DECIUS MUS (DIED 295 BC)

A plebeian who served as consul four times in 312, 308, 297 and 295 BC. He died leading the left flank of a Roman army against the Gauls. When his troops started routing, he dedicated himself and the Gallic army to the gods of the underworld and charged into the enemy ranks (as had his father famously done before him at the Battle of Vesuvius – see the rite of devotio page 114). The self-sacrifice inspired his men and they held formation long enough to win the battle.

PYRRHUS OF EPIRUS (318-272 BC)

Invited by the city of Tarentum in 281 BC to be their war leader, Pyrrhus consulted the Oracle of Delphi, who encouraged him to aid them against the Romans. He brought the first war elephants to Italy. After several costly battles which Pyrrhus won, his loses were so great he was forced to give up the campaign in the face of the Romans ability to draw upon seemingly endless reinforcements. He instead travelled to Sicily to drive out the Carthaginians and was declared king. However, the Sicilians fearing a despotic rule, eventually drove him out of the country. He returned to Italy but on facing vastly superior numbers of Roman troops and battling them to a standstill, he decided to return to Epirus and thereupon conquered Macedonia.

PUBLIUS APPIUS CLAUDIUS PULCHER (288-247 BC)

Rome's most inept admiral. Elected consul in 249 BC he sailed for the enemy held harbour of Drepanum but ignored a dire omen when the sacred chickens used for augury failed to eat and he had them all cast overboard. After which he sent his entire fleet into the harbour at dawn to crush the Carthaginian navy, keeping his own flagship at the rear. Thus he failed to notice that the Carthaginians had sailed clear and was thereby trapped against the shore when the enemy flanked his fleet from the open sea. Of his 120 warships he lost 93 and was charged with treason for his incompetence. His trial was delayed by a thunderstorm, but before it could resume Publius died suspiciously.

"Shall we remain unimpressed by the tale of the presumptuous conduct of Publius Claudius in the first Punic war, who, when the sacred chickens, on being let out of the coop, refused to feed, ordered them to be plunged into the water, that they might, as he said, drink, since they would not eat? He only ridiculed the gods in jest, but the mockery cost him many a tear"

Cicero - On the Nature of Gods

QUINTUS FABIUS MAXIMUS VERRUCOSUS, THE SHIELD OF ROME (275-203 BC)

A patrician general and politician, he was consul five times in 233, 228, 215, 214, and 209 BC and dictator twice in 221 and 217 BC. Although he was granted the derogatory epithet of 'Cunctator' (the delayer) for his scorched earth strategy and refusal to engage Hannibal's forces in the 2nd Punic War, after the crushing defeat of Cannae the Romans understood that it was a sensible tactic and not cowardliness and the title became a badge of honour instead. Tough and courageous, during his life he also gained the honours

of being elected censor, and achieving the joint religious offices of Chief Augur and Pontifex Maximus.

"When Hannibal had proved no match for Fabius either in character or in generalship, in order to smirch him with dishonour, he spared his lands, when he ravaged all others. To meet this assault, Fabius transferred the title to his property to the State, thus, by his loftiness of character, preventing his honour from falling under the suspicion of his fellow-citizens"

Frontinus - Stratagems

MARCUS CLAUDIUS MARCELLUS, THE SWORD OF ROME (265-208 BC)

A plebeian general in the 2nd Punic War, he was consul five times, 222, 215, 214, 210 and 208 BC, and was the third and last commander to win the Spolia Opima, by slaying the chieftain of the Insubrian Gauls in single combat at the Battle of Clastidium. Amongst other successes he conquered and sacked Syracuse after several years of siege against the defences of Archimedes. He was eventually killed by Hannibal's forces whilst scouting near Venusia.

GAIUS FLAMINIUS (265-217 BC)

Twice consul, Gaius was a popular leader and protector of the plebeians, establishing the first land reforms in a manner that would be copied by the Gracchi a century later – which earned him a reputation of being a demagogue. However, the land redistribution sparked a renewed war with the Gauls, who were eventually defeated at the Battle of Telamon. As consul he forced the Gauls into submission and created the province of Cisalpine Gaul. In 220 BC he was made censor and built the Via Flaminia, two new colonies at Cremona and Placentia, and cleared the Circus Flaminius on the Campus Martius. He was one of the few senators who actively supported the Lex Claudia which prevented senators from engaging in overseas trade. He was killed in 217 BC during his second consulship, leading an army into Hannibal's ambush at Lake Trasimene

"A few days after entering his second consulship whilst offering his sacrifice, the calf after it was struck, bounded away out of the hands of the sacrificing priests and bespattered many of the bystanders with its blood. Amongst those at a distance from the altar who did not know what the commotion was about there was great excitement; most people regarded it as a most alarming omen"

Livy - Ab Urbe Condita

TITUS MACCIUS PLAUTUS (254-184 BC)

One of the earliest Roman playwrights who specialised in writing farces. His career was a colourful one, starting out as a carpenter, becoming an actor and with the money he earned, a merchant. When his investments collapsed he was reduced to a labourer and wrote plays in his spare time. His comedies were very popular and frequently performed at the festival games.

POMPONIA (3RD-2ND CENTURY BC)

An equestrian who married into the patrician Scipio family, giving birth to the famous general Publius Cornelius Scipio Africanus. She was modelled as an ideal Roman wife, being both extremely pious and dedicated to hard work within the household.

HANNIBAL BARCA (247-183 BC)

One of the greatest military commanders in history, Hannibal was reputed to have sworn an oath to his father that as long as he lived, he would never be the friend of Rome. He subjugated Hispania and when Rome broke her treaty with Carthage, starting the 2nd Punic War, he marched his army (which included elephants) from northern Iberia, across the Alps and down into the Po Valley of northern Italy, in the face of active native opposition. Once in Italy he continuously crushed the Romans in battle, the most notable defeats being Trebia, Trasimene and Cannae – after which the Romans followed the Fabian strategy of non-engagement. Despite his successes Hannibal was unable to conquer Rome itself and lacking full support of the Oligarchy in Carthage, he was eventually forced to return to Africa to defend the capital. At the climactic Battle of Zama he was narrowly defeated by Scipio. After peace was reached Hannibal became the chief magistrate of Carthage and repaid the indemnities owed to Rome in record time by redirecting money which had previously been lost to corruption. Unfortunately he was so successful that Carthage once again became a threat to Rome and the Senate demanded Hannibal be handed over to them. He went into voluntary exile, hiring his skills as a general but was hounded from country to country by the Romans until he finally committed suicide by poison.

"When I was a small boy, Antiochus, my father Hamilcar took me up to the altar whilst he was offering sacrifice and made me solemnly swear that I would never be a friend to Rome. Under this oath I have fought for six-and-thirty years; when peace was settled this oath drove me from my native country and brought me a homeless wanderer to your court"

Livy - Ab Urbe Condita

QUINTUS ENNIUS (239-169 BC)

The father of Roman poetry, Ennius was from Salento, a Greek city in the south of Italy. His works influenced future Latin literature and ranged from satires to epics, on diverse subjects such as theology and history.

PUBLIUS CORNELIUS SCIPIO AFRICANUS, SCIPIO THE ELDER (236-185 BC)

A general of the 2nd Punic War, he gained fame for defeating Hannibal by adopting many of the Punic commander's own tactics against him. Devout and pious like his mother before him, he survived the disastrous defeats of Ticinus, Trebia and Cannae. He was granted the proconsulship of Hispania since he was the only one brave enough to take the position and successfully prosecuted a campaign against Hannibal's brother Hasdrubal. Elected consul in 205 BC he raised an army in Sicily, sailed to Africa the following year and in 202 BC finally defeated Hannibal at the Battle of Zama. He refused the honours of dictator or consul for life but in 199 BC was elected censor. Scipio was infamous for his love and appreciation of Greek culture, and spent many years magnanimously trying to prevent the (in his eyes) unjust persecution of Hannibal. He was exiled from Rome over charges of corruption brought by Cato the Censor and died a year later under suspicious circumstances.

"When people said of Scipio Africanus that he lacked aggressiveness, he is reported to have answered: 'My mother bore me a general, not a warrior'"

Frontinus - Stratagems

MARCUS PORCIUS CATO, CATO THE CENSOR (237-149 BC)

A politician of plebeian stock, he was a devoted farmer and holder to old fashioned ways of Roman life. A new man, he progressed through the offices of Cursus Honorum, as tribune in 214 BC, quæstor in 204 BC, ædile in 199 BC, prætor in 198 BC, consul in 195 BC and finally Censor in 184 BC. An orator of great skill and stern disciplinarian, he served with distinction in the 2nd Punic War; and repeatedly called for the destruction of Carthage delenda est Carthago "Carthage must be destroyed" before the outbreak of the 3rd Punic War. He was granted one triumph for a successful campaign in Hispania and was very generous with his distribution of the spoils, including the dedication of a small temple to Virgo Victoria in thanks for his success. During his censorship he was stringent against luxury, Hellenic culture, stamped out corruption (albeit temporarily) and even expelled a man from the Senate for kissing his wife in front of their daughter. Conversely he cleaned the sewers, repaired the aqueducts, cleared private properties which encroached on public streets and built a number of new buildings, including the first basilica. His ruthlessness, incorruptibility, misogyny and intransience earned him countless enemies; despite being viewed as an icon of impartial integrity. In his later years he was an author and historian of note and died of old age.

"On one occasion when Marcus Cato, who had lingered for several days on a hostile shore, had at length set sail, after three times giving the signal for departure, and a certain soldier, who had been left behind, with cries and gestures from the land, begged to be picked up, Cato turned his whole fleet back to the shore, arrested the man, and commanded him to be put to death, thus preferring to make an example of the fellow than to have him ignominiously put to death by the enemy"

Frontinus - Stratagems

AEMILIA PAULLA (230-163 BC)

The patrician wife of Scipio the Elder and mother of Cornelia Africana, she was noted for the unusual freedom given to her by her husband and her scandalous enjoyment of luxury.

TITUS QUINCTIUS FLAMINIUS (229-174 BC)

A military tribune in the 2nd Punic War, curule ædile in 203 BC, quæstor in 199 BC and consul in 198 BC at the young age of 30. During his consulship and following proconsulship, he defeated King Philip (the 5th) of Macedon using new legionary formations to defeat the obsolescent phalanx. An admirer of Hellenic culture, he proclaimed the freedom of the Greek States from Macedonian authority in 196 BC. With his Achaean League allies he conquered and plundered Sparta, returning to Rome to celebrate a triumph accompanied by thousands of freed slaves. In 189 he was elected censor, after which returned to Greece and on his own authority demanded the King of Bithynia to hand over the old general Hannibal, prompting the Carthaginian to commit suicide and costing Flaminius his political support in Rome.

POLYBIUS (203-120 BC)

A member of the Greek aristocracy, he was captured and held as a hostage by Rome for 17 years, after their war with Perseus of Macedonia. In Rome he was hosted by the Aemilius family, where he became a tutor to Scipio the Younger. A friendship formed between them and they travelled together during many of Scipio's military campaigns. He also used his patrician connections to organise new forms of government in the Roman conquered Greek cities. Polybius is famous for his written history, which he researched by speaking with veterans of the various wars, or by first-hand experience, being present at the destruction of Carthage.

PUBLIUS TERENTIUS AFER, TERENCE (195/185-159 BC)

Brought from Libya or Carthage as a slave and educated, he impressed his senatorial master Terentius Lucanus so much that was soon granted freedom. Famed as a playwright, he wrote six comedies, which were first performed in Rome between 170 and 160 BC.

CORNELIA AFRICANA (190-100 BC)

Mother of Tiberius and Gaius Gracchus, she was viewed by Roman women as a model of feminine virtues and stoicism, and loved by the plebeians for the efforts of her sons. After her death a statue was erected in her honour, an unusual honour for a woman.

PUBLIUS CORNELIUS SCIPIO AEMILIANUS, SCIPIO THE YOUNGER (184-129 BC)

Adopted from the Aemilian family into the Cornelius Scipio family, he distinguished himself in the 3rd Punic War as a junior officer, winning a Corona Muralis in Hispania for being the first man to crest the walls of an assaulted city. In 147 BC he was elected consul, conquered Carthage and by the order of the Senate, levelled it to the ground. He was said to have wept at the destruction fearing the same fate lay in wait for Rome. On his return he celebrated a triumph and was granted the same title of his adoptive grandfather, that of Africanus. In 142 BC he became a censor, piously repairing the stone bridge erected by his birth family and initiated a policy against luxury and immorality, dismissing several members from the senate. In revenge three years later, he was accused of treason but easily brushed off the case. During his second consulship in 134 BC he restored the discipline of the army, conquered the city of Numania and brought the province of Hither Hispania under Rome's dominion, for which he gained the second title of Numantius. He died mysteriously in his bed, probably assassinated; on the very day he was to make a speech against the agrarian proposals of the Gracchi.

TIBERIUS SEMPRONIUS GRACCHUS (163-133 BC)

The patrician who started the instability of the Republic, by circumventing certain Roman political conventions and twisting the law to his own purposes. He started his career as a military tribune on the staff of his brother-in-law Scipio the Younger. As quæstor in Hispania he saved the army from destruction by agreeing a peace treaty with the enemy but back in Rome was accused of cowardliness by Scipio and the treaty was nullified – thus starting the enmity between Tiberius and the Senate. After the long years of the Punic wars, most of Rome's middle class land owners had died or gone bankrupt whist serving in the legions. Since entry into the army was limited to land owning citizens, Tiberius recognised the future danger and as tribune proposed an agrarian land reform, granting land back to the dispossessed lower classes. Unfortunately the majority of Rome's public land was settled or rented by the richest citizens and the Senate turned down the proposal. Thus he started to legislate by bypassing the Senate entirely and placing proposals directly to the

popular assembly, incidentally violating the sanctity of, and deposing, a fellow tribune who was under the influence of the oligarchy. As a final act of defiance he used his tribunician powers and diverted a foreign king's legacy to pay for his land reforms, undermining one of the key areas of responsibility of the Senate. Surrounded by alienated political enemies, Tiberius attempted re-election as tribune the following year to avoid impeachment and pass further threatening policies. He appeared at the vote surrounded by armed guards but was mobbed and killed by the senators who feared he wished to make himself king. Many hundreds of his closest supporters also died in the attack, their bodies cast like criminals into the Tiber. Thus it was the Senate who began the use of open violence in Roman politics.

"The wild beasts of Italy have their caves to retire to, but the brave men who spill their blood in her cause have nothing left but air and light. Without houses, without settled habitations, they wander from place to place with their wives and children; and their generals do but mock them when, at the head of their armies, they exhort their men to fight for their sepulchres and the gods of their hearths, for among such numbers perhaps there is not one Roman who has an altar that has belonged to his ancestors or a sepulchre in which their ashes rest"

Tiberius Gracchus – Speech 133 BC

GAIUS GRACCHUS (153-121 BC)

Inheriting Tiberius's ideals, Gaius built upon his brother's efforts and pushed for more reforms popular with the plebeians. After serving as a quæstor he was elected to tribune and amongst others, introduced policies to redistribute lands illegally acquired by the wealthy, limit the time citizen's mandatorily served in the army, and regulate the price of grain (which had inflated during the wars). Like his brother he ran for a second consecutive term as tribune of the plebs, this time successfully. However, running for a third term failed and Gaius saw his new laws repealed by the consuls of that year. In frustration, he attempted to use mob violence and assassination to protect his hard work but the insurrection was suppressed by the Senate, which armed itself and declared him as an enemy of the Republic. In the resulting atrocities, Gaius was killed along with three thousand of his supporters, whose estates were confiscated. His head was taken to one of the consuls, who paid the promised reward of its weight in gold, despite it being deviously filled with lead.

"But you suffered Tiberius to be despatched with bludgeons before your eyes, and his dead body to be dragged from the Capitol through the middle of the city in order to be thrown into the river. Such of his friends, too, as fell into their hands, were put to death without form of trial. Yet, by the custom of our country, if any person under a prosecution for a capital crime did not appear, an officer was sent to his door in the morning, to summon him by sound of trumpet, and the judges would never pass sentence before so public a citation. So tender were our ancestors in any matter where the life of a citizen was concerned"

Gaius Gracchus – Speech 122 BC

MARCUS LIVIUS DRUSUS (?-108 BC)

Set up as a tribune of the plebs in 121 BC to oppose Gaius Gracchus. He undermined the land reform bills by suggesting instead to build 12 new colonies, each populated with 3,000 poor citizens and to relieve the rent on property distributed in the last decade. The new laws were never ratified since his purpose was simply to

Quod non est in actis, non est in mundo – What is not kept in records does not exist

reduce support from Gracchus, in which he was successful. In 112 BC he was elected consul and fought in Macedonia driving out the Scordisci. Three years later in 109 BC he was made censor but died the following year.

MARCUS LIVIUS DRUSUS THE YOUNGER (128-91 BC)

Following in his father's footsteps, Drusus was ultimately elected tribune of the plebs in 91 BC. He started out as a conformist, supporting the Senate but upset them first by alienating the populace of Asia Minor from extortionate tax collectors (for which he was exiled) and then by wanting to grant citizenship to the Italian allies. His arrogance eventually undermined all of his popular support in Rome and he was assassinated. However the death of their champion angered the allies, who desired more say in the policies of the Republic to which they lent the majority of military strength and thus precipitated the Social War of 91-88 BC. Ironically, the Senate eventually capitulated to the demands and opened up access to full citizenship.

GAIUS MARIUS (157-86 BC)

The equestrian general who was elected an unmatched seven times as consul in 107, 104-100 and 86 BC. As a 'new man' his early political career was mediocre but he served as a legate in the campaign against Jugurtha in Numidia. Apparently advised by a seer to trust the gods and pursue his desires, he ran for consul campaigning against the corrupt oligarchy and was elected. To campaign against Jugurtha he revolutionised the army by allowing landless citizens to join the legions and modified its equipment and tactics, thereby producing Rome's first professional army. Eventually Jugurtha was captured by his subordinate Sulla and Marius as the commander rightfully claimed the glory and celebrated a triumph. After several disastrous campaigns led by idiotic commanders against Cimbri and Teutones, causing the loss of several hundred thousand men, Rome elected Marius for five successive terms as consul in order to avert the Germanic tribes from invading Italy. Against superior numbers he completely annihilated the Teutones and followed up by defeating the Cimbri and enslaving the survivors. Another (joint) triumph was celebrated but the sixth consulship was marred by the necessity of suppressing a revolt led by his own political ally Saturnius – who after capture was murdered despite being placed under his protection. Marius retired but was drawn back to offer military advice to help put down rebelling cities during the Social War. After this the 1st Mithridatic War broke out and a jealous disagreement broke out over who should lead the army. The senate chose Sulla, but the Popular Assembly at Marius' urging chose him. Sulla travelled to his waiting legions, convinced them to follow him and then marched on Rome, an act forbidden by law and ancient tradition which started the first civil war of the Republic. Although Marius attempted to organise a defence using gladiators, he was defeated and fled to Africa. A death sentence was passed against him but once Sulla had taken the army to battle Mithridates of Pontus, Marius returned from exile with an army to intercede in the partisan fighting that had broken out between the two consuls, Octavius who supported Sulla and the Cinna who supported Marius. Some of his troops went on the rampage and killed Octavius, along with a dozen nobles, adherents of Sulla. The soldiers were put to death but the damage was done, establishing a precedent. Marius was elected consul for the 7th time but died a month later.

"Since he was naturally virile and fond of war, and since he received a training in military rather than in civil life, his temper was fierce when he came to exercise authority. Moreover, we are told that he never studied Greek literature, and never used the Greek language for any matter of real importance, thinking it ridiculous to study a literature the teachers of which were the subject of another people; and when, after his second triumph and at the consecration of some temple, he furnished the public with Greek spectacles, though he came into the theatre, he merely sat down, and at once went away"

Plutarch – Life of Marius

LUCIUS CORNELIUS SULLA (138-78 BC)

The eventual enemy of Marius and the first man to march a Roman army on Rome, he was consul twice in 88 and 80 BC and an unconstitutional dictator. Born to an impoverished patrician family, his early life was spent with the dregs of city life, including a Metrobius female impersonator with whom he held a livelong romantic attachment. Receiving two inheritances he used the money to pay his way up the Cursus Honorum till he became the quæstor to Marius in the Jugurthine War. Sulla captured Jugurtha by bribing King Bocchus to betray him. He next won the magistracy of Prætor Urbanus supposedly through bribery again and was given proconsulship in Cilicia where he first established relations with the Pontus and Parthia. His next major command was as a general during the Social War, being set up in opposition to Marius whom the Senate was beginning to fear and won for himself a Grass Crown (Corona Graminea) for saving a Roman army at Nola. After this the Senate elected him to command in the 1st Mithridatic War but after Marius jealously attempted to wrest the command for himself, Sulla took six of his most loyal legions, marched on Rome and ousted Marius. Sulla successfully defeated Mithridates earning the agnomen 'Felix' the lucky and although his rival was four years dead, returned to Italy to crush Marian support for once and for all. With the support of subordinate officers such as Marcus Licinius Crassus and Pompey, he overcame all opposition and concluded the civil war by assaulting Rome at the Battle of the Colline Gate. In 82 BC he was appointed dictator by his supporters in the Senate with no limit to his term in office and promptly engaged in a bloodbath of proscriptions, sentencing one and a half thousand nobles (senators, patricians and equestrians) to death and confiscating their property. After a sweeping series of reforms, new laws and returning political power firmly in the hands of the Senate, he resigned the dictatorship in 81 BC and restored normal consular government. He was elected to consul the following year and then retired, surrounding himself once more with the dancers and actors of his poor beginnings.

"When he was still young and obscure he spent much time with actors and buffoons and shared their dissolute life; and when he had made himself supreme master, he would daily assemble the most reckless stage and theatre folk to drink and bandy jests with them, although men thought that he disgraced his years, and although he not only dishonoured his high office, but neglected much that required attention"

Plutarch – Life of Sulla

Quos Deus vult perdere, prius dementat – Those whom god wills to destroy he first deprives of their senses (Euripides)

QUINTUS SERTORIUS (126-73 BC)

A successful jurist and orator Sertorius began a military career by surviving the Battle of Arausio, then served under Marius as a spy against the Germanic tribes and in Hispania as a military tribune. As a quæstor he lost an eye and on returning to Rome to run for tribune of the plebs he was thwarted by Sulla, starting an enmity between them. After Sulla precipitated the civil war by attacking Rome, Sertorius supported Cinna and criticised Marius for the actions of his unruly soldiers. In 83 BC Sertorius returned to Hispania as proconsul and fought a running war with Sulla's forces; and despite being forced to temporarily retreat to North Africa, he won the respect and support of Hispania, especially the Lusitanians who had been plundered by Sulla's supporters. His skill as a general was matchless and he persecuted a guerrilla war against Sullan forces under Quintus Caecilius Metellus Pius, winning many battles against armies several times his own in size. Fortified with refugees and deserters, he took back the province of Hispania Ulterior and started to civilise the region. Aided by a white fawn, supposedly a messenger from the Goddess Diana, he held Hispania and was reinforced by an army led by dissatisfied nobles from Rome. In 77 BC Pompey was sent to aid Metellus Pius conquer Sertorius but the latter proved far the superior tactician and repeatedly crushed his opponents in several battles. In 73 BC he was assassinated at a banquet, on the verge of creating Hispania as an independent Republic.

"He did not remit the activities of a daring soldier after he had advanced to the dignity of a commander, but displayed astonishing deeds of prowess and exposed his person unsparingly in battle, in consequence of which he got a blow that cost him one of his eyes. But on this he actually prided himself at all times. Others, he said, could not always carry about with them the evidences of their brave deeds, but must lay aside their necklaces, spears, and wreaths; in his own case, on the contrary, the marks of his bravery remained with him, and when men saw what he had lost, they saw at the same time a proof of his valour"

Plutarch – Life of Sertorius

SPARTACUS (120-70 BC)

A Thracian who served in the Roman army as an auxiliary but was sentenced or sold as a slave into a gladiatorial school near Capua belonging to Lentulus Batiatus. In 72 BC the slaves revolted, seizing knives from the kitchen and weapons delivered in a wagon, they broke free of the school and occupied the summit of Mount Vesuvius. To survive they began pillaging the local area until the Senate was roused and sent a legion of three thousand men under the command of a prætor, Claudius Glaber, to capture them. Spartacus sent some of his men down the cliffs on the opposite side of the caldera whom then flanked the unfortified Roman camp at night, killing most of the soldiers and their commander whilst they still slept. The victory drew runaway slaves from all over Italy to join the successful revolt. Spartacus trained his rabble army using the gladiators and under his tactical command, defeated two more legions sent to destroy them. Two consuls each with their own legion were sent to stop the slaves escape north and although a subordinate Crixus split off with 30,000 slaves to continue plundering, Spartacus defeated each consul's legion in turn and then the legion of the proconsul of Cisalpine Gaul. Although some of his non-combatant followers may have passed over the Alps to return to their homelands, Spartacus returned south, defeating a two legion army under Crassus,

and then wintered at the Straights of Messina negotiating with local pirates for transport to Sicily (the home of previous slave uprisings). Fate conspired against him, and breaking free of Crassus' eight legions, he was eventually trapped between the army of Pompey recently returned from Hispania and that of Lucullus from Macedonia. He died in a final battle against Crassus at the headwaters of the Siler River.

MARCUS TERENTIUS VARRO (116-27 BC)

An equestrian scholar and author, he served in the magistrate offices of tribune of the plebs, quæstor, curule ædile and prætor. He was a supporter of Pompey in the civil war but was pardoned by Julius Caesar. He was appointed to supervise the first public library of Rome in 47 BC but was later proscribed by Marc Antony, causing the loss of all his personal property. He eventually found favour under Augustus and wrote a great many works on amongst other things, agriculture, architecture, linguistics and satire.

MARCUS LICINIUS CRASSUS (115-53 BC)

A supporter of Sulla in the first civil war, he benefitted from the proscriptions to rebuild his family's confiscated fortune and then increased it by trafficking in slaves, silver mines, and property investments. His nickname was 'Dives' meaning rich. Crassus undertook at his own expense to raise, equip and train his own army to eventually defeat Spartacus in 71 BC, capturing 6,000 slaves alive and had them crucified along the Via Appia as a warning. Although he won the war, Pompey stole his glory by claiming credit for finishing it (by cleaning up the broken, fleeing survivors) and Crassus was only awarded an ovation because he had been fighting slaves. The animosity between the two grew, despite a joint consulship in 70 BC and later both forming the first Triumvirate with Julius Caesar. He was censor in 65 BC and when elected to a second consulship with Pompey in 55 BC, Crassus took Syria as his province in an effort to finally outshine Pompey in military glory; using it to launch a military campaign against Parthia. Cursed horrifyingly as he left Rome by the tribune Capito (who was later prosecuted for the act), Crassus was defeated at the Battle of Carrhae, where he and his legions were annihilated.

"Wealth is sought sometimes for the necessary uses of life, sometimes for indulgence in luxury. In those possessed of a higher order of mind the desire for money is entertained with a view to the increase of the means of influence and the power of generous giving. Thus, not long ago, Marcus Crassus pronounced no property sufficient for one who meant to hold a foremost place in the republic, unless its income would enable him to support an army"

Cicero – De Officiis

LUCIUS LICINIUS LUCULLUS (110-57 BC)

A patrician who began his political service as a military tribune in the Social War. In 88 BC, serving as prætor, he was the only officer to support Sulla on his march on Rome. He fought in all three of the Mithridatic Wars and as curule ædile in 79 BC he gave a lavish series of games. Lucullus inherited Sulla's memoirs and became guardian of his son. In 74 BC he was elected consul, initially receiving Cisalpine Gaul as his proconsular province but swapped it for Cilicia in order to prosecute the 3rd Mithridatic War and eventually defeated Mithridates at the Battle of Cabira, completing the conquest of Pontus. Following up on his successes he continued the campaign into Armenia defeating Mithridates again at the Battle of Artaxata in 68

Quot linguas calles, tot homines vales – You are worth as many people as there are languages that you speak

BC. At this point his brother-in-law Publius Clodius caused dissention amongst his troops, allowing the severely weakened Mithridates to briefly retake some of his lost territories. As a direct result of his attempt to reform the rapacious administration of Asia, which gained him enemies amongst the tax farmers of Rome, Lucullus was recalled and replaced by Pompey. On his return his well-earned triumph was maliciously delayed until 63 BC and he gave up pursuing a political career, instead living a life of indolent luxury, becoming known as a gastronome. He used part of his wealth earned in the wars to build famously beautiful gardens north of Rome and several lavish villas one of which sported fish ponds connected to the sea.

LUCIUS SERGIUS CATILINA, CATILINE (108-62 BC)

A patrician of an impeccable family but declining fortunes, Catiline served in the Social War and with Sulla in the later civil war. His reputation suffered a blow when he was accused of adultery with one of the Vestal Virgins. Acquitted of the charge he was elected to prætor in 68 BC and after a two year proprietorship in Africa, was charged with abuse of power, of which he was again acquitted. Charges of corruption prevented him from running for consul for two years. He was defeated in the consular elections of 63 BC, due to a lack of senatorial support and fear of his proposed universal cancellation of debts. He was once again brought to trail, this time for being one of the men who profited during Sulla's proscriptions and for killing his brother-in-law for financial gain. Again acquitted (although perhaps only because Julius Caesar was the judge), he ran for consulship in 62 BC. However, the constant blackening of his reputation undermined his political support and he failed to be elected. At this point he decided to seek the consulship via illegal means. Approaching other cast out and side-lined politicians, he gathered together conspirators who sought restoration to the Senate and those dispossessed and veteran soldiers who clung to his idea of debt relief. His subordinate Gaius Manlius organised the assembly of an army in Etruria and a slave revolt started in Capua. Catiline remained in Rome to lead the planned slaughter of senators and the burning parts of the city to cause disruption. Cicero, one of the targets, was warned of the plot and placed guards to defend himself. The following day Catiline was denounced in the Senate by Cicero and stormed off, seemingly leaving to a voluntary exile. Soon after letters were intercepted proving the conspiracy and the implicated conspirators were rapidly executed, terminating the insurrection in Rome. Driven to desperation, Catiline, along with his army of 10,000 men attempted to flee to Gaul but was forced to fight at the Battle of Pistoria and he died bravely with his men, whose bodies were noted for only bearing wounds to their fronts.

"He [Catiline] was intimate with many thoroughly wicked men; but he pretended to be entirely devoted to the most virtuous of the citizens. He had many things about him which served to allure men to the gratification of their passions; he had also many things which acted as incentives to industry and toil. The vices of lust raged in him; but at the same time he was conspicuous for great energy and military skill. Nor do I believe that there ever existed so strange a prodigy upon the earth, made up in such a manner of the most various, and different and inconsistent studies and desires"

Cicero – Pro Caelio

SERVILIA CAEPIONIS (107-AFTER 42 BC)

The half-sister of Cato the Younger, Servilia was married twice producing a son, Marcus Junius Brutus from the first marriage and three daughters named Junia in the second. Sometime prior to 64 BC she became the mistress of Julius Caesar and remained so until his death in 44 BC. She had no dealings in the assassination of Caesar and indeed resented the influence of Porcia, Cato's daughter over her son. After Brutus's death she retired to the guardianship and care of Titus Pomponius Atticus.

GNAEUS POMPEIUS MAGNUS, POMPEY (106-48 BC)

An equestrian from provincial eastern Italy, Pompey ascended the Cursus Honorum as quæstor in 104 BC, prætor in 92 BC and consul in 89 BC. A supporter of the Optimates, he sided with Sulla in the civil war and defeated Marian forces in Sicily and Africa. For his victories he was proclaimed 'Imperator' by his legions and sarcastically granted the cognomen 'Magnus' the Great by Sulla. He demanded a triumph which was eventually granted after he refused to disband his legions outside Rome and in retaliation Sulla celebrated his own triumph first, followed by one for Quintus Caecilius Metellus Pius, leaving Pompey's for last – much to the amusement of the populace when his elephant drawn chariot would not fit through the gates of Rome. Sent to help Metellus Pius against Sertorius in Hispania, for five years he was unable to achieve any victory until Sertorius was assassinated, at which point he helped pacify the province. On return to Italy with his army he came across the fleeing ragtag remnants of Spartacus' defeated army and promptly executed them – thereby claiming glory for ending the war. In 71 BC he celebrated a second triumph for his Hispanic success, and using his military victories to bypass the legal age requirement he was elected as consul with Crassus in 70 BC. Breaking with the Optimate party and supported by a young Julius Caesar, he passed a law restoring power to the tribunes of the plebs and re-shared jury positions between senators and equestrians. In 67 BC he was granted an extraordinary magistracy against the pirates that controlled the Mediterranean Sea. With his gift for logistics, he completed the task in only three months. He was then tasked to replace Lucius Licinius Lucullus in prosecuting the 3rd Mithridatic War and just as in the war against Spartacus he stepped in after Lucullus had successfully broken the power of Mithridates and then celebrated a third triumph for his pacification of the East. He joined the first Triumvirate in order to achieve the land settlements he had promised to his veterans and married Caesar's daughter. With the death of his wife, followed by that of Crassus in Parthia, the relationship between Caesar and Pompey became strained, and the Senate used him to undermine Caesar's growing power, resulting in another civil war. At their final confrontation at the Battle of Pharsalus in 48 BC, despite outnumbering his foe two to one, Pompey lost and fled to Egypt where he was assassinated by two old friends. His head was presented by a slave to Caesar who "turned away from him with loathing, as from an assassin; and when he received Pompey's signet ring on which was engraved a lion holding a sword in his paws, he burst into tears."

"Too long had great Pompeius from the height of human greatness, envied of mankind, looked on all others; nor for him henceforth could life be lowly. The honours of his youth too early thrust upon him, and the deeds which brought him triumph in the Sullan days, his conquering navy and the Pontic war, made heavier now the burden of defeat, and crushed his pondering soul."

Lucan – Pharsalia

MARCUS TULLIUS CICERO (106-43 BC)

The most famous author and orator of the late Republic, Cicero was an equestrian and self-styled champion of the Republic. An intellectual by nature, Cicero served the minimum necessary military service under Strabo and Sulla during the Social War. He then dedicated himself to a career as a lawyer. His first case in 79 BC was the defence of Sextus Roscius on a charge of patricide, chancing Sulla's disfavour. Although successful, he soon left for a philosophy tour of Greece, Asia Minor and Rhodes, learning from the greatest rhetoricians of the time. After his return he began his climb up the Cursus Honorum, elected as quæstor to the Sicilians in 75 BC, who impressed with his honesty, became his clients and asked him to prosecute Gaius Verres, who had illegally plundered the island during his governorship. As a 'new man', Cicero had problems finding political support in the Senate, despite the fact that he strongly supported the Optimates faction. However he struggled on, achieving curule ædile in 69 BC, prætor in 66 BC and finally consul in 63 BC. During his consulship he discovered and prevented a conspiracy led by Catiline, for which he was granted the cognomen 'Pater Patriae', father of the fatherland. However, despite physical proof, Cicero overstepped his authority by sentencing the conspirators to death by strangulation in the Tullianum without a trial. During the civil war between Caesar and Pompey, Cicero sided with the Pompeians but became disillusioned and was later pardoned by Caesar. After Caesar's assassination, Cicero rose to the forefront of the Senate in an attempt to preserve the Republic but in the process alienated Marc Antony, eventually naming him an enemy of the State. After Antony formed a second Triumvirate with Octavian and Lepidus, he proscribed Cicero, who was caught and murdered at his villa in Formiae. His hands and head were displayed on the Rostra.

"For this man beyond all others showed the Romans how great a charm eloquence adds to the right, and that justice is invincible if it is correctly put in words, and that it behoves the careful statesman always in his acts to choose the right instead of the agreeable, and in his words to take away all vexatious features from what is advantageous"

Plutarch – Life of Cicero

GAIUS JULIUS CAESAR (100-44 BC)

A patrician by birth, Caesar became the head of his family at the age of 16 and the Flamen Dialis at 17. However during Sulla's proscriptions, he was stripped of his priesthood, inheritance and his wife's dowry, but survived in hiding despite being Marius' nephew, via the intercession of his mother and the Vestal Virgins. Joining the army he served with distinction, winning for himself a Civic Crown at the siege of Mytilene. He was accused of a love affair with King Nicomedes whilst seeking to secure his fleet. After Sulla's death, Caesar returned to Rome and lacking funds, purchased a modest house in the Subura, the lowest class neighbourhood in the city. He took up legal advocacy and proved himself an excellent orator,and whilst travelling to Rhodes to perfect his rhetoric, was kidnapped by pirates – whom after being having his ransom paid, he captured and sold into slavery. He worked up the Cursus Honorum, starting as a military tribune, served a quæstorship in Hispania and borrowed massively to pay for public works and games during his ædileship. In 63 BC he became the Pontifex Maximus, and moved into the official residence. He was accused of being part of the Catiline conspiracy but was later cleared. Elected prætor in 62 BC he was suspended

from office by the Senate but public demonstrations helped return him to office. He also divorced his wife that year, because she was suspected of adultery. He was given the province of Hispania Ulterior as his proprætorship and conquered the local tribes, being heralded Imperator by his troops. Faced with either celebrating a triumph or standing for election as consul, he chose the latter. In 59 BC he was elected consul with Bibulus, his ineffectual colleague. Coordinating with Crassus, who had paid off many of Caesar's debts and Pompey who wanted land for his veterans, the three men formed the first Triumvirate. During the consulship he passed reforms to redistribute lands to the poor, which were forced through by the intimidating presence of Pompey's veterans. After his term in office Caesar was granted an extraordinary proconsulship over Cisalpine and Transalpine Gaul and Illyricum. Safe from prosecution, he began the conquest of the rest of Gaul in part to pay off his remaining debts. From 58 to 51 BC he conquered the entire region, drove off a Germanic incursion and invaded Britain. In the process he earned vast wealth from the plunder and enslavement of thousands of Gauls. In 50 BC the Senate, by manipulating Pompey, ordered Caesar to disband his army and return home since his extended term as proconsul had finished. Accused of treason, and fearing legal prosecution, he approached Rome with only a single legion, which sparked civil war. Pompey and the Senate fled, leaving Rome in Caesar's hands, who proceeded to confiscate the treasury and began hounding Pompey and his legions, first defeating the Pompeian subordinates in Hispania and then travelling to Greece to defeat Pompey himself. After the Battle of Pharsalus in 48 BC he was declared dictator, a position he resigned after 11 days, and stood for consul instead. He pursued the defeated Pompey to Egypt where he supported Cleopatra in the Alexandrian civil war. In 47 BC he suppressed uprisings in the Middle East, then travelled to North Africa in 46 BC to defeat Metellus Scipio and Cato the Younger and finally to Hispania in 45 BC to finish off Pompey's sons. During the last two years he was re-elected as consul for the third and fourth times and appointed dictator at first for 10 years and then for life. Showing unexpected leniency, Caesar pardoned his enemies and celebrated a great series of games on his return to Rome. He also started major works, building a new forum and a temple to Venus Genetrix. Despite being awarded many honours and titles by the Senate, his new reforms for the common good sewed fears amongst some senators that Caesar would undermine their wealth and power, prompting 60 of them to assassinate him in the Theatre of Pompey.

"But do you see what sort of man this is into whose hands the state has fallen, how clever, alert, well prepared? I verily believe that if he takes no lives and touches no man's property those who dreaded him most will become his warmest admirers"

Cicero – Selected Letters

TITUS LUCRETIUS CARUS (99-55 BC)

Lucretius was a poet and Epicurean philosopher, probably a wealthy dilettante. His prominent work was 'On the Nature of Things' (De Rerum Natura), which attempted to free the reader's mind of superstition and the fear of death by illuminating the philosophy of Epicureanism.

Romani ite domum – Romans Go Home! (Monty Python, Life of Brian)

MARCUS PORCIUS CATO SALONIUS, CATO THE STOIC (95-46 BC)

A passionate believer in the Republic and politician of famed tenacity, Cato was one of a few Roman politicians considered incorruptible and his completely objective opinion was decisive in the court or senate. Although wealthy, his lifestyle was austere conforming to his stoic philosophy, wearing the minimum of clothes and consuming the plainest of foods. As a military tribune in 67 BC, he was sent to Macedonia and led from the front, sharing the work and living standards of his men, who respected him greatly. After a private trip through the Middle East, Cato returned to Rome in 65 BC and was elected as quæstor, during which he prosecuted former quæstors for corruption. In 63 BC he became a tribune of the plebs, assisting Cicero in suppressing the Catiline conspiracy by arguing against Caesar's speech for the novel sentence of lifelong imprisonment for the conspirators, demanding execution instead. In possible vengeance for this, Caesar entrapped Cato by reading a personal note during a meeting of the Senate. Cato accused Caesar of involvement in the conspiracy and demanded that the message be read out, which turned out to be a love letter to Caesar from Servilia, Cato's own half-sister. The personal enmity continued when Cato attempted to unify opposition to the monopoly of the first Triumvirate, his favourite tactic being that of speaking until the sun set, preventing the Senate from taking a vote. After an immaculate quæstorship in Cyprus where he raised a huge revenue of silver by eradicating the normal graft and corruption, he was elected prætor in 54 BC. After the collapse of the Triumvirate when Crassus died, he then drove a wedge between Caesar and Pompey in order to weaken both parties. This disastrously failed, leading to the outbreak of civil war. Reluctantly supporting Pompey, he was initially given command of Sicily but withdrew when faced with superior forces. In charge of the camp at the Battle of Pharsalus, he survived and escaped to join Metellus Scipio in North Africa where they raised a new army. Despite outnumbering Caesar, this resistance was defeated in 46 BC and unwilling to surrender to his enemy, Cato killed himself by pulling out his own intestines after an initially failed suicide attempt.

> *"As for Cato, my affection for him is no less than yours; but even with the best will in the world, there are times when his high-mindedness is a positive danger to the state. He delivers opinions which would be more at home in the pages of Plato's Republic than among the dregs of Romulus here. "*
>
> Cicero – Letters to Atticus

CLODIA METELLI (95-? BC)

The elder sister to Publius Clodius Pulcher, Clodia was married as a young girl to Lucullus, then after being divorced in 66 BC due to arguments between her husband and brother, she was remarried to Quintus Caecilius Metellus Celer. Throughout this second marriage she engaged in many affairs with married men and slaves, and was notorious for drinking and gambling. When her husband died in 59 BC, Clodia was suspected of poisoning him. She refused to marry again but led a scandalous life with many more affairs during which she accused an ex-lover of attempting to poison her. The defence lawyer was Cicero, who slandered Clodia with an incestuous relationship with her own brother. After the case was overturned, Clodia vanished into obscurity.

PUBLIUS CLODIUS PULCHER (92-52 BC)

Descended from an illustrious patrician family, Claudius was a troublemaker during his undistinguished military career, stirring up rebellion and mutiny wherever he served. Returning to Rome in 65 BC, he entered politics and three years later caused an uproar when he was caught sneaking into the female-only religious rites of Bone Dea dressed as a woman. The event caused the divorce of Julius Caesar from his wife, who was rumoured to be in an adulterous affair with Claudius. In 61 BC to stand for election as tribune of the plebs, he voluntarily gave up his patrician rank by being adopted into the plebeian branch of the family – thus changing his name from Claudius to Clodius. Successful, he angered the Senate by granting a free grain dole, abolishing the right of magistrates to prevent the assembly of the comitia by taking unfavourable omens, preventing censors from excluding members from the Senate without trial and re-establishing the guilds. These changes made him very popular with the plebeians, so that he was able to abuse his tribuneship to exile Cicero, confiscate his property and burn down his house on the Palatine Hill. Clodius himself purchased the burnt out lot at auction via a proxy. Once Caesar had left for Gaul, no authority restricted Clodius; accompanied by a gang of thugs, he became the unspoken master of Rome using violence and intimidation to subdue his political opponents. He was eventually countered by Milo who procured his own gang of ex-gladiators and Cicero was recalled to the city. Despite this, the violence escalated, with Cicero assaulted in public and the house of his brother set fire. In 53 BC outright war erupted in the streets between the armed gangs of Milo and Clodius, who were both standing for magisterial office. When both passed each other on the Via Appia outside of Rome, Clodius was killed in the melee and at the funeral his clients used the Senate house for his funeral pyre, burning down the curia and part of the forum in the process.

GAIUS SALLUSTIUS CRISPUS, SALLUST (86-34 BC)

A plebeian from the Sabine region, he spent his youth as a wastrel and began his political career as a tribune of the plebs in 52 BC. A sympathiser of the populares, he became a loyal devotee of Caesar who became his patron. In 50 BC he was dismissed from the Senate for immorality but Caesar reinstated him the following year and he was elected quæstor. He managed to gain the office of prætor in 46 BC and accompanied Caesar on his African campaign, setting him up for the proprætorship of the province, which he extorted brutally. On returning to Rome he used part of his rapaciously gained wealth to lay out the Gardens of Sallust, near to those of Lucullus. Retiring from politics, he became an author of historical literature, including the 'Catiline Conspiracy' (De Coniuratione Catilinae) and the "Jugurthine War' (Bellum Juguthimun).

> *"Accordingly, when my mind found peace after many troubles and perils and I had determined that I must pass what was left of my life aloof from public affairs, it was not my intention to waste my precious leisure in indolence and sloth, nor yet by turning to farming or the chase, to lead a life devoted to slavish employments. On the contrary, I resolved to return to a cherished purpose from which ill-starred ambition had diverted me, and write a history of the Roman people, selecting such portions as seemed to me worthy of record; and I was confirmed in this resolution by the fact that my mind was free from hope, and fear, and partisanship"*
>
> Sallust – Conspiracy of Catiline

MARCUS JUNIUS BRUTUS (85-42 BC)

The descendant of the famed Brutus who started the Republic, Marcus Junius Brutus started his political career as an assistant to Cato during his governorship of Cyprus. He became rich by unscrupulously lending money at outrageously high rates of interest and aligned himself with the optimates in the Senate. When civil war broke out, Brutus followed Pompey against Caesar, despite the fact that Pompey had killed his father and Caesar was the love of his mother. After the Battle of Pharsalus, he wrote an apology to Caesar who pardoned him. In 46 BC he was then made governor of Gaul and in 45 BC made Prætor Urbanus. Moved by his loyalty to Cato (to whose daughter he was then married) and constantly reminded of his founding ancestor's acts, he joined the conspiracy to murder Caesar whom he feared was seeking kingship. After the assassination Brutus retired to Crete from 44-42 BC but when Octavian was elected consul and declared that Caesar's assassins were murderers, Brutus (at Cicero's urging), raised 17 legions with Cassius and marched on Rome. At the second Battle of Philippi Brutus was finally defeated and he committed suicide by falling on his sword.

> *"Brutus rose and said 'By all means must we fly; not with our feet, however, but with our hands.' Then, after clasping each by the hand, with a very cheerful countenance he said he rejoiced with exceeding joy that not one of his friends had proved false to him, and as for Fortune, he blamed her only for his country's sake; himself he regarded as more to be envied than his conquerors, not yesterday and the day before merely, but even now, since he was leaving behind him a reputation for virtue, which those who surpassed in arms or wealth would not do; since the world would believe that base and unjust men who put to death the good and just were unfit to rule. Then, after earnestly entreating them to save themselves, he withdrew a little way in the company of two or three friends, amongst who was Strato, whom had been his intimate since they studied rhetoric together. This man he placed nearest to himself, and then, grasping with both hands the hilt of his naked sword, he fell upon it and died"*
>
> *Plutarch – Life of Brutus*

GAIUS CASSIUS LONGINUS (85-42 BC)

A survivor of the military disaster at Carrhae, he managed to escape Parthia with 500 cavalry and defended Syria against Parthian incursions as proquæstor until the replacement proconsul arrived. He joined Pompey during the civil war, acting as commander of his fleet and successfully burned a large portion of Caesar's navy. After Pompey's defeat he was forced to surrender and in an act of mercy Caesar appointed him a legate in the Alexandrian War. Unable to face fighting Cato and Scipio in North Africa, he retired to Rome and two years later was made Prætor Peregrinus. Despite the clemency shown him, Cassius conspired to assassinate Caesar and led the physical assault on the dictator. When Marc Antony raised the populace against them, Cassius fled, turning down the province of Cyrene assigned to him, in favour of Syria. He raised an army of 12 legions to confront and defeat the legitimate governor Publius Cornelius Dolabella and joined forces with Brutus to oppose the second Triumvirate. Cassius was slain at his own request by his freedman Pindarus, when he lost the first Battle of Philippi against Marc Antony.

GAIUS VALERIUS CATULLUS (84-54 BC)

An equestrian poet from Verona, he travelled to Rome in 61 BC and fell in love with the 'Lesbia' of his poems, who is believed to have been Clodia Metelli. His brief affair ended when she spurned him for his friend Caelius Rufus. In 57 BC he served on the staff of a friend assigned as proprietor of Bithynia, then returning to Rome to spend the last two years of his short life there. His poetry concerned erotic love, rude or obscene invectives of friends or politicians, and condolences for the loss of loved ones.

MARCUS ANTONIUS, MARC ANTONY (83-30 BC)

A distant cousin of Julius Caesar, Antony's youth was a wild and unguided and he frivolously wasted money on gambling, drinking,and love affairs. He eventually was forced to flee to Greece to escape his creditors and there was conscripted to fight in the campaigns against Judea. Gaining a reputation for bravery and leadership of cavalry, he was admitted to Caesar's staff on his conquest of Gaul. Under his patronage, Antony was elected to the offices of quæstor, augur and tribune of the plebs. When Caesar became dictator, Antony was made Master of Horse and retained control over Italy until the last Pompeian dissidents were defeated. Despite being relieved of political responsibilities due to his administrative ineptitude, Antony remained faithfully loyal to Caesar and was joint consul with him in 44 BC. After Caesar's assassination, Antony professed the desire to seek peace and agreed to an amnesty for the assassins. However at Caesar's funeral, Antony gave a powerful eulogy and dramatically displayed Caesar's body, pointing at each stab wound and shaming the senator responsible. He also read Caesar's will, which left most of his property to the people of Rome, demonstrating the he had no desire to found a royal dynasty. The audience was roused to anger, attacking the homes of the assassins, forcing them to flee Rome. After warring over Cisalpine Gaul as his proconsular province, Antony joined forces with Marcus Aemilius Lepidus and Octavian, forming the second Triumvirate, in order to face the threat of Brutus and Cassius marching on Rome. Defeating Caesar's assassins, Antony travelled on to Egypt where his began an affair with Cleopatra. After Lepidus foolishly tried to usurp control, Octavian and Antony divided responsibility for the empire between them, with Antony taking the East. Disagreements over an ill-considered invasion of Parthia, further compounded by the revelation that he had illegally granted Roman provinces to his young children with Cleopatra and that Caesarion was the legitimate heir to Caesar's name and fortune (threatening Octavian's popularity and legal status as the adoptive son), caused the outbreak of hostile propaganda and eventually the Senate declared war on Cleopatra, giving Antony the chance to return to the fold. He refused and the two sides met at the naval Battle of Actium, where Marcus Vipsanius Agrippa defeated Antony. Fleeing to Egypt, Antony and Cleopatra lived their final months to the full before Octavian invaded. He committed suicide in despair after being falsely informed that Cleopatra was dead. At the time of his death he had been married five timesand had fathered dozens of children.

> *"For whenever he was going to be seen by many people, he always wore his tunic girt up to his thigh, a large sword hung at his side, and a heavy cloak enveloped him. However, even what others thought offensive, namely, his jesting and boastfulness, his drinking-horn in evidence, his sitting by a comrade who was eating, or his standing to eat at a soldier's table, it astonishes how*

much goodwill and affection for him all this produced in his soldiers. And somehow even his conduct in the field of love was not without its charm, nay, it actually won for him the favour of many; for he assisted them in their love affairs, and submitted pleasantly to their jests upon his own amours. Furthermore, his liberality, and his bestowal of favours upon friends and soldiers with no scant or sparing hand, laid a splendid foundation for his growing strength, and when he had become great, lifted his power to yet greater heights, although it was hindered by countless faults besides"

Plutarch – Life of Antony

Marcus Vitruvius Pollio (80/70-15 BC)

An architect, engineer and author, Vitruvius served as an artilleryman in the army. As a free but poor citizen he served in many campaigns across Gaul, Hispania, Aquitaine and Pontus and built various different artillery and siege machines. He wrote a comprehensive book on Roman architecture, including chapters concerning aqueducts, materials, surveying and central heating. He eventually found patronage under Augustus' family.

Fulvia (77-40 BC)

A strong willed woman, she was the offspring of a plebeian family and inherited the Gracchi fortune in 63 BC. She married three times. The first was with Publius Clodius Pulcher, whose political career she financed and possibly influenced. She had a daughter Clodia with him. Widowed in 52 BC she quickly married again to Gaius Scribonius Curio, a tribune of the plebs bribed by Caesar, who was killed in 49 BC leading an expedition to conquer Numidia. Her third marriage was to Marc Antony whose political career she also funded and bore him two sons. To solidify the second Triumvirate she offered Octavian her daughter Clodia in marriage. However when he later divorced her daughter, Fulvia took offence and together with Antony's brother (Antony at this time was settled in Egypt), she raised an army of eight legions to fight for her husband's rights. Despite the brief capture of Rome, she was forced to retreat to Perusia where they were starved into submission. Fulvia was exiled to Sicyon and died of an illness before Antony could join her.

Publius Vergilius Maro, Virgil (70-19 BC)

Born in Cisalpine Gaul, Virgil travelled to Rome to study rhetoric, medicine and astronomy, but abandoned these to study Epicurean philosophy. He soon began to write poetry and eventually published the classic epics known as the Bucolics, the Georgics and the Aeneid – which became the Roman national epic. The Aeneid took 10 years to write and recounts the tale of Aeneas the last hero of Troy, from the fall of the city to the foundation of Rome and the moral challenges he faces of whether to fulfil his desires as a man or act with virtue and pietas towards his ancestors and the gods. The work was left unfinished when Virgil died from fever but Augustus overruled the author's own wish that the poem be burned on his death.

Quintus Horatius Flaccus, Horace (65-27 BC)

The son of a freedman in Venusia, he was educated in Rome and Athens, subsisting as a middleman at auctions. He joined the army of Brutus as a staff officer after Caesar's assassination and survived the Battle of Philippi by shamefully throwing away his shield and running. He returned to Rome under Octavian's amnesty, but discovered his estate had been confiscated. Reduced to poverty he

purchased an appointment as an official in the State treasury and used his free time writing lyrical poetry.

Gaius Julius Caesar Octavianus, Octavian (63 BC – AD 14)

Born a mere plebeian, but gaining patrician status when he was adopted by his great uncle Gaius Julius Caesar, the young Octavian only started his political life after inheriting Caesar's estates in 44 BC. Returning from his military studies in Dalmatia, he was granted Imperium to legally command the legion of veterans he had raised on the way to Rome, and was sent with the consuls of that year to defeat Antony in Cisalpine Gaul. Although Antony was forced to retreat, both consuls were killed, leaving Octavian in command of the consular armies. The Senate attempted to transfer command to Decimus Brutus, the governor of Cisalpine Gaul, but since he was one of his great uncle's assassins, Octavian refused. Instead he remained in the Po Valley and demanded that he should receive one of the vacant consulships, and that Antony should be cleared of being a public enemy. When his demands were refused he marched on Rome with eight legions and the Senate capitulated. After this he joined forces with Antony and Lepidus to form the second Triumvirate, in order to fight off the combined armies of Brutus and Cassius. They enacted a series of murderous proscriptions in the manner of Sulla to remove their enemies from power and raise money for the legions. This purge of 300 senators and 2,000 equestrians permanently weakened the Senate. Eventually the Triumvirate collapsed and after another succession of civil war, Lepidus was allowed to retire in exile and Antony committed suicide following his defeat at the Battle of Actium. Octavian was left in sole command over Rome. Although appearing to restore the workings of the Republic, he retained autocratic power despite turning down the office of dictator. Instead he was voted both tribunate and censorship powers for life by the Senate and was continuously re-elected as consul. He held much of his power from financial domination won by conquest and by granting patronage to many loyal soldiers and veterans across the empire. With such irresistible popularity with the people and overwhelming military support, the Senate was forced to concede to his decisions. His authority was such that in 27 BC he was granted the titles 'Augustus' and 'Princeps', and declared the start of the Pax Romana, a peace which was to last (save for a single year) for two centuries.

"Although weakened by illness, being driven from his camp in the first battle [of Philippi] and barely making his escape by fleeing to Antony's division, he did not use his victory with moderation, but after sending Brutus's head to Rome, to be cast at the feet of Caesar's statue, he vented his spleen upon the most distinguished of his captives, not even sparing them insulting language. For instance, to one man who begged humbly for burial, he is said to have replied: "The birds will soon settle that question." When two others, father and son, begged for their lives, he is said to have bidden them cast lots or play mora, to decide which should be spared, and then to have looked on while both died, since the father was executed because he offered to die for his son, and the latter thereupon took his own life. Because of this the rest, including Marcus Favonius, the well-known imitator of Cato, saluted Antony respectfully as Imperator, when they were led out in chains, but lashed Augustus to his face with the foulest abuse"

Suetonius – Life of Augustus

MARCUS VIPSANIUS AGRIPPA (63-12 BC)

Agrippa began his impressive military career fighting under Julius Caesar against Pompey's son in Hispania, after which he was sent to Dalmacia with Octavian to study warfare, befriending him in the process. Following Caesar's assassination, he accompanied Octavian back to Rome where he assisted levying new legions in Campania. He was elected tribune of the plebs in 43 BC and the following year fought alongside Octavian at the Battle of Philippi. In 41 BC he helped put down a rebellion led by the brother and wife of Marc Antony and in 40 BC was left as Prætor Urbanus to defend Italy against Sextus Pompeius who had captured Sicily. In 38 BC he crushed an uprising in Transalpine Gaul and harried the Germanic tribes. Agrippa was made consul by Octavian in 37 BC in order to prepare for a war against Pompeius which he prosecuted the following year, and received a Naval Crown, a unique award. During the next few years he undertook a vigorous series of restoration and improvement projects in Rome. As ædile he repaired the streets, cleaned the sewers, restored and built new aqueducts, and constructed baths, porticoes and gardens. In 30 BC he was the commander of Octavian's navy, successfully winning several naval battles until his final confrontation with Antony at the Battle of Actium which he won.

TITUS LIVIUS, LIVY (59 BC - 17 AD)

A native of Cisalpine Gaul, he is famous for writing his huge historical work, 'From the Founding of the City' (Ab Urbe Condita). He used previous Roman annalists as his sources and openly mixed legendary stories with extant historical records. His history eventually comprised of 142 'books' (or more rightly scrolls) and was an instant success after its publication.

LIVIA DRUSILLA (58 BC - 29 AD)

After marriage to a patrician cousin and forced to flee Italy during the civil wars, her family returned to Rome under Octavian's amnesty. Already the mother of the future emperor Tiberius and six months pregnant, she was introduced to Octavian in 39 BC whereupon he immediately fell in love with her. Although already married to Scribonia his second wife, Octavian divorced her after only a year, on the very day she gave birth to his daughter. He then persuaded Livia's husband to divorce her and they were married three days after the birth of her second son. The marriage lasted a further 51 years and she played the part of a faithful matron, taking care of the household, weaving clothes and dressed modestly. In 35 BC she had a statue erected to her and was given the right to control her own finances, becoming a patron to her own circle of clients.

Scio me nihil scire – I know that I know nothing (Socrates)

TIMELINE

This chapter sketches out the history of Rome from its founding in 753 BC to the final fall of the Republic in 27 BC; a long and complex melange of wars, superstitions, politics, treachery and glory. So much information was recorded by the Romans themselves that it would take several books of this size just to cover it briefly, let alone comprehensively.

Therefore in order to give Games Masters a chance of locating happenings often overlooked in more in-depth reviews, the following table has been constructed to show interesting events in the categories of War, Politics, Religion and the City. Those who desire a slightly more detailed summary of early Roman history are encouraged to look to the internet or specialised history books for additional help.

As a final warning, the dates included are roughly correct to a year or so either way. Most of our knowledge comes from an amalgam of several historical authors whose annals, of course, do not quite match up. Thus each entry on the table is only as accurate as the source used.

Year	War	Politics & Law	Religion	City
753 BC				Traditional Founding of Rome by Romulus and Remus atop the Palatine Hill
753 - 716 BC	War and eventual peace with the Sabines	Rule of Romulus, after killing his own brother. Division of the people into curiæ	Romulus dedicates a temple to Jupiter Feretrius atop the Capitoline Hill	Rape of the Sabine women. Settlement of the Quirinal Hill
715-674 BC		Reign of Numa Pompilius	Construction of many shrines, including a temple to Janus at the foot of the Aventine Hill	The city spreads to the Aventine Hill
673-642 BC	Conquering of the Albans and the destruction of their city	Reign of Tullius Hostilius	Temples built to Pallor and Pavor	The Curia Hostilia is built. The dispossessed Albans are welcomed into Rome which expands to include the Caelian Hill
642-617 BC	Assault and conquest of the Latin city of Politorium and its population transferred to Rome	Reign of Ancus Marcius	The Temple of Jupiter Feretrius expanded	The city wall is extended and fortifications built to defend the lower regions of the hills. The Pons Sublicius is built spanning the Tiber River near the Forum Boarium downstream from the Tiber island
616-579 BC	Further conflict with the Sabines	Reign of Tarquinius Priscus	Lucius Tarquinius Priscus vows a great temple to Jupiter Optimus Maximus, Juno and Minerva in return for defeating the Sabines and begins to lay its foundations atop the Capitoline Hill, incorporating the existent shrines of Terminus and Juventas. The purchase of the Sibylline Books from the Sibyl	The area for the Circus Maximus is laid out and stands are built by members of the patricians and equites. The Forum Romanum is constructed with space allotted for arcades and shops, on drained land
578-535 BC		Reign of Servius Tullius	The construction of the Temples of Diana, Fortuna and Mater Matuta	Rome expands to incorporate the Viminal and Esquiline Hills. The Servian wall is built around the city

Year	War	Politics & Law	Religion	City
535-510 BC		Reign of Tarquinius Superbus	Work continues on the construction of the Temple of Jupiter Optimus Maximus. Introduction of the cult of Apollo	Construction of the Cloaca Maxima, the first major drainage ditch and eventual sewer
509 BC		Overthrow of Etruscan kings and destruction of the monarchy by L. Junius Brutus. Establishment of the Roman Republic	The temple of Jupiter Optimus Maximus is finally dedicated. First occasion of the Ludi Romani	The rape and suicide of Lucretia
508 BC	Invasion of the Etruscans under Lars Porsena		Creation of the position of Pontifex Maximus as an official, to oversee the Rex Sacrorum	
505 BC		First pair of consuls elected		
504 BC				Migration of the Claudii to Rome
502 BC	Battle of Pometia, the Latin League defeats the Romans, leaving one of the consuls badly wounded			
501 BC		Appointment of the first-ever dictator, T. Larcius	A temple to Saturn begins construction in the Forum Romanum	
498 BC			The Temple of Saturn is dedicated. Known as the Aerarium it is used to store the treasury of Rome, the state archives, and the insignia of the legions	
496 BC	Battle of Lake Regillus, where Rome under the command of Aulus Postumius Albus Regillensis finally defeats the Latins and the former king of Rome, Tarquinius Superbus	Carthage and Rome make a treaty whereby Roman ships undertake not to trade to the west of Carthage while the Carthaginians undertake not to interfere in Latin politics		
495 BC	Battle of Aricia, consul Publius Servilius Priscus wins over the Auruncans		Introduction of the cult of Hermes by Greek traders and a temple built to him in the Circus Maximus	
494 BC		First Secession of the Plebeians to the Mons Sacra where they threaten to found a new city. To end the crisis, the patricians allow the plebs to annually elect two leaders who are given the title of Tribune. Establishment of the aediles, magistrates originally in charge of the temple and cult of Ceres and also elected from the plebeian class		
493 BC	Gaius Marcius Coriolanus captures the Volscian town of Corioli.	A mutual defence treaty known as the Foedus Cassianum is agreed between Latin League and Rome, in which Rome abandons its claim to hegemony over the league in return for being recognised as the dominant city	Dedications of the Temples of Ceres, Liber and Libera built on the Aventine Hill	
491 BC	Gnaeus Marcius Coriolanus is exiled for withholding grain from the starving plebeians unless they agreed to the abolition of the office of Tribune. He then seeks refuge with the King of the Volsi and leads their army against Rome in retribution, turning back when his mother and wife entreat him		The Temple of Fortuna Muliebris is built	Famine in Rome

Semper inops quicumque cupit – Whoever desires is always poor (Claudian)

Year	War	Politics & Law	Religion	City
486 – 436 BC	War with the Aequi and the Volsci, which continues on and off for another 50 years	The proposal of an agrarian law by Consul Spurius Cassius Vecellinus to assist needy plebeians, is violently opposed both by the patricians and wealthy plebeians, who have Cassius condemned and executed		
484 BC			The temple of Castor and Pollux (the Dioscuri) in the Forum Romanum is completed and dedicated in honour of their aid at the Battle of Lake Regillus	
482 - 474 BC	Intermittent wars with Veii			
482 BC	The Volscians defeat consul Lucius Aemilius Mamercus at the Battle of Antium. The following day, he reverses his defeat, by winning the Battle of Longula			
480 BC	Battle of Veii in which the consuls Marcus Fabius Vibulanus and Gnaeus Manlius Cincinnatus win a heavy battle over the Veientes and their Etruscan allies			
477 BC	The Battle of the Cremera where all the members of the Fabii clan but one are killed in battle with the Veientes. Consul Gaius Horatius Pulvillus fights an indecisive battle with the Etruscans at the Battle of the Temple of Hope. This is rapidly followed by the Battle of Colline Gate where consul Gaius Horatius Pulvillus achieves an indecisive victory over the Etruscans			
474 BC	The Greek city-states in Italy win a naval battle at Cumae and crush Etruscan power in Campania			
471 BC		Creation of the Concilium Plebis. Office of the tribunes officially recognised		
460 BC	A revolt in Rome leads to the Capitoline Hill and most of the important temples there being occupied by the rebellious slaves. The revolt only ends with the intervention of an allied army from Tusculum, led by the Tusculan dictator Lucius Mamilius			
457 BC	Lucius Quinctius Cincinnatus is summoned by the Senate and declared dictator in order to rescue a besieged Roman army at Mt. Algidus. He musters the remaining men in Rome, marches all night and traps the besieging Aequi within hastily erected fortifications. The Aequi are then defeated by a double attack from within and outside their lines	Cincinnatus resigns his dictatorship after only 16 days and returns to his farm		Cincinnatus celebrates a Triumph

Sero venientibus ossa – The bones [leavings] for those who come late

Year	War	Politics & Law	Religion	City
456 BC		The plebeians of Rome are granted land in the Aventine		
451 BC		The patricians set up the decemvirate (council of ten) to establish the Code of the Twelve Tables, the foundation of Roman Law		A terrible pestilence kills half the citizens and almost all the slaves of the city
449 BC		The laws of the Twelve Tables are inscribed on ivory and posted in the Forum Romanum for all to read. Following a blatantly criminal decision upholding the kidnap and slavery of a young woman named Verginia, her father kills her to maintain her chastity and freedom, which leads to an uprising against the Decemvirate; forcing them to resign their offices and return to the previous system of elected magistrates		
449 BC		Secession of the plebs. The Lex Valeria Horatia grants the tribunes inviolability		
447 BC		Creation of position for two quaestors, elected by the tribal assembly		
446 BC	Titus Quinctius Capitolinus Barbatus leads Roman troops to win over the Aequi and the Volsci at the Battle of Corbione			
445 BC		Law passed by a tribune named Gaius Canuleius, the Lex Canuleia, removes the ban preventing inter-marriage between Plebeians and Patricians. Anger over this social reform, which the Senate sees as a threat to its authority results in the patrician consuls being replaced with three military tribunes (with consular powers), whom could be elected from the plebeian class		A spring emerges in the Forum Romanum after a divine thunderbolt strikes the ground there
443 BC		Introduction of the office of censor to the Cursus Honorum, to prevent plebeian military tribunes from having control of the census		
440 BC				Rome suffers a famine
439 BC		Gn. Spurius Maelius attempts to make himself king of Rome, by buying up a large amount of grain and selling it at a low price to garner votes from those suffering from the famine. He is summoned to face Lucius Quinctius Cincinnatus (made dictator to suppress any revolt by the plebeians) but refuses to appear. Maelius is killed by Quintus Servilius Ahala, his house razed and his wheat distributed amongst the people		

Si uno adhuc proelio Romanos vincemus, funditus peribimus! – Another victory like that, and I'm done for! (Pyrrhus)

Year	War	Politics & Law	Religion	City
435 BC	Q. Servilius Fidenas excavates a tunnel under the walls of the city of Fidenae in order to capture it			
434 BC		The terms of office for censors are fixed at four years		
433 BC				A pestilence strikes Rome
431 BC	The Aquei are driven from Mt. Algidius by M. Furius Camillus		The temple of Apollo Medicus (the doctor) built in the Flaminian fields is dedicated by Gnaeus Iulius Mento, in fulfilment of a vow to the god during the plague of two years earlier	
428 BC	Rome conquers Fidenae			
427 BC		Comitia Centuriata given final voice in the matter of declaration of war		
421 BC		The number of quaestors is increased to four, and it is opened to plebeians		
414 BC				The river Tiber floods causing destruction
409 BC		Three of the elected quaestors are plebeians		
406 BC	The city of Anxur is besieged and captured by the Romans			
405 BC	The beginning of the Siege of Veii, which lasts 10 years			
396 BC	Rome completes her conquest of the Etruscans when Veii is finally captured by M. Furius Camillus. Pay is introduced for Roman soldiers for the first time	Marcus Furius Camillus is made dictator		
394 BC	The Falerii surrender unconditionally to the Romans under M. Furius Camillus			
391 BC	Quintus Fabius Ambustus and his two brothers are sent as emissaries to parley for the relief of the town of Clusium with Brennus, chief of the besieging Gauls. When negotiations break down, Quintus Fabius kills one of the Gallic leaders. Outraged at the act Brennus demands that the Fabii brothers be surrendered to him, but the Romans refuse so the Gauls advance on Rome	Marcus Furius Camillus is accused of making an unfair distribution of the spoils of his victory at Veii and goes into voluntary exile. The three Fabii brothers are elected as military tribunes for their defiance of Brennus		
390 BC	Disaster at the Battle of the Allia River. The Roman army under the command of the military tribunes Q. Servius Fidenas, Q. Sulpicius and P. Cornelius Maluginensis are defeated by the Brennus of the Gauls. The Gauls then sack and burn the city of Rome and the inner capitol is besieged for seven months, before the invaders are bought off	A ransom of 1,000 pounds of gold is paid to Brennus who uses heavier weights than standard. When the Romans complain, Brennus throws his sword onto the scales and states 'Woe to the vanquished'	During the siege of the Capitoline Hill, the Gauls attempt a sneak attack up the steep cliff. Marcus Manlius Capitolinus is alerted to the Gallic attack by the sacred geese of Juno, which are honoured for their timely warning. Temple of Saturn burns down, causing the loss of all official records. It is rebuilt and dedicated by Lucius Furius	Rome is sacked and burned. Every following year on the anniversary of the sacking, guard dogs are crucified on the Capitoline Hill as punishment for their failure to alert the people of Rome to the Gallic sneak attack, whilst the Capitoline Geese watch
388 BC	The Aequi are defeated by the Romans at a battle near Bola			

Year	War	Politics & Law	Religion	City
387 BC			Marcus Furius Camillus introduces the Ludi Capitolini honouring Jupiter Capitolinus, in commemoration of Rome's Capitol not being captured by the Gauls	
386 BC	The combined Italian tribes, the Latins, Volscii and Hernici are defeated by the Romans			
				The censor Gaius Maenius has temporary wooden balconies built on top of the shops around the Forum Romanum, so increase the viewing area for spectators of public performances
381 BC	The district of Tusculum is pacified after a revolt against Rome and conquered	Tusculum becomes the first municipium		
378 BC				Rebuilding of the permanent Servian Wall
377 BC	The Latins are defeated after the capture of the city of Satricum			
376 BC		Gaius Licinius (Calvus) Stolo starts 10 years of successive election as tribune, during which he smoothes relationships between the patricians and plebeians		
375 BC		No curule magistrates are elected for this year		
367 BC		Gaius Licinius Stolo and Lucius Sextius Lateranus institute the Lex Liciniae Sextiae, which not only restores the Consulship but reserves one of the two seats for plebeians. It also limits the amount of public land any man might hold to 500 iugera (300 acres)	The Temple of Concord is vowed and built in the Forum Romanum by Marcus Furius Camillus to commemorate the political reconciliation between the patricians and plebeians	
366 BC		The first plebeian consul, L. Sextius Sextinus Lateranus, is elected. Offices of Praetor and Aedile added to the Cursus Honorum	The Ludi Romani games begin to be held annually	
365 BC				The first theatrical performances are held in Rome, by Etruscan actors
363 BC				The river Tiber floods
362 BC				A bottomless hole opens up in the Forum Romanum but closes up again after a young man named Marcus Curtius, dressed in armour and on horseback, casts himself into the chasm
361 BC	Rome captures the city of Ferentinum			
360 BC	War with cities of Tibur, Praeneste, and the Hernici tribe who advance to the gates of Rome but are beaten back			
359 BC	The town of Tarquinii revolts against Roman rule			

Sic semper tyrannis – Thus always to tyrants (Brutus)

Year	War	Politics & Law	Religion	City
387 BC			Marcus Furius Camillus introduces the Ludi Capitolini honouring Jupiter Capitolinus, in commemoration of Rome's Capitol not being captured by the Gauls	
386 BC	The combined Italian tribes, the Latins, Volscii and Hernici are defeated by the Romans			
				The censor Gaius Maenius has temporary wooden balconies built on top of the shops around the Forum Romanum, so increase the viewing area for spectators of public performances
381 BC	The district of Tusculum is pacified after a revolt against Rome and conquered	Tusculum becomes the first municipium		
378 BC				Rebuilding of the permanent Servian Wall
377 BC	The Latins are defeated after the capture of the city of Satricum			
376 BC		Gaius Licinius (Calvus) Stolo starts 10 years of successive election as tribune, during which he smoothes relationships between the patricians and plebeians		
375 BC		No curule magistrates are elected for this year		
367 BC		Gaius Licinius Stolo and Lucius Sextius Lateranus institute the Lex Liciniae Sextiae, which not only restores the Consulship but reserves one of the two seats for plebeians. It also limits the amount of public land any man might hold to 500 iugera (300 acres)	The Temple of Concord is vowed and built in the Forum Romanum by Marcus Furius Camillus to commemorate the political reconciliation between the patricians and plebeians	
366 BC		The first plebeian consul, L. Sextius Sextinus Lateranus, is elected. Offices of Praetor and Aedile added to the Cursus Honorum	The Ludi Romani games begin to be held annually	
365 BC				The first theatrical performances are held in Rome, by Etruscan actors
363 BC				The river Tiber floods
362 BC				A bottomless hole opens up in the Forum Romanum but closes up again after a young man named Marcus Curtius, dressed in armour and on horseback, casts himself into the chasm
361 BC	Rome captures the city of Ferentinum			
360 BC	War with cities of Tibur, Praeneste, and the Hernici tribe who advance to the gates of Rome but are beaten back			
359 BC	The town of Tarquinii revolts against Roman rule			

Year	War	Politics & Law	Religion	City
357 BC	Falerii revolts. Gauls raid Latium			
356 BC		The first plebeian dictator is appointed		
354 BC	Samnites sign a treaty of alliance with Rome to defend against the Gauls			
353 BC	Caere defeated			
351 BC	The Etruscans sue for peace	The office of censor is opened to the plebeians		
348 BC		Treaty with Carthage establishing non-aggression towards members of Rome's Latin League		
347 BC				Foreign coinage begins to be used in Rome
346 BC	The Romans defeat the cities of Antium and Satricum			
343 BC	Beginning of the First Samnite War. Romans occupy northern Campania, interceding on behalf of the city of Capua against the Samnites			
342 BC	Battle of Mount Gaurus in which the Roman general Marcus Valerius Corvus defeats the Samnites	Marcus Valerius Corvus made dictator		
341 BC	The Roman consul Marcus Valerius Corvus defeats the Samnites once more at the Battle of Suessola. End of the First Samnite War	A hasty peace treaty is signed with the Samnites, owing to the revolt of members of the Latin League. Rome retains control of Campania		
340 - 338 BC	Start of the Latin War. Rome conquers the Volsci seaport of Antium	The members of the Latin League request equal rights with Rome, including seats within the Senate. Rome refuses and war breaks out		
339 BC	Battle of Vesuvius, Romans under P. Decius Mus and T. Manlius Imperiosus defeat the rebellious Latins	Capua and Cumae are granted full citizenship, becoming part of the Roman State		
338 BC	Roman general T. Manlius Imperiosus decisively defeats the Latins at the Battle of Trifanum. End of the Latin War	Latin League dissolved but Latin rights and partial citizenship established, bringing many of the cities into the Roman State. The Volsci accept an alliance with Rome		The rostra, or speaking platform, is created by G. Maenius
337 BC		Office of praetor opened to plebeians		
336 BC	The Romans capture the town of Teanum Sidicinum			
335 BC	The Campanian city of Cales is conquered	Marcus Valerius Corvus is elected consul for the fourth time		
332 BC		Rome signs a treaty with the city of Tarentum		Creation of two new tribes at Rome, the Maecia and Scaptia
330 BC	The Italian cities of Fondi and Privernum, led by M. Vitruvius Vaccus, launch a revolt against Rome, which is quelled by the consul L. Plautius Venno			Ostia, Rome's coastal port, founded
329 BC				The Circus Maximus is completed in Rome
328 BC	Etruria and Campania annexed			

Stultum est timere quod vitare non potes – It is foolish to fear that which you cannot avoid (Publius Syrus)

Year	War	Politics & Law	Religion	City
327 BC	At the request of Neapolis, the Romans send an army, which evicts a Samnite garrison from the city	Neapolis becomes an ally of Rome		
326 BC	Start of the Second Samnite War. After the eviction of their garrison in Neapolis the Samnites declare war on Rome	Rome increases its influence in southern Italy by forging new alliances		
324 BC		Lucius Papirius Cursor appointed dictator	A temple to Quirinus vowed by Papirius Cursor	
321 BC	After failing to reach an agreement for a peace settlement, the Romans under Spurius Postumius and T. Verturius Calvinus are defeated and humiliated by the Samnites under Gaius Pontius at the Battle of the Caudine Forks	The Samnites sue for peace but the terms offered by Rome are so harsh the Samnites reject them and the war continues		
316 BC	Battle of Lautulae where the Romans are badly defeated by the Samnites, who march to within 20 miles of Rome			
312 BC		Censorship of Appius Claudius Caecus, whose political reforms; including the distribution of the landless citizens of Rome among the voting tribes, the admission of sons of freedmen into the Senate, and the right of freed slaves to hold office		Construction of the first aqueduct, the aqua Appia, and the first major road, the Via Appia, which connects Rome with southern Capua.
311 BC	Etruscans join the Samnites against Rome			
310 BC	The Romans, led by Lucius Papirius Cursor, defeat the Etruscans at the Battle of Lake Vadimo	The Etruscans are persuaded by the Samnites to break their alliance with Rome.		
309 BC	Lucius Papirius Cursor defeats the Samnites at Longula. He compels the city of Luceria (which had revolted) to surrender, thus recovering Roman hostages held there in captivity, the standards lost at Caudium, and makes 7,000 of the enemy pass under the yoke	Lucius Papirius Cursor appointed dictator		Lucius Papirius Cursor celebrates a triumph
308 BC	The Umbrians, Picentini, and Marsians join the war against Rome	The Etruscans sue for peace, which is granted under severe terms		
307 BC	The Italian tribe, the Hernici, revolts against Rome			
305 BC	Battle of Bovianum - Roman consuls M. Fulvius Curvus Paetinus and L. Postumius Megellus decisively defeat the Samnites			
304 BC	Aequi defeated. End of the Second Samnite War, Rome establishes many new colonies and gains control over much of central and southern Italy	Peace treaty made with the Samnites	A bronze shrine to Concord is erected by the aedile Gnaeus Flavius, in the hope of reconciling the nobility who are outraged by his publication of the calendar	Under the censor Fabius Maximus Rullianus landless new citizens are assigned to four tribes in the city
301 BC		Marcus Valerius Corvus made dictator for the second time		

Year	War	Politics & Law	Religion	City
300 BC		Lex Valeria passed by a tribune of the plebs granting the legal right to appeal against any capital sentence passed on a Roman citizen	Lex Ogulnia is passed, which states that half of the members of Rome's priestly colleges must be plebeian	
299 BC	The Romans capture the territory of Narnia			
298 BC	Start of the Third Samnite War. Gauls raid Roman territory. Battle of Camerinum in which the Samnites defeat the Romans under Lucius Cornelius Scipio. The Romans capture the Samnite cities of Taurasia, Bovianum Vetus, and Aufidena.	An alliance is formed with the Picentes		
296 BC			A Temple to Bellona is vowed by Appius Claudius Caecus after a victory over the Etruscans and is built outside the Pomerium but close to the Servian Wall	
295 BC	The Romans under Fabius Maximus Rullianus and Publius Decimus Mus are victorious over a coalition of Samnites, Gauls, and Umbirnas at the Battle of Sentinum	Fabius Maximus Rullianus elected consul for the fifth time		
294 BC	Samnite victory at Luceria		The Temple of Victory is built and dedicated by Lucius Postumius Megellus out of fines he levied during his aedileship	
293 BC	The Romans under Lucius Papirius Cursor achieve a decisive victory over the Samnite forces at the Battle of Aquilonia		After the pestilence the Sibylline Books are consulted which advise that a temple to Aesculapius be dedicated on the Tiber Isle. Completion and dedication of the Temple of Quirinus by Papirius Cursor	
292 BC	The rebellious city of Falerii is reduced by the Romans			
291 BC	The Romans storm the Samnite city of Venusia			
290 BC	The Sabines are conquered by Manius Curius Dentatus. End of the Third Samnite War	The territory of the Samnites is annexed. Establishment of the triumviri capitals (criminal magistrates) occurs in Rome		
287 BC		Introduction of the triumviri monetales (official mint supervisors) to control the minting of coins. Dictator Quintus Hortensius is appointed to deal with a secession of the plebeians and passes the Lex Hortensia, which gives plebiscites (plebeian referendums) power in law		
286 BC		The Lex Aquilia is passed, which provides compensation to the owners of property, including slaves and herd animals, injured as a result of someone's fault		
284 BC	Battle of Arretium where a Roman army under Lucius Caecilius Metellus Denter is destroyed by the Senones Gauls			

Sunt facta verbis difficiliora – Deeds are harder than words

Year	War	Politics & Law	Religion	City
283 BC	A Roman army under P. Cornelius Dolabella first repulses the Senones from Arretium, then defeats the Etruscans and the Gallic tribe of the Boii, at the Battle of Lake Vadimo		The Temple of Saturn burns down (again)	Rome burns
282 BC	Etruscan resistance to Roman domination of Italy is finally crushed at the Battle of Populonia. Rome conquers territory still held by the Gauls along the Adriatic. The Roman Fleet is attacked by Tarentum. Beginning of the war against King Phyrrus	King Phyrrus of Epirus offers his aid to defend Tarentum from the Romans		
280 BC	Battle of Heraclea the first engagement of Roman and Greek armies, in which Pyrrhus defeats a Roman force under the command of P. Valerius Laevinus, with the judicious use of elephants previously unknown to the Romans	Gaius Fabricius Luscinus, is sent to negotiate the ransom and exchange of prisoners. Pyrrhus is so impressed by Fabricius refusing to accept a bribe, that he releases the prisoners without the requirement for a ransom		
279 BC	Battle of Asculum in Apulia, where Pyrrhus defeats another Roman army under the command of Publius Decimus Mus but at great cost to his own force, giving rise to the phrase 'Pyrrhic victory'			
278 BC	Carthage invades Sicily and lays siege to Syracuse. Pyrrhus leaves Italy to help Syracuse and begins conquering Carthaginian held territory	The Carthaginians loan Rome money and ships in their fight against Pyrrhus		
275 BC	Increasingly despotic, Pyrrhus is asked to leave Sicily by the Syracusians and returns to Italy. But after an inconclusive battle against the Romans under Marcus Curius Dentatus at Beneventum, Pyrrhus decides to leave Italy for good			
273 BC		Impressed by Rome's defeat of Pyrrhus, Ptolemy II sends a friendly embassy, which is reciprocated		
272 BC	Surrender of Tarentum brings most of southern Italy under Roman control			A second aqueduct, the Anio Vetus, begins construction
270 BC	Capture of Rhegium and the subjugation of the Brutians, the Lucanians, the Calabrians and the Samnites	Rome effectively dominates the entire Italian peninsular		
269 BC				The first Roman bronze coinagen is minted
268 BC	Picentes conquered and granted limited citizenship			
267 BC	The Romans capture the city of Brundisium			
266 BC	Apulia and Messapia reduced to alliance securing the Italian Peninsula for Rome			

Year	War	Politics & Law	Religion	City
264 BC	Start of the First Punic War. Appius Claudius Caudex defeats the Syracusans in battle outside the Sicilian city of Messina; the first time Roman legions have fought outside of Italy. Razing of the Etruscan city of Volsinii	The Mamertines of Sicily form an alliance with Rome, hoping for protection against the Carthaginians	A temple to Vertumnus is built on the Aventine Hill	Introduction of the first funeral munera (gladiatorial combat) in the Forum Boarium. 2,000 bronze statues looted from Volsinii are melted down to make coins to help pay for the war
263 BC		Hiero of Syracuse becomes an ally of Rome		The first sundial is brought to Rome from Sicily
261 BC	Battle of Agrigentum during which Carthaginian forces under Hannibal Gisco and Hanno are defeated by the Romans, who attain control over most of Sicily			
260 BC	Rome builds its first navy based on the model of a captured Carthaginian quinquereme. At the Battle of the Lipari Islands part of the Roman fleet is defeated by the Carthaginians. The Romans under Gaius Duilius Nepos then defeats the Carthaginian fleet at the Battle of Mylae, giving Rome control of the western Mediterranean. However, the Carthaginian army under Hamilcar defeat the Romans at the Thermae of Himera with a surprise attack			
259 BC	Romans occupy Corsica. Hamilcar continues to defeat Roman forces, seizing the cities of Enna and Camarina			
258 BC	Minor naval victory against the Carthaginian fleet at the Battle of Sulci, near Sardinia. The Romans retake Enna and Camarina and capture the town of Mytistraton	In a rare honour Gaius Duilius Nepos, a novos homo (new man), is elected as censor		
257 BC	Naval victory of Tyndaris, over Carthage in Sicilian waters. Rome captures Sardina			
256 BC	Major naval victory at the Battle of Cape Ecnomus, over a Carthaginian fleet under Hamilcar and Hanno. An expeditionary force is sent to North Africa under Marcus Atilius Regulus, who then defeats the Carthaginians at the Battle of Adys			
255 BC	Battle of Tunis in Africa, in which the invading Roman army under M. Regulus is virtually destroyed and Regulus captured by the Carthaginians led by Xanthippus. The Roman fleet which rescues the few survivors is wrecked in a terrible storm off the coast near Pachynus, with the loss of 270ships and a 100,000 men	Carthage sues for peace, but during negotiations Marcus Atilius Regulus demands that Carthage agree to an unconditional surrender, cede Sicily, Corsica, and Sardinia to Rome, renounce the use of their navy, pay an indemnity, and sign a vassal-like treaty. The Carthaginians decide to keep fighting and hire the services of the Spartan mercenary Xanthippus		

Tempus fugit – Time flees (Virgil)

Year	War	Politics & Law	Religion	City
254 BC	Romans capture the city of Panormus but lose Agrigentum back to the Carthaginians			Birth of the Roman comedy playwright Plautus, in the town of Sarsina, Umbria, in Italy
253 BC	A second Roman fleet of 150 ships is wrecked off the coast of Sicily near the town of Palinurus		First plebeian Pontifex Maximus	
251 BC	Battle of Panormus at which the Carthaginian forces under Hasdrubal are defeated by the Romans under L. Caecilius Metellus			
250 BC		The Carthaginians send Marcus Atilius Regulus to Rome on parole to negotiate a peace or an exchange of prisoners. However, on his arrival, he urges the Senate to refuse both proposals and continue fighting. He then honours his parole, returning to Carthage where he is executed by being placed in a spiked barrel, which is then rolled down a hill		
249 BC	The Roman admiral Publius Claudius Pulcher loses 93 of his 123 ships, against the Carthaginians at the Battle of Drepana	Following his defeat Publius Claudius Pulcher is fined 120,000 asses and his colleague, Lucius Iunius Pullus, commits suicide. Aulus Atilius Calatinus is then elected dictator and leads an army into Sicily, the first dictator to command overseas		
247 BC	Hamilcar Barca begins offensive in Sicily	Hiero of Syracuse makes a treaty with Rome		Birth of Hannibal, the Carthaginian commander
242 BC	Gaius Lutatius Catulus constructs another major fleet of 200 ships and blockades the Sicilian cities of Lilybaeum and Drepanum			
241 BC	Battle of the Aegates Islands, in which the Roman fleet is victorious over Carthaginians who sue for peace, thus ending the First Punic War.	Occupation of Sicily which is made a Roman province	The Temple of Vesta burns down whereupon the Pontifex Maximus Caecilius Metellus enters the burning temple and rescues the holy Palladium	Construction of the Via Aurelia from Rome to Pisa
240 BC				The Roman poet and writer Livius Andronicus produces the first Latin literature in Rome
239 BC				Birth of the writer Quintus Ennius, born at the town of Rudiae in Calabria
238 BC	Annexation of Sardinia and Corsica		A new temple to Flora built on the Aventine Hill and the first instance of the Ludi Florales	
236 BC	Gallic raids in northern Italy			
235 BC			Consul Titus Manlius Torquatus presides over the first ever closing of the gates of the Temple of Janus, signifying peace	
233 BC	Peace ends. Roman general Q. Fabius Maximus Verrucosus wins a victory over the Gallic Ligurians			

Teneo te, Africa! – I have you, Africa! (Julius Caesar)

207

Year	War	Politics & Law	Religion	City
232 BC		T. Flaminius passes a law for the distribution of the ager Gallicus into smallholdings for those plebeians whose farms have fallen into ruin during the First Punic War		
230 BC		Envoys are sent to Illyria to end the killing of Roman merchants by Illyrian pirates. When one of the envoys is murdered for causing offence to Queen Teuta, Roman forces invade the island of Corcyra		
229 BC	First Illyrian War. Lucius Postumius Albinus and Gnaeus Fulvius Centumalus invade Illyria, capturing the Greek cities of Epidamnus, Apollonia, Corcyra and Pharos	Establishment of friendly relations between Rome and the Aetolian and Achaean Leagues, which approve of the suppression of Illyrian piracy		
228 BC	The Romans besiege Shkodra, the Illyrian capital			Birth of Titus Quinctius Flamininus
227 BC	Queen Teuta surrenders to the besieging Roman army and is forced to accept a crushing peace treaty. End of the First Illyrian War	Rome creates two new provinces, those of Sicily and Sardinia and Corsica combined. Each is assigned an annually elected Praetor with consular powers over his region		
226 BC		At the request of Greek merchants from Massilia, whom are worried by the Carthaginian conquests in Spain, a treaty is drawn up with Hasdrubal defining river Iberus (Ebro) as border of influence between Rome and Carthage		
225 BC	The Romans are defeated by a coalition of Gallic tribes of Cisalpine Gaul at the Battle of Faesulae			
224 BC	The Romans under Lucius Aemilius Papus and Caius Atilius Regulus defeat the Gauls at the Battle of Telamon			
223 BC	T. Flaminius is victorious in a war against the tribe the Insubres	The province of Cisalpine Gaul is created		
222 BC	At the Battle of Clastidium, the Roman general M. Claudius Marcellus kills Viridomarus, chieftain of the Insubres tribe, in single combat, causing the surrender of the Insubres and earning himself the spolia opima			
221 BC		After the assassination of the Carthaginian general Hasdrubal, the Spanish allied city of Saguntum appeals to Rome for help against Hannibal who succeeds to power in Carthaginian Spain		
220 BC	Start of the Second Illyrian War following renewed pirate attacks			T. Flaminius begins construction of the Circus Flaminius to be built on the Campus Martius, and the via Flaminia which connects Italy to northern Greece

Timendi causa est nescire – Ignorance is the cause of fear (Seneca)

Year	War	Politics & Law	Religion	City
219 BC	End of the Second Illyrian War, but the region remains rebellious. Hannibal captures the town of Saguntum.	Although in their treaty with Rome, the Carthaginians are permitted to conquer any territory south of the Iberus river (within which Saguntum lies), the Romans declare it an act of war		The first foreign surgeon to practice in Rome arrives in the city.
218 BC	Start of the Second Punic War. First naval clash between the navies of Carthage and Rome during the Second Punic War at the Battle of Lilybaeum. The Romans defeat Carthaginians at the Battle of Cissa and gain control of the territory north of the Ebro River. Hannibal crosses Alps and arrives in northern Italy. This is followed by the Battle of the Ticinus at which Hannibal defeats the Romans under Publius Cornelius Scipio the elder in a small cavalry fight and the Battle of the Trebia where he defeats the Romans under Tiberius Sempronius Longus with an ambush	Lex Claudia is passed, which prohibits senators from engaging in commerce and owning vessels with the ability to be launched at sea, thus establishing the social snobbery towards money made from trading	A new temple to Concordia is vowed by the praetor Lucius Manlius after quelling a mutiny among his troops in Cisalpine Gaul	
217 BC	Battle of Lake Trasimene at which Hannibal destroys the Roman army of Gaius Flaminius, who is killed. The Romans gain a victory in a naval encounter near the Ebro River	Elevation of Q. Fabius Maximus Verucosis (Cunctator) to Dictator. Later joined by Marcus Minucius Rufus also elevated to dictator	The Saturnalia festival is established. During the festival, masters are required to wait on their servants	
216 BC	Hannibal crushes a large Roman army at the Battle of Cannae under commanders G. Terentius Varro and L. Aemilius Paullus. He then marches through the district of Cannae into Campania and begins to plunder and ravage the countryside. Capua revolts against Rome. Marcus Claudius Marcellus holds off an attack by Hannibal at the first Battle of Nola. Two legions under praetor Lucius Postimus posted in Cisalpina Gall, are ambushed and destroyed by Gauls in Litanam Forest	Many of Rome's allies begin to defect to Hannibal's side	Beginning of the Ludi Plebeii. The new Temple of Concordia is built on the arx (atop the Capitoline Hill). The Roman historian Quintus Fabius Pictor is sent to Delphi in Greece to consult the Oracle for advice about what Rome should do after its defeat in the Battle of Cannae	
215 BC	Hasdrubal defeated by Cn. and P. Cornelius Scipio at Dertosa, Spain. Marcellus again repulses an attack by Hannibal at the Second Battle of Nola	The Lex Oppia, which not only restricts women's wealth but also the display of it, is instituted by the tribune Gaius Oppius. Excess jewellery and possessions are used to raise money to pay for the war and grain to feed the city	A temple to Venus Obsequens is dedicated outside the Colline gate on the Capitol, to commemorate the Roman defeat at the Battle of Lake Trasimene. It is built with money fined from women found guilty of adultery	
214 BC	Syracuse is persuaded by Carthage to revolt against Rome. Marcellus fights an inconclusive battle with Hannibal at the third Battle of Nola. Start of the First Macedonian War	The censors Publius Furius Philus and Marcus Atilius Regulus condemn and degrade senators and equestrians who have either… broken their parole as captured officers when the senate refuses to pay their ransoms, advocated surrender to Carthage after the disaster of Cannae, or who have made plans to flee Rome		Destruction caused by the Tiber flooding

Timeo Danaos et dona ferentes − I fear the Greeks, even when they bring gifts (Laocoon, Virgil's Aeneid)

Year	War	Politics & Law	Religion	City
213 BC	Siege of Syracuse in Sicily begins. Hannibal captures Tarentum		The temples of Spes, Mater Matuta and Fortuna burn down in a major conflagration	A fire rages for two days, consuming everything between the Aventine and Capitoline Hills and extending as far north as the Forum Romanum. In its path it destroys the Forum Boarium, the Forum Holitorium
212 BC	Romans besiege the city of Capua. during which Hannibal defeats the consuls Q. Fulvius Flaccus and Appius Claudius but the Roman army escapes. Hannibal then annihilates the army of the Roman praetor M. Centenius Penula at the Battle of the Silarus and destroys the Roman army of the praetor Gnaeus Fulvius Flaccus at Herdonia		The senate decrees the start of a new festival, the Ludi Apollinares on the instructions of a prophecy. Publius Licinius Crassus Dives is elected pontifex maximus, despite never having held any magisterial offices	The first silver coinage is struck in Rome
211 BC	Defeat of the Scipios in Spain. Publius and Gnaeus Cornelius Scipio are killed in the Battle of the Upper Baetis, against the Carthaginians under Hasdrubal Barca. Hannibal marches on Rome but fails to break the siege at Capua, which along with Syracuse, falls to the Romans	Rome enters into an alliance with the Aetolians against Macedonia		
210 BC	Following the deaths of his father and uncle, P. Cornelius Scipio (later Africanus) is given the command in Spain. The second Battle of Herdonia, Hannibal destroys the Roman army of Fulvius Centumalus, who himself is killed. Hannibal defeats Marcus Claudius Marcellus once more at the Battle of Numistro		Once again the temple of Vesta catches fire. The temple is saved by the bravery of 13 slaves who were all manumitted as a reward	Another great fire breaks out in the Forum Romanum burning the private houses and shops surrounding it, the Forum Piscarium, the eastern slope of the Capitoline. Famine and inflation in the city are eased by the re-pacification of Sicily
209 BC	Recapture of Tarentum. Capture of Carthago Nova. Battle of Asculum - Hannibal once again defeats Marcellus, in an indecisive battle. At the first Battle of Lamia the Romans are defeated by Philip V of Macedon. This is followed by the second Battle of Lamia where the Romans are defeated again			
208 BC	P. Cornelius Scipio the Younger defeats army of Hasdrubal Barca near the town of Baecula, in Hispania	Marcus Claudius Marcellus elected consul for the fifth time		
207 BC	Roman general Gaius Claudius Nero fights an indecisive mêlée with Hannibal at the Battle of Grumentum, then escapes north to confront Hasdrubal Barca, who has invaded Italy. At the Battle of the Metaurus River Hasdrubal is defeated and killed by Nero's army			
206 BC	Scipio again decisively defeats the remaining Carthaginian forces in Hispania at the Battle of Ilipa		The Temple of Quirinus is struck by lightning	The Pons Mulvius is originally built, spanning the Tiber north of the city as part of the Via Flaminia

Tunc tua res agitur, paries cum proximus ardet − It also concerns you when the nearest wall is burning

Year	War	Politics & Law	Religion	City
205 BC	Scipio travels to Sicily. End of the First Macedonian War, which concludes in a stalemate		The worship of the cult of Cybele is introduced to Rome from Phrygia. Scipio Nassica is ordered to take all the married women of Rome to Ostia to receive the statue of the Great Mother and a temple to hold her icon is started on the Palatine Hill	
204 BC	Battle of Crotona in which Hannibal fights a drawn battle against the Roman general Sempronius in Southern Italy. Scipio Invades Africa		First instance of the Ludi Megalenses	
203 BC	Scipio defeats Hasdrubal Gisco and Syphax, winning the Battle of Bagbrades. Hannibal recalled to Carthage. King Syphax of Numidia is defeated and captured in the battle of Cirta			Another conflagration erupts and destroys the densely built tenements of the Clivus Publicius, a street leading south from the Circus Maximus over the Aventine
202 BC	Scipio Africanus Major narrowly defeats Hannibal at the Battle of Zama. End of the Second Punic War		Beginning of the Ludi Cereales	The river Tiber floods
200 - 197 BC	Second Macedonian War			
200 BC	Roman forces defeat the Cisalpine Gauls at the Battle of Cremona. Romans sack the Macedonian town of Acanthus			Birth of the Greek historian Polybius, in Megalopolis, Arcadia, Greece
198 BC	Titus Quinctius Flamininus defeats the army of King Phillip in the Battle of the Aous River			
197 BC	Revolt of Turdenati in Spain. Second Macedonian War ends with defeat of Philip V by T. Quinctius Flamininus at Cynoscephalae, in Thessaly	Number of praetors is raised to six, to cover the growing number of Roman provinces		
196 BC	The city of Smyrna appeals to Rome for help against the attacks of King Antiochus III	Flaminius proclaims the liberty of Greece		
195 BC	Hannibal Barca, exiled from Carthage joins Antiochus			
194 BC	Roman victory over the Gauls at the Battle of Mutina.			
193 BC				Massive flooding by the Tiber. Construction of the Emporium
192 - 188 BC	Syrian War against Antiochus			
192 BC				The Tiber floods the city again for the second sequential year. The Forum Boarium erupts in a fire which lasts a day and a night, spreading along the warehouses bordering the Tiber and causing a great loss of life and valuable merchandise
191 BC	Antiochus defeated at Thermopylae by the Romans under Manius Acilius Glabrio. Antiochus' fleet defeated off Corycus. Defeat of the Boii by P. Cornelius Scipio Nasica, son of Gn. Scipio and cousin of Scipio Africanus. Rome conquers and annexes what becomes known as the province of Cisalpine Gaul		The Temple of Magna Matter on the Palatine Hill is dedicated and the ludi Megalenses are instituted in her honour	

Year	War	Politics & Law	Religion	City
190 BC	Roman forces under Lucius Aemilius Regillus defeat a Seleucid fleet commanded by Hannibal, at the Battle of the Eurymedon. Another Seleucid fleet is defeated by the Romans at the Battle of Myonessus. In the Battle of Magnesia Romans under Lucius Cornelius Scipio and his brother Scipio Africanus Major defeat Antiochus III the Great in the decisive victory of the war			
189 BC				Disastrous flooding of the Tiber
188 BC	Peace of Apamea ends the Syrian War			
187 - 173 BC	Ligurian Wars in Spain			
187 BC				Construction of the Via Aemilia Lepidi
186 BC			The Bacchanalian conspiracy	
184 BC		M. Porcius Cato the Elder is elected as censor, and is known afterwards as Cato the Censor		Construction of the first basilica, the Basilica Porcia in Rome. The censors cut off all water supplied to private homes from the public aqueducts
183 BC	Death of the Roman general P. Cornelius Scipio Africanus, in Laternium, Campania. Death of the Carthaginian general Hannibal Barca, who poisons himself in order to avoid capture by the Romans			
181 BC	Beginning of the First Celtiberian War		Dedication by prostitutes of the Temple of Venus Erycine built near the Colline gate	
180 BC		The lex Villia annalis is passed by a tribune of the plebs L. Villius	A shrine to Hygea (the consort or daughter of Aesculapius). Destruction of the Pythagorean Books discovered at the foot of the Janiculum	
179 BC	End of the First Celtiberian War			Censor Marcus Fulvius Nobilior builds the Basilica Fulvia in the Forum Romanum, along with the Macellum on the site of the Forum Piscarium. However, before they are completed he dies, leaving his colleague Marcus Aemilius Lepidus to finish construction and the Basilica is eventually known as the Basilica Aemilia. Aemilius also builds Rome's first stone bridge, the pons Aemilius
178 BC			The Temple of Venus near the Forum Romanum burns down	
175 BC				Expulsion of the Epicurean philosophers from Rome
174 BC				The Circus Maximus in Rome is rebuilt after suffering major structural damage. Walls are built around the Emporium to prevent thievery. The streets of Rome begin to be paved

Year	War	Politics & Law	Religion	City
171 - 168 BC	Third Macedonian War			
171 BC	Battle of Callicinus at which Perseus of Macedon defeats a Roman army under Publius Licinius Crassus			
169 BC		The lex Voconia de milierum hereditatibus is passed		The Basilica Sempronia is built by the censor Tiberius Sempronius Gracchus
168 BC	Defeat and capture of the Macedonian King Perseus at Pydna, by the Romans under Lucius Aemilius Paullus Macedonicus, thus ending the Third Macedonian War			Historian Polybius is brought to Rome as a hostage from Megalopolis in Greece and is made a guest of Scipio Aemilianus
167 BC	Epirus plundered. Macedonia divided into four parts, Illyricum into four	Taxation of Roman citizens is abolished. Taxation now falls only upon allies		
161 BC				Greek orators and philosophers are (vainly) expelled from the city
159 BC		Laws are passed against bribery		A water clock is installed in the Basilica Aemilia
157 - 155 BC	Campaigns in Dalmatia and Pannonia			
155 BC		Moratorium passed preventing the future construction of permanent theatres		The first stone theatre begins construction in Rome. However, the consul Scipio Aemilianus in his backlash against Hellenistic culture, appeals to the senate to pull the building down
154 - 138 BC	Lusitanian War			
154 BC		The King of Cyrene, Ptolemy VII Euergetes Physcon, makes his will, in which he promises to bequeath his kingdom to Rome		The via Cassia, is built
153 - 151 BC	Second Celtiberian War			
150 - 148 BC	Fourth Macedonian War			
149 - 146 BC	The Third Punic War. Siege of Carthage			
149 BC		The lex Calpurnia is passed, which establishes the first permanent law court		The Origines a history of Rome written by Cato the Censor, is published
148 BC	At the second battle of Pydna, the forces of the Macedonian pretender Andriscus are defeated by the Romans under Quintus Caecilius Metellus in the decisive and final engagement of the Fourth Macedonian War		The Regia (house of the Pontifex Maximus) burns down	
147 BC	Macedonia annexed as a Roman province			
146 BC	Scipio Africanus Minor captures and destroys Carthage, ending the Third Punic War. Africa annexed. Battle of Corinth - Romans under Lucius Mummius defeat the Achaean League forces of Critolaus, who is killed. Corinth is destroyed and Greece comes under direct Roman rule.	The senate publishes a set of regulations known as the leges provinciae, which were basically constitutions and laws for each province	The first Roman temple to be built from marble, the temple of Jupiter Strator, is dedicated and built by Q Caecilius Metellus Macedonicus after his Triumph, along with the Temple of Juno Regina and the enclosing Porticus Metelli. The 'evocation' of the Carthaginian deity Tanit to Rome	A great amount of Greek art is introduced to the city from the spoils of Corinth

Year	War	Politics & Law	Religion	City
144 BC				Construction begins on the Aqua Marcia, the longest aqueduct yet built, by the praetor Quintus Marcius Rex
143 - 133 BC	Third Celtiberian War (also called Numantine War)			
142 BC		Censorship of Scipio Aemilianus		The Pons Aemilius, the first stone bridge, is built over the Tiber
139 BC				Expulsion of eastern astrologers from the city
137 BC	Defeat and surrender of Mancinus in Spain			
135 - 132 BC	Slave revolts in Sicily			
133 BC		King Attalus of Pergamum bequeaths his kingdom to Rome in his will. After opposing the legislation of Tiberius Sempronius Gracchus, a fellow tribune named Octavius is voted out of office by Gracchus, setting a precedent in Roman history. Death of Ti. Gracchus, clubbed to death by the consul P. Cornelius Scipio Nasica and other members of the senate fearing a demagogic uprising		
131 BC		The leges tabellariae is passed by the tribune G. Papirius Carbo, allowing secret balloting in Rome for the first time		The 'Daily Acts', message boards which post the results of trials and other legal proceedings, are erected in the Forum Romanum
129 BC	Annexation of the Roman provinces of Asia and Illyria			
126 BC				Construction of the Aqua Tepula by the censors G. Servilius Caepio and L. Cassius Longinus
125 BC		M. Fulvius Flaccus, an adherent of the ideals of G. Sempronius Gracchus, proposes a bill to enfranchise the Latin citizens of Italy		
124 BC	War against Arverni and Allobroges in Gaul			
123 BC		Tribunate of Gaius Sempronius Gracchus, who introduces many social reforms benefiting the lower classes of Rome, including an agrarian policy to return ownership of public lands to the Plebeians – incensing the Senate		
122 BC	Gallia Narbonensis made a province. War again breaks out with the Arverni	G. Gracchus elected tribune for the second time. After passing a law in the plebeian assembly, he reduces unemployment with massive public works on roads, harbours and baths, at great expense to the State. For the first time, the juries of the courts are taken away from senators and given to the equestrians		

Ulula cum lupis, cum quibus esse cupis – Who keeps company with wolves, will learn to howl

Year	War	Politics & Law	Religion	City
121 BC	The Gallic tribe of the Arverni are subjugated by the Roman general Gn. Domitius Ahenobarbus	Failing to be re-elected for the third time due to a proposal of granting full citizenship to all the Italian allies, Gaius Gracchus leads a protest of thousands of his angry supporters in the streets of Rome. The Senate passes the Ultimate Decree of martial law (Senatus consultum ultimum de res publica defendenda) and leads an armed militia to slaughter the mob. G. Gracchus is murdered in the grove of Furrina and 3,000 of his suspected supporters are rounded up and executed by strangulation	The Temple of Concord rebuilt by the consul L. Opimius, after the murder of Gaius Gracchus	A road, the via Domitia, is built after the conquests of Gn. Domitius Ahenobarbus, running along the coastline of Italy and southern Gaul. Consul L. Opimius builds the Basilica Opimia
120 BC			Approximate date of the construction of the Temple of Hercules Victor in the Forum Boarium	
119 BC		Tribunate of G. Marius, and abolition of the Gracchus land reforms		
117 BC			The Temple of Castor and Pollux is reconstructed and enlarged by Lucius Cecilius Metellus Dalmaticus after his victory over the Dalmatians	
115 BC				The Pons Mulvius is rebuilt in stone
114 BC			A temple to Venus Verticordia is built and dedicated, at the instruction of the Sibylline Books to atone for the unchastely conduct of three Vestal Virgins	
113 - 101 BC	Germanic Cimbri and Teutones invade Roman territories			
113 BC	Cn. Carbo defeated at Noreia by the Cimbri			
112 - 106 BC	Jugurthine War. Jugurtha sacks Cirta			
111 BC			The Temple of Cybele burns down	
109 BC	The consul Q. Caecilius Metellus is appointed as the new commander in the Jugurthine War and has some success. A Roman force under Marcus Junius Silanus are defeated by the Helvetii at the Battle of the Rhone River		Metellus restores the Temple to Cybele	
108 BC	At the Battle of the Muthul, Roman forces under Caecilius Metellus fight indecisively against the forces of Jugurtha of Numidia			
107 BC	First consulship (of seven) of Gaius Marius, who is given command in war against Jugurtha. Consul L. Cassius Longinus is defeated by the Tigurini at the battle of Burdigala			
107 - 101 BC	G. Marius makes reforms in the Legions			

Year	War	Politics & Law	Religion	City
106 BC	King Jugurtha is betrayed by his brother-in-law King Bocchus of Mauretania. He is captured by the quaestor Marius, L. Cornelius Sulla			
105 BC	Cimbri and Teutones completely destroy the Roman army of Gnaeus Mallius Maximus at the Battle of Arausio			
104 BC		Death of King Jugurtha of Numidia		
104 - 100 BC	Second Sicilian slave war			
104 BC		The lex Domitia de sacerdotiis is passed		
				Riots instigated by Gaius Norbanus, a tribune of the Plebs
102 – 101 BC	Marius with Q. Lutatius Catulus Caesar defeats the Teutones at the battle of Aquae Sextiae, after which there are mass suicides amongst the captured women			
101 BC	Battle of Vercellae in which the Romans under Gaius Marius defeat the Cimbri, who are entirely annihilated. Cilicia is annexed as a province of Rome			
100 BC		After a failed insurrection, the demagogue Lucius Appuleius Saturninus and his surviving partisans are held captive in the Curia Hostilia awaiting trial, whereupon they are 'stoned' to death by a mob who cast down the roof tiles of the Curia upon the prisoners	Approximate date of the construction of the Temple of Portunus in the Forum Boarium	Riots of Saturninus, order restored by Marius
98 BC	Revolt in Lusitania, Hispania	Publius Furius is brought to trial for his acts whilst tribune and is murdered in the assembly. Riots follow		
97 BC	Q. Caecilius Metellus Nepos conquers Crete			
96 BC		The last Ptolemy ruler of Cyrenacia dies, and it is willed over to Rome		
95 BC		Sulla is sent to Cappadocia to place King Ariobarzanes on the throne after he is deposed by King Mithridates of Pontus		
93 BC	T. Didius completes a victory over the Celtiberians in Spain			
91 - 88 BC	Social War between Rome and its Italian allies			
91 BC	Second Sicilian Slave war ended by Roman general Manius Aquillius. The Italian city of Asculum massacres its Roman citizens and prepares for Roman reprisals	The tribune of the plebs M. Livius Drusus tries to legislate for total Italian citizenship		Adoption of the hypocaust
90 BC	The legate Gn. Pompeius Strabo creates a blockade around the city of Asculum	The consul L. Julius Caesar passes a law, the *lex Julia de civitate Latinus et sociis danda*, which gives citizenship to those Italian allies who have not taken up arms against Rome		

Ut amicum habeas, sis amicus – To have a friend, you should be a friend (Pylades)

Year	War	Politics & Law	Religion	City
89 - 85 BC	First Mithraditic War			
89 BC	Roman victories at Nola and Corfinium. L. Cornelius Sulla captures the rebel Italian city of Bovianum Vetus. Battle of Fucine Lake where Roman forces under Lucius Porcius Cato are defeated by the Italian rebels. The Roman army of C. Pompeius Strabo decisively defeats the rebels at the Battle of Asculum			
88 BC	Q. Caecilius Metellus Pius meets and is defeated by the army of the Italian Q. Pompaedius Silo. The proconsul M. Aquillius invades the Pontic territories with the militia of Asia Province and the army of King Nicomedes of Bithynia. King Mithridates of Pontus invades Greece and issues an edict that all Romans and Italians are to be killed. The number of dead reaches about 110,000 people.	Publius Sulpicius Rufus uses his tribune powers to eject Senators from the Roman Senate until insufficient remain to form a quorum. Violence erupts in the Forum as the senators attempt to publicly lynch Sulpicius, who protects himself with a large bodyguard of armed gladiators. L. Cornelius Sulla leads an army directly into Rome to restore control, the first Roman since the founding of the Republic to do so		
87 BC	Marius marches on Rome with L. Cornelius Cinna. After a short battle, he occupies the city and orders the deaths of the leading supporters of Sulla. However things spiral out of control and after five days of rioting, the rampaging soldiers are rounded up and killed, leaving 100 senators and equites dead, along with countless other citizens	Marius and Cinna are made joint consuls		A riot breaks out between the followers of the two consuls Gnaeus Octavius and Lucius Cornelius Cinna over land redistributions proposed by Marius. Over 10,000 die in the resulting insurgence
86 BC	Sulla conquers Athens, and defeats Mithridates' forces led by Archelaus at the Battle of Chaeronea	Proscriptions against Sulla's supporters cease when Marius dies of a third and fatal stroke, during his seventh consulship		The orator M. Tullius Cicero completes his first work on rhetoric, De Inventione Rhetorica. The historian Sallust using his wealth extorted as governor of the province of Africa Nova (Numidia), starts building landscaped pleasure gardens known as the Horti Sallustiani between the Pincian and Quirinal hills. They are finally finished in 34 BC
85 BC	Sulla again defeats Archelaus in the decisive battle of the First Mithridatic War	Treaty of Dardanus with Mithridates		
84 BC		The new Italian citizens enfranchised by the lex Julia, lex Pompeia and lex Papiria are redistributed throughout all 35 tribes of Rome		
83 BC	L. Cornelius Sulla lands in Italy at the port city of Brundisium, and wages a civil war against the remaining Marian forces. L. Licinius Murena starts a second war against Mithridates	The Roman governor of Spain and future triumvir M. Licinius Crassus joins forces with Sulla	The Temple of Jupiter Optimus Maximus burns down, consuming the Sibylline Books which are lost in the flames	Much of the city burns down as a result of civil unrest. Birth of Marcus Antonius

Year	War	Politics & Law	Religion	City
82 BC	The battle of Clusium, which is indecisive, occurs under the Marian general Gn. Papirius Carbo against L. Cornelius Sulla. Battle of Faventia where the Sullan general Q. Caecilius Metellus Pius defeats the army of Gn. Papirius Carbo. After suffering defeats by Mithridates, Murena is recalled to Rome on the pretext of celebrating a triumph. L. Cornelius Sulla emerges victorious in the decisive battle of the Civil War, when he recaptures Rome at the Battle of Colline Gate	L. Cornelius Sulla and Mithridates agree to a new peace treaty. Gn. Papirius Carbo flees to Sicily, where he is captured by the Sullan general Gn. Pompeius Magnus and executed in the town of Lilybaeum.	Start of the Ludi Victoriae Sullae	
81 BC		Sulla appointed dictator and reforms the constitution. Julius Caesar ordered to divorce his wife by Sulla. He refuses, flees to Asia and joins in the campaign against Mithridates		
80 - 72 BC	The start of the Sertorian revolt under Q. Sertorius in Spain, one of the remaining Marian generals			
80 BC	Rebel forces under Quintus Sertorius defeat the legal Roman forces of Lucius Fulfidias at the Battle of the Baetis River in Hispania. G. Julius Caesar goes with an army under L. Licinius Lucullus to suppress a revolt at the city of Mitylene on the island of Lesbos. He is awarded the corona civica (oak crown) for saving a cohort from destruction.	M. Tullius Cicero has his first major case defending Sextius Roscius against the proscriptions of Sulla. He wins, and publishes the trial as Pro Sextius Roscius Amerino		Lucius Cornelius Sulla restores and enlarges the Curia Hostilia
79 BC	The city of Nola surrenders during the Italian War and the city is razed to the ground	Sulla resigns the dictatorship		
78 BC	P.Servilis starts three year campaign against pirates, accompanied by Julius Caesar	Death of L. Cornelius Sulla, in a villa outside the city of Puteoli. Revolt of the anti-Sullan consul M. Aemilius Lepidus, who is routed by Q. Lutatius Catulus at a battle near the Quirinal hill at Rome		The Tabularium, the bureaucratic and official records office of Rome is built in the Forum Romanum, on the front slope of the Capitoline Hill
77 BC	The remnants of the defeated army of the rebel Lepidus join the forces of Q. Sertorius in Spain. Gnaeus Pompeius Magnus (Pompey) arrives in Spain	Julius Caesar conducts his first trial. He prosecutes the governor of Macedonia, Gn. Cornelius Dolabella Minor		
76 BC	Metellus Pius inflicts a minor defeat on the Sertorian lieutenant L. Hirtuleius. P. Servilius Vatia ejects the pirates from Pamphylia, destroying the stronghold of a pirate admiral known as Zenecities			
75 BC	Q. Caecilius Metellus Pius annihilates the army of the Sertorian lieutenant Lucius Hirtuleius at the Battle of Segovia. The Roman general Gn. Pompeius Magnus is defeated in a battle with Q. Sertorius near the River Sucro and later enters an indecisive battle near the town of Saguntum. Caesar captured by pirates			Civil discord erupts over a shortage of grain, prompting the consul Gaius Aurelius Cotta to make a speech to the assembly of the people to calm the plebeians

Ut sis nocte levis, sit cena brevis! – That your sleeping hour be peaceful, let your dining hour be brief!

Year	War	Politics & Law	Religion	City
74 - 64 BC	Third Mithradatic War			
74 BC	Creation of the new Roman province of Bithynia. Cyrenaica also made a Roman province. The Roman consular M. Aurelius Cotta is defeated in a battle near the town of Chalcedon and also loses his entire fleet. Roman forces under Lucius Lucullus defeat the forces of Mithridates VI of Pontus at the Battle of Cyzicus. M. Antonius makes slight inroads into the pirate menace in the western seas, thereby helping Pompeius Magnus against Q. Sertorius			
73 - 71 BC	Slave war of Spartacus			
73 BC	L. Licinius Lucullus defeats a Pontic squadron off Lemnos under an admiral named Archelaeus		The Temple of Castor and Pollux is restored by Gaius Verres	
72 BC	End of the Sertorian War. Q. Sertorius is killed in Spain, murdered by his legate M. Perperna Viento. Lucullus again defeats Mithridates at the Battle of Cabira, overrunning Pontus. M. Antonius transfers his fleets to the Aegean region, where he firstly suffers a naval defeat off the island of Crete and then is defeated again in a land battle on Crete. The slave revolt led by Spartacus defeats a Roman army led by Gellius Publicola and Gnaeus Cornelius Lentulus Clodianus at the Battle of Picenum. He then defeats another Roman army at Mutina			With the aid of his legions, Crassus builds a 60 kilometre long fortification and wall across Bruttium, from the Tyrrhenian to the Ionian Sea, to entrap Spartacus
71 BC	End of the Third Servile War, when Spartacus' army is defeated at the Battle of Silarus River in Lucania by M. Licinius Crassus. 6,000 survivors are crucified down the length of the Via Appia. Capture of the town of Heraclea by M. Aurelius Cotta			
70 BC	The defeat of Mithridates' forces near the fortress of Cabira. The kingdom of Pontus is annexed and added to the province of Bithynia by L. Licinius Lucullus	The consuls are M. Licinius Crassus and Gn. Pompeius Magnus, both elected for the first time. Passing of the lex Aurelia. Marcus Tullius Cicero prosecutes the governor G. Verres for over taxation on behalf of his Sicilian clients		Birth of the great Roman poet Virgil, near Mantua, in Cisalpine Gaul
69 BC	Pirates attack the port of Ostia. L. Licinius Lucullus invades Armenia and defeats the army of Tigranes II at the Battle of Tigranocerta, for harbouring his father-in-law Mithridates VI of Pontus. Pirates sack Delos			
68 - 67 BC	The ex-consul Q. Caecilius Metellus fights two hard campaigns against the pirates of Crete, subdues the island and annexes it as a Roman province			

Year	War	Politics & Law	Religion	City
68 BC	L. Licinius Lucullus defeats the combined forces of King Mithridates and King Tigranes near Artaxata	Julius Caesar marries Pompeia Sulla, the granddaughter of Sulla and a relative of Gn. Pompeius Magnus		
67 BC	Mithradates defeats Lucullus at Zela. Lucullus stripped of command. Pompey takes command in the east and creates the province of Syria.	The tribune A. Gabinius passes his lex Gabinia, granting Gn. Pompeius Magnus unlimited imperium on water to fight against the growing pirate menace		Following a law reserving the front 14 rows of seats at the theatre for the exclusive use of the equites, the plebeians start a riot, requiring a public address from the praetor Marcus Tullius Cicero to suppress
66 BC	Gn. Pompeius Magnus decisively defeats King Mithridates at the Battle of Dastria in the Lycus valley. Mithridates VI flees, effectively ending the Third Mithridatic War	A law passed by a tribune of the plebs, the lex Manlia, gives Pompey the command against the two kings Mithridates and Tigranes. Rioting occurs at the trial of Caius Cornelius when he is accused of sedition (maiestas) by the brothers Cominii. The trial is abandoned after the brothers are forced to flee the city		
64 BC		First Catilinarian Conspiracy, in which Lucius Sergius Catilina angered by his failure to be elected consul by accusations of ambitus (electoral corruption), conspires with other dissatisfied designates to slaughter the new consuls, then claim the consulships for their own		
63 BC		Death of Mithradates, who commits suicide. Cicero elected Consul. Caesar elected Pontifex Maximus		Birth of Octavian (Augustus) and Marcus Vipsanius Agrippa
62 BC	At the Battle of Pistoria the forces of the conspirator Catiline are defeated by the loyal Roman armies under Gaius Antonius. Pompey settles matters in the east, returns to Italy and disbands his army	Julius Caesar is elected as praetor. Still failing to win an election to consul, Cataline organises the second Catilinarian Conspiracy to overthrow the senate, is discovered and flees Rome to lead a military uprising		The Pons Fabricius a stone bridge connecting Tiber Island with the Campus Martius is built by Lucius Fabricius
60 BC				The Horti Lucullani, landscaped gardens, are laid out by Lucius Licinius Lucullus as an extension of his patrician villa on the Pincian Hill. A wooden theatre collapses during a violent storm
59 BC		Caesar elected Consul and the First Triumvirate is formed between M. Licinius Crassus, Gn. Pompeius Magnus, and G. Julius Caesar. Lex Vatinia was passed, which gives Caesar the governorship of Cisalpine Gaul and Illyricum for five years		Birth of the Roman historian Livy the Elder, born in the city of Patavium, Italy. Julius Caesar expands the content of the 'Daily Acts' message boards to include news about the games, gladiatorial contests, society gossip and astrological omens
58 - 51 BC	G. Julius Caesar wars against the Gauls			
58 BC	Cyprus annexed by Clodius, which is overseen by M. Porcius Cato. At the Battle of the Arar, Caesar defeats the migrating Helvetii, finally subjugating them at the Battle of Bibracte. He then decisively defeats the forces of the Germanic chieftain Ariovistus near modern Belfort	Cicero exiled. King Ptolemy Auletes of Egypt is driven out of Alexandria		During his Aedileship, Marcus Aemilius Scaurus erects a temporary wooden theatre which is criticised for its wasteful magnificence

Veni, vidi, vici! – I came, I saw, I conquered (Julius Caesar)

Year	War	Politics & Law	Religion	City
57 BC	G. Julius Caesar subdues the tribes of the Belgae. At the Battle of the Axona he defeats the forces of the Belgae under King Galba of Suessiones. After this Caesar defeats the Nervii at the Battle of the Sabis	Publius Claudius Pulcher purposely incites his partisans to violence to prevent the passing of a bill to recall Marcus Tullius Cicero to Rome. Many people die as the assembly flees the pre-planned bloodshed. Cicero eventually returns		Gangs under P. Clodius Pulcher and T. Annius Milo start open street warfare in Rome
56 BC	Caesar suppresses the revolt of the Gallic Morini	Conference of the First Triumvirate at Luca		
55 BC	Caesar defeats two immigrating German tribes, the Usipetes and Tencteri, and bridges the Rhine to invade Germania (the first Roman to do so). He then invades Britannia		Pompey dedicates a temple to Venus Victrix atop of his theatre in the Campus Martius	The river Tiber floods. Gn. Pompeius Magnus builds the first stone theatre in Rome near the Campus Martius. M. Tullius Cicero writes his work, De Oratore.
54 BC	Caesar's second invasion of Britannia. Crassus prepares for war against Parthia. A. Gabinius is sent to Egypt to restore King Ptolemy Auletes to his throne in Alexandria			Construction of the Forum Caesaris begins, extending the Forum Romanum further North and East
53 BC	The Nervii revolt in Gaul and others force Caesar to abandon Britain. Vercingetorix revolts in Gaul. Defeat of Roman Army at the Battle of Carrhae against the Parthians under the Triumvir M. Licinius Crassus, who is killed in the battle	The tribune P. Licinius Crassus Dives causes panicked riots after he proposes that Gnaeus Pompeius be appointed dictator to restore public order		Major rioting in Rome. Scribonius Curio hosts funeral games in memory of his father, erecting a pair of wooden theatres which can be rotated and joined together to form an amphitheatre
52 BC	T. Labienus defeats an army of Gauls under the command of Camulogenus near the site of Lutetia. Caesar builds two sets of fortifications 42 miles long and lays Siege to Alesia. Greatly outnumbered he besieges 100,000 Gauls within the fort and holds off 250,000 men in a relief force on the outside, defeating the Gallic rebel Vercingetorix. The provinces of Belgica, Aquitania and Lugdunesis are created	Gn. Pompeius Magnus is elected as consul without a colleague in an attempt to prevent him from assuming the dictatorship		Rioting runs rampant when the news of Clodius' death reaches Rome. The Curia Hostilia is burned down when a mob cremates the demagogue's body inside it. The flames spread and also consume the Basilica Porcia
51 BC	The Parthians invade the province of Syria after the defeat of Crassus			
49 - 45 BC	Civil War between Caesar and the Republican forces of Pompey			
49 BC	Caesar crosses the Rubicon and marches into Rome. He then surrounds the Pompeian commander L. Domitius Ahenobarbus and three legions at Corfinium. At the Battle of Utica in North Africa, G. Scribonius Curio defeats a large number of Numidian horse and foot sent by Juba I of Numidia to aid Attius Varus. However he is later defeated at the Battle of the Bagradas River by Pompeians under Attius Varus and commits suicide. The Pompeian legates M. Petronius and L. Afranius are defeated by Caesar at the battle of Ilerda		The temple of Quirinus on the Quirinal hill is again struck by lightning, burning down the temple and its surroundings	

Year	War	Politics & Law	Religion	City
48 BC	Caesar is defeated at the Battle of Dyrrachium in Macedonia but then decisively defeats Pompey at Pharsalus, who promptly flees to Egypt	Death of Pompey the Great, decapitated in Egypt by Ptolemy XII	Caesar vows the construction of a temple to Venus Genitrix at the Battle of Pharsalus	
47 BC	While in Alexandria to sort out the dynastic dispute between the Ptolemies, Caesar is attacked and trapped in the palace quarter of Alexandria by the young King Ptolemy XII. Battle of Zela, with Caesar and his army against Pharnaces II of Pontus, a son of Mithridates and his army. The tenth legion, Caesar's favourite from the Gallic Wars, mutinies and marches on Rome. Caesar stops the mutiny			
46 BC	Caesar loses a third of his army to Titus Labienus at the Battle of Ruspina. However, at the Battle of Thapsus, Caesar defeats the Pompeian garrison army of Q. Metellus Scipio in North Africa		Caesar reforms the Roman calendar via Egyptian astrologists. The Julian calendar is introduced, and the month of Caesar's birthday, Quinctillis, is renamed as Julius (July). The Temple of Venus Genitrix is completed and dedicated, accompanied by the Ludi Veneris Genetricis	The Forum Caesaris is finally completed and dedicated to the name and deeds of Julius Caesar. The Basilica Julia is initially dedicated by Julius Caesar but is not completed until the reign of Augustus. Caesar excavates an artificial lake on the Campus Martius upon which he displays a great naumachiae (naval battle). He also builds the first permanent wooden amphitheatre
45 BC	Battle of Munda, Ceasar defeats the Pompeian forces of Titus Labienus and Gnaeus Pompey the Younger in Hispania. Labienus is killed in the battle and the Younger Pompey captured and executed	The Lex Iulia Municipalis restricts commercial carts to night-time access to the city and within a mile outside the walls		Cicero publishes his work, Academica
44 BC		Caesar is murdered by Brutus, Cassius and their co-conspirators acting for the 'good of the Republic'. Octavian returns from Greece. M. Tullius Cicero delivers the '12 Phillipics' against M. Antonius, in order to urge the senate to declare war against him		Cicero completes his work De Officiis. Rioting follows the oration of Marcus Antonius at Julius Caesar's funeral, where he reads Caesar's will and displays the bloody toga, naming the perpetrator of each stab wound. The crowd assault the property of the conspirators who flee the city in fear of their lives
43 BC	Battle of Forum Gallorum in which M. Antonius, besieging Caesar's assassin Decimus Brutus in Mutina, defeats and kills consul Pansa, but is then immediately defeated by the army of the other consul, Hirtius accompanied by Octavian. In the following Battle of Mutina, Antony is again defeated in battle but Hirtius is also killed. Octavian takes control of the army and negotiates a truce with Antonius. Decimus Brutus' troops desert to Octavian and he himself is assassinated whilst leaving Italy	Murder of Cicero. Founding of the Second Triumvirate between Octavian, Antonius and Lepidus		Birth of the Roman writer Ovid, in the city of Sulmo, Italy

Verbum semel emissum volat irrevocabile – A word, once emitted, flies irrevocably (Horace)

Year	War	Politics & Law	Religion	City
42 BC	First Battle of Philippi where the Triumvirs Marcus Antonius and Octavian fight an indecisive battle with Caesar's assassins Marcus Brutus and Cassius. Although Brutus defeats Octavian, Antonius defeats Cassius, who commits suicide. At the second Battle of Philippi - Brutus's army is decisively defeated by Antonius and Octavian. Brutus escapes, but commits suicide soon after		Julius Caesar is deified and Octavian begins construction of a temple to him. Octavian vows to build a temple honouring Mars Ultor (Mars the Avenger) during the battle of Philippi	
41 BC	The Perusine war in Italy, Lucius Antonius (brother to Marcus) is defeated by Octavian. Although Lucius and his wife are pardoned, the town of Perugia is sacked and the town magistrates put to the sword			
40 BC	A Parthian invasion, under Pacorus of Syria takes place	Reconfirmation of the Second Triumvirate between Octavian, M. Antonius, and Lepidus. Herod is appointed as king of Judaea by the Senate		
39 - 38 BC	An army of reinforcements under P. Ventidius defeats the Parthian invasion at the battles of Mt. Amanus and Mt. Gindarus			The Hut of Romulus on the Palatine burns down
37 BC		Antony marries Cleopatra at Antioch		The Roman poet Horace begins writing his Satires
36 BC	The son of Pompey, Sex. Pompeius Magnus Pius is defeated by M. Vipsanius Agrippa, the legate of Octavian, at the naval Battle of Naulochus. Battle between M. Antonius and a Parthian army under the command of King Phraates IV near Phraaspa	Triumvirate breaks up when M. Aemilius Lepidus is removed from power by Octavian	The Regia once again burns down and is rebuilt by Gnaeus Domitius Calvinus. Consecration of the site of a Temple to Apollo on the Palatine	
34 BC			T. Statilius Taurus begins building the first stone theatre in the Campus Martius	
33 BC			L. Marcius Philippus builds temple and portico of Heracles Musarum in the Campus Martius. L. Cornificius builds a temple to Diana on the Aventine	Expulsion of the Chaldean Magi from Rome. As Aedile Marcus Agrippa repairs the aqueducts, sewers, fountains and streets of the city; and starts the construction of the Aqua Julia
32 BC			Octavian rebuilds the temple of Jupiter Feretrius on the Capitoline Hill	Destructive floods wash away the Pons Sublicius
31 BC	At the naval Battle of Actium, Agrippa defeats Antonius and Cleopatra, and Octavian effectively takes control of the entire empire		A great conflagration consumes the temple of Ceres, the temple of Spes and the temple of Janus	During riots, a fire begun in the shops of the Circus Maximus spreads up the Aventine hill, burning numerous residential buildings and continues between the Aventine and Palatine hills destroying everything in its path, including the Forum Holitorium, till it reaches the Tiber

Year	War	Politics & Law	Religion	City
30 BC	Egypt is annexed as an imperial province of Rome	Death of Antony and Cleopatra in Alexandria	Dedication of the Taurus Theatre. Triumphal arch built by Octavian in the Forum Romanum	The Roman writer and poet, Horace, completes his work the Epodes
29 BC			For only the second time in Rome's history the doors of the temple of Janus are closed ushering in a well-deserved period of peace. Dedication of Temple of Divus Julius	
28 BC		Octavian named Princeps Senatus	Restoration of 82 temples in the city. Dedication of the Temple of Apollo	
27 BC		Octavian named Augustus and declares the Pax Romana. Establishment of the Praetorian Guard		Destructive flooding as the Tiber overflows its banks. Restoration of the Via Flaminia

APPENDICES

APPENDIX I - BIBLIOGRAPHY

The following is a list of different media and entertainments which cover the subject of pre-Imperial Rome.

ANNALS

The annals are Roman written histories. This list focuses on the earliest surviving works by authors who wrote about periods contemporary to their time. Online copies may be found at the websites given further down. All of these works are great sources for NPCs, surprising anecdotes, and scenario ideas.

Caesar – The Gallic Wars and The Civil Wars, which cover both politics and military campaigns

Livy – Ab Urbe Condita, from which most of our knowledge of early Rome comes from

Plutarch – Parallel Lives, although written post Republic, it contains many entertaining biographies

Polybius – The Histories, good coverage of the military campaigns about the time of the Punic Wars

Sallust – Catiline's War, the political machinations and growing social unrest which led to the ineffectual coup

BOOKS

This list covers the key scholarly books used to research this supplement, which might interest Games Masters wishing to do greater research on specific subjects.

A History of Rome – Marcel Le Glay, Jean-Louis Voisin, and Yann Le Bohec. A general and easy to read book covering the whole of Roman History.

Ancient Rome on Five Denarii a Day – Okay, it's not a book on the Republic but great fun to read and presents a view of Rome from a tourist's perspective, rather than a scholar's.

Atlas of the Roman World – Tim Cornell and John Matthews. Full of political and geographical maps covering the growth of the empire and an in-depth history explaining it all.

Chronicle of the Roman Republic – Philip Matyszak. A useful series of biographies of the foremost Romans of the Republic. Illustrates the political and family connections linking the period, which can be mined for campaign ideas.

Gladiators and Caesars – The best book I have read on the whole subject of gladiatorial combat, beast hunts and chariot racing. It strips out the sensationalist hype and presents the facts.

Greece and Rome at War – Peter Connolly. The classic source book for military information, covering everything from individual battles to equipment and includes lots of pretty illustrations.

Religion and the Romans – A thin, but very academic book whose value lies in the fact it talks about real Roman religion and does not just regurgitate the usual Hellenic excuses.

Rome in the Late Republic – Mary Beard and Michael Crawford. Another scholarly work, which explains in greater detail the political, religious and cultural drives of the Republic.

FICTION

The next list contains historical, Sci-Fi and crime novels set in Republican Rome.

The Eternal City – Edited by David Drake. A collection of Sci-Fi stories which spread across Roman History.

The Last King: Rome's Greatest Enemy – Michael Curtis Ford. A novel covering the Mithridatic Wars, depicting Mithridates as a heroic liberator seeking freedom from the Republic. Lots of battles.

Imperium – Robert Harris. The entertaining novelisation of Cicero's rise to the consulship.

The Emperor series – Conn Iggulden. A romanticised story of Julius Caesar's life, of dubious historical accuracy and rather superficial style. Not really recommended, but may be a gentle introduction to Roman history to hook players. The books are The Gates of Rome, The Death of Kings, The Field of Swords and The Gods of War.

The Masters of Rome series – Colleen McCullough. Excellently researched historical novels covering the period from the rise of Marius to the defeat of Antony. Lots of wonderful plot ideas and an accessible insight into the gritty, self-serving details of Roman politics. The books are *The First Man in Rome, The Grass Crown, Fortune's Favourites, Caesar's Women, Caesar, The October Horse,* and *Antony and Cleopatra*.

Hannibal's Children, The Seven Hills – John Maddox Roberts. Two alternate history books set in a timeline where Carthage won the 2nd Punic War.

The SPQR series – John Maddox Roberts. Very fun crime novels set at the end of the Republic. The writing style is punchier than the Roma Sub Rosa novels but squeezes in more information about everyday Roman life. Its fictional hero Decius Caecilius Metellus is a better representation of the Roman attitudes at the time. The books are ***The King's Gambit, The Catiline Conspiracy, The Sacrilege, The Temple of the Muses, Saturnalia, Nobody Loves a Centurion, The Tribune's Curse, The River God's Vengeance, The Princess and the Pirates, A Point of Law, Under Vesuvius,*** and ***Oracle of the Dead.***

The Roma Sub Rosa series – Steven Saylor. An enjoyable and evocative series of crime novels centring about a man called Gordianus, who seems to get involved in every major event in late Republican history. Many of the novels are useful in illustrating the depth of superstitious fear and belief the Romans had towards the supernatural. The books are ***Roman Blood, The House of the Vestals, Arms of Nemesis, A Gladiator Dies Only Once, Catilina's Riddle, The Venus Throw, A Murder on the Appian Way, Rubicon, Last Seen in Massilia, Mist of Prophecies, The Judgment of Caesar,*** and ***The Triumph of Caesar.***

Roma – Steven Saylor. Although not part of his Sub Rosa series, this stand-alone novel covers Rome from the founding of the city to the end of the Republic, in a series of snapshots of critical points in its history. A must read for Games Masters who want to select which precise period of early Rome they wish to set their campaign in. Also an excellent insight on the growth of myth from mundane events.

MOVIES

Very few good movies have been set in Monarchic or Republican Rome. Most of the big productions are set in later periods but since they are still very enjoyable, I have included the best of them below.

A Funny Thing Happened on the Way to the Forum – The musical epitome of the plays of Plautus. Funny and fun, with wild chariot pursuits and the first depiction of Rome as a real, dirty and cluttered city.

Barabbas – The 1962 epic starring Anthony Quinn, where the convict freed in place of Jesus becomes a gladiator in Rome; the movie has some excellent arena scenes.

Ben Hur – Mandatory viewing for those Games Masters wishing to run a chariot race, both the 1959 Charlton Heston version, and the 1925 silent movie which actually killed several horses and a stuntman during the filming of the racing scenes.

Cleopatra – One of the most expensive movies ever made, the production is an amazing spectacular epic. Paying lip service to real history, it is still an entertaining introduction for players.

Demetrius and the Gladiators – The 1954 sequel to The Robe, where Victor Mature (the now freed slave of the previous movie), loses his Christian faith and becomes a successful gladiator. No historical accuracy, but lavish gladiator scenes.

Duel of Champions – Another sword and sandal movie retelling the legendary tale of the three Horatii brothers sent to duel the Curiatii triplets in order to determine the fate of Rome and Alba.

Hero of Rome – A sword and sandal epic staring Gordon Scott as the assassin Mucius Scaevola striving against the Tarquins at the start of the Republic.

Gladiator – Russell Crow in the striking remake of The Fall of the Roman Empire.

Quo Vadis – The colourful story of the Christians plight under Nero, it does however have an excellent sequence where Rome burns, which should be educational to players about exactly how frighteningly dangerous city fires were.

Satyricon – Loosely-based on Petronius's book, it is an outrageous depiction of decadence and debauchery at the time of Nero.

Scipio Africanus – This 1937 fascist Italian epic depicts the story of the one Roman general able to defeat Hannibal. Vaguely faithful to history, it is one of the most accurate movies in terms of costume, architecture and military tactics, and presents truly violent and epic battles with many of the elephants reputed to have been actually butchered.

Spartacus – A cast of thousands, Spartacus is one of Hollywood's greatest classics. Once again not true to history, it still engenders the salient points and is a great introduction for campaigns focussing on slave rebellions.

The Fall of the Roman Empire – The original movie which inspired Gladiator. Also some excellent chariot racing outside of a stadium and well as glorious battle scenes.

The Robe – Set in the Rome of Caligula, it concerns the redemption of an army tribune who believes himself cursed by the robe Jesus wore to his crucifixion, which he wins in a gambling game. More watchable for the stunning visual aspects, rather than its attention to detail.

POETRY

Reading poetry? You have to be kidding. Well, that is what I thought before writing this supplement. Although most available translations of Latin poetry use the flowery old fashioned language of the 18th and 19th centuries, some modern versions are more accessible. The best Latin poetry to read is probably the satires and the obscene, erotic poetry. Both types are highly amusing revelations of Roman gripes and crudity – which seem little different to those of our modern society.

The most readable Republican poets are:

Catullus – Love poetry which includes some very obscene and erotic verses.

Horace – The odes are very mythic but a little hard to begin with, but the satires are very good

Virgil – The classic Aeneid tells one of the founding stories of Rome

These next poets lived after the Republic but their work is very entertaining and evocative:

Ovid – Another erotic poet, whose Metamorphosis is an epic concerning witchés, magical transformations and mythology

Juvenal – Somewhat sexist satires reflecting male attitudes of the time

Martial – Wonderful satires of city life and a lot of humorous obscene epigrams

Petronius – The Satyricon is a comic look at faithfulness and lower class life

TV SERIES

Unfortunately as with epic movies, only a single TV series has focussed on early Rome. However, the following are the best of the bunch, illustrating politics, warfare, and everyday Roman life.

Rome – The stunning production depicting the end of the Roman Republic. Although the first series took some liberties with recorded history and the second cut out huge swathes, both were generally excellent in terms of portraying Roman social life, beliefs, slavery, celebrations, costumes, furniture, architecture and graffiti. As an introduction to role-playing in ancient Rome it is perfect and reflects the colourful, crowded, dirty and quite frankly brutal nature of city life. A must-watch.

Vincit qui patitur - He who perseveres, conquers

I Claudius – The British TV series, which focussed on character acting rather than visual sets, illustrating the labyrinthine machinations of early Imperial affairs of state, which are the fading shadow of Republican politics

Masada – Although overly patriotic, the siege and fall of Masada is an excellent series showing life as a soldier, and illustrating the fight for independence against Roman rule

Quo Vadis – Although set at the time of Nero, the 2001 Polish production is far better than the original movie and contains good portrayals of various aspects of Roman life

WEB SITES

There are countless web sites devoted to Roman history, mostly focussed on the Imperial period. A few are good but most are pretty awful. If Games Masters need such things as a list of consuls and the years they ruled, then it is easy enough to find something applicable. The following websites give free access to English translations of Latin works.

The Lacus Curtius site < http://penelope.uchicago.edu/Thayer/E/Roman/home.html > is by far the best online resource for interesting historical texts. It includes invaluable cross-linking with William Smith's Dictionary of Greek and Latin Antiquities, making it easy to look up quotes and references.

The Perseus Digital Library < http://www.perseus.tufts.edu/hopper/ > is another valuable site for translations of lesser known Latin works. The server is rather slow though, so it is best to temporarily save individual pages if you need to repeatedly reference them.

The Roman Law Library < http://droitromain.upmf-grenoble.fr/ > is the best place to find complete copies of Rome's leges, especially the Laws of the Kings and the Twelve Tables which are fundamental parts of Roman law. Make sure you select 'Lingua Anglica' for the English translations.

Note that the web addresses of these sites may change over time. If they don't work for you, try searching by name.

APPENDIX II - LATIN PROFANITY

Swearing in most cultures is a de facto part of life and the Romans were masters of it. Many examples have come down to us from the myriad of graffiti, which was continually daubed upon the walls of their cities, and the obscene poetry they published. This section is included for mature players who wish to add an element of fun into their games and learn a bit of Latin on the side.

Although it is common to insult those of high rank by associating their name with that of a famous prostitute, stronger slurs can be implied by naming a person directly as a type of whore. Many of the names for types of prostitute (see Prostitution page 31) are utilised for such foul slander.

"Atia amat omnes" - Atia 'loves' everyone.

To escape possible censorship, the English versions of some of these insults have been given a rather dry translation... But most readers should be able to figure out the correct stronger phrasing.

GENERAL INSULTS

These are common everyday gibes which can be used without being overly crude.

Arde in regnum phasmatis – burn in hell
Barcala – idiot
Baro – blockhead
Bustirape – tomb robber
Caenum – scum
Fur – thief
Hircus – lecherous goat
Lupa - slut
Lustror – haunter of brothels
Lutum lenonium / lenarum – filthy pimp / madam
Matris prolapsus – son of a female dog
Merda – excrement
Moecha – adulteress
Perite – drop dead
Plenus stercoris es – you are full of faecal matter
Porcus obesus – fat pig
Puellarius – effeminate
Sociofraude – backstabber
Spurius – bastard
Stultus - stupid
Trahax – sticky-fingered
Vae – damn

SEXUAL ACTS

Insulting graffiti often utilises the sexual acts. Whilst a man may freely perform penetrative sex (on men or women), it is unmanly for a male to take the submissive or feminine position and hence many insults revolve about the role taken during intercourse. All oral sex was frowned on by polite society, due to its fouling of the mouth, an important consideration since public kissing was the common form of greeting.

Catamitus – a catamite
Cevens – a man who shakes his buttocks invitingly
Cinaedus – an effeminate man who takes the passive role during sex
Cunnilingus – a man who is orally 'penetrated' by women
Fellator – a man who is orally penetrated by men
Futue te ipsum – go have intercourse with yourself
Fututor – a vaginal penetrator in its crudest sense
Irrumator – an oral penetrator. In an odd way the Romans sometimes considered the irrumator to be the passive role (if the partner was performing the motion) and thus being branded as an irrumator could be worse than being a fellator
Matris fututor – someone who copulates with their mother
Mulier secutuleia – nymphomaniac
Obscenus – pervert
Pathicus – one who submits to anal copulation
Pedicator – an anal penetrator
Scortari - to prostitute oneself
Tribas – a lesbian, viewed as distasteful by Romans
"An refert, ubi et in qua arrigas?" - Does it make any difference to me who made you horny, or when?

ORGANS AND BODILY FUNCTIONS

Other obscene words mainly involved reproductive body parts, and the natural processes of excretion.

Cacare – to defecate

Clunes – buttocks

Coleus – the scrotum

Culus – the behind

Cunnus – vagina

Fimus – bodily filth

Landica – the clitoris (very obscene in ancient Latin)

Lotium – urine

Mentula – penis, but often used to indicate someone is a dick

Mingere – to urinate

Pedere – to fart

Podex – anus

Sopio – an abnormally large penis

Sputare – to spit

Stercus – manure

"Culus tibi purior salillo est, nec toto decies cacas in anno" - *Your arse is purer than the salt-cellar; you probably don't even take a dump ten times a year.* Catullus

APPENDIX III - THE TWELVE TABLES

The following are the remaining fragments of the Twelve Tables, Rome's original laws. They are presented to help Games Masters visualise the oddities and strictness of Roman rules and give some devious ideas for scenarios based around an unusual point of law.

TABLE I. CONCERNING THE SUMMONS TO COURT

Ω When anyone summons another before the tribunal of a judge, the latter must, without hesitation, immediately appear

Ω If, after having been summoned, he does not appear, or refuses to come before the tribunal of the judge, let the party who summoned him call upon any citizens who are present to bear witness. Then let him seize his reluctant adversary; so that he may be brought into court, as a captive, by apparent force

Ω When anyone who has been summoned to court is guilty of evasion, or attempts to flee, let him be arrested by the plaintiff

Ω If bodily infirmity or advanced age should prevent the party summoned to court from appearing, let him who summoned him furnish him with an animal, as a means of transport. If he is unwilling to accept it, the plaintiff cannot legally be compelled to provide the defendant with a vehicle constructed of boards, or a covered litter

Ω If he who is summoned has either a sponsor or a defender, let him be dismissed, and his representative can take his place in court

Ω The defender, or the surety of a wealthy man, must himself be rich; but anyone who desires to do so can come to the assistance of a person who is poor, and occupy his place

Ω When litigants wish to settle their dispute among themselves, even while they are on their way to appear before the Prætor, they shall have the right to make peace; and whatever agreement they enter into, it shall be considered just, and shall be confirmed

Ω If the plaintiff and defendant do not settle their dispute, as above mentioned, let them state their cases either in the Comitium or the Forum, by making a brief statement in the presence of the judge, between the rising of the sun and noon; and, both of them being present, let them speak so that each party may hear

Ω In the afternoon, let the judge grant the right to bring the action and render his decision in the presence of the plaintiff and the defendant

Ω The setting of the sun shall be the extreme limit of time within which a judge must render his decision

TABLE II. CONCERNING JUDGMENTS AND THEFTS

Ω When issue has been joined in the presence of the judge, sureties and their substitutes for appearance at the trial must be furnished on both sides. The parties shall appear in person, unless prevented by disease of a serious character; or where vows which they have taken must be discharged to the Gods; or where the proceedings are interrupted through their absence on business for the State; or where a day has been appointed by them to meet an alien

Ω If any of the above mentioned occurrences takes place, that is, if one of the parties is seriously ill, or a vow has to be performed, or one of them is absent on business for the State, or a day has been appointed for an interview with an alien, so that the judge, the arbiter, or the defendant is prevented from being present, and the furnishing of security is postponed on this account, the hearing of the case shall be deferred

Ω Where anyone is deprived of the evidence of a witness let him call him with a loud voice in front of his house, on three market-days

Ω Where anyone commits a theft by night, and having been caught in the act is killed, he is legally killed

Ω If anyone commits a theft during the day, and is caught in the act, he shall be scourged and given up as a slave to the person against whom the theft was committed. If he who perpetrated the theft is a slave, he shall be beaten with rods and hurled from the Tarpeian Rock. If he is under the age of puberty, the Prætor shall decide whether he shall be scourged, and surrendered by way of reparation for the injury

Ω When any persons commit a theft during the day and in the light, whether they be freemen or slaves, of full age or minors, and attempt to defend themselves with weapons, or with any kind of implements; and the party against whom the violence is committed raises the cry of thief, and calls upon other persons, if any are present, to come to his assistance; and this is done, and the thieves are killed by him in the defence of his person and property, it is legal, and no liability attaches to the homicide

Ω If a theft be detected by means of a dish and a girdle, it is the same as manifest theft, and shall be punished as such

Ω When anyone accuses and convicts another of theft which is not manifest, and no stolen property is found, judgment shall be rendered to compel the thief to pay double the value of what was stolen

Ω Where anyone secretly cuts down trees belonging to another, he shall pay twenty-five asses for each tree cut down

Ω Where anyone, in order to favour a thief, makes a compromise for the loss sustained, he cannot afterwards prosecute him for theft

Ω Stolen property shall always be his to whom it formerly belonged; nor can the lawful owner ever be deprived of it by long possession, without regard to its duration; nor can it ever be acquired by another, no matter in what way this may take place

TABLE III. CONCERNING PROPERTY WHICH IS LENT

Ω When anyone, with fraudulent intent, appropriates property deposited with him for safe keeping, he shall be condemned to pay double its value

Ω When anyone collects interest on money loaned at a higher rate per annum than that of the unciae (twelfth part), he shall pay quadruple the amount by way of penalty

Ω An alien cannot acquire the property of another by usucaption; but a Roman citizen, who is the lawful owner of the property, shall always have the right to demand it from him

Ω Where anyone, having acknowledged a debt, has a judgment rendered against him requiring payment, thirty days shall be given to him in which to pay the money and satisfy the judgment

Ω After the term of thirty days granted by the law to debtors who have had judgment rendered against them has expired, and in the meantime, they have not satisfied the judgment, their creditors shall be permitted to forcibly seize them and bring them again into court

Ω When a defendant, after thirty days have elapsed, is brought into court a second time by the plaintiff, and does not satisfy the judgment; or, in the meantime, another party, or his surety does not pay it out of his own money, the creditor, or the plaintiff, after the debtor has been delivered up to him, can take the latter with him and bind him or place him in fetters; provided his chains are not of more than fifteen pounds weight; he can, however, place him in others which are lighter, if he desires to do so

Ω If, after a debtor has been delivered up to his creditor, or has been placed in chains, he desires to obtain food and has the means, he shall be permitted to support himself out of his own property. But if he has nothing on which to live, his creditor, who holds him in chains, shall give him a pound of grain every day, or he can give him more than a pound, if he wishes to do so

Ω In the meantime, the party who has been delivered up to his creditor can make terms with him. If he does not, he shall be kept in chains for sixty days; and for three consecutive market-days he shall be brought before the Prætor in the place of assembly in the Forum, and the amount of the judgment against him shall be publicly proclaimed

Ω After he has been kept in chains for sixty days, and the sum for which he is liable has been three times publicly proclaimed

in the Forum, he shall be condemned to be reduced to slavery by him to whom he was delivered up; or, if the latter prefers, he can be sold beyond the Tiber

Ω Where a party is delivered up to several persons, on account of a debt, after he has been exposed in the Forum on three market days, they shall be permitted to divide their debtor into different parts, if they desire to do so; and if anyone of them should, by the division, obtain more or less than he is entitled to, he shall not be responsible

TABLE IV. CONCERNING THE RIGHTS OF A FATHER, AND OF MARRIAGE

Ω A father shall have the right of life and death over his son born in lawful marriage, and shall also have the power to render him independent, after he has been sold three times

Ω If a father sells his son three times, the latter shall be free from paternal authority

Ω A father shall immediately put to death a son recently born, who is a monster, or has a form different from that of members of the human race

Ω When a woman brings forth a son within the next ten months after the death of her husband, he shall be born in lawful marriage, and shall be the legal heir of his estate

TABLE V. CONCERNING ESTATES AND GUARDIANSHIPS

Ω No matter in what way the head of a household may dispose of his estate, and appoint heirs to the same, or guardians; it shall have the force and effect of law

Ω Where a father dies intestate, without leaving any proper heir, his nearest agnate, or, if there is none, the next of kin among his family, shall be his heir

Ω When a freedman dies intestate, and does not leave any proper heir, but his patron, or the children of the latter survive him; the inheritance of the estate of the freedman shall be adjudged to the next of kin of the patron

Ω When a creditor or a debtor dies, his heirs can only sue, or be sued, in proportion to their shares in the estate; and any claims, or remaining property, shall be divided among them in the same proportion

Ω Where co-heirs desire to obtain their shares of the property of an estate, which has not yet been divided, it shall be divided. In order that this may be properly done and no loss be sustained by the litigants, the Prætor shall appoint three arbiters, who can give to each one that to which he is entitled in accordance with law and equity

Ω When the head of a family dies intestate, and leaves a proper heir who has not reached the age of puberty, his nearest agnate shall obtain the guardianship

Ω When no guardian has been appointed for an insane person, or a spendthrift, his nearest agnates, or if there are none, his other relatives, must take charge of his property

TABLE VI. CONCERNING OWNERSHIP AND POSSESSION

Ω When anyone contracts a legal obligation with reference to his property, or sells it, by making a verbal statement or agreement concerning the same, this shall have the force and effect of law. If the party should afterwards deny his statements, and legal proceedings are instituted, he shall, by way of penalty, pay double the value of the property in question

Ω Where a slave is ordered to be free by a will, upon his compliance with a certain condition, and he complies with the condition; or if, after having paid his price to the purchaser, he claims his liberty, he shall be free

Ω Where property has been sold, even though it may have been delivered, it shall by no means be acquired by the purchaser until the price has been paid, or a surety or a pledge has been given, and the vendor satisfied in this manner

Ω Immovable property shall be acquired by usucaption after the lapse of two years; other property after the lapse of one year

Ω Where a woman, who has not been united to a man in marriage, lives with him for an entire year without the usucaption of her being interrupted for three nights, she shall pass into his power as his legal wife

Ω Where parties have a dispute with reference to property before the tribunal of the Prætor, both of them shall be permitted to state their claims in the presence of witnesses

Ω Where anyone demands freedom for another against the claim of servitude, the Prætor shall render judgment in favour of liberty

Ω No material forming part of either a building or a vineyard shall be removed there from. Anyone who, without the knowledge or consent of the owner, attaches a beam or anything else to his house or vineyard, shall be condemned to pay double its value

Ω Timbers which have been dressed and prepared for building purposes, but which have not yet been attached to a building or a vineyard can legally be recovered by the owner, if they are stolen from him

Ω If a husband desires to divorce his wife, and dissolve his marriage, he must give a reason for doing so

TABLE VII. CONCERNING CRIMES

Ω If a quadruped causes injury to anyone, let the owner tender him the estimated amount of the damage; and if he is unwilling to accept it, the owner shall, by way of reparation, surrender the animal that caused the injury

Ω If you cause any unlawful damage... accidentally and unintentionally, you must make good the loss, either by tendering what has caused it, or by payment

Ω Anyone who, by means of incantations and magic arts, prevents grain or crops of any kind belonging to another from growing, shall be sacrificed to Ceres

Ω When a patron defrauds his client, he shall be dedicated to the infernal gods

TABLE VIII. CONCERNING THE LAWS OF REAL PROPERTY

Ω A space of two feet and a half must be left between neighbouring buildings

Ω Societies and associations which have the right to assemble, can make, promulgate, and confirm for themselves such contracts and rules as they may desire; provided nothing is done by them contrary to public enactments, or which does not violate the common law

Ω The space of five feet shall be left between adjoining fields, by means of which the owners can visit their property, or drive and plough around it. No one shall ever have the right to acquire this space by usucaption

Ω If any persons are in possession of adjoining fields, and a dispute arises with reference to the boundaries of the same, the Prætor shall appoint three arbiters, who shall take cognizance of the case, and, after the boundaries have been established, he shall assign to each party that to which he is entitled

Ω When a tree overhangs the land of a neighbour, so as to cause injury by its branches and its shade, it shall be cut off fifteen feet from the ground

Ω When the fruit of a tree falls upon the premises of a neighbour, the owner of the tree shall have a right to gather and remove it

Ω When rain falls upon the land of one person in such a quantity as to cause water to rise and injure the property of another, the Prætor shall appoint three arbiters for the purpose of confining the water, and providing against damage to the other party

Ω Where a road runs in a straight line, it shall be eight feet, and where it curves, it shall be sixteen feet in width

Ω When a man's land lies adjacent to the highway, he can enclose it in any way that he chooses; but if he neglects to do so, any other person can drive an animal over the land wherever he pleases

TABLE IX. CONCERNING PUBLIC LAW

Ω No privileges, or statutes, shall be enacted in favour of private persons, to the injury of others contrary to the law common to all citizens, and which individuals, no matter of what rank, have a right to make use of

Ω The same rights shall be conferred upon, and the same laws shall be considered to have been enacted for all the people residing in and beyond Latium, that have been enacted for good and steadfast Roman citizens

Ω When a judge, or an arbiter appointed to hear a case, accepts money, or other gifts, for the purpose of influencing his decision, he shall suffer the penalty of death

Ω No decision with reference to the life or liberty of a Roman citizen shall be rendered except by the vote of the Greater Comitia

Ω Public accusers in capital cases shall be appointed by the people

Ω If anyone should cause nocturnal assemblies in the City, he shall be put to death

Ω If anyone should stir up war against his country, or delivers a Roman citizen into the hands of the enemy, he shall be punished with death

TABLE X. CONCERNING RELIGIOUS LAW

Ω An oath shall have the greatest force and effect, for the purpose of compelling good faith

Ω Where a family adopts private religious rites every member of it can, afterwards, always make use of them

Ω No burial or cremation of a corpse shall take place in a city

Ω No greater expenses or mourning than is proper shall be permitted in funeral ceremonies

Ω No one shall, hereafter, exceed the limit established by these laws for the celebration of funeral rites

Ω Wood employed for the purpose of constructing a funeral pyre shall not be hewn, but shall be rough and unpolished

Ω When a corpse is prepared for burial at home, not more than three women with their heads covered with mourning veils shall be permitted to perform this service. The body may be enveloped in purple robes, and when borne outside, ten flute players, at the most, shall accompany the funeral procession

Ω Women shall not during a funeral lacerate their faces, or tear their cheeks with their nails; nor shall they utter loud cries bewailing the dead

Ω No bones shall be taken from the body of a person who is dead, or from his ashes after cremation, in order that funeral ceremonies may again be held elsewhere. When, however, anyone dies in a foreign country, or is killed in war, a part of his remains may be transferred to the burial place of his ancestors

Ω The body of no dead slave shall be anointed; nor shall any drinking take place at his funeral, nor a banquet of any kind be instituted in his honour

Ω No wine flavoured with myrrh, or any other precious beverage, shall be poured upon a corpse while it is burning; nor shall the funeral pile be sprinkled with wine

Ω Large wreaths shall not be borne at a funeral; nor shall perfumes be burned on the altars

Ω Anyone who has rendered himself deserving of a wreath, as the reward of bravery in war, or through his having been the victor in public contests or games, whether he has obtained it through his own exertions or by means of others in his own name, and by his own money, through his horses, or his slaves, shall have a right to have the said wreath placed upon his dead body, or upon that of any of his ascendants, as long as

the corpse is at his home, as well as when it is borne away; so that, during his obsequies, he may enjoy the honour which in his lifetime he acquired by his bravery or his good fortune

Ω Only one funeral of an individual can take place; and it shall not be permitted to prepare several biers

Ω Gold, no matter in what form it may be present, shall, by all means, be removed from the corpse at the time of the funeral; but if anyone's teeth should be fastened with gold, it shall be lawful either to burn, or to bury it with the body

Ω No one, without the knowledge or consent of the owner, shall erect a funeral pyre, or a tomb, nearer than sixty feet to the building of another

Ω No one can acquire by usucaption either the vestibule or approach to a tomb, or the tomb itself

Ω No assembly of the people shall take place during the obsequies of any man distinguished in the State

TABLE XI. SUPPLEMENT TO THE FIVE PRECEDING ONES

Ω Affairs of great importance shall not be transacted without the vote of the people, with whom rests the power to appoint magistrates, to condemn citizens, and to enact laws. Laws subsequently passed always take preference over former ones

Ω Those who belong to the Senatorial Order and are styled Fathers, shall not contract marriage with plebeians

TABLE XII. SUPPLEMENT TO THE FIVE PRECEDING ONES

Ω No one shall render sacred any property with reference to which there is a controversy in court, where issue has already been joined; and if anyone does render such property sacred, he shall pay double its value as a penalty

Ω If the claim of anyone in whose favour judgment was rendered after the property had been illegally seized, or after possession of the same had been delivered, is found to be false, the Prætor shall appoint three arbiters, by whose award double the amount of the profits shall be restored by him in whose favour the judgment was rendered

Ω If a slave, with the knowledge of his master, should commit a theft, or cause damage to anyone, his master shall be given up to the other party by way of reparation for the theft, injury, or damage committed by the slave

APPENDIX IV - MINOR ROMAN DEITIES

The following is a fairly comprehensive list of the minor deities recorded in Roman annals, tomb inscriptions and shrines. Since Romans are openly polytheistic they are free to make sacrifices to whichever gods they wish. Daily life is a constant succession of prayers for aid or protection, from the gods of the household to the multitudes of small shrines scattered throughout the streets of the city.

In the beliefs of the time, no particular god or goddess is stronger or more powerful than another. Basically the city has an egalitarian divine ecology. The major gods are elevated in their worship only because they are specifically sponsored by the State, in return for which Rome is granted their blessing.

By the end of the Republic, most of these deities have at least a single shrine in the city, and some have many. A few are important enough to have small temples built to them, Heracles for example. Games Masters are encouraged to prompt their players into building shrines to show their piety and characters could even claim a particular god as the founder of their family.

Abeona - *protector of children outside the home*
Abundantia - *goddess of abundance and prosperity*
Acca Larentia - *goddess of wheat fields*
Adeona - *protector of children returning home*
Aeolus - *god of winds*
Aera Cura - *goddess of the underworld*
Aequitas - *goddess of fair trade*
Aesculapius - *god of health and medicine*
Aeternitas - *goddess of eternity*
Africus - *god of the southwest wind*
Alemonia - *goddess of pregnancy*
Angerona - *goddess of pain relief*
Angita - *goddess of witchcraft*
Angitia - *goddess of snakes*
Anna Perenna - *goddess of the year*
Antevorta - *goddess of the future*
Apeliotus - *god of the southeast wind*
Aquilo - *god of the north wind*
Arimanius - *god of the underworld*
Aurora - *goddess of the dawn*
Auster - *god of the south wind*
Averna - *goddess of the underworld*
Averruncus - *god of childbirth*
Bellona - *goddess of war*
Bromius - *god of wine*
Bubona - *goddess of cattle*
Caca - *goddess of the hearth*
Cacus - *god of fire (See Creatures page 155)*
Caelius - *god of the northeast wind*
Camenae - *the four goddesses, Carmenta, Egeria, Antevorta, and Postvorta.*
Candelifera - *goddess of childbirth*
Cardea - *goddess of thresholds*
Carna - *goddess of the heart and organs*
Caurus - *god of the northwest wind*
Cinxia - *goddess of marriage*
Clementia - *goddess of mercy*
Cloacina - *goddess of sewers*
Concordia - *goddess of harmony*
Consus - *god of grain storage*
Convector - *god of the harvest*
Cuba - *goddess of sleeping infants*
Cunina - *protector of infants*
Cupid - *god of love*
Cura - *goddess who created humans*
Dea Dia - *goddess of growth*
Dea Tacita - *goddess of the dead*
Decima - *measurer of the thread of life*
Dei Lucrii - *gods of commerce and trade*

Devera - *goddess of purification brooms*
Deverra - *goddess of midwives*
Dius Fidus - *god of oaths*
Disciplina - *goddess of discipline*
Discordia - *goddess of discord*
Dis Pater - *god of wealth and the underworld*
Domiduca - *protector of children returning home*
Domiducus - *goddess of brides travelling to their husbands' house*
Domitius - *god of respectful wives*
Edusa - *goddess of nourishment*
Edesia - *goddess of banquets*
Egeria - *water nymph*
Empanda - *goddess of generosity*
Epona - *goddess of equines*
Eventus Bonus - *god of agriculture and commerce.*
Fabulinus - *god of children*
Facunditas - *god of bountiful harvests*
Fama - *goddess of fame*
Fauna - *goddess of vegetation*
Faunus - *god of flocks*
Faustitas - *protector of livestock*
Favonius - *god of the west wind*
Febris - *goddess of fevers*
Felicitas - *goddess of success*
Feronia - *goddess of woods and fountains*
Fides - *goddess of loyalty*
Fontus - *god of wells and springs*
Fornax - *goddess of bread and baking*
Fraus - *goddess of treachery*
Fulgora - *god of lightning*
Glycon - *god of snakes*
Gratiae - *The Graces*
Hercules - *god of strength*
Herulus - *god of underworld darkness*
Hespera - *goddess of dusk*
Hippona - *goddess of horses*
Honos - *god of military honours*
Hora - *Quirinus' wife*
Imporcitor - *god of harrowing*
Indiges - *the deified Aeneas*
Insitor - *god of crop sewing*
Intercidona - *protector against evil spirits*
Inuus - *god of sexual intercourse*
Invidia - *goddess of envy*
Justitia - *goddess of justice*
Juturna - *goddess of fountains, wells, and springs*
Juventas - *goddess of youth*
Lactanus - *god of prospering crops*
Larentina - *goddess of death*
Lares - *the household gods*
Laverna - *goddess of thieves*
Levana - *goddess of newborns*
Liber - *god of fertility*
Libera - *goddess of earth*
Liberalitas - *goddess of generosity*
Libertas - *goddess of freedom*
Libitina - *goddess of death and funerals*
Lima - *goddess of thresholds*

Varium et mutabile semper femina – Woman is always a changeable and capricious thing (Virgil)

Lua - goddess of captured weapons
Lucina - goddess of childbirth
Luna - goddess of the moon
Lupercus - god of shepherds
Mana Genita - goddess of burials
Manes - the souls of the dead
Mania - goddess of the underworld
Mantus - god of the underworld
Mater Matuta - goddess of mariners
Mefitis - goddess of poisonous and volcanic vapours
Mellona - goddess of beekeeping
Messor - god of harvesting crops
Moneta - goddess of prosperity
Mors - god of death
Morta - severer of the thread of life
Murtia - goddess of sloth
Muta - goddess of silence
Mutinus - god of fertility
Naenia - goddess of funerals
Necessitas - goddess of destiny
Nemesis - goddess of revenge
Nemestrinus - god of woods and forests
Nerio - goddess of martial valour
Nixi - goddesses of childbirth
Nodutus - god of wheat stalks
Nona - spinner of the thread of life
Nox - goddess of night
Obarator - god of agriculture
Occator - god of harvesting
Orchadis - god of olive groves
Orbona - goddess of orphans
Pales - god of shepherds and livestock
Parcae - the goddesses of destiny, Decima, Morta, and Nona
Partula - goddess of the length of pregnancy
Patalena - goddess of flowers
Paventia - goddess of comforting frightened children
Pax - goddess of peace
Penates - household gods of the storage cupboard
Picumnus - god of matrimony
Pietas - goddess of duty
Pilumnus - protector of infants at birth
Poena - goddess of punishment
Porus - god of plenty
Porrima - goddess of the future
Postverta - goddess of the past
Potina - goddess of children's drinks
Priapus - god of the shade
Promitor - god of growing crops
Prorsa Postverta - goddess of women in labour
Providentia - goddess of forethought
Pudicita - goddess of chastity
Puta - goddess of pruning
Quiritis - goddess of motherhood
Redarator - god of ploughing
Robigo - goddess of blight
Robigus - god of blight
Roma - personification of the Roman state
Rumina - goddess of breastfeeding

Runcina - goddess of reaping and weeding
Rusina - protector of fields
Rusor - god of agriculture
Salus - goddess of public welfare
Sancus - god of oaths
Sarritor - god of weeding
Securita - goddess of security
Semonia - goddess of sowing
Sentia - goddess of mental development
Septentrio - god of the south wind
Silvanus - god of woodlands and forests
Somnus - god of sleep
Sors - god of luck
Spes - goddess of hope
Spiniensis - god of thorny bushes
Stata Mater - protector against fires
Statanus - god of standing up
Statina - wife of Statanus
Sterquilinus - god of fertilisation
Strenua - goddess of endurance
Suadela - goddess of persuasion
Summanus - god of nocturnal thunder
Tellus - goddess of the earth
Tempestes - goddess of storms
Terra - goddess of the land
Terminus - god of boundaries
Tiberinus - god of the River Tiber
Tibertus - god of the River Anio (a tributary of the Tiber)
Tranquillitas - goddess of peace
Trivia - goddess of magic
Ubertas - god of prosperity
Unxia - goddess of marriage
Vacuna - goddess of sheep
Vagitanus - god of children
Vediovus - god of the underworld
Venti - the gods of the winds, Africus, Apeliotus, Aquilo, Auster, Caecius, Caurus, Favonius, and Vulturnus
Veritas - goddess of truth
Verminus - god of cattle worms
Vertumnus - god of the seasons
Vervactor - god of the first ploughing
Victoria - goddess of victory
Viduus - separator of the soul from the body
Virbius - god of forests
Viriplaca - goddess of marital strife
Virtus - god of strength and bravery
Volumna - goddess of nurseries
Voluptas - goddess of pleasure
Vulturnus - god of the east wind

Vulpem pilum mutat, non mores – A fox may change its hair, not its tricks

INDEX